Sunbelt Rising

POLITICS AND CULTURE IN MODERN AMERICA

Series Editors: Margot Canaday, Glenda Gilmore, Michael Kazin,
and Thomas J. Sugrue

Volumes in the series narrate and analyze political and social change in the broadest dimensions from 1865 to the present, including ideas about the ways people have sought and wielded power in the public sphere and the language and institutions of politics at all levels—local, national, and transnational. The series is motivated by a desire to reverse the fragmentation of modern U.S. history and to encourage synthetic perspectives on social movements and the state, on gender, race, and labor, and on intellectual history and popular culture.

Sunbelt Rising

The Politics of Place, Space, and Region

Edited by
Michelle Nickerson and Darren Dochuk

University of Pennsylvania Press

Philadelphia

Published in Cooperation with the William P. Clements Center for Southwest Studies, Southern Methodist University

Copyright © 2011 University of Pennsylvania Press

All rights reserved. Except for brief quotations used for purposes of review or scholarly citation, none of this book may be reproduced in any form by any means without written permission from the publisher.

Published by
University of Pennsylvania Press
Philadelphia, Pennsylvania 19104-4112
www.upenn.edu/pennpress

Printed in the United States of America on acid-free paper
10 9 8 7 6 5 4 3 2 1

Library of Congress Cataloging-in-Publication Data

Sunbelt rising : the politics of place, space, and region / edited by Michelle Nickerson and Darren Dochuk.
  p. cm. — (Politics and culture in modern America)
"Published in Cooperation with the William P. Clements Center for Southwest Studies, Southern Methodist University."
  Includes bibliographical references and index.
  ISBN 978-0-8122-4309-3 (hardcover : alk. paper)
  1. Sunbelt States—Politics and government—20th century.
  2. Political culture—Subeslt States.   3. Regionalism—Sunbelt States.
  4. Sunbelt States—Economic conditions—20th century.   5. Sunbelt States—Race relations—Political aspects—History—20th century.
  I. Nickerson, Michelle M.   II. Dochuk, Darren.   III. William P. Clements Center for Southwest Studies.   IV. Series: Politics and culture in modern America.
F787.S85   2011
979—dc22   2010039358

Contents

Introduction 1

I. Constructing Region

1 Sunbelt Boosterism: Industrial Recruitment, Economic Development, and Growth Politics in the Developing Sunbelt 31
   Elizabeth Tandy Shermer

2 Strom Thurmond's Sunbelt: Rethinking Regional Politics and the Rise of the Right 58
   Joseph Crespino

3 Big Government and Family Values: Political Culture in the Metropolitan Sunbelt 82
   Matthew D. Lassiter

4 Religion and Political Behavior in the Sunbelt 110
   Lyman A. Kellstedt and James L. Guth

II. Civil Rights in the Sunbelt

5 From the Southwest to the Nation: Interracial Civil Rights Activism in Los Angeles   141
   Shana Bernstein

6 Sunbelt Civil Rights: Urban Renewal and the Follies of Desegregation in Greater Miami   164
   N. D. B. Connolly

7 Racial Liberalism and the Rise of the Sunbelt West: The Defeat of Fair Housing on the 1964 California Ballot   188
   Daniel Martinez HoSang

III. Contingent Places

8 Sunbelt Lock-Up: Where the Suburbs Met the Super-Max   217
   Volker Janssen

9 Sunbelt Imperialism: Boosters, Navajos, and Energy Development in the Metropolitan Southwest   240
   Andrew Needham

10 Real Estate and Race: Imagining the Second Circuit of Capital in Sunbelt Cities   265
   Carl Abbott

IV. The Global Sunbelt

11 The Marketplace Missions of S. Truett Cathy and Chick-fil-A   293
   Darren E. Grem

12 Tortilla Politics: Mexican Food, Globalization, and the Sunbelt   316
   Laresh Jayasanker

13 Latinos in the Sunbelt: Political Implications of Demographic Change   335
   Sylvia Manzano

Notes   361

List of Contributors   447

Index   449

Acknowledgments   469

Introduction

One week before the 1976 presidential election, evangelicals gathered in Dallas, Texas, for the National Prayer Congress sponsored by Campus Crusade for Christ. Thirty-two pastors, lay leaders, Christian celebrities, and housewife activists gave warmly received talks on different facets of prayer, but two Texans with California ties stood out. Fifteen years earlier, the Reverends E. V. Hill and W. A. Criswell could not have shared the same stage; the former black radical and founding member of the Southern Christian Leadership Conference from Houston and the white fundamentalist Baptist from Dallas were ideological foes in the early 1960s and stark reminders of a polarized South. Yet in 1976, the two spoke passionately and in unison about the virtues of a Sunbelt South and its spiritual and political mandate to lead the nation.

Much as he had done since the early 1970s, when speaking on behalf of Richard Nixon's "black silent majority," Hill offered a message of racial reconciliation through changed hearts and minds. "I'm a Texan. . . . I breath [sic] comfortably in Texas," he announced, before recounting his struggles with poverty and discrimination as a child growing up in a South Texas hamlet, his personal embrace of Jesus and reliance on family in times of need, and his move to Los Angeles to guide Mount Zion Missionary Baptist Church out of the Watts race wars of the mid-1960s. These were testimonial signposts evangelicals already recognized, but they nevertheless allowed the famous black preacher to reiterate his parable for the nation. There was no social welfare in his childhood hometown, just a lot of neighborly love, he explained, no government handouts, just an abundance of faith in human potential. It was through spiritual supplication, he charged, that this potential was realized; prayer brought comfort, a sense of direction, and proof of an active God. In light of the nation's crises, Hill concluded, it seemed about time for the lessons of his life to be replicated, for citizens to begin trusting again, for America to turn its heart toward heaven.[1]

The other Texan to address the crowd took a sharper tack. In his signature fire-and-brimstone style, Criswell thundered, "Uncle Sam is on his knees," unable to rise from under the burden of "desperate trial" because "he" has stopped praying. A Puritan could not have stated it with such blunt force, but then the Baptist turned contemporary. "If you want to see what America is twenty years [from now]," look at New York City, he cried out. America's own modern Gomorrah was now "the place of rendezvousing for the pimp and procurer and the prostitute and the drug pusher and the pornographic peddler."[2] Criswell contrasted this hell to a place of godliness he once knew intimately, the Northwest Texas plains, "Texahoma." There he had grown up amid scarcity worsened by dust storms. "I have seen the sky, the heavens turn into brass and the earth into iron," he recalled. "I have heard the cattle lowing, thirsting for water." The preacher then talked about his father, a failed farmer who had struggled to survive before moving west to California. Through plague and pestilence, the poor Texan had remained dedicated to God; he prayed for relief from hard times but endured whatever the weather brought him and rejoiced when divine blessing seemed to shine down. How stark the difference, Criswell declared with a quivering voice, between this man's faith and the prevailing winds of lasciviousness that now blew over the spiritually and politically barren soil of American society. It was time for Christians to pray for rain—for revival, for reformation, for a reconstituted nation: "Oh for the floods on the thirsting lands."[3]

Sunbelt Rising

American jeremiads in the classical sense, Hill's and Criswell's sermons were also quintessential Sunbelt anthems commissioning conservatives along the southern rim of the country to change their nation from the bottom up. Like countless other homilies delivered at similar "congresses" held during the Bicentennial year, Hill and Criswell's were layered with transparent political meaning. As calls for religious awakening, they certainly spoke a theology heard for centuries in American revivalism. Yet as social commentaries, they represented something unprecedented. Fundamentally, these sermons prescribed an agenda of free market capitalism and decentralized government, patriotism and family values, but there was more to them than this. Thanks to the colorful oratory of skilled preachers who used the occasion to reminisce about their own odysseys, these prescriptions were delivered with heavy doses of sentimentality—poignant tales of a fabled, hardscrabble past and enchanted future. In their sacred discourse, these booster-minded clerics turned shared plain-folk legacies into superlatives of regional privilege; in their political discourse, they turned them into leverage for power. Altogether, their religious politicking made the intended point that self-made "southerners" and a rags-to-riches "South" had finally earned the right to lead the nation. And by referencing the plight of a Rustbelt north, where wayward cities like New York tempted God's wrath, these preachers argued that, for the good of America, this power shift could not come too soon. Their earnestness, effort, and ability to recast an age-old Puritan dispensation in a blueprint for mass political mobilization would soon pay off in Ronald Reagan's 1980 election win, a victory legitimizing years of grassroots work by a Baptist and Pentecostal rank-and-file.

The story behind a rising Sunbelt, of course, is much more complex than any sermon reveals and involves a host of characters and influences that far exceed the constituency to which Criswell and Hill belonged. These right-wing prophets, in fact, spoke for one Sunbelt only; there was another Sunbelt every bit as animated and powerful, one that leaned to the political left. Witness to the Reagan insurgency, Sunbelt liberals and Social Democrats stepped up their long-standing efforts to make this region a bastion of progressive thinking. Drawing on their own logic and narrative of mission and destiny, they revamped their quest—begun decades earlier—to make the Sunbelt a place where citizens encountered a future of corporate accountability, responsible urbanism, environmental concern, and multicultural exchange. In contrast to their conservative counterparts, they lobbied for more, not fewer, state regulations; championed an expansive internationalism rather than assertive nationalism; and looked for ways to enlarge the boundaries of the body politic and hasten change in American attitudes, values, and vision. And so, even in the late 1970s, when evangelicals from Miami to Los Angeles took to the streets to protest high taxes and moral decline and, in 1980, rushed to the polls to elect a cowboy president, these denizens marched with their own political momentum, certain that the "City on a Hill" conservatives promised to build in the Sunbelt presaged the nation's damnation, not its salvation.

Separated by a deep ideological divide, these colliding Sunbelt societies nevertheless shared two traits: an all-or-nothing, political discourse of ultimate consequence, and a political conviction that as the Sunbelt went, so would go the nation. *Sunbelt Rising* not only appreciates the complexities and paradoxes that emerge when studying this dynamic give-and-take but accentuates them as a way to gain fresh perspective on post-World War II America writ large. One of the underlying premises of this volume, in fact, is that American society's most heated and significant political struggles in the postwar era grew out of the passionate and sometimes violent clashes that played out on this political turf. Regardless of their political perspectives, rightly or wrongly, Americans saw this terrain as a blank slate upon which a prosperous future could be built; naturally, then, this frontier-for-the-taking elicited strong political emotions and stirred up a relentless string of political contests and crusades. The rising Sunbelt, in this sense, came to embody all the country's unbridled hopes and unremitting despairs and encourage its utopian dreams and dystopian nightmares to flourish alongside each other in perpetual tension. In scholarly speech, the Sunbelt became the lens through which citizens everywhere could readily see the momentous socioeconomic, cultural, and political forces redefining their lives. In evangelical idiom, it became the nation's window onto its soul.

Sunbelt Origins

We see these instructive juxtapositions in the origins of the "Sunbelt" concept itself. The Sunbelt first captured national attention because of the provocative works of Kevin Phillips and Kirkpatrick Sale. It was Phillips, in fact, who resurrected a 1940s Army/Air Force term—"sunshine belt"— used to describe favorable testing and training conditions south of the thirty-seventh parallel and applied it to the new realities of late 1960s American politics.[4] In his 1969 bestseller *The Emerging Republican Majority*, the Republican strategist described a new alloy of conservatism that united voters across the southern rim of the country behind a pro-growth, pro-family, pro-defense, antilabor, antistatist agenda.[5] Whereas Phillips heralded this developing trend as a potential boon to the GOP, Sale decried it. In his book, *Power Shift*, published in 1975, Sale spoke critically of the way a new class of regional boosters had pried "the balance of power in America away from the Northeast and toward the Southern Rim."[6] This rim of influence, Sale explained, began as a "rival nexus" that competed with the Northeast for economic supremacy in the post-World War II years. Here, along the "broad band of America that stretches from Southern California through the Southwest and Texas, into the Deep South," a

> power base took shape, built upon the unsurpassed population migrations that began to draw millions and millions of people from the older and colder sections of the Northeast to the younger and sunnier sections of the South and Southwest . . . [and] upon an authentic economic revolution that created the giant new postwar industries of defense, aerospace, technology, electronics, agribusiness, and oil-and-gas extraction.[7]

Sale, along with so many other prognosticators, saw clearly that this "Southern Rim" had achieved supremacy by the early 1970s and would dictate American politics for the "foreseeable future." From his perspective, the rise of the Sunbelt portended the nation's decline.

Despite their differences of opinion, Phillips and Sale crafted the outlines of a concept and a region that cohered, in their minds, around a unique amalgam of economics, metropolitan spaces, community life, culture, and politics. Postindustrial in its new dependence on service and leisure industries, high-tech manufacturing, information, extractive, and defense sectors, Phillips's Sunbelt (or Sale's Southern Rim) was also poststructural in its urban layouts, with communities sprawling out from the city's edge rather than concentrating in its core. A distinctive climate of political thought settled over this sprawling landscape. Residents of this corporate dreamland internalized the pro-growth, antiregulatory, free market assurances of venture capitalism and sought to limit the reach of the federal state in sectors that did not serve these interests. The myth and ethic of self-help and independence matched the surroundings, as did the culture of localism and community protectionism that grew up alongside it.[8] By the time Phillips and Sale wrote, partisan change was catching up to these larger trends. After decades of dormancy, the one-party Democratic South was finally fragmenting along class and cultural lines and becoming a competitive two-party place. Phillips wrote about the Sunbelt in part to make sure that the Republican Party recognized and took full advantage of this seismic shift.

Phillips, Sale, and their cohort of journalists accentuated this Sunbelt storyline throughout the 1970s. This popular narrative reached its crescendo in 1976. During the same week as the National Prayer Congress in Dallas, *Newsweek* featured a front cover that blared "Born Again!" and a lead story that declared 1976 "The Year of the Evangelical."[9] The article singled out the reconstructed "Bible Belt" as the seedbed of this revival and Jimmy Carter as it personification. This same year, Carey McWilliams, the California expatriate and editor of the *Nation*, asked rhetorically, "Who are the evangelicals"? They live in the "missile crescent," stretching from "Florida . . . to Southern California," he answered, and they "are by no means exclusively white; thousands of Blacks, Chicanos, Orientals, Indians and White ethnics are also members." Together, these "God-fearing, up-and-coming types" constitute a "movement" ideally suited to their "jerry-built suburban" communities built on "cheap land" with the aid of "tax inducements, lower wage scales, less union activity . . . [and] defense spending." The "God factor" now taking the country by storm, McWilliams summarized, was a producer and product of the Sunbelt economic juggernaut, and it promised to have a commanding presence under the leadership of a "twice born" politician—Ronald Reagan.[10] Other journalists were less concerned with the Sunbelt's spiritual politics than they were in explaining its socioeconomic roots. The *New York Times* encouraged this conversation by publishing a series of articles in 1976 that stressed regional economic change in a national context of financial strain. Reporting from Huntsville, Alabama, Wayne King opened the discussion by announcing, "The factors behind the emergence of the Sunbelt as a powerful and cohesive region are multiple rapidly changing industrial, economic and population patterns, new living styles, a balmy climate."[11] King's piece, along with McWilliams's and the countless others that appeared during America's Bicentennial year, made it clear that, even as the country paused to commemorate its past, impatient, ambitious citizens clustered along its southern rim were far out ahead in imagining an illustrious future.

Even as these pundits continued to posit the new American politics in this light, scholars began to question the usefulness of their lexicon. Did a "Sunbelt" actually exist, and if so, how could it be quantified? Qualified?

At least two fields of analysis emerged shortly after public interest in the Sunbelt peaked in 1976, both of which held this regional concept up to scrutiny. Drained of the polemics pulsating through Phillips's and Sale's works, these scholarly treatments nevertheless embraced the Sunbelt synthesis while also grounding it in social science research. In an effort partly to soften Sale's thesis that the Sunbelt was stealing the Rustbelt North's resources, influence, power, and confidence, economists Bernard L. Weinstein and Robert E. Firestine published *Regional Growth and Decline in the U.S.: The Rise of the Sunbelt and the Decline of the Northeast* (1978). Weinstein and Firestine traded in Sale's notion of an economic shift but not in his screed against the Southern Rim's exploitive tactics. In their estimation, Sunbelt prosperity did not come from the influx of northern businesses looking for low taxes and a union-free corporate environment as much as it came from the natural evolution of a new consumer-based economics and corporate restructuring, much of it precipitated by northern-based companies. The Sunbelt and Rustbelt (or, alternatively, "Snowbelt") need not see themselves in opposition, Weinstein and Firestine concluded; it was simply time for the Rustbelt to learn from and adjust to the new economic strategies to which the Sunbelt laid claim.[12]

Whereas Weinstein and Firestine spoke the language of public policy, David C. Perry and Alfred J. Watkins used their study of the Sunbelt to talk about new urban forms. Like their economic counterparts, Perry and Watkins saw in the Sunbelt coherent patterns of development that stood at odds with what was going on elsewhere around the country. Particularly striking, in their mind, was the Sunbelt's organization of metropolitan space. In contrast to linear, contained, core-attentive cities like Chicago and New York, Buffalo and Cleveland, the Sunbelt boomtowns of Charlotte, Atlanta, Houston, Dallas, and Los Angeles claimed very different arrangements, with self-sufficient communities scattering on their periphery and impacting environments that "far exceed their metropolitan hinterlands."[13] Perry and Watkins's edited volume also contained and elaborated on other distinctive features of the region Phillips and Sale helped delineate. Six economic "pillars" of post-World War II growth (mirroring Sale's six-pronged powerbase) contributed directly to Sunbelt urban growth: agriculture, defense, advanced technology, oil and natural gas, real estate and construction, and tourism and leisure. According to Perry and Watkins, these economic forces, combined with an inordinate amount of federal funding funneled into the region's infrastructure, provided Sunbelt cities with the means to flourish in a postindustrial economy, even as their counterparts in the north struggled to recalibrate their floundering, industrially based financial, spatial, and political mechanisms.[14]

Perry and Watkins's anthology set the trend for Sunbelt studies during the following two decades, even as some of its basic suppositions were undermined. In the 1980s and early 1990s, urban historians took the lead in fleshing out distinctions between and tensions within Sunbelt cities in hopes of illuminating the inconsistencies of this regional designation. Richard M. Bernard and Bradley R. Rice's edited volume *Sunbelt Cities: Politics and Growth Since World War II* provided a general but valuable overview of twelve southern rim cities, ranging in size and influence from Houston, Miami, Dallas, and Atlanta to New Orleans, Oklahoma City, Tampa, and San Diego. Eclectic and only loosely connected, this anthology's individual essays highlighted the ways in which these cities similarly strove to balance boosterism and new wealth with extant and deep-seated traditions of community, race, and ethnicity, but also hinted at the difficulties associated with the Sunbelt label: these metropolitan complexes were different enough to beg the question whether a Sunbelt urban form actually existed.[15] A number of historians continued the conversation into the late 1980s and early 1990s, with some holding on to the Sunbelt thesis first laid out by Perry and Watkins and others returning to more conventional regional designations of "South," "Southwest," and "West."[16]

The fragmentation of a Sunbelt thesis was announced in 1990, when Raymond A. Mohl published a collection of essays stemming from a conference held a few years earlier. Aptly titled *Searching for the Sunbelt: Historical Perspectives on a Region*, the volume contained scholars that ran the gamut between those who still felt comfortable with the Sunbelt analytic category and those who believed recent study had shown this to be a tenuous concept, too imprecise to be useful. Besides stressing the differences in metropolitan and economic growth evidenced in Bernard and Rice's edited collection, the doubters in this group also pointed to the lack of clear geographical boundaries as reason to jettison (or at the very least, severely limit) the use of the Sunbelt label. If, as was commonly assumed at this time, the Sunbelt's border ran east-west from North Carolina to Southern California, how could one account for the notable disjuncture between the underdeveloped metropolitan centers of Alabama and Mississippi and the mature metroplexes of Los Angeles and Atlanta? And what about San Francisco and Seattle on the West Coast, Baltimore and Washington on the East

Coast, and cities caught in the middle like Denver and Colorado Springs? Were these Sunbelt cities?[17] A few of the skeptics had the last word in the volume. In their essay "The Vanishing Sunbelt," Howard N. Rabinowitz and David R. Goldfield left room for a Sunbelt journalistic past but little for a Sunbelt scholarly future. They argued that the sectional animosities that pitted Sunbelt boosters against the Rustbelt's beleaguered supporters during the 1970s—and that enlivened the journalism of Phillips and Sale and the scholarship of Weinstein, Firestine, Perry, and Watkins—had abated, rendering "Sunbelt" a remnant of a fizzled "public relations ploy." "In the end it is the uneasy alliance of South and West in the Sunbelt and the equally simplified view of the Frostbelt that exposes . . . the [Sunbelt] concept," they wrote. "We can more profitably understand America in terms of North, South, and West, or urban, rural, and suburban. Either of these more traditional models works better than the Sunbelt stereotype of more recent theorists."[18]

Rabinowitz and Goldfield's essay helped set the tone for the 1990s, when historians seemed eager to retreat from the notion of a coherent, concrete Sunbelt entity (and the Phillips and Sale narrative that bolstered it) back inside the bounds of traditional regional history. Southern urban, social, cultural, and political historians saw a renaissance in their field, which selectively incorporated dimensions of the 1970s and 1980s Sunbelt literature but focused almost exclusively on developments east of the Mississippi River.[19] Historians like James Cobb and Bruce Schulman offered broad treatments of post-New Deal developments that connected the South to the nation and foregrounded southern interests in the unfolding of the nation's recent past. Both historians showed how the New Deal offered the best of both worlds for the Sunbelt South's rising entrepreneurs: guaranteed low-interest capital invested in a union-free, deregulated economic climate with promises of social stability, racial accord, and maximum profit.[20] The same style of regional boosterism that appeared in Cobb's and Schulman's examinations of the South also found its way into studies of the post-World War II California and the West. In keeping with the larger historiographical pattern of the 1990s, however, this literature too remained regionally specific and self-contained. A renewed interest in Los Angeles and, more generally, Southern California was, perhaps, the most intense and exciting dimension of this scholarly reawakening. With a critical eye and sharp rhetorical edge, Mike Davis's *City of Quartz: Excavating the Future in Los Angeles* turned historians' attention (at least those working in that part of the country) to this quintessentially booster-controlled, postindustrial, postsuburban—dystopic—Sunbelt city and in the process encouraged a new generation of historians to study this region. As dynamic as it was, this scholarship tended to mirror trends in Southern historiography by highlighting the exceptionalism of a place bounded by a unique process of mythmaking and distinctive patterns of racial, cultural, geographical, economic, spatial, and political interaction. In the 1940s, Carey McWilliams wrote about his native southern California as an "Island on the Land"; and though enlivened by a new, intense level of scholarly engagement, through the 1990s historians seemed ready to acknowledge that it was indeed so, that California's Southland was a strange and peculiar place set apart from the nation.

Despite what Goldfield suggested and historians seemed to imply in the 1990s, the concept of a Sunbelt is not dead, nor should it be. Recent trajectories in historical scholarship in fact point to a coming together of West and South in fresh and innovative ways and suggest that Kevin Phillips and Kirkpatrick Sale's journalistic treatments are not so easily shelved as entertaining but antiquated opinion pieces from a bygone era. The study of conservatism is an obvious case in point. Since the 1990s, historians have begun uncovering and unpacking the ways right-wing parents, mothers, grassroots activists, interest groups, political action committees, businessmen, corporations, intellectuals, preachers, churches, parachurch organizations, alternative media, research institutes, powerbrokers, and politicians worked diligently (and quietly) through the Cold War years to lay the foundation for a right-wing movement that would surge in the late 1970s and become entrenched thereafter. Each new article and monograph published in this expansive (and rapidly expanding) field has suggested that Phillips and Sale were, to a large degree, correct—that a new transregional nexus of ideology and institution building did indeed transpire along the southern section of the country, thus uniting citizens from South Carolina and Southern California, Atlanta, Dallas, Miami, and San Diego, behind a shared economic, cultural, and political vision. Though their political attentions were often cast locally, suburban conservatives in Cobb County, Georgia, and Orange County, California, encountered their immediate spatial, racial, fiscal, familial, and cultural realities in very similar ways, and out of this they forged an agenda for national action, one that was on display in Dallas at the 1976 National Prayer Congress.[21]

As other historians are increasingly emphasizing—and as the essays in this volume will illuminate—there are many other Sunbelt political strands that intersect with or run parallel to the conservative movement, all worthy of further attention. Since its very beginnings in the late 1930s and early 1940s, the Sunbelt has, in fact, exported to the nation a remarkable range of left-wing political ideologies every bit as vibrant as those on the Right. Urban historian (and contributor to this volume) Carl Abbott once asserted in the early 1980s that the "typical sunbelt politician" and typical Sunbelt politics were not easily distilled into Kevin Phillips's Republican majority: Jesse Helms, John Tower, Barry Goldwater, and Ronald Reagan may have legitimized Phillips's point, but what about Andrew Young, Tom Hayden, and Jerry Brown?[22] These politicians rode waves of Social Democratic politics generated at the grassroots level as early as World War II, both in conjunction with and response to the coast-to-coast changes in American demographics and political economy. California's evolution suggests a clear example. With wartime defense buildup came population explosion and with that phenomenon, a "white flight" to the "jerry-built" suburbs that Carey McWilliams decried. The white-only suburb quickly became the face of the Cold War, Sunbelt lifestyle, but behind this façade stirred a vibrant, multiracial, urban-based civil rights movement eager to shock the status quo. By the late 1940s, California's Social Democrats were using coalition building and the courts to attack the de jure and de facto underpinnings of Jim Crow in housing, labor, and education, and—thanks to Supreme Court rulings like *Mendez v. Westminster School District* (1946), *Shelley v. Kraemer* (1948), and *Barros v. Jackson* (1953)—the nation was beginning to feel the effect. Similarly, California's rising techno-hubs—evidenced in the aerospace industries and university campuses that encircled its cities—seemed to demand conformity; but in reality, they also spawned a generation of nonconformists who, following Hayden's lead, loudly and effectively objected to the military-industrial complex they believed was running their state and ruining their society.

Situated elsewhere on the political spectrum, liberals and libertarians also shaped and were reshaped by the Sunbelt experience. The California that produced Tom Hayden also produced liberal Democrats Edmund (Pat) Brown and Jesse Unruh, who blended a Social Democratic vision into a more expansive and flexible challenge to right-wing assumptions about economic growth. Between Pat Brown's years as governor during the early 1960s and his son's administration in the late 1970s, Californians helped build a dynamic environmentalist movement by providing models of political advocacy and public policy. Richard G. Lillard's treatise *Eden in Jeopardy: Man's Prodigal Meddling with His Environment—The Southern California Experience* (1966), for instance, implored Americans to learn from the mistakes of the first U.S. Sunbelt experiment. For years, Southern California had become entangled in a "self-fulfilling set of paradoxical assumptions" rooted in the circular logic of progress and an insatiable booster mentality: the more it grew the more it came to believe that only growth was good. The problem, historian Kevin Starr points out, was that "progress . . . could only feed on more progress, lest it fail to believe in itself; and boosterism . . . could only fuel itself with more boosterism, lest it suddenly disbelieve the story it was telling itself."[23]

As new scholarship has shown, Lillard's opinions were echoed by countless other Sunbelt critics in the day. Many faced the prospects of runaway growth, overpopulation, and the exploitation of natural resources head on by building alternative structures of communal thinking and being. Some of the greatest innovations came from "countercultural libertarians" and hip, "lifestyle liberals" who spent the 1970s chasing dreams of the innovative, creative, and environmentally sustainable "micropolitan" city. As Amy Scott asserts in her recent study of Boulder, Colorado, new-generation liberals in emerging communities like Austin, Texas, Santa Fe, New Mexico, and Asheville, North Carolina, melded the participatory democracy and liberation politics of the 1960s with the 1970s socially conscious entrepreneurialism and environmentalism into a broad campaign for organic, holistic cityscapes that encouraged capitalist growth only to the degree it minimized "environmental damage" and maximized "individual and community health." The result of these experiments in freethinking, citizen diplomacy, and cutting-edge planning, Scott states, was a foil to the conservative imperative: "Citizens of these culturally and politically creative cities generated a useful opposition political ideology about the culture and economy of America, the future of American democracy, and America's role in the world."[24] What deeper probing of the Sunbelt political nexus makes clear, then, is that conservatism is hardly the only player in the game. When we explore urban geographies of power, growth ideology, corporatism and the state, political and religious culture, race relations, globalization, and other formative dynamics of change that forged America's southern crescent, we also gain new insight into the way liberalism itself—the arbiter of postwar American politics—was tested, tweaked, and, in some cases, completely reconstituted.

At the very least, these exciting new trends suggest that a moment has arrived for historians to revisit the Sunbelt as an analytic category. This volume works from the premise urban historians agreed on in the 1980s—that the Sunbelt is difficult to pin down as a geographically bounded, culturally and historically unified regional entity. Certainly, concrete markers of something approaching this type of entity exist. Census data, for instance, demonstrate that southern rim states between South Carolina and California have far outpaced the nation since 1950 in population growth (sometimes measuring growth rates ten times the national average), gross domestic product, and investment dollars from the federal government. Beyond demographics, we also see polling data that suggest some level of unity in political behavior across this region, particularly in its sprawling suburban communities. Yet, there is little question that census and polling data only get scholars so far when evaluating the Sunbelt. Scholars regularly point to the fluidity and contingency and abstractness of regional identity; even the West—a land more easily united by myth and natural environment—and the South—more clearly bound by encounters with history, culture, and race—are (and should be) subject to critical review. In the Sunbelt—where unities of myth, environment, history, culture and race are harder to identify—the lack of absoluteness is even more problematic, hence its definition more difficult. But this does not mean that a definition does not exist and is not worth pursuing. In fact, as the essays in this volume underscore, there is something especially intriguing and potentially useful about the Sunbelt because it at once begs for a reworking of the very notion of regionalism in post-World War II America and demands that this notion be flexible and inclusive of the nation, not firm, static, and insular.

Space, Place, and Region

Indeed, the Sunbelt does not describe a regional identity like the modifiers "Southern," "Western," or even "Midwestern; after all, nobody would say, "I am a Sunbelter" or "Damn Sunbelter." But the Sunbelt is a region, nevertheless; and its impact on late twentieth-century America demands that scholars wrestle with its conceptual challenges. Many of the essays in this volume suggest, in fact, that we might better understand certain historical transformations since the mid-twentieth century if we yield the "regional concept" to the "conceptual region." As Robert Goldfield, Matthew Lassiter, Joseph Crespino, political historian Robert Johnston, and others have rightly noted, regional categories often inhibit useful scholarly analysis. However, only by interrogating, historicizing, and naming forces that historical actors inscribe on landscapes can we identify certain patterns of change—patterns described best, though not perfectly, in regional terms. Specifically, this volume of essays finds unity and meaning in the "Sunbelt" through the transformative processes of space making and place making.

As politically and economically created *spaces*, regions represent landscapes with nebulous and constantly shifting boundaries drawn by institutional and individual actors who, over time, create patterns that mark a geography as distinct—as a recognizable region. The following essays will show how a history of industrial-labor relations, infusions of military-industrial complex dollars, post-World War II in-migration, prison construction, Indian policy, and other developments became not only systemic but also embedded into the built environment of the Sunbelt.[25] Authors in this volume study the raised highway, the bulldozed "slum," the sprawling prison complex, and the fast food restaurant as texts for identifying the material contours of a region. They delineate the Sunbelt in corporate, government, organizational, and criminal justice models that replicated themselves most noticeably in the region's metropolitan corridors. By establishing their political economic dominance in the nation's southern rim, these models came to shape urban policy, entrepreneurialism, labor relations, penal management, residential development, and numerous other aspects of political and economic culture for the rest of the country. The Sunbelt thus acted as a national pacesetter.

We also probe the Sunbelt as a culturally defined *place*—a set of ideas born from the spatial transformations just described. Urban historian Dolores Hayden has written that place represents a "powerful source of memory, as a weave where one strand ties to another."[26] But places similarly shape ideas, hopes, identities, visions, and beliefs as concrete physical markers that humans rely upon to make meaning of the world around them. Street names, topographical variations, seasonal climate, and architectural features pattern thought as they pattern landscapes. "Generic Americans become real people in particular places," note Edward Ayers and Peter Onuf; "they put down roots, acquire accents, assume historic burdens."[27]

The Sunbelt started to become a place within the nation's collective imagination decades before it was actually named. Much like the "frontier" of the nineteenth century, push-and-pull factors gave the Sunbelt gravitational force, rendering movement and influx into part of its essence.[28] The migration vectors established during World War II forged imagined links between the region's economic expansion and the hopes for retirement, family life, employment, and recreation that transplants brought with them to their homes in the warmer climate. The Sunbelt of the American mind came to represent a settlement destination—a late twentieth-century frontier wrought by cutting edge military-industrial, information, and telecommunications technology.

As we have already illustrated, however, more than fifty years of debate over urban planning, crime prevention, the civil rights movement, and public education have assigned inconsistent and often contradictory meanings to the place-name Sunbelt. As pundits like Sale and Phillips portrayed competing visions of growth and decline while Weinstein, Firestine, Perry, Watkins, and other scholars debated nuances of the Sunbelt thesis, policymakers involved in acrimonious disputes brought real stakes to the concept. Visions of progress represented by the region's boosters, for example, have become the subject of comic irony in the hands of contemporary artists interested in the noir that lurks right in the midst of that glaring sun. Del Webb, who developed the first iconic Sun City retirement communities in the 1960s, promoted clean, orderly, peaceful, and friendly tract housing to draw senior citizens into the Arizona desert.[29] In the 2007 film *The Savages*, however, that same Sun City landscape represents a veneer rather than a reality of tranquility. Opening images of palm-lined streets, ranch homes, and swim-suited active elders humorously foreshadow the gloomy family drama about to unfold. *The Savages* relies on a Sunbelt irony that has become so ubiquitous in American culture that artists need only show the landscape to evoke paradoxes. Films like *Paris, Texas*, *Little Miss Sunshine*, and *Transamerica* similarly juxtapose desertscapes against highways and big skies to highlight tensions between superficial light and stalking darkness.[30]

The Sunbelt also came into focus as a result of acrimonious political disputes in the late 1970s on the release of President Carter's Commission for a National Agenda for the Eighties, which pitted the economic interests of Northern and Sunbelt cities against each other. Carter's appointed panel, one of nine constituting the Commission, issued recommendations for promoting migration to the region as a catalyst for economic growth. The ensuing outburst of disagreement over the "Policies and Prospects for Metropolitan and Nonmetropolitan America" fueled rivalries between congressional "Sunbelt" and Frostbelt" or "Rustbelt" caucuses. Though these coalitions dissolved by 1990, regional contests over resource allocation nevertheless reinforced the Sunbelt's associations with economic growth and the spectrum of values that Americans ascribed to the transformations wrought by this growth. Proponents championing Sunbelt development and critics lamenting a rootless Sunbelt culture of consumption all shaped the Sunbelt's meanings as a place that coevolved with the material transformations of space. Political-economic structural formations and ideological formations thus shaped and reshaped each other.[31]

The patterns that define the Sunbelt as a political-economic space and imagined modern place fall within the geographic boundaries of the South, West, and Southwest, but two-dimensional maps cannot render the nuances that distinguish these regions from and relate them to one another. Such a perspective fails to conceptualize relative life spans of regions, their competing significance to national identity, their relationships to each other, or the recipes of history, landscape, and culture that define each. The conceptual Sunbelt, in other words, stands on borrowed, refurbished, and rejected mythologies of the South, West, and North. The much talked about "blight" of Rustbelt decay and southern poverty dating back to the nineteenth century, for example, shaped late twentieth-century articulations of imagined Sunbelt progress—how visions of advancement would be realized on the modern infrastructure of Atlanta, Houston, Phoenix, and other metropolitan centers. Some authors in this volume explicitly frame the political, racial, industrial, and entrepreneurial ideals they study as "Sunbelt" developments to characterize how those ideals formed in dialectic with or in opposition to other regional mythologies. These scholars examine discourse—from political speeches and corporate rituals to military parades and neighborhood activist meetings—alongside action, demonstrating how their subjects relied on historical assumptions about the South and West to develop both the ideas and material structures that became the Sunbelt. Whether pushing urban renewal policies to disassociate their cities explicitly from the backwardness of Jim Crow segregation or invoking symbols from western history to represent self-reliance as an anti-statist virtue, Sunbelt powerbrokers drew from established notions of regional exceptionalism to envision a new place of the future.

The South and the West shaped conceptions of the Sunbelt with their deeper roots in national history. James Cobb, C. Van Woodward, and others have traced ideas about Southern backwardness not only back to the all-too-real history of plantation slavery, rural poverty, and racial violence but to an oppositional counternarrative of northern success:[32] "that mythical non-South," writes Cobb, "had become virtually synonymous with America itself."[33] The racial, social, economic, and cultural progress of Northern states came to stand as the history of the United States, casting the South as a degenerate regional aberration to the national paradigm. Regional analysis shows that a mythical non-West, to borrow Cobb's model, also represents the nation, as encapsulated by the expression "back East," with its implications of a universal non-western point of national origin. As New Western historians of the 1980s and 1990s vigorously debated the material questions of where, when, and what defined their region, they also deconstructed the myths of "westernness," particularly the concept of the frontier, what cultural historian Patricia Nelson Limerick has playfully referred to as the "f-word."[34] Limerick notes that as "prosaic" as she and many Westerners may tend to be, she has learned from scholars of Southern exceptionalism that we can study region seriously as a something both "real" and "imagined." "Region is a mental act and region is real," she writes, "at one and the same time."[35]

The Sunbelt maps over the South and West because its conceptual basis in the future has relied on myths that historians of these regions have struggled to problematize. With slogans like "the Charlotte Way" and Atlanta, the "city too busy to hate," economic boosters promoted their cities with indirect references to the virtues of prosperity, tranquility, modernity, and good living associated with the Sunbelt.[36] The word "hate" jettisons associations with the white supremacist South to an imaged past. The Sunbelt of the American mind similarly relies on what Robert Alan Goldberg calls the "cult of true westernness."[37] Stock western heroes of American print and cinema made Stetsons, bolo ties, and cowboy boots into symbols of independence, valor, and authenticity. Historians have documented the ways that politicians, oilmen, and farmers adopted these symbols into their clothing, rhetoric, and lifestyles to associate themselves with the attributes of the western hero. The "cult of true westernness" shaped the Sunbelt as a mythic version of regional history that evoked ideals identical to or in line with Sunbelt boosters.[38] Industrial expansion and metropolitan development could transform the open spaces of the West because the architects of Sunbelt infrastructure wove the "cult of true westernness" into their ideology of growth. Senator Barry Goldwater and Ronald Reagan, moreover, successfully incorporated cowboy imagery in their political personas to portray themselves as embodiments of conservative antistatism and private enterprise.[39]

The efflorescence of scholarly work on urban and metropolitan history in the Southern Rim demands a reassessment of the Sunbelt as a category of historical analysis. Essays that follow will reckon with the particularities of space and place from Atlanta and Miami to Phoenix and Los Angeles. Together, they show how the Sunbelt, as a conceptual category, can reveal historical actors, institutions, relationships, and developments that would be invisible to us without its analytic light (smog-choked as it might be).

Sunbelt Sojourns

The volume's four thematically organized sections highlight new understandings of the Sunbelt. Each part probes a similar set of political, economic, or spatial dynamics and introduces fresh analytical approaches, drawn from recent developments in fields of American race relations, cultural history, conservatism, religion and politics, labor history, business history, Latino politics, and other areas. In one context, these essays reflect the interest among urban historians in the role played by federal and state governments in local, metropolitan growth. In another, they scrutinize racial ideologies and show how the Sunbelt has sparked the formation of "colorblind conservatism," a late twentieth-century means of entrenching racial inequality in the logic of economic and civil rights. Building on the work of environmental historians, a few authors examine relationships between cities and their hinterlands by probing how bureaucracies, migration networks, prison systems, and patterns of land ownership link urban centers with their rural peripheries. Some essays examine how evangelicals defined prosperity as a Christian principle, preached against government "handouts," and sought to make the Sunbelt a "moral geography."[40] The volume also considers how globalization has influenced regional growth in a transnational context, the application of Sunbelt business practices in an international context, and the political impact of demographic change in the Sunbelt's Latino community.

Part I of *Sunbelt Rising*, "Constructing Region," consists of four essays that measure political realignment since the mid-twentieth century. Each contribution addresses a cluster of concerns that operate at the core of Sunbelt studies: can the Sunbelt be thought of as a politically distinctive region, and if so, on what basis and since when? In looking for answers to these related questions, each author points to an evolving conservatism as the axis around which this region came to revolve.

Elizabeth Shermer's "Sunbelt Boosterism: Industrial Recruitment, Economic Development, and Growth Politics in the Developing Sunbelt" documents the probusiness ideology, policies, and political climate metropolitan "boosters" cultivated across the mid-century South and Southwest. After the New Deal and wartime defense spending brought federal dollars and workers southward, Shermer explains, local businessmen sought to recruit manufacturers from "the well-regulated, progressively-taxed" sections of the country by advancing antiunion "right-to-work" legislation and tax breaks, and offering other free enterprise incentives. These boosters also used their power in government to raise revenues for "services, perks, and guarantees" necessary to meet the needs of the highly skilled work force, educate a managerial class, and attract and retain businesses. Shermer's essay asserts that concrete and identifiable political-economic forces at work in Phoenix—her case study—reflected a pattern of regional development across the Sunbelt.

Joseph Crespino's essay, "Strom Thurmond's Sunbelt: Rethinking Regional Politics and the Rise of the Right," shows how the Senate Armed Services Committee's "Muzzling the Military" hearings in 1961–62 rallied Sunbelt citizens behind a potent anticommunist conservatism. The hearings had two purposes: first, to investigate the circumstances that led to General Edwin Walker's admonition by the Defense Department for indoctrinating troops with right-wing propaganda; and second, to explore the Defense Department's alleged censorship of anticommunist statements by high-ranking military officers. Strom Thurmond, a member of the Armed Services Committee, traveled between Washington and Southern California rallying right-wing activists in hopes of defending Walker and pressuring the Kennedy administration to encourage hard-line anticommunism. By doing so, Crespino argues, Thurmond helped destabilize a Southern conservative order previously animated by race and forge a new synthesis that married South and West in the politics of national security. This fusion, strengthened by interlocking ties connecting grassroots activists to structures of power within the nation's capital, allowed the Sunbelt to play a central role in federal politics by the late 1960s.

"Big Government and Family Values: Political Culture in the Metropolitan Sunbelt," by Matthew Lassiter, sheds light on a maturing conservative movement. This study of Cobb County, Georgia, highlights the fusion of defense interests and popular evangelicalism in suburbia, while measuring this amalgam's effect on national politics. Lassiter's exhaustive research documenting change through three decades challenges three theses: the "'Southern Strategy' thesis" that white backlash against civil rights "led directly to a Republican takeover of the region"; the "New Right thesis" that draws "too sharp of a distinction between anticommunist conservatism in the West and racial conservatism in the South"; and the "Religious Right thesis" that overstates grassroots support for "culture war" crusades in conservative-leaning suburbs. He demonstrates that the influx of middle-class migrants from the American Northeast (not just anxious, rank-and-file whites from Atlanta) played a vital role in Cobb County's right turn. This pivot, however, was not decisive. Within the county itself, there occurred a lively contestation between competing political voices, most moderately conservative and a few stridently conservative. Lassiter thus tempers popular assumptions about Cobb County as a natural bastion of the Religious Right and "Republican Revolution" engineered by local U.S. Representative Newt Gingrich. When viewed across time in one place, he suggests, the story of Sunbelt conservatism's ascendancy becomes one of chance and contingency rather than inevitability.

In "Religion and Political Behavior in the Sunbelt," social scientists Lyman Kellstedt and James Guth use statistical analysis to ascertain voting patterns across the South and Southwest from World War II to the present day. Relying on the National Election Studies data, state-level metrics, and their own surveys, they assess the linkages between matters of faith and government in this region, asking all the while what overriding trends allow us to see this political landscape as a whole. Their conclusion for today is that the Sunbelt's religious residents lean slightly more "to the Republican and conservative side" than their counterparts around the country and, by extension, work harder to sustain a more conservative political environment. But they also underscore the problems that arise when trying to map this region as a whole. "From a religious and political perspective," they note with a cautionary tone, the Sunbelt "does not hang together all that well as a single region." While subregions and individual states within this nexus often reveal considerable difference in political behavior, Sunbelt religious adherents now look, think, and act very much like their fellow believers across regions and states. What these two scholars make clear is that the soul of the Sunbelt now looks like the soul of the nation, making it "frustratingly elusive" to quantify, measure, and scrutinize as any type of traditional region.

Part II, "Civil Rights in the Sunbelt," features three essays about race relations that transport their readers from the 1940s to the 1970s, the West Coast to East Coast, and the politics of civil rights to color-blind conservatism. In each case, race serves as the dominant analytic category, bringing attention to the nuances of the Sunbelt's modern, cosmopolitan, multiethnic landscape. This section studies dynamic grassroots campaigns to reconfigure the racial composition of neighborhoods and communities—involving conflict and cooperation between multiple groups operating within different layers of government.

Shana Bernstein launches this section with her essay "From the Southwest to the Nation: Interracial Civil Rights Activism in Los Angeles." Drawn from original research on Los Angeles in the World War II and postwar eras, this essay describes the ways Mexican, Japanese, and Jewish Americans united with other black and white Angelenos to create a progressive alliance that would wield power on behalf of civil rights initiatives. This coalition grew out of the tumult of wartime mobilization, when the city's status as a West Coast arsenal of democracy confronted its citizens with the realities of a pluralism and globalism. Out of shared experiences with localized racial politics and their cosmopolitan and internationalist perspectives, activists joined together in organizations like the Jewish Community Relations Committee, the Community Service Organization, and the National Association for the Advancement of Colored People to promote the common objectives of fair employment, open housing, and racial tolerance, all in hopes of spurring the rest of the nation on toward the same goals. Bernstein thus highlights a different narrative of twentieth-century civil rights activism, one that moves past the southern black-white binary toward a new Sunbelt regionalization marked by interracial cooperation.

In "Sunbelt Civil Rights: Urban Renewal and the Follies of Desegregation in Greater Miami," N. D. S. Connolly also calls for a new regional framework to characterize the racial politics at the center of his study, but to scrutinize the market-driven agenda driving reform in South Florida. At first glance, Miami's would seem to mirror other American tales of urban renewal that posit white city leaders against black residents and business owners against neighbors who lack the political muscle to stop the bulldozers from leveling their communities. Connolly posits another narrative, however. He shows how South Florida's urban renewal campaigns and civil rights movement intertwined, championing race reform and economic development as part and parcel of the same project. Spearheading these efforts, a liberal interracial coalition acted on blended—and somewhat blurred—interests. Black civil rights activists, on one hand, supported renewal as a way to rectify the indignities of segregation through innovative uses of eminent domain and aggressive action against white slumlords. White urban planners and corporate leaders, on the other hand, saw urban renewal as a way to increase tourism while solving the problem of Jim Crow. Connolly characterizes this approach to race reform through land reform as a "Sunbelt" solution—a strategy that ultimately succumbed to the weaknesses of its internal contradictions by entrenching discrimination in subtler market logic.

Daniel HoSang's essay, "Racial Liberalism and the Rise of the Sunbelt West: The Defeat of Fair Housing on the 1964 California Ballot," takes readers back to the West Coast and the politics of race in the Golden State. HoSang examines the debate surrounding Proposition 14, passed by Californians in 1964 before the U.S. Supreme Court ruled it in violation of the Fourteenth Amendment. Rendering all "forced housing" measures illegal in the state, "Prop 14" temporarily barred antidiscrimination laws passed on behalf of nonwhites without making references to race. HoSang's scrutiny of the campaigns for and against the proposition reveals how both sides contributed to conservative racial economic relations, practices, and ideology by reinforcing "color blind conservatism." Even as progressives fought vigorously on behalf of the measure targeted by Prop 14 advocates—the Rumford Fair Housing Act—their defensive campaign affirmed the racial fears and sense of entitlement that caused white property owners to segregate themselves in the first place. HoSang suggests that the "Sunbelt" might be a useful framework for understanding the convergence of conservative and liberal race politics in the postwar era, as well as a lens into the ways history acts as an ideology of political and economic transformations.

In Part III, "Contingent Places," three historians examine how webs of ideas and institutions in the Sunbelt linked central and peripheral places together in unequal relationships of power. Through the study of corporations, prison systems, Indian tribal lands, energy grids, and literature, they show how prosperity and power, from California to Arizona to Georgia, were negotiated on shared and always politically contested physical and cultural planes. The essays collectively argue that to understand the postwar growth of metropolitan regions, analytic focus needs to broaden beyond the perimeters of suburbs and exurbs.

"Sunbelt Lock-Up: Where the Suburbs Met the Supermax," by Volker Janssen, studies the rapid growth of prison populations from California to Florida since 1960. Janssen is interested in how a Sunbelt "culture of control," forged out of Southern and Western penal traditions and emphases on law and order, have made prisons and prison politics a central feature of the modern American state. Besides analyzing incarceration rates, the disfranchisement of felons, sentence lengths, and rates of prison construction, he also tracks geographic patterns and ideological and institutional trends in the growth of the "hyper-carceral state." In the case of California, his focus, he explores the processes by which once isolated, rural prisons have become suburban satellites of urban poverty—opening a new front for racial antagonisms and political struggles over the welfare state. With more than a hint of irony, "Sunbelt Lock-Up" accentuates the fact that the turn to mass incarceration and escalation of prison construction in the Golden State has actually created "penal sprawl." White-flight, middle-class suburbanites now find their residential paradises bordering "on the very institutions meant to render the urban plight of crime, poverty, and racial inequality invisible." Alongside the shopping mall, military installation, and megachurch, Janssen argues, the "supermax" prison needs to be considered an essential feature of life in Sunbelt suburbia.

Andrew Needham builds on Janssen's study of urban sprawl and its impact on rural hinterlands, only with attention to native populations disenfranchised by subtler metropolitan grabs for resources, financial gain, and power. In "Sunbelt Imperialism: Boosters, Navajos, and Energy Development in the Metropolitan Southwest," he examines the layers of bureaucracies involved in constructing the electrical infrastructure stretching from the Navajo Nation to the Sunbelt cities of Phoenix, Albuquerque, and Los Angeles. Needham accounts for the personalities and policies responsible for these energy grids and, in the process, tracks the connections between the material infrastructure that emerged in the postwar Southwest and the networks of political power that gave this region's boosters greater influence in and because of Washington, D.C. With this leverage in hand, these powerbrokers stretched their authority over neighboring Navajo and Hopi lands in hopes of "civilizing" and "modernizing" their inhabitants and gaining access to their resources, both necessary requisites for the realization of a prosperous, sparkling Sunbelt cityscape. Needham thus proves that the study of metropolitan inequality in the Sunbelt must reach beyond urban corridors and suburban borders to include the predominantly rural, native populations living far from the urban core.

The section concludes with Carl Abbott's "Real Estate and Race: Imagining the Second Circuit of Capital in Sunbelt Cities," which examines the construction of a Sunbelt in American fiction published since 1970. Abbott studies the competing claims of indigenous peoples and the modern real estate industry through four key texts: John Nichols's *The Milagro Beanfield War*; Rudolfo Anaya's *Alburquerque*; T. C. Boyle's *The Tortilla Curtain*; and Leslie Marmon Silko's *Almanac of the Dead*. In different ways, these novels explore flows of people and investment across regional and national boundaries, placing New Mexico, Arizona, and California within the emerging postindustrial economy. Just as "southern" and "western" genre categories link works of fiction together based on the ways authors fuse regional landscape and history to imagery, character development and other literary devices, we can now see the contours of recognizable Sunbelt themes in literature as well. The essay also contextualizes this imagined Southwest within a larger Sunbelt literature by drawing comparisons and contrasts to fictions that evoke similar regional themes but in the Southeast, such as Tom Wolfe's *A Man in Full*, Peter Matthiessen's *Lost Man's River*, and the Louisiana novels of James Lee Burke.

Part IV, "The Global Sunbelt," concludes the volume with three essays that examine the Sunbelt's relationship to foreign nations. The studies of demography, globalization, religion, and entrepreneurialism in this section investigate the importance of the national borders to the region's development—how flows of people, capital, and goods across that border have contributed to the business-friendly political-economic conditions that mark the Sunbelt as a borderland region. This section also explores the ways in which the Sunbelt has, most recently, served as the way station for capital investment and workers moving from Latin America into the rest of the United States. Analysis of recent census data and economic and political trends suggests that this shifting trajectory is reconfiguring the political, cultural, and economic patterns of the Sunbelt, even as it is beginning to transform the nation.

"The Marketplace Missions of S. Truett Cathy, Chick fil-A, and the Sunbelt South," by Darren Grem, studies the spiritual, regional, and spatial dimensions of Atlanta-based Chick-fil-A's rise to success. S. Truett Cathy, a devout Southern Baptist, developed a coherent corporate ethos for the company he founded in 1946 out of postwar zeal for development and traditional evangelical values of patriarchy, family, and measured charity. Juxtaposing a "Sunbelt South" against "the other South," Grem examines how Chick-fil-A opened restaurants to capitalize on suburban prosperity while taking advantage of the depressed land values, low wages, and political powerlessness of rural hinterlands to build a deunionized poultry industry. The essay also examines Chick-fil-A's relationship with non-U.S. institutions and actors by following the company's expansion into other countries and documenting its dependence on immigrant laborers. Grem probes Chick-fil-A's Christian volunteer organizations, hiring practices, and meeting rituals, studying how S. Truett Cathy and his family created a moral universe in which their global business ventures represented virtue rather than exploitation.

"Tortilla Politics: Mexican Food, Globalization, and the Sunbelt," by Laresh Jayasanker, examines how patterns of political-economic growth that mark the Sunbelt have spilled across the U.S.-Mexican border. Focusing on a Mexican-owned tortilla monopoly that dominates both the U.S. and Mexican markets, Jayasanker shows how industry leaders learned to capitalize on the border. Companies like GRUMA, Bimbo, Walmart, and ADM took advantage of laws, trade agreements, government connections, and agribusiness technology to consolidate the tortilla market. Operating mainly in Texas and California under American names, these Mexican corporations thrived in large part on Mexican-origin laborers and consumers that put smaller manufacturers out of business. Neoliberals in the Mexican government with ties to GRUMA, moreover, facilitated amalgamation of the tortilla market by eliminating the National Company of Popular Subsistence (CONASUPO), a federal agency that subsidized food consumption. Jayasanker also probes how migration propagated "formula retail" patterns modeled by Walmart that homogenized shopping experiences in U.S. and Mexico for regular border crossers.

Political scientist Sylvia Manzano concludes the volume with a study of the Sunbelt's growing Latino population. "Latinos in the Sunbelt: Political Implications of Demographic Change" tracks this growth, evaluates its political implications, and considers its possible impact on the future political landscape. Relying on data from the U.S. Census Bureau to document the changing racial composition of the Sunbelt between 1970 and the present,

Manzano measures how patterns within the Latino community intersect with the demographic trajectories of other racial minority groups and how unique circumstances in the South and Southwest present different political challenges for Latinos. With the help of data drawn from the registrar of voters, the Voter News Service, and offices of the secretaries of state, she also reveals the impact of demographic changes on voting patterns, policy, and political coalition formation—how, for instance, issues like bilingual education, health-care funding for immigrants, and anti-immigration campaigns encourage Latinos to form voting blocs and defend and advance their political interests. "Latinos in the Sunbelt" concludes by projecting the long-term impact of the aforementioned demographic changes, since naturalization rates and a comparatively youthful population reaching voting age promise to increase Latino representation in the electorate.

Manzano's essay is an appropriate way to end this volume's historical sojourn along the country's southern rim, for it returns us to the present, and in this sense, it is also incredibly well timed. Even as we put the final touches on this volume, we are inundated with news of the latest political crusades sweeping across the Sunbelt, stirring its residents and the entire nation up in another all-or-nothing political discourse of ultimate consequence. Arizona Governor Jan Brewer's signing of a new stringent immigration law, making it easier for police to "identify, prosecute, and deport illegal immigrants," has reignited a firestorm of protest, including from President Barack Obama, who has said this action threatens "to undermine basic notions of fairness that we cherish as Americans, as well as the trust between police and our communities that is so crucial to keeping us safe."[41] During the last ten days, multiracial coalitions of students have picketed the Sunbelt's sprawling, high-tech college campuses and rights activists have marched on its palm-tree-lined, sun-drenched boulevards, begging for this "spiral of pervasive fear" toward immigrants to end. One religious leader in Los Angeles likened Arizona's measure to "Nazism," and Mexico's Foreign Ministry has decried the act as one that promises to harm citizens' rights and American relations with his country.[42] Meanwhile, Phoenix's basketball team promised to don its "Los Suns" jerseys for Game 2 of its quarterfinal series against the San Antonio Spurs, a game to be held on Cinco de Mayo.[43] An act of solidarity with these protestors, Suns management also saw it as good business. In quintessential Sunbelt fashion, the Suns team sought to comment on social policy while ensuring its market shares—to denounce the "mean spirit" of Arizona's immigration law by appealing to the wants (and pocketbooks) of what it hopes will remain an expanding consumer base. Truly, as Connolly shows in this volume, this is market-driven, color-blind, "Sunbelt civil rights" in motion.

As striking as this gesture is and as dramatic as these outpourings of opposition have been, they are not the only recent Sunbelt statements of note. No one, in the summer of 2010, can avoid the latest word about a devastating oil spill in the Gulf of Mexico. With millions of gallons of oil washing up on the Louisiana, Texas, and Alabama shores, and promising to invade Mexico, this catastrophe serves as a reminder that one of the principal sectors on which the Sunbelt was built—energy—knows no boundaries, either in good times or in bad. Always a boon to the Southern Rim's economy, oil has also been a burden at times to its metropolitan residents, hinterlands, natural environment, and international neighbors to the global South. Although trumped by this latest development, another political happening stole the headlines during tax time. A few weeks before Arizona's governor passed her controversial bill, the state's most revered Republican—John McCain—toured locally with Sarah Palin to drum up support for a resurging grassroots Right. On March 27, fresh from her trip with McCain and an appearance in Nashville, Tennessee, Palin addressed a crowd of eight thousand at a Tea Party rally in Nevada. "We're sending a message to Washington," she declared. "It's loud and it's clear, and in these upcoming elections we're saying that the big-government, big-debt, Obama-Pelosi-Reid spending spree is over. You're fired." Anxious to get in one last fiery sound bite, Palin announced to her supporters, "It's not a time to retreat. It's a time to reload."[44] In much the same way populist conservatives stormed the Sunbelt in the late 1970s during California's People's Initiative to Limit Property Taxation (Proposition 13) and other grassroots, antitax campaigns, Palin and Tea Party advocates underscore the fact that as internationalist as one side of the Sunbelt can (and wants to) be, the other side remains decidedly localist. Much like earlier generations of Sunbelt citizens rallied behind Strom Thurmond, Barry Goldwater, and Ronald Reagan, Sunbelt citizens in Palin's and McCain's orb remain steadfast in their belief that a "pristine" frontier freedom is reliant on America's diligent protection of private income, private space, and the free market imperative.

So it is that the multifaceted, polarized politics of place, space, and region have reloaded and resurged in the ever-evolving American South and Southwest. Of course, the impetus and momentum behind Sarah Palin's Tea Party and against Governor Brewer's immigration bill stem from a much larger movement of people and affect a much broader constituency of citizens; after all, Palin and the Tea Party are favorites in Ohio, Montana, and Massachusetts, too, and President Obama—Brewer's most powerful critic—earned his political stripes in Illinois, once the epitome of Rustbelt decline. Yet even in this moment of incredible political ferment and partisan realignment, so much about the future trajectories of Left, Center, and Right—liberalism and conservatism—remain tied to developments along the California-Texas-Florida nexus. In a way, not much seems changed from 1976, when Kevin Phillips and Kirkpatrick Sale debated the merits of a Sunbelt rising and the likes of W. A. Criswell and E. V. Hill heralded its divine destiny. Reading the newspapers and watching the nightly news today, one can't help but conclude that as the Sunbelt goes, still goes the nation.

PART I

Constructing Region

Chapter 1

Sunbelt Boosterism: Industrial Recruitment, Economic Development, and Growth Politics in the Developing Sunbelt

Elizabeth Tandy Shermer

> Few Northeasterners realize the new prominence of the South and West or appreciate that a new political era is in the making.
> —Kevin P. Phillips, *The Emerging Republican Majority,* 1969

In 1969, Kevin P. Phillips earned national recognition with *The Emerging Republican Majority.* He spent more than 500 pages outlining a century of presidential voting patterns and concluded that Richard Nixon's 1968 triumph symbolized the overthrow of an "obsolescent 'liberal' ideology." Many have forgotten the countless charts and maps, but Phillips's five-page section on the "Sun Belt Phenomenon" has had a lasting impact. The amateur statistician argued, "the huge postwar white middle-class push to the Florida-California Sun country (as well as suburbia in general)—seems to be forging a new, conservative political era in the South, Southwest and

Heartland." At the heart of this phenomenon were the blossoming metropolises, "centers of commerce, light industry, military preparedness, defense production and space-age technology, vocational seedbeds of a huge middle class . . . a century removed from the Allegheny-Monongahela Black Country and the dun-colored mill canyons of the Merrimack."[1]

Since *The Emerging Republican Majority* first appeared, scholars have sought to define the boundaries and characteristics of this region. There has been little agreement. Some dismissed outright the assertion that the Sunbelt was, at its essence, conservative. "Sunbelt voters have been inconsistent in enlisting in Phillips' emerging Republican majority," historian Carl Abbott asserted. "The typical sunbelt politician of the last decade may have been Jesse Helms, Jeremiah Denton, John Tower, or Barry Goldwater. It may also have been Tom Hayden, Jerry Brown, Harry Cisneros, or Andrew Young." Many also concluded that the country's southern half was not uniformly vibrant. There were select "sun spots," but, as a whole, the region had not undergone any radical economic or demographic transformation. These experts pointed out that most Sunbelt cities, though admired for their growth and wealth, retained stark inequalities of income and power. With few exceptions, non-Anglo residents and working-class Anglos struggled in this supposedly new South and Southwest.[2]

The true Sunbelt encompassed those large metropolises, Charlotte, Atlanta, Phoenix, and San Diego, where an urban, business-oriented cohort of civic leaders and local and state officials had worked to transcend the authority of the region's old commodity-based production regime. During the 1930s and through the 1950s, a younger generation of boosters marginalized the influence of those elites whose power depended on fortunes made in agriculture, ranching, or mining. As Phillips inferred, relatively advanced manufacturing, a military presence, and a sophisticated set of service and recreational industries displaced traditional sectors. External capital investment proved essential to this development, which, in turn, reinforced an aggressively anti-New Deal, probusiness, progrowth politics. There remained, of course, many smaller cities and towns that received far less warmth from the heat generated by this hyperactive Sunbelt capitalism. In these communities, new manufacturing was often connected to the traditional commodity-based economy, which continued to tether these areas to low-wage, labor-intensive industry and leave them devastated when these textile or low-skill manufacturing enterprises relocated outside the U.S. in the late twentieth century.[3]

A young cohort of well-networked, politically aroused businessmen proved central to Sunbelt growth. Because their fortunes were tied to the fickle commodities market, many urban and small-town professionals, storeowners, and bankers had a vested interest in diversifying area economies, especially after the Great Depression ravaged these sectors. World War II made clear what might be accomplished with enough money and manpower. Under the direction of liberals eager to use industrialization to build a modern Southwest and to restart the South's reconstruction, New Dealers and war planners poured billions of dollars into the military outposts and war production plants. As well-paid military personnel and factory workers spent their paychecks in these cities, bringing these towns out of the Depression, local entrepreneurs and professionals became enthusiastic proponents of a locally based investment strategy that might extend this prosperity into the postwar years.[4]

Demobilization proved a moment of crisis and opportunity for boosters. To attract firms eager to leave the union strongholds in the nation's industrial core, local business leaders endeavored to make their hometowns into oases from the powerful, intrusive liberal regulatory state through local and state policies to create and sustain a "business climate." A business-friendly environment included, generally, low taxes, minimal regulation of business activity, and the enactment of legislation that weakened or discouraged trade unionism. Boosters perfected a language of hypergrowth that enticed a majority of enfranchised voters to grant business carte blanche in the name of economic progress. Stalwarts also created and utilized ostensibly nonpartisan civic reform movements and machines to upend long-standing regional political traditions and ultimately transform mainstream national politics. This new civic elite's industrialization rhetoric stood squarely against the New Deal regulatory ethos. By the early 1950s, liberalism in the developing Sunbelt was already associated with red tape, retarded development, and economic stagnation.

Phoenix, Arizona, was no exception to this regional trend. In 1910, this small town had but 11,000 residents. By 2000, it was a part of a metropolitan region of more than four million people. Led by Barry Goldwater and other leaders of the Chamber of Commerce, the Phoenix elite came to embrace government power and planning in order to reconstruct a developmental state that privileged business by insulating the government from the electorate, weakening organized labor's strength, curbing regulatory restrictions, and reversing progressive tax policies. In the face of greater competition from other cities, the Chamber, through both its private industrial development program and its control over the city government, expanded its efforts to develop a business climate that offered recreational opportunities, top-notch schools, higher education options, and anything else high-tech industrialists demanded. By 1964, more than 700 firms had relocated, started up, or established branch plants in the Phoenix Valley. Such success not only positioned local boosters as leading figures in a national network of likeminded businessmen but also made them key spokesmen for an economic philosophy incongruous with modern liberalism.

An Oasis from the New Deal

The rise of the Sunbelt makes clear the extent to which America's New Deal moment proved but a transitory and contested episode in the construction of late twentieth-century capitalism. Roosevelt Democrats did much to transform the nation's politics and economy. The labor movement, though often embattled, negotiated high-wage and high-benefit contracts in key industries and pushed to expand on progressive federal and state wage, hour, and employment laws. In Congress and in the federal bureaucracy, a cohort of Keynesians and racial progressives made slow but steady progress even in the face of red-baiting and massive resistance to civil rights. This liberal-labor polity was most entrenched in the Northeast, in the industrial Midwest, and along the Pacific Coast but did make inroads in the underdeveloped South and Southwest.[5]

Indeed, the 1930s were a watershed moment that reshaped much of the old South and the Southwest. The Roosevelt era had a dramatic impact on the region's infrastructure and economy. Both the West and the South were undeveloped regions that needed water and power projects as well as investment funds and credit. The South was almost uniformly monocultural, with specific subregions dependent on cotton, sugar, rice, or tobacco. The western economy was more diverse but also linked to the land: The economic pillars were some combination of ranching, mining, farming, and tourism. Both regions had little manufacturing. Southern planters exhibited a sustained hostility toward industry because urbanism and wage work seemed a threat to the regional caste system that kept African Americans at the lowest rung in the suthern cultural hierarchy but that also stopped poor whites and the small class of urban professionals and shop owners from challenging the rule of the old southern elite.[6]

From Washington, liberals recognized the potency of these regional roadblocks to democratic progress in the South and West. They dared not directly confront racial hierarchies or the power of the southern plantation elite, whose representatives maintained a veto over virtually every piece of progressive legislation making its way through Congress. Instead, New Dealers thought that economic development and the modernization of agriculture would eventually ameliorate the racism and gothic poverty of the region. New Dealers preoccupied with the West did not see its institutionalized racism as clearly as that manifested in the South's Jim Crow system. Instead, developmental liberals, in Washington and in the region, worried over the aridity and poor infrastructure that limited the West's entrepreneurial promise. New Dealers did not envision the money sent to relieve southwesterners, water the desert, or bring electricity to the frontier as having much impact on Western racial norms or class hierarchies. Public projects were about improvement and possibility. The 20-million acres of land the New Deal watered in the mountain and Great Basin states created new settlement and farming opportunities throughout the region, or, as one National Reclamation Association president explained, ensured "a new West—a bountiful dwelling place—using the natural resources of a pioneer empire."[7]

These federal efforts coexisted with a complementary private drive for investment and economic diversification. The push, which varied in scale, scope, and possibility, arose from the regions' small coterie of small town professionals, businessmen, and storeowners. Most wanted to supplement or supplant the farming, mining, and ranching economies. They often worked with New Dealers to recruit new industries, but that cooperation was always tempered by a profound and growing mistrust of the Rooseveltian state and the social liberalism it fostered.[8]

Thus, local boosters relied on home-grown investment. Some experimented with community drives to raise capital on the assumption that such contributions would yield benefits for the entire community. In Albany, Georgia, boosters raised $10,000 from residents with a public subscription drive to underwrite a new hosiery plant. Executives promised the facility would provide jobs for local high school graduates. There were a few dynamic southern cities, most notably Atlanta and Charlotte, that began to separate themselves from agricultural interests, mostly through their ability to tap into government coffers. By the end of the 1920s, banking, aviation, and recreation had already come to Charlotte. The Federal Reserve had a branch in the town, which made it the Carolinas' financial center. The city's airport provided both passenger and mail services. Because of the Chamber's aggressive efforts to promote the city, Charlotte emerged out of the 1930s with more than seventy-five new manufacturing outfits. Boosters made good use of federal programs, which included lobbying for New Deal monies to expand the airport and stumping for war production facilities and military bases. Charlotte was clearly one of the exceptions. Most community development initiatives merely reproduced the low-wage economy in an urban setting. Industrialists interested in moving to the South wanted cheap, unskilled, white laborers, whose employment in textile mills, sawmills, and foundries could do little to transform or expand the South's still primitive economic base or mitigate its systemic, jarring inequalities.[9]

The most successful Southwest boosters were those who embraced lucrative manufacturing, reform, and politicking. The San Jose City Council gave its Chamber of Commerce public funds for a national publicity campaign in 1938. In an effort to join the emerging West Coast industrial garrisons, the San Jose boosters targeted high-tech electronics firms. In 1938, the founders of Hewlett-Packard arrived. IBM, General Electric, and Kaiser began operations with ten years. In Austin, a new cohort of young businessmen overthrew the chamber's Old Guard who had opposed industry during the interwar period. The upstarts forced the resignation of the organization's secretary and embarked on a publicity campaign similar to that of San Jose. The new leadership worked willingly with liberals, including Texas congressmen like Lyndon Baines Johnson, who helped direct federal projects to the area.[10]

World War II wrought the most dramatic efforts to industrialize and modernize the South and Southwest along New Deal lines. Liberals wanted to disperse industries, both as a defense measure and as a tool to develop the nation's hinterland. In May 1940, President Roosevelt decreed that the bulk of war production would occur in the nation's interior. Such investment, as Matthew Lassiter describes in his essay in this collection on the Bell Bomber plant in Marietta, Georgia, depended on a joint effort among townspeople, business groups, city fathers, and federal officials, whom local congressional representatives often lobbied, to secure military contracts. Development was decidedly uneven. By and large, labor-intensive projects, military bases, airframe factories, ship fabrication, and munitions came to the South, whereas the Southwest housed these and more sophisticated, high-tech initiatives, including radar and navigation systems.[11]

Southern and southwestern towns blossomed. Downtown merchants, bar owners, restaurateurs, and hoteliers reaped the benefits of the deals to open military bases and manufacturing facilities. Yet, even before the war's end, demobilization threatened to bring this region-wide boom to an end and thus inaugurated a concerted effort from many in the South and Southwest's larger cities to attract manufacturing. Boosters, who had lobbied for investment during the 1930s and 1940s, now used their economic power to transform local, state, and regional politics to privilege business and keep manufacturing investment coming in the postwar years. Hypergrowth policies were not grounded in a crude antistatism. Though some business groups experimented with private industrial recruitment through Chambers of Commerce or trade associations, they found these methods increasingly ineffective. Instead, local business and civic leaders sought to use governmental power to redraft laws and ordnances to create a business climate amenable to industry and enterprise.[12]

Capital's postwar internal movement depended on both local initiatives to diversify the economy and corporate interest in moving. Both parties had material and ideological motives. Many retailers and professionals had a vested interest in building a more stable work force with more disposable income. Yet many were also ideologically opposed to modern liberalism, much like the executives whom they lured to the emerging Sunbelt. These CEOs also benefited from uprooting or establishing new operations in their hinterlands where they could better serve emerging markets and enjoy significant savings in overall operating costs. Surveys of manufacturers even indicated that corporate officers often conflated ideological and material reasons for the closure of Northern plants and the dispersal of industry. "Property taxes are important," one Northeastern business owner noted, "but greater importance is given to Massachusetts politicians['] desire to initiate and implement legislation which will get them votes from the labor unions. . . . The legislators must be made to realize that they cannot kill the 'Goose that lays the golden egg.'"[13]

The postwar, business-led drive for investment in the developing Sunbelt ranged widely. Often, boosters secured land, offered specific tax breaks, or pursued a new recruitment policy as a part of a general attempt to attract one specific firm. Local initiatives also included a broad overhaul of the area's "business climate," a term that economists, industrial relations experts, executives, and boosters employed to describe the general effort to make a locale attractive to all investors and, hence, competitive with other developing areas. Scholars defined this "business-friendly" ethos as more than just material advantages. By the mid-1950s, analysts concluded that firms sought such an environment, which included not just taxes and restrictions on union security but also the kinds of public services, including roads and schools, that were necessary for a firm to attract the desired work force. The elements that composed a good business climate multiplied throughout the postwar period as recruitment drives intensified throughout the South and Southwest, especially after Steelbelt boosters also began to adopt similar promises and policies in order to retain existing industry.[14]

The construction, maintenance, and expansion of the business climate required southern and southwestern businessmen to have real political power. From the 1930s through the mid-1950s, a business-driven wave of municipal reform placed the urban economic elite in control of the regions' cities and towns. Within the broad rubric of good government reform, Anglo businessmen started nonpartisan civic reform leagues, displaced an older generation of politicians with a new industry-minded cohort, and drafted new or extensively-revised city charters. In general, the goals were the same: economic growth, urban dynamism, and political change through concerted efforts from business owners, professionals, and upwardly mobile middle-class suburbanites. The desired effect, if not the actual outcome, was to put these industry-minded, largely Anglo businessmen in charge of municipal affairs. With both public and private resources at their disposal, these businessmen-politicians had the political power and financial backing to undertake expansive development initiatives. Moreover, their growth politics were steeped in antiliberal rhetoric, which made the New Deal regulatory state and an empowered trade union movement anathema to economic dynamism and affluence.[15]

From the standpoint of the Anglo economic elite, municipal reform in the name of industrialization proved most successful in the Southwest. Across the arid states, municipalities mandated at-large elections and abandoned commission-style government for an appointed, powerful city manager-based governmental structure. Though cities were racially and economically diverse, the majority of votes and elected officials came from affluent, Anglo neighborhoods because at-large voting arrangements stopped poor, working-class, or minority communities from sending representatives to city hall. Thus, between 1931 and 1971, 157 of 182 Dallas City Council members had the Citizens' Charter Association's endorsement; between 1955 and 1971, San Antonio Good Government League candidates only lost four City Council races; the Albuquerque Citizens' Committee never lost a race between 1954 and 1966; and Phoenix's Charter Government Committee enjoyed victories in every City Council race for twenty-five years. In contrast, southern white businessmen found themselves with less power and control. Southern municipal politics were also transformed during the 1930s and 1940s. An early challenge to the urban, white businessmen came from the Supreme Court, which ruled consistently against white-only primaries in the mid-1940s. These decisions triggered voter registration drives in the urban South. In Atlanta, activists tripled the number of black registrants in Fulton County in just three weeks. By decade's end, Atlanta's white political elite had to respond to these constituents' demands, particularly the most affluent and influential. Throughout southern cities, there were similar biracial coalitions. Though these political arrangements left African Americans, for all intents and purposes, as junior partners and second-class citizens, white southern businessmen-politicians still had less overall control over their cities than their southwestern counterparts, whose machinations occurred outside the national spotlight on southern race relations.[16]

State legislatures also became incubators for conservative, pro-growth, anti-New Deal policies. High taxes and union power, which local governments could not fully control, were key considerations for local boosters. A wave of probusiness tax legislation sought to improve the business climate in order to lure industry out of the Northeast and coastal California. In 1949, for example, the Reno Chamber of Commerce pushed a "free-port" bill through the Nevada legislature, which permitted manufacturers to avoid property taxes on goods officially "in transit" from or en route to California ports. The State Assembly relaxed these rules throughout the decade, which allowed companies to process materials or engage in some manufacturing without fear of such levies. This loophole soon made the Nevada-California border a center of warehousing, wholesaling, and light manufacturing. As competition between burgeoning Sunbelt metropolises increased, local and state governments crafted numerous policies to reduce other taxes, including: property and sales tax exemptions for new industry, tax "freezes" for new businesses, negotiations on local property tax rates, guaranteed write-offs, and even promises of favorable assessments.[17]

This regional investment drive led to an overall reduction in corporate taxes in the early postwar years, especially as rusting Steelbelt communities emulated their Sunbelt competitors in order to retain industry. Nationwide, companies paid 46 percent of federal revenues in 1950 and 40 percent in 1964. There was a similar drop in business contribution to state and local treasuries. Tax payments to nonfederal governments rose from $5.7 billion to $14.5 billion but still represented an overall drop in responsibility (from 39.9 to 34.6 percent). Companies did spend $500 billion on new plant and equipment during this period, but taxes accounted for only 22.6 percent of revenue in 1950 and just 18 percent in 1964. Moreover, the end of wartime price controls in 1946 allowed businesses to pass on expenses to customers, which generated an inflationary spiral that business blamed on organized labor's demands for higher wages and benefits. At the same time, individual taxpayers assumed a much larger share of the burden because of increased property, sales, and income taxes.[18]

"Right-to-work" legislation was also vital to Sunbelt business climates. These antiunion statutes, passable by the individual states under the 1947 Taft-Hartley Act, prohibited unions from making membership a requirement for work in an organized shop. In much political rhetoric of the time, this arcane legal language was often simplified to a ban on the union shop, which captured the outright hostility to labor power as a whole. The earliest right-to-work referendums were in the South and Southwest. Floridians and Arkansans passed the first of such statutes in 1944, even before Taft-Hartley permitted states to legislate such restrictions. By 1960, most Sunbelt states had such provisions; only Colorado, California, and New Mexico did not have a broad right-to-work law.[19]

During the next two decades, with fierce, national competition for investment, Sunbelt boosters used more than low taxes and union avoidance legislation to attract Northern industry. They raised some local and state government taxes on homeowners in order to provide the services, schools, and investment guarantees that they thought necessary to compete for enterprises on the move. Chamber men eager to attract firms with a well-educated, highly skilled workforce often had to spend money on cultural and recreational opportunities, such as golf courses, tennis courts, theaters, museums, and sports teams. Thus, the money and power necessary to compete for industry, particularly the lucrative high-tech manufacturing outfits, increased. To compensate for these costs, state expenditures, across the country, rose almost 10 percent per year during the 1960s, while continued pressure to cut taxes on industry slowed revenue growth.[20]

Because coffers did not fill at the same rate that the government spent, Sunbelt businessmen-politicians championed the physical growth of their municipalities. Boosters needed suburban property owners to tax in order to fund their corporate welfare states. Across the nation, cities found that their dwindling tax revenues were often a consequence of their inability to tax subdivisions that sprouted up outside their borders and took advantage of municipal services and infrastructure. Many local governments looked to take possession of ballooning, parasitic suburbs beyond city limits to secure more revenue but also to control sprawl and increase the number of affluent, white voters, who were the electoral base for these chamber political machines. Such annexation policies were most successful in the developing Sunbelt. Most regional metropolises, and even the smaller cities that lay in their shadows, more than doubled in land and population. Vast stretches of farmland or empty territory, which surrounded these towns, provided ample area for expansion. The suburbs annexed were relatively new developments in which most residents lacked any real civic investment. State laws also provided fewer barriers toward annexation than in the Northeast and Midwest. North Carolina and Tennessee statutes enabled automatic incorporation of an adjacent territory when an outlying area's population reached a set threshold. In Texas and Arizona, businessmen-politicians pushed through annexation laws that allowed big cities to expand their borders without the consent of the affected property owners.[21]

With a growing homeowner tax base, local elites continued to build their business climates. Education emerged as a critical, costly item in industrial recruitment packages. Good schools and advanced educational opportunities were requirements for light electronics, aerospace, and high-tech industries. These firms needed a research university as a part of their local research and development nexus and had become increasingly eager to hire locally to save the added expense of importing talent from top schools. For many Sunbelt cities, higher education promised not only to diversify the local economy but also to transcend an area's traditional base. Boosters, then, were key to the postwar development of, as Margaret Pugh O'Mara deemed them, "cities of knowledge." California's Silicon Valley, with Stanford University at its center, stands out as the example of such a scientific hub. In the early Cold War period, the school received a significant share of federal research monies, began an aggressive effort to recruit top engineering and scientific faculty from the Ivy League, and poured portions of its substantial endowment and land holdings into faculty housing and an early research park.[22]

Few public or private universities could compete with this archetype, but higher education seemed imperative for growth and dynamism. By the mid-1960s, expenditures were high throughout the Southwest and select parts of the South that had prioritized a move toward the most lucrative, manufacturing industries. Research institutions by themselves did not guarantee high-tech investment. Booster activism was key, even in North Carolina's much-celebrated region of knowledge. The Research Triangle, situated in the pastoral area between the three major research universities in Raleigh, Durham, and Chapel Hill, had a tumultuous start. In the late 1950s, a University of North Carolina faculty member, backed by Governor Luther Hodges, a former textile executive, proposed an industrial park to help the area move past its traditionally low-skill, low-capital manufacturing base. Interest was low. Hodges left public office in 1963 to dedicate himself to the Research Triangle Foundation. He relied on his contacts in the textile industry to attract IBM, which led to a marked increase in corporate investment in the region. By the 1970s, the foundation began to turn away business, particularly from manufacturing outfits. During this decade, the Triangle emerged as a leader in medical technologies and research, which positioned it perfectly to survive the coming manufacturing crisis and thus thrive in the lucrative, late twentieth-century knowledge economies.[23]

"The Prototypical Sun Belt City"

Before the Research Triangle emerged as a force in biotech, Phoenix had spent twenty years at the forefront of the high-tech manufacturing economy. The town with little industry and just 11,000 residents in 1910 emerged as a force in light electronics and aerospace during the 1950s and 1960s and took its place among the ten largest cities in the U.S. by 1980. Hence, Phoenix loomed large in the creation of a Sunbelt ethos. Journalists called it "a developer's city, a pivot in the Southwest's growth machine, . . . [and] the prototypical Sun Belt city."[24]

Within both the South and Southwest, Phoenix's businessmen-politicians stood out in the vigorous, regional campaigns to remake local and state politics, create a competitive business climate, and transcend the tumultuous commodity-based regional economy. Overall, the Southwest reached Sunbelt status first. National attention to conflicts over civil rights in the South directed national attention away from similar abuses in the systematically segregated West. Southern boosters struggled to attract the high-wage, high-skill industries, whose educated work forces bristled at moving South at the moment when residents were closing schools rather than integrating them. The West was decidedly more dynamic. In regard to the nationwide surge in trade, services, and government employment, the Southwest was responsible for the lion's share, with California, Texas, and other Western states responsible for 30.5, 15.9, and 14.2 percent of the increase between 1939 and 1954 respectively. Industrialization was still uneven in the Sunbelt West. Even Boulder, Colorado, renowned for its leadership in space-age technology and research, developed its science economy more slowly. In the early 1950s, Boulder boosters were eager for some type of investment but did not begin pursuing high-tech industries aggressively until later in the decade, when they worked in partnership with University of Colorado officials to capitalize on the town's open skies, proximity to Denver, and research university.

Coastal California and Phoenix stood out as the early leaders in the most lucrative sectors responsible for the region's dynamism. The West Coast's industrialization had begun in the interwar period. Indeed, Phoenix boosters initially considered themselves to be in metropolitan California's hinterland and looked on the Los Angeles, San Diego, and San Francisco chambers of commerce as models for attracting lucrative industries. By 1962, Phoenix had emerged as a Western center for electronics and aerospace. The two giants in the region were still Los Angeles and San Francisco. Both Phoenix and San Diego were well behind but essentially tied in overall productivity and sales. Phoenix, unlike military-dominated San Diego, was more than just a fortress city. Only half the firms in Phoenix produced products under government contracts because boosters had sought a diversified industrial base, which further distinguished the Arizona metropolis from most cities in the South and many in the West. Politics had been the key to Phoenix's rise. The Valley's top professionals and entrepreneurs had far more control over the City Council and state legislature. Throughout the Sunbelt, most famously in the South and California, but not in Arizona, malapportionment stymied much of the urban vote to structure a business climate for manufacturers, not agriculturalists, miners, or ranchers.[25]

Local boosters had worked through the Phoenix Chamber. In the territorial period, members busied themselves with promoting the area as a tourist destination, urging Arizonans to buy locally, and trumpeting central Arizona's agricultural bounty. The Great Depression transformed this organization. The next generation of businessmen was convinced that the leadership, who had resisted large-scale outside investment and development of a manufacturing base, would prevent Phoenix from growing into a real metropolis. One lawyer later reflected, "There was a feeling that we had work to do to make it a bigger and better town."[26]

The founding group of booster-modernizers came from the city's most profitable businesses, particularly its banks, law firms, newspapers, and major stores. Like other southern and southwestern professionals and owners, they perfected an anti-New Deal growth politics that relied on bringing businessmen from out behind their office doors and into the very public, visible, political work of attracting industry, overturning liberal reforms, and convincing the local electorate to embrace the boosters' path toward prosperity and investment. The Phoenix's chamber's political program and its underlying business philosophy cannot be explained by its place in the West. The young upstarts who took over the association in the 1930s were not all from the region. Some traced their families back to the state's territorial days. Others migrated to Phoenix with hopes of escaping the Northeast and Midwest, over which these transplants thought the New Dealers exercised too much control. A few also came for the weather and their health. Plus, many of these leading figures, including the Arizona natives, received their bachelors, law, and business degrees from universities in the East and Midwest, including George Washington University, the University of Michigan, and Harvard University.[27]

The city's top young newsmen, lawyers, bankers, and retailers were awakened politically in the 1930s and began actively working against both the liberals and the city's older coterie of politicians in the 1940s. Each played a vital role in the broad movement. "You can't do it individually," a leading litigator explained, "It was a network." Journalists, newspaper owners, and radiomen had a monopoly on news sources, which allowed them to set the debate over Phoenix's economic and political future. The most powerful, Eugene Pulliam, had a media empire in the Southwest and Midwest, which was infamous in liberal circles for its conservative slant.

Lawyers drafted new legislation, including the state's right-to-work referenda, and defended them in the courts. Bankers financed the Chamber's industrial recruitment campaigns and broad political initiatives. The retailers, recognizable because of their stores throughout the state, served as the face of the Chamber's industrialization initiative and its political work.[28]

Among this Chamber elite, Barry Goldwater was the most famous and played an early, outsized role in this general effort to remake Phoenix. Arizonans knew of him before he ran for public office because of his family's department store chain and his thrill-seeker persona. His notoriety grew during the Depression when he made a name for himself as a guest editorialist for the *Phoenix Gazette*. Within its pages, he urged business owners to band together in order to challenge liberal politicians and programs. In one of his earliest editorials, "Scaredee-Cat" (1939), he lashed out at businessmen for not challenging the "minority groups who are causing the tax increases" and for not "wagging their tongues where they will do the most good: in political offices." His disgust for the "American businessman," "the biggest man in this country . . . afraid of his own shadow," was palpable. "He is the man who condemns, and sometimes justly so," the Phoenician charged, "the politician over his luncheon tables and his desks and in his other very private conversations, but never in the open where his thoughts and arguments would do some good toward correcting the evils to which he refers in private." Goldwater also directed his rage at New Dealers and union leaders. In "A Fireside Chat with Mr. Roosevelt" (1938), Goldwater questioned

> just where you are leading us. Are you going further into the morass that you have led us into or are you going to go back to the good old American way of doing things where business is trusted, where labor earns more, where we take care of our unemployed, and where a man is elected to public office because he is a good man for the job and not because he commands your good will and a few dollars of the taxpayers' money?

The worst move, from Goldwater's standpoint, was "turn[ing] over to the racketeering practices of ill-organized unions the future of the working man. Witness the chaos they are creating in the eastern cities. Witness the men thrown out of work, the riots, the bloodshed, and the ill feeling between labor and capitol [sic] and then decide for yourself if that plan worked."[29]

This clarion call energized Valley businessmen. Out of this rage grew a veritable juggernaut of boosters dedicated to reengaging with politics, overhauling the Chamber, and embarking on large-scale industrial recruitment. They reasserted themselves into politics vigorously. In the 1930s and 1940s, Democrats seemed unchallengeable; there were four registered Democrats for every Republican. During the war, the outnumbered GOP met at a local hotel. One member recalled, "We had a room that was, ohhh, very, very small, for the state meeting." Yet, the Democratic Party was hardly a monolith. Many members did not identify with the New Dealers and found themselves more in line with the Phoenix business-minded Republicans who were reshaping and reinvigorating the organization through impressive campaigns and registration drives. Republican membership rose steadily during the 1950s, while the number of Democrats increased at a much slower rate. Democratic ranks even declined during the mid-1950s. Indeed, by 1960, the GOP had chipped away at the Democratic Party's tremendous number of registrants.[30]

The Chamber of Commerce men also threw themselves into city politics. Since the early 1940s, they had tried to exert more control on local affairs but found themselves stymied by an old charter that vested power in city commissioners who served staggered two-year terms. There was already conflict between the city's Old Guard of small storeowners, mostly the city's suppliers of construction materials and other necessities, and liberal Democrats. These local New Dealers hated the spoils system that seemed to stymie their efforts to democratize and build modern Phoenix. Yet these liberals' schema for governmental reform clashed with the chamber leadership's plans for the city, which mirrored other Sunbelt boosters' policies that constrained popular participation by empowering unelected city managers and championing at-large, not ward, elections.

The Phoenix Chamber men went beyond just campaigning for reform: they ran for and held public office under the newly formed Charter Government Committee (CGC) in order to carry out their vision for Phoenix. The first meeting was held in the summer of 1949. Among the eleven assembled, four ran on the CGC's first City Council ticket. From this initial meeting, the CGC grew from a reported twenty-nine activists to nearly 300 members by the 1960s. Most hailed from the more prosperous parts of town, over 90 percent resided in the wealthy, Anglo northern enclaves. In the 1949 election and through most of the CGC's twenty-five-year reign, the ticket was weighted with successful Anglo businessmen. The leadership constructed a ticket to mask their intent to ensure their control over the city. In 1949, they consciously chose one woman and balanced the committee between six different religious denominations, including Judaism, Catholicism, and Mormonism. The illusion of bipartisanship and nonpartisanship was also critical. Though all candidates ran without a listed party affiliation, the CGC carefully selected known Democrats, but half of the candidates were businessmen Republicans, which was not an accurate reflection of the partisan split in Phoenix or Arizona.[31]

Although the CGC celebrated its lengthy membership rolls in its campaign literature, the Selection Committee, which put together the ticket every two years, was much smaller. One founding member later explained that only toward the end of the CGC's reign did it grow to twenty-two members. CGC higher-ups later admitted that the organization was very exclusive. "It was all done in secret," one remembered, "and behind—or [in] the smoke-filled room, we would go after [candidates] and get them—persuade them to run." "We had no on-going organization. We had no by-laws. We had no dues. We had no permanent staff," one recounted. "It was very much ad hoc." While jurors insisted on term limits for candidates, the Selection Committee imposed no such restrictions on themselves. "In a sense we'd start up all over again," another later clarified, "but it was generally pretty much the same group that came together."[32]

In newspaper coverage and campaign ads, a vote for the CGC slate in 1949 was lauded as a measure to ensure that Phoenix had a "sound business basis." As in other emerging metropolises, this common refrain emphasized businessmen's ability and right to rule and to emphasize the need for public support for the Chamber's industrial recruitment initiative. Besides their campaign rhetoric, the four CGC-endorsed ballot initiatives encapsulated the committee's broader agenda. The first three proposals focused on increasing the City Council's power and efficiency over municipal affairs, thus strengthening the businessmen's political power. The final proposition was a part of the Chamber men's long-standing opposition to taxes and redistribution. This Chamber-drafted and -recommended measure eliminated taxes on inventory, both for raw goods used in manufacturing and for finished products ready to be shipped, and also scaled back the tax on equipment used in manufacturing. This proposal had no other purpose than to attract industrialists and wholesalers, whom the chamber had identified as central to its plans for Phoenix. The CGC deemed these levies bad for the economy because "these taxes cause production costs to be higher here than in other areas, making it undesirable for manufacturers to locate here. Thus these two taxes have been keeping many manufacturers out of Phoenix, thereby robbing us for jobs for people and of increased prosperity."[33]

The CGC's resounding 1949 victory only set the stage for the Chamber's broad industrial recruitment efforts. Over the next thirty years, members concerned themselves with a general drive both to build a good business climate and to negotiate specific deals with major corporations. The Chamber's Industrial Development Program began formally in March 1948. This project inaugurated an even more cohesive, systematic effort to industrialize the Phoenix area. Leading Chamber members, including Goldwater, worked on the Industrial Development Committee, which shouldered the larger organization's direct investment efforts and cooperated with other committees focused on complimentary projects and organizational goals. Within the main taskforce, subgroups tackled compiling information for new firms, advertising and publicity, industrial outreach, coordination with other Arizona business organizations, and fundraising for recruitment campaigns.[34]

From the outset, the Industrial Development Committee focused on providing a diversified, "well balanced" economy based on industrialized agriculture, tourism, wholesaling, distribution, and manufacturing. Boosters prioritized light electronics and aerospace manufacturing and research and development because they worried over keeping their outdoor playground pristine, protecting the water supply, and controlling who would live beside them. High-tech enterprises were lucrative, high profile, and, relative to heavy industry, modest in their needs for water and power. A leading member stated that the Chamber "did not want dirty industries." "There was talk of a refinery in this area," he remembered, "and . . . we did our best to kill it." This concern for "clean industry," as one lawyer called it, also went to the heart of the Chamber elite's vision for an Anglo, affluent, industrial Phoenix with no dependence on agriculture and mining. Electronic firms, he explained, were "inclined to bring people with somewhat higher income—engineers and people who had somewhat higher income than you might otherwise have." The Chamber, in fact, only entertained the oil company's offer if the factory was more than thirty miles outside the city limits.[35]

Throughout this period, boosters also crafted specific policies to maintain their area's competitiveness with other emerging Sunbelt metropolises.

Politics, labor, and taxes were the Phoenix Chamber's core concerns. Unlike in the South and parts of the Southwest, Phoenix boosters had a strong voice in the legislature. Moreover, the Industrial Development Committee's first chairman recognized the importance of adequate representation. He warned executive officers, "industry must have the assurance it will receive a fair deal from the locality in which it locates" and thus prioritized explaining the importance of industry to voters, especially since their support was needed to elect businessmen, or their preferred candidates, and pass local initiatives to change the tax code, amend labor statutes, or overturn city ordinances. Antiunion legislation stood out as a major facet of the Phoenix business climate. Arizonans passed the first right-to-work law in the Southwest and then further strengthened management's hand in the 1950s when the legislature passed laws restricting picketing and the negotiation of collective bargaining contracts.[36]

Boosters also constructed a particularly inviting tax code. The Chamber of Commerce targeted levies in and around the city of Phoenix and the state of Arizona. For example, in 1952, the organization fought the county inventory tax on wholesalers and retailers. The reduction or elimination of this duty required working with other business groups around Arizona because the decision was left to the Arizona County Assessors Association. The Phoenix Chamber led the way in organizing statewide support. With this pressure to bring county taxes in line with Phoenix duties, the Association agreed to cut the valuation from 45 to 35 percent of the cost in January 1953. At the state level, businessmen pushed through impressive breaks for aerospace, electronics, and computer manufacturers. Legislators signed off, for example, on a repeal of the tax on sales to the federal government, an exemption on inventory, and a loophole that permitted businesses to subtract the amount firms paid to the federal government when figuring what they owed Arizona.[37]

These provisions were particularly important to the high-tech companies that Phoenicians courted. Arizona's tax code privileged these industries because it exempted inventory when figuring property taxes, a bonus for firms that maintained a large stock of high-value products. Computers, semiconductors, electronics, and other scientific instruments were often worth much more than a plant's other equipment or property. Utah, New Mexico, and California, comparatively, levied more overall dues on electronics and aerospace manufacturers than Arizona. In terms of total tax burden, across the board, Arizona fared well in comparison to these Sunbelt

West states. Arizona's corporate income tax was less than California's and Colorado's. Utah and New Mexico had a lower rate but did not allow companies to deduct their tax payments to the federal government. Arizona was also competitive with those outside the Southwest. In 1957, Arizona firms paid just 32.7 percent of the tax burden, which was just 0.5 percent higher than the South's overall average and much lower than the tax burden for New England, Mid-Atlantic, and Great Lakes regions, as well as for the nation as a whole. In 1962, property taxes on businesses accounted for 4.9 percent of the state's tax revenue, just above the traditionally low-tax Southeast states.[38]

Higher education became a cornerstone of the Phoenix Chamber's industrial development initiative. As regional competition increased, Phoenix boosters faced increasing difficulties satisfying firms who wanted a scientific community to better aid technological innovation. By the mid-1950s, many of the city's money-making firms, most notably AiResearch and Motorola, had tired of importing engineers, scientists, and skilled laborers. Potential investors began to demand a research university to compliment their research and development facilities. In contrast to other cities that sought knowledge-based industry, Phoenix seemed at a tremendous disadvantage. The city had neither a research university nor a tradition of technical education at the local teacher's college.

Arizona State University (ASU) emerged out of a broad confluence of forces, interests, and political ambitions. In 1945, Arizona's largest postsecondary schools were in Flagstaff, Tempe, and Tucson. The latter housed the state's only university, the land grant, agriculturally oriented University of Arizona, so its representatives had the most seats on the Board of Regents. By the mid-1940s, the Phoenix Valley had grown into the state's population center, but there were few educational options. Returning servicemen were especially frustrated that Maricopa County could not provide them with the educational opportunities the GI bill guaranteed. A broad coalition formed after the war, including not only local chapters of the American Legion but also farmers who hoped for a closer agricultural research station, the local newspaper, and the Chamber, which now included electronics manufacturing executives in its top leadership.[39]

Phoenix boosters had the political influence and the deep pockets needed to build ASU and its high-profile engineering department. Two leading Chamber men joined the Regents in the late 1940s. Another served as governor in the early 1950s and provided the crucial vote when, in 1954, the Regents finally agreed to expand Arizona State's curriculum, which made it, because of the new emphasis on graduate and undergraduate education in the hard sciences and engineering, a college in name only. To facilitate development of a first-rate engineering program, Phoenix aerospace and electronics manufacturers helped start a private organization, the ASU Foundation, which prioritized science and engineering through contributions to supplement state funds for expensive equipment, top-notch lab space, and faculty wages in order to attract respected researchers from Ivy League and other top schools. The university proved a boon to high-tech industries and to the chamber's drive to foster a modern, heavily Anglo, professional, technocratic metropolis. Shortly after the school began granting graduate degrees in the hard sciences and engineering, more than 150 students enrolled. Over the next few years, Motorola and General Electric employed more than two-thirds of these advanced students.[40]

Advanced technical education was vital but could not, solely, account for the staggering level of postwar investment in Phoenix. Between 1948 and 1964 alone, more than 700 firms relocated to, opened branch plants in, or started up in Phoenix. For many American CEOs, Phoenix had set the standard for industrial recruitment. Executives always attributed location decisions to a variety of the Chamber-built business climate's defining features. "Basic economic reasons influenced the choice of a Phoenix site for this division of our fifty-year-old corporation," Cannon Electric Company's Phoenix general manager explained; "availability of land and labor; suitable subcontractors and suppliers to support our type of manufacture; good housing and climate, an inducement to the recruitment of employees." The vice president and general manager of National Castings Company, Capitol Foundry Division, regarded Phoenix as "ideal due to the climate, the availability of skilled and unskilled personnel, the fine transportation facilities and the availability of utilities and service facilities." "Of no less importance," he noted, "is nearby Arizona State University, which afford[s] a reservoir of new talent as well as the means for continuing training and development."[41]

The Sunbelt Men of Power

The Phoenix miracle made local boosters into prominent figures in national business and political circles. Even the mainstream media took notice of the city's growth, leadership, and politics. In a 1947 *Saturday Evening Post* profile, Milton MacKaye called Phoenix, "Palm Beach, Red Gap and Mr. Babbitt's Zenith all rolled into one." "Neither the very rich nor the very poor are truly representative of Phoenix," he claimed. "The city itself is middle class and commercial, and much more vigorous than its annual mean temperature would suggest." Though MacKaye lavished praise on the agricultural harvests, rugged mesas, and breathtaking deserts in the surrounding lands, Phoenix's rapid modernization impressed him the most: "within the span of a single lifetime, this townsite had on it only one building, a crude one-story adobe," but now "Phoenix is hard to distinguish from New York, Miami and Los Angeles."[42]

The *Wall Street Journal* also featured Phoenix in its March 9, 1953, "Arizona Survey." Staff dedicated more than two full pages to the state's dude ranches, mines, cotton fields, saddle shops, cactus candy entrepreneurs, and squaw dress designers, but the majority of the spread celebrated Arizona's industrial present. Journalists lauded its new aircraft industry, transport facilities, and the rapidly growing Valley National Bank. "The six-gun clutched in the capable fist of a Wyatt Earp . . . was pretty much the symbol of this youngest of the states only a generation ago," a staff reporter mused, but the technicians, scientists, and researchers "may well be the new symbols" and "they're likely to be far more lasting." He lavished the most attention on CEOs, not their employees, including the heads of AiResearch and Motorola, who claimed that Arizona's climate, natural and business-friendly, was a boon to themselves and their work forces.[43]

Phoenix also kindled envy among boosters in the developing Sunbelt's smaller, less vibrant cities. Phoenix's development, for example, dismayed El Paso business leaders whose town had once been the rail center and dominant commercial hub for the desert lands. In the early 1960s, an El Paso booster envied his Phoenix counterparts who could introduce industrial scouts to the Goldwater family, promise them land, and guarantee them tax concessions because they had an "electorate willing to approve $209 million in business-backed bond issues in two years." "El Paso does nothing to get new industries," he lamented, "We are likely to give executives the cold-shoulder treatment. Instead of luring them with special tax deals, we're likely to push them away by throwing all kinds of problems at them. Zoning, water, things like that." An El Paso bank president confided, "our leadership has been sort of mediocre. We didn't have the influx of well-educated people in the industrial and commercial world. Phoenix did."⁴⁴

The mighty California chambers of commerce were also covetous of Phoenix's success. For many business owners and executives, the Golden State stood for everything that they despised about doing business in modern America. It had a strong union movement, a relatively high level of taxation, and a state government that was dominated either by moderate Republicans or liberal Democrats. California, of course, had continued to prosper, but an increasingly large cohort of conservative businessmen, especially in Southern California, thought the Arizona model superior. A leader of the San Bernardino Chamber of Commerce, for example, hoped to meet with the Chamber's leadership personally. "California does not have the best business climate desired by industry," he explained. "We would consider this trip very beneficial and at some later date maybe legislation could be introduced at our own State Capitol."⁴⁵

Such admiration helped propel Phoenix Chamber members into leadership roles in national business organizations. Two of the most powerful were Walter and Carl Bimson, brothers who saved Phoenix's struggling Valley National Bank (VNB) in the 1930s and remade it into the largest bank in the Rocky Mountain West. Both had broad political influence. Walter directed the Los Angeles branch of the Federal Reserve Bank of San Francisco, served on the American Bankers Association's Small Business Commission, and also joined the Department of Commerce's Business Advisory Committee. In all these roles, he protested, vigorously and effectively, state regulation of the financial sector. Bimson dismissed the efforts of liberal policy-makers to convert war production plants into centers for consumer goods and congratulated "the American businessman," who "constructed new plants, re-equipped his factories with new machines, built millions of new homes, and poured out an endless stream of cars, radios, [and] refrigerators." In celebrating postwar affluence, Bimson credited the "system of democratic capitalism and individual freedom" and thus condemned liberals who "attempt to make America over along lines that have failed again and again."⁴⁶

Walter Bimson basked in a highly favorable public image of himself and his bank. In 1945, Keith Monroe penned a celebratory look at Walter Bimson's banking philosophy for *American Magazine*. The journalist dubbed Bimson the "Bank Knight in Arizona" and heralded his faith in private investment and dogged efforts to attract investment. Monroe lauded the banker for "sen[ding] emissaries all over the country to bring new businesses, army bases, flying schools, branch factories, government housing, and other wealth-producing operations into the desert. And . . . laying vast, finely detailed plans to make Arizona bloom in the postwar period as never before." "All of which is unorthodox banking," Monroe observed, "but profitable." "Bimson has brought banking down to earth and created a thriving money oasis in the Southwest."[47]

Bimson's brother Carl also became a major figure in American banking. Throughout the 1950s and 1960s, the younger Bimson espoused the Phoenix business elite's antiliberal modernization doctrine before fellow Westerners as well as peers in the South and Northeast. In Arizona, he continued to work for VNB but also held leadership positions in Phoenix's Chamber of Commerce, Credit Bureau, Better Business Bureau, and YMCA, as well as in the Arizona Bankers Association. On the national level, he spoke before business groups to advocate political activism and the rollback of liberal-regulatory economic policy. In 1960, for example, he appeared before the Ohio Bankers Association to advocate that financiers take a greater role in politics. Echoing Goldwater's Depression-era remonstrations against apathetic business owners, Bimson called the assembled executives "Probably the best hope for stopping the present political drift toward a government-controlled economy." When traveling, he also advocated bankers' active involvement in making communities hospitable to industry. He argued that a financier "should muster the economic power of his business behind causes, activities, and organizations designed to improve the efficiency of government and the climate of business."[48]

The most renowned booster was Barry Goldwater. His rise to national prominence was built on a decidedly antiliberal politics, particularly a critique of the empowered labor movement, which echoed much of the antiunionism within Sunbelt boosterism. During his first term, Goldwater spent much of his time traveling the country to deliver speeches for the Republican Senate Campaign Committee. He advanced a Phoenix, rather than a Dwight Eisenhower, Republicanism. Goldwater's attacks traversed party lines: he defamed anyone still promoting the expansion, no matter how limited, of the welfare state. When Goldwater did speak before the Senate, he preached the developing industrialization gospel that he and his compatriots honed in Phoenix. Goldwater found himself exasperated that the first Republican president in two decades seemed to embrace the New Deal state. To his friends, he wrote, "It's obvious that the Administration has succumbed to the principle that we owe some sort of living, including all types of care to the citizens of this country, and I am beginning to wonder if we haven't gone a lot farther than many of us think on this road we happily call socialism."[49]

Goldwater staked out his most distinctive and politically consequential positions when he challenged both Eisenhower moderates and Democratic Party liberals on issues that touched on the radical reform of federal labor policy. Goldwater was the Republican Right's most outspoken and effective critic of what, he called, "monopoly unionism." He clashed publicly with supporters of the Eisenhower administration's labor policy. In the summer of 1954, the Arizonan sponsored an amendment to the 1947 Taft-Hartley Act, which would give much of the federal government's power over industrial relations to the states. He argued that, with these proposed revisions, states could, conceivably, pass laws that would require 95 percent, not just a majority, of the work force to support a union before certification. One liberal senator believed Goldwater's proposals "are determined . . . to drive a blow at organized labor that will send it rolling and rocking for weeks and months and years to come."[50]

Increased public concern over labor's power gave Goldwater a chance to make himself a household name and spread the antilabor message that had laid the foundation for hypergrowth, antiliberal Sunbelt politics. In 1957, the U.S. Senate created a Select Committee on Improper Activities in the Labor or Management Field (also known as the McClellan or Rackets Committee) after headline-grabbing scandals, especially those involving the Teamsters, seemed to tie the labor movement to a vast network of organized crime interests. Goldwater and other Republicans on the Rackets Committee were critical of Teamster leaders, but they targeted Walter Reuther, the ambitious, visionary United Auto Workers (UAW) president. Goldwater expended little energy exposing Reuther's earlier radical political affiliations but grilled him about UAW contributions to and influence on state and national Democratic Party leaders, the aggressive and sometimes violent nature of UAW organizing efforts, and Reuther's larger ideological and political ambitions.[51]

For the senator, Reuther seemed to embody labor's increasing power on both the shop floor and on Capitol Hill. Goldwater disliked Reuther's "bold statements on matters of domestic, foreign, and political policy which have only a most obscure bearing on the interests and welfare of labor union members." This last concern was Goldwater's greatest. He pushed Republicans to ask, "Do these statements of Walter Reuther constitute a proper function of his responsibility to the members of these unions? Indeed, what is Walter Reuther's job?" In January 1958, Goldwater flew to Detroit, where he chastised an Economic Club audience, well marbled with executives from the Big Three automakers, for their unwillingness to curb UAW economic or political ambitions. In a critique, which was reminiscent of the complaints he lodged against other timid businessmen in his Depression-era editorials, Goldwater declared Reuther "more dangerous to our country than Sputnik or anything Soviet Russia might do." A week later, Goldwater told the press, "This man cannot meet the charges that I, as well as others have made about him and his obsessive drive for political power." The antagonism between both men reached its zenith during a well-noted exchange at Reuther's three-day interrogation before the Senate Rackets Committee, when Goldwater told the UAW president that he would "rather have Hoffa stealing my money than Reuther stealing my freedom."[52]

Goldwater's 1958 reelection campaign became, in effect, a national showdown with Reuther, a state-level referendum on the empowered Arizona GOP, and a test of the boosters' industrialization philosophy. Arizona Republicans and Phoenix boosters did well: Valley propane retailer and former IDC head Paul Fannin was elected governor. He brought the Chamber's vision for a statewide industrial hinterland for the Phoenix metropole to the governor's mansion. Pundits considered this and other Arizona GOP victories as evidence of a profound shift in the state's political character. Goldwater's victory also had national ramifications. The first, prominent cowboy conservative earned new respect and acclaim. Major news outlets such as *Time* and *Saturday Evening Post* took notice of this rugged Westerner and devoted pages to the Republican who had defied labor and the Democrats. Republican Senator Everett Dirksen praised Goldwater openly for his "courage, your singleness of purpose and your determination to get a job done in a field of endeavor which has frightened so many in public life because they were afraid of reprisal." Richard Nixon reached out to the reelected Senator in the hope that Goldwater could help revitalize the GOP. Soon after, when Goldwater accepted the chairmanship of the Republican Senate Campaign Committee, he announced that he was "proud of being a conservative" and demanded "the party quit copying the New Deal." His new power and prestige provided the fuel that fired the first "Draft Goldwater" movement.[53]

By the time Goldwater accepted the presidential nomination in 1964 and Kevin Phillips outlined the broad contours of the Sunbelt phenomenon in 1969, Sunbelt boosterism had already transformed the South and Southwest. Phoenix Chamber of Commerce men, and their successful contemporaries in San Jose, Atlanta, Charlotte, and Houston, had excelled at attracting and keeping industry, refashioning the regulatory state, and decoupling regional industrialization from the liberal reconstruction of the South and Southwest. The scope, scale, and cost of their efforts show explicitly that air conditioning was not responsible for the Sunbelt's emergence. Its creation was a part of a region-wide, anti-New Deal developmental politics that redrew the boundaries of American capitalism and reoriented American politics toward the idea that the chief purpose of government, on both the local and the national level, was to sustain and advance business interests and those who presided over America's great corporations.

Chapter 2

Strom Thurmond's Sunbelt: Rethinking Regional Politics and the Rise of the Right

Joseph Crespino

The history of American politics is full of odd alliances and strange bedfellows. In the decades following World War II, however, few seemed more unusual than the coalition signaled by an anticommunist speaking tour Strom Thurmond made through Southern California in late 1961. The former Dixiecrat presidential candidate from South Carolina addressed largely Republican crowds in his five-day swing through Los Angeles and surrounding suburbs. He kicked off the campaign in a press conference at the Ambassador Hotel, where he denounced "pussyfooting diplomats" and defended the right of military leaders to speak out against communism. He addressed a noontime crowd of 500 at the Sportsman Lodge in the San Fernando Valley. Two thousand people showed up that night at the Coast Cities Freedom Program in Santa Monica. Thurmond's speech at the Hollywood Palladium was televised locally, and he spoke in venues that ranged from the Cocoanut Grove to the La Puente High School gymnasium.[1]

Thurmond's tour came on the heels of his campaign in the Senate to have Congress hold hearings on the alleged "muzzling" of military officers. The issue crystallized around the figure of General Edwin Walker, the army officer who had come under fire for his use of anticommunist material as part of a troop indoctrination program. Thurmond called for an investigation of Walker's reprimand, of troop education programs more generally, and of attempts by Kennedy administration officials to censor statements by military officers. Thurmond's California trip was bracketed by speeches in front of anticommunist groups in other Sunbelt locales. In September, he was scheduled but had to pull out of an appearance at a two-day anticommunist seminar in San Antonio. He addressed the Freedom Forum in Dallas in November.[2] He left California for speeches before the American Legion in Little Rock and a group called "Survival U.S.A." in Memphis.[3]

Thurmond's supporters in South Carolina hailed his antimuzzling campaign and pointed to the California trip as a turning point in Southern and national politics. It was a "story of major importance" said the *Charleston News and Courier*. The paper marveled that "Americans in Santa Monica turn out to listen to counsel of a Southern conservative." It was just as notable that South Carolinians turned out to hear "a Republican from Arizona," an obvious reference to several recent trips that Barry Goldwater had paid to the Palmetto State. For the *News and Courier*, Thurmond's muzzling campaign had "helped bring South Carolina back into the mainstream of American political affairs."[4]

The trip was equally auspicious for Southern California's hard-line conservatives. Thurmond's muzzling campaign was one of the key efforts in a revitalized right-wing, anticommunist movement that was remaking conservative politics in the United States. Reporters in Los Angeles speculated about Thurmond's potential in harnessing this movement to transform national politics. Perhaps Thurmond was gearing up for a third party run in 1964, some speculated, this time heading not a regional racial movement but a national right wing crusade. "If the hundreds of new rightist organizations ever unite and form a major political party," a reporter noted in February 1962, "Thurmond might very well be their first choice for president."[5] A more likely scenario, however, had Thurmond helping bring southern conservative Democrats into Barry Goldwater's camp, should the Arizona senator win the GOP nomination in 1964.[6] Several years before the term had yet to be coined, commentators were noting the potential of a Sunbelt coalition of hard-line conservatives that could remake the political map.

Thurmond seems an unlikely figure to have led a Sunbelt anticommunist crusade. He is more commonly associated with what the journalist

Robert Sherrill described as the "gothic politics of the Deep South."[7] Thurmond's anti-civil rights resume was unparalleled. As the Dixiecrat presidential candidate, he was an early and articulate opponent of antipoll tax legislation, a federal antilynching law, and the permanent establishment of the Fair Employment Practices Committee. He was the instigator of the 1956 Southern Manifesto, the anti-Supreme Court statement written in protest of the *Brown* decision. And during his one-man filibuster against the 1957 Civil Rights Act, Thurmond set the record for the longest single speech in Senate history, a mark that still stands.

Yet recasting Strom Thurmond as a Sunbelt politician rather than a mere Dixie demagogue helps us think in new ways about the history of both the South and the Sunbelt. Too often scholars have seen southern conservative reaction as driven solely by racism. Historians have viewed white southerners' Americanism and staunch anticommunism as a mere cover for their racial beliefs, a convenient and politically respectable means of opposing civil rights changes.[8] Sunbelt conservatism, by contrast, has been figured as racially innocent, characterized by a moderation that contrasted sharply with the massive resistance politics that Strom Thurmond pioneered. In her study of Orange County conservatism, for example, Lisa McGirr argues that "racial issues were far more central to the texture and fabric of southern politics and to that region's conservatism." It is true that white residents of southern California were not reared in the mythology and memory of racial struggle in the same way that white South Carolinians were. Yet McGirr asserts that in Southern California racial issues "did not occupy the same prominence in the life, ideas, and politics of Southern California as they did in the former confederate states." Opposition to civil rights, she writes, "was only one of a host of issues in a broader conservative package."[9] In the South, we are to assume from this formulation, racism was not merely "one of a host of issues" but was *the* issue. Conservative white southerners' Cold War anticommunism, their antilabor politics, their conservative religious beliefs and staunch opposition to liberal church groups, their criticism of judicial activism, their hypermilitarism—all this was merely a function of their desire to maintain white supremacy. Even if one admits the unusually powerful role of race in Southern politics, it does seem an odd distinction to make given the generally lily-white character of the communities that McGirr describes. Indeed, much of the new work emerging on Southern California conservatives goes much further than

McGirr in showing the centrality of racial concerns in postwar California politics.[10]

The muzzling hearings show how insufficient regional identification or segregationist politics are in explaining the new political alliances that emerged in the 1960s and 1970s. The four key figures involved in the hearings were southerners, all of whom signed the Southern Manifesto: Strom Thurmond; Richard Russell of Georgia, chair of the Senate Armed Services Committee; John Stennis of Mississippi, chair of the subcommittee that ran the muzzling hearings; and J. William Fulbright of Arkansas, who authored a confidential memo critical of right-wing anti-communist generals that precipitated Thurmond's interest in the matter. All of them, with varying degrees of commitment, were segregationists.[11] And yet, on the issue of national security, Thurmond was poles apart from Fulbright and clearly to the right of such staunch military advocates as Russell and Stennis. In fact, the muzzling hearings marked Thurmond's emergence as a key figure in an inchoate, ideologically charged, right-wing Sunbelt constituency.

Scholars have provided important studies of these communities at the grassroots level. They have shown how "modern" these actors were and how their politics emerged out of specific aspects of the suburban, Sunbelt communities where they settled.[12] But it is important to link studies of the grassroots with how powerful political actors mobilized and put into action the sentiments of right-wing Sunbelt constituencies. A close examination of the muzzling hearings helps connect grassroots political mobilization in the Sunbelt with politics inside Washington. It reveals how popular anticommunist movements in the postwar period destabilized traditional regional alliances and opened the door for a new southern and western coalition that would go a long way in shaping the character of modern conservative politics.

The Dixiecrats and the Proto-Sunbelt

In recasting Thurmond from a Southern demagogue to a Sunbelt politician, the place to begin is with Thurmond's quintessential act of regional racial defiance: his 1948 campaign for the presidency as the nominee of the States' Rights Democratic Party, or as it is more commonly known, the Dixiecrat Party. Thurmond's decision to accept the presidential nomination of the States' Rights Democratic Party would come to be seen later by many of his political friends as one of the biggest mistakes of his career. As the Dixiecrat candidate, Thurmond won four Deep South states. His appeal was confined largely to the Black Belt, the traditional cotton plantation belt with the largest African American population and home to most virulent and reactionary racist politics. Thurmond became the face of a reactionary movement that was fueled by racist and Neanderthal forces in southern politics, one that would alienate Thurmond from established southern Democratic leaders both in South Carolina and across the South.

Yet Thurmond's leadership of the Dixiecrat's also set the stage for his later Sunbelt ambitions. Throughout the 1948 campaign, Thurmond struggled—and largely failed—to define his presidential run as one not of regional racial defiance but national conservative revolt. His most conspicuous and important failure was with the very nickname of the party—the Dixiecrats. The term is used unthinkingly today. It is worth noting, however, that, at least from Thurmond's perspective, it was an epithet. A waggish newspaper editor coined the term. Thurmond himself never used it and during the campaign objected whenever someone else did.[13] Thurmond always made clear that he headed the National States' Rights Party. He was keen to define the movement as a national conservative reaction against the statist and socialistic tendencies of the Truman administration. Without a doubt, it was white southerners' opposition to Truman's civil rights stands that was the precipitating factor and the driving force behind the Dixiecrat revolt. Yet it is important to recall the battle of the party name because it reflects in microcosm the unsuccessful struggle Thurmond waged in defining the political movement as one about not merely segregation but broader issues of national concern.

One of the most important of those issues was economics. As Dixiecrat presidential candidate, Thurmond became the face not merely of the forces of racist reaction in the South but also of the Dixie dissenters from liberal New Deal labor and economic policy. Here is an important tie for understanding the origins of Thurmond's Sunbelt conservatism. The Dixiecrats failed as a third party movement, but they encompassed the procorporate, antiunion conservative economic forces that would eventually find a home in the Sunbelt-based GOP. The Black Belt, which held the highest percentage of African American population and typically was home to most vehement antiblack sentiment, was the main source of Dixiecrat support in 1948. Yet in his recap of the significance of Thurmond's run, Kevin Phillips rightly pointed out that the Black Belt also had a heritage of economic conservatism.[14] Before the Civil War it was the home of much of the southern Whig support. In the postwar period, economic elites from the Black Belt were among the industrial boosters that actively courted Northern industries.[15]

When we think of economic developments in post-World War II America uniting Sunbelt states we think of National Security Council Report 68 (NSC-68) and the growth of the Cold War state and the military contractors that congregated in Sunbelt states. We think of the flight of capital from the rustbelt to the Sunbelt and the rise of a white collar, high-tech, high-wage industries that brought new migrants to the region. But chronologically speaking, the first post-World War II Sunbelt industry—the one that oriented states around a comprehensive economic logic connecting states as diverse in their social and historical orientation as Louisiana, Texas, and California—was oil and gas. The fight between Sunbelt states and the federal government over control of the tidelands—the areas off the coast of California, Texas, and Louisiana rich in oil and mineral deposits—played a prominent role in the 1948 Dixiecrat campaign. Dixiecrat support for states' rights fit perfectly with conservative oil men who wanted to have individual states rather than the federal government control access to these valuable areas.

Dixiecrat critics contended that the movement was primarily a front for wealthy oil interests out of Texas. They pointed to the fact that Houston oil executive H. R. Cullen and Humble Oil Company flew Strom Thurmond to the States' Rights Democratic convention in Houston in a private plane and chartered a special train for the Mississippi delegation.[16] Leander Perez, the boss of Plaquemines Parish in coastal Louisiana, was a leading Dixiecrat and one of the nation's most fervent opponents to federal control of the tidelands.[17] Thurmond denied that oil interests played a controlling role in the Dixiecrat movement, and leaders worked hard to portray the party as fed by broad grassroots reaction.[18] Few financial records of the party survive, and scholars have had a hard time documenting any undue influence that oil interests might have had on party strategies.[19]

Regardless of how directly a role oil interests played in Dixiecrat finances, conservative Sunbelt economic forces were in the driver's seat in the Dixiecrat campaign, whether or not they were in the oil industry. According to Alexander Heard, in addition to Black Belt planters, the party's leadership was dominated by "corporation lawyers, wealthy businessmen, [and] industrial captains."[20] If it was not oil money exactly that fueled the party, it was what Thomas Sancton writing in the *Nation* called the "investing and managing communities"—"the oil and cattle men of Texas, the oil men and sugar planters of Louisiana, the mercantile and shipping interests of New Orleans, Houston, Memphis, and Atlanta, the steel and coal operators of Alabama, the textile manufacturers of the whole South Atlantic region"—a whole range of business interests that stretched from "the southern industrial metropolis to Old Man Johnson's 'furnish' store at the unnamed crossroads."[21]

The Dixiecrat campaign signaled a growing consolidation of the forces of economic and racial reaction in the region. The midterm elections of 1950 provide a good example. Thurmond's narrow defeat for a U.S. Senate seat in South Carolina at the hands of Olin Johnston, an ardent New Dealer, was the exception that proved the rule of conservative ascendancy. Willis Smith defeated Frank Graham for a Senate seat in North Carolina, and George Smathers beat the liberal stalwart Claude Pepper in Florida. It was enough to lead the political scientist Samuel Lubell to characterize the 1950 election cycle as a "conservative revolution." Lubell pointed not just to electoral results but to the broader set of economic and social factors transforming southern politics: agricultural diversification beyond cotton and tobacco, the mechanization of traditional crops, urbanization, the growth of manufacturing, and the rise in personal incomes. Three factors in particular, however, stood out: the failure of southern labor organizing efforts, the rise of a new urban middle class, and the intensification of racist sentiment following the extension of civil and political rights for southern African Americans.[22]

Cold War Anti-Communism

Thurmond's 1950 defeat for a U.S. Senate seat coincided with the end of his term as South Carolina governor. In his return to private life, Thurmond's choice of residence marked another step in the development of his Sunbelt orientation. Thurmond was originally from Edgefield, South Carolina, a venerable old town where his family had lived for generations. Edgefield is renowned in South Carolina for being the home to eleven governors, as well as such fiery politicians as Preston Brooks, the South Carolina representative who attacked the abolitionist Charles Sumner on the floor of the Senate, and the notorious demagogue "Pitchfork" Ben Tillman.

Vernon Burton, a native of the region as well as its most distinguished historical chronicler, has noted how Edgefield was remarkable for distilling distinctive qualities commonly associated with white southern temperament, sensibility, and culture.[23] When Thurmond returned to private life in 1950, however, he moved not to Edgefield but to Aiken, an expanding community along the Savannah River just across the state line from Augusta, best known as a winter vacation spot for wealthy northerners. Edgefield and Aiken are separated by just over twenty miles. But in 1950, when Thurmond moved there, they were at the beginning of a process that would leave them worlds apart.

Aiken lay at the center of the Savannah River Site, a nuclear materials processing center established in 1950 by the Atomic Energy Commission. The federal government contracted the Dupont Corporation to build and operate a plutonium production plant along the Savannah River. "It is as if Scarlett O'Hara had come home from the ball, wriggled out of her satin gown, and put on a space suit," wrote the journalist Dorothy Kilgallen, describing the transformation of the bucolic southern town into a modern Cold War production center.[24] The scale of the project was monumental; as an industrial and engineering feat, it rivaled the construction of the Panama Canal. Its impact on the local area was equally vast. During the peak of the construction period, the project employed over 38,000 skilled and unskilled laborers.[25]

One of South Carolina's chief postwar industrial boosters—Charles Daniel, a close political friend of Thurmond's and the owner of Daniel Construction Company of Greenville, South Carolina—called the Savannah River Site "the beginning of the industrial revolution in South Carolina."[26] Daniels overstated the point but only slightly. South Carolina's industrial past was comprised largely of textile mills in the Piedmont. By 1950, Strom Thurmond and other political leaders were actively recruiting northern industries based on the South's unique "business climate," the chief attribute of which was the region's historic resistance to labor unions, yet the Savannah River Site was the best example of how the exigencies of the Cold War transformed isolated areas of the Deep South into dynamic modern centers of the nation's military-industrial complex.[27] Southern committee chairmen in Congress were particularly well placed to direct Cold War defense dollars southward. South Carolina Representative Mendel Rivers, chairman of the House Armed Services Committee, was a good example. Rivers's predecessor once joked that "you put anything else down there in your district, Mendel, it's gonna sink."[28]

In Aiken, Strom Thurmond became a leading citizen of an expanding postwar Sunbelt community. He and his young wife built a brick, ranch-style home in a newly developed neighborhood. He helped bring a federally charted savings and loan association to Aiken, which sold mortgages to the engineers and white-collar, college-educated employees that flooded the area. And he paid off campaign debts with profits from his booming law practice, a firm that presaged the anti-federal government stance that became a staple of Thurmond's political life: Thurmond's office specialized in representing local landowners forced to sell their property to the government to make way for the new construction.[29]

Thurmond's residence in Aiken alone would have disposed him toward issues of national security and Cold War military funding, yet additional factors contributed to this orientation. Thurmond amassed a distinguished record of military service during World War II. In his early forties, Thurmond abandoned a job as a civil affairs officer to volunteer with the Eighty-Second Airborne Division then in preparation for the D-Day invasion at Normandy. He crash-landed a glider behind German lines, was wounded in action, and received sixteen different medals, decorations, or awards for his service. After the war, Thurmond played a leading role in the Reserve Officers Association. He won election as president of the organization in 1954 and would later retire as a major general in the U.S. Army Reserves. In the early 1960s, during the muzzling hearings, Thurmond was the highest-ranking reserve officer in the Senate (Barry Goldwater, an Air Force Reserves officer, held the second-highest rank).

All these associations made Thurmond eager to get involved in foreign and military affairs on his arrival in Washington. He initially sought a place on the Foreign Relations Committee. His brash ways as a junior senator, however, did little to endear him to Democratic Party leadership. Not until 1959, after Thurmond agreed not to oppose a compromise on cloture rules, did Majority Leader Lyndon Johnson pass along the plum of a Senate Armed Services Committee seat.

Thurmond's new position of influence in military affairs coincided with a dramatic upswing in popular anticommunist sentiment. The development could be traced in numerous ways, but one of the most important was the formation of the John Birch Society. The organization's initial meeting took place in Indianapolis in December 1958, but the society spread quickly across the South and Southwest. One prominent southern conservative believed that the Birch Society provided an outlet for the "temperate Conservative Southerner," a group that was joining the Birch Society "in droves."[30] Strom Thurmond never joined the John Birch Society and turned down a position on the organization's board. To a letter writer who inquired about his relationship to the group, Thurmond defended Birch Society members' freedom of speech but questioned the effectiveness of Robert Welch's extreme statements. Yet Thurmond was also irked by the public reaction against the Birch Society. "In order to get any sympathetic consideration in this country any more one must be either black or red," Thurmond wrote; "no other color seems to matter."[31]

Strom Thurmond did not believe everything the Birch Society did, but the group seemed to at least address some of the growing fears of many conservative Americans. One such fear involved the Supreme Court and internal subversion. On June 17, 1957, the Supreme Court issued decisions in three cases that pitted civil liberties against congressional attempts to police Communism. A number of books appeared in the late 1950s that stoked anticommunist popular reaction. Rosalie M. Gordon's book *Nine Men Against America*, published in 1958, presented in lay terms the conservative case against the Supreme Court. W. Cleon Skousen's *The Naked Communist* became a common sourcebook for hard-liners likely to join one of the new anticommunist organizations springing up. The most influential anticommunist book by far, however, was J. Edgar Hoover's widely read *Masters of Deceit*. Hoover soberly warned of the continuing communist threat—and the important role the Federal Bureau of Investigation played in combating it. The FBI chief's book was a number-one bestseller for six weeks in the spring and early summer of 1958.[32]

For many hard-line anticommunists, American leaders simply did not grasp the seriousness of the problem. Ongoing efforts by the Eisenhower administration to conduct peaceful negotiations with the Soviets drew the ire of many. Soviet premier Nikita Khrushchev's visit to the United States in 1959 provoked widespread reaction among right-wing anticommunists. Equally important in stoking right wing sentiment was the controversy surrounding a short documentary film, *Operation Abolition*, produced by the House Un-American Activities Committee (HUAC). The film showed footage of civil libertarian protestors at HUAC hearings in San Francisco in May 1960. It alleged to document how covert communist agents had stirred up naïve students into attacking the one government agency dedicated to exposing the communist threat. Interspersed were talking head committee members and congressmen who marveled at the brazenness of subversives in their midst.[33] HUAC printed two thousand copies of the film. By mid-1961, it was estimated that some 15 million people had seen it. Liberals were outraged at HUAC's heavy-handed tactics, as well as the fact that tax dollars were spent spreading what it viewed as right-wing propaganda.[34] Conservatives were equally horrified at the nightmarish scenario that the film claimed to depict. Strom Thurmond was in San Francisco at the time of the HUAC hearings. He saw firsthand the demonstrations at City Hall and, as he told a constituent, was "sickened" by "the spectacle of those young people and their faculty leaders participating in what I considered to be communist activity."[35] He protested a Defense Department policy banning the film as required training material for military personnel. To another constituent, he confided that the Defense Department seemed "to be under heavy pressure from the left wing, and, as you know, the left wing seems to have the upper hand in this country these days."[36] Thurmond would later cite the prohibition of the film as an example of military muzzling. The replacement film the military chose, "Communism on the Map," seemed to Thurmond, by comparison, "a namby-pamby, gutless film."[37]

The Fulbright Memo

The circumstances that led to the muzzling hearings began in the earliest days of the Kennedy administration. During delicate negotiations between the Kennedy administration and the Soviets over the return of two American pilots who had been imprisoned for seven months, Republicans charged the new president with imposing a "dictaphone type of 'gag rule'" on military leaders. These were the words of Barry Goldwater, who took the lead in attacking the Kennedy administration's decision to delete sharp anticommunist statements in a speech by Admiral Arleigh Burke, chief of naval operations.[38]

While the Burke incident raised the issue, no event dramatized the matter of military muzzling more dramatically than the case of General Edwin Walker, commander of the Twenty-Fourth Infantry Division in West Germany. *The Overseas Weekly*, a newspaper for American GIs abroad, first reported in April 1961 that soldiers under Walker's command were being indoctrinated with John Birch Society materials. This set off an army investigation that culminated in June when the commander in chief of the army in Europe officially "admonished" General Walker for indoctrinating his troops with partisan anticommunist political material. Walker denied any direct connection with the Birch Society, but the information for his "Pro Blue" troop education program was drawn from the febrile conspiratorial literature that fed the radical Right. Walker saw himself on the frontlines of the Cold War battle (it was generally presumed that, should the opening blow come, the Twenty-Fourth Infantry would be the first to meet the Soviets). He was determined that his men would understand the totalizing threat posed by the communists. Walker's superiors, however, saw a military commander who had crossed the line that separated troop education from partisan political advocacy.[39]

Walker's situation was not an isolated case. Under the 1958 National Security Council resolution, it was the policy of the U.S. government to use military personnel and facilities to arouse the public "to the menace of the cold war." By the early 1960s, with the John Birch Society and similar anticommunist groups in full flower, this policy had created a volatile situation. Military leaders were spicing their speeches with analyses and speculation drawn from right-wing propaganda. High-ranking officers who repeated these ideas and accusations seemed to give official military approval for far-right conspiracy theories.

One of the first and most influential people to recognize the extent of the problem was J. William Fulbright, the Democratic senator from Arkansas and chairman of the Senate Foreign Relations Committee. In the summer of 1961, Fulbright sent a confidential memo to President Kennedy that outlined the dangers involved in the military's education and propaganda activities. "There is little in the education, training, or experience of most military officers," the memo argued, "to equip them with the balance of judgment necessary to put their own ultimate solutions . . . into proper perspective in the President's total strategy for the nuclear age." Fulbright scoffed at the notion that American ignorance of the communist threat created a challenge for political leaders. He believed that, given the simplistic slogans of the Right and the ongoing hostilities around the world, the real problem for officials was how "to restrain the desire of the people to hit the Communists with everything we've got."[40]

In the early 1960s, J. William Fulbright was the Senate's leading voice of liberal internationalism. A Rhodes scholar and president of the University of Arkansas by age thirty-four, Fulbright was elected to the Senate in 1944 after one term in the House. His greatest legacy was the eponymous foreign exchange program that President Truman signed into law in 1946. He chaired the Senate Foreign Relations Committee for fifteen years. By the mid-1960s, he would become his party's and the Senate's most withering critic of Lyndon Johnson's Vietnam policies. Admired by his colleagues for his intellect, he was also resented for his superciliousness. Harry S. Truman once called him "an over-educated S.O.B." Lyndon Johnson said he was "unable to park his bicycle straight."[41]

The Fulbright memo included an attachment that detailed eleven instances of military programs operating under the 1958 National Security Policy. The courses used "extremely radical rightwing speakers and/or materials" that explicitly condemned foreign and domestic policies of the Kennedy administration. The seminars ridiculed foreign aid and cultural exchanges as wasteful, and they tended to conflate social legislation with socialism and socialism with communism. The graduated income tax, social security (medical care in particular), federal aid to education—the memo noted that all such programs were characterized in many troop education programs as "steps toward communism."[42]

Fulbright's memo was directly responsible for a Defense Department directive in July 1961 that restricted the right of military personnel to participate in right-wing seminars. Defense Secretary Robert McNamara had requested a meeting with Fulbright after reading the memo. McNamara had been concerned for several months with reports of high- and middle-ranking officers indoctrinating their troops and civilian populations with right wing materials.[43] McNamara issued the new directive shortly after the meeting with Fulbright.[44] Fulbright and McNamara were accustomed to receiving the scorn of conservative hard-liners, but neither man anticipated the reaction that ensued. Fulbright's assistant wrote a whimsical message to his boss summarizing the situation. The Fulbright memo, he noted, had succeeded in "arousing the ire of practically every organized segment of world public opinion." This included "John Birchers, McCarthyites, Goldwaterites, Thurmondites, Dixiecrats, militarists, isolationists, Zionists, Germans, Catholics, Chinese Nationalists, Koreans, NAACP-ers, ADA-ers, Communists, private powerists, veterans, farmer cooperativites."[45]

Fulbright's chief nemesis in the Senate was Strom Thurmond. Arriving at his Senate office on the morning of July 21, 1961, Thurmond discovered what he described as the shock of his Senate career. An aide came in with a copy of the *Washington Post* that carried a story of excerpts leaked from Fulbright's month-old memo. Thurmond immediately phoned Fulbright's office to request a copy of the memo. None were available, he was told. A Fulbright staffer who came over to explain the situation "was promptly chewed into small pieces." Thurmond immediately fired off a letter to Fulbright addressed "Dear Bill," requesting a copy of the memo before he left Washington after lunch. Fulbright responded the same day in an equally blithe letter that refused to supply the memo. It was private correspondence with the secretary of defense, Fulbright wrote, not a public committee document.[46] The casual politeness of the two letters hardly masked the fact that neither man had much regard for the other. In a Senate speech a week and a half later, Fulbright dismissed Thurmond's "ultimatum" that he receive a copy of the memo within the hour. "I was unwilling to open my private files in response to so impertinent a letter," he said.[47]

In a press conference on the morning of July 21, Thurmond denounced the Fulbright memo as "a dastardly attempt to intimidate the commanders of United State armed forces" and "a serious blow to the security of the United States." Rejecting Fulbright's assertion that military leaders were not trained to educate the public, Thurmond argued that the military was "the real bastion of knowledge and understanding of the Communist threat."[48] As for anticommunist criticism of domestic social programs, Thurmond believed that "if the military teaches the truth, it must necessarily teach that communism is fundamentally socialism." "Many of the domestic programs advocated and adopted fall clearly within the category of socialism," Thurmond argued.[49] He finally obtained a copy of the memo on August 2, which he immediately placed in the *Congressional Record*. Republican senators Barry Goldwater, Karl Mundt, and Carl Curtis joined Thurmond in denouncing the Fulbright memo. In response to the memo's assertion that military men were not trained to instruct the public on Cold War matters, Goldwater gibed, "I don't know: perhaps one must be a Rhodes scholar in order to be able to state what is good for this Republic of ours."[50]

In pushing for the muzzling hearings, Thurmond worked closely with right-wing conservatives across the Sunbelt. He contacted Dan Smoot of Texas to beat the drums in his anticommunist newsletter.[51] Anticommunist evangelist Billy James Hargis of Tulsa, Oklahoma, recorded a special radio program urging listeners to write their congressmen in support of the

Thurmond's resolution.[52] Thurmond met with Kent and Phoebe Courtney of New Orleans, publishers of the *Independent American* and probably the most vigorous defenders of Edwin Walker.[53] Richard Morphew of the Citizens' Council of America, based in Jackson, Mississippi, got Thurmond to contribute an article on the muzzling issue for the Council's monthly magazine and pledged to keep the issue before his readers.[54] An aide to a rival senator cited "a number of suggestions" that Thurmond's material in these weeks was "written, produced or developed by persons who are members of or associated with the John Birch movement."[55] In fact, it was not. Thurmond had no direct connection with the John Birch Society, but he was drawing from the same well of right wing anticommunism.

Thurmond's efforts to build up support for hearings were clearly paying off in the mail received by Richard Russell, chairman of the Armed Services Committee, which would be responsible for hearings on the subject. More than 18,000 letters, telegrams, and postcards urged prompt inquiry into Thurmond's charges of military muzzling.[56] Most of them were belligerent and accusatorial. A remarkable number posed the same peppery question to Russell: ADA or USA—which are you working for? A Russell aide soon discovered that the inspiration for the missives was a John Birch Society newsletter. It surely was a disorienting experience for Russell, one of the Senate's stalwart conservatives, to experience such withering skepticism from the Right.[57]

The Muzzling Hearings

On September 20, 1961, the Armed Services Committee approved an inquiry into alleged muzzling in the military. Thurmond's original resolution called for "complete study and investigation" into the Pentagon's policy. This language caused dissension among committee members. Senator John Stennis of Mississippi was one of two committee members who argued that the term "investigation" implied wrongdoing. He substituted the phrase "study and appraise," which the committee eventually supported by a 15 to 1 vote.[58] Part of the problem was senatorial courtesy; it was considered improper for a group of senators to "investigate" Fulbright, a colleague.[59] But the amendment also betrayed an important difference in approach from Thurmond's bombastic tack. An editorial in the *Washington Post* noted the "anxiety and confusion" that Thurmond had stirred up. It called the change in language "a welcome sign of sobriety." "Study is what is needed," the editorial concluded, "Not vilification."[60]

The wrangle over wording foreshadowed other antagonisms to come. Armed Services Committee Chairman Russell, alarmed by the frenzied letters he had been receiving, made sure that things did not get out of hand. Rather than naming a special select committee that Thurmond might have headed, Russell assigned the study to the preexisting Military Preparedness Subcommittee, chaired by Mississippi Senator John Stennis. Russell added Thurmond to the panel, but Stennis remained as chair.[61] Russell, having already been burned by Thurmond's grandstanding during debate over the 1957 civil rights bill, was not about to give Thurmond free rein with an issue as explosive as military muzzling.

Washington insiders saw Russell's move coming. Earlier in September, when Thurmond first pushed for an investigation, the journalist William S. White believed that Russell and Stennis would bring a sense of responsibility to such hearings. He contrasted Thurmond with the "calm Southern conservatives of the Russell-Stennis stamp," who were indispensable to the Kennedy administration and the Democratic Party because they could mediate between a liberal internationalist like Fulbright and a hard-line anticommunist like Thurmond.[62]

John Stennis was one of Richard Russell's closest allies in the Senate. Stennis's voting record was hardly less conservative than Thurmond's, but Stennis shared Richard Russell's low-key temperament and deep reverence for Senate traditions. Stennis had a reputation among his colleagues for diligence and honesty. He also had a history of taking a strong stand against anticommunist grandstanding in the Senate. Stennis made a name for himself in 1954 when he became the first Democratic senator to speak out against Joseph McCarthy. As a junior member, he was named to the committee that investigated charges against the Wisconsin senator.[63]

Though they both were quick to downplay it in public, Stennis and Thurmond clashed continually over the administration of the hearings. The fact that Thurmond was so zealous in agitating right-wing sentiment prejudiced Stennis against him to begin with. For his part, Thurmond was annoyed with Stennis for ignoring his suggestion for chief counsel of the subcommittee.[64] Thurmond and his supporters measured Russell's and Stennis's distaste for the investigation by the amount of resources committed to it. The committee had only five investigators and an initial appropriation of $30,000. By comparison, a House public works subcommittee had

$774,000 and a staff of 20 to make a highway investigation. Robert Kennedy had been given more than 100 investigators and $1.7 million to expose labor-management racketeering. Thurmond complained to Stennis in early November about the lack of investigators. "I am ever conscious of my responsibility in this matter in which, as you stated, I am the moving party," Thurmond wrote. "To fulfill this responsibility I do need more investigators."[65]

On November 20, Stennis announced that the hearings, scheduled to begin the following week, would be postponed until January. Stennis had Thurmond's approval for the holdup, but news reports covering the delay only inflamed right-wing suspicions of a whitewash in the making. Willard Edwards of the *Chicago Tribune* characterized the subcommittee staff as "noticeably apathetic." Stennis, the article said, was "known to dread the controversy" and "would like to get the job over with quickly."[66] The conservative columnist Holmes Alexander implicitly criticized Stennis for wanting to conduct the hearings on "a semi-judicial plane." "A Congressional probe ought never to be compared with a court of law," Alexander wrote. "Investigations, to be effective, must be expensive and must get very rough." He lauded Thurmond for the South Carolinian's dogged pursuit of the matter.[67]

In late November and early December 1961, Thurmond made his California speaking tour. The intensity of Thurmond's schedule during this period led one political columnist to wonder, "What is Strom Thurmond running for?"[68] His numerous appearances laid the groundwork for the muzzling hearings, which opened to great fanfare on January 23, 1962. One source billed the muzzling panel as the most exciting congressional hearing since a labor-racketeering investigation that featured Robert Kennedy trading icy barbs with Teamster President Jimmy Hoffa. Newsmen and spectators swarmed inside the cavernous, red-carpeted Senate caucus room, with its suspended crystal chandeliers. All 250 public seats were filled early; other observers stood wedged in along the edges of the room. Seven of the eight senators were seated at the front, looking out at the audience. Chairman John Stennis, described as having "the air of a country judge at a big trial," sat in the middle. To his right was Strom Thurmond, who was expected to "act as a sort of prosecuting attorney." Thurmond looked "thin, studious, serious" as he carefully took notes during the opening testimony.[69] Barry Goldwater, who had petitioned to get on the subcommittee but was denied out of fear of weighting the panel too heavily toward military interests, sat in on the hearings and was invited to ask questions.[70]

A showdown quickly emerged between Thurmond and Defense Secretary Robert McNamara. On January 31, Thurmond questioned Willis D. Lawrence, assistant director of security review at the Pentagon, about deletions in a statement by an army lieutenant general before the House Science and Astronautics Committee the previous year. Lawrence was the chief of the army security review, and Thurmond wanted to know which of his staff members had handled this particular speech. After consulting with Cyrus Vance, general counsel for the Defense Department, Lawrence declined to answer the question. He cited an order from Secretary of Defense McNamara not to identify reviewers in respect to particular speeches.

Thurmond immediately protested and asked Stennis to "require" Lawrence to answer the question. Thurmond cited the testimony of high-ranking military officers who said that certain deletions in their speeches had led them to "wonder" about the "motivation" of the reviewers. Without questioning reviewers about specific deletions, Thurmond argued, the committee could not do its work. He noted that executive privilege, the principle that private deliberations and communications related to the president's duties were confidential, had not been invoked by the administration, nor, he argued, would it apply in this instance.[71] Stennis was unsure about the applicability of executive privilege but was inclined to agree with Thurmond. Stennis delayed ruling on Thurmond's request until he had time to study the issue further.

The following day, McNamara sent a letter to the committee explaining his instructions to Lawrence. He noted his department's extensive cooperation with the committee and said that he was reluctant to invoke executive privilege. Individual censors may have made mistakes in their deletions, McNamara admitted, but he did not see how linking specific censors with particular acts of censorship would advance the inquiry. He feared the effect such revelations would have on morale in his department.[72]

This was not mere posturing by McNamara. For several observers, Thurmond's campaign to investigate Defense officials evoked memories of Joseph McCarthy's crusade against the State Department less than a decade earlier. Then the State Department, under intense scrutiny from McCarthy, had difficulty defending specific decisions by mid- and low-level officials. Taken out of their policy context, McCarthy mischaracterized the actions as part of a larger conspiracy and in the process defamed innocent government employees. State Department officials were "sacrificed with little or no attempt to show what their duties and responsibilities had been in the Executive branch," wrote journalist Marquis Childs. "This was one reason for the disastrous drop in State Department morale from which, as [the Kennedy] Administration is well aware, the Department and the Foreign Service have never fully recovered."[73]

President Kennedy eventually took McNamara off the spot by invoking executive privilege, ordering the Defense officials not to answer Thurmond's questions.[74] This made things a bit easier on Stennis, who was unlikely to confront the president directly over a constitutional principle as well established as executive privilege. Yet it only confirmed suspicions among right-wingers—a significant number of them in his home state of Mississippi—that Stennis was a tool of appeasers inside the Kennedy administration.

In drafting his decision respecting executive privilege, Stennis drew on the example of his mentor Richard Russell. Stennis had already contacted one of Russell's old advisors from the MacArthur hearings, and he saw parallels between his work guiding the muzzling inquiry and Russell's earlier efforts. President Truman's decision in 1951 to remove General Douglas MacArthur from his command during the height of Korean hostilities was one of the most controversial presidential orders in twentieth-century American politics. For millions of Americans, MacArthur returned home a hero, a giant of a man undermined by the timid Truman. Many expected and hoped that MacArthur would run against Truman for the presidency in 1952. Republican opponents immediately called for a full-scale congressional investigation into MacArthur's dismissal. Both the Armed Services and Foreign Relations Committees claimed jurisdiction, but Russell's reputation for firm but fair leadership led his colleagues to choose him to head the hearings. With an intelligent, orderly approach, Russell quietly deflated MacArthur's balloon. He revealed the dangerous ends to which MacArthur's military decisions might have led had President Truman not stood firm. By the end of the hearings, even MacArthur's strongest supporters were forced to admit that the general's moment had passed.[75]

In that earlier showdown, Russell had ruled in favor of Truman's right to protect private deliberations. Stennis did the same in the muzzling hearings, announcing his decision on February 8. He cited a long list of precedents in which the executive branch had invoked its privilege against the legislative. He quoted Richard Russell directly in a statement Russell had given sustaining a plea of executive privilege during the MacArthur hearings: "The future freedom and security of our country depend as much upon the maintenance of the delicate system of checks and balances designed by the Founding Fathers as upon our armies, our navies and our fleets of airplanes. Among the most valuable of those checks and balances yet devised are those which prevent one of the branches of the government from imposing its will upon the other." Stennis sent a copy of the statement to Russell with a brief note attached: "You blazed the trail, and I was following it."[76]

As the hearings progressed, the cracks that had already surfaced between Thurmond and subcommittee chairman Stennis soon spread into open fissures. On April 7, Stennis consulted with the subcommittee counsel over how to speed up the remainder of the investigation. He was concerned about the many minor witnesses that Thurmond was calling and vowed to have a conference with the senator.[77] Tempers flared between Stennis and Thurmond during hearings in June. In questioning Assistant Secretary of Defense Arthur Sylvester, Thurmond inquired about Sylvester's knowledge of "revolutionary anti-militarism" used by communists against American military personnel. This was a good example of the kind of the right-wing jargon that dotted Thurmond's questions and statements during the hearings. Stennis surely was familiar with Thurmond's usual practice of asking witnesses questions prepared in advance by his staff. This query perhaps came from Fred Buzhardt, Thurmond's chief military advisor who read widely in far-right anticommunist literature. Whether or not he was attempting to tweak Thurmond is unclear, but Stennis interrupted him, said that he was unfamiliar with the term, and asked Thurmond to define it. "I am not a witness," Thurmond shot back. "If you are trying to cross question me, this is not the time and place." Stennis said that he was certainly not trying to cross-examine a colleague. "Well it looks very much like it," Thurmond replied testily.[78]

The acrimony lingered. In an executive subcommittee meeting a few days later, Stennis and Thurmond disagreed on almost every point under discussion.[79] The two men and their staff continued to argue over the shape and the makeup of the final committee report. Stennis was careful to have staff members distinguish between Thurmond's conclusions and those drawn by the rest of the subcommittee members.[80]

The Legacy of the Muzzling Hearings

In August 1962, Willard Edwards of the *Chicago Tribune* reported that the delay in the committee's final report was "unprecedented" for a major Washington investigation on such an important subject. A "mantle of silence" descended since the end of the hearings in June, Edwards argued, contributing to public disinterest. Strom Thurmond proudly noted one development that he claimed was a direct result of the hearings. On August 13, Secretary of State Dean Rusk told reporters that in the fight against the Soviets, "it goes without saying that our purpose is to win." Thurmond claimed that before his antimuzzling drive, this kind of direct, confrontational language had fallen prey to conciliatory liberal censors in the Kennedy administration.[81]

Thurmond believed that events in Cuba in the fall of 1962 further underscored his charges of the Kennedy administration's Cold War complacency. Thurmond had warned as early as January 1962 that the Soviets were building up a supply of missiles in Cuba that could strike the United States. The Soviet Union had continued to send arms aid to Cuba over the summer. In early September, Moscow openly announced new shipments of arms and military technicians, signaling its firm commitment to defend Castro's regime in Cuba against what it saw as hostile American intervention. What the Soviets portrayed as defensive actions, many Americans saw as naked aggression. Numerous senators criticized Kennedy for his failure to confront the Soviets directly over the military buildup. New York's two Republican senators, Kenneth B. Keating and Jacob Javits, urged the president to take action; Keating said the administration was guilty of a "do nothing" attitude.[82] John Tower urged the president to recognize a Cuban government in exile. Barry Goldwater criticized Kennedy for "a policy of indecision and timidity." Strom Thurmond, however, was the only senator to issue an unequivocal call for invasion. "The time has come for Cuba to be decontaminated" of Communism, he said.[83] Thurmond criticized Kennedy for what he characterized as an abandonment of the Monroe Doctrine.[84]

The final report from the muzzling hearings was issued in October 1962 during the height of the Cuban Missile Crisis. Willard Edwards saw this as yet another attempt by the administration and its allies on the Armed Services Committee to downplay the issue.[85] The report found ineptness and capriciousness in Pentagon censoring of military officers but no evidence of appeasement. According to chairman John Stennis, the report had the "solid agreement" of all members of the committee save for Thurmond, who issued a 157-page minority report.[86] Thurmond's report was a wide-ranging summary, but at least one news report picked up on evidence that linked the State Department speech review program directly to events in Cuba. Thurmond cited instances in which portions of speeches by Admiral Arleigh Burke and Lieutenant General Jospeh F. Carroll that referred to Fidel Castro's communist connections were cut. Thurmond charged that State Department officials repeatedly tried to "play down the Soviet threat" because "they don't understand it."[87]

Right-wing leaders were disappointed with the tameness of the committee report. Robert Welch urged John Birch Society members to write letters to Senator Thurmond "congratulating him on and thanking him for his courage, determination, perseverance and skill in having this investigation carried out; and on accomplishing as much as he did, against such heavy odds and powerful opposition."[88] Edward Hunter of the Anti-Communist Liaison urged his readers to request copies of Thurmond's report. As for the muzzling hearings themselves, Hunter wrote, "In a generation connected with the press, I have never seen a news story so unethically and dishonestly covered in the U.S."[89]

In the end, the muzzling hearings initiated no significant change in American military policy. Yet the hearings marked a clear turning point in Thurmond's career. They further eroded Thurmond's relationship with the powerful pragmatic southern Democrats that dominated the Southern Caucus. Thurmond's 1948 Dixiecrat run along with his record filibuster over the 1957 civil rights bill had already marked him as a renegade among his fellow southerners. Richard Russell's wariness of Thurmond, combined with Thurmond's altercations with John Stennis over the administration of the hearings, widened an already existing rift. Stennis and Thurmond's clashes during the muzzling hearings showed dramatic differences in style and political temperament. The two would work together on plenty of issues to come, but the muzzling hearings confirmed Thurmond's sense that, as conservative as they may have been personally, many of his fellow southern Democrats were too willing to placate liberals in their own party, fellow Democrats that Thurmond had come to see as dangerous appeasers.

The muzzling hearings solidified Thurmond's leading role in a Sunbelt-based, ideologically charged right-wing anticommunist movement. In February 1962, he was a guest, along with Barry Goldwater, Robert Welch, Billy

James Hargis, Edwin Walker, and others, on a *CBS Reports* episode titled "Thunder on the Right."[90] The following month he received an award from the Young Americans for Freedom at their "Conservative Rally for World Liberation from Communism" at Madison Square Garden.[91] Thurmond joined, among others, Roger Milliken, John Dos Passos, M. Stanton Evans, Ludwig Van Misees, John Wayne, and Richard Weaver at the event, which brought in 18,000 conservative activists and received front page coverage in the *New York Times*.[92] Thurmond became a frequent guest on right-wing radio programs, such as the Clarence Manion radio forum and the Citizens' Council Forum Film and Radio series, where he addressed not only civil rights issues but defense and foreign policy concerns as well.[93]

The muzzling hearings provide crucial context for understanding Thurmond's party switch in 1964. If Thurmond's overriding political concern had been merely to maintain white supremacy in his native South, there would have been no reason for him to leave the Democratic Party. Since the 1930s, conservative Southern Democrats had successfully used their power in the Senate to block or dilute civil rights measures. With the power they held on numerous Congressional committees, southerners such as Russell and Stennis would continue throughout the 1960s to extract civil rights concessions from Democratic and Republican administrations alike. The Republican Party, moreover, included many of the same "problems" as the Democrats—civil rights moderates and liberals—without any of the benefits of the Democratic Party—namely, seniority power.

When Thurmond switched to the GOP in 1964, the central element in the deal he worked out with Republican leadership was that he would not only maintain his position on the Senate Armed Services Committee but also keep his seniority.[94] With Barry Goldwater's temporary retirement from the Senate following his unsuccessful presidential run, Thurmond became the leading voice of right-wing anticommunism in the GOP. He dominated conservative Republican foreign policy circles for the remainder of the Cold War. He was one of the harshest congressional critics of Lyndon Johnson's handling of the Vietnam War. He was a major supporter of the antiballistic missile system throughout the 1960s and the most consistent enthusiast of Richard Nixon's hard-line Vietnam policies.

The muzzling hearings opened up to Thurmond the electoral potential of popular, right-wing anticommunism that was rooted in the Sunbelt. They certainly deepened Thurmond's political relationship with the Sunbelt's leading politician, Barry Goldwater; the two men went further in attacking the Kennedy administration than any other senators. But more importantly, the hearings endeared Thurmond to the constituency that fed Goldwaterism. It was a group that in many ways Thurmond had been courting since 1948. For activists on the right, the muzzling hearings transformed Thurmond's political profile. He was no longer merely a regional figure defending white southern interests: he was now a serious conservative critic on issues of foreign policy and national security. With his muzzling campaign, Thurmond joined in spirit if not yet in political identification a small but feverish clan that was remaking the Republican Party, one whose influence on national politics was just beginning to be felt.

Chapter 3

Big Government and Family Values: Political Culture in the Metropolitan Sunbelt

Matthew D. Lassiter

In the mid-1990s, Cobb County in suburban Atlanta gained national prominence and notoriety as a grassroots bastion of the Religious Right and as a Sunbelt base of the "Republican Revolution" engineered by local U.S. Representative Newt Gingrich. The GOP takeover of Congress in the midterm elections of 1994 depended on the mobilization of conservative activists and suburban voters throughout the nation, with particular strength in the fast-growing Sunbelt metropolises of the New South, the Rocky Mountain states, and the Southwest.[1] In the "Contract with America," Republican candidates pledged to replace the Great Society with a new Conservative Opportunity Society by slashing government spending, reforming welfare, cracking down on crime, cutting middle-class taxes, strengthening the military, and liberating corporations from bureaucratic regulations and consumer lawsuits.[2] During the campaign, Gingrich labeled Democratic President Bill Clinton "the enemy of normal Americans," whom he defined as middle-class suburbanites who "still believe—and are working toward—the American Dream of owning our own home, raising our families, giving our children a better life with safe streets, and a future built on self-reliance and hard work." The self-described visionary championed Cobb County as

Table 3.1. Population of Cobb County and State of Georgia, 1900–2000

Year	Cobb Population	% Increase	Georgia Population
2000	607,751	35.7	8.2 million
1990	447,745	50.4	6.5 million
1980	297,718	51.3	5.5 million
1970	196,793	72.4	4.6 million
1960	114,174	84.7	3.94 million
1950	61,830	61.6	3.44 million
1940	38,272	8.1	3.12 million
1930	35,408	16.3	2.91 million
1920	30,437	7.2	2.90 million
1910	28,397	15.1	2.61 million
1900	24,664	10.7	2.22 million

Sources: Digital Library of Georgia, http://georgiainfo.galileo.usg.edu/countypop/cobbpop.htm; Historical Census Browser, University of Virginia, Geospatial and Statistical Data Center, http://fisher.lib.virginia.edu/collections/stats/histcensus/index.html.

the ideal suburban synthesis of traditional family values and the futuristic Sunbelt economy, a booming destination for migrants from across the nation who "want safety and . . . believe big cities have failed." "What they find here," Gingrich enthused, "is a sort of Norman Rockwell world with fiber optic computers and jet airplanes."[3]

Cobb County, a linchpin of metropolitan Atlanta's extraordinary growth during the second half of the twentieth century, represents an archetype of the national power shift to the metropolitan Sunbelt.[4] Cobb's total population increased from 61,830 in 1950 to 297,718 in 1980 to 607,751 in 2000, with white-collar families from the Northeast and Midwest making up a significant majority of these newcomers (see Table 3.1). By century's end, only 37.4 percent of Cobb residents had been born in the state of Georgia, and a substantial number of these natives were the children of recent arrivals. In evidence of the highly mobile work force of the Sunbelt corporate economy, 51.5 percent of Cobb residents in 2000 lived at a different residence than they had only five years earlier. These trends reflected the broader demographic patterns across the booming suburbs located north of Atlanta, which trailed only Phoenix for the nation's highest rate of growth among large metropolitan regions during the 1990s (38.9 to 45.3 percent, respectively). In another illustration of the dynamic expansion of the Sunbelt, the state of Georgia ranked fourth in the U.S. for total population increase during the decade, following California, Texas, and Florida. In percentage terms, Georgia grew faster than every state east of the Rocky Mountains between 1990 and 1999, including a net increase in domestic migration of 665,000 people (second highest in the U.S. behind Florida).[5] Many white middle-class residents of Atlanta's northern suburbs "have come from Rustbelt cities to find opportunity," the local *Marietta Daily Journal* proclaimed at the dawning of the so-called "Gingrich Revolution" of 1994. "With job growth outpacing population growth, Cobb is a prosperous destination." "I came here in 1973," recalled a Little League father from an affluent East Cobb subdivision. "It was paradise. It was vibrant, growing. Detroit was stagnant. You can travel around the whole world and not find a better place to live than this."[6]

Placing demographic and economic transformations at the center of political history recasts conventional narratives of electoral realignment in the modern South and in the broader Sunbelt region.[7] A closer examination of Cobb County challenges and complicates three influential models of political change in modern America: the "Southern Strategy" thesis that the white backlash against the civil rights movement led directly to a Republican takeover of the region; the New Right thesis that has drawn too sharp a distinction between anti-communist conservatism in the West and racial conservatism in the South; and the Religious Right thesis that overstates the grassroots support for "culture war" crusades in conservative-leaning suburbs.[8] In Cobb, white middle-class migrants born outside the South played the dominant role in the ascendance of the local Republican Party, which did not achieve a critical mass until the county's greatest population surge during the post-1970 period. This timing reflected a second wave of Sunbelt growth, when many southern and western metropolises located away from the coasts underwent the scale of suburbanization that Southern California and Florida had experienced in previous decades. Although considerable political, ideological, and racial diversity has always existed within the metropolitan Sunbelt as a whole, the clustering of white-collar Republicans in suburban areas such as Cobb County provided the demographic and economic foundations for what Kevin Phillips labeled "The Emerging Republican Majority"—the "rising insurgency of the South, the West, . . . and white middle-class suburbia." In Cobb County and throughout metropolitan Atlanta, the direct link between GOP fortunes and the middle-class corporate economy reflected a broader pattern of New Right mobilization in sprawling Sunbelt suburbs such as Orange County, California; Phoenix and Colorado Springs in the West; the Dallas-Fort Worth metroplex; and "New South" destinations such as Virginia Beach, Charlotte, and Orlando.[9]

The modern political culture of Cobb County evolved from its overlapping roots in the Cold War, the New South, and the nationalization of suburban patterns of residential growth and racial/economic segregation in the post-World War II period. Investigating Cobb County from each of these perspectives highlights the forces of convergence, but also the different paths of political development, in the ascending Sunbelt that has captured the attention of scholars and journalists since the 1970s. Defense spending by the federal government galvanized Cobb County's postwar growth, like many other Cold War suburban landscapes that were disproportionately but by no means exclusively located in the Sunbelt South or West.[10] Timing and existing historical conditions shaped Cobb's political trajectory as well, since the dynamics of the one-party South and the relatively limited white-collar population growth before 1970 delayed grassroots Republican expansion, in comparison with suburban Phoenix or Los Angeles. Among other variations, this meant that right-wing anticommunist groups such as the John Birch Society played a much smaller role in the rise of southern Republicanism than they did in the origins of the New Right in the Southwest during the 1950s and 1960s.[11] Instead, the GOP's ascension in Atlanta's white-collar suburbs intersected most directly with the mobilization of the Religious Right in the 1980s and 1990s, similar to other high-tech and defense-oriented Sunbelt centers such as Colorado Springs and Virginia Beach/Hampton Roads. The polarizing politics of the Christian Right, however, revealed the dynamic nature of the metropolitan Sunbelt once again, as the Democratic party has achieved recent success by appealing to moderate white-collar professionals, as well as the growing Latino and Asian-American populations, in the increasingly diverse suburbs of the South and West.[12]

The political history of Cobb County is therefore a thoroughly national story about suburban development, as much as it is a regional story about the emergence of the two-party South and the booming Sunbelt. During the postwar era, when federal policies and real-estate corporations standardized the all-white suburban landscapes built across the United States, the politics of anti-communism and the politics of racial segregation converged in the national defense of private property rights.[13] Whether in the West, the South, or points beyond, conservative activists from the Birchers to the Religious Right have influenced party politics through effective grassroots organizing, but in ideological terms their agendas have been subordinate to the mainstream suburban issues of maintaining low taxes, defending homogeneous neighborhoods, preserving property values, ensuring children's security, and rejecting social welfare programs for cities and the minority poor—all while favoring government spending on entitlements and infrastructure for the middle class. In the mid-1990s, when Newt Gingrich's Cobb County came to symbolize a rising Republican tide of hard-edged southern/Sunbelt conservatism, the middle-class transplants in Atlanta's upscale suburbs repeatedly insisted that they were the same as other Americans, and indeed prototypically American, in their dedication to capitalism, patriotism, and family values. "The people here have the same concerns that most Americans have—good schools, [low] crime and their economic future," explained an IBM executive who relocated to Cobb from the similar Dallas suburb of Plano. "In our neighborhood, we're just regular people," insisted a suburban mother of two. "We want to invest ourselves in our families, and we don't want to be taxed to death. I think most Americans feel this way."[14] Beyond the "culture wars" that raged in the 1990s, this political culture of middle-class family values was deeply structured by the big-government policies that produced the political economy of Cold War investment, Sunbelt-style sprawl, and the racially segregated suburban dream.

Cold War Suburb

Wars created and sustained the conditions for Cobb County's economic dynamism and population influx, as with many of the high-growth and high-tech places in the region eventually labeled the Sunbelt. The military policies of the federal government made the settlement and expansion of Cobb possible, from the U.S. army campaign that drove out the Cherokee Indians in the 1830s to the aerospace industry that dominated the local economy during the early decades of the Cold War. Before World War II, Cobb was a mostly rural agricultural county with a few small furniture and textile factories, a shortage of decent roads, and a streetcar line connecting the seat of Marietta to downtown Atlanta twenty miles away.[15] Then in late 1941, following the Japanese attack on Pearl Harbor, a group of Cobb business leaders convinced federal officials to convert Marietta's small municipal airport into a massive B-29 bomber plant. The War Department constructed the Marietta facility for the Buffalo-based Bell Aircraft Corporation, and the *Atlanta Constitution* celebrated the "beginning of a new industrial era which will directly or indirectly affect the present and future of every one in the Empire State of the Southeast." When the war ended in 1945, the Bell plant had produced almost seven hundred B-29 Superfortress bombers and provided skilled jobs with decent wages to nearly 100,000 Georgians, "recruited from the fields, the soda fountains, grocery stores and even housewives." Flush with federal money, Marietta also paved many local roads and supplied Bell workers with 2,500 new brick homes in single-family subdivisions. Wartime prosperity had provided the infrastructure for family-oriented suburban growth in the future, a local businessman observed. "We're only 20 minutes from Atlanta, the community is new and clean, and living conditions are excellent."[16]

Boosters in Cobb County turned the success story of the Bell Bomber Plant into a broader crusade for economic development, part of the regional trend of promoting the New South to federal officials and corporate investors.[17] Before World War II, Cobb's national profile was almost nonexistent, except for the infamous lynching of Jewish factory manager Leo Frank by Marietta citizens in 1915. During and after the war, business leader James V. Carmichael became Cobb's most prominent advocate of the New South model of rapid economic development through policies of racial moderation and pledges of national reunification. In 1941, Carmichael spoke at a local Confederate Memorial Day ceremony while helping to lead the recruitment drive for the federal military airfield. He praised the courage of those who "built a new South" out of the ruins of the Civil War but promised that "we do not live in the past. . . . We have long since dedicated ourselves unreservedly and whole heartedly to the United States of America."[18] Carmichael served as the general manager of the Bell factory until its closure in 1945, following V-J day and the cancellation of the military contract. He reassured Cobb's boosters that the future remained bright because the pool of newly skilled workers offered "a blazing invitation to other industries to come in here and take advantage of that force."[19] The next year, Carmichael ran for governor on a New South platform of modernization and industrial growth, winning the metropolitan counties and the popular vote but losing the election because of Georgia's malapportioned, rural-dominated county unit system.[20] In a 1950 commencement speech at Emory University, Carmichael lambasted the racial demagogues who were holding back industrial progress by "always waving the Confederate flag and telling us what a glorious heritage the South has." To overcome the region's "inferior economic position in the Nation," he called for high-wage manufacturing jobs, recruitment of white-collar corporations, and the educational and cultural advancements necessary to lure middle-class families away from the "congested industrial centers of the East and Midwest."[21]

The outbreak of military conflict in Korea turned Cobb County into a thriving hub in the national military-industrial complex, a microcosm of the Cold War's dramatic effects on proto-Sunbelt landscapes from California to Texas to Florida. In 1951, the U.S. Air Force and the Lockheed Corporation, based in suburban Los Angeles, reopened Marietta's dormant Bell plant under the auspices of the Lockheed-Georgia Company, which quickly became the largest employer in the state. At the renamed Dobbins Air Force Base, the massive Lockheed-Georgia factory churned out thousands of aircraft during the national security escalation of the 1950s, including B-47 Stratojet bombers and C-130 Hercules transport planes. Lockheed selected James Carmichael as the first manager of its Marietta subsidiary, and he issued the call for "patriotic" employees who wanted to "serve your country by becoming an important part of its defense activities!" Carmichael pledged to hire black and white applicants "according to their ability," although they would work on segregated assembly lines and use "separate but equal" rest rooms and dining facilities. By the end of the decade, Lockheed-Georgia employed 15,000 people, fully half of Cobb's manufacturing workforce, with 45,000 more dependents living in "Lockheed families" and another 10,000 hired by subcontractors. A 1958 report in *Manufacturer's Record* praised the county's new business climate, including the highways, shopping centers, "wholesome recreation" for youth, and single-family subdivisions "of the sort which may be seen in many parts of the country." Lockheed's arrival "set off a small economic revolution," the *Marietta Daily Journal* observed on the tenth anniversary. Property values quadrupled and southern traditions receded during the 1950s, as the "plant became a mecca for the world's scientists, engineers, skilled mechanics and technicians. The pilgrimage to Cobb by highly trained people from all over the world began [in 1951] and has been going on ever since."[22]

The Cobb County Chamber of Commerce moved aggressively to make Lockheed the foundation of a suburban political economy organized around white-collar employment, a diversified industrial base, single-family homeownership, residential segregation, and "progressive" national values.

In the early 1950s, Cobb's marketing campaign displayed the awkward tensions between the Confederate past and the Cold War present, with both defined by an intensely martial ethos. Chamber of Commerce pamphlets portrayed Cobb as the gateway for tourists heading to the mountains of North Georgia, where they could spend a day in "Gone With the Wind Country" and visit the Civil War museum at Kennesaw Mountain National Battlefield Park. After traveling down memory lane, visitors might consider "joining us in gracious living in Cobb County," the home of "friendly, progressive people," "moderate temperatures at all seasons," and the Lockheed airplanes that "circle the earth."[23] By the early 1960s, the Chamber of Commerce had abandoned nostalgia altogether, urging prospective corporations and residents to "Invest in the Future" of a suburban county filled with "good homes, good schools, good churches, good transportation, good roads." Business leaders promised that exclusionary zoning would protect residential neighborhoods and also highlighted a new industrial park and two large shopping centers located along the commuter highways that offered easy access to downtown Atlanta. Marietta, which claimed to be "America's fastest growing city," boasted of "good neighbors, clean government, easy access, beautiful homes" as the center of a "prosperous and progressive" county—92 percent white in 1960, with 87 percent owner-occupied housing. Smyrna, located between Marietta and Atlanta, also claimed the title of fastest growing city in the nation as well as the "only 100 per cent white populated city in Georgia" with at least 10,000 residents.[24]

In 1964, *Time* magazine highlighted Lockheed and NASA in an article linking economic development in the South and the West to federal government contracts and regional strategies to "lure industry with sunshine, low-wage labor, and generous tax concessions." Rates of expansion in the Midwest and Northeast were lagging behind this proto-Sunbelt nexus, especially because "aerospace and defense have drifted to areas that boast a gentler climate and more persuasive Congressmen."[25] That same year, Cobb industrialist James Carmichael celebrated the New South miracle: "In a period of thirty years, the Nation's Economic Problem No. 1 has become the Nation's Economic Opportunity No. 1. Two world wars and the absolute necessity to utilize all available manpower triggered the movement of industry into the South."[26] Cobb County leaders found a new reason to rejoice in 1965, when the Air Force awarded the multibillion dollar contract for the new C-5A Galaxy airplane to the Lockheed-Georgia Company. Local boosters labeled the C-5A contract "the best thing that ever happened to

Cobb County," a guarantee of further migration by highly desirable newcomers: "engineers, designers, scientists and other technical people." Ernest Barrett, the chair of the Cobb County Commission, reported "hundreds of new homes and apartments being constructed, new shopping centers, and new businesses of all types. Lockheed and the C-5A have given us all the push we needed, and now I believe we are on our way to a great future." Barrett, a pro-growth politician with close ties to the Chamber of Commerce, implemented an expansionist program that included major road construction projects and the comprehensive sewer and water systems necessary for outlying subdivisions in unincorporated areas of the county. In 1969, developer Tom Cousins opened the first major residential neighborhood in East Cobb, a golf course community called Indian Hills that eventually encompassed more than 1,600 homes built for the affluent corporate transplants who would become a driving force behind the local GOP.[27]

In Cobb County, as in other sprawling Cold War suburbs from Orange County to Norfolk/Hampton Roads, the direct link between federal defense spending and local economic prosperity structured a bipartisan political culture of hawkish conservatism and material self-interest on issues of national security. "War has played a major part in the financial seesaw of Cobb County," the Board of Commissioners declared in the late 1960s. The Civil War left the area "charred and penniless," but World War II followed by the Korean War and two decades of uninterrupted growth for the aerospace industry "saw the County flourishing again."[28] The Vietnam era, however, shattered the Cold War consensus in Washington in favor of escalation of the national security state, which brought new challenges to Cobb County's share of the federal government's military-industrial largess. Local politicians and aerospace workers expressed outrage in 1969, when liberal Democrats in the U.S. Congress began investigating cost overruns and quality defects in the production of the C-5A. Lockheed-Georgia mobilized its supporters by warning that cancellation of the contract could result in 30,000 layoffs in Cobb and reminding residents that locally built airplanes had helped keep the nation "out of a disastrous World War III for almost 25 years."[29] In the early 1970s, the Nixon administration engineered a $250 million taxpayer bailout to prevent the bankruptcy of the parent Lockheed Aircraft Corporation, but the end of the Vietnam War and the concurrent economic recession caused Lockheed-Georgia to slash its local workforce from 33,000 to 9,000.[30] Cobb County emerged relatively unscathed, thanks to its recently diversified economy and a population base that nearly tripled between 1960 and 1980, but the ritual retelling of the Cold War origins story remained a potent element of local political culture. To commemorate every major anniversary, the Cobb Chamber of Commerce and the *Marietta Daily Journal* organized "Salute to Lockheed" celebrations praising the company for "its notable contributions to the community and the nation's defense."[31]

While federal programs built the modern landscape of Cobb County, the political ethos of local boosters and corporate leaders combined considerable pride regarding their participation in the national security state with an equally forceful defense of free-market capitalism. In addition to the heavily subsidized aerospace industry, the federal government paid for the highways that connected Cobb to downtown Atlanta and other suburban destinations, including the I-75/I-285 interchange that anchored the "Platinum Triangle" of shopping malls, upscale hotels, and office parks. Federal agencies provided mortgage loans or insurance for most of Cobb's housing stock, and they paid for much of the sewer and water services that facilitated suburban growth. The national government also dammed the rivers that provided electric power, drinking water, and two recreational lakes (Lanier and Allatoona) for Cobb residents.[32] Yet in 1965 the Cobb Chamber of Commerce saw a synthesis rather than a contradiction when the group launched a "free enterprise" educational program for local public schools while calling for more military spending and federal highway dollars. For the next two decades, as part of the national mobilization of corporate lobbies to advance the New Right economic agenda, the Cobb Chamber sent business executives into classrooms to "explain and promote our American free enterprise system . . . that has endowed the average American with the highest standard of living in the world."[33] During the early 1980s, the Cobb business alliance openly endorsed the Reagan administration's national security escalation and the president's "Program for Economic Recovery." The Chamber praised Reagan's promise to cut taxes, domestic spending programs, and bureaucratic regulations, which would "nurture the strength and vitality of the American people by reducing the burdensome, intrusive role of the Federal Government." Without missing a beat, the group simultaneously pledged to "utilize all applicable sources of federal and state assistance" for the expansion of transportation networks and other forms of infrastructure essential to corporate expansion and suburban development.[34]

Cobb's political and business leadership also adopted the Reagan slogan

"Peace Through Strength" for the celebration of Armed Forces Week in 1982, and the county commissioners called on all residents to "join in the effort to keep America strong, proud, and free." Dozens of local corporations joined in praising the Dobbins Air Force Base for its defense of national security and for the "economic impact of the military presence" in Cobb County.[35] Officials of Lockheed-Georgia and military officers at Dobbins likewise contributed to the nationalistic and militaristic political culture of their Cold War suburb, especially during the annual Armed Forces Day that offered citizens a chance to tour the facilities and view an acrobatic air show. "A strong and ready national defense posture is mandatory," the Dobbins commander insisted in the early 1980s, "to project our national will and protect our interests around the world." "Pride in America and what she stands for is a way of life" in Cobb County, the Lockheed-Georgia Company agreed. "Waving the American flag or getting a lump in your throat when singing the Star Spangled Banner is not out of style."[36] Lockheed's president observed that the corporation did not even have to lobby the elected officials who represented Cobb because support for defense spending remained robust, bipartisan, and indeed automatic.[37] The Cobb County Chamber of Commerce expressed its own full confidence in the future at the dawn of the Reagan era, with little visible anxiety about local consequences from the ongoing national recession or spillover effects from the widely acknowledged urban crisis just down the highway in the city of Atlanta. "The Sunbelt is still the growth area of the next decade," Cobb's corporate establishment proclaimed in 1980, "and we are in the #1 spot in the South."[38]

Shades of Conservatism

James Carmichael, the Cobb native who managed the aerospace plants for Bell and Lockheed, championed a metropolitan vision of New South progress and Sunbelt prosperity. "Whether we like it or not, we are a part and parcel of metropolitan Atlanta," he told the Cobb Chamber of Commerce in 1966. Thousands of residents of Cobb's bedroom communities commuted to work in the central city, and corporate growth in the suburbs would never have happened without their proximity to Atlanta. "Our destiny lies with Atlanta, and it ill becomes us to oppose and refuse to cooperate in things which will help Atlanta just because we are a separate political entity and because a river separates us." During the civil rights era, when he served as the president of the Atlanta-based Scripto Company, Carmichael also took the booster story of the New South miracle on the road. Metropolitan regions from Atlanta to Houston offered "unlimited opportunity for future growth and development," he informed business groups across the country, as long as national corporations overcame their "preconceived ideas of what life in the deep South is like." Carmichael explained that economic progress required enlightened race relations, the formula that had made Atlanta "the dream city of the great Southeast." Agreeing that "the Negro has a good cause," he called for the replacement of Jim Crow segregation with a color-blind and merit-based American Dream that provided "equal economic opportunities" (but specifically not affirmative action) to black citizens.[39] Carmichael also remained active in electoral politics by endorsing moderate Democrats at the state level, supporting Richard Nixon in 1960 in an effort to "establish a true two-party system" in Georgia, and joining forces with a group of national business leaders to back Lyndon Johnson as the "conservative" alternative to what he considered the extremist Goldwater movement of 1964.[40]

During the civil rights era, when grassroots conservatives in Southern California were mobilizing against powerful liberal forces in state politics, Republican politics in suburban Atlanta revolved around a very different reaction against the conservative Democratic leadership of a one-party state.[41] In the 1960 presidential campaign, nearly 200,000 people turned out for Vice President Richard Nixon's appearance in downtown Atlanta, where he declared that "it is time for the Republican candidates to stop conceding the South to the Democrats." In an effort to build on Eisenhower's inroads in the metropolitan South, the GOP nominee promised military strength in the struggle against communism, free enterprise and limited government at home, and enforcement of racial equality under the law. According to the *Saturday Evening Post*, the white middle-class voters at the Nixon rally carried their Republicanism with an "air of fashionable defiance" because they "hate the state machine, the redneck gang from the Talmadge family which denies suffrage or voice to the new and growing cities of Georgia." The emergence of a competitive two-party system seemed inevitable, given all the "new industry and a naturally conservative middle class" in Atlanta and its surrounding suburbs.[42] During the 1950s and 1960s, however, Cobb's support for Republican candidates in national contests lagged behind more established suburbs on Atlanta's northside. Nixon received 39

Table 3.2. Partisan Trends in Presidential Elections in Cobb County, 1960-2008 (percent)

Year	Republican	Democratic	Independent	Total Votes
1960	39.0 (Nixon)	61.0 (Kennedy)		21,146
1964	55.6 (Goldwater)	44.4 (Johnson)		37,510
1968	41.3 (Nixon)	19.4 (Humphrey)	39.4 (Wallace)	45,209
1972	85.1 (Nixon)	14.9 (McGovern)		51,665
1976	43.3 (Ford)	56.7 (Carter)		79,326
1980	54.2 (Reagan)	40.9 (Carter)	3.4 (Anderson)	94,363
1984	77.4 (Reagan)	22.6 (Mondale)		125,843
1988	73.1 (Bush)	26.9 (Dukakis)		145,918
1992	52.8 (Bush)	32.6 (Clinton)	14.6 (Perot)	196,441
1996	57.6 (Dole)	37.2 (Clinton)	5.3 (Perot)	198,376
2000	60.5 (Bush)	37.3 (Gore)	2.2 (Libertarian)	232,094
2004	62.1 (Bush)	37.5 (Kerry)	0.7 (Libertarian)	279,473
2008	54.1 (McCain)	44.7 (Obama)	0.9 (Libertarian)	316,589

Sources: Atlas of U.S. Presidential Elections, USelectionatlas.org; Georgia Secretary of State Elections Division, http://www.sos.ga.gov/elections/.

percent of 21,146 ballots cast in Cobb in 1960, ten points below his totals in the nearby counties of Fulton and DeKalb. Because of rapid population growth, almost twice as many Cobb voters participated in the 1964 presidential election, when Goldwater's conservative national security platform and his opposition to civil rights laws carried the county with 55.6 percent. Cobb split down the middle in 1968, with Nixon edging the segregationist third-party candidate George Wallace by a 41–39 margin. Democratic nominee Hubert Humphrey received only 19 percent, while Wallace ran twice as strong in Cobb as he did in the more affluent and populous suburbs of Fulton and DeKalb (see Table 3.2).[43]

Although Cobb's population remained around 90 percent white between the 1950s and the 1980s, substantial political diversity existed within the county throughout this period, most notably because residential growth patterns established significant electoral divisions based on socioeconomics and geography. Three distinct processes drove suburban expansion during Cobb's long postwar boom. In the earliest phase, developers and planners created blue-collar and white-collar subdivisions inside and around the towns of Marietta and Smyrna for the managers, engineers, and assembly line workers drawn by Lockheed and related Cold War industries. While most residents of Cobb's working-class neighborhoods were Georgia natives, a large percentage of the county's white-collar work force migrated from outside the state. Next, in the 1950s and early 1960s, "white flight" from residential integration in southwest Atlanta brought thousands of working-class and middle-income families to new subdivisions located in the Smyrna section of South Cobb or near the previously rural towns of Mableton and Austell in West Cobb. And then, starting in the late 1960s, upscale subdivisions located in the unincorporated areas of East Cobb attracted tens of thousands of non-southern transplants and their families. Residents of these new white-collar neighborhoods, as with similarly situated Atlanta suburbs in North Fulton and Gwinnett County, rarely worked in the defense industry and instead commuted to downtown skyscrapers or to the new suburban office parks sprouting up along the interstate corridors. The 1970 census revealed that East Cobb and the white-collar pockets around Marietta contained the county's highest median family incomes and thousands of recent arrivals from the Northeast and Midwest. These demographic gaps widened during the next two decades, as the population boom brought the median income in East Cobb to double the national average and the ratio of county residents born outside Georgia to 56 percent by 1990.[44]

Rather than a uniform politics of suburban conservatism or a wholesale defection of white Democrats during the civil rights era, partisan divisions in Cobb County reflected the demographic trends of a rapidly expanding electorate sorted out by socioeconomic class and geographic background. In statewide elections from the 1940s through the early 1960s, Cobb consistently backed business moderates such as James Carmichael over rural traditionalists in the factional battles of the Georgia Democrats. Then populist segregationist Lester Maddox won 57 percent of the vote in the 1966 Democratic primary for governor, thanks largely to blue-collar workers and recent white refugees from racial transition in Atlanta but also to nonparticipation by white-collar voters who finally had Republican options in statewide elections. Republican residents of East Cobb, who supplied Nixon's plurality in 1968, enabled GOP candidates for governor to carry the county narrowly in 1966 and 1970 (although each lost the statewide election). Nixon swept Cobb by an 85–15 margin against liberal Democrat George McGovern in 1972, when issues of national security, crime, and "forced busing" predominated. Moderate southern Democrats fared much better, as Jimmy Carter won back most of the Wallace Democrats in the 1976 presidential election, when he received 57 percent of Cobb's ballots and polled especially well in blue-collar and middle-income white areas. In 1980, an influx of new voters helped Ronald Reagan defeat Carter by 54–41 percent in Cobb, before he trounced Walter Mondale by a 77–23 margin in his 1984 reelection campaign.[45] Presidential results, however, tell only one slice of the story of political culture and electoral realignment in the suburban South, as building a Republican party at the grassroots took a substantial amount of time and a certain amount of patience in order for migration patterns to reach critical mass. Although Cobb's electorate overwhelmingly rejected liberal Democrats in national elections, residents of South and West Cobb continued to display high levels of support for conservative and moderate Democrats well into the 1990s, while East Cobb emerged as a dependable GOP stronghold of the type found in many of the nation's affluent suburbs.[46]

"Cobb needs two parties," an unsuccessful Republican candidate for the Georgia state legislature informed Marietta voters in 1962. Lockheed engineer Warren Herron, a typical early Republican activist in the Sunbelt South, campaigned on a platform of industrial development, increased funding for public schools and delinquency prevention, and county management by professional civil servants rather than the corrupt courthouse politics of a one-party system.[47] Real estate broker Johnny Isakson offered the same critique of the Marietta "courthouse crowd" in his breakthrough campaign of 1976, when he won a seat in the Georgia House of Representatives as a Republican from East Cobb. Isakson, a native of Atlanta's elite Buckhead enclave who had recently moved to the suburbs, campaigned on intensely local issues of property values and quality-of-life regulations such as infrastructure development for East Cobb and restrictive zoning to keep multifamily apartments out of single-family neighborhoods. A self-defined "moderate conservative," Isakson became one of the most influential architects of the modern Republican Party in Georgia, eventually serving in the U.S. House of Representatives before winning election to the Senate in 2005. He maintained that the "party base was built primarily with newcomers . . . from outside the state of Georgia that moved from areas where Republicans and Democrats ran competitively." Roy Barnes, a moderate Democrat from Mableton who represented West Cobb in the state legislature from 1975 to 1990 (and served as governor from 1999–2003), agreed with this demographic analysis of the roots of Cobb's political transformation and the nature of the county's partisan divide. The challenge for local

Democrats, Barnes said in 1990, came from the fact that new migrants were "bringing their politics from other states to Georgia with them. . . . The typical voter has probably lived here less than ten years . . . and is upper income—upper middle income—and more affluent, very concerned about education and typically a Republican voter."[48]

Democratic politicians in Cobb County spanned a broad spectrum from New Deal populists to suburban moderates to right-wing ideologues. The most reactionary Cobb-based politician was Larry McDonald, a fiercely anti-communist member of the John Birch Society and a Democrat of convenience who served in the U.S. House from 1975–1983. But McDonald frequently failed to carry Cobb and stayed in power only with wide margins in the rural parts of his congressional district, as a majority of suburban voters seemed satisfied with the mainstream versions of conservative anti-communism that enjoyed bipartisan support throughout the county.[49] Roy Barnes and George (Buddy) Darden, who succeeded McDonald in Congress from 1983–1995, were moderate Democrats with bases in West Cobb who campaigned as fiscal conservatives and endorsed the military-industrial complex and traditional family values.[50] Joe Mack Wilson, usually described as a "yellow-dog Democrat," represented Marietta in the state legislature from 1961–1988 until losing his seat, according to his hometown newspaper, "to a county that was filling up with transplants from the Northeast and Midwest." Wilson believed in the redistribution of wealth, considered Franklin Roosevelt to be "the greatest man that ever lived," and credited federal mortgage policies with allowing working-class families to achieve "the American Dream, a part of the Franklin Roosevelt era, that gave a lot of folks hope and made them realize those dreams . . . about having a home." An equally outspoken segregationist during the civil rights era, Wilson also played a critical role in curtailing suburban annexation by the city of Atlanta and in preventing Cobb County from joining metropolitan ventures such as the MARTA mass transit system. And in a reflection of the class rifts among white areas of the county, Joe Mack Wilson scorned his East Cobb opponents as "snobbish type Republicans, . . . country club types, . . . It all boils down to greed, . . . the rich taking advantage of the poor. . . . There's more to life than a tennis court or golf club or Saab."[51]

Between 1970 and 1990, Cobb's population increased by more than 250,000 residents at a growth rate of more than 50 percent per decade, turning the county into a pacesetter of the second-wave Sunbelt boom. As a result, local politics shifted decisively from a one-party system to a competitive two-party environment. By the mid-1980s, the GOP consolidation of the affluent subdivisions of East Cobb had produced a distinct countywide advantage for Republicans in national and statewide elections, while the Democratic resilience in the middle-income areas of West Cobb had maintained almost evenly divided delegations to the state legislature and Board of Commissioners.[52] At the same time, elected officials and ordinary voters in both parties continued to operate within a broad consensus framework on the fundamental issues that energized suburban political culture: the defense of property values and residential segregation, the provision of quality schools and family-friendly consumer spaces, and the policing of the actual and symbolic boundaries separating Cobb from the city of Atlanta. Cobb politicians Johnny Isakson, Roy Barnes, and Joe Mack Wilson differed on many matters, but each cited neighborhood battles over zoning as the initial catalyst for his involvement in electoral politics. "Zonings—that's what's the real power in this county," Wilson explained in an incisive summary of Cobb's modern transformation—and of American suburban politics writ large. "It ain't goodness and kindness and sweetness. It's who can zone what where and when and for how much."[53] Exclusionary zoning combined with pervasive racial discrimination in housing to make Cobb a typically segregated American suburb by the end of the 1960s, a decade when the county's net increase of 82,619 people included only 148 African Americans. Outside Marietta, where longtime black residents were concentrated in neighborhoods near the town center, most census tracts in East Cobb contained populations more than 99 percent white in 1970. The high-growth neighborhoods of East Cobb (and Smyrna in South Cobb) remained more than 97 percent white at the time of the 1980 census, while the black population in the West Cobb tracts located closest to the city of Atlanta had increased to about 8 percent.[54]

As Atlanta became a majority-black city in the 1970s, Cobb's politicians and business leaders embraced an explicitly suburban political consciousness, often portraying their county as "adjacent to" but independent from a metropolitan region that provided economic benefits without cultural risks or political responsibilities. "The county enjoys every advantage of the metropolis," the Cobb Chamber of Commerce proclaimed in 1969, "but retains its separate identity in an atmosphere of unhurried, uncongested suburban living." "Despite a record rate of growth and its proximity to a huge metropolitan area," the Board of Commissioners promised in 1974, "it has succeeded in maintaining its own identity, and been able to offer all of its citizens the comforts and conveniences of a metropolitan center while keeping a measure of community life."[55] Disregarding James Carmichael's counsel against adopting a "selfish attitude of self-containment," Cobb's leaders refused to join the MARTA light rail system established in the early 1970s, partly because of an unwillingness to share in the tax burden but largely because of the specter of black crime invading the white suburbs.[56] The Chamber of Commerce published literature that portrayed Cobb County as a place "where property rights are still respected . . . and law and order continue to remain a way of life!" The cover image of this document showed a young white girl with a baby doll talking to a friendly police officer, with houses and a church steeple in the background and the tag line: "Another reason for coming to Cobb with confidence!"[57] In addition to equating racial security with the suburban good life, Cobb's business and political leaders presented a comprehensive agenda of protecting middle-class family values by promoting "a pleasant atmosphere for youthful citizens to grow up in"—a civic program to distribute "Neighbors Against Crime" signs, safe and wholesome "family entertainment" at the Six Flags over Georgia amusement park, "one of the best public school systems" in Georgia, the traditional "charm of small community living."[58]

Beyond the Culture Wars

During the postwar era, the Protestant churches that dominated religious worship in Cobb County actively embraced the consensus politics of the Cold War mission, the gospel of suburban growth, and the culture of traditional family values. Residents of Cobb were "a church-going and church-supporting people," the Chamber of Commerce boasted in a 1960 promotional pamphlet that seamlessly portrayed single-family homes, military-industrial employment, and plentiful houses of worship (both mainline and evangelical) as the mutually reinforcing pillars of the utopian suburban dream.[59] Booster literature in the 1950s and 1960s sought to encapsulate Cobb's essence with recurring images of a police officer holding the hands of white children in front of a Protestant house of worship—a powerful message that parents could count on both church and state to protect suburban youth and uphold family values.[60] Prominent ministers also drew a direct connection between suburban expansion and evangelical growth, with every new business and resident considered a welcome opportunity for increased membership. The opening of the Bell Bomber Plant in 1943 had brought a rapid influx of members at each of Cobb's major houses of worship, including the First Presbyterian Church of Marietta and the Marietta First Baptist Church, which promptly split its congregation to create the Roswell Street Baptist Church. "How fortunate we are to live in such a delightful community as Marietta," the First Baptist Church announced in 1959, thanks in large part to the Lockheed prosperity. "The new growth has presented us with what has been called 'a nice problem to have.' . . . We are in the heart of a growing city and our growth has kept pace with our community."[61] Even as they expanded their own facilities, Southern Baptist ministers in Cobb continued to spin off new churches such as Eastside Baptist, which started in 1961 and soon ministered to the county's second-largest congregation at its upscale East Cobb location with a preacher from Iowa.[62]

The Roswell Street Baptist Church, located near Interstate 75 on the outskirts of Marietta, became Cobb County's largest and most influential house of worship during the Sunbelt boom that accelerated dramatically during the 1970s. The Reverend Nelson Price, who arrived from Louisiana in 1965, oversaw the transformation of Roswell Street Baptist from a mostly blue-collar congregation of 1,900 to a prosperous megachurch of 10,000 members three decades later. He deliberately recruited middle-class youth and "new families moving to Cobb" through a fundamentalist message presented with the flair of a self-described "showman" in charge of a "spiritual mall [with] a smorgasbord of programming." Price preached the doctrine of biblical inerrancy, expressed sympathy for teenagers caught in the Sixties "generation gap," and adopted a Cold War stance of firm anticommunism and fervent patriotism. Marketing literature in the 1970s portrayed the preacher denouncing evolution, leading teenagers to salvation, and standing in front of a church sign congratulating Lockheed employees for their contributions to Cobb's economic success. Price also understood that churches such as Roswell Street Baptist could provide a sense of community on Cobb's rootless landscape, where middle-class family values were strained by economic recession and rising divorce rates, where constant population turnover worked against stable neighborhood-based institutions, and where teenagers often went unsupervised because their parents worked long hours and/or let them consume too much television instead of "spend[ing] time" with their children. As white-collar transplants flocked to Cobb during the 1980s and 1990s, Roswell Street Baptist advertised the structured community of a church "big enough to provide for you, small enough to care who you are." "Get off of lonely street," commanded one flyer featuring a sad-looking man in an isolated subdivision setting, "and into Roswell Street Baptist Church." With plenty of social, recreational, and entertainment options, Roswell Street Baptist was just the place for anyone "looking for friends" and ready to "become part of the 'family.'"[63]

Nelson Price and many of his congregants at Roswell Street Baptist eventually became key players in the rise of the so-called Religious Right, the fundamentalist takeover of the Southern Baptist Convention, and the grassroots outbreak of "culture wars" over the politics of family values. Like other prominent evangelical preachers, Price had supported Jimmy Carter as a designated "prayer partner" during the 1976 election, but the conservative faction of the Southern Baptist Convention moved into open if unofficial alignment with the Republican Party during the Reagan era. In 1979, Sunbelt televangelists took the lead in organizing two new political lobbies, the Moral Majority and the Religious Roundtable, each of which enlisted Southern Baptist ministers from megachurches in high-growth metropolises such as Atlanta, Fort Lauderdale, Dallas-Fort Worth, Los Angeles, and San Diego. These national organizations reflected a broader mobilization of grassroots activists in the nascent Religious Right, including the anti-feminist network that defeated the Equal Rights Amendment and the moral crusades against gay rights that arose in rapidly diversifying Sunbelt centers such as Southern California and South Florida. As much as any other issue, the "Save Our Children" campaigns led by popular singer Anita Bryant and Virginia televangelist and Moral Majority cofounder Jerry Falwell catalyzed the national emergence of the Religious Right, especially as suburban conservatives fought back against urban-based gay rights movements in Miami, Atlanta, Los Angeles, and other big cities. Across the United States, leaders and grassroots activists pledged to defend traditional family values by resisting what they viewed as the external threats of feminism, the gay rights movement, and the cultural consequences of the sexual revolution.[64]

Along with other Religious Right leaders, Nelson Price's political concerns revolved around what he called the "moral breakdown in the American family," a diagnosis that reflected the widespread sense that the postwar consensus surrounding suburban cultural values had entered a period of profound crisis in the 1970s and 1980s. On one hand, Roswell Street Baptist sought to buttress the traditional nuclear family through internally focused programs that provided marriage counseling to forestall divorce, a broad array of wholesome activities for youth, and alternatives to abortion such as a pregnancy counseling center and a home for unwed mothers.[65] Despite the provision of such social services by multiple suburban churches, public health studies in the 1980s and early 1990s revealed that Cobb County led the metropolitan Atlanta region in teenage abortions per capita, along with high rates of divorce, underage alcohol consumption, and marijuana use in the high schools.[66] Activists from the Cobb chapter of the Christian Coalition, a new Christian Right organization founded in the late 1980s by Virginia televangelist Pat Robertson, responded by launching a campaign for an abstinence-only curriculum in the public schools. But about 90 percent of families in Cobb County elected to participate in opt-in sex education courses, providing clear evidence that a suburban supermajority did not support the full-scale family values crusade of the Religious Right.[67] The local Christian Coalition also joined forces with conservative preachers such as Nelson Price to trigger a series of controversies over gay rights and Cobb County's persistent (and unconstitutional) efforts to teach creationism in public schools and post the Ten Commandments on public property. When the County Commission terminated public funding for a Marietta community theater that allegedly promoted "the homosexual lifestyle," Price applauded political leaders for sending a strong "pro-family" message against art that "glamorize[s] sexual distortion."[68]

During the early 1990s, a number of up-and-coming Sunbelt boomtowns became embroiled in nationally publicized culture wars, most notably the effort sponsored by evangelical groups in Colorado Springs to amend the state constitution to ban laws protecting gay rights, a referendum narrowly approved by voters in 1992 but then overturned in the courts.[69] In Cobb County, the Republican-dominated commission approved an anti-gay rights resolution in 1993, leading to a bitter local debate and an avalanche of negative national publicity portraying Newt Gingrich's district as a conservative bastion of Christian fundamentalism and suburban intolerance. Although the origins of Cobb's resolution are murky, the initial catalyst appears to have been the Clinton administration's ill-fated attempt to lift the ban on the service of gay men and women in the military, followed soon after by the city of Atlanta's passage of a law recognizing domestic partners. For conservative religious activists in Cobb County, the gay rights movement was directly challenging the sanctity of all three of the longtime pillars of local political culture: the U.S. military, the free-enterprise economy (by seeking government subsidy of "alternative lifestyles"), and the heterosexual nuclear family. The resolution, sponsored by Commissioner Gordon Wysong of East Cobb with the collaboration of Reverend Price, labeled the "traditional family structure" to be the "primary and best method of fostering a positive development in children" and "the best mechanism for maintaining a lifestyle which leaves citizens independent of their government for support." The most controversial section declared that "lifestyles advocated by the gay community . . . are incompatible with the standards to which this community subscribes." Wysong, a small business owner with ties to the Christian Coalition, soon upped the ante by stating that regular people in Cobb County and the rest of America were "fed up with having the gay agenda crammed down their throat." "They're going after my kids," he claimed, "and I'm not going to surrender my kids."[70]

Cobb's "traditional lifestyle" resolution unleashed a public backlash that its sponsors did not anticipate and revealed that many, and perhaps most, of the county's residents preferred a less confrontational approach to the defense of their family values. Critics charged that "a fringe element of the population" had manufactured the controversy in service of a narrow political agenda, with frequent claims that a "silent majority" in Cobb opposed the politicization of Christianity by the Religious Right. Cobb County was a "very loving, wonderful place to live," explained a mother from Marietta, but this "makes us look like a bunch of bigoted jackasses. . . . This is not Christianity that I know, that I've been raised to believe in, and I think there's a silent majority that knows it." The longtime publisher of the *Marietta Daily Journal* argued that most Cobb residents were "embarrassed" by the controversy because they were "mainstream people. Balanced budgets and cuts in taxes are their issues, not gays or school prayer." Two new local groups emerged to demand repeal of the resolution: a grassroots gay rights organization called the Cobb Citizens Coalition, and a confederation of thirty-seven mainline and liberal congregations named the Marietta Interfaith Alliance. The ecumenical group reflected the increasing religious diversity brought by the county's rapid growth; its leader, Rabbi Steven Lebow (of an East Cobb synagogue), denounced the commissioners for "tearing apart the social fabric" and encouraging "hatred and bigotry against gay men and women." Two hundred preachers from conservative churches responded by holding a counterdemonstration for traditional family values.[71] Gay rights activists based in Atlanta also formed a movement called Olympics Out of Cobb and successfully pressured the Atlanta Olympic Committee to ban venues in the county from hosting the 1996 Summer Games.[72] This rebuke and other boycott threats caused the Cobb Chamber of Commerce and Republican state senator Johnny Isakson to push for a compromise that would end the saga, but the county commissioners refused to back down.[73]

Whether viewed as an "anti-gay" or a "pro-family" measure, the Cobb resolution revealed that political efforts to restore the suburban consensus of the post-World War II era had backfired, by exposing the impossibility of defining uniform moral values in an increasingly diverse county of more than 500,000 residents. When opponents of gay rights gathered at a rally featuring the Rev. Nelson Price of Roswell Street Baptist and the Rev. Charles Sineath of the First United Methodist Church, a leader of the Cobb Citizens Coalition warned that "families will be split, churches will be split," if the Religious Right did not back down.[74] A few years later, Sineath's Methodist congregation experienced a major schism over abortion and gay rights, with the minister and one-third of the members leaving to protest the liberalization of their denomination.[75] The most extraordinary moment in Cobb's protracted controversy came at a County Commission hearing in 1995, when the sister of Representative Newt Gingrich and the daughter of chairman Bill Byrne each appealed, as lesbians, for the county to repeal the resolution.[76] After Shannon Byrne publicly confronted her father, he confessed responsibility for causing a "dysfunctional family" by divorcing her mother when she was young. "My lifestyle wasn't one of choice," she replied. "I am a lesbian. The divorce did not cause me to 'go homosexual.'"[77] Bill Byrne's mea culpa reflected the still widespread belief among social conservatives that parenting practices within the home as well as the cultural influences of the sexual revolution caused the homosexual "lifestyle." In the broader context, the political defense of traditional moral values on dynamic and rootless landscapes such as Cobb County suggested that the crusades of the Religious Right resulted as much from an internal crisis of the nuclear family as from the perceived external threats to middle-class suburban utopias.

The national furor generated by the culture wars and the "Gingrich Revolution" also distracted attention from the diverse and at times oppositional strains of conservative politics in sprawling Sunbelt suburbs that trended Republican. A public opinion survey in the mid-1990s revealed that 45 percent of GOP voters in Gingrich's congressional district labeled themselves moderates and 43 percent identified as conservatives. During Cobb's gay rights controversy, the Christian Coalition claimed to represent 100,000 voters in the state of Georgia—only 10 percent of the total electorate but, more significantly, up to one-third of the swing vote in any contested Republican primary. The leaders of the Christian Coalition acknowledged that they did not speak for a popular majority, even in New Right strongholds such as Cobb County and even among the subset of Republican Party members in the Sunbelt suburbs. But activists on the Christian Right realized that they could wield disproportionate influence in party politics by mobilizing conservative evangelicals in low-turnout primaries, especially through the grassroots infrastructure of alternative media and suburban megachurches. In the 1988 presidential contest, Virginia Beach televangelist Pat Robertson won only 16 percent of the Republican vote in Georgia, but his supporters proceeded to swamp the state GOP convention and initiate a drawn-out power struggle with the party establishment. Then, during the early to mid-1990s, the Georgia branch of the Christian Coalition successfully targeted a number of pro-choice Republicans for primary defeats. In the 1996 U.S. Senate primary, for example, intervention by the Christian Coalition helped social conservative Guy Millner win the nomination over Johnny Isakson, his pro-choice rival. Isakson denounced the "extremists" who believed he was "not Christian enough for their litmus test," and he did carry Cobb after appealing to pro-choice women and GOP centrists. Millner lost the general election to Democratic candidate Max Cleland, who asked for the support of "all those moderate Republicans who backed a good man in Johnny Isakson."[78]

When Newt Gingrich championed family values, he appealed not only to the Religious Right but also to the much broader group of middle-class Republicans whose priorities revolved around the same economic issues that made Ronald Reagan so popular in the suburban Sunbelt: slashing taxes for corporations and affluent households, cutting federal spending for cities and minorities and the poor, and building up the national security state. A Pennsylvania native, Gingrich originally represented a blue-collar congressional district southwest of Atlanta, becoming the state's only Republican member of the House of Representatives on his third try in 1978. He moved to Cobb County fourteen years later, in search of a safe seat after the Georgia state legislature enacted a redistricting plan designed to end his career. Longtime Republican leaders in Cobb initially opposed the outsider who described himself as a "conservative revolutionary," and Gingrich narrowly survived the 1992 primary against an equally conservative opponent. In the general election, Democratic challenger Tony Center received 44.4 percent of the Cobb vote by labeling Gingrich a right-wing carpetbagger who opposed reproductive freedom for women and whose messy divorce revealed a flawed personal character. Gingrich won more easily in the landslide of 1994, with 64 percent of the vote in his heavily Republican district, followed by a 58–42 margin in a hotly contested 1996 campaign.[79] Another GOP firebrand, the Iowa-born Bob Barr, narrowly unseated five-term Democratic incumbent Buddy Darden in 1994 in Cobb's other congressional race. Barr, who welcomed endorsements by the Christian Coalition and the National Rifle Association, was a polarizing figure who repeatedly secured barely half of the vote in the South Cobb portion of his district. A more moderate Republican, Johnny Isakson, garnered 75 percent of the ballots from East Cobb when he replaced Gingrich after the Speaker of the House's resignation in 2000.[80]

Critics often portrayed Newt Gingrich, and by extension his constituents in the sprawling suburbs of Cobb County, as hypocritical ideologues regarding the twin pillars of the "Republican Revolution"—opposition to liberal big government and support for traditional family values. Gingrich presented the GOP's ascendancy in 1994 as both a moral and a political awakening by the suburban majority: "middle-class Americans [who] want a neighborhood where their children are safe, a school where they can actually learn, an opportunity to work, a chance to save what they earn, the right to spend it themselves." But "how normal is Newt," *Newsweek* asked in response, if he declined to serve his country in Vietnam, initiated divorce proceedings while his first wife was recovering from cancer surgery, and violated ethics guidelines with his political fundraising machine?[81] Gingrich portrayed the "liberal welfare state" as the enemy of Middle American voters, charged that taxpayers in the suburbs were fed up with "sending more money to inner-city mayors," and insisted that the "government is too big and it spends too much, and the government clearly should be put on a diet." Then why, *Time* wondered while naming Gingrich "Person of the Year" for 1995, did the Republicans diligently protect middle-class entitlement programs such as the home mortgage deduction and enthusiastically distribute corporate welfare through pork-barrel subsidies and wasteful military projects? Cobb had flourished thanks to "white-picket welfare," according to an expose by the watchdog group Common Cause, as the recipient of more federal dollars per capita than every other suburban county in the nation except for Arlington County in Virginia (home of the Pentagon and the CIA) and Brevard County in Florida (NASA Space Center). In a biting episode of *TV Nation*, guerilla filmmaker Michael Moore traveled to Cobb to confront Gingrich and yell at suburban residents to stay off the highways and away from the lakes and to stop using the sewer system in order to "get the big, bad federal bogeyman off their backs."[82]

The GOP capture of both houses of Congress in 1994 transformed Gingrich into a temporary visionary and confirmed the conservative Republican surge across Georgia, and the party's other strongholds in the suburban Sunbelt, during the final decades of the twentieth century. The sources of political transformation are always multifaceted, but the demographic trends of white middle-class migration to metropolitan Atlanta and other pacesetting Sunbelt centers laid the essential foundation. Cobb's population increased by 310,000 during the 1980s and 1990s, and Republicans dominated election returns from the County Commission to the national level. Building on Reagan's success in Cobb, Vice President George Bush defeated Democratic nominee Michael Dukakis by a 73–29 margin in 1988. Bush carried Cobb with only 53 percent in 1992, when independent candidate Ross Perot siphoned off almost 15 percent of the county electorate (especially fiscal libertarians and cultural moderates who disliked the Religious Right). In 1996, 2000, and 2004, each of the Democratic presidential candidates received 37 percent of the ballots (see Table 3.2).[83] In statewide elections, the Georgia Democrats remained competitive but rarely proved able to reach a majority in Cobb County, although they did win half of the gubernatorial and U.S. Senate elections held between 1990 and 2006. Johnny Isakson and Paul Coverdell, two relatively moderate Republicans with deep roots in the Atlanta suburbs, secured more than three-fifths of the Cobb tally in their successful Senate campaigns. But Guy Millner, a wealthy Atlanta businessman with close ties to the Christian Coalition, failed to capture enough suburban moderates and barely carried Cobb on his way to losing three statewide contests in a row between 1994 and 1998. Millner lost his final election to Roy Barnes, the centrist Democrat from West Cobb, who became governor in 1998 after a campaign that promised to address traffic jams, school overcrowding, and other consequences of suburban sprawl (see Table 3.3).[84]

Beneath the surface of the Republican consolidation during the 1990s, the center of gravity was shifting again in Cobb County, driven as always by changing demographics and neighborhood-based politics. Growth patterns

Table 3.3. Partisan Trends in Cobb County
in Statewide Elections, 1990–2008 (percent)

Year	Office	Republican	Democratic	Georgia Winner
1990	Governor	64 (Isakson)	36 (Z. Miller)	Z. Miller (D)
1990	Senate	None	100 (Nunn)	Nunn (D)
1992	Senate	62 (Coverdell)	38 (Fowler)	Coverdell (R)
1994	Governor	57 (G. Millner)	43 (Z. Miller)	Z. Miller (D)
1996	Senate	56 (G. Millner)	44 (Cleland)	Cleland (D)
1998	Governor	54 (G. Millner)	46 (Barnes)	Barnes (D)
1998	Senate	62 (Coverdell)	38 (Coles)	Coverdell (R)
2000	Senate	46 (Mattingly)	54 (Z. Miller)	Miller (D)
2002	Governor	54 (Perdue)	46 (Barnes)	Perdue (R)
2002	Senate	60 (Chambliss)	40 (Cleland)	Chambliss (R)
2004	Senate	65 (Isakson)	35 (Majette)	Isakson (R)
2006	Governor	66 (Perdue)	34 (Taylor)	Perdue (R)
2008	Senate*	53 (Chambliss)	42 (Martin)	Chambliss (R)

Source: Georgia Secretary of State Elections Division, http://www.sos.ga.gov/elections/.
*General election (Chambliss defeated Martin in Cobb in a run-off (63.6 to 34.4) with reduced voter turnout.

took three distinct forms during the decade: white-collar migration from outside the state continued in the upscale parts of East Cobb, middle-class black families moved from Atlanta into the older suburbs of South and West Cobb, and Latino immigrants flocked to the county and especially to the town of Marietta. The 2006 census update revealed that white residents constituted only 63 percent of Cobb's total population, which had become 23 percent black, 11 percent Latino, and 4 percent Asian.[85] As in diversifying suburbs across the nation, the Latino population clustered in Marietta has generated the most friction, as elected officials have banned day laborer hiring sites, local law enforcement raids have swept up undocumented workers in construction and landscaping jobs, and homeowners' associations have launched "save-the-neighborhood" campaigns to restrict multifamily occupancy of single-family homes.[86] Black homeowners in the formerly all-white strongholds of South Cobb have transformed suburban politics more successfully, electing African Americans to the County Commission, the state legislature, and the House of Representatives—in the congressional district previously represented by right-wing Republican Bob Barr.[87] U.S. Representative David Scott of South Cobb, who labels himself a pro-business Democrat and once worked on the assembly line at Lockheed, promptly pledged that he would be as committed as any Republican to maintaining the county's share of federal defense spending and defending the F-22 Raptor fighter jet from its many critics.[88] In the clearest sign of the changing times, Barack Obama won 44 percent of the Cobb vote in 2008, the best Democratic showing in three decades, and part of the party's new inroads into the increasingly multiracial Sunbelt suburbs, from northern Virginia and North Carolina's Research Triangle Park to former GOP strongholds in Colorado and Southern California.[89]

In the late 1990s, Republican moderates and independent swing voters in Cobb's white-collar suburbs also began to fight back against the doctrinaire conservatives and confrontational culture warriors who took control of county politics during the Gingrich era. In 1998, centrist Republicans defeated Christian Coalition-endorsed candidates in multiple primary elections in the Atlanta suburbs, and a longtime GOP consultant warned the party to address voter anxieties about the environmental and social costs of unchecked sprawl because "you can't win these counties as a gun-toting, anti-abortion Republican anymore." Cobb "is still a conservative place," Representative Johnny Isakson remarked, but the culture wars over abortion and gay rights were receding. "Now people are more concerned about quality-of-life issues, education, and transportation."[90] That same year, a Jewish Republican and corporate transplant named Sam Olens easily unseated incumbent Gordon Wysong, the sponsor of the anti-gay resolution, in a 1998 race for the County Commission. Olens first entered local politics as head of the East Cobb Civic Association, an alliance of one hundred subdivisions that engaged in frequent zoning battles with real-estate developers. Among its major campaigns, the East Cobb Civic Association demanded that fiscal conservatives on the County Commission raise the sales tax in order to build more sidewalks, soccer fields, and parks for suburban youth. Olens ran for office on a "Neighborhoods First" platform of curbing sprawl, and he labeled Wysong a "rampantly homophobic" embarrassment whose alliance with the Christian Coalition had distracted attention from the most critical issues facing Cobb County as a built-out suburb. As chair of the County Commission from 2002–2010, Olens championed the latest version of Cobb's always dynamic newcomer politics, a slow-growth "save the neighborhood" movement in favor of government spending and regulation to preserve the quality of life for middle-class suburban families.[91]

Chapter 4

Religion and Political Behavior in the Sunbelt

Lyman A. Kellstedt and James L. Guth

For many years, social scientists have explored in great depth the social divisions that influence American political behavior, such as region, class, race and ethnicity, age, gender, and marital status.[1] Region has always been near the top of the list, given historic sectional divisions going all the way back to the founding. The Civil War left its mark on the culture, the economy, the politics, and even the psyche, of southern states that persisted well into the twentieth century. If the South is no longer "solid," it still retains certain characteristics that differentiate it from the rest of the country. Where else can you find grits and "moon pies" in almost every restaurant and a Southern Baptist church in every town, if not on every street corner?

Scholarly literature on the South is voluminous. In political science, V. O. Key's 1949 *Southern Politics* remains a classic that Ph.D. students avoid at their peril.[2] Despite the attention given to the South, other regions have received little attention.[3] In addition, social scientists have been slow to provide adequate conceptualization for *region*. Nicole Mellow's *The State of Disunion* is an exception. She argues that regions can be viewed in material or economic terms as well as cultural and demographic phenomena.[4] Such a conceptualization clearly fits the states of the Old South. But does it fit other possible "regions" historically or presently? And, in particular, does it fit the "Sunbelt"? Is the Sunbelt a viable region with common historical roots, economic and cultural similarities, and unique demographic characteristics? In particular, does religion provide one element of the glue that distinguishes the Sunbelt? Or is the Sunbelt simply a figment of our imagination, a series of states, or parts of states, across the southern tier of the country where the weather is warm and the living is easy?

This chapter will not answer these questions with any finality, but it will take a careful look at the role of religion in the political behavior of Sunbelt states. Only in the past few decades have scholars become interested in the role that religious factors may play in contemporary American elections. Although there is still much dispute about the relative power of various social traits (class, race, ethnicity, religion, gender, region) in describing American political behavior, there is a growing consensus that religion has played an increasing role, perhaps eclipsing the impact of other demographic influences.[5] But virtually all the massive literature on the role of religion in American electoral politics has been national in focus. Although most analysts recognize that religious groups are not evenly distributed across the country, the tendency is to assume that their behavior does not vary significantly by region. Although there are a few exceptions, we have very few efforts to consider the way that religion and politics interact in identifiable regions.[6]

We start with the assumption that the Sunbelt is a meaningful political entity.[7] If the Sunbelt is truly "a unified region rivaling traditional centers of power in the East" or, for that matter, matching the distinctiveness of the Old South, that unity must subsist in a degree of social and political homogeneity. Much of the early discussion of the concept found the Sunbelt distinctive in its religious and political conservatism, reflecting on the one hand the cultural dominance of evangelical religion and, on the other, the increasing political dominance of the GOP.[8] Indeed, for many scholars, these two developments were intertwined aspects of the same larger trend. For other analysts, these features represented the extension of distinctively "southern" religious and political traits into the burgeoning regions of the Southwest and southern Pacific coast—or even the entire country.[9] Although some authors have insisted that both religious and political conservatism were transformed in that transition, others argue that they maintained their distinctive features.[10]

Despite these differences in interpretation, one thing is clear—the population in Sunbelt states has grown at the expense of the rest of the country in the years since World War II. These changes have enormous political implications. For example, representation in the Congress has been transformed by these changes. After the 2010 Census, the Sunbelt will almost match non-Sunbelt areas in the number of U.S. House seats, giving it the potential to be a powerful force in American politics—if it musters a certain amount of unity.

We address that question of Sunbelt unity from the perspective of both religious traits and political characteristics—and their intersection. Although one body of thought continues to insist on considering the Sunbelt a meaningful analytic category, other scholars would argue that the Sunbelt states are better thought of in subregional groupings. For example, a mid-2000s series on American religious regionalism has divided the Sunbelt into at least four regions: the South, the "Southern Crossroads," the "Pacific Region" of California and Nevada, with Arizona, Colorado, and New Mexico relegated to the "Mountain West."[11] Still others would argue that, as political, economic, and cultural units, even this level of aggregation hides important social and political traits and that individual states maintain a considerable degree of religious and political distinctiveness.[12] Finally, many scholars are much more impressed with the impact of regional convergence, producing an increasing nationalization of politics.[13]

In our analysis, we focus on the question of religious and political change in the Sunbelt, with a view to determining whether the concept has clear meaning in these respects. This essay, then, has several objectives: (1) to describe the religious composition of "Sunbelt" states; (2) to consider the way that religious affiliation influences electoral behavior in the same area; and (3) to compare our Sunbelt findings to the those of various "subregions," as well as the rest of the country, to put the purported distinctiveness of the geographical entity into focus.

Religious Traditions in the Sunbelt States

Although there are a number of religious variables that are relevant to political analysis,[14] we start with religious affiliation and its key concept—religious tradition. By "religious tradition," we mean a group of "religious communities that share a set of beliefs that generates a distinctive worldview."[15] In a larger historical and theoretical sense, these are the communities identified by *ethnoreligious theory*, which emphasizes the historic

European religious groups that migrated to America and often multiplied on reaching her shores. Nineteenth-century party politics consisted largely of assembling winning coalitions of contending ethnoreligious groups.[16] Well into the twentieth century, the GOP represented historically dominant mainline Protestant churches, such as Episcopalians, Presbyterians and Methodists, while Democrats spoke for religious minorities: Catholics, Jews, and evangelical Protestants (especially in the South).

By the 1980s, these configurations had shifted, as Mainline Protestants dwindled in number, Evangelicals moved toward the GOP, the ancient Catholic-Democratic alliance frayed, and Black Protestants became a critical Democratic bloc. Growing religious diversity added Latino Catholics and Protestants and even groups like Muslims, Hindus, Buddhists, and others to the equation, usually on the Democratic side. Still, even today many analysts think in ethnoreligious or ethnocultural terms, referring to the "Evangelical," "Catholic," "Jewish," or "Muslim" vote. And as we shall see, these religious traditions are indeed often distinctive in contemporary electoral politics.

Data Sources

Our first task, then, is delineating the religious composition of the Sunbelt states. There are a number of potential data sources for estimating that religious population. One frequently used source is the well-known Glenmary Research Center series that uses official denominational counts to depict the membership of religious bodies by counties across the United States.[17] Although the decennial Glenmary surveys are useful for many purposes, they have a number of drawbacks for ours. Not surprisingly, given their sources, the Glenmary studies are usually quite good at portraying the membership of religious bodies that keep good statistics, that is, the mainline Protestant denominations and the Roman Catholic Church. They are much less accurate in estimating the numbers in less centrally organized religious bodies, such as the great variety of fundamentalist, evangelical, and Pentecostal churches, many of which are functionally independent of any centralized organization, and Black Protestant churches, which share the same decentralization and lack of denominational bureaucracy. Although Glenmary researchers have made valiant efforts to compensate for such deficiencies, their efforts have not been entirely successful.[18]

Another source widely used in recent years to describe the religious composition of the American public has been the national surveys carried out by Barry Kosmin and his colleagues at the Graduate Center of the City University of New York: the National Survey of Religious Identification (1990) and the American Religious Identification Project (2001). In one important respect, these are attractive data sources: they are based on very large samples derived from random digit dialing procedures.[19] Unfortunately, the surveys used an open-ended question on respondents' affiliation—"What is your religion?"—that makes it quite difficult to determine denominational membership or make correct assignments to religious traditions. Although these surveys do provide some purchase on religious change over time, they provide relatively little information about the political traits of respondents. Other specialized surveys, such as the quadrennial network exit polls, though useful for limited purposes, lack both religious and political details.[20]

To address both religious and political questions simultaneously, we rely on the National Survey of Religion and Politics (NSRP), conducted by the Survey Research Center at the University of Akron during the presidential elections of 1992, 1996, 2000, 2004, and 2008. These large national studies have the major advantage of well-developed affiliation questions and substantial batteries of other religious and political items. At times, we use the combined 1992–2004 file to aggregate sufficient cases to provide comparative data for the Sunbelt, various subregions, and the rest of the country. To extend our political analysis over time, we also use that standard data source for political scientists, the American National Election Studies (ANES). Although the religious affiliation measures in ANES have changed over time, careful use of the presidential election year studies since 1964 provides us with time series data for our analysis.[21] Using both ANES and NSRP data allows us to compare the partisan proclivities and vote choices of religious groups in the Sunbelt over a fifty-year period.

Whenever possible, we compare ANES and NSRP results with data from the Pew Forum on Religion & Public Life U.S. Religious Landscape survey, a massive study conducted in 2007 with more than 35,000 respondents.[22] This data set has a religious affiliation measure that is directly comparable to those in the ANES and NSRP surveys. The extremely large sample size provides numerous respondents in even the smallest Sunbelt states, increasing confidence in our findings.[23]

The Religious Composition of the Sunbelt

Is the Sunbelt a homogeneous religious entity? Does it share religious characteristics that differentiate it from the rest of the country? Or is there more diversity than unity? Table 4.1 reports the proportion of the population that falls within various religious traditions for the Sunbelt,[24] various subregions, and the rest of the country, using data from the 2007 Pew Forum Landscape Survey. We have ordered the states in Table 4.1 by size of the white evangelical Protestant population, often thought a marker of Sunbelt religion. As the data reveal, there is some truth to that characterization: while slightly less than one-quarter of the national population are evangelical Christians, that percentage rises to 27 percent in the Sunbelt, compared with only 20 percent in the non-Sunbelt states. Certainly, evangelical religion and, presumably, its political manifestations are more evident in the Sunbelt than elsewhere.

Perhaps even more striking than the differences between Sunbelt and non-Sunbelt states, however, is the wide range in evangelical numbers in the Sunbelt states. Evangelicals make up more than half the populations of Arkansas and Oklahoma—with Tennessee, Alabama, Mississippi, and South Carolina following closely behind—but less than a fifth in a composite of the four Southwest states, as well as California. Evangelicals are obviously most numerous in the "Old South" (with the exception of Louisiana) and decline in proportions in the "Rim South" states of Virginia, Texas, and Florida. The Southwest and California actually look more like the rest of the country than like the "Old South" states. Thus, any "evangelical" predominance in the Sunbelt is mostly the statistical artifact of averaging the highly evangelical Old South with the rather different states of the Southwest and West.

The story for other Protestants is also one of diversity. Mainline Protestants are considerably less numerous in the Sunbelt states (about 15 percent) than in the rest of the country (about 20 percent), but once again the population varies dramatically, from a 20 percent in North Carolina to 8 percent in Louisiana. Of course, mainline Protestants are still overrepresented among the political elites of Sunbelt states (as elsewhere), but that advantage is shrinking with their population. Black Protestant numbers are also larger in the Sunbelt than in the rest of the country, but they vary even more by state. They are largest in the Old South (Alabama, Georgia, Louisiana, and Mississippi), where they make up at least one-fifth of the

Table 4.1. Religious Traditions in the Sunbelt States—2007 (Percent of Population)

	Evangelical Protestant	Mainline Protestant	Black Protestant	Latino Protestant	White Catholic	Latino Catholic	Jewish	Not Affiliated	N
Total U.S.	23.1	17.3	8.4	2.8	16.5	7.0	1.7	16.2	35556
Non-Sunbelt	19.7	19.7	6.7	1.7	22.4	4.1	2.0	16.7	19452
Sunbelt	27.0	14.7	10.4	4.1	9.8	10.2	1.4	15.7	16104
Oklahoma	50.9	15.2	2.9	6.9	4.8	0.4	11.8	465	
Arkansas	50.4	15.5	12.0	1.1	2.8	1.8	0.0	12.7	378
Tennessee	48.9	17.8	10.7	0.5	4.4	2.0	0.2	11.9	837
Alabama	45.3	14.0	21.3	1.7	4.0	1.5	0.1	8.3	681
Mississippi	42.8	9.4	28.1	0.9	4.4	3.4	0.0	5.8	333
S Carolina	42.8	17.7	17.2	1.1	6.2	1.4	0.8	9.9	570
N Carolina	37.1	20.0	15.5	2.7	5.4	3.5	0.5	12.2	1166
Georgia	32.3	16.0	20.0	2.5	6.4	4.5	0.7	12.9	967
Louisiana	27.9	7.6	22.5	2.1	23.5	1.3	0.3	7.8	528

Virginia	27.4	19.0	12.6	2.2	11.0	2.7	1.0	18.0	997
New Mexico	21.8	14.3	2.0	4.6	7.9	18.5	1.8	21.0	228
Colorado	21.3	18.8	2.6	1.8	12.3	7.2	2.1	25.3	590
Texas	20.6	14.0	10.9	7.8	7.6	16.2	0.8	12.1	2266
Florida	20.6	14.3	9.8	3.9	15.2	10.8	3.4	16.5	1694
Arizona	20.6	15.1	1.7	4.2	11.3	13.1	1.1	22.7	578
California	14.0	12.1	4.0	6.1	11.9	18.6	2.3	20.7	3574
Nevada	10.5	10.6	4.5	1.3	13.5	13.6	1.3	21.6	252
Summary of Sunbelt									
South	38.6	16.3	16.0	1.9	7.6	2.8	0.5	12.0	6922
Texas	20.6	14.0	10.9	7.8	7.6	16.2	0.8	12.1	2266
Florida	20.6	14.3	9.8	3.9	15.2	10.8	3.4	16.5	1694
Southwest	19.4	15.6	2.5	2.9	11.6	11.7	1.6	23.2	1648
California	14.0	12.1	4.0	6.1	11.9	18.6	2.3	20.7	3574

Source: Pew Forum on Religion & Public Life, *U.S. Religious Landscape Survey*, 2008. States are ordered by percent evangelical Protestant. Smaller groups such as non-Christians and Latter-day Saints are omitted from the table. "South" includes Arkansas, Tennessee, Oklahoma, Alabama, North Carolina, Mississippi, South Carolina, Georgia, Virginia, and Louisiana. "Southwest" includes Colorado, Arizona, Nevada, and New Mexico.

citizenry, but much less numerous in the western Sunbelt states. As in the case of evangelicals, Black Protestants are a larger part of Sunbelt populations only by virtue of averaging highly varying regional figures. Finally, Latino Protestants are becoming a significant population group in the Sunbelt, more than twice as numerous there as in the rest of the country. They are especially evident in Texas and California, where they have already demonstrated considerable political clout, but they are only a minor, if growing, presence in the Old South.

In some ways, the Sunbelt is better characterized by the status of other religious traditions. If the Sunbelt is more evangelical than other regions, it is distinctively less Anglo Catholic than the non-Sunbelt states (9.8 to 22.4 percent). Of the Sunbelt states, only Louisiana has more than one-fifth of the population identifying as white Catholic and with only a handful of other states rising above 10 percent. The small proportions of Anglo Catholics contrast with the substantial numbers of Latino Catholics, especially in New Mexico and other Southwest states, as well as in California and Texas. The Latino Catholic population is very small in Old South states, although percentage increases in these states are substantial (as documented by the Manzano chapter in this volume). But even combining the two Catholic groups leaves the Sunbelt much less Catholic than the rest of the country (20 percent to 27 percent). In the same vein, the Jewish populations of Sunbelt states are small, from virtually undetectable in the Old South to 3.4 percent in Florida.

Finally, the table also reports the proportion of respondents with no religious affiliation whatever. Recent surveys have led some analysts to argue that this number is increasing nationally and may especially characterize rapidly growing regions.[25] Once again, we discover more diversity than unity in the Sunbelt. Southern states range from 5.8 percent unaffiliated in Mississippi to 18 percent in Virginia, but that number rises to over one-fifth of the population in California, with similar proportions in the Southwest. Thus, the presumably "secular" population varies considerably across the putative Sunbelt—and may be increasing rapidly in the western regions. If this is the case, the subregions of the Sunbelt have even less in common religiously.

To make this point more concisely, in the last section of Table 4.1, we summarize religious affiliation by subregion, separating the Old South; the "Rim South" states of Texas and Florida; the Southwest states of Arizona, Colorado, New Mexico and Nevada; and the Pacific monolith of California.

Evangelical populations decline dramatically from the Old South to California; mainline Protestants have a roughly similar presence across these areas; Black Protestants are much more numerous in the Old South than in the other regions; Catholics—Anglo and Latino—are concentrated in Florida, the Southwest, and California; and the unaffiliated are more numerous in the western Sunbelt, that is, the Southwest and California. Thus, the component parts of the Sunbelt have quite distinctive religious configurations.[26]

And it is important to remember that those religious populations are ever-changing. Over the past fifty years, there has been an impressive increase in the number of Latinos, regardless of religious persuasion. If the major demographic movement in the Sunbelt from the end of World War II through the 1980s was the migration of Rustbelt whites to Sunbelt states, the key population changes since that time resulted from the immigration of Latinos and the high birth rates of U.S.-born Latinos. These increases have been particularly large in Florida, Texas, and California and the states of the Southwest. By the beginning of the twenty-first century, moreover, Latino numbers were growing even in the Old South, in particular, Georgia, North Carolina, and Virginia. Population projections are always tricky, but the Pew Hispanic Center estimated in 2008 that the Latino population in this country will triple by 2050, making Latino population growth in both the South and Southwest a major demographic factor in the next few decades.

Party Affiliation in the Sunbelt

Is the same kind of diversity characteristic of the political affiliations of Sunbelt residents? To provide a comparable summary measure of Sunbelt political characteristics, we turn to an assessment of party identification among Sunbelt residents over time. Table 4.2 reports the Republican and Democratic Party identification percentages of the U.S. electorate, the non-Sunbelt states, the Sunbelt states, and the subregions we reported on previously. (For simplicity, "Pure Independents" are left out of the table.) As political scientists have long known, party identification is the best predictor not only of voting decisions but of a host of other political choices as well. It is, thus, the central variable in electoral analysis. To provide the longest possible time span for our analysis, we have added data from the American National Election Studies going back to 1960 to our information

Table 4.2. Partisan Identification in Sunbelt, 1960–2008 (Independents Excluded)

	1960–1978		1980–1988		1992–1996		2000–2004		2007		2008	
	R	D	R	D	R	D	R	D	R	D	R	D
Total U.S.	32	53	37	50	39	44	41	44	35	47	36	45
Non-Sunbelt	36	50	39	48	39	44	40	45	35	48	35	45
Sunbelt	27	58	34	53	39	45	43	43	36	45	37	45
Summary of Sunbelt												
South	23	59	28	58	41	44	44	41	39	45	36	44
Florida	38	50	38	47	37	51	40	42	35	47	39	49
Texas	16	70	32	53	41	42	45	39	39	41	41	42
Southwest	37	50	41	45	34	46	47	41	36	42	43	41
California	32	57	43	45	39	45	37	50	30	49	30	49

Sources: ANES1960–1988; National Surveys on Religion and Politics (merged file) 1992–2004; Pew Forum, U.S. Religious Landscape Survey, 5th National Survey on Religion and Politics, 2008.

from the 1992–2004 NSRP, the 2007 Pew Forum Landscape Survey, and the 2008 NSRP. As the number of respondents in the ANES studies is relatively small, we have combined several elections to produce large enough numbers in the subregions for stable estimates.

As is evident from the first row in Table 4.2, the nation as a whole gravitated in a Republican direction from 1960–78 to 2000–2004, moving from a 21-point deficit in the earliest period to almost a tie in 2000–2004. Most of that change, however, was concentrated in the Sunbelt, where partisanship shifted dramatically toward the GOP, with the percentages identifying with the two parties at an exact tie in 2000–2004. Pro-Republican change in the rest of the country was much more modest, with the Democrats maintaining a 5-point edge in 2000–2004. To this point, at least, some of the old conventional wisdom about the Sunbelt's being a source of "rising Republicanism" is correct. The bottom portion of Table 4.2 forces some revision in that picture, however, as partisan change is dramatically different by subregion. By 2000–2004, Texas had shifted from being the most Democratic area of the Sunbelt (to some extent reflecting identification with a favorite son, Lyndon Johnson) to one of the most Republican, while the Old South moved almost as strongly in the same direction. Florida and California, on the other hand, as well as the Southwest states, experienced more modest net Republican gains. Note the dramatic pro-GOP move by Californians in the 1980s, during the Reagan White House years, a move that was reversed in later periods. Still, although the partisan change pattern is quite different by subregion, the end result is somewhat less variation across the Sunbelt in 2000–2004 than was present in the earliest period, when Texas and the Old South still represented the remnants of the historically Democratic "Solid South."

Table 4.2 also demonstrates that the Republican gains over the forty years beginning in the 1960s came to a screeching halt by 2007. The extremely large sample numbers in the 2007 Landscape Survey give us confidence that the GOP losses are not illusory; data from the 2008 NSRP election survey seem to confirm the 2007 results. Republican losses in partisan identification occurred all across the Sunbelt's subregions, but particularly in the Old South. Clearly, the pattern in California is very different from that in other Sunbelt areas, with the Democrats holding a wide margin in partisan identities. In terms of geography and weather, California fits conceptions of a Sunbelt state, but it does not seem to fit politically with the remaining states and subregions.

Religion and Partisanship in the Sunbelt

The preceding section shows a movement over time in the Sunbelt toward the Republican Party, a movement slowed somewhat since 2000–2004. How did religious traditions participate in these partisan shifts? Did Sunbelt residents behave differently from those outside the region? Or were partisan changes by religious groups similar across regions? Table 4.3 provides the answers to these (and other) questions. We begin our analysis with evangelical Protestants. As the table shows, evangelicals became substantially more Republican over the period, particularly in the Sunbelt, moving from the Democratic side of the scale to the Republican. GOP identification peaked in 2004, then fell off slightly in 2007 and 2008. However, Democratic identification dropped as well, actually reaching its lowest point in 2008. Although there has been an overall decline in Republican identification since 2000–2004 (see Table 4.2), evangelicals have not contributed to that decline. In addition, within-Sunbelt differences among evangelicals are minimal, with large margins in favor of the GOP in every region. In sum, evangelicals everywhere look much alike by 2008, solid identifiers with the Republican Party. They have truly become a "national" religious bloc, as is readily apparent when comparing evangelicals with other religious groups in Table 4.3.

Mainline Protestants, on the other hand, have been quite stable politically, at least at the national level, resting solidly on the GOP side of the scale through 2004. In 2007, however, this historic Republican group (once dubbed "the Republican Party at prayer") had moved toward the Democrats, but they shifted back toward the GOP in 2008. In the Sunbelt, mainliners had begun the time period as Democrats, although not as staunch as evangelicals, but quickly jumped to GOP partisanship in the 1980s, joining the Reagan Revolution and maintaining these ties thereafter. In recent years, Sunbelt mainliners have been somewhat more Republican than their non-Sunbelt counterparts. Whatever their partisan ties, the declining number of mainliners across the nation reduces their significance compared to a generation ago. White Catholics have also shifted away from their historic Democratic affiliation at the national level, but that change was greatest in the Sunbelt where the Anglo Catholic presence tends to be small, with partisanship running in favor of the Republicans in 2000–2004 and again in 2008.

What about smaller religious groups? We combined Latino Protestants

Table 4.3. Party Identification by Religion over Time in the Sunbelt

	1960–1978		1980–1988		1992–1996		2000–2004		2007		2008	
	R	D	R	D	R	D	R	D	R	D	R	D
Evangelical	32	53	44	43	52	32	59	29	54	31	57	27
Non-Sunbelt	41	45	53	34	51	31	59	29	53	32	58	27
Sunbelt	26	59	37	49	52	32	59	30	56	30	56	27
South	26	58	33	53	50	33	56	32	53	33	49	27
Florida	22	67	36	48	48	37	54	29	52	35	59	32
Texas	14	70	40	48	56	31	64	23	62	25	70	25
Southwest	45	40	47	28	44	34	70	25	61	25	63	31
California	41	46	62	26	62	27	62	33	60	26	67	23
Mainline	**50**	**38**	**53**	**36**	**48**	**36**	**48**	**39**	**43**	**42**	**46**	**40**
Non-Sunbelt	53	34	54	35	49	35	45	42	40	45	44	42
Sunbelt	42	46	52	40	48	36	51	36	46	38	49	38
Anglo Catholic	24	63	35	52	39	46	42	45	40	46	38	47
Non-Sunbelt	24	63	33	54	38	45	39	47	39	47	34	51
Sunbelt	23	65	42	45	40	47	49	39	42	43	49	36
All Latinos	13	73	24	59	28	53	28	56	21	49	24	54
Non-Sunbelt	12	66	22	60	32	50	34	51	20	54	21	55
Sunbelt	13	77	25	59	26	54	26	58	22	46	24	54
South		+	+		35	57	35	44	25	33	11	51
Florida		+	+		40	40	36	44	30	32	55	
											27*	

124 Lyman A. Kellstedt and James L. Guth

Table 4.3. (Continued)

	1960–1978		1980–1988		1992–1996		2000–2004		2007		2008	
	R	D	R	D	R	D	R	D	R	D	R	D
Texas	+		+		22	52	26	61	21	42	32	48
Southwest	+		+		27	63	14	65	21	41	23	54
California	+		+		21	54	25	62	17	46	21	64
Black Protestant	8	79	8	82	11	81	11	78	9	79	9	79
Non-Sunbelt	8	82	5	87	7	82	10	80	8	81	6	75
Sunbelt	8	76	10	80	13	81	11	77	10	77	11	82
Jewish	16	72	20	68	22	69	20	70	24	66	12	71
Non-Sunbelt	17	70	15	73	25	62	21	69	26	65	13	74
Sunbelt	8	80	31	58	17	79	19	73	10	20	68	11
											68*	
Unaffiliated	27	52	33	49	34	45	31	46	23	55	24	48
Non-Sunbelt	28	50	32	49	30	48	28	47	21	57	21	51
Sunbelt	25	55	34	49	38	41	34	45	25	52	27	42

Sources: ANES 1960–1988; National Surveys on Religion and Politics (merged file) 1992–2004; Pew Forum on Religion & Public Life, 2007 U.S. Religious Landscape Survey;; 5th National Survey on Religion and Politics, 2008.
* N < 20; + N too small.

and Catholics in the table because of the small numbers in the earliest eras (the 1960s, 1970s, and 1980s). Latinos follow the trajectory discussed above—toward the Republican Party through the 1990s—but stabilizing thereafter.[27] The failure of the GOP to make further gains is no doubt due to Latino frustration with the Republican Party's recent immigration stands and some attraction for minority candidate Barack Obama in 2008. Although differences between Sunbelt and other Latinos are generally not large, subregional differences among Sunbelt Latinos are evident, with the small subsample of Latino Floridians identifying as Republicans, while in other parts of the Sunbelt Latinos are almost a mirror image of Sunbelt evangelicals. Given the growing demographic importance of Latinos, especially in the Sunbelt (see Table 4.1), their partisan preferences are of considerable, and increasing, importance.

Black Protestants, the nation's most Democratic religious group, hardly shifted at all over this period, in the Sunbelt or elsewhere. Sunbelt Jews may have become a little less Democratic than their counterparts elsewhere, but their numbers are too small to be very confident about this. Finally, the religiously unaffiliated, solidly on the Democratic side of the scale, nevertheless joined the general movement away from the Democrats from the 1960s until 2000–2004, with those in the Sunbelt more prone to do so. However, like most other groups, the unaffiliated moved back to the Democrats more recently.

All in all, then, we find that, among most religious groups, Sunbelt residents moved more in a Republican direction than their counterparts elsewhere. In the case of evangelical Protestants, this really represents a kind of nationalization of their political profile, as regional differences among coreligionists were reduced or virtually eliminated. Among mainline Protestants and white Catholics, however, the processes of change opened a partisan gap where none existed previously, as Sunbelt residents moved more decisively in a Republican direction, although admittedly these groups are relatively small in the region. In sum, Table 4.3 suggests that religious differences are much more important in explaining partisan preferences than regional distinctions.

Regional Religious Party Coalitions

Over time, these partisan changes have altered the coalitional character of the Republican and Democratic parties. More than a few observers have argued that the growth of the Sunbelt has increased its political weight, especially in the Republican Party, and that the increasing Sunbelt influence in the national GOP has been accompanied by a new conservative religious constituency, dominated by evangelical Protestants, who have moved party policy sharply to the Right, especially on moral issues. The Texas GOP's declaration that the United States is a "Christian Nation" is often cited as an example of such impact. Some observers have even seen the need to compete in the Sunbelt as a "conservative" force in the Democratic Party, especially in the form of the New Democratic centrism advocated by the Clinton-Gore wing of the party or by the so-called Blue Dogs and New Democrats in the Congress.

Table 4.4 provides an overview of the religious composition of the Republican and Democratic party coalitions in the Sunbelt and Non-Sunbelt, giving us a wealth of insight into interregional battles within the parties, especially those tied to religious divisions. First of all, note the major differences between the religious coalitions of the two GOP regional wings. At the beginning of the period, the dominant non-Sunbelt GOP reflected the religious dominance of mainline Protestants, the party's historic religious base, with almost half of all Republican identifiers affiliated with that tradition. Evangelical Protestants were no more numerous than Anglo Catholics, and both were distinct minorities. By the end of the period, evangelicals had more than doubled their share of GOP identifiers in the non-Sunbelt, and Anglo Catholics had slipped past mainliners for second place by 1992–96. Latino contributions to the party coalition were negligible in the earliest period and are still small. Unaffiliated citizens were about as numerous in the GOP coalition in the first period as in the last (slipping only 4 percentage points). In sum, the Republican Party coalition outside the Sunbelt went from mainline to evangelical Protestant dominance.

The coalition pattern for the Republicans in the Sunbelt is somewhat different. At the beginning of the period, the still relatively small Sunbelt Republican party was based almost equally in the two white Protestant traditions, with mainliners having a slight edge, while Catholics, Latinos, the unaffiliated, and other religious groups combined for a little over a third of the GOP constituency. As in the rest of the country, over the coming decades, the evangelical community increased its share of the GOP, and mainline Protestants lost ground. As elsewhere, white Catholics became a somewhat larger component over time, as did "all others." By 2000–2004

Table 4.4. Party Coalitions over Time in Non-Sunbelt and Sunbelt (Column Percents)

	1960–1978		1980–1988		1992–1996		2000–2004		2007		2008	
	R	D	R	D	R	D	R	D	R	D	R	D
Non-Sunbelt												
Evangelical	16	12	20	11	27	14	32	14	30	13	34	13
Mainline	47	22	35	18	24	16	22	19	23	18	21	16
Anglo-Catholic	16	30	21	27	26	27	23	25	25	22	22	27
All Latinos	0.3	1	2	3	3	5	4	5	3	7	3	6
Black Protestant	1	8	1	12	1	13	2	12	2	11	1	9
Unaffiliated	14	18	18	23	12	17	12	18	10	20	10	19
All Others	5	9	3	6	6	8	6	9	7	9	9	10
Sunbelt												
Evangelical	31	31	31	26	40	22	42	21	42	18	43	18
Mainline	36	18	24	12	18	12	20	14	19	13	16	11
Anglo-Catholic	8	11	9	6	12	12	14	11	11	9	13	8
All Latinos	1	3	6	9	6	11	5	13	9	15	10	20
Black Protestant	4	16	5	23	4	20	3	18	3	18	4	24
Unaffiliated	16	17	21	19	15	14	12	16	11	18	9	12
All Others	4	4	4	5	5	9	5	8	5	9	5	7

Sources: ANES 1964–1988; National Surveys of Religion and Politics: 1992, 1996, 2000, 2004 (Merged File). Pew Forum, U.S. Landscape Survey 2008, 5th National Survey of Religion and Politics, 2008. R = Republican, D = Democratic. Column percentages for both the Non-Sunbelt and the Sunbelt do not always add up to 100 due to rounding. **All others** include Latter-day Saints, Jehovah's Witnesses, Unitarians, Jews, Muslims, and all other religions.

these changes had created a Sunbelt GOP in which evangelicals outnumbered mainliners by more than 2 to 1, and Catholics by 3 to 1. In 2007 and 2008, evangelical domination of the GOP coalition became even more evident, as the party lost adherents from other religious groups. Thus, although evangelicals were the largest single GOP religious constituency in both regions, their position was more entrenched in the Sunbelt. In non-Sunbelt areas, they were merely the senior partners in a three-way alliance with mainline Protestants and Anglo Catholics.

What about the Democrats? Here, too, we see major changes in religious coalitions, as well as rather different regional alliances among religious groups. In the earliest period, the regional bases of the party are quite different, reflecting some of the historic splits among Democrats between the urban, ethnic, and Catholic north and the rural, WASP, and Protestant South, as well as the party's historic role as a haven for ethnic and religious minorities.[28] Outside the Sunbelt, the Democratic coalition in the first period was a broad alliance of Catholics, with almost a third of the party, and almost equal-sized groups of mainliners, unaffiliated citizens, and religious minorities (including, of course, Jews and Black Protestants). Evangelical Protestants were a *small* Democratic constituency outside the Sunbelt. Within the Sunbelt, however, evangelicals replaced Catholics as the centerpiece of the Democratic alliance, followed by other religious groups, the unaffiliated and mainliners (both at about one-sixth of the party's base), with Anglo Catholics only a small Democratic group.

By the twenty-first century, the Democratic religious coalition had changed dramatically in the Sunbelt, with smaller changes in the rest of the country. In the non-Sunbelt states, the Catholic plurality was reduced somewhat, while the mainline Protestant portion of the coalition fell more dramatically. Note the sizable number of Latinos, Black Protestants, and the "all others" classification (Jews and other small religious groups). What is noteworthy about the non-Sunbelt Democratic coalition is its religious diversity and "balance" among groups. Democratic electoral appeals must be made to a broad array of groups.

The Sunbelt Democratic coalition looks different. The 1960–78 evangelical contribution to the coalition declined significantly over the period. Mainline, Catholic, and unaffiliated Democrats also declined somewhat in importance across the era. The dramatic change is, of course, in the proportion of Sunbelt Democrats drawn from among Latinos.[29] By 2008, the Black

Protestant contribution to the Sunbelt Democrats had also increased, making the coalition a minority-based phenomenon. The result of these transformations, as well as those on the Republican side, is twofold. First, the Sunbelt GOP and Democratic parties still look somewhat different from their Non-Sunbelt counterparts: the Sunbelt GOP is more evangelical, less mainline and Catholic, while the Sunbelt Democratic coalition is more "minority" religion, and less mainline and Catholic. And a glance at the last period also reveals that there is less religious "overlap" between the Republicans and the Democrats in the Sunbelt than present elsewhere, with the largest religious groups in each—evangelicals in the GOP and minorities in the Democratic Party—in a more dominant position.[30] These religious differences in party composition may well contribute to the much-noted political polarization characterizing modern American politics.

The religious composition of the GOP and the Democratic Party constituencies is important for a variety of reasons. First, of course, most voters usually make their electoral choices in accordance with their long-term identification. This "standing decision" is an important constraint on election outcomes. In addition, party identifiers are much more likely to participate in other decisions: to vote in primaries and caucuses choosing party candidates for office, to influence party platforms, or to contribute money or energy to campaigns. Those who participate in these ways are much more likely to shape party operations and their ideological bent.

Religion, Region, and the Presidential Vote, 1960–2008

Of course, people sometimes deviate from their identification in making electoral choices. Various short-term forces may lead a voter to choose a candidate of the other political party. Indeed, such deviating choices may take place over a string of elections, eventually leading the voter to reassess his or her party identification. Thus, we need to look also at the electoral decisions of voters in different regional and religious groups. Table 4.5 reports the Republican vote for president, using the same sources as our previous tables. Once again, our interest is in both the electoral propensities of religious groups and how those vary by region and subregion.

We begin with observations of all voters before turning to religious groups, finding that, since the 1990s, the Sunbelt has provided somewhat

Table 4.5. Republican Presidential Vote by Religion over Time (percent)

	1960–1976	1980–1988	1992–1996	2000–2004	2008
All Voters	51	56	47	50	46
Non-Sunbelt	51	57	45	48	45
Sunbelt	51	55	50	54	48
South	49	51	45	57	49
Florida	66	76	52	54	51
Texas	39	50	52	60	53
Southwest	52	56	47	55	54
California	52	58	49	45	34
Evangelical	61	71	68	75	76
Non-Sunbelt	65	73	65	73	72
Sunbelt	57	69	70	77	79
South	56	66	62	74	84
Florida	72	89	62	69	70
Texas	42	64	73	85	87
Southwest	64	69	67	83	64
California	66	81	82	79	60
Mainline	66	69	56	54	50
Non-Sunbelt	66	69	51	50	46
Sunbelt	65	67	62	59	56
Anglo Catholic	39	55	46	52	51
Non-Sunbelt	38	53	44	48	47
Sunbelt	42	67	50	59	60
All Latinos	40	40	23	36	30
Non-Sunbelt	29	43	22	24	27
Sunbelt	46	39	24	44	31
Black Protestant +	11	9	10	9	5
Jewish	19	29	13	28	23
Unaffiliated	46	55	39	30	27
Non-Sunbelt	45	51	38	29	22
Sunbelt	49	62	40	32	34

Sources: ANES 1960–1988; National Surveys on Religion and Politics (merged file) 1992–1004; Pew Forum, U.S. Religious Landscape Survey, 5th National Survey on Religion and Politics, 2008.

greater support for Republican presidential candidates than has the rest of the country. Florida and Texas were more likely to support the GOP than other parts of the Sunbelt in the 1992 and 1996 elections, while Texas led the way in 2000 and 2004 with George W. Bush as the candidate. In 2008, there was little variation in support for John McCain within the Sunbelt, except in California where Barack Obama won handily.

The observant reader will have noted that evangelical Protestants were voting Republican before they began to identify with the GOP (cf. Table 4.3). In particular, Richard Nixon in 1960 and 1972 received strong support from evangelicals. Nationally, the evangelical vote for Republican presidential candidates reached its peak in the twenty-first century, with an impressive average of 75 percent going to George W. Bush in 2000–2004 and with an even higher 76 percent going to John McCain in 2008. In 2008, evangelicals were the only religious group to increase their support for the GOP over 2000–2004 figures. And although evangelical voting did not vary enormously by region, during the first two periods, "Northern" evangelicals were slightly more likely to vote Republican than their Sunbelt brethren, but this pattern reversed later, as Sunbelt evangelicals took the prize for GOP voting.

The subregional breakdown among evangelicals shows the reason for the global change. In the earlier periods, the Old South ran only slightly behind non-Sunbelt evangelicals, but Texas lagged far behind, no doubt reflecting native son Lyndon B. Johnson's candidacy in 1964 and Jimmy Carter's "southern" candidacy in 1976. By the most recent period, however, the Old South's GOP vote had risen considerably, Florida's had remained fairly high, and Texan evangelicals went overwhelmingly for their former governor in 2000 and 2004 and for McCain in 2008. Note also that California evangelicals became regular Republican voters by 1980–88, perhaps reflecting the Reagan appeal. The support for Bush and McCain by California evangelicals is also quite impressive given the minority support McCain received by voters in the state as a whole.

Mainline Protestants have a different story but one that parallels their changes in party identification. Their propensity to vote Republican has dropped fairly consistently in both regions, although Sunbelt mainliners remained more likely to choose the GOP than their northern brethren. And as we might expect from the partisan change data reported above, Anglo Catholics have shown a slowly increasing propensity to vote Republican in presidential elections. Indeed, in 2000–2004, they gave a majority of their votes to George W. Bush and did the same for John McCain in 2008. Throughout the period covered in Table 4.5, Sunbelt Anglo Catholics have outpaced their northern counterparts in voting for the GOP.

Latino support for Democratic candidates has remained strong throughout the time period, increasing in importance as population percentages have increased. Throughout the past half century, Sunbelt Latinos have been somewhat more prone to support GOP candidates than their non-Sunbelt compatriots, particularly in 2000–2004.[31] And we note that Black Protestants and Jews have remained very Democratic throughout the time period, with Blacks and Latinos giving Democratic candidates a large edge, particularly in the Sunbelt. The unaffiliated also join the Democratic voting coalition, except for the 1980s (where an attachment to Reaganomics seemed to motivate this group to vote Republican). Since that time, the unaffiliated have moved rather dramatically toward the Democrats in presidential elections, although once again, the Sunbelt contingent lags slightly behind in this tendency.

Religion, Region, and Political Issues

Politics is about more than which candidate wins elections. Winning candidates and parties make important decisions on a wide range of public policy issues. Public opinion on these issues may well shape which candidates win elections, and may influence the decision-makers once in office. There is some conventional wisdom that the shift in political power to the Sunbelt has had a conservative impact on a range of public policy issues, from abortion to tax policy to free trade to national defense. Other analysts doubt that such regional differences exist.[32] In this section of the chapter, we look at the configuration of regional and religious group opinion on seven issues in 2008. In Table 4.6, we report the results for questions on abortion, gay rights, national health insurance, preference for lower taxes and fewer public services, support for Israel over the Palestinians in the Middle East, approval of free trade,[33] and backing for a strong military. We have reported "conservative" responses to each question. (Remember that, on all questions, a varying number refuse to answer or are "not sure," so that 46 percent may actually represent a plurality response or even a majority of those with an opinion.)

Table 4.6. Religion and Issue Positions in the Sunbelt in 2008

	Pro-Life	Anti-Gay Rights	Oppose National Health Plan	Fewer Public Services	Favor Israel over Palestinians	Favor Free Trade	Favor Strong Military
All Respondents	48	26	38	34	40	32	52
Non-Sunbelt	44	23	37	33	37	31	47
Sunbelt	53	28	40	34	44	33	56
South	60	37	46	36	49	28	57
Florida	40	23	41	33	41	33	65
Texas	52	28	44	28	46	32	60
Southwest	48	19	31	38	39	44	52
California	44	16	29	31	37	39	48
Evangelical							
Non-Sunbelt	63	38	50	41	49	27	51
Sunbelt	69	49	56	43	62	28	67
Mainline							
Non-Sunbelt	35	20	41	33	39	33	42
Sunbelt	30	21	53	40	44	37	56
Anglo Catholic							
Non-Sunbelt	50	19	34	31	35	32	52
Sunbelt	52	26	45	43	42	49	59

Table 4.6. (Continued)

	Pro-Life	Anti-Gay Rights	Oppose National Health Plan	Fewer Public Services	Favor Israel over Palestinians	Favor Free Trade	Favor Strong Military
Black Protestant							
Non-Sunbelt	37	33	14	30	31	15	56
Sunbelt	61	31	35	21	28	11	58
Latino Protestant							
Non-Sunbelt	69	36	32	32	19	22	52
Sunbelt	78	34	30	16	49	29	46
Latino Catholic							
Non-Sunbelt	55	16	24	15	20	30	45
Sunbelt	62	13	12	19	31	44	50
Jewish *	4	5	25	26	78	55	42
Unaffiliated							
Non-Sunbelt	20	11	29	29	33	31	38
Sunbelt	22	11	32	32	36	39	43

Source: Pew Forum, 5th National Survey of Religion and Politics, 2008.
* Almost no Non-Sunbelt/Sunbelt differences among Jewish respondents.

First, are Sunbelt residents more conservative than Americans elsewhere? The first section of Table 4.6 would suggest that the answer is "yes, but not by a whole lot." The conservative margin in the Sunbelt on these seven issues runs from a high of 9 percentage points on pro-life and strong defense to a single point advantage on national health insurance. Indeed, the variation is much greater within subregions. Old South residents are much more pro-life and opposed to gay rights than Californians, and Texans stand out in opposition to increased government spending.

In fact, a quick glance at the table suggests that religion is a much better explanation for ideological differences than region is. Evangelicals consistently demonstrate the greatest conservatism across the board, with Sunbelt evangelicals leading the way. And, in data not shown, the subregional differences among evangelicals are relatively small and apparently random in nature except for California evangelicals who hold slightly more liberal views than their counterparts elsewhere (data not shown).

Mainline Protestants are much more liberal on these issues than evangelicals. Within the mainline tradition, there are few differences by region, with a slight tip to the conservative side by the Sunbelt respondents, except on abortion and gay rights. Anglo Catholics tend to be more liberal than evangelicals and more conservative than mainline Protestants with Sunbelt Catholics often much more conservative than their brethren elsewhere. Black Protestant stances vary rather dramatically by issue area. Sunbelt Black Protestants do have strong pro-life attitudes, while in both regions the group is more opposed to gay rights than the national average. Both non-Sunbelt and Sunbelt Black Protestants favor a strong military, but are less likely to favor Israel than most other religious groups. Both groups are very skeptical about free trade but are fairly liberal on national health care and government services.

We also note the greater political conservatism of Latino Protestants as opposed to Latino Catholics, particularly on abortion and gay rights with the former resembling evangelicals on these two issues. There is a slight tendency for Sunbelt Latinos to hold more conservative attitudes than do their counterparts in the rest of the country. Table 4.6 also shows the strong and unsurprising liberalism of Jewish respondents, with the exception of massive support for Israel over the Palestinians. Finally, unaffiliated respondents support liberal policy attitudes with little variation between regions.

Have these issue positions changed over time? The NSRP time series has data for most of these issue variables going back to 1992, and the results are revealing. In data not shown, they indicate that Americans have become more pro-life with the Sunbelt leading the way. At the same time, attitudes toward gay rights are more favorable in 2008 than in 1992. In addition, opposition to a national health plan has increased, spurred by evangelicals, while, at the same time, Americans are now more favorable to increased government services. Favorable attitudes toward Israel have increased, led by the Sunbelt and by evangelicals in that region. Finally, negative attitudes toward free trade have increased, while a strong national defense is viewed more favorably. As this review suggests, there appears to be no broad, consistent ideological direction to these changes.

Is there an "issue basis" for maintaining that the Sunbelt is a viable region? Yes, the Sunbelt does exhibit more conservative attitudes than the rest of the country, but the results in Table 4.6 do not provide as much support for regional issue differences as for religious polarity. If the Sunbelt is to achieve political viability in the manner of the old "Solid South," it must foster a set of issues that exhibit strong support across the region among elites, political parties and interest groups, and the mass public. An earlier effort among elites, the so-called Sunbelt Caucus, formed in 1981 in the U.S. House of Representatives, suggested the possibility that a set of issues might bind together states in the Sunbelt. It is interesting that California was not represented in the caucus, although Kentucky, Missouri, and West Virginia were. The caucus went out of existence in 1995.[34] Despite increased numbers of legislators from Sunbelt states, there is no congressional caucus representation from this "region" today. This suggests that the dominant issues of contemporary American politics do not generally divide citizens along Sunbelt/non-Sunbelt lines.

Summary and Implications

No observer of American political history would deny that regionalism has been a powerful force from the very beginning of the nation. Political conflict between regions was evident in the Constitutional Convention, in the struggle over slavery, in the great battles over economic expansion and regulation, and in the partisan warfare of the New Deal period. Even as late as the 1960s, a vast literature in political science explored the distinctive politics of one region, the American South, in large part occasioned by the great struggle over civil rights. Indeed, this large body of literature continues to this day.

Despite this historic concern for regional explanations, the dominant perspective in contemporary American political science strongly favors what might be called the "nationalization" hypothesis: the notion that with economic growth in formerly disadvantaged regions, the nationalization of the media, massive population movements, and the creation of a national legal regime by the federal courts, the once great disparities in political behavior among regions has been eliminated.[35] Yet this contention has often been challenged by those who see continuing regional differences or even distinctive state political cultures. Certainly, the much-touted "red state, blue state" political labels are a popular expression of such continuing assumptions.

What do our findings on the interaction of religion and politics contribute to this debate? First, our data certainly support the nationalization hypothesis in a number of ways. Most importantly, the last fifty years have produced a major homogenization of political orientation among most major religious groups, but especially in the large evangelical Protestant community, so important in many parts of the Sunbelt. Evangelicals now behave politically in very much the same way whether they live in the North, the Old South, or California. The same tends to be true of other religious groups as well, although in a few cases Sunbelt residents do lean slightly to the Republican and conservative side. Thus, from the perspective of religious factors, differing regional politics are largely the effect of the composition of their religious communities—not the result of some distinctive "regional" culture on all religious groups.

And those differing religious populations do create differing political environments. As we have argued, from a religious and political perspective, the Sunbelt does not hang together all that well as a single region. The religious composition of the area differs in major ways as one moves from the Old South to the Pacific coast. And the political choices made by Sunbelt residents are quite different as well. Indeed, the subregions and individual states we were able to examine often reveal considerable individuality in political behavior, providing some comfort to those theorists who note that it is still American states that are the basic political units, with their own history, culture, and traditions. But it is important to note that individuality may be a thing of the past, as adherents to any single religious tradition now look very much alike across regions and states.

All this is not to say that the Sunbelt is not a political entity for certain purposes. For example, members of Congress from rapidly growing regions often share similar views on the allocation formulas for federal program expenditures.[36] Political and religious conservatism in much of the region provides additional incentives for cooperation. And in some instances, Sunbelt states may exhibit a greater preoccupation with other problems occasioned by rapid economic and population growth or more immediate concerns with immigration from Latin America. But such occasions for a common political agenda within the Sunbelt have not brought about much cooperation across state lines on matters of common interest. The same growth in size and economic power that makes the Sunbelt a potential powerhouse in national politics also produces a diversity that makes regional cooperation frustratingly elusive.

PART II

Civil Rights in the Sunbelt

Chapter 5

From the Southwest to the Nation: Interracial Civil Rights Activism in Los Angeles

Shana Bernstein

In 1946, Gonzalo and Felicitas Mendez initiated a lawsuit after Westminster Elementary School denied admission to their children, Sylvia, Gerónimo, and Gonzalo Jr., because of their dark skin color and Spanish surname. Four other Mexican American fathers joined Gonzalo in filing suit against their respective school districts in Orange County, California, for discriminating against children of "Mexican and Latin descent." While California schools were not segregated as entirely or as clearly as southern schools, they were segregated in ways unique to California's multiracial environment, targeting Japanese, Chinese, and Mexican children to different degrees.[1] A judge ruled in favor of the plaintiffs, and a federal court of appeals held that segregating Mexican Americans violated California's Constitution. The appeals court affirmed that California law, which permitted the segregation of people of Asian descent (Chinese, Japanese, and "Mongolian"), forbade the segregation of Mexican Americans. Unlike the national desegregation victory later achieved in *Brown v. Board of Education*, the *Mendez v. Westminster* judgment did not rule against segregation per se. The appeals court sidestepped the issue of race by ruling that the California Constitution prohibited the segregation only of Mexican-origin children, not any ethnoracial group.[2]

Mendez, though, distinguished itself from earlier desegregation cases as a federal rather than a state or local court ruling. Supporters, thus, hoped to challenge *Plessy v. Ferguson*, the 1896 Supreme Court case that had originally established segregation's legality.[3] They reasoned that school districts appealing on the ruling's legality would invite the Supreme Court to decide on the constitutionality of segregation itself. But the school districts did not file appeals, so *Mendez* never became the test case for segregation; that had to wait for *Brown v. Board of Education*. Nevertheless, *Mendez* stands as the first federal court decision and the first use of the Fourteenth Amendment to overturn the widespread segregation of a minority group. Legal and educational scholars suggest that *Mendez* was the first step toward overturning the *Plessy v. Ferguson* doctrine of "separate but equal."[4]

Despite the case's failure to achieve complete desegregation on a national or even statewide level, the *Mendez* case was a success in terms of collaborative interracial activism among Mexican, Anglo, African, Jewish, and Japanese Americans. While Mexican Americans' initiative lay at the heart of the case and provided its foundation, cooperation from other communities was crucial to Mexican Americans' success. For instance, a Jewish American civil rights attorney represented the plaintiffs; an Anglo American field worker for the American Council of Race Relations (ACRR) joined Mexican Americans to protest the Santa Ana Board of Education's lack of compliance with the judge's initial ruling; and Jewish American, African American, Japanese American, and other groups filed friends of the court briefs to support this case, which they collectively hoped would provide the Supreme Court an opportunity to review *Plessy v. Ferguson*'s long-standing precedent of "separate but equal."[5]

The collaborative struggles of the *Mendez* supporters reflect more than an interesting local or state story of Mexican Americans' challenge to desegregation and more than an example of the importance of interracial collaboration to this challenge. This and other examples of interracial activism in Southern California and particularly in Los Angeles, like the cooperation between Jewish Americans and Mexican Americans that helped launch the Mexican American civil rights group the Community Service Organization (CSO), raise questions about our understanding of civil rights activism in mid-century America, and in the Sunbelt more specifically. The story of civil rights activism in this racially diverse metropolitan region suggests we re-examine narratives of civil rights activism, which have developed from understandings of southern and, more recently, northern civil rights resistance.

Southern California's significant populations of Mexican, Japanese, and Jewish Americans and their relationship to black and white residents shaped a different civil rights narrative from the black/white axis that engendered the southern and northern struggles for racial equality. This activist history in Los Angeles subverts understandings of civil rights as either southern or northern and reveals the limits of the binary black/white history of twentieth-century civil rights activism that emerges from studies of southern, northeastern and midwestern regions. While L.A. was clearly not the South, where urban and rural African American communities launched the civil rights movement, it was also not the North. African Americans in Los Angeles, unlike in northern cities like New York, Chicago, and Detroit, were not a significant enough presence to act on their own or with sympathetic white support, composing only approximately 8.7 percent of the total population in 1950. Moreover, the city's other main minority groups, of Jewish, Mexican, and Japanese origin, were a significant fraction of the population—12.7, 8, and just over 1 percent respectively—and were themselves active in equality struggles.[6]

In a city and region with no majority minority, the various ethnoracial groups relied on each other to advance certain shared goals, making finding common ground particularly crucial. Jewish and Mexican allies, with their relatively large populations and political potential, were especially important to the city's African Americans. Moreover, many of these groups lived in proximity to each other during this mid-century period, and this shared space—including the conflicts that frequently emerged from it—facilitated finding common ground. Rarely were civil rights struggles in mid-century Southern California the product of a single ethnic community, as the actors in this study neither practiced ethnic particularism nor related exclusively to dominant white society. Rather, different racialized and subordinated groups engaged each other and often worked together to achieve some common goals, defining their strategies in relation to each other as well as to the dominant society. Northern cities were similar to Los Angeles in the sense that they also operated to some degree as laboratories of interracial civil rights activism, as northern urban African Americans' frequent cooperation with Anglo and Jewish activists illustrates.[7] But the extreme ethnoracial diversity of mid-century Los Angeles meant that coalitions there were particularly crucial to racial equality campaigns. Its multiracial complexity, moreover, made the city a bellwether that gave Americans a glimpse of where their soon-to-be multiracial nation would head in decades to come. The city, in a sense, modeled interracial activism among diverse populations for a future generation.

Most important for our understanding of the significance of the postwar Sunbelt, the cooperative interracial initiatives that emerged in Southern California helped shape the emergent liberal civil rights agenda that produced legal transformations in issues like school and housing segregation. The school desegregation struggles of Southern California Mexican Americans and their multiracial allies in *Mendez* provided a training ground for activists who later took the fight to the Supreme Court, where it culminated in the 1954 *Brown* decision. Activists like the National Association for the Advancement of Colored People (NAACP)'s Loren Miller, an African American who emerged from Los Angeles's interracial milieu where he worked through organizations like the predominantly Mexican American CSO, also helped shape national policies against widespread restrictive housing covenants that forbade many minorities from buying houses in white neighborhoods. This essay first explains how and why conditions during World War II and especially the early Cold War facilitated the development of interracial initiatives like *Mendez* and others, focusing in particular on the CSO. It then illustrates how these interracial postwar struggles and the activists who emerged from them helped shape national school and housing desegregation outcomes, in the process recentering Los Angeles in a national civil rights narrative.

The CSO and the Struggle to Forge an Interracial Political Culture in Los Angeles

Postwar interracial collaboration built on an earlier tradition of interracial activism in the City of Angels, which World War II era tensions in particular facilitated.[8] Wartime racial tensions climaxed in Los Angeles with the Sleepy Lagoon case and the "Zoot Suit" Riots. First, in late 1942 and early 1943, seventeen Mexican American boys were tried and unjustly convicted for the death of another teenager who died of wounds whose cause was never actually determined. Police arrested the entire group of boys (in addition to five others whom they later released), who had attended a party with the victim the night before he died. Anti-Mexican sentiment helped convict the boys in the largest mass conviction in California history to that point, with the judge sentencing three of the boys to life in prison for first degree murder, finding nine guilty of second degree murder, and convicting five of assault.[9] Then from June 3 through June 13, 1943, the Zoot Suit violence between the Mexican-origin community and servicemen from local military installations raged on the streets of downtown and East Los Angeles. Racist white servicemen stripped and beat young Mexican American (as well as some African American) men wearing zoot suits, a style of clothing popular in the Mexican community. Although nobody died, many Mexican Americans suffered violence. The police later unfairly arrested the victims and charged them as the instigators, and contemporary press reports also blamed Mexican American "Zoot Suiters" for the violence.[10]

The rapid growth and increasing ethnoracial diversity that the war brought to Los Angeles fueled such tensions. Part of this growth stemmed from federal investment in the defense and related industries. Migrants flooded in from the South, the Midwest, the East, and Mexico to take advantage of the West's growing economies, especially opportunities created by the defense industry. Los Angeles provided more jobs than any other American wartime production center, and the area had scores of military bases and installations by the beginning of the cold war.[11] Los Angeles led the way in western cities' population growth, with a 31 percent general population increase from 1940 to 1950, making it the largest city in the West and the fourth largest nationwide.[12] The minority populations grew even faster than the rest of the population, except for Japanese Americans, whom immigration restrictions and internment—from which many residents did not return—limited.[13] The black population increased by almost three times between 1940 and 1950. African Americans migrating from the South and Southwest helped their community's population surge from 4 percent to almost 9 percent of the total population.[14] The Mexican-descent population, which came both from across the international border and other southwestern states, grew by about half between 1940 and 1950, though this population's growth is difficult to track accurately. While the census indicates the Mexican-origin percentage of the larger population remained steady, approximately 8 percent, it undoubtedly undercounted this difficult-to-categorize population.[15] The city's Jewish population, which came from Europe, the Midwest, and the East Coast, had nearly doubled from the prewar period by 1948.[16] Observers estimated 168,000 Jews,

200,000 African Americans, 235,000 Mexican-origin people, 5,000 Chinese-origin people, and 12,000 Japanese-origin people lived in the city by 1946. Some locals believed that minorities composed 40 percent of the city's population by 1950, though 30 percent is probably a more accurate figure.[17] Whatever the number, Los Angeles was no longer the heavily white, Midwestern Protestant city it had been in prewar decades, and postwar Angelenos navigated a multifaceted racial terrain.

As the city's economic and defense importance grew, particularly in the context of the Pacific Front war, conflicts among increasingly diverse populations assumed new significance. Domestic eruptions like the Sleepy Lagoon case and the Zoot Suit Riots, which exposed deep anti-Mexican discrimination, became both a national and an international issue. They drew negative attention from domestic and global audiences, especially Latin American countries, at the same time the United States relied more on its alliances with Latin America, China, and European nations. When exposed to an increasingly attentive world, Los Angeles and national discrimination created an international public relations fiasco and jeopardized U.S. alliances with countries like Mexico, for whom these incidents illuminated the hypocrisy of fighting a "good war" against Hitler's racism yet permitting racial discrimination in the United States. Racial discrimination drew negative attention from American enemies, too, including Japan, who used the hypocrisy to underscore the importance of beating the United States. This international significance continued during the Cold War as the Soviets used discrimination to shore up communist claims that democracy was morally bankrupt.[18] Los Angeles played a particularly important role in this ideological battle as its multiracial residents heralded from locations around the globe and drew the attention of Latin American, Asian, and other countries.

Events like the Sleepy Lagoon case and Zoot Suit Riots also brought the relatively parallel struggles of minority groups into greater contact with each other. Mexican, Jewish, African, Japanese, and Anglo American activists recognized that local and national officials feared that incidents of racism endangered the city's defense production capacities and damaged the United States' global reputation, and they used the attention to make common cause and advance their proequality agendas. The birth of interracial committees like the Coordinating Council for Latin American Youth (CCLAY) and the Citizens' Committee for Latin American Youth reveals how the connection between discrimination and wartime defense facilitated interracial civil rights efforts.[19] One of the best-known examples is the Sleepy Lagoon Defense Committee (SLDC), the group of Mexican Americans, Anglos, Jewish Americans, and African Americans who fought on behalf of the unjustly incarcerated Mexican American boys. SLDC and other civil rights coalition activists successfully used the United States' wartime aims to legitimize and facilitate their work, eventually convincing the court to overturn the guilty verdict against the Sleepy Lagoon defendants. SLDC members seized upon Mexico's concern for the defendants—illustrated most visibly by the Mexican Consulate's retention of a lawyer for them—as fodder for their cause. They articulated a "Double V" strategy, arguing that fighting discrimination at home was essential to winning the war abroad because it would alleviate the violence that undermined the domestic war effort and project a better image of democracy to U.S. allies. Committee lawyers opened the trial by arguing that racism jeopardized the hemispheric solidarity required to defeat the Axis powers. They argued that all of Latin America and the Good Neighbor Policy stood trial along with the Mexican American defendants. The fight for civil rights, the Committee claimed, was "an integral part of the welding of Allied unity for the winning of the war."[20]

Memories of the damage the Zoot Suit violence inflicted on multiracial Eastside neighborhoods also spurred some of the collaborative momentum that continued to build during the postwar years, particularly Jewish community support for the Community Service Organization. The CSO, one of the most important mid-twentieth-century civil rights organizations for Mexican Americans, emerged out of a coalition of Mexican, Jewish, African, Japanese, and progressive "Anglo" Americans that came together to elect Edward Roybal, a local social worker and community organizer, to the Los Angeles City Council in 1949. Roybal became the first Mexican American City Council member since 1881—and the council's only nonwhite member—in a district in which fewer than one-fifth of voters were of Mexican origin.[21] Mostly Mexican American supporters had failed two years earlier but succeeded in 1949 after recognizing the importance of building ethnoracial coalitions. Mexican American activists involved in Roybal's first election coalition who hoped to continue this kind of activism began to form the CSO in that same year, 1947. By 1963 the CSO had established thirty-four chapters across the Southwest, primarily in California, with more than 10,000 paid members.[22]

The CSO's main purpose was to encourage civic participation among

Eastside residents, who increasingly were of Mexican origin (citizen and immigrant) but also Jewish, Japanese, Italian, Filipino, and African American, as well as white. The CSO concentrated on issues such as health care; neighborhood improvement projects like adding street lights to the area's dark, often unpaved roadways; housing, including fighting against restrictive covenants and for public housing; fair employment; voter education; voter registration; police brutality; and civil rights more generally. The organization played an instrumental role in achieving two particularly important Mexican American civil rights victories during its first decade. First, the CSO helped secure the conviction of five Los Angeles police officers and the dismissal or suspension of seventeen others who had severely beaten seven young men, five of whom were Mexican Americans, during a station Christmas party in the 1951 "Bloody Christmas" incident.[23] Then, in the 1956 Hidalgo case, the CSO helped convict two Los Angeles County deputy sheriffs for the unprovoked beating of a thirteen-year-old boy, the first such police brutality verdict in Los Angeles history.[24] Voter registration became a top CSO priority too. The CSO registered 15,000 Spanish-speaking people in the city's ninth district alone by 1949 and launched the career of Roybal and other local Mexican Americans.[25] Its membership was equally male and female, and the majority—about three-fourths—were citizens. Though a small minority of professional and small business people joined, most members were field and factory workers, simultaneously belonging to labor unions like the American Federation of Labor (AFL) and the Congress of Industrial Organizations (CIO), organizations that also frequently supported CSO efforts.[26] The CSO efforts were all part of what the *Los Angeles Daily News* characterized at the time as a "great upsurge of inter-group cooperation."[27]

This great upsurge of intergroup cooperation is crucial to understanding the CSO. Scholars usually recount the story of the CSO's early years as a central episode in twentieth-century Chicano history and debate whether the organization represents a form of accommodation or resistance to the surrounding culture. This discussion affirms the CSO's importance to Mexican Americans but obscures the significance of its multiracial foundation.[28] While the organization served mostly Mexican-origin Los Angelenos, it worked for all the Eastside's diverse residents and, significantly, drew on interracial cooperation for its foundation and sustenance.

The CSO's founders benefited from connections arising from shared neighborhoods and, in some cases, memories of recently shared space—

especially in the case of the Jewish community, which through its Community Relations Committee (CRC) provided disproportionate support to the CSO. In the years following World War II, the Eastside neighborhoods where the CSO emerged were still significantly multiracial, with Jewish, Mexican, Japanese, black, and other residents sharing streets, schools, work places, and social venues, though during the 1950s many of the non-Mexican residents left. African Americans concentrated increasingly in the city's poor and segregated south side and its adjacent poor suburbs like Compton. Many Jews, who were becoming more upwardly mobile socially and economically despite instances of ongoing housing restrictions and employment discrimination they confronted, increasingly left the Eastside behind as they moved westward to the city's wealthier Westside and to surrounding areas like the San Fernando Valley, San Gabriel Valley, and the South Bay. As Japanese Americans' social, economic, and political status began to improve, they too moved to similar neighborhoods.[29] This accelerating exodus left the Eastside significantly Mexican-origin, and increasingly marginalized. The Mexican-origin population was "Southern California's largest and, in many ways, most disadvantaged minority," according to a 1949 report by the Industrial Areas Foundation, the organization formed by Chicago's prominent Jewish activist Saul Alinsky, whose wartime visits to Los Angeles as a good will ambassador for the Department of State sparked his interest in the city's Mexican population. The group's poverty, lack of networks to other communities, low voter turnout, and high percentage of noncitizens, according to reports like these, impeded attempts at securing financial backing to pressure politicians to improve their conditions.[30] A 1946 investigation of racial minorities' conditions by the Chicago-based race relations group the American Council of Race Relations (ACRR) concluded that the Mexican American community was even worse off than other poor Los Angeles minorities.[31] Despite Mexican Americans' increasing marginalization, though, in the late 1940s, Jews and Mexicans shared enough common interests and common space to inspire their collaboration.

The multiracial CSO formed when the Roybal election coalition joined forces with Alinsky who, after the war, used his community networks to help secure funding and support, especially from the local Jewish community. He used the money he raised from the CRC and from Hollywood film star Melvyn Douglas and his wife, the "pink lady" Congresswoman Helen Gahagan Douglas, who were both politically left-leaning, to hire Fred Ross as a full-time assistant to work with the CSO. Ross, a white social justice activist who had built a good reputation among Mexican Americans, a couple of years earlier had supported the *Mendez* effort. Ross joined local Mexican Americans who had been active in Roybal's campaign and together, with support from the local Jewish community, they turned the CSO into a long-lasting organization.[32]

The CSO began and remained multiracial into the 1950s, though later it became more exclusively Mexican American. Early CSO organizers encouraged multiracial membership and were happy to note that 1948 meetings maintained and deepened racially diverse attendance. "Although the great majority of CSO members are Mexican Americans, we have gradually had members of other groups come in," Executive Director Ross reported. "At the last meeting, for instance, we had 15 reps from the adjacent Jewish community, 4 Negroes and around 18 so called 'Protestant Anglos'."[33] In 1949, Ross reported that "Orientals, Negroes, Jews and Christians [Anglos]" composed the approximately 12 percent of membership who were not Spanish-speaking.[34] According to the organization's chairman Tony Ríos, percent of its more than 3,500 members in the early to mid-1950s (approximately 3,000 from three Los Angeles County branches and 500 from San Jose) were from the "Negro, Jewish, and the so-called Anglo American communities."[35] The CSO also appointed leaders of African American organizations to its own committees. For instance, the NAACP's West Coast Legal Committee chairman Loren Miller, who had been active in *Mendez* and later struggled to achieve the *Brown* decision, also later chaired the CSO's own Legal Aid Committee.[36] The CSO emphasized the importance to the Mexican American community of cross-ethnic ties. It highlighted comments the NAACP's field secretary Lester Bailey made at its 1955 national board meeting, where Bailey emphasized collaborative interracial efforts by groups like the CSO and the NAACP to fight segregation, pass fair employment practices legislation, and increase minority voter registration. The CSO noted Bailey's observation that these ties were particularly significant in the West where, unlike the South, the African American was not "alone in his battle against discrimination" because of the large presence of groups like Mexican Americans in the region.[37] Bailey especially emphasized that collaborative efforts between African and Mexican Americans, including CSO efforts, had been central to the national desegregation campaign and to *Brown v. Board of Education*. "It has been through the combined efforts of these types of organizations that have made this history-making decision possible," Bailey stated.[38]

The CSO turned its attention to the Jewish community in particular, and its initial success especially depended on this collaboration. Mexican Americans appointed Fred Herzberg, the executive director of the CRC, as the only non-Mexican American member of its seven-person Advisory Committee.[39] The CSO invited Jewish groups to attend its community civil rights meetings, where they discussed housing, police brutality, and other vital civil rights issues.[40] Ralph Guzman, a CSO vice president, asked Jewish community representatives to help his organization gain tax exempt status.[41] Furthermore, from 1947 to 1950, the Jewish community provided critical financial contributions to the CSO, particularly through the CRC. Jewish-community financial assistance continued, though in smaller amounts, for a few years after.[42] Some early CSO meetings were held in Jewish community leaders' offices.[43] Jewish community members supported the CSO's civil rights work in the Mexican-origin community because they believed it was important. As they explained at a CRC meeting, it carried the "greatest impact . . . of any project submitted" in 1948.[44]

The Zoot Suit Riots' legacy factored prominently into postwar calculations about the value of cooperating across community divides, especially as mounting employment discrimination and a housing crunch escalated racial tensions in minority areas. The transformation to a peace-time society meant the end of the wartime employment boom. Jobs disappeared and unemployment rose. The contraction hit the defense industry particularly hard. Ten percent of unemployed Americans were in California in May 1949, making it one of the hardest hit areas in the country, and more than half of these unemployed Californians resided in Los Angeles.[45] Los Angeles also faced a housing shortage unequaled elsewhere in the U.S., according to the Los Angeles Housing Authority's director who "conservatively estimated" a one hundred thousand unit shortfall.[46] Both housing and employment problems were exacerbated for minorities, given employers' tendency to hire them last and fire them first, and the prevalence of restrictive housing covenants. Economic tensions fueled racial tensions and stirred Jews', Mexicans', and other Angelenos' fears that violence would once again erupt. East Los Angeles Jewish and Mexican communities, among whom relations were particularly strained as the two groups' financial, social, and geographic distance increased, viewed potential violence as an especially salient issue.

Class difference increasingly estranged Jewish and Mexican Americans from each other. In the schools, the ACRR's report *The Problem of Violence* observed, "The great barrier to the acceptance of Mexican children by Jewish children is the middle-class bias of the Jewish parents expressed in excessive concern over dirt and disease." Divergent police action toward the two groups also "contribute[d] to the increase of community tension between middle-class Jews and lower-class Mexicans."[47] This "class bias" was intertwined with a racial bias, as Jewish Americans were becoming increasingly integrated into American society and accepted as white, while Mexicans increasingly faced categorization as brown "others." Mexican Americans saw their Jewish neighbors moving to nicer neighborhoods, while their own conditions stagnated or deteriorated, breeding "frustration and bitterness." Alinsky's Industrial Areas Foundation reported, "These, in turn, found expression in intergroup hostility and scape-goating with particular reference on the Eastside to the adjacent Jewish Community."[48] Jews who moved west frequently kept Eastside businesses and rental properties, which sometimes provoked charges of exploitation from their former neighbors.[49] Associating Jews with exploitation sometimes stemmed from anti-Semitic assumptions, since many non-Jews also became absentee landlords.[50]

This growing divide between the two communities, which seemingly had little in common after the war, counterintuitively helps explain their interest in collaboration. Because Mexican Americans' daily struggle for survival left little money to fund organizations such as the CSO, they sought support from other Los Angeles ethnic communities, including Jews. The Jewish community's motives for assisting a group increasingly distant from its own population seem less apparent. CRC leaders, discussing the Mexican American community, justified support for the CSO by explaining that it "deflects the hostility which exists in that community against the Jews, to constructive social issues of benefit to the Mexican American and the Jew alike." The CSO could "by its very existence . . . prevent race riots such as have happened before in this city." CRC leaders claimed it already had "no doubt prevented serious repercussions which might have otherwise happened on the East Side."[51] CRC Executive Director Herzberg countered a member's protest that the CRC should stop funding the CSO, since it was not "closely related enough to the activities of the Jewish community," by explaining that its "prophylactic value" was "a relatively cheap investment" for the Jewish community. Herzberg's comment that the CSO would help prevent "gang fights and similar anti-social acts" also reveals underlying assumptions about Mexican Americans' violent potential.[52]

Amid these complex attitudes, which reflect some prejudice and misunderstanding, both Mexican American and Jewish American communities viewed bridge-building projects as critical for their mutual survival. The CSO particularly hoped to secure Jews' participation since, as Ross explained, "this is the other large group on the East Side and Jewish–Mexican American relations have left a good deal to be desired for some time."[53] Ross attempted to obtain Jewish-community support by emphasizing to the CRC how the CSO's work improved "deplorable" East Los Angeles neighborhood conditions that "had been reflected in a history of hostility between Spanish speaking colonies and the Jewish Community surrounding Temple Street."[54] The CSO reported in 1949 that two years of efforts had redirected the "scape-goating" of nearby "disadvantaged groups" (specifically the "adjacent" Jews) and had "pav[ed the way] for cooperation with other groups particularly with those in the Jewish Community."[55] In short, memories of World War II era violence and fears of its recurrence helped inspire postwar collaboration represented by organizations like the CSO.

Besides social and economic conditions, postwar political conditions motivated the two communities' collaboration through organizations like the CSO. Cold War red-baiting, which often targeted such civil rights activists because of similarities between their racial equality agendas and those of the communists, encouraged them to maintain their effectiveness by reinforcing their reputations as "acceptable" anti-communists. They did so in part by seeking and strengthening alliances with seemingly "safe" civil rights proponents, those with established anti-communist credentials. In this way, postwar interracial cooperation was a pragmatic strategy for self-protection and, to some degree, success.[56]

CSO members and their partners actively sought cooperation from allies whom they believed would shore up their legitimacy. For instance, Fred Ross decided to respond proactively rather than defensively to rumors that the CSO was a "Communist outfit" by pursuing alliances with other well-reputed interracial groups. He eagerly accepted an invitation from the Council for Civic Unity, an anti-communist civil rights group, to attend a conference of agencies working in the "minorities field."[57] When Roybal first inquired how Ross expected, as a white person assisting Mexican

Americans, to "escape the red label," Ross replied that he would seek backing from "legitimate," noncommunist organizations like the Catholic Church and "a number of respected, prominent Mexican American business and professional men."[58] When Los Angeles organizations started rumors that Ross and the CSO were communist, Ross immediately sought the support of Bishop Joseph T. McGucken, who wrote letters of introduction to priests in Mexican American parishes.[59] Herman Gallegos, the vice president of the San Jose, California, CSO branch during this period, later remembered how much the CSO relied on the Catholic Church's reputation as a bulwark against anti-communism.[60] The CSO's anti-communist stance inspired and reinforced the Jewish community's interest in collaborating with the CSO. Leonard Bloom stated his admiration for the CSO' efforts to "protect itself from being captured or exploited by Stalinist and Trotskyite elements" and urged the CRC's executive director to support an even "larger and more expensive [CSO] enterprise" in the future.[61] Joining forces decreased both organizations' susceptibility to red-baiters. Ross reported that when some people attending an interracial activist meeting on youth issues voiced the opinion that the CSO's "pressure tactics" indicated it was too far Left, Jewish community agency representatives rushed to the CSO's defense. The CSO's Jewish defenders fortified the agency by "promptly point[ing] out that such tacts [CSO tactics] rather than being a 'neighborhood liability' . . . were definitely wholesome and indispensable."[62] Such alliances with other ethnic and racial communities were crucial to the CSO's survival during the early Cold War.

Other factors besides fears of neighborhood violence and fortification against red-baiting motivated Jewish and Mexican activists to join forces through the CSO. Jews and Mexicans recognized that they had too little influence to achieve certain goals without assistance from other excluded groups, realizing that they needed each other to create a society that would treat them all more fairly. Jewish community leaders, for instance, believed that improving the status of other minority groups would also help Jews. In later years, the CRC's postwar director Joe Roos reflected on his organization's postwar policy of supporting organizations like the CSO, which he had encouraged by emphasizing that other people's problem was "our problem." "I think we would have defeated ourselves," he continued, "if we would only have screamed for the poor Jews who were being discriminated against." Roos believed that fighting general intolerance and convincing Americans to judge individuals on a merit basis would gradually eliminate prejudice against Jews.[63] Herzberg, the CRC's executive director before Roos, articulated this same philosophy in 1948. He wrote in a letter to a CIO representative, "We [the organized Jewish community] realize that those things which are good for the greatest number of people would also be good for us."[64]

Jews' unusual social and political position "in-between" two poles of Los Angeles society helps explain their active role in interracial civil rights initiatives like the CSO. On the one hand, mainstream Americans increasingly accepted Jews, whose political and economic status gained them more access to avenues of power than African or Mexican Americans. The status of many CRC members who were judges or other prominent citizens illustrates this access, as does the move of many Jews toward the city's affluent westside. Yet on the other hand, the anti-Semitism that marked the era left Jews feeling uneasy. Many whites still considered Jews hated outsiders, and many Jews themselves persisted in thinking of themselves as an outsider minority group.[65] Jews' physical whiteness and ability to change their names to sound less Jewish if they wished—as many Jewish Americans did, especially in the wake of the Holocaust—provided a cover, allowing them to conceal their activism by instigating interracial efforts.[66] As they moved between minority and white majority, Los Angeles Jews' in-between status placed them in a unique position to negotiate between the mainstream polity and minorities. They used their in-between status and political, economic, and social connections behind the scenes by serving in a way as civil rights brokers, as with the CSO.

Jews' decision to serve as civil rights brokers through organizations like the CSO was not a foregone conclusion, despite their pervasive fears about their safety and status. Unlike more unambiguously racialized groups like African Americans, who generally had no choice but to fight for more equality, Jews' ambiguous social and racial status between mainstream and minority confronted them with a dilemma. They wondered whether they should join forces with other minorities to address discrimination or shun civil rights activism for fear collaboration would "lower" their status even further by association. Many postwar Jews did not agree with their community's ultimate decision to collaborate with other minorities to fight common discrimination. "Some of my super-white Jews [were] not happy" with the policy the CRC adopted, the CRC's then-executive director Joe Roos later noted.[67] But other Jewish community members, especially the influential ones whose opinions prevailed, agreed that Jews must develop a pro-civil rights policy, highlighting the danger that they still faced. Roos and other CRC members criticized other Jews who rejected their duty to fight discrimination and who refused to join forces with other oppressed peoples to save their own skin as "trying, in fact, to appear to society as 'white Jews'" and contributing to the racial oppression that affected them too. These Jews should "never forget that the fate of our people is inseparably linked with that of all racial and religious minorities and with the future of progressive democracy," and they must uphold their responsibility to oppose injustice.[68] Coalition-minded Jews sometimes even protested when non-Jews classified them as "Anglo," as when Herzberg responded to the ACRR's report about Los Angeles Mexican Americans' conditions. Herzberg thought the report was spot on, he wrote, but qualified his enthusiasm by saying that he wished it could use "a term other than 'Anglo.' Most of us [Jews] ain't Anglos."[69]

Jews were not the only Los Angeles minority group to find they occupied an in-between position that presented them with a choice of civil rights avenues. Their in-betweenness also structured Mexican Americans' involvement in organizations like the CSO. While Jews navigated between white and minority, Mexican Americans, particularly those with light skin, navigated between white and black. Mexican American actors like Rita Hayworth and Anthony Quinn found success in Hollywood, attracting a wide following in the American public, by downplaying their Mexican heritage and embellishing their whiteness.[70] Societal power structures sometimes deemed Mexican-descent people white, as revealed by legal categories and decisions including *Mendez*, which ruled that segregating Mexican children was unconstitutional because they were "white." Mexican Americans' census categorization as white, except in 1930, also underscores their ambiguous status.[71]

Their ambiguous status drove Mexican Americans to take different approaches. Like some Jews, some sought to claim the advantages of white racial status and shunned cooperation with other minority groups. Such Mexican Americans distanced themselves, for instance, from African Americans for fear of lowering their status by association, as the ACRR observed in a postwar report. Some of these Mexican Americans, who were especially likely to be middle-class, "opposed cooperation with Negro groups, believing that the Mexican caste advantage would be compromised by any identification with Negroes."[72] But other times Mexican Americans' attempts to claim whiteness, as with some Jews, reflected an assertive claim to equality with other Americans more than a desire to separate from other more "tainted" groups, as certain CSO decisions reveal. This quest manifested itself clearly through the CSO's late 1940s struggle to force the military to classify them as white rather than Mexican. CSO members supported CSO Vice President Ralph Guzman's brother when he walked off the air force voluntary enlistment line after the recruiter refused to accept a claim by the Spanish-speaking man in front of Guzman that he was "white." The recruiter crossed out "white," which the man had marked as his racial category on the applications and replaced it with "Mexican." This incident reveals that Mexican Americans often did not have a choice of how to identify, as dominant society ascribed them an identity regardless of their own self-perception. Southern California Air Force officials responded to protests by the CSO, which argued that Mexicans were white, by explaining that appropriate racial categories included "Negro, Mexican, Puerto Rican, Cuban, East Indian, Hawaiian, etc.," and that Mexicans needed to mark "Mexican."[73] The CSO emerged victorious in 1950, with the help of politicians Helen Gahagan Douglas and Chet Holifield. The Secretary of Defense conceded that the Army, Navy, and Air Force would begin using the racial categories of "Caucasian, Negroid, Mongolian, Indian (American), [and] Malayan" and that selection would be left to the applicant. Mexican, Puerto Rican, Cuban, and others were conspicuously absent from these new categories.[74] The Frank Guzman incident aligns with postwar Mexican American attitudes about the relationship between their racial identity and rights. The CSO argued that their community deserved rights not because they were Latin Americans or Mexican Americans but because they were part of an American population that deserved equality.[75] But their claim to whiteness left intact the categories of blackness, "yellowness," and "redness," suggesting either that they did not always view their own quest for equality as part of a broader transminority struggle or that they did not want to join the fight for other minorities if it might jeopardize their own.

Mexican Americans, though, had a harder time blending in—when they wanted to—than Jews, despite these limited victories and generally faced more extreme discrimination. Socially, most Mexican Americans lived the experience of "otherness" despite their legal whiteness. Their more fixed minority status, combined with their less organized and less financially secure community structure, meant that they could not claim the same role as "race brokers" that Jews could. Mexican Americans' marginality also meant that they, even more than Jews, relied on external support from other communities to achieve their goals. The nebulous in-between status of Los Angeles Jewish and Mexican Americans, somewhere between white and black, heightened both groups' commitment to building bridges across communities.

Such cooperation did not necessarily reflect political relations among similar ethnic groups in other parts of the country. In fact, collaboration between Jews and Mexicans was particular to Los Angeles and attributable to the city's unusual demographics. Its concentration and overlap of both groups were unique, though some of the same philosophies that inspired Los Angeles Jews to collaborate across ethnic lines with other groups produced similar relationships in other cities, particularly with African Americans.[76] Evidence suggests, however, that Mexican Americans elsewhere did not act as collaboratively as they did in Los Angeles. Separation rather than alliance more often marked the efforts of Texas Mexican Americans, for instance, who feared that visible association and collaboration with other minority groups—namely, African Americans, the other prominent minority group in the region—would lower their status even farther.[77]

Even in Los Angeles, Jews, Mexicans, African Americans, and other minorities did not always cooperate. Tensions between the groups brought conflict, sometimes violent. Their various interests often did not coincide, in part because groups experienced different kinds and levels of exclusions.[78] Nonetheless, in the postwar era, they all found themselves excluded to some degree and recognized they likely would achieve more progress toward equality together than alone and that, at this point in time, they needed each other to achieve some common goals.

The kind of interracial collaboration embodied by the CSO in the years following World War II also characterized the activity of the NAACP, the Japanese American Citizens League (JACL), the CRC, and many others as they combated issues of mutual concern like discriminatory laws, police brutality, and poor neighborhood conditions like inadequate sewage and street lights.[79] Interracial political collaboration did not necessarily translate into deeper relationships. Some of the activists who worked together in political coalitions undoubtedly developed meaningful bonds across ethnoracial divides, but, for the most part, the postwar contact among these groups' members did not extend beyond the organizational realm. As the neighborhoods became increasingly segregated and Jewish and Japanese Americans increasingly integrated while African and Mexican American "ghettoes" grew, the groups' political interests diverged. Issues like police brutality and discrimination in housing and employment became almost exclusively Mexican and African American issues. The evaporation of shared minority political districts, moreover, eliminated bases for collaborative election campaigns. Diminished common causes lowered the incentive for coalition building. The moment for collaboration proved fleeting, since group interests increasingly diverged as the postwar era progressed; but, for the late 1940s and early 1950s, interracial cooperation provided an opportunity for various marginalized minority groups to fight for their own advancement and each other's.

Los Angeles to the Nation: School Segregation and Housing

Despite the short life of Los Angeles civil rights coalitions, their impact on national politics was lasting. Activists and strategies that emerged within the city's multiracial political culture significantly influenced national struggles seemingly rooted exclusively in an African American, eastern context. Collaborative interracial networks like the CSO that emerged from multiracial Los Angeles helped shape the strategies and arguments that transformed the national civil rights scene, specifically on school and housing desegregation.

The activists involved in the *Mendez* case and the strategies they developed reveal the national reach of Southern California's multiracial political culture. In certain respects, *Mendez* provided a training ground for lawyers active in *Brown v. Board of Education* seven years later, some of whom worked on both cases. The American Jewish Congress, NAACP, and others who first tested their strategies, tactics, and abilities in *Mendez* also represented the *Brown* plaintiffs. Individuals who argued both cases included Robert Carter and Thurgood Marshall, who became two of the most prominent attorneys in the *Brown* case. Carter, an African American attorney, eventually became head counsel of the NAACP's Legal Defense and Educational Fund, and Marshall became the first African American justice on the U.S. Supreme Court. Local NAACP activist Loren Miller assisted in filing the *amici curiae* briefs in both *Mendez* and *Brown*, as did the JACL's Saburo Kido and the American Jewish Congress's Will Maslow.[80] *Brown* lawyers followed the lead of *Mendez* lawyers who set a precedent by using social scientists to offer "expert" testimony against segregation. Carter, Marshall, and others arguing *Brown* relied on the same arguments articulated by experts testifying in the *Mendez* case. Carter was so impressed by how social science knowledge had been used to criticize segregation in *Mendez* that he suggested to Marshall that the "social science approach would be the only way to overturn segregation in the United States." The *amicus curiae* brief Carter and Marshall filed in the appellate court in support of *Mendez*, Carter explained, was a "dry run for the future." David Marcus, the attorney for the *Mendez* plaintiffs, provided Marshall with all the briefs and notes he had compiled during the case, further reinforcing the link between the state and national desegregation cases.[81] *Mendez* clearly helped prepare activists for a national stage.

Contemporaries of the *Mendez* plaintiffs, including legal scholars nationwide, recognized the historical and national significance of this struggle for full citizenship by Mexican Americans and their multiracial allies, even if popular culture and scholars, until recently, have not. Such venerable legal journals as *Columbia Law Review* and *Yale Law Journal* in 1947 reported on its significance. *Columbia Law Review* discussed the case as breaking sharply with the past approach that authorized the existence of separate but equal facilities as "not in itself indicative of discrimination." In *Mendez*, the court instead "finds that the 14th Amendment requires 'social equality' rather than equal facilities."[82] *Yale Law Journal* reported that *Mendez* "has questioned the basic assumption of the *Plessy* case and may portend a complete reversal of the doctrine." It wrote, "Modern sociological and psychological studies lend much support to the District court's views. A dual system even if 'equal facilities' were provided does imply social inferiority."[83] The *Yale Law Journal* article concluded by predicting, "There is little doubt that the Supreme Court will be presented with a case involving segregation in the schools within the next year or two."[84] Contemporary observers recognized the national significance of the *Mendez* decision, a victory that rode on the shoulders of interracial activism in mid-century Southern California.

This still underappreciated connection between Mexican American and African American school desegregation struggles highlights how local incidents in the multiracial Southwest influenced the shape of national reforms. While the Supreme Court likely would have overturned *Plessy* regardless and though *Brown* emerged in significant part from African Americans' long struggle against racial injustice, Mexican Americans' fight against school segregation in *Mendez* helped provide the *Brown* lawyers with a strategic foundation for their arguments. The *Mendez* decision, which built on a long history of Mexican and Asian origin parents' desegregation challenges in the Golden State and on Southern California's early to mid-twentieth-century political culture of multiracial collaboration, shaped legal and political understandings of segregation in California and nationwide even if it did not succeed in reaching the Supreme Court. The case also set an important precedent for similar cases involving Mexican Americans elsewhere, particularly Arizona and Texas.[85]

Alongside the fight against school segregation exhibited by *Mendez*, campaigns against housing discrimination during the 1940s and 1950s further extended the influence of civil rights activists shaped by Southern California's multiracial political culture. The career of Loren Miller, the NAACP's West Coast Legal Committee chairman who also chaired the CSO's Legal Aid Committee and assisted with the collaborative *Mendez* and *Brown* efforts, is emblematic. Miller's Los Angeles experience, rooted both in local interracial activism and in the African American community, launched him in the decade after World War II to help lead the national housing struggle.

In the years following World War II, Miller worked closely on housing issues with Southern California allies like A. L. Wirin, the Jewish American representative of the American Civil Liberties Union who fought restrictive covenants for that organization as well as for the JACL. Rampant housing shortages and the intensity of overcrowding in Los Angeles, whose conditions were the worst in the West and among the worst anywhere, generated widespread protest.[86] In 1946, Miller and Wirin together successfully fought restrictive covenants on publicly owned land in South Pasadena, and in 1946 and 1947, Miller consulted on JACL lawsuits involving restrictive covenants against Chinese and Korean American ex-GI's. The interracial collaboration of L.A. activists like Miller, Wirin, and others helped shape African American and other communities' legal approaches to housing discrimination.[87]

Los Angeles's serious housing problems motivated local black activists like Miller and other NAACP members to build on their experience fighting for racial equality with and among the city's multiracial populations and lead the national campaign to eliminate restrictive housing covenants. After investigating Los Angeles conditions, they urged the local, regional, and national housing authorities to oppose such covenants.[88] The Los Angeles

NAACP alone filed more suits against them between 1945 and 1948—the first Supreme Court victory against restrictive covenants, *Shelley v. Kraemer*—than were filed in any other part of the country. The determination of Los Angeles African Americans helped win the 1948 *Shelley v. Kraemer* case, which outlawed restrictive covenants.[89] Loren Miller was central to the local efforts and also became one of the primary attorneys in *Shelley*, together with the national NAACP's Thurgood Marshall.[90] Miller and other Los Angeles NAACP members continued to fight after the inadequacy of the *Shelley* decision became clear, as whites continued to evade the court's restraints by filing damage suits against other whites who violated their original commitment to restrictive covenants by selling to African Americans. Some state and local courts even upheld such damage suits.[91] Miller and other Los Angeles NAACP members joined and led teams lobbying the Supreme Court to close these last loopholes in restrictive covenant legislation. Miller and Marshall's defense of whites whose neighbors had sued them for breaking neighborhood covenants resulted in the 1953 *Barrows v. Jackson* decision, which ruled that damage suits against these white sellers were illegal because they forced the sellers to violate *Shelley*.[92]

Miller's role in national housing cases underscores the crucial influence exerted by Los Angeles activists rooted in collaboration among Mexican Americans, African Americans, Jews, and other minority groups, as well as some whites. While African Americans from other parts of the nation deserve significant credit for these struggles, Southern California residents like Miller gained important civil rights experience both from African Americans nationwide and by cooperating with a multiracial spectrum of the Los Angeles population. Los Angeles thus produced activists and approaches that helped shape national school desegregation and fair housing outcomes.[93]

What we previously have assumed to be black and white initiatives rooted in an eastern/southern context derived in part from collaborative activism in a multiracial Southern California context. Activism by, on behalf of, and among multiracial southwestern populations provided an important foundation for American rights struggles and helped shape the emergent liberal agenda that produced national postwar civil rights transformations. In other words, mid-century civil rights outcomes were not only the culmination of battles by African Americans and their allies in Selma, Birmingham, Detroit, New York, and elsewhere; they also emerged from collaborative struggles among Mexican, Jewish, Japanese, and African

Americans in Los Angeles.[94] This story of multiracial mid-century Los Angeles thus re-centers Southern California in a national civil rights narrative. Moreover, it hints at how struggles in this mid-century Southwestern city with no majority minority, which made finding common ground particularly crucial, foreshadowed the future of a multiracial nation. In the twenty-first century, collaborative multiracial political support has become crucial to national political victories, as the black, Latino, Asian, and white support of Barack Obama in the 2008 presidential election so recently demonstrates.

Chapter 6

Sunbelt Civil Rights: Urban Renewal and the Follies of Desegregation in Greater Miami

N. D. B. Connolly

When the Republican National Convention came to Miami Beach on August 5, 1968, the Grand Old Party had hoped to profit from the political center's shift farther to the Right and deeper into America's emergent Sunbelt. Over the next four days, Republicans articulated a law-and-order platform aimed at winning the country's white suburbs. They nominated Richard Nixon as that platform's standard-bearer. And in Liberty City, a distant black Miami neighborhood, two thousand citizens, immigrants, and police officers clashed in a frenzy of riotous violence. By week's end, Republicans had unified their party for a run at the White House. Five miles away, three people lay dead, dozens injured, and hundreds in jail.[1] The press portrayed these events as unrelated, claiming that typical urban problems—such as unemployment and high crime—led to the unrest.[2] While these and other hardships no doubt plagued the neighborhood, explanations of an "urban crisis" seemed oddly out of place, for Liberty City was and is a decidedly *suburban* community, a Sunbelt community consisting mostly of single-family homes and duplexes.

Whether discussing residential life in or outside the Sunbelt, historians rarely speak of anything resembling a violent "suburban crisis." Nevertheless, August 1968 saw Liberty City join Los Angeles's Watts (1965), Atlanta's Summerhill neighborhood (1966), and Louisville's Parkland (1968) as the latest in a series of suburban riots. These and the many riots to hit the South and West during the 1970s, 1980s, and 1990s made a lie of "color-blind" Sunbelt prosperity.[3] In fact, the violence that ripped through Miami's black suburbs in 1968 echoed a growing and ultimately racist trend whereby municipal authorities routinely instituted policies of black suburban containment, often in the wake of widespread demolition or mass urban displacements. Around the country, in fact, state and local officials commonly followed their failed urban renewal efforts with a reduction in government assistance and an expansion of the state's putative powers.[4]

For most of the twentieth century, Miami's blacks lived in the city's congested Central Negro District, located blocks from downtown but a world away from the beachfront where so many blacks worked. By the mid-1950s, a growing number of black suburbanites bestowed on the community a new name—Overtown. Migrating out of the city and into new bedroom communities, more and more blacks talked of having to travel "over town" to maintain social and economic ties to the old neighborhood. Despite all its charms, Overtown's crowded "colored" slums increasingly represented Miami's Jim Crow past. By contrast, Liberty City, since the late 1940s, seemed to represent what black suburbs symbolized throughout the country—a racial Promised Land. But if Liberty City's concrete ranch homes and green spaces reflected blacks' residential hopes for life after Jim Crow, the clouds of tear gas and throngs of riot police enveloping the neighborhood in the summer of 1968 sounded the end of that promise.

Like increased black suburbanization, the Republican Party of 1968 was supposed to represent a break with times past or provide, in the words of Nixon's convention speech, a "new road to progress." Never quite the party of George Wallace and not yet the party of Ronald Reagan, Nixon's GOP vowed to challenge the criminality and "welfare ethic" many believed at fault for the riots in Miami and in metropolitan areas around the country. The party also promised to invigorate so-called "forgotten Americans" who increasingly complained of being harried by taxes, spooked by hippies and radicals, and ignored by elite intellectuals.[5] As delegates from New York to California whisked from Miami International Airport to their beachfront

Figure 6.1. The single-story ranch homes and green spaces of Liberty City served as the backdrop for a clash between black Miamians and police in early August 1968. Like many suburbs to which nonwhites migrated during the 1950s and 1960s, Liberty City, part of unincorporated Dade County, suffered from insufficient city services, spotty zoning enforcement, and absentee profiteering from white landlords. The unidentified youth being arrested was one of nearly 200 people taken into police custody on August 8, the heavier of the two days of unrest. © Bettmann/CORBIS

convention, they never had to behold the hidden slums and distant, downwardly mobile suburbs housing the region's other "forgotten Americans." That is because, by 1968, state and local planners had laid their own "road to progress"—Interstates 95 and 395—carrying visitors straight through and over what was once Overtown's most densely populated corridor.[6] In both literal and figurative terms, the Republican Party traveled to Miami Beach on a road liberals built right on top of black poverty. Despite the undeniable size and heft of bulldozers or highways, this kind of land-based racism remained invisible to most white Americans, especially when compared to the Old South white supremacy of cross burnings, "Whites Only" signage, or the Wallace campaign. Yet, it was precisely this invisibility that made Greater Miami at once appealing to the GOP's moderate whites and irritating to the region's poor blacks—fertile ground for both the Republican National Convention and the Liberty City riot.

This essay remains less concerned with the GOP Convention or Miami's suburban riot as such and more determined to explore the political and economic road South Florida's liberals took in the decades-long lead up to those sister events. Many observers associate the weakening of antipoverty measures or militarization of law enforcement with some kind of post-1968 "conservative counteroffensive," but these processes first emerged as handmaidens to liberal programs of urban growth and neighborhood reform, some occurring twenty years before political strategists ever discerned a region they would later name the "Sunbelt." It would indeed take years—and several missteps during an ill-conceived "Southern Strategy"—before Nixon and other Republicans would effectively appropriate liberal attacks on the poor on their way to hastening the nation's rightward turn. In fact, what the GOP came to advocate was essentially a long-standing, centrist position on the race question, a commitment to what I call "Sunbelt civil rights."

Advocates of this politics argued that civil rights rested on property rights. More pointedly, adherents of Sunbelt Civil Rights sought to attain suburban property and/or preserve suburban privileges by steering the fast growing economies of America's postwar South and West. Since at least Lisa McGirr's study of religious conservatism in Orange County, California, historians have placed heavy emphasis on conservative expressions of what could easily be described as a postwar property rights movement. They have interrogated, for instance, the grassroots activism of white suburbanites who, in the midst of massive demographic and economic transformations, relied on the discourses of civil and property rights to oppose everything from property tax increases in California to school desegregation efforts in North Carolina or Georgia. In crafting what were essentially right-wing protections of liberalism's racial preferences, these activists used a language of "freedom of choice" and "personal responsibility" to meet simultaneously white America's changing material needs and the rhetorical needs of a country forever changed by the black freedom struggle.[7]

Yet, in all the intellectual excitement generated by scholarship on "The Rise of the Right," we have generally ignored a progressive property rights movement at least as old as its right-wing counterpart and one equally implicated in furthering American capitalism's undemocratic tendencies. In many ways, the twin of white property interests on the center-right,

Sunbelt civil rights from the center-left likewise relied on blending traditions of racial and spatial liberalism. It drew on the kinds of race-neutral language that was rapidly becoming the national currency of postwar urban development policy. And, I argue, it was a politics at the foundation of black suburbanization, slum clearance, and the tragic outcomes of urban renewal. In fact, as part of a broader effort to maintain the racial peace in America's immediate postwar years, this strain of liberal reform remained nominally committed to desegregation and sympathetic to modernizing the Jim Crow South through the expansion of African American property rights. But such commitments would change only the form, not the fact, of white suburban privilege and racial violence in the Sunbelt era.

In postwar Florida, liberal advocates of Sunbelt Civil Rights employed slum clearance and urban renewal as weapons against the symbolic and material ills of Jim Crow segregation. Like more familiar civil rights movements, the architects of this politic used a combination of elite-level statesmanship, grassroots organizing, litigation, and legislation to expand the power of the liberal state and widen the discursive openings and economic possibilities provided by World War II and the Cold War. However, unlike more traditional forms of civil rights activism, which tended to level state power directly at inequalities in education, employment, or voting rights, the self-styled progressives of the emergent Sunbelt sought to unmake Jim Crow at the spatial level, believing they could redress any range of social problems by democratizing American's access to suburban real estate and weakening the property rights of powerful urban landlords.

To be sure, the South in the immediate postwar years was, by and large, a land of urban and rural slums. In 1960, housing officials found over 1.2 million dilapidated dwellings in the South, with more than 3 million lacking basic plumbing facilities; both these numbers roughly equaled those of the North and West combined.[8] Also in 1960, seven of the ten cities with the highest percentage of nonwhite poor were in the South, with over half the nonwhite population in Little Rock, Memphis, Tampa, and New Orleans living below the poverty line ($3,000/year). The look and feel of Miami's poverty was in keeping with that of the broader South. Forty-two percent of Miami's nonwhite families lived below the poverty line, and some 83 percent of black Miamians worked either as domestics or unskilled laborers (a figure only surpassed by New Orleans's 84 percent). A weak seasonal economy and segregationist real estate practices left tens of thousands underemployed and largely confined to weatherbeaten wooden shacks infested with every manner of vermin.[9]

Because southern cities like Miami had much of their physical layout determined by capitalists in need of unskilled labor and landlords in search of sustained profits, two sets of interracial interests ventured to unmake the Jim Crow city—housing advocates, on the one hand, and growth politicians and their allies in southern chambers of commerce, on the other. In the eyes of housing reformers, the postwar state was supposed to help blacks attain the autonomy and security provided by a single-family home. Historian Andrew Weise describes, for instance, how, during the 1940s, blacks and whites negotiated "Negro expansion" by relegating upwardly mobile blacks to the suburban fringes of southern cities like Atlanta or Memphis.[10] Yet even in national conversation of housing reform, progressives such as Robert Weaver and Charles Abrams believed that greater black access to suburban mortgages, home equity, and equally funded public education could right the ship of America's democracy and assure racial equality, if not integration. The modernization of the South also required new infrastructural investments, such as highways, rebuilt downtowns, and clean industries. So, in the name of this vision, captains of the South's growing white-collar and tourist economies looked to expansive federal and state redevelopment programs to liquidate the substandard rental properties creeping across the face of southern cities. Prior to the 1950s, the need to battle Jim Crow and spatially modernize the metropolitan South represented parallel and distinct liberal visions. Thus, during Greater Miami's immediate postwar years, city building in South Florida, like most of the country, remained beholden to openly segregationist practices of urban and suburban development.[11]

Through Progressive Era segregation mandates, increases in wartime spending, and the expansion of professional networks of urban planners, Miami's bureaucrats perfected techniques wherein they used infrastructural improvements to provide services for whites while consolidating and isolating black housing. During the 1940s, South Florida's city and county officials sought out planning experts across the western and northern United States, taking their cues especially from planners who favored suburbanization and mass expulsions of the urban poor as the default approach to American city building. Men like Harold Bartholomew of St. Louis; New York's legendary master-planner, Robert Moses; and a slew of West Coast city builders from Los Angeles and San Diego proved instrumental for Miami's planning community.[12] Miami's city builders and those of the American West found common purpose in their need to increase tourism and encourage new forms of capital investment. And California's city planners, in particular, showed South Floridians how to expand "clean" industries like garment manufacturing and aviation without compromising the attractiveness of beaches and seaside hotels. Robert Moses likewise provided, in the words of one Miami planner, "much valuable advice as to practical procedure in accomplishing best results."[13] Indeed, none had proven better than New York's "Power Broker" at mixing corporate capital with federal and municipal funding lines for long-term growth initiatives, even as his housing and road building projects almost always came at the detriment of poor and nonwhite populations.[14]

This impulse for growth in the late 1940s, combined with right-to-work campaigns and speculative real estate development across the South and West, would lay the foundation for the Sunbelt growth era to come.[15] In Miami, as with much of the South, growth meant building the urban infrastructure of the New Deal era on top of the social infrastructure of Jim Crow. Greater Miami's housing officials attempted to orchestrate regional prosperity by providing Miami's blacks essentially two options: to live either in cramped slums or in distant unincorporated areas underserved by city services. The foundation of this practice was, of course, the mortgage programs of the Federal Housing Administration (FHA), which wrote segregation into national housing policy and relied on local staffers to move mortgage finance along established color lines.[16] The most inventive real estate entrepreneurs took advantage of captive populations of black renters by throwing up tenements backed by FHA-secured mortgages. And in what was often a pain-free movement of capital from one set of investors to another, banks gave loans freely to those engaged in even the most egregious forms of slum development or racially restrictive suburbanization. With the federal government having underwritten the placement of suburbs and rental housing, city and county planners contained black residential expansion by manipulating tax laws, zoning regulation, and eminent domain.[17]

Of these, eminent domain enjoyed perhaps the most increasing use in the postwar period because it granted governments the power to make quick and direct interventions on residential patterns. By definition, the power allowed officials to expropriate legally private property for the building of public use projects. But in practice, it empowered city officials to raze black rental housing or liquidate blacks' homes—under the guise of slum clearance—whenever residential growth threatened to cause racial unrest. Eminent domain proved an especially useful market "corrective" in Jim Crow cities. For despite being so-called experts of city design, southern planners found themselves often having to heed the whims of local white homeowners who commonly had their own designs for "progressive" residential growth.[18]

In 1942, white citizens from a mostly rural Miami suburb called Allapattah lobbied city planners to expel the residents of a nearby black homeowner community called the Railroad Shop Colored Addition. Having grown from a single plat of black-owned land in the nineteenth century, Railroad Shop boasted over one hundred homes during the war years, with most having been built by Caribbean- and American-born blacks whose families descended from railroad workers. Edward Braynon, only a child at the time, remembered how his family, under threats of bodily harm, came to settle in Railroad Shop in the 1920s. "My family was chased out of what is now Little Havana . . . They called it South Miami."[19] Some twenty years later, the Braynons had to contend with Allapattah's whites, newly organized into several neighborhood associations. The white residents demanded the Miami City Commission use the authority of eminent domain to redraw the residential color line, have "the negroes in this addition removed," their homes leveled, and their property turned into a park, elementary school, or some other municipal property for "whites only." The Miami City Commission unanimously supported the motion. And, in August 1947, once city coffers could afford the demolition and construction costs, local law enforcement initiated a series of successive mass evictions, tossing out as many as thirty-five households at a time. "They did not need those schools," Braynon recalled. "The schools were practically unused for years but that was the only way they could legitimately get those black families out of there."[20]

These kinds of expulsions proved a defining feature of postwar urban and suburban growth. In 1945, local planning officials aimed to push black housing into the distant unincorporated areas that would eventually become Liberty City. In the small "colored" outpost of Nazarene, white homeowners and city planners chipped away at dozens of black-owned homes, building a park here and expanding a street there. And shortly before the evictions at Railroad Shop in August 1947, the City of Miami confiscated twenty black homes in Sanford's subdivision to build a park for whites just south of downtown.[21] Only in 1948, with the Supreme Court ruling restrictive covenants unconstitutional in *Shelley v. Kraemer*, would housing reformers employ eminent domain as a tool for seeking racial equality in housing. Such progressive uses, however, would prove even more destabilizing for blacks attempting to preserve and improve their communities.

In 1948, a handful of domestics, chauffeurs, and other working blacks in Miami's Coconut Grove neighborhood joined white reformers and a young activist priest named Theodore Gibson in trying to halt slum building in their community. Gibson, a black Episcopalian of Bahamian heritage, tried to kill a real estate deal that would have allowed two rent-seeking developers to build tenements in what was, to Gibson's mind, an already overcrowded section of the neighborhood. Just southwest of Miami's downtown, Coconut Grove consisted of larger homes for affluent whites and a nearby quarter of "colored" residents who worked mostly as whites' servants. The whites of Coconut Grove came mostly from the Northeast and Midwest. And, yet, "The Grove," in its spatial layout and its culture of racial interdependence, was the kind of community one commonly found in the Jim Crow South. Whites in the Grove, in other words, lived closer to blacks than the average northerner and often believed themselves more progressive than the average southerner. The blacks of Coconut Grove were mostly a generation or two removed from the Bahamas. Their poverty—housed, at times, seven to a room in shotgun shacks without plumbing—stood as part of a regional black experience stretching from New Orleans, over the Caribbean, and into South America.

This blend of southern geography, northern white sensibilities, and tropical poverty in many ways captured the essence of Miami's history. And when Gibson roused about a dozen whites to join blacks in forming the Coconut Grove Citizens' Committee for Slum Clearance, he helped set the course for Greater Miami's Sunbelt future.[22] Many of Coconut Grove's whites saw the state of black housing as pivotal to their own residential futures, both in paternalistic terms about the moral fate of "The Negro" and in public health terms about domestics bringing "Negro" disease into white homes. It also mattered that the developers planned the new tenement project on a vacant lot that previously served as a buffer zone between blacks and whites, a line few whites wanted to see crossed.[23] Elizabeth Virrick, a white Grove resident and well-connected wife of a prominent Russian architect, became the de facto leader of the movement by virtue of her ability to press white Miami officials into action. The younger Gibson provided much of the group's grassroots muscle and moral leadership.

After twenty-four months of constant petitioning and voting drives, the Coconut Grove Committee for Slum Clearance helped pass a city referendum condemning the proposed rental project. In its place, city officials helped fund a nursery for the children of the Grove's black domestics. The slum clearance committee also gained enough broad white support to force the city to supply black tenants with new plumbing protections and trash collection services.[24] Contrary to the group's name, though, the committee proved ineffective at clearing actual slums. Landlords, preserving their own property rights, were still a force far too powerful. The committee, therefore, began lobbying for an expanded definition of acceptable eminent domain uses in hopes of moving against the further development and deterioration of shotgun shacks and other forms of substandard housing.[25] Such a move represented one of the earliest expressions of a biracial effort to appropriate eminent domain as a weapon against urban real-estate developers. And it would place Miami squarely within a growing national movement that saw expanding state powers over the land as central to civil rights reform.

Though rarely discussed as such, the Housing Acts of 1949 and 1954—which established national programs of slum clearance and urban renewal, respectively—were in many ways intended to serve as important pieces of civil rights legislation in the wake of the Supreme Court's decisions in *Shelley* and in *Brown v. the Board of Education* (1954). With restrictive covenants barred and school desegregation seemingly imminent, housing reformers in Washington bureaucracies, the National Urban League and the National Association for the Advancement of Colored People (NAACP) believed that slum clearance and urban renewal would hasten the "all deliberate speed" of desegregation. Suburbia, and all its benefits, would become available.

In Miami, such logic seemed to bear out. Through the committee's efforts, the spirit of Cold War race reform and desegregated economic growth spread outward from Coconut Grove. Realizing blacks' robust demand for better housing in 1952, white developers opened the all-black bedroom community of Richmond Heights fifteen miles outside the city. Residents who once lived in Coconut Grove quickly elected to name one of the streets after Theodore Gibson. Thelma Anderson, who married Gibson many years later, was one of those Grove residents who moved to Richmond Heights. She remembered having to leave home at 5:30 a.m. and take three buses to get to her downtown job.[26] She nevertheless recalled "how thrilled I was that we were finally moving from a rented house . . . into our own home."[27] In the meantime, chamber-of-commerce types around the city continued to lobby with Virrick and Gibson to fund sanitation efforts in the black ghetto. In 1954, Theodore Gibson would assume stewardship of the Miami chapter of the NAACP, making slum clearance part of that chapter's official platform. That same year, the slum committee's attorney, Abe Aronovitz, used his ties to the group's reform efforts to become Miami's first Jewish mayor and, eventually, the first politician ever to court black tourism openly and successfully.

Virrick would later recall helping improve blacks' housing quality and building an interracial movement: "We felt that this [was] a wonderful way to counteract Red propaganda."[28] The committee contended, further, that black-occupied slums greatly detracted from Miami's reputation as a tourist mecca. Both arguments resonated with a growing white-collar business culture that increasingly saw desegregation, slum clearance, suburbanization, and regional prosperity as intertwined. Slum clearance, in short, was rapidly becoming a consensus issue.

Yet, in this growing consensus lay dormant the seeds of a reform discourse that proved racist in its consequences if not its intent. Indeed, by casting ghetto clearance as both quintessentially American and necessary for the preservation of regional economic interests, the Grove committee's campaign cultivated at least four profound assumptions shaping Sunbelt Civil Rights. First, the slum clearance committee treated black housing, and by extension black people, as a direct threat to progress in a tourist-dependent South Florida. Second, the group's threatened use of a seemingly altruistic eminent domain affirmed a problematic assumption evident in the Railroad Shop evictions and elsewhere, namely, that condemnation was often the most effective response to the problems of black housing. Third, in the still ill-formed discourse of postwar racial justice, Miami's early slum clearance campaigns set slumlords alongside violent segregationists as the greatest enemies to equality. This insulated more liberal forms of economic and racial discrimination—such as affluent homeowner politics and corporate, pro-growth agendas—from any meaningful leftist critique. Last, because the group proved ineffective at actually increasing the stock of black housing within Miami's city limits, the Grove committee urban reforms actually helped move Miami's housing battle into the suburbs.

In 1951, the very developers Virrick and Gibson defeated in Coconut Grove moved their housing development to a historically impoverished white inner-ring suburb called Edison Center. After a brief and heated exchange between local politicians and white residents, the Miami City Commission refused to meet the request of whites demanding the condemnation of "encroaching" Negro-occupied housing. This denial must have been confusing given the widely known precedent for dramatic black expulsion carried out at Railroad Shop and elsewhere just a few years earlier. However, nonstop suburbanization beyond Miami's borders and almost no infusion of federal slum clearance monies meant city coffers simply could not afford another series of condemnation payouts to property owners. The whites of Edison Center grew frustrated by municipal inaction and the limits of Florida's eminent domain laws. In response, militarily trained members of the Ku Klux Klan allied with a white homeowner's association to conduct a string of bombings that, even in the absence of casualties, generated enough negative publicity to threaten Florida's entire 1951–52 tourist season.

Many believed the violence at Edison Center, while occurring far from downtown, was largely the fault of slumlords whose profiteering continued to foment destructive myths about the inferiority of black people across the metropolitan South. In 1952, the Southern Regional Council, an Atlanta-based racial justice group, drew a direct link between racial terrorism and slum housing. Slums, the group argued, fomented "distrust, fear, rumor, and ultimately open violence" more than the Ku Klux Klan or any race-baiting politicians.[29] And slums, unlike the postwar Klan, still enjoyed the legal and political protections of cities, states, and a nation committed to protecting landlords' property rights.

Across Greater Miami, a combination of political bribery, rapacious construction, and the federal underwriting of housing segregation allowed landlords and rental developers to build row upon row of one-story shotgun shacks and low-rise wooden and concrete tenements. Their profits hovered between 10 and 15 percent annually, and at least one property manager made, in late 1950 dollars, upward of $640,000 a year.[30] With their money, landlords bought off city councilmen and housing code enforcers, while expanding their share of the black rental market. In Overtown, slum housing stretched over 130 blocks, wrapping around the homes of affluent blacks, "Colored Only" hotels, churches, and small businesses. For blacks living on the ground, the richness of Overtown's music, culture, and community building hardly fit liberal definitions of a "slum" existence. And many landlords knew how to contribute to blacks' cultural tapestry, trading donations to "Colored Only" hospitals and schools for votes favorable to slumlords' chosen candidates.[31]

Landlords' mastery of hard and soft power made them more powerful than any overt white supremacist would ever be. Across Florida, property management firms, rental owners, and even a few unapologetic segregationists organized into formal and informal business networks, mostly in the form of lobbying groups staffed by developers and their attorneys. Their singular purpose was to attack any progressive housing legislation that, in the words of one lobbyist, "would have seriously hurt us" or "put us out of business."[32] Sam Gibbons, a state representative who failed to pass urban renewal legislation in 1959, accused "Miami slum owners" of repeatedly throwing tons of cash and legal motions in the way of his housing bills. *Miami Herald* reporter James Russell complained that slum clearance programs, in place for over a decade in northern cities, "never got to first base in Miami because the people who own the city slums fought it with a vengeance." In one year alone, lobbyists killed twelve separate pieces of state legislation that would have improved housing code, increased fire hazard protection, provided rent control, and offered other kinds of tenant protections.[33]

Landlords' stonewalling of urban renewal and slum clearance efforts during the 1950s proved an integral part of the "southern" prologue to the political transformations of the Sunbelt era. Certainly, in an age of massive resistance and widespread political race baiting, many legislators argued that expelling blacks from slums would hasten racial integration or, worse, miscegenation.[34] Nevertheless, landlords usually framed their opposition to federal clearance efforts and public housing programs as part of wider rebuttal to Washington's increased interest in southern affairs. Never mind that many Miami landlords were born in and still lived in the North. In statewide political debates, landlords cast themselves as aggrieved southerners who, as a 1957 *New Orleans Times-Picayune* editorial noted, "don't wish to get all their orders from Washington." This rhetorical strategy made sense with Florida's State Legislature still dominated by rural, "States Rights" Democrats. It also made sense, in the context of the Cold War, to argue, as many real estate interests had, that slum clearance advocates overstated black destitution and created a "sentimental smoke screen" to close the eyes of the American people "while socialism takes over the country."[35] It seemed to matter little to such arguments that tenements routinely burned down around the ears of slum dwellers, killing more than a few children in the process.

Landlords' negotiation of racial poverty and political power also provided early inflections of the self-interested, color-blind populism Republican strategists would articulate a generation later—that of big government and big capital versus small business. By and large, landlords and their allies talked about protecting the livelihoods of hardworking, yeoman entrepreneurs from the "socialistic" machinations of downtown boosters and pie-in the-sky liberals.[36] "These do-gooders," one property manager queried, "how many houses have they built?" "If it were not for the guy trying to make a profit," he continued, "there would be no housing at all built in these [black] areas."[37] Indicting affluent white housing reformers, in particular, one regional commissioner of the Federal Housing Administration suggested that what might look like benevolence actually functioned "to eliminate minorities from specific areas under the guise of a slum clearance program."[38] Such critiques bore a ring of truth in the wake of the Coconut Grove Slum Committee's ability to block, but never build, new black housing.

In strict legal terms, landlord opposition to slum clearance meant restricting eminent domain's use to "governmental functions of public concern" while patently opposing the involvement of "private enterprise" in any redevelopment efforts.[39] The exclusion of any and all private investment made it almost impossible for cash-strapped southern cities like Miami to initiate even modest slum clearance projects, much less massive Robert-Moses-style redevelopment efforts. Moreover, Miami's landlords had been remarkably successful at stopping civilian public housing projects. Between 1937 and 1952, not a single unit of non-veteran public housing was built anywhere in Greater Miami. This maintained the region's dependence on private rental speculation as cities struggled to alleviate blacks' constant housing shortage and meet the needs of South Florida's growing postwar population more broadly.

With slum conditions continuing to fester around Greater Miami, newspaper reports of tenement fires and vice-related crime in black neighborhoods regularly christened the breakfast tables of visitors coming to Greater Miami. The hidden underside of high-end beach leisure during the 1920s, Negro slums by the 1950s housed in their abject poverty "a deplorable and dangerous situation" that could potentially deter tourist travel to South Florida or, worse, explode into racial unrest.[40] Importantly, Miami's Overtown neighborhood, by virtue of its location, was among the most valuable stretches of real estate in all Florida. With 290 acres of non-right-of-way living space in the heart of downtown, the neighborhood, in 1949, had been assessed by local tax collectors at over $12.1 million dollars, or a little more than $47,000 an acre.[41] Still, those politicians, boosters, or housing reformers with visions for a more modern Miami found themselves trapped between the Scylla of surrounding white suburbanites who still used zoning laws and realtor prejudice to keep blacks out and the Charybdis of legislators who, under the influence of statewide landlord lobbying groups, would not provide Miami with the slum-clearance legislation necessary for purging downtown of its black ghetto. Answers to this impasse would come from the state level via the Florida Supreme Court and the governorship of LeRoy Collins.

Collins, Florida's governor in 1956–1960, was perhaps the most influential figure in helping the state access federal urban renewal monies. Popularly remembered for his public support of racial peace and civil rights, Collins's vision of a progressive and profitable Florida also depended on his efforts to modernize the Jim Crow landscape through urban renewal and a strengthening of eminent domain policy. With the South's reputation mired in a history of racial violence, one of Collins's greatest fears was that black pursuits for racial justice would be "banged out on the street corners by the worst educated sections of the population." No matter the depth of white racism or black poverty, street corner solutions, by Collins's estimation, were unacceptable. They would drive up police costs, polarize residents, and cause statewide economic decline. Collins, therefore, pursued urban renewal as a means to preempt the formation of a racially antagonistic and radical political ethos among poor, uneducated, impassioned Floridians. And he orchestrated the formation of interracial urban affairs committees that, like modern city planners, would espouse a "professional educational approach" that could ease race anxiety and place the responsibility for progress and reform "on [the] shoulder[s] of community leaders."[42]

Capitalizing on funds provided by the Civil Rights Act of 1957, Collins set up "biracial commissions" around the state. And through these groups, he aggressively pushed his urban renewal agenda, fusing statewide slum clearance and racial reconciliation into a single project. Members of the Collins administration searched for the right language to sell their program of reform and craft the governor's public positions on race, pouring over the black journal *Phylon* and the writings of liberal housing experts like Charles Abrams and Robert Weaver.[43] Like Collins, Weaver was among those liberals who believed one could not legislate integration and should not tamper with the broader workings of American capitalism. Both men also believed governments—in "progressive" hands—could effectively use eminent domain to bring about a kind of spatial uplift for the Negro.[44] Weaver spent a lifetime supporting black suburbanization and expanded eminent domain powers against slumlords, first as staffer at the Housing and Home Finance Agency, then as national head of the NAACP, and, eventually, as the first secretary of Housing and Urban Development. And the Collins administration found in Weaver's work the kind of black liberalism that promised to save the South from its Jim Crow past and further racial violence.[45]

Of his various commissions, Collins asked city leaders to take a multifaceted approach to urban reform. He charged them with creating black/white consensus around the need for slum clearance, generating litigation in the state courts that might strengthen eminent domain law, and, if necessary, developing "home rule" charters to circumvent property rights lobbyists stalling the housing debate in the state capitol. Miami-Dade County actually took the lead on "home rule" by creating America's first metropolitan county government in 1957. But because this experiment in political centralization was still years from providing a functional model for regional governance, Miami was nowhere near developing a comprehensive land use plan that could meet the requirements of federal urban renewal policy.

Moreover, it quickly became evident that Collins's approach to civil rights—namely, professional "conversations" and slum clearance—had little to offer Miami's blacks in the way of immediate steps toward equality. In the wake of the Cuban Revolution and a long history of anti-Semitism in South Florida, Miami's mayor, Robert King High, turned Collins's "Biracial Affairs" committee into the "Community Relations Board," appointing a wealthy corporate attorney from Cuba to its chairmanship. The mayor, a protégé of Abe Aronovitz, hoped to squelch the spike in Cuban-on-Cuban street violence resulting from conflicts between supporters of Fidel Castro and Fulgencio Batista in 1958–59. The name change to "Community Relations Board" was also meant to reflect Miami's destiny as "a growing cosmopolitan center whose population is composed of numerous and differing social, racial, religious, linguistic, cultural and economic groups."[46] By 1960, the pursuit of racial justice for those bearing the "colored" burden seemed doubly undone by the establishment of a communist republic next door and a newfound commitment to "diversity" among Greater Miami's white officials. Before it even got off the ground, the City of Miami's new race committee, in the words of one black leader, was "not worth a dime."[47]

But if the civil rights side of the committee approach proved weak, its urban renewal component enjoyed a dramatic boost thanks to a landmark case the Florida Supreme Court decided in 1959. In November of that year, the state's highest court handed down new eminent domain powers to Florida's cities through its decision in *Grubstein v. Urban Renewal Agency of the City of Tampa*. With a 4–3 vote, the Florida Supreme Court ruled in *Grubstein* that a city government could condemn any slum area en masse with little regard for individual properties within a designated urban renewal zone. Properties so designated could be sold to private interests for redevelopment if the city could prove said area to represent a clear detriment to public health and the community's general morality and welfare. Perhaps the most decisive line came in the consenting opinion of Justice Campbell Thornal. "It is simply my view here that the elimination of slum areas is in and of itself a 'public use' which may be accomplished through the exercise of the power of eminent domain." The day after a ruling he called "most encouraging," Governor Collins pushed urban renewal forward at the legislative level, strengthening Florida's eminent domain law to reflect the new latitude granted in *Grubstein*. At the local level, municipal leaders in the state's largest slum-riddles cities—Jacksonville, Daytona Beach, Tampa, and Miami—began looking for all the "public good" renewal jobs that they could afford to initiate.[48]

There also remained a curious fact about the *Grubstein* ruling that would set the racial tone for Sunbelt-style urban redevelopment. The court's decision came on a case involving a "colored" community in Tampa that, since its founding some seventy years earlier, had been used by local whites for the explicit purpose of containing migrating Afro-Cuban and

American Negro workers. Across all fourteen pages of the *Grubstein* ruling, however, the words "blacks," "Negroes," or "Coloreds" never once appeared. It was a completely color-blind ruling discussing a neighborhood steeped in a decidedly color-conscious history.[49]

In place of overt racial signifiers, the court used a term that proved increasingly indispensible for its remarkable ability to take the politics out of planning and control public opinion on slum clearance: "blight." "Blight," on its face, was an economic descriptor in real estate parlance that denoted property in which value no longer appreciated, regardless of that property's appearance or structural integrity. It was a term Robert Weaver and other liberal reformers used quite frequently. But, despite its strict *economic* meaning, "blight," in America's racial context, served as a *cultural* signifier for a people—usually black people—who themselves had no value, or at least no values.[50]

In Miami, claims of "blight" allowed city officials to condemn Railroad Shop in 1947, parts of the black Grove in 1948, and, in 1960, massive stretches of the Central Negro District. Once Miami's city government deemed a neighborhood blighted, it could lawfully deny residents access to building or repair permits. Without permits, deterioration in so-called blighted neighborhoods would worsen. This deterioration would further drive down property values and reduce the city's condemnation costs when eminent domain proceedings began.[51] "Blight," in short, became a handy cost-cutting tool for Miami's planners and bureaucrats in other cash strapped cities. It allowed them to begin ambitious interstate highway construction, postindustrial distribution centers, and other the kinds of land-modernization projects that would soon entice northern capital to help construct the Sunbelt.

In 1960, local planners and politicians used the precedent of the *Grubstein* ruling, the arrival of the Dwight D. Eisenhower Interstate Highway System, and a growing black frustration with deplorable housing conditions to craft the "Magic City Center Plan." This was a top-to-bottom urban renewal agenda that was supposed to unmake the Jim Crow city and create a new era of color-blind prosperity for Miami. The "Magic City" plan pulled funds from public housing, highway-building, and urban renewal budgets, in addition to enjoying funds from a score of local and state budget lines. The result was the grandest land initiative South Florida had ever seen. "Magic City" promised to bring in suburban consumers, tourists, and potential downtown investors once scared off by "colored" slums. And the plan hearkened to a new age wherein, to quote one *Herald* reporter, "urban renewal will have beaten its land lord opponents."⁵²

The centerpiece of "Magic City" was the placement of the I-95/395 interchange. The interstate highway boasted an unequalled ability to connect South Florida's suburbs to its cities, its beaches to its airports. It would make Greater Miami an international convention center, cement South Florida's claim as the Western Hemisphere's preeminent trade hub, and move Miami one step closer to becoming what the Miami Chamber of Commerce hoped it would be—"The Capital of the Caribbean." Yet, the highway's "magic" was its ability to make the Central Negro District disappear. Concept drawings detailed parkland, office space, and a web of highways imposed over a sea of emptiness where the black Miami's downtown enclave used to be.

However, based on road officials' conservative estimates of displaced residents (only some 5,000 people), some journalists worried that, even after the proposed highway was built, the bulk of the Negro slum area and its moral evils would remain "in full view of the tourist hordes that will be driving on the expressway." The black downtown, all 136 blocks of it, had been, in one *Herald* reporter's words, "a blight on the glittering metropolis of Miami during the years of its phenomenal growth as the resort capital of the nation." And many feared that one, two, or even three highway interchanges might not be enough.⁵³

Despite all the development wishes coming from pro-growth politicians or the press, it seemed perhaps no group believed more in the promise of the Sunbelt and its new landscape than the black middle class. Trapped for decades in close proximity to the poverty of the Central Negro District, upwardly mobile blacks often fled to suburbs whenever money, real estate developers, or white flight allowed. The suburban home represented escape from landlord paternalism, substandard housing, and the stigma of race.

Even beyond the South, where slumlords exercised far less power at the state level, liberal solutions to America's slum problem required tapping the suburban dreams of aspiring blacks and their white allies. In St. Louis, for instance, slum clearance would never have gotten off the ground without support from the League of Women Voters, local reporters at the St. Louis *Post Dispatch*, and organized labor. In Flint, Michigan, Negro residents of the city's St. Johns neighborhood proved instrumental in helping General Motors move forward with its plans to demolish massive sections of Flint's black community. And even when accounts of blacks losing their homes or unjust evictions began circulating the country in the wake of mass displacements, proponents of urban renewal cast condemnation, demolition, and social disorientation as a natural, if at times inconvenient, consequence of the nobler aim to end blacks' collective housing woes.[54]

In contrast to NAACP chapters in Baltimore or Birmingham, Miami's NAACP, with Theodore Gibson in charge, chose to support urban renewal's higher ideals, though Gibson would repeatedly denounce the disruptive process of displacement. The local Urban League chapter followed suit in its qualified support. Miami's black press also endorsed South Florida's urban renewal efforts, arguing in 1960, "We are living in a progressive state. We cannot afford to take a backward step."[55] And once the first urban renewal project broke ground in 1966, many black elites still believed in the power of urban renewal as a means of spatial uplift, arguing that it saved both the race and the wider region from the destructive habits of black slum-dwellers.[56]

In addition to urban renewal's elite black support, city officials played to the imagination and material needs of poorer blacks to preempt the possibility of resistance from the grassroots. They presented conceptual drawings depicting the highway connecting—rather than dividing—Miami's black communities and the rest of South Florida. "Everybody was excited," remembered Sonny Wright, one former Overtown resident. "They had all these pretty pictures, renderings of how the area is going to look. It's going to tear down this and build that." Wright also recalled how black leaders, bearing promises from white city officials, "sold us on Urban Renewal. That was supposed to be the big savior." T Willard Fair, head of Miami's Urban League and one of those who helped pitch the project intimated, "The Overtown community did not fight back because . . . the Wall Street packaging of the product said that things are going to get better. That if you are to be relocated, you will be relocated into better housing."[57]

Promises included financial incentives newly available to displaced blacks. City officials offered low-income families "$200 federal relocation payments" and access to "new homes constructed with FHA . . . long-term mortgages," a first for most living "over town." Further, local officials promised black businesses in the projected path of the highway a measure of federal and state assistance, partly intended to grant black entrepreneurs access to new suburban markets and to "remove the stigma of 'Negro Business'" in the coming, post-Jim Crow economy. Dade County's urban renewal program also paid money directly into local civil rights organization;

T. Willard Fair's Urban League received over $56,000 in direct government payouts "to implement community organization activities in Central Miami, Coconut Grove, and Coral Gables."[58] Then there was just the simple matter of a limited imagination. Prior to the 1950s, no project the scale of urban renewal or the size of the interstate highway had ever been executed in Miami or, for that matter, in America. Few could even conceive of its magnitude, in general terms or on the actual face of the neighborhood. This led to many misconceptions at the black grassroots.[59]

Miami's more influential black property owners seemed to be among the few to learn the true scale of urban renewal. Oral histories of the period suggest blacks with substantial rental holdings or connections in the real estate business made early preparations to move their investment into Miami's suburbs. "They had a master plan," recalled George Littlefield. "I was permitted to see it one time. All of this [black downtown] was . . . the object of the developers and the realtors to get a hold of this property." Leome Culmer, black rental property owner, recalls how her white property manager—well connected in Miami housing circles—told her and her husband about the city's plan well before politicians and planners ever revealed it to the public. "My husband asked [our manager,] 'What are you going to do with all these people, you talking about doing this and that?' [the manager] said, well the plan a long time ago was [that] you'll be going to Carol City, you'll be going to Opa-locka and you'll be going here and there." Mrs. Culmer then corroborated what a number of Miamians suspected, that "these plans were made many, many, long years ago." According to one resident, some owners with particularly strong ties to Miami's white bureaucracy were "able to hold off some of the eminent [domain] actions for a while." Others, in the absence of an organized freeway revolt or similar protest, were not interested in fighting.[60]

Once the federal bulldozer came to downtown Miami, the combination of black flight and federal construction projects caused the Central Negro District to lose some 12,000 residents in the short term and nearly 20,000 more over the subsequent decade. Overtown housed more than 60 percent of Dade County's total black population in 1950. The marriage of growth liberalism and housing reform reduced that proportion to 28 percent in 1960, 11 percent in 1970, and less than 5 percent in 1980.[61] As generations of reformers had hoped, black Miamians, by the end of the civil rights era, had become a suburban people. But it soon became evident that suburban life in the Sunbelt did not mean an escape from poverty.

The flight of rental capital from the Central Negro District taught many black homeowners a sobering lesson about the economic power of slums during the Jim Crow era: proximity to certain slum housing could actually save your home. While generally concerned about the prevalence of slums in their communities, many black homeowners had no idea that it was actually powerful lobbyists who, through their resistance to condemnation legislation, had been protecting black homes from demolition since at least the late 1930s. For decades, Miami's slumlord lobby had provided a hedge of legal protection around black homeowners in the Central Negro District. With that hedge removed, most blacks found themselves having to negotiate with a battle-hardened bureaucracy that had become all too efficient at closing condemnation deals with staggering legal precision. "When we really understood what was happening," remembered Marian Shannon, an Overtown homeowner, "people . . . almost gave their homes away because there was nobody to advise them on how to deal with these people who were buying it up." Rachel Williams recounted, "They sent us [a] notice and a check for $7,000 for two double lots . . . and most of us got these checks from the city and we thought we just had to move." Learning later that she sold her house and adjoining family residences at a significant loss, she continued, "At the time, we were not educated to the point to know that we didn't have to take that." Many onetime black property owners joined the ranks of the landless tenantry when their condemnation payments fell short of what was needed to buy a new home.[62] Remembered Dorothy Graham, who was in her fifties at the time of her expulsion, "I was too old to start over again, trying to get comparable living accommodations . . . it just sort of wrenched you apart. They didn't cut you apart, you just wrenched apart."[63]

By contrast, white tenement owners often had the attorneys, capital, and awareness of certain bureaucratic loopholes to make eminent domain far less jarring and far more lucrative. On average, rental owners profited at rates significantly higher than those homeowners caught in the path of urban renewal or highway building. This was because state appraisers took both the *current* value of a structure and its *projected* revenue potential into account when considering condemnation payouts. A corporation of eight white investors packed ninety-two separate units on a lot equal in size to that owned by Rachel Williams. By the time the State Road Department bulldozers had arrived, they had received a government payout of over $340,000 for their property (compared to Williams's $7,000). One wealthy white landlord received nearly $215,000 for a stretch of eighty-six units consisting mostly of dilapidated thirty-year-old shotgun shacks. Some enterprising developers even began buying up land and erecting apartments directly in the path of the proposed expressway so they could then sell their property to the government at an inflated price. In light of the fantastic sums gained by landlords, a *Herald* editorial commented, "landlords who own property in Miami's Central Negro District slum area in the path of the North-South expressway are discovering 'gold' in their land."[64]

Enriched yet again by the government—first, by FHA segregation mandates and, then, by urban renewal—white property managers moved their operations out of the Central Negro District and into Miami's suburbs with no remarkable slowdown in their monthly cash flow. White landlords followed, buying up suburban homes, renting them out, and, when possible, rewriting zoning laws to allow for the occasional low-rise apartment buildings. During the 1960s and 1970s, the suburbanization of black Miami's population actually allowed white landlords to increase their stake in the black rental market. In 1950, white absentee landlords owned 70 percent of all the rental property in Overtown. Some twenty years later, whites collected 92 percent of all the rent in the suburb of Liberty City.[65] Whites would also own 97 percent of the businesses in Liberty City. For many, the movement of capital from black hands into white ones was a holdover from the Jim Crow era, one that fueled anger at the source of South Florida's first suburban riot.[66]

Florida's urban and suburban progressives tried to redefine the cultural and economic meanings of private property under Jim Crow, and, to do that, they fought to replace the slums of the Old South with the suburbs of the New.[67] Both black activists and growth politicians held suburbs out as the logical residential endpoint of economic modernization and civil rights activism. Suburbs, in short, represented the "End of History" for the movement and for Dixie.[68] And while we now call that end of history "The Sunbelt"—laden with all the progressive baggage that term connotes—the asymmetries of power governing black and white life in Jim Crow's America all but guaranteed that pursuits of suburbia would carry very different consequences for blacks and whites in the Sunbelt era.

As for much of the Sunbelt, the ability to access suburbia has mattered little to South Florida's blacks, for, as historian Andrew Weise notes, black suburbanization tends "to extend rather than erode historical patterns of spatialized inequality in the metropolitan United States."⁶⁹ During the Reagan years, stadium construction and the expansion of rental housing into Miami's black suburbs only hastened middle-class out-migration, turning neighborhoods once built for homeowners into bigger cash cows for rental entrepreneurs and absentee landlords.⁷⁰ During the Clinton years, blacks suffered continued displacements for public transportation projects "to nowhere" and government buildings. And under the weakened oversight of President George W. Bush's Justice Department, Miami saw profiteers engage in rampant real estate speculation and the blatant mismanagement of Hope IV and other projects. The Bush era, in fact, saw black Miamians erect an actual shantytown where Liberty City's 1968 riot once occurred.⁷¹ As of 2010, the widespread faith in the social merits of suburban expansion—the backbone of Sunbelt civil rights—has left California and Florida racked with more consumer debt and foreclosures than any other part of the country.⁷² Combined with the poverty broadcast out of New Orleans in the aftermath of Hurricane Katrina, much of Sunbelt's promise still lies out of reach.

It is hard to imagine that this was the future Florida's progressives imagined when they fused the politics of civil rights liberalism and the economics of urban growth into a single spatial agenda—an urban renewal agenda. Yet, as with the checkered history of voting reforms, failed school desegregation efforts, and other aborted affirmative actions, interests on neither the left nor the right—neither Democrats nor Republicans—addressed urban renewal's most tragic consequences—hypersegregated urban neighborhoods, downwardly mobile black suburbs, or the modernization of white supremacy. Still, we should not take the profane making of the Sunbelt in South Florida as an affirmation of dominant scholarly opinion on urban renewal, which tends to characterize the program as a top-down imposition from banks, large corporations, or newspaper publishers. Neither should we accept uncritically the popular jeremiad evident in the oral history record, that about highway development or urban renewal killing the Civil Rights Movement in Miami. The point, rather, is to take a fresh look—a long historical look—at the political assumptions activists and boosters incubated at the grassroots a full generation before the massive land projects of the 1960s broke ground or a single federal dollar was spent.⁷³ The point is to broaden our understanding of "The Movement" and its suburban visions and to see both as part and parcel of the Sunbelt's remarkable and unfortunate history.

Chapter 7

Racial Liberalism and the Rise of the Sunbelt West: The Defeat of Fair Housing on the 1964 California Ballot

Daniel Martinez HoSang

The November 1964 election in California included two events that would help shape Kevin Phillips's vision of the political alignment he would soon describe as "the Sunbelt" in *The Emerging Republican Majority*. In the presidential election, California voters followed the national trend in decisively rejecting Senator Barry Goldwater in favor of Lyndon Johnson by a two-to-one margin. But Goldwater's primary triumph over moderate New York Governor Nelson Rockefeller, a scion of the GOP's Northeast establishment, and the extraordinary enthusiasm evidenced for actor Ronald Reagan as he stumped for the Arizona senator, portended a decisive reemergence for conservative interests within a state that had elected liberal Democrats to nearly every statewide office just a few years earlier.[1]

Equally important for Phillips's purposes, however was the outcome of a highly controversial statewide ballot measure during the same election. Proposition 14 was a six-sentence constitutional amendment that sought to exempt the real estate industry, apartment owners, and individual homeowners from nearly all the antidiscrimination legislation recently passed by the state legislature, enshrining an unprecedented "right to discriminate" in housing sales and rentals within the state's highest law. A month before the election, *Time* magazine described Proposition 14 as "the most bitterly fought issue in the nation's most populous state," interest that overshadowed "that of such relatively piddling contests as the one between Johnson and Goldwater."[2] On election day, California's overwhelmingly Democratic electorate endorsed Proposition 14 by a margin of nearly forty points. Millions of Democratic voters who supported the pro-civil rights Johnson cast ballots in favor of making racial discrimination in housing a constitutionally protected practice.

This essay explores the high-profile debates over Proposition 14 to reveal the central role played by race in binding self-identified liberals and conservatives to the political formation Phillips would soon describe as the Sunbelt. For Phillips, attachments to white political authority were as important to fashioning a Republican electoral bloc in California (and especially Southern California) as they were in the South. He noted with approval in *The Emerging Republican Majority* that "given the ethnocentricity of white Southern California, the Negro–Mexican population is large enough to provoke white anger and counter-solidarity but seemingly not large enough to achieve a balance of power."[3] The Proposition 14 campaign and its outcome reveals the ways that developments on the Left and Right converged to make race a central determinant of political community and authority during this period, transcending many partisan, class, and geographic fissures. Proposition 14 did not simply represent a backlash among disaffected white voters against civil rights, the Democratic Party, and liberalism more generally. Instead, it signaled the triumph of a particular kind of liberal racial politics, one that fixated on individual attitudes and beliefs at the expense of structural and historical dynamics. The triumph of these decidedly liberal ideas, I argue, was central to the electoral realignment that Kevin Phillips anticipated.

The Emergence of California's Fair Housing Legislation

In April 1963, Democratic Governor Edmund "Pat" Brown capped the first legislative session of his second term in office by signing the Rumford Fair

Housing Act. Narrowly passed by the legislature, the Rumford Act empowered the state's new Fair Employment Practices Commission (FEPC) to receive, investigate, and adjudicate claims of racial discrimination in housing. The measure was named after its sponsor, Assemblyman William Byron Rumford of Berkeley, one of the first African Americans to serve in the State Assembly and a central figure among a coalition of labor unions, civil rights organizations, and activist Democratic organizations that championed the measure. These groups had worked for the passage of antidiscrimination legislation in housing and employment since the mid-1940s. The passage of the Rumford Act, in the wake of Brown's successful gubernatorial campaigns in 1958 and 1962, marked a high point of their influence in state politics (see Shana Bernstein's chapter in this volume for a fine-grained account of the emergence and constitution of this multiracial alliance).[4]

To be sure, the Rumford legislation had significant limitations. Most of the housing included in the Act was already covered by previous state and federal civil rights legislation, and complainants still faced a lengthy process to have their cases adjudicated.[5] One estimate suggested that the Act covered only about twenty-five percent of the nearly 3.8 million single family homes in the state and less than 5 percent of the 857,000 duplexes, triplexes, and four-plexes. Other than vesting authority with the FEPC, its primary impact was to extend coverage to 99 percent of the 738,000 apartment buildings of five units or more. Because vacant or rented single family homes (for example, an investment property) were exempted from the Rumford Act's coverage even if they were publicly financed, most individual homeowners remained entirely unaffected by the provisions of the legislation.

Still, the Rumford Act signaled that the state would no longer sanction or enforce the rigid patterns of racial segregation in housing that typified California since the early twentieth century. In 1921, California courts became the first in the nation to rule that racially restrictive housing covenants and occupancy clauses were enforceable. Realtors, as represented by the powerful California Real Estate Association (CREA) and its more than one hundred local affiliates, moved quickly to expand the use of such covenants to neighborhoods across the state. Combined with patterns of discriminatory federal lending policies institutionalized since the New Deal and the segregationist commitments made by large-scale suburban housing tract developers and many local homeowners' groups, patterns of racial segregation endured even after the U.S. Supreme Court outlawed the enforcement of racially restricted covenants in the 1948 *Shelley v. Kramer* decision.[6]

When Brown was elected in 1958, the systematic exclusion of African American residents from the vast majority of white neighborhoods was remarkable. The chair of the San Fernando Valley Fair Housing Council told a state commission in 1960 that he knew of only a single black family able to purchase a home in a new housing tract during the last ten years in an area with a population approaching 750,000 residents.[7] A 1963 estimate put the black population in the valley outside the segregated city of Pacoima at .0015 percent. The first black resident to buy a house in the community of Sun Valley remarked, "I didn't know California had become Mississippi."[8] While Mexican Americans and Asian Americans buyers and renters typically faced less rigid and totalizing exclusions, they too were effectively barred from many all-white communities.

By the early 1960s civil rights groups took more forceful action to confront these patterns of discrimination. E. J. Franklin, a member of the National Association for the Advancement of Colored People (NAACP), told a gathering of more than 1,100 civil rights supporters assembled in the Beverly Hills High School auditorium in 1963: "Everybody is upset about conditions in Mississippi and Birmingham; but they should be upset about conditions in Los Angeles." Another NAACP leader explained, "There is more racial residential segregation in Los Angeles than in any major Southern city in the United States."[9] Chapters of the Congress of Racial Equality (CORE) in San Francisco, Berkeley, Oakland, and Los Angeles increasingly used direct-action tactics such as sit-ins at segregated subdivisions and "window-shopping days" to test whether realtors showed properties for sale on a nondiscriminatory basis. In 1962 and 1963, an interracial group of several hundred protesters regularly picketed segregated-housing tracts in the city of Torrance outside Los Angeles; many hundreds were regularly arrested, including actors Marlon Brando and Rita Moreno.[10]

To the vast majority of its backers, fair housing legislation like the Rumford Act represented a logical and relatively uncontroversial extension of antidiscrimination principles to the field of housing, a development already affirmed in John F. Kennedy's 1962 executive order. Thirteen other states and at least ten other municipalities around the nation had already adopted similar legislation, and while the final vote in the state legislature was close, no wave of angry homeowners descended on Sacramento to protest the new law. Indeed, when a Berkeley group attempted to qualify a referendum to force a public vote on the adoption of the Rumford Act, they fell 60,000 signatures short, suggesting grassroots opposition to the open housing legislation was not automatically guaranteed.[11]

Bringing the "Forced Housing" Question to the Ballot

The Supreme Court ruling against the enforcement of racially restrictive covenants in 1948 marked a slow but deliberate withdrawal of formal state support for discrimination in housing. In response, organized groups of realtors, apartment owners and developers continued to actively mobilize to preserve their authority to use race to organize housing markets. As historian Robert Self argues, since the New Deal, federal policy actually encouraged realtors "to treat black and white housing markets as entirely distinct entities."[12] From their perspective, open housing policies and practices risked triggering wide fluctuations in property values instead of the steady increases that the industry most prized. Self concludes that "the real estate industry came to see the promotion, preservation and manipulation of racial segregation as central—rather than incidental or residual—components of their profit-generating strategies."[13] After the Supreme Court's ruling against covenants in 1948, the all-white Los Angeles Realty Board urged "a nationwide campaign to amend the United States Constitution to guarantee enforcement of property restrictions" that they argued provided "a traditional element of value in home ownership throughout this nation." The Board drew up a proposed amendment and advocated for its adoption before the National Association for Real Estate Boards (NAREB) for more than a decade. The CREA and its local affiliates pursued a number of other tactics, including disciplining realtors who violated the implied racial restrictions of particular neighborhoods and organizing neighborhood associations to defend racial restrictions in order to "protect" their property.[14]

By the early 1960s, however, the NAREB, CREA, and other organized realty groups concluded that defending explicit housing segregation was proving ineffective. The courts had increasingly determined that state enforcement of such claims was constitutionally suspect, and public opinion, especially outside the South, was becoming more sympathetic to the broad mantle of "civil rights." A California poll taken in 1964 found "civil rights and the race problem" to be the most important issue in the presidential election.[15]

As open housing legislation like the Rumford Act continued to win support at the state level, the CREA, as well as the NAREB, decided to abandon their long-standing efforts to defend the legality of racially restrictive covenants and choose a new tact to reverse the tide of these laws. Rather than politically defending the necessity or inevitability of segregated neighborhoods per se, realty groups focused instead on challenging fair housing laws as an abridgement of fundamental "homeowners' rights," asserted without an explicit reference to race. The NAREB concluded that defeating fair housing laws in California—the nation's most populous state and one that often regarded itself as the antithesis of the Jim Crow South—could reverse the national proliferation of open housing laws.[16]

While the NAREB, the CREA, and the California Apartment Owners' Association were resolutely committed to taking the Rumford Act off the books, they faced a vexing tactical dilemma. In the Democratic takeover of 1958, Brown and other Democrats effectively portrayed their Republican opponents as atavistic extremists who were out of touch with the state's liberal and forward-looking electorate. When Brown won reelection in 1962 against Richard Nixon, he candidly expressed his support for additional civil rights legislation, including open housing measures, with little apparent "backlash" from voters.[17]

To rollback the Rumford Act would require the realtors to steer clear of any language, symbols, or inferences that suggested that their opposition to open housing was motivated by segregationist commitments. Since CREA specifically sought to protect a policy and practice of racial segregation, their campaign stood on unstable political terrain.

As early as March 1963, three months before the Rumford Act was adopted, CREA president L. H. Wilson had proposed that a ballot initiative that incorporated the association's newly adapted "Property Owners Bill of Rights" be placed before voters. Soon after, at least 20 realty boards took out full-page ads posting his Bill of Rights in their local newspapers.[18] Calling itself the "Committee for Home Protection" (CHP), the CREA ultimately drafted an initiative that adopted much of the document's language. Concise and cleverly crafted, the declaration made no mention of race. Its operative first paragraph instead focused on the seemingly transparent and fundamental notion of property rights:

Neither the State nor any subdivision or agency thereof shall deny, limit or abridge, directly or indirectly, the right of any person, who is willing or desires to sell, lease or rent any part or all of his real property, to decline to sell, lease or rent such property to such person or persons as he, in his absolute discretion, chooses.[19]

While the initiative would come to be identified as a straightforward "repeal" of the Rumford Act, the constitutional amendment actually eviscerated most (but not all) of Rumford's provisions and also invalidated components of earlier laws banning discrimination in public housing, apartment rentals, and housing construction. An analysis authored by the deans of UCLA, University of Southern California, and UC Berkeley's law schools concluded that the measure "would establish constitutional immunity for those who discriminate in the sale or rental of their property and would exempt them from present and future fair housing laws."[20]

The CREA quickly retained a campaign management and public relations consultant (funded in part by a $10 assessment paid by member realtors), but decided to forgo the customary practice of retaining paid signature gatherers. The group instead mobilized its membership of nearly 45,000 members, organized into 171 local realty boards, to the immense task of gathering at least a half-million signatures within 150 days.[21] A February 20, 1964, advertisement in the *Oakland Tribune* seeking volunteers to circulate petitions revealed the careful construction of the issue the realtors intended to bring before voters:

> "RUMFORD ACT FORCED HOUSING"
> COMMITTEE FOR HOME PROTECTION
> In September 1963, the Rumford Act became state Law. Heretofore, a man's home was his castle. The Rumford Act makes a man's home subject to the whims of a politically appointed State Board. . . . The politically appointed Commission can FORCE you to sell or rent your home to an individual NOT OF YOUR CHOICE. Most people believe that a man has the right to sell, rent or lease his property to whomever he wishes; consequently they OPPOSE the Rumford Act . . . VOLUNTEERS NEEDED TO CIRCULATE PETITIONS.[22]

Neighborhood realtors, joined by committed political and religious conservative activists, mobilized an enormous grassroots operation, delivering and collecting petitions from thousands of volunteers through designated "area captains."[23] Local realty boards assumed responsibility for coordinating petition gathering in their areas and pressed individual realtors to collect signatures and make additional contributions to the CREA to defray campaign expenses.[24] Apartment owners also played a significant role in this effort. The Apartment Association of Los Angeles urged its members to "regain and keep control of your property" and to protect the "American right of freedom of choice" by distributing petitions widely.[25] By late March, the CHP, now headed by former CREA president L. H. Wilson, submitted 633,206 valid signatures to Secretary of State Frank Jordon, reportedly the largest number ever certified for an initiative measure.[26]

The narratives in clear sight in the *Oakland Tribune* advertisement would be rehearsed throughout an intensely fought campaign during the next ten months. The "Committee for Home Protection" identity (first developed by political consultants in a 1948 ballot initiative campaign against public housing) continued to draw on a powerful Cold War narrative of home and civilian defense against a menacing outsider—"the home as a man's castle" evoking threats to a collective domestic security. The campaign materials, news accounts, and other public discourse developed by the CHP assiduously avoided most direct mentions of race, civil rights, or segregation. In their published communications, few claims were ever made that the Rumford Act would drive down property values, lead to racial strife, or sacrifice any natural orders of segregation—arguments that circulated widely in open housing conflicts in other parts of the country at the same time.[27]

Instead, in their campaign materials, public talking points, organized letters to newspaper editors, and fundraising appeals, Proposition 14 supporters steeped their arguments in the rhetoric of egalitarianism and even *anti-racism*. Incorporating dimensions of emergent liberal civil rights discourse, they portrayed racial discrimination as a regretful but individually rooted problem of morality and tolerance, one the state could or should do little to address, incorporating some of the emergent rights-based language popularized by the burgeoning civil-rights movement. These arguments were not entirely novel; business groups deployed similar claims to fight fair employment laws since the 1940s. But the California realty groups went further by incorporating some of the emergent rights-based language popularized by the burgeoning civil rights movement.

The CREA had begun to deploy the language of tolerance and antidiscrimination in early 1963. As it was lobbying vigorously to defeat the Rumford Act and other civil rights legislation, the CREA Board of Directors formed an "Equal Rights Committee" to "inform and assist members of the Association in their understanding and responsibility in giving equal service to all clients." In June 1963, the CREA and NAREB adopted a new policy declaring that realtors "have no right or responsibility to determine the racial, creedal or ethnic composition of any area or neighborhood" and that the realtor should "exert his best efforts to conclude the [real estate] transaction irrespective of the race, creed, or nationality of the offeror."[28] The CREA further amended its constitution to include language prohibiting member boards from imposing "any limitation upon membership because of race, color, creed or national origin" and adopted new guidelines prohibiting realtors from promoting panic-selling or "blockbusting."[29] Thus, a year before the public battle over Proposition 14 had begun, the realtors had already incorporated some of these liberal rights-based claims.

A pro-Proposition 14 editorial in the *Los Angeles Times*, which had supported earlier desegregation measures in employment and education, articulated the propositions espoused by the CREA clearly. The editorial decried "Artificial laws designed to hasten the process of social, as distinct from civil, justice" insisting that "Discrimination will disappear only when human prejudice succumbs to human decency." The editorial criticized the Rumford Act for "seeking to correct such a social evil while simultaneously destroying what we deem a basic right in a free society." Proposition 14, the paper declared, "should relieve tensions between ethnic groups, leaving human decency and good will as powerful allies in overcoming prejudice.[30] The CHP never represented its opposition as agitating civil rights organizations and almost never as people of color per se but as a government controlled by an unaccountable cadre of elites determined to dispossess a silent but fair-minded majority.

Situating Proposition 14 in the spirit of an inclusionary Americanism built on freedom and opportunity over exclusion and hierarchy, the CREA's "Property Owners Bill of Rights" asserted that Proposition 14 was indeed the rightful heir to the nation's history of pluralist inclusion. It referenced the "Forty million immigrants [who] gave up much to come to this land . . . for the precious right to live as free men with equal opportunity for all" and celebrated the passage of the Fourteenth Amendment as "a new guarantee of freedom . . . to guard against human slavery. Its guarantees were for equal protection of all."[31]

Proposition 14, they insisted, would restore a divine, eternal, preternatural "property right"—held to be the bedrock of American freedom—that the Rumford Act had abridged. The headline of a typical CHP pamphlet announced "OWNERS! TENANTS! NEIGHBORS! GET BACK YOUR RIGHTS! VOTE "YES" ON PROPOSITION 14."[32] Mobilizing Cold War anxieties over a "creeping socialism," another "Yes on 14" pamphlet titled "That Long, Long Arm of the Law" warned that: "The Rumford Forced Housing Act's police arm is long and strong. It can reach almost any Californian—almost anyone who owns or rents a place to live.[33] The pro-14 ballot argument stated bluntly that "The Rumford Act establishes a new principle in our law—that State appointed bureaucrats may force you, over your objections, to deal concerning your own property with the person they choose." Such a policy "amounts to seizure of private property."[34]

While the CHP carefully avoided explicit references to race during the campaign, as another article in the *Los Angeles Times* put it: "Anyone who thinks that [Proposition 14] doesn't have anything to do with the racial issue just hasn't been paying attention."[35] An NAACP lawsuit seeking to prevent the initiative from qualifying for the ballot because it violated the Fourteenth Amendment captured the issue clearly. In response to the argument advanced in the Proposition 14 statement of purpose that the initiative would restore a constitutionally guaranteed right, an NAACP attorney argued:

> If the asserted right is already "constitutionally guaranteed" the Legislature could not take it away. . . . The [initiative's] statement of purpose is but a disguised appeal to racial prejudice, because the only part of the right to decline to sell or rent real property abridged by "recently enacted laws" is that based on race, color, creed or religion.[36]

In other words, Proposition 14's backers were, in fact, referring to a historically specific *racial* right: a white right to discriminate against and exclude people of color in general and black people in particular. The rights and freedoms voters were being exhorted to defend were not generic or abstract—they referenced specific historic constructions and narratives recognizable to white voters even when asserted in the language of individual rights and opportunities. They were unmistakable appeals to the political interests of white voters.[37] The CHP sought to frame the Rumford Act as an assault on the very foundations of this privilege, asserting that the right to discriminate by race was not only rooted in "natural law" and guaranteed by the Constitution but a cornerstone of American prosperity writ large. Proposition 14, they argued, would simply return the state to a "neutral" position of protecting this right.[38]

In addition, if proponents declared that Proposition 14 had nothing to do with race or civil rights, they also clearly signaled that the Rumford Act would implicitly and necessarily dispossess white homeowners. A CREA pamphlet explained: "The Rumford Act, by granting one group of citizens' rights for reason of race, color, religion, national origin or ancestry, necessarily takes equivalent rights away from the rest of the citizenry. This is denying equal protection under the law."[39] Another realtor argued that "the issue is not one of property rights versus human rights, but of the human rights of one person in the community versus the rights of another."[40] References to the Rumford "*Forced* Housing" Act, racialized a prevailing antistatist discourse: innocent white families would be *compelled* to cede their neighborhoods and homes, and the status and value they embodied, against their wishes. These references to the dispossession of "one group" reveal that it was a specific "racial right" that was being asserted. The claims again naturalized the proposition that such a racial right was foundational and beyond any state action. CHP spokesperson L. H. Wilson argued that "Forced housing is like forced religion. An apartment owner may be honestly afraid of members of some particular race. Such a person should have the right to be a conscientious objector to people who he fears."[41]

This discourse fashioned an identity position that would prove enormously appealing to white voters: it legitimated a historic "right to discriminate" as beyond the regulation of the state while disavowing any complicity in or responsibility for prevailing inequalities, an unapologetic racial innocence.

Challenges Facing the Proposition 14 Campaign

The CHP's campaign initially won few endorsements, even among recognized conservative groups and opinion leaders. Other than the realty boards, only a handful of organizations and individuals formally supported Proposition 14. The Republican State Central Committee refused its endorsement of Proposition 14, as did George Murphy, the Republican candidate for the U.S. Senate. Caspar Weinberger, a former GOP chairman of California and future member of Ronald Reagan's cabinet, declared that the issues at stake were "settled 100 years ago by a civil war."[42] Rockefeller suggested that the Rumford Act was a "start in the right direction for civil rights and a step ahead for us all."[43]

The initiative did receive enthusiastic support from a growing cadre of activist conservatives, including the California Republican Assembly, the Young Republicans, and many smaller churches and conservative political groups concentrated in Southern California.[44] Both Goldwater and Ronald Reagan, the cochairman of Goldwater's California campaign, endorsed the measure. Even the Goldwater campaign, however, did not make Proposition 14 a central part of its California strategy. Reagan did not mention Proposition 14, the Rumford Act, or "homeowner's rights" in his famous "A Time for Choosing" speech at the 1964 Republican National Convention in San Francisco, and it was not until Reagan's gubernatorial bid two years later that the term became a central part of his political vocabulary.[45]

Other than these deeply conservative organizations, the large majority of the state's political, civic, and religious organizations opposed the initiative. The debate that unfolded within the Los Angeles County Chamber of Commerce reveals the apprehension evinced by many traditionally conservative groups. Staunch and reliable foes of almost every piece of civil-rights legislation in the postwar period, the Chamber's 12 member Board of Directors took months to study and deliberate on Proposition 14 during the summer of 1964. Some board members concurred with a subcommittee report that cited the threat the Rumford Act posed to property values and property rights, the potential negative impact it could have on the business climate, and the fallacy of government intervention into the realm of personal sentiments.

An equally strident opposition countered with serious concern that the Chamber risked assuming a morally dubious position. As one board member explained, "The right we are giving up is the right to discriminate on the basis of race. Is that a right we want to bat for? I don't think this is a thing we should do a lot of breast-beating about. It is not a laudable right in the first place." Another inquired, "I wonder if we are not in favor of this type of legislation because we are men of property and men who have not ever been discriminated against?" Other members cited opposition to the initiative within their church and worried that the chamber would be going against "the so-called official moral leaders in the community." The group remained deadlocked as the election approached, and Proposition 14 was the only measure among the 17 statewide initiatives that appeared on the November ballot that the Chamber did not endorse or oppose.[46]

Even some CREA members sounded similar sentiments. At least ten local realty boards, including those in San Francisco and Ventura, voted to oppose the measure. Floyd Lowe, president of the CREA in 1955, thanked the anti-14 campaign for "saving the Realtor's profession from its leadership" and insisted that realtors "are not now and never have been recognized as spokesmen for property owners' rights." In Oakland, realtors committed to the fair-housing law organized a "League for Decency in Real Estate" to persuade other realtors to publish nondiscriminatory listings and oppose Proposition 14.[47] Earle Vaughan asked his fellow apartment owners in an article in the trade magazine *Apartment Journal*: "If all other types of business can prosper under integration, why can't we?"[48]

Lacking elite endorsements, the Committee for Home Protection continued to organize through its vast network of local realtors and neighborhood activists around a framework of property owners' rights and home protection. This grassroots approach urged supporters to hold "coffee klatches" in their homes, talk to their friends and neighbors about the dangers the Rumford Act posed, and to monitor news, radio, and television coverage of the initiative and write letters to the editor when appropriate. Apartment owners distributed pro-14 literature to their tenants signed "Your Landlady."[49] A letter delivered to renters in Belford Gardens, a Los Angeles apartment complex, asked "ARE YOU PARTICULAR WHO YOUR NEIGHBORS ARE?" The letter implored tenants to sign the petition so that the apartment management could continue to ensure the complex would not "become filled with undesirables" to whom "all Belford residents would violently object."[50]

In short, Proposition 14's proponents incorporated, rather than rejected, much of the prevailing language of racial liberalism and civil rights as they made their case to voters. They argued, implicitly, that one could favor the broad and abstract principle of "civil rights" while supporting Proposition 14 and its evisceration of antidiscrimination laws. These claims were not entirely unique to California; challenges to open housing laws in cities such as Detroit, Tacoma, and Milwaukee drew on similar narratives, though on a much smaller stage. What made the California struggle particularly instructive and distinct was the response of Democratic leaders and white liberal activists. While vehemently opposing Proposition 14, they endorsed many of the same ideas and commitments that fueled the realtors' effort, a paradox explored in the next section.

Organizing the Campaign to Defeat Proposition 14

At the end of the legislative session in June, 1963, supporters of the Rumford Act grew increasingly concerned about the CREA's intentions to launch an initiative campaign to roll back open housing legislation and began to plot their own organizing strategy. The influential grassroots California Democratic Council (CDC) declared defeat of the "segregation initiative" to be the top civil rights priority for 1964.[51] Civil rights groups such as CORE and the NAACP conducted regular pickets at CREA events and local realty board offices, demanding the withdrawal of the initiative petition.

After the secretary of state assigned the measure a ballot number in June 1964, civil-rights, labor, religious and Democratic activists along with elected officials formed Californians Against Proposition 14 (CAP 14) as an umbrella group to defeat the initiative. Governor Brown dispatched some of the leading figures in his administration to work on the campaign. Richard Kline, the deputy director of the Department of Motor Vehicles, resigned from the Brown administration to run CAP 14's day-to-day operations. Max Mont, a longtime organizer affiliated with the Jewish Labor Committee and a veteran of the campaigns to win a statewide FEPC, signed on to coordinate the activities in Southern California. Lucien Haas, who helped develop the Unruh Civil Rights Act in the late 1950s as an assistant to the Assembly leader before becoming Brown's press secretary, assumed responsibility for media relations. Marvin Holden, another stalwart in the Brown administration, became the campaign's treasurer. William Becker, a long-time organizer who worked on farmworker and fair employment issues and had joined the Brown administration as a human relations assistant, kept close track of the campaign's daily progress on behalf of the governor. Brown made the defeat of Proposition 14 a leading priority for the November election and appointed a "blue ribbon" commission of other high profile officials to lend their names to the anti-14 campaign.[52]

Collectively, the leadership of the newly formed CAP 14 brought decades of experience in California politics to the campaign. All the central figures appointed by Brown played a critical role in the landmark 1958 Democratic takeover of the Legislature and governor's office, as well as the subsequent passage of several important pieces of antidiscrimination legislation during Brown's first five years in office. They had a clear-cut mandate: persuade Brown's Democratic base to reject Proposition 14 as an illiberal assault on the state's progressive ideals.[53]

In the 1958 and 1962 elections, Brown successfully stigmatized his Republican opponents as out of step with the state's progressive and forward-minded electorate. The team put in place to defeat Proposition 14 plotted a similar strategy. CAP 14 sought to portray the proposition as a bigoted and extremist measure designed to serve the narrow concerns of realtors over the best interest of all Californians. In its communications with voters, CAP 14 framed the initiative as a contest between realtors, John Birch Society members, and other racial extremists on the one hand and a broad range of labor, civic, business, religious, and civil rights groups and elected officials—the authentic protectors and representatives of the Californian populace—on the other. As Haas would later describe, the campaign was intended to be "based pretty much on organizing the liberal and moral base of the state of California."[54]

The main image and logo selected to represent the "No on 14" campaign signified these intentions clearly. Conceptualized by Martha Holden, the wife of the CAP 14 treasurer, it featured stately sketches of Abraham Lincoln and John Kennedy. The tagline read, "Don't Legalize Hate: Vote No on 14." The California Democratic Council used this image to launch a statewide "Bucks for Billboards" campaign to secure grassroots contributions that would pay for a series of hand-painted billboards in prominent locations. The billboards added an American flag in the background and were eventually placed in 51 locations across the state. A CDC memo explained that "the symbolism of the flag was chosen by the artist to reflect the basic nature of a vote against Proposition 14 as being in the American tradition of equal rights for all citizens."[55]

Governor Brown repeatedly emphasized this theme in a series of speeches he delivered before the election. Addressing a Jewish women's group in August, he explained that the initiative represented the voices of "a minority of the angry, the frustrated, the fearful. They do not represent California or its people." He predicted that as "Americans we will heed our

Figure 7.1. "Don't Legalize Hate," Californians Against Proposition 14 campaign brochure, 1964. Courtesy of Max Mont Collection, Urban Archives Center, Oviatt Library, California State University, Northridge.

great Judeo-Christian heritage. . . . we will choose love over hate and concern over indifference." At another Los Angeles rally in October, he announced that the "issue here is not legislating morality; it is the controlling of anti-social behavior."[56] The ballot argument against Proposition 14 expressed the dividing line clearly: "For generations Californians have fought *for* a tolerant society and *against* the extremist forces of the ultra-right who actively are behind Proposition 14."[57]

Anti-14 forces often used the perceived baseness and bigotry of the South as a foil to contrast the high-minded ideals that Proposition 14 threatened to undermine. Lieutenant Governor Glenn Anderson addressed the Los Angeles area "Mar Vista-Westside Citizens Against Proposition 14" before the election and explained that, if the amendment was adopted, California would "be accepting the leadership of states like Mississippi, the poorest, most badly educated and in my opinion, amongst the most badly governed states in the nation." He continued: "If we now ally ourselves with the south in the civil rights struggle, the future of this state will be in serious jeopardy. California did not achieve her present wealth and importance by becoming a symbol of fear and hate."[58]

The mainstream CAP 14 message that emphasized tolerance and open-mindedness resonated deeply with a core set of religious, labor, Democratic Party, and other liberal activists, and the campaign mobilized thousands of volunteers among these groups. By late August, CAP 14 had secured dozens of high-profile commitments to oppose the initiative, and its endorsement list read as a who's who of California public life. The list included every significant Democratic official in the state, the California Council of Churches and the liberal Protestant denominations it represented, the American Jewish Congress, the California Teachers Association, the California Labor Federation, the State Bar of California, and every major African American, Asian American, and Mexican American civil rights organization.[59] A "Performing Arts Division" of CAP 14 won the support of stars including Richard Burton, Lucille Ball, Dinah Shore, Carl Reiner, Joan Baez, Nat King Cole, Burt Lancaster, Gregory Peck, James Garner, and Elizabeth Taylor, among others. Taylor and Burton headlined a "Night of Stars" fundraiser for CAP 14 in early October at the Hollywood Bowl; Baez and Pete Seeger led a fundraising concert in the same venue a week earlier.[60]

CAP 14's decision to focus on the white voters that made up Pat Brown's electoral base, however, meant that groups such as the NAACP, the Los Angeles-based United Civil Rights Committee, and the Mexican

American Political Association (MAPA) would play only a marginal role in the official anti-14 campaign. CAP 14 steered some funding to the groups to join in voter outreach and education efforts; the United Civil Rights Committee mobilized 2,000 volunteers to register some 40,000 voters in heavily African American and Mexican American precincts in Los Angeles and MAPA distributed more than 100,000 bilingual anti-14 materials in the Bay Area alone.[61] In many black communities in particular, mobilizing to defeat Proposition 14 was the singular political issue of the day, with opposition to the measure expressed in forceful, often outraged tones.

Whereas the majority of CAP 14's materials emphasized the ideals of tolerance and fairness, civil rights groups tended to focus on the concrete experiences of discrimination and segregation. An NAACP flyer circulated during a protest outside a CREA meeting in September 1963 declared, "We will no longer tolerate segregated housing as a way of life, and demand that housing in California be made available immediately without discrimination because of race, color or religion."[62] Materials produced by CORE similarly urged voters to "Register and Vote against this Jim Crow Amendment! Don't let our hard-won progress go down the drain!"[63]

Civil rights groups expressed frustration about their exclusion from the CAP 14 campaign. Education and mobilization efforts targeting black voters in Los Angeles funded by CAP 14 only provided for a single part-time staff person working with the NAACP, who had to furnish and supply the campaign office using his own money. The organizer complained bitterly to CAP 14 coordinator Max Mont about the lack of resources he received. Another African American lawyer organizing against Proposition 14 cut his ties with the CAP 14 organization because of its refusal to bring Hollywood stars opposed to the initiative into the black community for fundraising events.[64]

MAPA noted its displeasure that CAP 14 coordinator Max Mont claimed he could not find any "'eligible' Mexican-American to do full time staff work for Californians Against Proposition 14." When CAP 14 finally hired an organizer to do field work among Mexican American voters in August, MAPA informed its members sarcastically that "someone finally passed Max Mont's acceptability test."[65] MAPA leaders were particularly irritated by CAP 14's decision not to spend money on Spanish language radio advertisements, especially in comparison to the "thousands spent by the Real Estate interest for Spanish radio coverage." It noted in a newsletter that "As the vote draws to a close, the gravity of this mistake becomes more evident. Spanish radio, throughout the State of California, including Los Angeles, has been virtually bought out by the proponents of the Proposition. Up and down the San Joaquin Valley, all that is heard is Yes on 14, and the same is true for Los Angeles." As a result, only "a few valiant voices" were left on the airwaves to explain "the real meaning of the Proposition."[66]

Ambivalent Allies: The Case Against Proposition 14

Why would CAP 14 leaders so committed to defeating Proposition 14 distance the campaign from the communities, organizations, and leadership that bore the brunt of segregated and inferior housing? The omission was largely intentional. Early in the campaign, CAP 14 leaders made a strategic decision to attack the abstract ideas and extremist actors animating Proposition 14 rather than defending the Rumford Act or asserting the widespread prevalence of housing discrimination and segregation. As an organizing manual prepared in February 1964 by the California Committee for Fair Practices explained, "it would be a mistake to gear our campaign primarily to a defense of the Rumford Act. This is what the amendment's proponents desire." It continued: "Of course, we will speak for anti-discrimination legislation, but the issue at hand is the constitutional amendment. We are defending the American system of representative government." The committee also counseled against demonstrations or pickets against realtors, which might suggest Proposition 14 was a "minority rights" issue alone.[67]

Indeed, CAP 14 leaders became convinced that specific references to the existence or prevalence of racism would only hurt the campaign's fortunes among the white voters who dominated the electorate. In April 1964, Bill Becker, the human relations assistant for Governor Brown, came upon a flyer produced by an unidentified group that criticized Proposition 14 in strident anti-racist terms, declaring "HUMAN RIGHTS are NOT subject to a VOTE." It asked: "Shall tax dollars be spent for Jim Crow housing? Shall de facto segregation in schools be constitutionalized?" Fearful of the reaction the flyer might cause among white voters, Becker wrote to Max Mont and black Assembly member Mervyn Dymally asking if they knew who was behind the "frightening movement" that produced the materials with such a "negative approach."⁶⁸ Becker, like many CAP 14 leaders, concluded that white voters would not respond to a direct appeal to defend the Rumford Act or the specific protections it provided.

Most CAP 14 leaders and activists also proved deeply ambivalent about asserting the importance of antidiscrimination laws or highlighting the crisis in housing faced by hundreds of thousands of Californians. Many opponents of Proposition 14 placed a repeated emphasis on assuaging the fears of white voters by asserting that the Rumford Act would not upset the character of their neighborhoods or violate their "property rights" in any significant way. A memo to Episcopal lay leaders in Los Angeles insisted that the "Rumford law is *not* a 'special privilege' law for the minorities. It does *not* give minorities any special claim on housing in any way, shape, or form. It merely attempts to give them an equal chance for housing if they are fully qualified." The memo declared that the "law was *not* passed for the benefit of the minorities, but for the benefit of the health, welfare, prosperity and peace of the whole community. Delinquency, slums, social welfare programs, reduced community business and income, bitterness and strife—all of which are destructive to total community life—are at stake."⁶⁹

A brochure against Proposition 14 produced by the liberal Council of Churches offered similar reassurances, explaining to parishioners who feared that the fair housing laws might upset the composition of their neighborhood that "Economic inequalities over our long history of discrimination make it impossible for most minority citizens to buy homes of their choice." The council assured its audience that among the relatively small black population in California, "probably not more than 1% or 2% ... can afford to buy houses in all-white areas. Of those who can afford to do so, experience shows only a small percentage choose to do so, even though they should have this right." The fair housing act, they promised, would not "basically change racial housing patterns."⁷⁰

When CAP 14 and its affiliated groups did mount a defense of the Rumford Act, it was also framed within the expectations of white political identity. Brown warned that "the ancient problems of segregation and discrimination" would be "settled in the streets, with blood and violence" if Proposition 14 passed.⁷¹ A fundraising letter to support anti-14 work from the ACLU asked if Proposition 14 were to become law, "How much will California's spreading slums and their accompanying evils cost us and our children in the interim?" It warned ominously, "What will the minority ghettos do to the newly-planted hopes and the age-old angers of their chief residents?"[72] Opponents also frequently sought to downplay the impact of the Rumford Act itself, pointing out that, during its first year of implementation, no fines had been issued by the FEPC and that only one of the complaints filed had led to an administrative hearing. Thus, when the Rumford Act was referenced, it was either to emphasize its limitations and feebleness or to argue that its repeal risked inciting explosions in the "ghetto" that might spill into white communities.[73]

In focusing almost entirely on the contradictions and dangers of Proposition 14, CAP 14 declined to endorse or defend the original purpose of the Rumford Act in any meaningful way. Liberal activists rarely mentioned the housing crisis that drove civil rights organizations to demand the passage of the legislation in the first place or referenced the overwhelming levels of discrimination many home buyers and renters still faced. Only when the housing crisis might erupt beyond the "walls of the ghetto" was the necessity of the Rumford Act invoked. Whereas civil rights groups intentionally sought to link Proposition 14 to a longer history of racial subjugation, the CAP 14 campaign asserted a much different position, largely suggesting that no such tradition of discrimination had existed in the state until the arrival of Proposition 14. Like the CHP, CAP 14 affirmed the basic privileges white homeowners had come to expect as natural and unassailable—they simply argued that Proposition 14 itself represented a greater attack on those interests than the Rumford Act. The two competing campaigns actually shared important ground. Ultimately, the liberal campaign to defeat Proposition 14 was itself segregated, subordinating and marginalizing the claims of those facing housing discrimination in favor of addressing and validating the perceived needs and interests of white voters.

The Election and Its Aftermath

CAP 14 mobilized at a furious pace in the two months leading up to the election, organizing endless press conferences and fundraising events, participating in televised debates and community forums, and running a series of television and radio advertisements. Campaign materials from both sides inundated voters, and the measure received extensive media coverage. At the same time, many property owner associations took up the issue aggressively, continuing door-to-door organizing on behalf of Proposition 14 in suburban subdivisions across the state.[74]

Polls conducted throughout the campaign identified two trends. First, contrary to the claims of CAP 14 that the ballot language was deceptive and misleading, voters seemed to increasingly understand that a vote for Proposition 14 meant the evisceration of the Rumford Act. Second, as the campaign wore on and both sides had an opportunity to present their case, support for Proposition 14 grew.[75]

Voters ultimately approved Proposition 14 by a 65 to 35 margin. Nearly 85 percent of registered voters in the state cast their ballots on the measure, the highest number for any proposition on the ballot and just below the number cast in the presidential contest. While President Johnson secured almost 4.2 million California votes in his landslide defeat of Goldwater, only 2.4 million votes were cast against Proposition 14. The California poll conducted a week before the election suggested that white voters supported the measure by a three to one margin—black voters rejected it nine to one—and that union voters and Protestant voters favored Proposition 14 by more than 60 percent.[76] In Los Angeles County, where registered Democrats outnumbered Republicans by three-to-two and cast ballots for Johnson by the same margin, Proposition 14 won by 35 points and nearly a million votes.[77]

It would be difficult to overstate the profound sense of defeat and anguish that gripped the anti-14 forces after the election. In retrospective assessments, many of the CAP 14 leaders candidly acknowledged that they had simply been out-organized. Richard Kline, the Pat Brown aide assigned to head CAP 14 campaign, confessed, "I made a huge strategic misjudgment which was, in my naiveté, that if you could only explain this issue to people, raise enough money, have enough good media campaigns, organization and everything, if you'd explain the issue to people, people in the goodness of their hearts would vote no on 14."[78]

Lucien Haas, the press secretary dispatched by the Brown administration to work on the campaign, suggested that the outcome of the election shattered his understanding of race relations in the state. Before the initiative, he imagined that "We had Mexicans, we had blacks, everything like that and we were all mixing it up and getting along fine. Everybody was working and happy and so on." Proposition 14, he said, "shattered [the myth] for me" as he realized, "My God, we're facing racism in the state of California."[79] Part of the reason that many leaders and supporters of the CAP 14 campaign likely shared Haas's lack of knowledge of the housing crisis and discriminatory barriers facing so many other Californians was because they also lived in segregated white communities. Indeed, the West Los Angeles communities that voted strongly against Proposition 14 were as deeply segregated as pro-14 areas in the San Fernando Valley.[80]

CAP 14 never offered a forceful defense of the Rumford Act or attempted to tie the legislation to the broader vision that animated the Brown administration's other policy commitments during the period—such as the expansion of the state infrastructure and higher-education system—that drew on shared aspirations for a society with greater possibilities and opportunities for all Californians. They sought to paint neighborhood realtors and their organizations as racial extremists, a strategy that hardly resonated with the sensibilities and experiences of most white homeowners. These homeowners might not trust Barry Goldwater's finger on the atomic button, but that did mean they were ready to believe that their local realtor was shilling for the Ku Klux Klan. Following the dominant logics embedded in the postwar liberal civil rights discourse, they attacked Proposition 14 on the grounds that it used race to justify inequality, a violation of the nation's civic creed. This discourse drew simple contrasts between tolerance and bigotry and asserted that racism was a matter of individual belief and mindset rather than structure. The realtors defended Proposition 14 not by challenging this framework but by articulating their vision for homeowners' rights within its terms.

As a matter of law and public policy, Proposition 14 had only a fleeting impact. In May 1966, the State Supreme Court ruled in *Mulkey v. Reitman* that Proposition 14 was unconstitutional because it involved the state in encouraging discrimination by "making it at least a partner in the instant act of discrimination."[81] The court rejected the claims of the realtors, as represented by future Reagan Attorney General William French Smith, that "the People" had determined it "in the public interest" to protect a private right to discriminate.[82]

The most enduring impact of the Proposition 14 election was not the policy it enacted during the two years between the election and the Supreme Court's ruling but the way it helped valorize a set of ideas about the "rights" particular homeowners possessed. If before the election, the large majority of elected officials were unwilling to assert that a right to discriminate existed, in the wake of Proposition 14's overwhelming passage, they eagerly embraced this position. During the 1966 election, multiple Republican candidates for the State Assembly attacked their incumbent opponents simply as "Rumford Act supporters," a designation that operated as racial shorthand for a politician who failed to champion "homeowners' rights."[83] Los Angeles Mayor Sam Yorty similarly condemned Governor Brown during the Democratic gubernatorial primary in 1966 for his continued opposition to Proposition 14, though Yorty also had opposed the measure. Yorty's attack anticipated relentless criticisms made by Republican gubernatorial candidate Ronald Reagan in the general election. Reagan had supported Proposition 14 in 1964, but the majority of his attention in that election was devoted to Goldwater's candidacy and to a broader criticism of the excesses of liberal government. In his successful campaign against Brown, Reagan used the ideas animating the Proposition 14 campaign to bring these themes together, declaring that "the right of an individual to the ownership and disposition of property is inseparable from his right to freedom itself."[84] Even Governor Brown began to genuflect before the altar of "homeowners' rights." In the wake of the State Supreme Court's ruling against Proposition 14, Brown maintained that the FEPC should utilize conciliation rather than strictly enforce the fair housing laws recently restored by the Court, prompting newly elected Assemblyman Willie Brown to remark that the governor was beginning to "sound like Reagan."[85] Thus, the Proposition 14 campaign increasingly bound both liberals and conservatives to a political discourse centered on white racial identity.

Like the leaders of the CREA, Reagan also steadfastly maintained his own racial innocence. During the 1966 gubernatorial campaign, Reagan identified civil rights as "one of the three or four most important issues," labeled "bigots" as "sick people," and vociferously objected whenever he was accused of supporting or tolerating bigotry; he famously stormed out of one campaign event during his first gubernatorial bid when such an insinuation was made. Yet Reagan also depicted a political environment in which hard-working and independent white Californians had to remain vigilant against the ominous and conceited attempts of the liberal state and its racialized clients to undermine their way of life. Like the realtors, he insisted that significant housing discrimination did not exist, telling an audience in South Carolina, "There is no law saying the Negro has to live in Harlem or Watts." And he too mastered the subtle vocabulary of white political identity: "We all have the responsibility to work to end discrimination and insure equal opportunities for all. . . . But I am opposed to trying to get this with legislation that violates basic tenets of individual freedom."[86] Kevin Phillips commented on the racial basis of Reagan's political support explicitly. He noted that in Southern California during the 1966 gubernatorial campaign, "Not only did Reagan sweep the country club, retiree and ex-naval precincts, but he won all of the white working-class suburbs" that had traditionally voted Democratic.[87]

After winning office, Reagan continued to sustain and address this political identity even as he quietly ended his support for future legislative action to repeal the Rumford Act. While the signifiers "Rumford Act supporter" and "homeowners' rights" became deeply influential in California political discourse and many Rumford opponents denounced the State Supreme Court decision invalidating Proposition 14, voter response to the future of the Rumford Act itself was more ambivalent. After the Court's decision, Reagan spent little political energy on trying to repeal the Rumford Act through the Legislature, and the CREA was forced to end its support for a repeal by 1967.[88]

Ultimately, Kevin Phillips's prediction that the growth of the Sunbelt would deliver electoral control of California to the GOP for decades to come did not fully materialize. The centrist character of the state's political culture largely endured, and while Republicans certainly dominated many of the suburban areas of Southern California for many years, some Democrats were still elected from the region, and Democrats still enjoyed a significant voter registration margin across the state.

Phillips was entirely correct, however, that white political identity and authority would continue to structure political discourse in the state, as it did across much of the Sunbelt. An important dimension of the principles advanced by the realtors during Proposition 14 was carried on by the neighborhood associations that proved so critical in defining the measure as a natural, populist response to an unlawful government incursion on property rights. These neighborhood and homeowner organizations, populated by Democrats and Republicans alike, continued to grow in influence and power, nourished by the experience of "defending their homes" during the Proposition 14 campaign. These associations would play a large role in the 1970s struggles over school busing and property taxes, employing much of the same political grammar in these campaigns. Twenty-six years after Proposition 14, Mike Davis would argue that the "most powerful 'social movement' in contemporary Southern California is that of affluent homeowners, organized by notional community designations or tract names, engaged in the defense of home values and neighborhood exclusivity."[89]

Ultimately, while many communities across the state experienced some modest integration in the decade after Proposition 14, the naturalized notions of inequality and restrictive notions of collective responsibility embraced by so many white Californians only grew in power. Proposition 14 valorized a sensibility that would prove enormously influential in state politics for decades to come. The same regions of the state—and the Sunbelt—that enthusiastically championed Proposition 14 also voted for ballot initiatives in 1972 and 1979 to prohibit the desegregation of California schools. They backed ballot measures in 1984 and 1986 to end bilingual voting materials and declare English the state's "official language." And they voted for ballot measures during the 1990s eliminating all public services and education for undocumented immigrants (1994), eliminating affirmative action (1996) and bilingual education programs (1998), and massively expanding the state's prison system (1994 and 2000).[90]

As a prognosis of long-term political realignment, *The Emerging Republican Majority* ultimately had considerable shortfalls. But in its observations about the central role that race would play in the political development of California and much of the Sunbelt, it was unsettlingly accurate.

PART III
Contingent Places

Chapter 8

Sunbelt Lock-Up: Where the Suburbs Met the Super-Max

Volker Janssen

Inventor and freelance writer Andrei Moskowitz wanted to do something about the overcrowded prisons spreading across the country in the 1990s. To civilize the "social jungles" of the institution, he thought up his own prison. Called "self-sufficient isolation," Moskowitz's prison plan looks more like a traditional postwar suburb than a place of punishment. Each prisoner would live in his own "studio-style cabin" on a grassy plot of 40 by 80 feet surrounded with chain-link fence and razor wire. Here, he would prepare his own food and engage in productive but solitary work like gardening, learning to read, or acquiring other skills by computer or television. His imprisoned neighbors would be right across the four-foot walkways separating the little plots. Each block would measure 10 by 2 units separated by service roads, multiplied a thousand-fold, and surrounded by walls and gun towers. "I'm not saying this has to be built in New Jersey or Rhode Island," Moskowitz told the *New York Times*. "This would work best in the West," he suggested.[1] Penal sprawl?

It is doubtful that Mr. Moskowitz ever found a financier. Most—except for the most cynical postmodern critics—consider Moskowitz's penal colony a poor way of marking the difference between freedom and confinement. Gated communities, yes; but carceral suburbs? Most Americans consider suburban settings as liberation from urban confinement and rural isolation—as different from the prison's punishing fortresses of brick, steel, and pain as the garden from the machine. Suburban life is a privilege to be desired, not a punishment to be feared. Suburbs house families of diverse, but still predominantly white, working and middle classes, not felons. They breed college graduates and corporate white-collar citizens, not gangs. Indeed, when the time came to separate "law-abiding, tax-paying Americans" from the criminal disorder of rioting cities, suburban communities of the Sunbelt were first in line to fight for law and order and protect their prosperous garden communities from the urban jungle.[2]

Moskowitz's penal suburb appears an unlikely bulwark of the Sunbelt state. And yet, over the past fifteen years, Sunbelt suburbanites have increasingly caught glimpses of the nation's expanding prison systems. In Southern California, for example, golfers at the Los Serranos Golf Club of Chino Hills enjoy not just "million dollar" valley vistas but also views of the California Institution for Men. A few miles southeast, fellow golfers at El Prado are almost a powerful swing away from California's women's prison in Corona. The prisons of Chino, Corona, and other institutions in the carceral complex of the "inland empire" are not the only ones in suburban settings. In the age of megasprawl, the urban flight of Sunbelt suburbanites reaches so deep into the hinterlands that they now border on the very institutions meant to render the urban plight of crime, poverty, and racial inequality invisible.

As with all historical ironies, there is much reason to suspect that the meeting of suburbs and prisons has not been one of chance but that the modern carceral landscape is as proprietary to the Sunbelt as its suburbs. After all, historians have identified contract prison labor with the Northeast during the Market Revolution, tied convict leasing to the Jim Crow South, associated the industrial prison with the early twentieth-century North and Midwest, and have placed state-use industries and the correctional treatment philosophy within the New Deal state. Just as these political economies produced distinct modes of punishment, the Sunbelt, too, possesses its own carceral regime.[3] Neoliberal forms of state governance that have shaped the region's post-Fordist economies, housing, education, politics, and public spaces have also born strange fruits in American punishment—like private corrections, supermax prisons, and soaring incarceration rates.

Not just a program embedded in distinct political economies, incarceration marks spaces. The bodies it removes from one site, it hides in another.

The patterns of displacement through prison, thus, sever social ties at the same time that they connect distinct places. Society's margin set in stone, prisons render invisible the mix of poverty, crime, and racial inequality that mark actual punishment and put in its place a compelling mythology of law and order. To be sure, segregating complex social realities behind prison walls in order to produce a more clarified political discourse over deviance and normality has been a bourgeois project ever since the emergence of the American middle class.[4] And we know that conservative suburbanites forged a secessionist stance toward cities and deployed their ideology of individualism, privatization, and pick-and-choose libertarianism in defense of school and neighborhood segregation, with great effect on states and the nation. But did Sunbelt suburbanites shore up bastions of privilege only in private schools and gated communities? Or could the suburban landscapes of the Sunbelt, which are so deeply invested in fantasies of growth and consumption, have fostered a political approach to crime and social disorder that drove the prison boom of the last quarter century?[5]

The late modern "culture of control," I argue here, has indeed been the culture of a Sunbelt that melded together the distinct penal traditions of the South with the American West of the postwar years. Whereas much of the South continued to base its penal discipline on Jim Crow institutions such as state farm and chain gangs, California's new department promised reform and raised prisoners' expectations for expanded civil rights. Just as racial fault lines between law enforcement and poor communities in Los Angeles and other southern cities disturbed the appearance of peace and prosperity in the Sunbelt, so did the conflict between black power activist prisoners and guards contradict the Golden State's claim for a historical departure from both northern and southern penal practice. The failure of the prisoner rights' movement and rehabilitative reform in the institution paralleled the transition from a war on poverty to an urban war on crime. The struggle for prisoner rights in the courts and in the yard invigorated a law-and-order backlash, but it also led to the end of the treatment model, the involvement of federal courts in penal policy, and the nationalization of imprisonment standards. Thus, as Sunbelt suburbanites took a punitive turn with popular tough-on-crime measures, they triggered a federally mandated expansion of an increasingly militarized supermax prison complex, one that particularly Sunbelt states sought to drop from their portfolio of governmental responsibilities through privatization.

Sunbelt politics in and outside prison walls played a crucial role in formation of the late twentieth-century carceral state. With its pronounced prison expansion and particularly vigorous sprawl, the carceral state also took distinct shape in the region. Thus, while Sunbelt states have been more likely to concentrate prisoners in rural isolation, they have also pushed suburban tract development close to its carceral belts. States of the Sunbelt did not all partake in this development in the same measure. And many states in the Midwest and Northeast have followed a similar path. As is the case with the other distinct features of the region's built environment such as suburbs, malls, and military installations, the Sunbelt did not deviate but led the nation in the politics of mass incarceration.

Worlds Apart: California Corrections After World War II

At the eve of World War II, there was little to suggest that the prisons and gallows stretching from Florida to California would come to share much common ground. The South had early on developed a mode of punishment distinct from prison reforms elsewhere in the country. Southern punishment, by and large, served as an institutional extension of racial slavery. In contrast to the northern fortresses that had so much in common with factories and garrisons, most penal discipline in the South remained tied to racial apartheid and the plantation.[6] The lives of southern convicts remained consistent in its harsh discipline through World War II. The violence and exploitation of southern convicts was indeed so brutal that it prompted prisoners in Texas to cut their own Achilles heel strings to escape forced labor. An inquiry by the American Correctional Association revealed only more gruesome details about the practice of punishment in Texas. The scandal prompted some modest reforms to limit the corruption and capriciousness of individual wardens. Hoping to trigger investigations and reforms in their prisons, convicts elsewhere in the South copied the self-mutilation of "heel-stringing," but nowhere in the South did prison reform bring about an end to plantation labor.[7]

Southern tradition and western innovation stood at polar opposites in their penal ideology in the postwar years. The economic boom of the war years had catapulted California from the margins to the center of a national economy. In the process, it also brought convicts from the shadows of the Depression to the forefront of an ambitious postwar welfare state. Lax order and scandalous escapes had led Governor Earl Warren to completely refashion the state's prison system into the California Department of Corrections. His postwar planning program—which the *New York Times* praised as the most "farsighted, intelligent, and thorough"—included not just aggressive investments in public education and infrastructure but also the state's first prison building boom. California added a dozen new "correctional facilities" between 1944 and 1966. California's postwar prisons complemented familiar labor discipline in diversified prison industries with recreation, education, counseling, and visits. Such reforms sought to restore prisoners to the life that white industrial workers led in suburbs like South Gate or Torrance.[8]

California's prison reformers thought of themselves as pioneers on a new frontier in the postwar welfare state: that of rehabilitation to work and citizenship through modern correctional science and statecraft. They were also heirs to a long tradition in penal reform that had been centered in eastern urban centers like Philadelphia and New York since the revolution. After World War II, however, the Golden State surpassed New York as the internationally recognized model for correctional reform. Industrialization, immigration, and urban growth had produced growing prison populations, and the various (mostly futile) progressive reform efforts had resulted in the era of "the big house" in mid-twentieth-century America marked by corrupt patronage, deep racial divides, and tight connections to the urban ethnic working class. The New Deal state had laid down new laws for the nation's prison administrations by banning most profitable forms of prison labor. The federal protection of workers' rights and restriction of states' abilities to exploit cheap convict labor united the nation's prison administrations in a sense of crisis, as they were not used to interventions by state governors, not to mention the federal government. While a wave of northern and midwestern prison riots in 1952 and 1953 gave ample testimony to the difficulties "big house" prisons in the industrial belt had with the transition from labor-based discipline to the carceral welfare state, both southern penal systems and California's new regime of therapeutic rehabilitation remained virtually untouched by the disorders.[9]

Surveys among corrections experts and workers in 1950 and 1964 confirmed that the Golden State had embarked on a path of penological reform radically different from that of the South and the Northeast. California's prison system was considered the best in the nation, while those of the South and Southwest stood at the bottom of the scale virtually en bloc.[10] Bold behavioral experiments in the Golden State actively encouraged prisoners to identify as a community and develop an awareness of the rights of citizenship. Housed "in pastel-colored cell blocks named Cyprus and Madrone," prisoners "were bombarded with sophisticated tests administered by young, congenial, 'college types'," recalled prisoner-turned-sociologist John Irwin. "During the rest of the day we played basketball, sat in the sun, worked out, or engaged in other recreation. . . . In this relatively agreeable environment, we became convinced that the staff . . . was going to make new people out of us." Indeed, after World War II, many Americans were inclined to imagine delinquents as "rebels without a cause" whose families had been torn apart during the war. Despite considerable anxiety about juvenile delinquency, a sense of kinship prevailed. In addition, professionals in public service had successfully managed other postwar—and wartime—challenges. There seemed to be no apparent reason why the rehabilitative capabilities of law enforcement and criminal justice had to be doubted.[11]

Ideological legacies of World War II and Cold War rivalries set new expectations among citizens for the role of the state but also raised hopes for recognition among prisoners. Legal imprisonment simply could not mean "the forfeiture of citizenship," concluded the U.S. Supreme Court when it declared in 1944 that "[a] prisoner retain[ed] all the rights of an ordinary citizen, except those expressly, or by necessary implication, taken from him by law." Its decision in *Coffin v. Reichard* for the first time opened the door for legal claims against prison administrations and signaled an end to the long-standing hands-off doctrine. Beginning in the 1950s, Black Muslims outside the South began to ground their litigation on this precedent. Their struggle for recognition as a religious organization with constitutional rights succeeded eventually, and their litigation in *Cooper v. Pate* (1964) ultimately caused the U.S. Supreme Court to permit prisoner litigation against state corrections officials.[12]

Just as important as these early legal victories, however, was the opposition to expanding civil rights to prisoners, which contradicted rehabilitative ambitions nowhere more glaringly than in California. While the prison administration advertised Chino's minimum security prison as a representative case of prison life in the state, tensions between the treatment model and the prisoner rights claims of black inmates were boiling under the surface. Guards successfully defended their right to discriminate openly against Muslims *In re Ferguson* (1961) on the grounds that their religious practice threatened institutional order.[13] Muslim prisoners responded with peaceful labor stoppages, demonstrating the discipline and resolve of a nascent black power movement.[14] A tightly organized community with a strict moral code, racial pride, and chauvinist ethos, Muslims challenged a rehabilitative program blind to the racial inequality between California's urban and suburban communities. California guards and prison investigators began to target Black Muslims and responded most suspiciously to any form of civil rights activism among prisoners, no matter how benign. While rumors about a Muslim assassination plot against Los Angeles Police Chief William Parker and a San Quentin guard heightened suspicions of the Nation of Islam as a terrorist organization in the spring of 1963, guards seemed to pose a much larger danger to Black Muslims. Just a week before the assassination plot came to light, a coroner's jury called the fatal shooting of prisoner Booker T. Johnson, a twenty-seven-year-old Louisiana native (A45941), by an unnamed officer from the balcony an "accident and misfortune." About 75 "well-dressed, well-disciplined" members of the Nation of Islam filled the courtroom for the coroner's inquest, "made no protest or any outward emotional signs, and did not leave "until dismissed by the person in charge."[15]

In August 1965, African American Angelenos in Watts were less patient with police violence. Black Californians from Oakland to Compton were fed up with police officers acting like occupying forces that prevented the realization of legal victories in the civil rights movement, just as guards from Folsom to Soledad blocked prisoner rights. African Americans who had come to Los Angeles during and after the war in hope of a future with different economic prospects found that the City of Angels, like other Sunbelt metropolises, showed little immunity to the trends in deindustrialization that marked the urban crises of the North.[16] Those who had hoped for better race relations saw in Proposition 14 evidence that, in fact, Jim Crow had followed them westward. As Daniel HoSang explains in this volume, this initiative passed with the votes of the white suburban majority and nullified the prohibition against racial discrimination that the Rumford Housing Act had introduced the year before. Martin Luther King and Bayard Rustin had been "completely nonplussed" by Police Chief Bill Parker's and L. A. Mayor Samuel Yorty's assertion that the proposition protected "not prejudice" but "personal choice." "While the rest of the North was passing civil rights laws and improving opportunities for Negroes," wrote a frustrated Bayard Rustin in the wake of the Watts Riots, "their own state and city were rushing to reinforce barriers against them."[17]

For white Californians, on the other hand, the Watts riots suggested that California had lost its place as a world apart from the racial urban conflicts that seemed to mark the gradual decline of the Northeast.[18] Suburban Californians had put a benign façade on the Sunbelt phenomenon only a few miles further south in Orange County's residential fantasy landscapes.[19] Redlining, blockbusting, and restrictive covenants had given this prosperity a racial exclusivity and a place apart from the urban center where African Americans stayed behind after white flight. The Rumford Housing Act had threatened that separation, and Californians had rejected it forcefully with the passage of Proposition 14. The cores of Sunbelt cities like Los Angeles were supposed to develop as different societies—"separate and unequal."[20] Just as prison riots in the later 1960s would make the true tensions between convicts and guards visible, so did the riots reveal the violence of racial inequality that Southern California had so long been able to whitewash.

The urban unrest also shattered an "ideological touchstone" of California's rehabilitative ideology—that there was a place to return to after prison—and it stimulated an increasing convergence of the discourses on the urban and the penal crisis. In their testimony before the McCone Commission charged with investigating the riots, urban sociologists and poverty experts formulated pathologies for the ghetto and its inhabitants strikingly similar to those ascribed to convicts and their prisons. Both places, in their estimations, suffered from lack of employment opportunities, overcrowding, poor health care, a severe lack of education, and particular dangers to family stability and for youth. And both prisoners and ghetto-dwellers were sexually deviant, poor, and corrupted by their state of dependency, and they brought violence on each other, formed gangs, remained hostile to law enforcement, and resistant to reform.[21] If the rehabilitation of the ghetto was failing, what hope was there for those taken captive in the same neighborhoods? Little, suggested gubernatorial candidate Ronald Reagan: "We must return to a belief in every individual being responsible for his conduct and his misdeeds with punishment immediate and certain. With all our science and sophistication . . . the jungle still is waiting to takeover. The man with the badge holds it back."[22]

White Californians who had understood their suburban homes as safe havens in residential gardens tended to agree with Reagan. Far quicker than experts to willfully conflate civil unrest with street crime, suburban and rural Californians deciphered media images of young black men rioting in distant cities as another threat to the principles of good citizenship.[23] Gone was the empathy with kids in trouble and working men fallen on hard times. Crime gained a different complexion. Some Californians came to look with envy at southern penal servitude. "Your legal system is obviously not killing the criminals it should kill, not locking up the revolutionaries who break all kinds of laws and then are released on bail," wrote an angry Californian. "I'm beginning to think, for the first time in a long life, that maybe the wrong side won the Civil War." In 1966, Reagan steamrolled incumbent Democrat Pat Brown with the campaign promise to wage a "war against the tax taker," winning all but three counties. California's legislature also turned "South" in the 1966 elections, since legislative reapportionment in the wake of the Warren court's "one man, one vote" decision in *Reynolds v. Sims* gave the more heavily populated Southern California new weight. The eight southern counties from Santa Barbara to San Diego held more Senate and State Assembly seats than the rest of the state combined. Put on the defensive, the Democratic Party struggled to gain ground on the law-and-order issue. By 1978, there was little choice for Reagan's successor Jerry Brown, son of the once venerated liberal Pat Brown, but to abolish California's indeterminate sentencing law, effectively closing the book on the state's commitment to correctional rehabilitation.[24]

White reactions to the Watts Riots also derailed federal efforts to incorporate a war on crime within the war on poverty. In its report *Crime in a Free Society*, the President's Commission on Law Enforcement and Administration of Justice still promised a reduction in "poverty, discrimination, ignorance, disease, and urban blight" instead of stricter enforcement and longer sentences. Both liberals and conservatives had believed that the newly created Law Enforcement Assistance Administration (LEAA) could "conquer crime as they had conquered space." The escalation of the riots in the 1960s, however, jeopardized the political legitimacy of rehabilitation for the urban poor as well as the delinquent. Liberties seemed to have turned into license. As welfare programs failed to solve the problems born out of segregation and industrial restructuring, law and order looked increasingly appealing. A 1968 Gallup Poll found that Americans saw crime and lawlessness as the single most pressing domestic problem. On the eve of the Democratic National Convention in 1968, another poll found, nearly

81 percent of Americans believed that law and order was in jeopardy. And most white voters looked at the city as the center of crime and disorder.[25]

President Lyndon Johnson's task force report, *Crime and Its Impact*, made the first step from the war on poverty to the war on crime when it interpreted the Watts riots as "a criminal sort" of social protest. "Thousands of acts of assault, or arson, of theft, of vandalism are what a riot is," it stated bluntly, adding that it could not be mere "coincidence that riots take place in just those neighborhoods where there is the greatest amount of everyday crime." Democratic presidential candidates in the 1968 race did not ignore this connection between urban crisis and the riots. But they disagreed on whether to respond with force or with aid. A candidate as liberal as Robert Kennedy thus rejected fellow contender Eugene McCarthy's suggestion that a mass transit system ought to connect the unemployed urban poor with suburban jobs as taking "ten thousand black people and move them into Orange County," something that certainly would have roused white suburban fears.[26] But it was Richard Nixon's demand for "freedom from fear" in 1968 that turned the urban crisis into a promise to white working- and middle-class suburbanites to protect them from criminal invasions and a preservation of the sanctity of neighborhood and home. During his administration, the LEAA budget grew fourteenfold. An experiment in new federalism, it strengthened state's particular law enforcement policies and played a crucial role in undermining the legitimacy of rehabilitative corrections.[27]

The growing number of disturbances in the nation's prisons in the late 1960s looked to many like an extension of the second wave of urban riots. In fact, prisoners themselves had compared the prison to a "City of Men," replete with the same problems they had known in their urban environments.[28] There were five prison riots in 1967; fifteen in 1968; twenty-seven in 1970; thirty-seven in 1971; and forty-eight in 1972. Two thousand Folsom prisoners in California shocked the state with a manifesto of demands and the formation of a prisoners' union. Reagan's director of corrections Raymond Procunier and his administrators explained the increase in prison violence in the late 1960s with a "new type of inmate": angry, young, black, and radical. Researchers for the California legislature found, however, that the type of person sent to prison had not changed significantly in the 1960s. It was the prison that politicized prisoners and motivated their protest and disobedience—just as the ghetto had stirred unrest in Watts and other cities, both in the North and in the Sunbelt.[29]

California's newly formed United Prisoners Union, for example, increasingly "took on the character of a civil rights advocacy organization for prisoners." At the same time, a number of legal decisions in the Sunbelt states of California, Arkansas, Texas, North Carolina, but also in Ohio, Pennsylvania, New Jersey, and New York, forced the courts to abandon judicial restraint and determine which rights were abridged by necessity in imprisonment and which were constitutional rights. They also forced on the state the question whether inmate workers were in a state of enslavement or whether they were public employees with the constitutional rights to free speech, assembly, and equal protection of the law on which unionization rested.[30]

In the legal contests of the 1970s, the prisoners' claim to the right of unionization quickly fell apart, along with the hope for other labor rights. Worse, the call for workers' rights among convicts invigorated the opposition of guards who forged a union in immediate opposition and shored up job security and benefits for union members who walked the state's "toughest beat." On the other hand, a series of victories for the prisoner rights movement over the indeterminate sentence had broad repercussions for the prison building boom in California, Texas, and other southern prison systems—fifteen years after the first calls for law and order. In response to the complaints of African American prisoners, the federal courts ordered an equitable application of the discretionary practice of indeterminate sentencing, the foundation of California's parole system since 1917. Instead, the state in one stroke abolished indeterminate sentencing entirely and relieved the Department of Corrections from the legal responsibility to rehabilitate. Celebrated by both prisoners and critics of California's failed rehabilitative system, the path for future mandatory minimum sentencing laws was now open.[31]

Federal courts demanded not just equitable justice but minimum standards in corrections as well. Overcrowding, thus, became not just an administrative challenge within prison walls; it also exposed states to litigation, federal oversight and receivership, and a cut in funding assistance. Thus, when Governor Jerry Brown's modest prison expansion plans became part of a fear-mongering campaign against drug crime and "street terrorism" under successor George Deukmejian, California found itself squeezed between punitive, penny-pinching taxpayers and prisoners and federal courts demanding appropriate prisons. The Golden State avoided the conflict between fiscal conservatism and an expansive carceral state with the use of special lease-revenue bonds that did not require voters' approval. By the end of the 1980s, California's debt for prison construction had expanded from $763 million to $4.9 billion.[32]

Prison Modernization in the South: The Convergence of a Carceral Sunbelt

In the 1970s, the South, too, reaped what California's prison activists and conservative suburbanites had sowed. Court-ordered reform became a hallmark of the South's late modern prison systems. On behalf of prisoner rights activists, the courts began to order the comprehensive reformation from southern penal servitude to modern standards of corrections. Until then Texas had shielded off most reform pressures from prison experts and had prided itself on plantation farms, chain gangs, and minimum expenditures on criminal justice at a time when states like New York and California spent five times as much on each prisoner for a rehabilitative program that produced unionization efforts and riots.[33]

Texas and five other southern states ultimately had to face prisoner rights litigants in federal courts, however, where they found the legitimacy of their penal state disassembled. The case of *Ruiz v. Estelle* identified overcrowding as a serious violation of prisoners' basic human rights to body and mind.[34] In response, the state of Texas launched a prison-building program even larger than in California. Within five years, Texas expanded its prison system from 18 to 27 and legally committed itself to a maximum occupancy rate of 95 percent. By ordering more official control over prisoners and an abolition of the old con-boss system, federal courts on behalf of imprisoned litigants pushed Texas from the punitive practices of a southern institution straight to the practice of modern mass incarceration. Federal pressure for reform also affected other southern states, including New Mexico which had only organized into a modern Department of Corrections in 1970 and which was the site of the deadliest prison riot in American history.[35]

Court-ordered improvement of correctional standards in the South and California is one side of the story of carceral expansion since the 1970s. The other one is the dramatic increase in imprisonment over the remainder of the century, a trend only loosely related to a growing crime rate but thoroughly tied to political activism for tougher sentencing measures. Following

Reagan's charge in the war against the street drugs of the poor, state lawmakers identified law-and-order initiatives and sentencing enhancements as a winning ticket, especially with the white conservative electorate of the Sunbelt. In California, this meant that, between 1977 and 1990, the share of drug offenders in the system increased from 10 percent to 34.2 percent.[36]

Sunbelt suburbanites emerged as key policy initiators in a new politics of fear, preferring "broad and extreme penal measures rather than individualized penalty decisions." The popular revolt of white suburbanites against property taxes and the welfare state also included popular "tough on crime" initiatives, often receiving the rubber stamp approval of legislatures without consideration for feasibility or cost. Stripped of their legitimacy, the experts that had accompanied the penal-welfare framework since World War II had little chance of holding up populist legislation such as California's Three Strikes Law. Public media campaigns for anti-crime measures have benefited from the abstract nature of the law-and-order discourse, allowing powerful symbols of racial and gendered threats (the gang member) and sexual dangers to family (the menacing child predator) to fill the conceptual void of abstract categories like "violent crime."[37]

Campaigns for law and order bank on the fact that voters almost never identify themselves, a friend, or a relative as a possible suspect. As was the case in the bussing and housing controversies of the Sunbelt, the fear of crime and the quest for a more punitive state rested on a profound sense of victimization and a strong identification with home, property, and family. It did not matter that the increase in the victimization of white suburbanites was bound to be less pronounced than that of black Americans who were still five times as likely as whites to be murdered and four times as likely to get robbed. Taking their cues from the rights struggles of the truly disenfranchised who learned to empower themselves, victims' rights groups have joined forces with guards unions and corporate sponsors to exercise political pressure on behalf of longer sentences. The intense discourse about crime and danger in press and television strongly casts suburban families as victims of spilled-over urban violence.[38]

The national increase in crime from the late 1960s through the 1980s certainly did not leave middle-class suburbs untouched. Recreational drug use, domestic conflict, and widespread gun ownership resulted in an increase in property crimes and violence even in sheltered enclaves. It appears, however, that suburbanites responded more to an increasing "ontological insecurity" as their ever more precarious lifestyles required intense management of time and resources—leaving them with a constant sense of vulnerability—and less to their increasing exposure to crime in the 1970s and 1980s. The militarization of urban spaces and the defensive enclosure of suburban communities are well documented. Gated communities, private security services, hi-tech alarm systems, closed circuit television cameras, and other private safety technologies have mostly provided "a sense of safety." In fact, the same could be said about mass incarceration. Placed in the context of Sunbelt suburbanites' sense of victimization in interracial housing, busing, and affirmative action, it appears they were less often victims of crime and more frequently disgruntled with the expanding state and the attention it paid to the welfare and civil rights of the discriminated and underprivileged. Urban communities, on the other hand, were most hard hit by gang warfare and an underground drug economy. Leading politicians from crime-stricken communities like Maxine Waters from Los Angeles saw no other recourse than to join in the call for tougher sentencing measures, which by the 1990s had become as popular a political agenda as tax cuts.[39]

Where the Lockdown Takes Place

The formulation of a more severe practice of punishment did not happen only in the Sunbelt's state legislatures, its press and television, and the home but in actual prisons. It was not enough for Sunbelt Americans to want "something done" about crime. Punishment also had to take place somewhere, literally. States have typically found it difficult to locate suitable sites with cooperative neighbors but have rarely imposed their will on local communities through eminent domain. In the 1960s, however, California communities began to court the state for prisons. Since then, the growing corrections industry has compared itself to another rural economic booster of special importance to the Sunbelt: "Prisons are like military bases," its advocates like to claim. In this logic, imprisonment might be considered a recession-proof service profession, offering steady sources of income and employment, no pollution, and no threat of downsizing. These statements are as misleading and unreliable for prisons as for military installations. Nonetheless, faith in such economic benefits encouraged hundreds of rural communities across the country, particularly in the Sunbelt superstates of

California, Texas, Florida, North Carolina, Georgia, and Colorado, to deputize themselves in the war against crime.[40]

The methods for determining prison sites vary from state to state. In North Carolina, the state has been inviting rural counties to apply for prison locations. Interested communities began to offer economic incentives, such as tax breaks, infrastructure support, and free land. In some cases, communities even build prisons on their own account. What virtually all host counties share, however, is a surplus in cheap land, a surplus in labor, and a lack of alternative economic growth centers such as manufacturing establishments, telemarketing, reservation, or online and catalog sales centers, or casinos and other recreational and resort facilities. Left behind in the postindustrial information economy much like the urban poor, a marginal labor force in the rural fringe earns its keep in custody. "More than a Wal-Mart or a meat-packing plant, state, federal and private prisons, typically housing 1,000 inmates and providing 300 jobs, can put a town on a solid economic footing," suggested Calvin L. Beale, senior demographer at the Economic Research Service of the U.S. Department of Agriculture. Under those circumstances, it is not surprising that unionization efforts among prison guards face stiff opposition. With the exception of the powerful California Correctional Peace Officers Association (CCPOA), prison guards experienced the same lack of labor organization as the rest of the Sunbelt labor force.[41]

Local communities hope for steady jobs and the revenue government payrolls bring to local businesses and real estate; and since prisoners are counted in the census, they can count on an increase in per capita distribution of state funds for services prisoners don't have access to. Beale noted that "communities become increasingly adept at maximizing their windfall through collecting taxes and healthy public service fees." And indeed, by 1998, more than fifty nonmetropolitan counties had rebounded from population losses in the 1980s thanks to prison construction. The actual benefits these communities received were mixed at best, however, both because the economic boom anticipated with supply contracts, new payrolls, and new residents did not happen—staff too often moved their families far away from the host community—and because communities suffered unexpected disadvantages (consider the declining appeal of the host community's residential areas, for example). Prisons seem to have improved local economies in persistently poor rural counties, which are overwhelmingly located on the edge of the Sunbelt region in the Deep South; the Indian

Reservations of New Mexico, Arizona, and Nevada; and the Appalachians in Kentucky and West Virginia. More often, however, prisons seem to have blocked other economic development opportunities. Despite our attention to the prosperity and inequality of metropolitan regions, then, poor counties are an important part of the political dynamic of the "lockdown" Sunbelt.[42]

Isolation from family and community has, of course, been a persistent part of carceral punishment throughout the history of prisons. And with the exception of the plantation South, prisons had historically removed convicts from their urban neighborhoods to places far enough "up the river" from the city so as not to raise safety concerns but still close enough to maintain political control over the institution and discourage open rebellion. The locations of California's San Quentin and Folsom, New York's Sing Sing, and Illinois's Stateville prisons are just a few examples. Prisons were both from the city and of the city, tightly linked to metropolitan might and city-centered politics rather than a placeless and amorphous state. The prison construction boom of the past twenty-five years has produced a distinct carceral geography, however, that is noticeable across the nation and most pronounced in the Sunbelt.[43]

Isolation seemed to be the very purpose of the recent concentration of penal populations in rural counties. At the very least, it has meant the deliberate and purposeful abandonment of any rehabilitative intent. The importance of family for the success of the treatment model of punishment after World War II was clear to experts. They specifically raised objections against the severe isolation prisoners and families experienced in the emerging system of satellite prisons. "Real hardships [were] going to be imposed upon the inmates' families in the urban centers," warned staff member John Conrad at the height of California's rehabilitative regime, and he predicted that prisoners would resist transfer or cause disciplinary problems in other ways. Just ten years later, in their investigation of a black prisoner strike in rural Susanville in 1972, both the NAACP and the *Sacramento Bee* identified rural isolation as the main cause for the prisoners' unrest. Similarly, sociologist Daniel Glaser blamed the spreading prison riots at the same time on prison locations in rural areas that required the employment of guards unable to relate to inmates from urban areas.[44]

Between 1985 and 1995, over half of all new prisons opened in nonmetropolitan counties. In 2000, Texas and Florida had counties with prisoner population shares of 30 percent or more; 10 of 13 counties with prisoner population shares of 20 percent, 38 of 47 counties with at least 10 percent of their population imprisoned, and 80 of 114 counties with prisoner populations of 5 percent were in the Sunbelt. Lassen County in northeastern California resembles a virtual penal colony almost completely occupied with prisoners from the Los Angeles area. Since the county has bolstered its economy with three state prisons and one federal facility, almost 30 percent of its population—and 90 percent of the county's black population—are prisoners. This is more than just a curious disproportion since prisoners count in the place of imprisonment. What Los Angeles lost, for instance, Kern, San Bernardino, and Lassen Counties have gained in census-based funding streams and political representation.[45]

Next to distant rural concentration, a new and seemingly contradictory trend has emerged in the nation's carceral geography, however. Since the 1990s, more and more prisons appear not in rural but in metropolitan counties. In fact, the rate of growth for rural prisons is declining. The five counties with the largest growth in prisons between 1990 and 2000—Los Angeles County, Miami Dade County, Fremont County in Colorado, and Coyrell and Jefferson Counties in Texas—were all metropolitan. In the wake of the Sunbelt conversion of surplus land, labor, and capital into a prison industrial complex, state governments may be recognizing new marginal lands not in the rural fringes with potential for suburban expansion, but in urban regions.[46]

In addition, a growing number of prisons originally built in rural settings are now squarely within larger metropolitan regions. In the 1940s, California's San Bernardino County was half cattle country, half desert, sprinkled with a few hamlets and small towns dependent on the dairy industry. When the state's Board of Prison directors decided to build Southern California's first prison here in the 1930s, in Chino, it envisioned a variety of agricultural occupations for rural prisoners. And when the new Department of Corrections moved its women's prison from the then still remote high desert town of Tehachapi to Corona in 1954, few people would have considered the new location metropolitan; prisoners and their families certainly did not. Even in 1963, when the department decided to add the state's first prison specifically for drug offenders near Norco, the county still counted as rural. The region that has now merged with Riverside County to form the so-called inland empire remains the nation's largest center for dairy production. But the suburban bedroom communities of middle-and lower-income service workers of the Los Angeles basin have since covered the ground all the way to San Bernardino.[47]

It appears that at least two sterile and marginally productive "second circuits of capital" revolve around Sunbelt metropolitan regions—those of suburban housing developments and those of the prison industrial complex. The suburban and carceral belts of sprawling metropolitan areas begin to rub against each other elsewhere in the Sunbelt, too. In the Denver suburb of Lakewood, surrounding residential development and the proximity of a large shopping mall across from it forced the Colorado Department of Corrections to reduce its operation at its Camp George West. Denver's Reception and Guidance Center, the system's entry prison, lies on the city's eastside between commercial districts and suburban tracts. Prisoners in the high desert town of Lancaster, north of Los Angeles, can see the new tract housing of Providence Ranch across the street from the perimeter fence.

Further north in the Golden State, snail-shaped suburban clusters of cul-de-sacs move all the way up to Vacaville Medical Facility. What had been factories in the fields in the days of Carey McWilliams have become suburban satellites, as more than one million people moved to the Central Valley, transforming rural into metropolitan counties.[48] Here, new developments are not quite as close to the sprawling state prison complex, but close enough. That is at least how the Department of Corrections advertises the master-planned housing developments it constructed in Clovis and Lemoore with Silver Oak Communities, "a distinguished new home builder with a reputation for providing exquisite European style architecture." Within thirty minutes, residents of Davante Villas can reach prisons in Pleasant Valley, Coalinga, Avenal, and Corcoran. Another five prisons in Chowchilla, Delano, and Wasco are a one-hour drive through California's agricultural heartland, in which all counties now count as metropolitan. Thus, even if suburbs do not spread toward and around the prisons, suburban architecture and lifestyle will come to the prisons—through state-subsidized housing producers.

The irony of this development lies not merely in the fact that the race to the suburbs has overtaken the race to incarcerate, producing suburban fantasy-scapes in the shadows of the largest prison complex in history. The construction boom and housing bubble of the early 2000s has also increasingly lured low-income families and increasingly Latinos and African Americans to the more marginal suburban properties that first fell victim to the 2007 mortgage crisis and economic downturn. And that is not the final irony of the overlapping developments of Sunbelt suburbanization and neoconservative fight against crime. As prison complexes and suburban communities threaten to compete over the same landscape on the urban-rural fringe, suburbanites of the South and Southwest also seem to have failed at their original mission—fighting crime. Although low density, car-dependency, and de facto segregation of Sunbelt cities have fed their reputation for relative safety, higher-density Frostbelt cities are not more crime-ridden. And, what is even more relevant for advocates of Sunbelt cityscapes, the very city that has made "isolation and suburban privacy" its mission statement is also the one with the most dangerous suburbs. The six most dangerous suburbs are all in Sunbelt metropolitan areas, followed by seven metropolitan regions outside the region.[49]

How Tight Is the Sunbelt?

Like any other historical region, the Sunbelt contains a large degree of diversity and at the same time shows many similarities with other neighboring regions. Distinctions that may be pronounced in the historical record may appear as gradual differences at best in the broader quantitative picture. Clearly defining the Sunbelt also offers a challenge. Those caveats aside, there are several ways to gauge the extent and intensity of punishment.[50]

Carceral capacities of both North and Sunbelt show a shared national trend, but a reversal of the roles of North and Sunbelt. The low number of prisons in the early twentieth century in the South indicates the prevalence of the convict lease system. By the beginning of World War II, Sunbelt prisons still offered only two-thirds of the space of northern prisons. Starting in World War II, Sunbelt prisons began closing the gap, and after 1980 the Sunbelt began its ascent as the region with the highest number of prisons. At the end of that decade, Sunbelt prisons housed roughly 170,000 prisoners more than the North—more than the entire prison system of California or Texas. Looking at the number of incarcerated prisoners rather than capacity, the growth of prison populations in the rest of the nation closely matched that of the Sunbelt until as recently as 1993. While California's prison population has grown steeply and surprisingly steadily since about 1980, Texas lagged behind the growth of prisons nationwide until

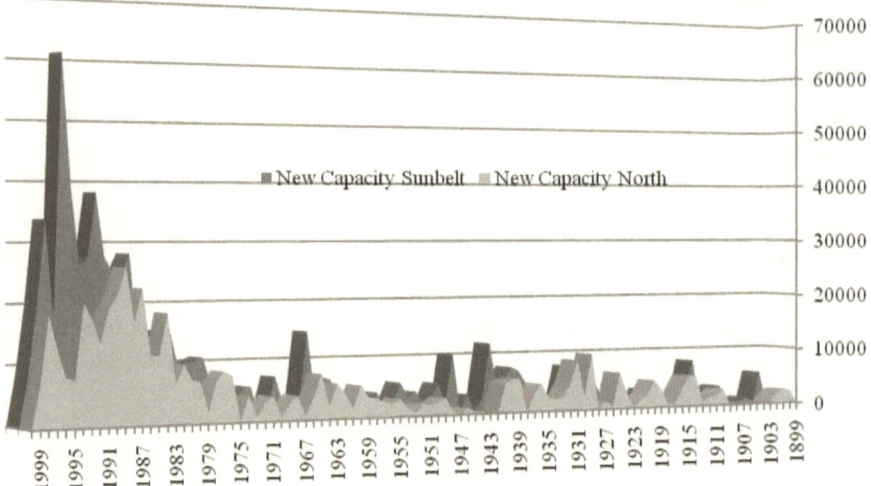

Figure 8.1. New carceral capacity, Sunbelt and North 1900–2000.

about 1990. To avoid measuring only the obvious growth of a state institution that comes with the region's demographic growth, we look at incarceration rates. The Sunbelt stands out clearly in this picture, and a comparison of the lowest and highest trend in incarceration rates further cements the distinction of the Sunbelt. In 2006, eight of the ten states with the highest rates of incarceration were in the Sunbelt, imprisoning between 509 and 883 of every 100,000 residents. Only one Sunbelt state—Utah—ranked among the states with the lowest rates of incarceration.

Further differences between the prisons of the Sunbelt and the rest of the nation support the claim that the South and Southwest turned more punitive since the 1960s. Large prisons of 1,000 inmates or more, which tend to imprison at higher security levels, are more widespread in the Sunbelt than the North. In 1928, the American Prison Association warned that no prison should house more than 1,200 inmates. By 1970, 45 prisons in the United States were larger than that. But the "vastly overcrowded" super-max prisons of the early 1970s look tame compared to the enormous dungeons that would emerge in the thirty years since. Of those, the majority would emerge in the South and West. Today over 58 percent of those types of prisons, and more than 63 percent of inmates in those institutions are in the Sunbelt. Of

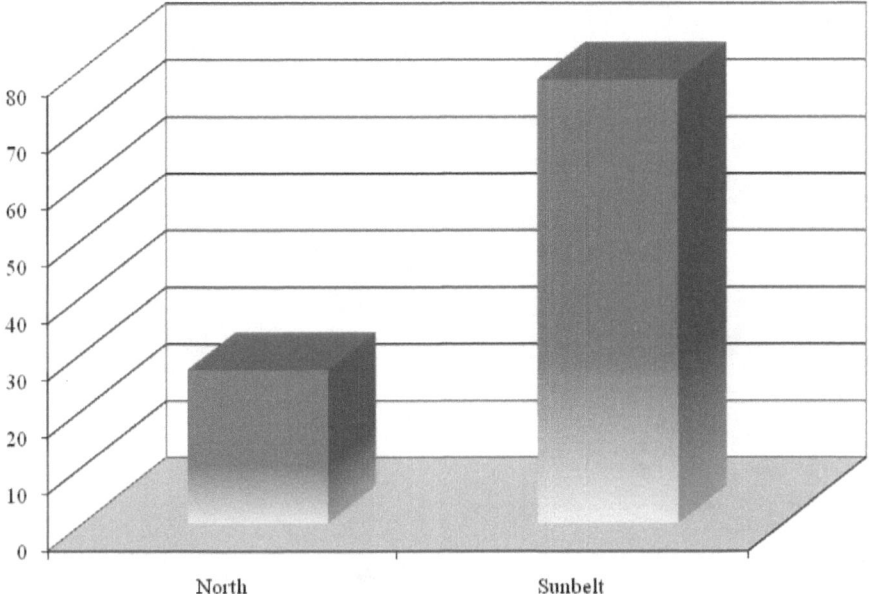

Figure 8.2. Super-max prisons (2000 plus), Sunbelt and North.

super-max prisons with 2,000 inmates or more, 78 out of 105 such facilities stand in the Sunbelt, with more than four times the population.[51]

The prevalence of private prisons in the Sunbelt has been a result of the fiscally conservative free market ideology and relative weakness of unions in the Sunbelt. By the year 2000, the Sunbelt hosted 189 private prisons with a total population of almost 78,000 prisoners. In the North, less than half the number of private prisons (73) house less than a quarter of their Sunbelt counterparts (15,600). One of the most important and easily identifiable indicators for a punitive state is the number of death sentences it metes out and executions it performs. With the exception of Pennsylvania, the Sunbelt has shown itself solidly more punitive than the rest of the country, with California leading the way in condemning convicts to death between 1974 and 2005. Sunbelt states condemn more often, and they also follow up with executions. Here, however, the Sunbelt contains significant discrepancies. Whereas Texas alone executed 139 people in the first five years of this century, the entire southwest region killed only nine.

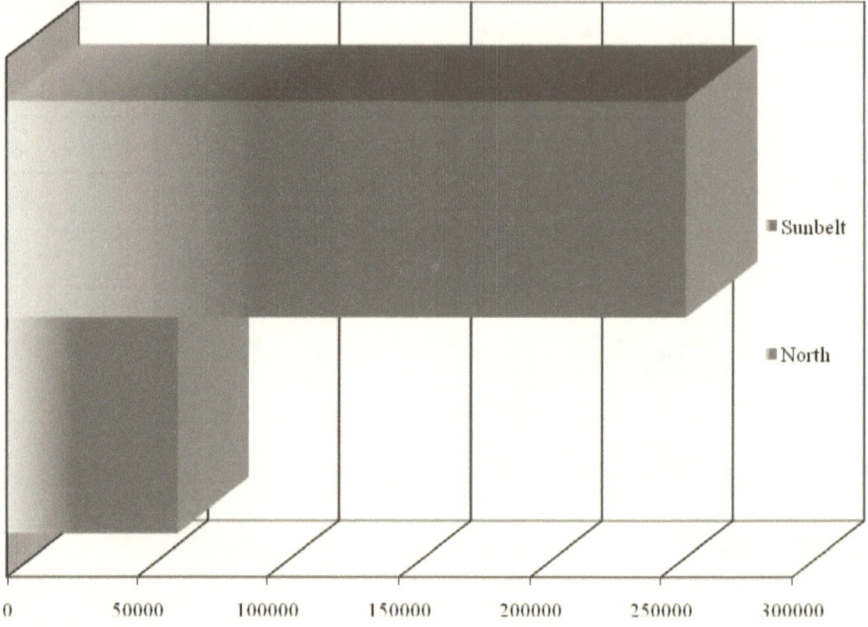

Figure 8.3. Prisoners in private facilities, Sunbelt and North.

The punitive nature and carceral geography of the Sunbelt, thus, suggests a leading role for the region in what David Garland has termed "punitive segregation," a disruptive practice with devastating social and political consequences.[52] The war of suburbanites on crime, and especially on drugs, has wrought casualties on urban communities and families that still demand further study but that most certainly include severed parent-child relationships, lowered reemployment prospects, weak holds on property, and restricted access to health care and welfare programs. At the same time, incarceration has politically empowered rural/suburban host communities and counties. Thus, while Los Angeles provides roughly a third of California's prison population, it has long been host to only about 3 percent of the state's prisoners. In contrast, Kings County in the Central Valley counts only .33 percent of the Golden State's free population but 12 percent of its convicts. Counted at their site of imprisonment rather than their last home address, prisoners enlarge that small county presence in the census from 112,000 to almost 130,000. Census figures determine the shape of legislative districts and affect political representation, but they also determine claims on a variety of state and federal funding sources.[53]

The political repercussions of mass incarceration carry further still. In this volume, Shana Bernstein alerts us to the diversity of the civil rights movement within the Sunbelt. She and other scholars have rightly drawn attention to the democratizing effects of civil rights activists not only in the Deep South but the Southwest as well. While not the only measure of civil rights, the right to vote certainly constitutes an important way of measuring the "progressive" nature of the Sunbelt. The advances in prisoners' rights have also been the product of activists' litigation efforts in California and the South. At the same time that civil rights movements could chart significant successes in expanding the franchise across the Sunbelt, however, a growing number of Americans have been losing their vote through incarceration and felony convictions.

Today, mass imprisonment has become the chief reason for the disenfranchisement of Americans. The practice of incarceration and parole has overtaken any progress civil-rights changes made to felony voting laws in the 1960s and 1970s. While some midwestern states feature some of the most dramatic disfranchisement rates for African Americans, the Sunbelt still remains the strongest bulwark in political exclusion. The significance of this is not purely academic. If ex-felons had been allowed to cast their votes in the presidential elections of 2000, Jeff Manza has calculated, the Democratic Party would have carried Florida with a margin of 31,003 votes. Instead, the Republican Party won the state with a slim, and famously disputed, margin of 537. One would be hard pressed to find a more dramatic expression of the powerful impact of the Sunbelt's mass incarceration politics than George W. Bush's ascendancy to the presidency.[54]

Chapter 9

Sunbelt Imperialism: Boosters, Navajos, and Energy Development in the Metropolitan Southwest

Andrew Needham

What is the Sunbelt? Is it a region or a type of metropolitan development? Neither answer seems satisfying. Spreading from northern Virginia to an indefinite terminus in California, the Sunbelt does not possess the levels of cultural identity or cohesion we have come to expect from the traditional "regions" in American history: the South or West. As Lyman Kellstedt and James Guth's essay in this volume illustrates, even political arguments for regional cohesion frequently crumble on examination. The metropolitan answer is more seductive. Taken together, essays in this volume show that Los Angeles, Miami, and Atlanta experienced similar processes of urban growth, suggesting that we should understand "Sunbelt" as a shared ideology and process of metropolitan growth. The benefits of this approach lie in understanding metropolitan growth within broader patterns of political economy. In largely ignoring region, however, these metropolitan histories miss key elements of Sunbelt growth that reached beyond metropolitan borders. From the 1930s forward, Sunbelt strategies of growth produced new demand for water and energy resources located on federally controlled lands, demand met through new production located on resource-rich spaces far from metropolitan borders. In the Southwest, this production occurred largely on Native American lands, especially the Navajo Reservation, while consumption took place in rapidly growing metropolitan areas hundreds of miles away in Phoenix, Los Angeles, and Albuquerque.

The creation of the Navajo Reservation as the Southwest's energy hinterland was not simply an economic process connecting production and consumption. It was fundamentally a political project in which metropolitan representatives claimed authority over distant lands and resources. Throughout the postwar years, Sunbelt cities became imperial entities; their demand for natural resources created far-flung, overlapping empires that connected rapidly growing metropolitan regions with hinterland resources. In the process, new regions took shape, tied together by aqueducts, power lines, and highways. Metropolitan growth and regional development in the Sunbelt depended on the increasing connection of metropolis to hinterland and the expropriation of hinterland resources for the benefit of metropolitan capital and consumers.

Understanding these connections requires broadening our understanding of the politics of Sunbelt boosters. Boosters have been vital actors in Sunbelt histories. Indeed, a central narrative of Sunbelt history focuses on the efforts of booster-led growth machines—Chambers of Commerce, real estate and commercial developers, newspapers, and local electrical utilities—to control local government and to use the local state to attract capital.[1] Indeed, such a narrative explains much about Phoenix's growth. Dominating local politics between 1949 and 1975, Phoenix's Chamber of Commerce transformed local policies to lure industries and promote growth: reducing taxes on business and manufacturing, passing laws that hamstrung union organizing, and offering land grants and issuing industrial development bonds to support prospective businesses. Boosters' control of the local state, however, explains only so much about the breadth of the growth machine's project. American government is organized into a series of overlapping scales—ward, city, state, federal—with each level confining its authority within spatially defined boundaries and offering particular levels of power over that space.[2] Concentrated only at the municipal level, boosters faced significant "city limits" in their pursuit of growth. Local authority could alter zoning laws and reduce local taxes; however, local governments provided little claim on energy resources located on federally controlled land that boosters desired to power their growth machine.[3]

In order to bring these resources to their cities, boosters worked to implement policies at the varying levels of the America polity, reshaping the policies governing natural resources as a central part of the political project of Sunbelt growth.

This essay explores the journey of three prominent boosters from Phoenix to Washington, examining how their activities as legislators and bureaucrats brought ideas about growth and government forged in metropolitan politics into federal policy-making. In November 1952, Barry Goldwater, Phoenix city councilman, was elected Arizona's junior senator. In December 1952, Orme Lewis, a corporate attorney and former head of the Arizona Republican Party, was appointed assistant secretary of the interior for Public Lands. Shortly after taking office, Lewis appointed Walter Bimson, president of Valley National Bank, to head a commission investigating the possible reorganization of the Bureau of Indian Affairs. Examining the actions of Goldwater, Lewis, and Bimson reveals how Sunbelt actors reshaped the American state even as existing federal policies produced Sunbelt growth. As numerous studies have shown, federal mortgage underwriting, transportation funding, and military spending created the structural conditions that led to the Sunbelt's rise.[4] Even as new subdivisions, highways, and industrial parks boomed in Phoenix, however, its boosters inserted their beliefs about economic growth into federal policy.

While advocates of "free enterprise," Phoenix's boosters were far from libertarian. Their experience recruiting industry to Phoenix led them to understand government action as central to economic growth, which emerged, in their eyes, from policies that created a healthy "business climate." They paired support for low taxes on business and barriers to union organizing with opposition to public entities that competed with private enterprise. Believing the growth of private enterprise brought broad public benefits in the form of jobs, population growth, and increased tax revenue, these boosters put the local state at the service of capital, spawning, as scholars have recently argued, a new neoliberal political economy in the Sunbelt.[5] Such views were not contained in the local state, however. With their influence in the Eisenhower Interior Department, Phoenix's boosters attempted to reorient natural resource policy around the demands of metropolitan growth.

These demands represented a dagger aimed at the heart of New Deal natural resource policy. New Deal agencies such as the Rural Electrification

Administration and the Tennessee Valley Authority (TVA) aimed to introduce public competition into electrical supply and generation, providing electricity to underserved populations. New "preference policies" governed dams built by the Bureau of Reclamation, giving publicly owned entities first claim on power generated at federally controlled facilities. This New Deal support for the public control of resources was not limited to electrification. The Indian Renewal Act (IRA) reversed the Dawes Act policy of privatizing Indian land holdings. In its place, the IRA empowered tribal governments to control lands under the trusteeship of the secretary of the interior, thus rejecting the incorporation of Indian lands into local economies. In short, New Deal resource policy aimed to develop hinterland communities through increasingly close relations with federal agencies, protecting them from the abuses that private development had often created.[6]

Southwestern boosters offered a much different view of hinterland resource development. In the eyes of Southwestern boosters, New Deal policies threatened to lock the private sector out of access to valuable resources while introducing "socialistic" competition that threatened metropolitan growth and private enterprise. On entering the federal bureaucracy, Lewis and Bimson championed "land freedom," a U.S. Chamber of Commerce-led project focused on opening the public domain to private development. Challenging the New Deal's equation of public ownership with the public good, "land freedom" made the claim that private development brought broad public benefit in the form of metropolitan economic growth. Public resource management, in their account, isolated the public domain from its potential beneficiaries, leaving it under the control of bureaucrats in far off Washington who knew little of local needs. Private development, by contrast, would allow resources to be put to beneficial use in metropolitan areas.

Phoenix's boosters aimed to transform Indian policy along much the same lines. Claiming that Bureau of Indian Affairs (BIA) paternalism represented the cause of Indian underdevelopment, Lewis, Bimson, and other boosters posed the Sunbelt metropolitan economy as the cure. In their eyes, the metropolitan Sunbelt's unfettered private enterprise could both free Indians from dependency and utilize reservation resources for the mutual benefit of Indians and metropolitan consumers alike. The most extensive development efforts focused on the energy resources of the Navajo and Hopi reservations. For boosters, such developments seemed to offer broad mutual benefit, bringing low-cost power to the metropolitan Sunbelt while providing jobs and revenue to the tribes. Indeed, shortly after taking office, Barry Goldwater wrote to Arizona's governor, Howard Pyle, "One of your first and most important measures should be to unlock the natural resources known to exist on the reservations. . . . In mineral wealth alone there is enough in reserve within the reservation boundaries to make our so-called Indian problems simple enough."[7]

The interest of boosters like Lewis, Goldwater, and Bimson in the development of Indian resources thus points to little recognized connections between metropolitan growth and the Indian policy known as termination, which aimed to eliminate tribal jurisdiction and bring Indian lands into the market. Indeed, during his term as assistant secretary of the interior, Orme Lewis was responsible for preparing and presenting termination bills to Congress.[8] While presented as a means to assimilation, the ideas underlying termination were paternalist in their own right. Southwestern boosters argued for the right to control land use and resource development on Indian lands, especially the Navajo Reservation. In much the same way that segregationist politicians claimed to understand the best interests of African-Americans while bolstering their own power, Phoenix's metropolitan boosters portrayed the best interest of Navajos as the incorporation of their land and labor into the metropolitan economy even as Navajo resources allowed metropolitan growth to continue apace. Examining these developments sheds new light on the long-term effects of the termination era. Recent histories of termination have concluded with the rise of "Red Power" and tribal resurgence, painting a broadly positive political narrative in which termination mobilized Indian people to protect their rights.[9] Emphasizing the material changes in Indian lands that accompanied termination, this article contends that termination's effects continued to structure both the political economy of energy in the Southwest and Indian lives long after the federal renunciation of termination in the mid-1960s.

The energy development that resulted from policy changes initiated by Lewis and Bimson created a new map of the Southwest, a map in which Phoenix, Los Angeles, and Albuquerque drew much of their power from Navajo lands while the negative externalities of metropolitan energy production—nitrous oxide, fly ash, and mercury emissions—were exported to Indian lands. The connections of the Navajo Nation to the metropolitan economy, then, were profoundly unequal. These unequal connections, however, suggest an answer to the lingering question of the Sunbelt's status.

If we think of the Sunbelt both as an ideology of growth and as a number of emerging places, a compelling dialectic emerges. As the Sunbelt's logic of growth began to hold greater and greater sway within the federal state, the South and West were spatially transformed. As the demands of metropolitan industry and consumers for resource supplies became vital federal interests, new material connections grew between cities and hinterlands, eventually tying multiple cities to resource-rich public lands. In these connections, a number of regional Sunbelts emerged, in which hinterland residents increasingly saw nearby resources transported to satisfy distant demand. It is to one of these networks of land, resources, and politics we now turn.

The Growth of Phoenix and the Search for Power

Born in Phoenix in 1902, Orme Lewis grew up swimming in the canals of what was a small agricultural town. The son of a local lawyer who represented some of the state's largest cattle ranchers, Lewis was raised among Phoenix's elite. Lewis followed in his father's footsteps, and by the late 1930s, his clients included the three largest ranchers in Arizona, as well as many large farms. His practice reflected the state's economic base—the "three Cs" of cotton, cattle, and copper. By the late 1940s, however, Lewis's practice began changing as he courted the manufacturers and real estate developers flocking to the desert Southwest from World War II onward. In 1950, he founded a new firm with his friend Paul Roca, aiming to establish "modern corporate representation" in a town dominated by small practices. Lewis and Roca quickly grew into one of the state's largest and most influential firms, the local representative of Honeywell, Sperry Rand, and Northrup Grummond, as well as the plaintiff's counsel for Arizona in the state's long-lasting litigation with California over the distribution of Colorado River water.[10]

The transition of Lewis's clients from farmers and ranchers to military contractors charted the broader course of Phoenix's economy. In 1940, manufacturing generated less than $5 million in Phoenix. The city's major manufacturers included canneries and broom factories.[11] The heart of Phoenix's economy lay in agricultural supply and in winter tourism. By 1960, manufacturing income had risen to $600 million and had surpassed tourism as the city's industry. In addition to the firms Lewis represented,

Phoenix was home to branch plants for Goodyear Aviation, Alcoa, Motorola, and numerous smaller suppliers. In those same years, the city's population rose from sixty-five thousand to over four hundred thousand residents.[12] These changes were not merely the result of broad structural forces, such as the rise of a military-industrial complex, the widespread use of air-conditioning, or a cultural preference for spacious western cities. Phoenix's transformation was also the result of a deliberate campaign by local businessmen to create political conditions that would attract and benefit manufacturers disenchanted by the New Deal state.

In the immediate postwar era, Phoenix's business elites consolidated control of local politics. They relied on structural reforms that limited or discouraged participation in local politics to insulate Chamber of Commerce-approved candidates from local opponents of growth, aggressively annexed peripheral areas, and pursued steady reductions in property taxes to ensure political support throughout the city. These structural changes were so successful that no candidate won election to Phoenix's City Council between 1949 and 1975 without the backing of the Chamber.[13] The Chamber used its control over municipal politics to direct the region's economic expansion, combining tax cuts on manufacturing and the nation's strongest "right to work" law with an aggressive recruitment campaign aimed at the branch plants of major defense contractors.[14] In this process, Phoenix's boosters, along with other Sunbelt advocates, developed ideas about economic growth that were strikingly different from the ideas that governed federal policy in the postwar years.

Scholars have used "growth liberalism" to describe a broad set of postwar federal economic policies meant to spur aggregate demand. Connecting a number of programs emerging from New Deal and postwar federal policy—social security, unemployment insurance, mortgage underwriting, and military spending—"growth liberalism" entailed a broad federal commitment to both Keynesian fiscal policy and public subsidies within private markets. In the minds of its advocates, growth liberalism simultaneously created economic prosperity and alleviated inequality.[15] And Phoenix would not have grown nearly as rapidly or extensively as it did without money from the Pentagon, the Federal Housing Authority, the Federal Highway Administration, or Social Security.

At the same time, metropolitan boosters, primarily in the Sunbelt, developed an alternate philosophy of growth grounded in metropolitan competition for capital and industry. At the center of this philosophy was use of state power over taxation, land use, and labor laws as recruitment tools to attract and benefit capital. These metropolitan growth politics existed within and relied upon growth liberalism's Keynesian policies. Metropolitan growth politics, however, operated with radically different goals in mind. Where growth liberalism sought to use economic demand-driven growth to create broad middle-class consumption and affluence, metropolitan growth politics envisioned economic development as inherently uneven. Regions grew or declined, in boosters' eyes, not because of national policy, but because of local attempts to generate economic activity. Where growth liberalism measured success nationally through broad measures such as GNP and GDP, the success of metropolitan growth politics could be measured by the attraction of new companies, demographic growth, and the spatial expansion of the metropolis. Seeking to attract increasingly mobile capital to fuel regional economies, metropolitan growth policies met capital's demands for less regulation, lower taxes, and limits on workers' rights. Actively using the local state to meet the demands of capital owners, Sunbelt boosters planted the seeds of American neoliberalism. Within a political economy where many businessmen contested the legitimacy of the New Deal state, Sunbelt boosters increasingly posed their region as a refuge not only from cold northeastern winters but also from northeastern "business climates" shaped by the New Deal's accords between capital, labor, and the state.

The influence of metropolitan-growth politics reached far beyond local administration, however, into attempts to reshape the administration and goals of federal resource policy. In Arizona and Phoenix, administration of natural resources produced deep conflicts between federal policy and local development. Even before the New Deal, officials in Arizona had challenged federal decisions regarding resources. Most strikingly, officials from Arizona had contested that the federal development of water and power resources on the Colorado River unfairly benefited California at their state's expense. In relatively undeveloped Arizona, state officials feared that federal resource conservation guidelines that stressed, in the words of Gifford Pinchot, "the greatest good for the greatest number for the longest time," would lead federal officials to channel resources to booming California.[16] In 1933, Governor Benjamin Mouer went so far as to create an "Arizona Navy" of two ferryboats crewed by the state militia to prevent the Bureau of Reclamation from completing Parker Dam and opening the Colorado River Aqueduct, the infrastructure built to bring the river's water to Los

Angeles.[17] During the late 1920s, Arizona had been at the center of claims that the states, not the Department of the Interior, should control the administration of range lands in the public domain.[18] At the heart of these disputes was a fundamental question of who was the rightful owner and distributor of natural resources located on the public lands.

Phoenix's boosters engaged these questions as a fundamental component of their campaign to draw industry and capital. The Bureau of Reclamation's projects on the Colorado River, especially Hoover Dam, represented a massive investment in Southwestern economic development. In the eyes of most Arizonans, Hoover Dam, like other Bureau projects on the river, seemed to benefit California at their state's expense. Such beliefs were not mere parochialism. While Arizona was entitled to 18 percent of the dam's power, the state received none as of 1937. Due to an attempt to mollify public and private power interests, the Bureau of Reclamation had leased Boulder Dam's power plant to the Los Angeles Department of Water and Power (LADWP) and Southern California Edison while allowing utilities from Arizona and Nevada to purchase electricity at cost, provided the utilities built their own power lines to the dam. Fearing that this arrangement would allow California utilities to monopolize the dam's power, a group of Phoenix businessmen attempted to claim Arizona's share. Calling themselves, rather awkwardly, the Boulder Dam Power Transmission Association of Arizona, they linked Boulder Dam's massive supplies of power with the potential economic transformation of the state.[19]

Opening its publications with the bold-faced statement that "ELECTRIC ENERGY IS AS NECESSARY AS WATER AND AIR FOR THE EXISTANCE OF MODERN ECONOMIC LIFE," the Association envisioned a future for Arizona in which vast amounts of cheap electricity created rapid modernization and industrialization without the pollution and environmental destruction that had accompanied earlier industrial eras.[20] Hydroelectric power, according the Richard White, solved the problem of "industrial capitalism itself with the degradation of work and nature," a special concern in Phoenix where manufacturing advocates had to manage the concerns of the region's resort and tourist industry.[21] As one booster recalled, "Everyone was afraid of smokestacks that would dirty up the beautiful open skies."[22] Hoover Dam's potential to bring a massive influx of electricity allowed booster dreams of "modern factories powered by . . . clean energy," factories that would not damage the city's reputation for clean air and open skies.[23] Despite the efforts of the Transmission Association, those dreams would have to wait. Given the mandate that utilities build their own power lines to Hoover Dam, Arizona utilities would have needed to expend $25 million, capital that they sorely lacked in the midst of the Depression. While the Association failed in its efforts to bring Colorado River power to Phoenix, it did not abandon contentions that such power was the rightful possession of the state of Arizona, to be used for its improvement. Indeed, the Association's final bulletin asserted that "Arizona can never reach its full development as a State until we have utilized to the greatest possible extent our natural power resources." In the larger picture, participation in the Association led Phoenix's boosters to conceive that the distant generation of massive amounts of electricity could resolve any dilemmas that existed between the city's status as a winter tourist haven and the growth of manufacturing.[24]

Phoenix's two electrical utilities—the public Salt River Project and the private Central Arizona Power and Light Company (CALAPCO)—continued to lack generating capacity through the 1940s. The Salt River Project relied on several dams on the Salt and Verde Rivers to generate electricity, rivers that had a small fraction of the Colorado's flow. The high prices natural gas garnered in California limited potential expansion of CALAPCO's Phoenix Power Plant.[25] During the war, these limits became severe constraints. As Phoenix became home to multiple aviation firms, utilities were forced to scramble to generate sufficient power. The navy loaned the city an experimental diesel generator, and the Phoenix Power Plant, at times, was reduced to burning sawdust when natural gas supplies ran low. While wartime shortages eased somewhat with the funding and construction of a transmission line connecting Phoenix with Parker Dam on the Colorado, power remained short in the postwar years, and the city experienced four blackouts between 1946 and 1948.[26]

By the late 1940s, electrical shortages seemed to threaten Phoenix's future as a site of "modern economic life." Power shortages coincided with reconversion from World War II; and the manufacturers that had flocked to Phoenix during the war—Alcoa, Goodyear Aviation, AiResearch—had shuttered their plants by 1948. The confident proclamations of its boosters, such as Chamber President Sylvan Canz who stated in 1941 that "It seems that the ice has been broken and that from now on Phoenix will become increasingly important, and properly so, as an industrial center," seemed in danger of coming to naught.[27] While the state and region possessed ample energy resources—hydropower from the Colorado River, natural gas in the San Juan Basin, and coal on the Navajo and Hopi reservations—Phoenix's boosters controlled none of them. The vast majority of the Southwest's energy-rich landscapes fell under the jurisdiction of federal agencies, such as the Bureau of Reclamation, the Bureau of Land Management, and the Bureau of Indian Affairs, which limited and regulated their development. As Phoenix boosters strove to attract and support new industry, they came to see federal public land policy as standing athwart the path of Phoenix's industrial future.

"Land Freedom" and Navajo Development

The year 1952 was a very good one for Arizona Republicans. Dwight Eisenhower won Arizona's four electoral votes. Howard Pyle won reelection as governor. And Barry Goldwater stunningly upset Ernest MacFarland, Senate minority leader, to become Arizona's junior senator. These electoral victories represented a stunning turn of events for Arizona's tiny Republican Party, which registered a scant 18 percent of Arizona voters in 1948. The 1952 elections did more, however, than just bring Goldwater to office. They also catapulted Orme Lewis and Walter Bimson into important positions within the Department of the Interior. With new federal authority, Phoenix's boosters began efforts to reorient federal policy in a metropolitan-friendly direction.

Goldwater's campaign epitomized the new political appeals of Phoenix's boosters. The scion of a department store fortune, Goldwater became politically active in the late 1930s, writing anti–New Deal editorials in the *Arizona Republic* that urged businessmen to enter politics and challenge Roosevelt's policies.[28] After a wartime stint in the Army Air Corps, Goldwater followed his own advice. In 1946, he spearheaded the campaign to pass Arizona's right-to-work law, a law so draconian that one labor leader recalled that "Phoenix was to labor organizing what Mississippi was to the civil rights movement."[29] In 1949, Goldwater won election to Phoenix's City Council as a part of a ticket sponsored by the Chamber of Commerce that promised "business-oriented government." As city councilman, Goldwater led the charge for tax cuts on manufacturing and worked to draw new manufacturing to the city. Running for Senate three years later, Goldwater proclaimed that the success of "business-oriented government" in Phoenix stood in stark contrast to the big government policies of Harry Truman's Fair Deal. Traveling across the state, he asked audiences "Do you believe in expanding federal government? Are you willing to surrender more of your liberty? Do you want federal bureaus and federal agencies to take over an ever increasing portion of your life?"[30]

These appeals reflected not only Goldwater's broad antipathy toward the New Deal but also on his particular departure from its natural resource policies. Rather than regarding such public lands as federal property in perpetuity, the policy since Roosevelt's inauguration, Goldwater contended land management should be left to the states or private owners, arguing that federal control blocked private development. Arriving at the Senate, Goldwater endorsed state control of offshore oil sites, encouraged the sale of timber lands to lumber companies, and, as we have seen, urged Arizona's governor to push for the development of Indian mineral resources.[31] In making these claims, Goldwater echoed calls by the U.S. Chamber of Commerce for "land freedom." In the words of U.S. Chamber president Laurence Lee, the Interior Department should "seek ways to dispose" of public lands and "return the land to private ownership." While cloaking "land freedom" as the legacy of the Homestead Act, its advocates envisioned the new policy as applying almost exclusively to lands containing timber and energy resources. Stressing the rapid development and use of resources on public lands, the Chamber claimed resource development was in the broader public interest of stimulating local economies through private enterprise. "Land freedom" represented an ideal vehicle for the ethos of Sunbelt growth, stressing the resource needs of local economies and state policies oriented around the distribution of resources to private enterprise.[32]

While Goldwater supported such ideas, as a freshman senator, his ability to implement them was limited by power and custom. Orme Lewis, however, faced no such barriers. The chair of the Arizona Republican Party from 1948 to 1950, Lewis oversaw an aggressive campaign to register Republic migrants who arrived in Phoenix from the Midwest and Northeast. This campaign, which eventually boosted Republican registration to 32 percent, brought Lewis to the attention of officials directing the Eisenhower transition. In December 1952, Eisenhower offered Lewis a position of Assistant Secretary of Public Lands, with authority over all public land agencies within the Department of the Interior. Among a Republican Party that had not controlled the executive branch for twenty years, Lewis's experience representing ranchers and miners left him one of few Republicans with extensive knowledge of federal public land policy.[33]

That experience had also made him sympathetic to conceptions of "land freedom." Representing ranchers and farmers had led him to view Interior policies with great suspicion. Shortly after taking office, Lewis wrote that "the Federal government is not the sole and only competent manager of our resources." Indeed, he claimed that Harold Ickes's policies withdrawing public lands from private sale went against the historic purposes of the public lands. "Sometimes our lands are more valuable in private hands, contributing more to the national economy, than in those of the federal government. This was the thinking which guided Congress into the enactment of laws by which individual Americans could acquire lands and homes and futures in the public domain."[34] At his confirmation hearings, Lewis posed the private development of natural resources as in the broad public interest. He especially criticized the "preference policies" of several agencies that gave public utilities priority in the use of federally developed electricity. Such policies, he stated, pointed "in the direction of nationalization of power" while giving excessive power to bureaucrats who favored public entities for ideological reasons. As he testified, "I would like to see the Government get out of ownership of lands that do not benefit everyone."[35]

Lewis's notion of resource management thus was diametrically opposed to New Deal policy. New Deal reforms subjected utilities to increased regulation while introducing public competition. Policies giving private utilities preference in purchasing federally generated power also supported New Deal conceptions of competition, allowing public utilities' generating capacity to compete with private utilities. In short, New Dealers conceived that increased regulation and support for public power would lead to social benefits in the form of lower prices and more widespread consumption. By contrast, Lewis argued that the public benefited when resources were not reserved for use by only public entities. Broadening the users of public resources to include individuals and private companies would result in greater capacity for economic growth. Giving private entities "access to the public domain where it appears that placing of such lands in private hands will best serve the national economy and long-term public interests" represented the public good. Rather than reserving resources for eventual public development, Lewis argued that resources should be freed for private use.

As he wrote, "Use is the very essence of the concept of conservation prevailing today in the Department of the Interior."[36] Private resource development, in short, promised rapid and widely distributed economic growth. In his term as assistant secretary, Lewis's understanding of the benefits of private resource use reshaped the Department of Interior's policies on Indian economic development. Most dramatically, it brought private electrical utilities and multinational coal companies to the Navajo Reservation under terms notably favorable to those companies.

Navajo economic development became a burning question in the years immediately following World War II as population growth and land degradation created a crisis of sustainability. In 1946, Clyde Kluckhohn, a Harvard professor and the president of the American Anthropological Association, declared the tribe "America's foremost Indian problem."[37] Navajos had the nation's highest rate of tuberculosis and its lowest life expectancy. Infant mortality was ten times the national average; nearly one-third of children born on the Navajo Reservation died before reaching school age. Despite such statistics, the Navajo population had grown rapidly, from just under 35,000 in 1928 to almost 70,000 in 1950. And Navajos seemed to have few economic options. Federal stock grazing policies in the 1930s had devastated the Navajo pastoral economy, leaving Navajos dependent on federal welfare payments.[38] While more than 12,000 Navajos had been employed in off-reservation war work in the early 1940s, fewer than 500 retained such jobs as of 1946.[39] As Kluckhohn wrote despairingly of the tribe's uncertain economic future, "Their rapid increase in numbers continues, and the adjacent areas can no longer absorb the overflow. Moreover, the resources of their own ancient lands have been shockingly depleted by erosion. How are The People to make a living?"[40]

Kluckhohn articulated the central questions in larger debates about the fate of Navajos within the postwar Southwest. How was it that an impoverished population of almost 70,000 people lived in the midst of the world's most powerful nation? What had caused this situation? How would Navajo society change in order to survive? And who would control those changes? Since 1946, federal policy had directed the BIA to seek the assimilation of Indians into American society. But what did this mean in the case of the Navajos?

BIA and Interior officials in the Truman administration envisioned extensive efforts to educate Navajos. Influenced by early work in modernization theory, they argued that Navajos were a primitive people suffering a sudden confrontation with modernity. Kluckhohn's 1946 ethnography had painted the Navajos as undergoing social and psychological breakdown due to incursions by what he termed "white American society." As he wrote, "An appreciable number of Navajos are so confused by the conflicting precepts of their elders and their white models that they tend, in effect, to reject the whole problem of morality as meaningless or insoluble."[41] BIA officials broadly accepted this portrait of social disconnection and dislocation. Assistant Secretary of the Interior William Warne (occupying the post that Lewis would later serve in) stated in 1949 that Navajos were "going through a stage of development that the rest of American society experienced fifty to one hundred years ago."[42] Warne's statement reflected modernization's understanding that economic progress occurred in a linear fashion, with different societies existing at different points on a continuum from primitive subsistence agriculture to advanced industrial economies.[43]

Warne's statement also implied modernization's faith in the ability of experts to speed development, in effect advancing "primitive" people rapidly toward modernity. After a brief dalliance with a proposal to create industrial villages on the Navajo Reservation, BIA efforts came to focus on preparing Navajos to work in the broader American, and particularly the Southwestern, economy.[44] By the late 1940s, BIA officials and legislators had concluded that large numbers of Navajos would have to leave the reservation in order to survive. "Even with full development of the reservation resources, . . . there will still remain some 27,000 Navajos with no adequate means of making a living on the reservation." Warne argued, "We feel that even using adequately the resources of the area . . . that we will still not be able to take care of all of them."[45] Other officials appeared to advocate the use of force, if necessary, to induce Navajos to abandon the reservation. James Preston, another Interior official testified, "They are very much attached to their country. You know, it is the Painted Desert type of country. It is a unique area, a picturesque and beautiful area, and they are very much attached to it. They're starving, but they'll stay there unless something forces them to leave."[46] Representative John Murdock of Arizona responded, "If men could live on scenery alone they would be rich indeed, but that country does not make it possible for them to live on scenery alone."[47] Unlike modern Americans, Navajos did not migrate toward opportunity but remained on the unproductive land of the Colorado Plateau unless some outside force compelled them to move.[48] BIA officials, thus, developed plans that aimed to train Navajos gradually under expert supervision and then gradually introduce them into the wider economy.

Such educational efforts were central to the Navajo-Hopi Rehabilitation Act, passed in 1950. The $88 million law appropriated money for construction of road, school, and communication infrastructure, as well as authorizing a revolving loan fund and a mineral survey of the two reservations. While seemingly stimulating development on Indian lands, the BIA's primary interest in the act lay in the industrial education it facilitated. Supporting the infrastructure projects, William Warne stated, "Every single road camp we set up where these men are employed in putting these new roads through ought to have its night classes in English and all of the various and sundry things that it will be advantageous for these people to know." Once Navajos had received the education available from improving the reservation's infrastructure, they would be prepared to move into jobs off the reservation. Warne continued, "If we follow . . . our work with an appropriate off-the-reservation employment program, we can put groups of them at satisfying and pleasurable employment for them, in road building and elsewhere in the Southwest."[49]

Supporters of termination found such plans fundamentally misguided. In their view, it was not the confrontation with white society that caused Navajo destitution but the debilitating effects of federal paternalism. Articulating their cause largely through the language of the Cold War, termination advocates argued for the "liberation" of Indians from reservations they compared to "concentration camps."[50] On the campaign trail in 1952, Barry Goldwater stated that "if you want to see the effects of welfare paternalism, just look at our Indian tribes."[51] The work programs of the Navajo-Hopi Rehabilitation Act, in the views of the most ardent supporters of termination, would be just one more form of expensive paternalism. For these supporters, the rapid extension of the region's economic and political structures formed the most effective means of assimilation.

The extension of state jurisdiction over Indian reservations formed the core of their program for developing Indian economies. By eliminating reservations' separate political status, by subjecting reservation lands to state taxation and regulation, and by opening reservation land to sale and development by private interest, termination supporters hoped to accomplish the rapid assimilation of Indians into regional economies. Such policies had broad support from metropolitan politicians from the Southwest. The initial version of the Rehabilitation Act, passed by Congress in 1949, contained an amendment introduced by Albuquerque's congressional representative, Antonio Fernandez, extending state jurisdiction over the Navajo and Hopi reservations, in effect, proposing the division of the Navajo Reservation between Arizona, Utah, and New Mexico. Fernandez argued that state jurisdiction would enable greater development of reservation resources and thus convey broad benefit to Navajos and Hopis, as it would encourage capital investment and secure credit on the reservation.[52]

President Truman vetoed the bill due to Navajo opposition. While some Navajos, along with the tribe's attorney, favored the extension of state authority, mainly for the financial incentives Fernandez raised, a majority of the Tribal Council rejected the proposal, citing fears of the loss of control over reservation land, distrust of Arizona and New Mexico for their long standing refusal to allow Navajos to vote, and, ironically, the specter of state taxation. After the Fernandez Amendment was excised over the objections of most legislators from Arizona and New Mexico, the Navajo Tribal Council voted to support the bill, and Truman signed the Rehabilitation Act into law.[53]

Tribal officials did not object only to the extension of state jurisdiction over Navajo land; they also rejected BIA officials' suggestions that the reservation was no longer economically viable. While Navajo officials welcomed the Rehabilitation Act's development projects, they found them minimal compensation for the BIA destruction of Navajo herds during the 1930s.[54] Navajos also compared the destitution of the Navajo Reservation with the recent passage of bills funding overseas development. As Lilly Neil, the first woman elected to the Navajo Tribal Council, complained in 1947, "The government is making all these big loans to foreign countries. . . . I doubt very much if there's a European or Asiatic country who are very much if any poorer than our own Navajo Indian tribe and none of them who need help any worse, and they owe their obligations to us North American Indians first."[55]

In the mind of most Navajo officials, such obligations should take the form of a consistent program of reservation development. At hearings on the Rehabilitation Act, Tribal Council member Joe Duncan contended that the Navajo economy remained stagnant because of the rapidly shifting advice offered by BIA officials. "I believe the blame lies a great deal with the Department educators. . . . They start something among the Navajos, 'Here is the way you should make a living,' and then before the man has finished the course or has gone far enough to realize what it is all about they change the course and start something else again. In that way we are all confused about just what is the right thing to do."[56] Similarly, Tribal Chairman Sam Ahkeah criticized the minimal training offered to Navajo workers before beginning off-reservation wage work. "I would say give us the right training first before anyone sends us out so that we can compete with the outside." Navajo concerns about wage work were not assuaged by their experiences in the early 1950s, where the BIA placed the vast majority of Navajo workers as seasonal laborers on Southwestern farms, in many cases replacing Mexican *braceros*.[57]

At the same time, Navajos argued that the reservation had vital resources whose development could support the tribe. "All effort should be put forward to utilize the land that we have," Duncan argued. "We have an immense reservation which we feel should be utilized. After we have exhausted every effort on the reservation, then it will be time for us to send our Navajos somewhere else, but we have not done that yet."[58] Duncan claimed that a great number of resources remained underutilized on the reservation, mainly irrigated farmlands and timber resources, and that such resources could provide a basis for the Navajo economy that would allow most Navajos to remain on the reservation. As Orme Lewis assumed office in 1953, then, Navajos laid out a different version of development than did BIA officials or termination supporters. Rather than potential workers in the lowest rungs of the Southwestern economy, tribal officials sought economic development strategies that would allow both Navajo individuals and the Navajo Reservation to remain economically viable.

"Land Freedom" in Indian Country

From within the Interior Department, Lewis and his advisors sought to resolve these disputes by creating new connections between the Navajo Tribe and key institutions of metropolitan growth. Judging from his actions toward other tribes, Lewis agreed in theory with extending state jurisdiction over Indian groups. As the official in charge of public lands legislation, Lewis guided bills terminating the federal relationship with the Menominee and Klamath tribes, thus extending the jurisdiction of Wisconsin and Oregon over those two groups. Lewis, however, never directly contemplated such actions toward the Navajos or any tribe within Arizona. At the same time, the policies that Lewis advanced within the Interior Department attempted to use the demand of the growing metropolitan Southwest for natural resources to resolve the dilemmas of both Navajo development and metropolitan growth. Rather than thinking of termination as limited to the few tribes actually "terminated" by the federal government, then, Lewis's actions demonstrate the policy as part of a broader pattern of transferring resources from public to private control. In short, termination became "land freedom" for Indians.

Walter Bimson played the key role in merging these two concepts. Bimson, president of Valley National Bank, was arguably the most important metropolitan booster in Phoenix. Later described by *Arizona Highways* magazine as "Arizona's Indispensible Man," Bimson underwrote the key industrial development initiatives of the Phoenix Chamber of Commerce both by keeping the Chamber's industrial scouts on the bank's payroll and by freely advancing credit to new industries and their employees.[59] Soon after taking office, Lewis appointed Bimson to chair a nine-member panel, a panel that featured no Indians, to direct the reorganization of the Bureau of Indian Affairs. The panel's subsequent report suggested a number of changes, all designed to connect Indian peoples more closely to regional metropolitan economies.

In some cases, these policy changes meant extending existing programs but tying them more closely to metropolitan areas. Most prominently, Bimson's panel suggested the expansion of an existing voluntary program of relocation from reservations to urban areas. Bimson saw the relocation program as essential to Indian welfare and believed locating training facilities in metropolitan areas rather than on the reservation allowed cost savings and less of a social service burden. As he told an audience at Phoenix's Paradise Inn, "If the Indians remain [on the reservation] they will always live in sub-standard conditions and need government subsidy. The only sensible answer is to relocate the excess population . . . to our city and elsewhere."[60]

Bimson's panel also suggested restructuring the BIA to increase connection between its officials and metropolitan boosters. While the report praised BIA personnel, writing that "many of them lead lives dedicated to Indian welfare," it charged that the BIA's structure hampered efforts to improve Indian welfare by removing authority to officials in Washington with little sense of the regional economies in which Indian reservations were embedded. The report recommended delegating almost all decision-making authority to the regional offices, located in Albuquerque, Phoenix, Denver, Los Angeles, and other western cities. From those locations, "The area office directors can best make decisions about economic integration, the capacity for independence, and the development of reservation resources." Following the decentralization of operations, each area office would create a timetable for transferring responsibility over Indians from the federal to local governments. Bimson's report thus envisioned a fundamental spatial reorientation of Indian policy away from Washington and to the local level.[61] Following a suggestion from Lewis that "perhaps it will be useful to think about the Indian problem in terms of the local economy," Bimson's report implicitly argued that a unified Indian policy directed from Washington harmed Indian economic and social progress. These goals could be met, in the commission's conclusions, by connecting Indian economies and politics with those of metropolitan areas. As Bimson wrote to Lewis, "One of the great benefits of such a reorganization will be the opportunity for connections between BIA officials and those of us working to attract industry and commerce."[62]

The transformation of leasing policy, allowing electric utilities to develop energy resources on the reservation, represented the most important element of the report. Immediately before Lewis's term, Arizona's electric utilities began studying the possibility of developing energy resources on the reservation. As part of the Rehabilitation Act, the Arizona School of Mines conducted a survey of the reservation's mineral resources. The report, released in 1952, concluded that the tribe possessed substantial recoverable oil, coal, and natural gas reserves but that the market for these resources was uncertain.[63] In the wake of the mineral survey, Arizona Public Service (APS) commissioned a study by the Stanford Research Institute about the feasibility of using the reservation's coal for electricity production. The report determined that the reservation's coal could be used to power "up to seven large power plants" that would "allow the dramatic expansion of southern Arizona's industrial capacity." The report sounded warning bells, however, about locating production on the Navajo Reservation, stating that "a confusing welter of jurisdiction and policy directions . . . leaves such development . . . highly questionable."[64] Federal leasing regulations for locating private business on the Navajo Reservation seemed to preclude possibilities for energy development. These regulations, part of the Rehabilitation Act, limited leases with non-Indian concerns to five years. Leases could be renewed, but such renewal required approval from both the secretary of interior and the Navajo Tribal Council. The short term of the leases and the frequent rules for renewal contained in the Rehabilitation Act reflected the beliefs of previous Interior officials that non-Indian enterprises on the reservation would be low-capital enterprises such as arts and crafts manufacturing that the tribe itself might want to run. While these rules kept private business from crowding out tribal enterprises, they also prevented capital intensive enterprises from locating on the reservation, a consideration that Lewis certainly realized as a former APS board member.

Bimson's report proposed a wholesale transformation in Indian leasing policy. The report called for much longer leases, recommending that standard leases run for twenty-five years with an option to negotiate up to fifty-year leases. It also recommended that the private companies entering into leases, rather than tribal governments, have the right to renew leases as long as businesses remained productive. Lewis endorsed the changes wholeheartedly, writing Bimson his thanks "for suggestions that will allow our state's Indians to participate fully in our free enterprise system."[65] Bimson's suggestions were enacted in a 1955 revision of the Rehabilitation Act sponsored both by John Rhodes, Phoenix's congressional representative, and by Barry Goldwater. Little noticed at the time, Bimson's changes fundamentally changed the intention of leasing provisions of the Rehabilitation Act. Initially, those provisions intended to draw small-scale enterprises that could provide instruction in industrial work discipline to Navajos in preparation for leaving the reservation for work in the broader Southwest. As such, the BIA had conceived as Navajos primarily as potential laborers who required extensive preparation for industrial work. After Bimson's revisions, Navajo leasing policy came to focus on the attraction of capital intensive enterprises aiming to put the resources of the Navajo Reservation into production. No longer a population requiring education by federal authorities, this new leasing structure conceived the Navajo Tribe as resource owners who would draw royalty payments from material resource extraction. Economic development of the reservation no longer possessed an educational role; instead, it became conceived as primarily on a contractual basis, bringing monetary returns to the tribe but requiring little action by federal officials.

Faced with an Indian policy that stated its aims as the termination of federal financial support for the tribes, Navajo officials initially embraced these new leasing terms. Negotiations of new leases followed quick on the heels of the Rehabilitation Act's revision. Wildcat oilmen flocked to new fields opened near Aneth, Utah; and the tribe negotiated a coal lease with Utah International, one of the nation's largest mining conglomerates, in 1957, allowing mining across 24,320 acres of reservation land near Farmington, New Mexico. In 1959, the tribe entered into a fifty-year agreement with Arizona Public Service to allow construction of a coal-fired power plant abutting Utah International's Navajo Mine. Tribal budgets increased exponentially in the wake of these leases, from just over $1 million in 1954 to almost $13 million in 1958. Thanking "divine Providence" for bringing tribe mineral wealth, Tribal Chairman Paul Jones stated in 1959 that the oil, gas, and coal leases signed over the previous four years portended the modern future of the Navajo. Addressing the Tribal Council, Jones stated, "Working together with the companies developing these resources, we will move into a future of self-determination and self-sufficiency. These resources will provide the funds, employment and energy that will make the Navajo Tribe a force in the Southwest."[66] The leases, however, brought few new jobs to the reservation. It was far cheaper for companies to bring trained workers in from outside the reservation than to train Navajos, even given the lower wages Navajo workers demanded. In any case, this lack of Navajo employment meant that the tribe and its members received few ancillary benefits from the economic activity occurring on their land. The boom of energy development represented the ironic conclusion to the termination era on the Navajo Reservation, mocking earlier promises of welcoming Navajos into metropolitan space. While Navajo resources became assimilated into the metropolitan Southwest, Navajo workers remained peripheral.

Navajo Coal and the Sunbelt Southwest

A 1970 map of the Southwestern electrical grid produced by the Department of Energy revealed the new geography that energy leasing had created in the Southwest. The region's major metropolitan areas lay on the map's margins: Salt Lake City to the north, Albuquerque to the east, Phoenix to the south, and "to Los Angeles" on the map's western edge. A maze of lines representing high-voltage transmission lines—eight heading toward Los Angeles alone—linked those cities to dark dots arranged in a rough circle near the maps center. Those dots represented the region's coal-fired power plants—Four Corners, Navajo, Cholla, Mohave—together producing almost 15,000 megawatts of electricity, enough energy to power twelve million homes. Had the map included the borders of the Navajo Reservation, it would have fit neatly between those power plants. Missing also were the locations of Black Mesa and Navajo Mines, both among the five largest strip mines in the world in 1975. The map represented the material changes that occurred in the years after 1955, as Navajo resources increasingly came to provide power not only to Phoenix but to the entire Sunbelt Southwest. Indeed, the power lines stretching forth from Four Corners created the Sunbelt Southwest as a material region, its peripheral metropolitan areas tied indelibly to the energy-rich Navajo landscape at its center.[67]

While Arizona Public Service's Four Corners Power Plant shipped the vast majority of its electricity to Phoenix in the early 1960s, it joined a consortium of ten Southwestern private utilities in 1964 in a vast expansion of coal-fired electricity generation. At the press conference announcing the formation of that consortium, Chairman D. W. Reeves announced Western Energy Supply and Transmission Associates (WEST) would be "the largest regional electrical power development program ever planned anywhere in the world," with a generation capacity three times the size of the TVA. Newspaper photos of the event show Reeves gesturing toward a map of the western United States, which read, "WEST Associates: 36,000,000 new kilowatts by 1985." On that map, a great circle reached from Los Angeles to eastern Colorado, encompassing almost all of Nevada, Utah, Colorado, Arizona, and New Mexico.[68] WEST immediately began an expansion of the Four Corners Power Plant, tripling its capacity, while building new power lines to transmit Four Corners power to the distribution systems of Public Service Company of New Mexico and Southern California Edison, the utilities serving Albuquerque and suburban Los Angeles and Orange Counties. By generating electricity for multiple metropolitan load centers, WEST could take advantage of the economies of scale created by running its coal-fired plants at maximum capacity, thus lowering the cost of "base" power to member utilities.

WEST's expansion plans continued into the late 1960s and early 1970s. Peabody Coal's massive Black Mesa mine, developed after a 1964 lease with the Navajo Tribe, supplied the newly built Navajo and Mojave Generating Stations. During those same years, WEST opened its membership to the region's public utilities—the Los Angeles Department of Water and Power and the Salt River Project—and even signed a contract to generate power for the Bureau of Reclamation. With the construction of those plants and the combination of public and private utilities into a single coordinated grid, electricity generated from Navajo coal became the base power source for the entire metropolitan Southwest, a reliable pool of low-cost power that metropolitan consumers could draw from with no sense of their power's ultimate source.

WEST represented an ironic outcome to the political project of Lewis and Phoenix's other booster bureaucrats. Lewis, Bimson, and others created legal and political conditions to enable energy development on the Navajo Reservation at least in part to give Phoenix competitive advantage over other Sunbelt metropolises. Those conditions, however, led to a rapid rise in utilities' demand for Navajo coal as a source of electrical generation. While some of this new demand arose from improvements in generator and transmission technology, which lowered the price of production and long-distance transfer of electricity, it also reflected the ways in which booster uses of the state provided material advantage—generous leasing terms for coal—to private enterprise. Occurring at the federal level, these benefits reached far more broadly across space than did boosters' power over the local state. Very rapidly, electrical utilities from across the region began drawing electricity from power plants located on the reservation, creating new material links not only between metropolis and hinterland but between metropolitan areas themselves.

While Paul Jones had celebrated energy resource development as a gift of "divine Providence," most Navajos developed a decidedly different view of energy development by the 1960s, as tailing piles, air pollution, and high-voltage power lines became ubiquitous on their landscapes. Navajos objected to their lack of control over the landscapes with intense personal and cultural meaning. As Many Mules' Daughter, a resident of Black Mesa, stated, "Where they are mining now is my land. My father is buried there. His grave was torn up in the strip mining. I never approved of anything in the agreement to mine this area."[69] At the same time, Navajo youth activists developed a broad critique that cited the dynamics of energy development as evidence of the colonization of Navajo land by imperialistic metropolitan actors. As one writer argued, "Our water and our land resources will be drained . . . and in exchange we get a handful of jobs and a small payoff. . . . They say the Indians must join the market economy, but they force us into a colonial economy. This is not economic development. This is economic termination."[70] Indeed, combating energy development became the main goal of Navajo nationalism from the 1960s forward. Peter MacDonald, tribal chairman in the early 1970s, embraced this rhetoric, telling audiences, "For too long we have seen unfair contracts for the exploitation of our resources and our people. We have seen our land scarred by mine sites . . . so that the giant cities of our country can be too cool in summer and too warm in winter."[71] While these critiques point to broad inequalities within the metropolitan Southwest, they also illustrate that Navajos increasingly saw themselves as part of a new region created, in part, by the power lines that marked their landscape. Indeed, Phoenix and Los Angeles joined the Bureau of Indian Affairs as the main sources of oppression cited by Navajo political actors.

Navajos' critique of energy development and identification of Phoenix and Los Angeles as sources of oppression suggests the spatial inequalities created in the processes of Sunbelt growth. While literature on spatial inequality has largely focused on the dichotomy between suburban development and urban underdevelopment, residents of metropolitan hinterlands experienced unequal incorporation into the Sunbelt economy as well. In the Southwest, Navajo Indians saw their landscape become the location of the negative externalities of the power production needed to sustain metropolitan economies. Such dynamics are not limited to the Southwest. In December 2008, a flood of fly ash from the TVA Kingston Fossil Plant breached its containing wall and rushed down the Emory River, rendering much of rural Harriman, Tennessee, temporarily uninhabitable due to contamination from mercury, cadmium, and other hard metals.[72] This event suggests that a similar narrative of state power and hinterland underdevelopment could be told about the TVA's connection of multiple metropolitan areas and the environmental costs that the rise of the Sunbelt has imposed on rural southerners. Such environmental costs have frequently been disguised through labels of rural backwardness or Indian primitivism or through a reductionist economic logic that ignores the vital ways in which the state has been shaped toward the benefit of metropolitan growth and consumption. By refusing to think of the Sunbelt as only urban and suburban, by seeing hinterlands as indelible components of both metropolitan space and modern life, we can move toward an understanding of the costs and scope of the Sunbelt's growth.

Chapter 10

Real Estate and Race: Imagining the Second Circuit of Capital in Sunbelt Cities

Carl Abbott

Kyra Menaker-Mossbacher is a whiz at selling real estate on the west side of Los Angeles. Working out of her Lexus and a Woodland Hills office, she's the "undisputed volume leader at Mike Bender Realty, Inc." Real estate is her life (apart from husband, son, cat, and Dandie Dinmont terriers). She knows how to put the best light on low-ball offers, how to charm buyers out of sudden jitters, and how to "keep the avenues open" with former clients (31, 36).

At the same moment in fictional time, Frank Dominic is cooking up plans to remake Albuquerque. Land developers have been buying up parcels in Old Town and low-lying barrio properties near the Rio Grande. Dominic is a banker and deal maker with mayoral ambitions who has a scheme to help these real-estate speculations pay off by diverting the river through a set of newly dug canals in imitation of San Antonio. There'll be tourists, casinos, and entertainment. Look out, Las Vegas!

Two decades earlier, Ladd Devine the Third had floated a similar plan to transform disused farmland in northern New Mexico into the Miracle Valley Recreation Area. He has inherited untilled grazing and farm land that his grandfather bought from Hispano farmers at bargain-basement prices in the 1930s and has been profiting from tourism with the Dancing Trout dude ranch. Now he hopes that a planned Indian Creek Dam will allow the "abandoned and apparently worthless land" to transmute into "a ritzy subdivision molded around an exotic and very green golf course" (23).

Most impressive of all is Leah Blue, wife of a mafia boss transplanted from Cherry Hill, New Jersey, to Tucson. Leah is into every dimension of real estate. Her starting capital is a reward for putting up with the cross-country move after Max Blue is nearly killed by an assassin and decides to downsize operations to a simple killer-for-hire business. Leah buys and sells and gets a rush that is almost like sex when she outsmarts a broker. She knows that "the real estate market in Tucson and southern Arizona was wide open, ripe for development" like San Diego and Palm Springs. She canvasses neighborhoods on the edge of town, "leaving her business cards in case large parcels of desert became available" (359, 361). She has a scheme for developing a desert Venice every bit as audacious as Frank Dominic's and as large in acreage as Ladd Devine's Miracle Valley.

Four Sunbelt Novels

Each of these characters—Kyra, Frank, Ladd, Leah—figures in a novel set in the contemporary Sunbelt Southwest. The books, in order of publication, are John Nichols, *The Milagro Beanfield War* (1974) for Ladd Devine; Leslie Marmon Silko, *Almanac of the Dead* (1991) for Leah Blue; Rudolfo Anaya, *Alburquerque* (1992) for Frank Dominic; and T. Coraghessan Boyle, *The Tortilla Curtain* (1995) for Kyra Mossbacher. The central role of real estate as both a background feature and plot element—its culturally embedded valuation, buying, selling, development, and protection—offers an entryway for understanding how important and influential writers have imagined and delineated one of North America's most rapidly changing regions.

The four books range from near a best seller (*Tortilla Curtain*) and a cult favorite (*Milagro Beanfield War*) to semipopular fiction (*Alburquerque*) with limited sales and self-consciously experimental fiction (*Almanac of the Dead*).[1] *The Tortilla Curtain* and *Alburquerque* are tightly structured as traditional well-made novels, focusing on limited sets of protagonists who interact through rising action and find themselves in a conflict that resolves with a decisive ending. *The Milagro Beanfield War* is a community picaresque with adventures and misadventures observed over the shoulders of multiple characters, a few of whom may not actually exist.² The two New Mexico books are also comedies in the formal sense of stories that end with at least partial restoration of social balance and harmony (*The Milagro Beanfield War* is also uproariously funny). *The Tortilla Curtain*, on contrast, follows the classic trajectory of tragedy. Its characters act with good intentions but, flawed by stubbornness or moral blindness and buffeted by circumstance, move inexorably toward disaster. *Almanac of the Dead* is harder to categorize. It is a sprawling, multivocal amalgam with enough story lines for half a dozen more compact novels, causing reviewers for standard sources like *Publisher's Weekly* and *Library Journal* to throw up their hands in confusion.³ Silko introduces and drops characters as her needs change, flips among half a dozen settings, and shifts tone from down-and-dirty realism to something akin to the semifantastic imagination of Latin American fiction. The modern West, she implies, is too complex and too unformed to sit still for a traditional novelistic portrait.⁴

Critics have most commonly approached these books with an eye to tensions and conflicts around race and ethnicity, for each author places Anglo Americans in confrontation and conflict with people of color and their communities—Hispano farmers, Mexican Americans, Indians, Mexican immigrants. Anaya and Nichols depict long-rooted natives, whether urbanites or country people, who respond to the intrusive demands of Anglo American society to remake specific places in the interests of monetary profit. Boyle sees two migratory peoples (educated Anglos and Mexican workers) colliding in Southern California. Both have claims to the same landscape that may be equal in right but are unequal in power. Silko casts the widest net as she depicts all of western America, from southern Mexico to Alaska, as a single Indian Country whose future is weighed down by European Americans in both Mexico and the United States and where multiple Indian peoples, Mexican American proletarians, and African Americans are potential allies for a utopian apocalypse.

Within this broad framework, it is striking that each novelist places *land* at the center of the racial conflict. These are not stories that hinge on the problems of love across racial barriers. They are not about traditional class conflict and labor organizing. They do not try to explore the ways in which the natural resources of western North America have been developed and misused. They are not about heroic individuals seeking self-realization and redemption in the wild. In short, the authors are not rewriting *Ramona* or *The Grapes of Wrath*, nor are they crafting fictions in parallel to *Angle of Repose* or *Sometimes a Great Notion*. Race and ethnicity are certainly obvious and vital factors in the history and future of the Southwest, but the dimension of land and landscape suggests an additional way to read these fictions, viewing them not so much as "western" or "frontier" stories of conquest and resistance than as *Sunbelt stories*—stories in which the particular processes of late twentieth-century growth are central.

In this reading, a central goal of the books is to unmask the processes through which Anglo Americans have asserted and established claims to the land. The attention to real estate makes visible what was previously concealed or invisible (the "invisible hand" of the market). The process of land conversion—the political deals and financial arrangements that underlie the development of the visible, physical metroscape—is front and center in the novels about the mid-sized cities of Tucson and Albuquerque and the ritzy side of megametropolis Los Angeles. The same factors are also at work in efforts to incorporate Milagro into the recreation hinterland of Denver, Dallas, and Albuquerque. John Nichols thus addresses the same broad issue as Andrew Needham and Volker Janssen, whose studies in this volume of Arizona energy development and California prison location also deal with entities that have utilized distant hinterlands for their own purposes. As they show, attempts to make the problems of both pollution and criminal populations invisible by displacing them dozens and hundreds of miles away fail as brown clouds show up on satellite images, coal trains rumble through tourist country, and suburban sprawl engulfs formerly isolated prisons.[5]

In using narratives to describe, embody, and make visible the pathways through which capital accumulates in real estate, these novels offer insight into the social and political dynamics of the modern southwestern Sunbelt. In particular, they highlight ways in which Anglo Americans continue to act as if western North America is *terra nullius*, land without prior ownership that is open for the taking. The action in all four stories is driven, at least in part, by the efforts of indigenous peoples to assert or reassert their own claims. The authors thus make visible the morally tottery foundation for the "white politics" that dominated the twentieth century Southwest, whether as regional development policies of the New Deal regime or the laissez-faire policies of southwestern conservatism.

The Second Circuit of Capital

Spanning the different settings, plots, and styles of writing is a concern with the differences between land as *place* and *commodity*—another way to phrase the effects of running land through the real estate development machine. In each case, the complex trajectories of economic development, cultural adaptation, and demographic change are condensed and represented as land development. The wheeler-dealers in Alburquerque (using Anaya's spelling to differentiate the fictionalized city from the real place) want to evict residents in the long-established barrio to construct tourist attractions. Ladd Devine wants to see a golf course and condominiums on land that was once a part of the agricultural base of the Milagro villagers. Kyra Mossbacher sells houses in subdivisions that encroach further and further along chaparral-clad ridges, paving over the natural landscape that provides the raw material that her nature-writer husband mines for magazine columns. Leah Blue plans to use legal maneuvers to appropriate Indian water rights in order to adorn fantasy subdivisions. In every case, a landscape that might well be understood as an ecological whole is commoditized for nonproductive or marginally productive uses.

It is useful here to utilize the idea of a "second circuit of capital" as introduced by sociologist Henri Lefebvre in *La Révolution urbaine* (1970) and *La Production de l'espace* (1974).[6] When capitalist production matures, according to traditional Marxism, opportunities for profitable industrial production fall as a result of overproduction, increased competition, resource depletion, and work force unionization. Owners of capital seek to restore profits by extracting additional surplus value from labor, leading to more and more intense conflict between workers and owners. Alternatively, however, capital can flow from industrial production (the first circuit of capital) into the built environment of housing, commercial space, and physical infrastructure (anything from freeways to golf courses). This creation of monetary value in real estate has its own dynamics of finance and its own logic of booms and busts and, therefore, constitutes a distinct, *second* circuit for capital circulation and accumulation. In addition, capital can also move into education, scientific research, and health care to constitute a third circuit that feeds back into the primary industrial sector through innovation, product development, and increases in the productivity of labor.[7]

The second circuit of capital depends on the availability of surplus capital whose owners are seeking profitable investments, but money does not "flow" of its own accord. The second circuit requires an elaborate system of financial institutions to assemble and redistribute investment funds. It also depends on government facilitation. The state works to stabilize the financial system, fund certain types of real estate investment such as transportation and utility infrastructure, and direct capital in particular directions (as through urban redevelopment programs). It may also be enlisted in corrupt alliances in which government authority favors particular interests (as Leah Blue well knows).[8] Finally, it depends on the real estate development and sales industries themselves to keep capital in motion by continually offering up new products and opportunities for investment.

In this analysis, the second circuit is the most sterile and least productive. Development of real estate does help to maintain the industrial sector by housing its activities and workers. It also provides the systems of physical circulation that make necessary connections between producers and consumers. However, projects in the second circuit do not put labor to work in the long haul, nor do they lead directly to technological change and industrial revitalization. Real-estate capital can transform places like a New Mexico village or a California canyon rim into a marketable commodity, but it has little ability to add permanently to productive capacity.

Real estate development is also "faddish." Cities such as Houston or Las Vegas gain reputations as "hot" investment opportunities and attract real estate investment beyond the absorptive capacity of the local economy. As Feagin argues, "development and finance capitalists frequently make decisions about urban development which are irrational from a tough cost-accounting, profit-making approach. . . . There is a social psychological dimension to capital investments flowing into the secondary circuit."[9] Feagin's comments about Houston have fictional counterparts in Frank Dominic; in Charlie Crocker, the self-deluding Atlanta office tower entrepreneur who's center stage in Tom Wolfe's novel *A Man in Full*; or in the urban renewal schemers who hope to benefit from the abandonment of entire St. Louis neighborhoods in Jonathan Franzen's *The Twenty-Seventh City*.[10]

All the writers under scrutiny tell stories that we can analyze in terms of the second circuit. They find it appropriate to contrast a natural, traditional, and sometimes spiritual connection to the landscape with artificial, profit-driven development. They also see the developments themselves as embodiments of fads and fashions—stoking a taste for conspicuous leisure, for conspicuous water consumption in the desert, for conspicuously gated enclave communities. Indeed, the real estate developers and sales people who populate these Southwest stories are themselves aware that they are dealers in fantasies and perhaps even scams. In contrast, the indigenous characters are more closely connected in community and more "in tune" with the land. Mysticism and mystery lie on one side of the economic and cultural divide. Markets lie on the other.

The idea of challenged authenticity places the Southwest in double juxtaposition to the rest of the United States. At the end of one axis are the gritty cities of the Rustbelt, which are "real" places that may be economically depressed and physically squalid but are no longer weighted down by myths of the future. Their residents know to cut through any illusions that might mask the exercise of power. In contrast, the Anglo American cities of the Southwest are commonly regarded as rootless, shallow, superficial. After all, French philosopher Jean Baudrillard traveled to Los Angeles in search of stage-set society (simulacra and simulation in his jargon), not to Akron or Allentown.

At the end of another axis is the Sunbelt Southeast. Because black and white southerners arrived at the same time, neither group have prior rights to the land (neither is more authentic than the other). Members of each, nevertheless, have moral relationships to the land that are shaped and burdened by centuries of shared history (contrast the heritage of slavery and sharecropping with the dubious ideology of the Southern Fugitives and other romantic regionalists). In the Southwest, the indigenous folk are not only visibly present but also stand in obvious and troubling contrast to the waves of Anglo newcomers. In Tucson and Albuquerque and Los Angeles, indigenous people are "authentically" present to challenge superficiality by participating in the politics of development and shaping what our authors hope may be more equitable futures.

Capital and Community in Four Imagined Communities

Across variations in style and tone, we find some common elements among the four novels. Indigenous characters in various ways have rooted or "authentic" connections to the land. The forces of Sunbelt change, as represented by the real estate sector, are never the good guys. They are variously venal in *The Milagro Beanfield War*, vacuous in *The Tortilla Curtain*, mildly villainous in *Alburquerque*, and vulturine in *Almanac of the Dead*.[11]

John Nichols provided an early and straightforward version of this Sunbelt narrative with his fast-paced, often side-splitting portrait of Hispano and Anglo cultures in unanticipated collision. Two different views of the world are at play and in conflict. The people of Milagro do not see much reason to hurry into the modern world, and they find their strength in an intricate web of community connections. Ladd Devine, his local allies (notably a real estate dealer), and his more powerful friend in the state government see the benefits of greater participation in the national economy. The cultural difference is summed up with the saga of Milagro's single parking meter, a brainstorm of Mayor Sammy Cantu, Councilman Bud Gleason (the real-estate man), and Sheriff Bernabé Montoya. Installed in front of the all-purpose General Store + Frontier Bar + Pilar Café, its purpose is to earn a few dollars for the financially strapped Sheriff's Office. But ancient and irascible Onofre Martinez regularly pulls his battered Chevy pickup into the metered space and tears up the parking tickets that appear like clockwork on his windshield. Installation, repairs, and the paper and ink required for the tickets have so far cost the city $553.13, while the meter has taken in exactly $1.91. As long as Onofre claims the space, no stray tourist can park there and naively feed the meter. Community values, in short, trump economic rationalization.[12]

The plot kicks off with Joe Mondragon, an otherwise ordinary and sometimes boneheaded member of the local community. Joe decides on impulse to chop a trench into the Miracle Valley's main irrigation canal, divert water onto an arid field, and plant beans. The first problem is that it may be his field but it is not his water. The second problem is that his action threatens Ladd Devine's plans for a dam in Milagro Canyon. Devine is the area's closest version of a land baron. His grandfather had bought up large tracts of land in the 1930s and 1940s when economic stress combined with new water laws to make subsistence farming problematic. But a planned conservancy district and new dam could restore actual H_2O to Devine's holdings, providing the water to go with his water rights. The improvement district will spread the costs, in effect taxing away surplus value from local residents, but most of the water will flow to Ladd Devine's lands and benefit the Anglo investment community. Joe's action in illegally diverting a tiny fraction of water threatens the entire scheme from is foundation, like a gopher gnawing a hole in the side of a canal.

Over the course of the book, Joe's initial, individual action gathers force. Ladd Devine enlists the forces of the state, particularly in the form of state police detective Kyril Montana. Townspeople slowly overcome their reluctance to get involved and their fear of public officials. "Despite building tensions, hardly anybody had even admitted to Joe that they knew the beanfield existed. Most people still did not want to get involved. . . . They wanted to see if Joe could get away with it" (116). Nevertheless, folks in town begin to see the symbolic power of the single beanfield, gradually and sporadically rallying to the cause. There is a community meeting, a petition that few people want to sign, a bit of mild monkey-wrenching of signs announcing Ladd Devine's business interests. Tensions escalate, Joe is arrested, townspeople surround the jail in their dusty trucks, and the governor decides to put things on hold before outside agitators decide to show up from Denver.

Nichols wrote as a fierce 1960s liberationist and an adopted New Mexican. He had attended schools in half a dozen states, experienced the headlong gentrification that turned New York's South Village into trendy SoHo, had a transformative experience observing capitalism up close in Central America, and arrived in Taos in 1969 sensitized to look for the same patterns.[13] Three years later he penned *The Milagro Beanfield War* in a feverish eleven-week burst. He has made no secret of his political leanings, publishing an admiring essay on Reies Tijerina and writing that the world needs more examples like Che Guevara and Mother Jones. One of his models for novel writing is Emile Zola's *Germinal* (1885) with its politically passionate drama of labor conflict in French coal mines.

Nichols is clear that the underlying issue that he addresses in his entire New Mexico trilogy, which also includes *The Magic Journey* (1978) and *Nirvana Blues* (1981), is an overabundance of money seeking investment bargains. The region's problem, he wrote in a later essay, is too much outside money: "Excessive capital, wielded by middle-class newcomers, has created harsh division between locals and immigrants. It has highlighted ethnic tensions, destabilizing ancient communities and their value systems."[14] Ladd Devine's desire to keep making money for its own sake drives the conflict in the novel, but he operates in a larger economic world. The politicians and string-pullers in Santa Fe want to keep New Mexico open and inviting to outside investors. The vacationers and condo buyers will come from Boston and Dallas. From the governor's point of view, "development swung votes . . . and Ladd Devine's Miracle Valley project was the kind of thing people considered progress; it would bring outside money into the state" (433).

The novel follows a large cast of characters who weave in and out of the action and play out side stories. In action, the villagers are cantankerous and only occasionally cooperative. They are impulsive and unpredictable and largely contemptuous of bureaucratic society (like Onofre Martinez and the parking meter). Joe Mondragon decided to irrigate his beanfield on a whim, and he adamantly refuses to lead the growing resistance. Ladd Devine's side includes his various employees, state officials, Forest Service personnel, and a reluctant sheriff. Attorney Charlie Bloom, a newcomer who edits a radical regional newspaper, is a stand-in for Nichols himself (who contributed articles to a similar publication) and functions as an occasional commentator on the action. Herbie Goldfarb, a bumbling VISTA volunteer, is a comic mirror whose misadventures simultaneously demonstrate the practical competence of the Milagro's people and points up their hit-and-miss approach to the growing crisis.[15]

Embedded in the contrast between homeland and real estate are other differences. The story weighs the value of large-scale institutions (state government, Forest Service, conservation district) against the small-scale interests of the town. It pits progress, defined as economic growth, against tradition. The Anglo world embraces change, whereas the Hispano community is skeptical out of long experience. The Anglo world is rational, never more so than in the form of detective Kyril Montana, who is a sort of applied sociologist who tries to figure out all the social gears and levers that make Milagro tick and fails completely. The residents, of course, have a deep affection for their home community. Even cynical Joe Mondragon holds on to memories of summer nights in the mountains with his father, helping to drive their sheep across the river, fishing in autumn, hunting through snowy hills, cleaning the ditches in the spring: "No getting around it, though: suddenly he held a profound tenderness for his people, that's what it was. His people. His gente. . . . Suddenly he loved the people he lived with, he cared about their lives. . . . His childhood, something he had all but forgotten, drifted out of a dim misty place" (116–17).[16]

In *The Tortilla Curtain*, T. C. Boyle offers a harder-edged narrative of the tension between land and real estate. Twenty years after Nichols wrote, it was difficult for Boyle or his readers to be quite so celebratory of traditional community. Los Angeles itself, of course, has long been a favored setting for cynical and satirical novels. Just compare the "noir" Los Angeles constructed in the work of James Cain, Nathaniel West, and Raymond Chandler and the alienating Los Angeles of Chester Himes, Budd Schulburg, and Joan Didion to the deeply rooted New Mexico pictured by Mary Austin, Oliver LaFarge, and Frank Waters. Boyle wrote as a relatively new Angeleno who grew up in suburban New York and came west in 1978 by way of Iowa City. He has a penchant for satire, and *The Tortilla Curtain* is filled with Los Angeles stereotypes deftly pinned to the specimen mat.

The novel opens with a literal competition for space. Nature writer Delaney Mossbacher in his freshly waxed Japanese sedan is speeding up Topanga Canyon. The illegal immigrant Candido is trying to sprint across the road when Delaney clips and injures him. Along with fright and worry about legal liability, Delaney is annoyed that those people are "camping out down there . . . crapping in the chaparral . . . thoughtless people, stupid people, people who wanted to turn the whole world into a garbage dump, a little Tijuana" (11). Soon thereafter, however, the tables are turned. Walking through his own upscale subdivision of Arroyo Blanco Estates after an evening property owners' meeting, Delaney finds himself shadowed by a big boat of a car with mag wheels, smoked glass, and ka-thumping stereo. The car paces him, then turns to freeze him in its headlights before driving off. "Who would be up here at this hour in a car like this? Was it burglars, then? Muggers? Gangbangers?" (64).

In fact, both of the men who collide on the Topanga highway are newcomers to Los Angles, Delaney since two years and Candido for a matter of days. Each is looking for a way to stake a claim on the landscape. For Delaney, it is through his *Wide Open Spaces* magazine column "Pilgrim at Topanga Creek" where he records his observations of nature. Arroyo Blanco Estates is up the canyon, allowing Delaney to wander out his back door along the ridge lines of the Santa Monica Mountains. He found it hard to feel bad, "not up here where the night hung close around him and the crickets thundered and the air off the Pacific crept up the hills" (63). Candido's personal connection to the canyon and mountains is far more practical. On a side ravine, he has made a camp for himself and his wife América. It is far better than the streets of Los Angeles, for "the water was still flowing, the sand was clean, and the sky overhead was his, all his, and there was nobody to dispute him for it" (26). He finds a way to make the polluted stream, which first gives him terrible diarrhea, work for him. When their first campsite is discovered and trashed, he discovers an even more secluded place protected by an overhanging cliff and the pooled stream. Here he envisions a facsimile of a real home—a place where they can feel comfortable enough to express their mutual affection and physical love.

The conceptualization of land as refuge (spiritual or practical) runs up against the realities of land as real estate. The most effective claims are not those of hidden immigrant or sensitive writer. Instead, Arroyo Blanco claims the most power. The name itself appropriates Topanga Canyon for people on one side of the social divide, and its residents have the power to control uses of land inside and outside the community. They can build gates and then walls. They can decide to shut down a gathering place for day laborers to protect the value of their houses. In the form of college students with a chip on their shoulder, they can invade the little corner of the canyon where Candido and América are trying to turn a camping spot into a home. The superficial argument for these actions is to make residents feel that Arroyo Blanco Estates is a safe place (to enhance its "use value" in the jargon), but the underlying concern is also to maintain its exchange value as a real estate investment.[17]

In contrast, neither wife has a connection with landscape. América does not share Candido's feelings of pride in finding a secluded campsite, which is just another place of drudgery and danger. She wants a house with a roof, a refrigerator, a bathroom, beds. What she wants is what Kyra has for sale. Kyra defines herself in terms of real estate. She deals with jet set money (one client has just moved back to Italy and left a multimillion-dollar house for sale) and she knows all the techniques for moving inventory. She knows how to display a house, psych out clients, and find exactly the right moment "to talk the place up, rhapsodize over the views, the privacy, the value and exclusivity" (107). She knows how to manipulate people with handwritten notes and housewarming gifts: "She knew that people in her area changed their place of residence once every 3.7 years, and that they had cousins, children, parents and old college roommates who needed housing too. And when the time came to list their property, they would go to Kyra Menaker-Mossbacher, the empress of goodwill" (156).

As a manipulator of symbols, Kyra is right at home in Arroyo Blanco. Her clients are musicians, television writers, investment company executives. Her neighbors range from lawyers to a corporate executive under house arrest for chicanery. One of the loudest voices for walling and protecting the community belongs to Jack Cherrystone, whose considerable wealth comes from doing the voice-overs for movie trailers. Just as trailers are manipulated and often misleading simulacra of cultural products that are themselves fictions, Jack is about as fake as a human can be yet becomes the "voice-over" for the community.

The Anglos have the literal high ground, the ridge tops and view lots as opposed to the canyon grotto. Hilltops are refuge against invaders, for many of Kyra's clients "wanted something out of the way, something rustic, rural, safe—something removed from people of whatever class or color, but particularly from the hordes of immigrants" (107). In spite of Delaney's liberal scruples, the Arroyo Blanco homeowners decide first to install gates to their private development, then to build a wall to keep out "coyotes," community shorthand for frightening humans as well as animals. Indeed, for Kyra, "the invasion from the South had been good for business to this point because it had driven the entire white middle class out of Los Angeles proper and into the areas she specialized in: Calabasas, Topanga, Arroyo Blanco. She still sold houses in Woodland Hills . . . but all the smart buyers had already retreated beyond the city limits. . . . There had to be a limit, a boundary, a cap, or they'd be in Calabasas next and then Thousand Oaks and on and on up the coast until there was no real estate left" (158–59).

Things go wrong when up-canyon and down-canyon interpenetrate. Delaney parks in the lower canyon for a hike only to have his car stolen and to encounter predatory criminals (who merely make him uneasy but who have raped América). The Da Ros house, with its magnificent view, is invaded by the same bad guys coming up the canyon. They do no direct harm when Kyra confronts them, but they return to deface the house with graffiti. Later, all Arroyo Blanco is threatened by a fire that sweeps up the canyon with a storm of rising heat, started when one of Candido's fires leaps out of control. It dies down only after consuming the Da Ros mansion, leaving Kyra fearing that "real estate had gone bad" and that the invaders are winning (310). Thereafter, things go from bad to very bad. Delaney becomes obsessed with immigrant refugees driven out of the canyon, seeking to find and root out shacks and shanties (real estate claims!) that have popped up in unburned scrub—nature writer turns vigilante. Fire season turns to rainy season. Flash floods rip the landscape. Delaney dies in the surging waters, closer to nature than he has ever been before. Candido and América survive, but América's child does not.

The novelist's satire throws off more barbs than an angry porcupine. As a morality play, the message is clear: nature dwarfs individual aspirations. Liberals are hypocrites. Environmentalists are romantic racists who prefer the idea of nature to its reality and choose nature in either form to other human beings. Delaney the nature writer becomes alienated from the land of benign flowers and birds. As if it has read Mike Davis's *Ecology of Fear* (1998), the commoditized landscape fights back with its natural systems. Fire and flood in succession undermine the hopes and plans of all four central figures.

As a real estate fable, the novel hammers home the shallowness of house buyers who see an investment rather than a home. Kyra knows that she is serving vanity rather than practical need when she peddles hilltop mansions. Delaney fights his neighbors' fetishizing of property values, then goes along with the gate and wall schemes, and finally falls for the rationalizations about property values even when he knows better. The novel implicitly attributes the contradiction between use and exchange values to the excess of available cash that is sucked into Los Angeles bank accounts through the entertainment industry and spurts out again in search of lucrative real estate deals by which individuals can try to skim some benefit as capital circulates through the built environment.

Like T. C. Boyle, Rudolfo Anaya is a seasoned writer who can craft a well-structured novel. He grew up in Santa Rosa (New Mexico) and Albuquerque and has spent much of his career at the University of Mew Mexico. He made his reputation with *Bless Me, Ultima* (1972), described by one commentator as a story of a young man's "bittersweet negotiations with family, church, peers, sexuality, and ethnic and cultural traditions as he stumbled toward adulthood."[18] Critics tend to dismiss *Alburquerque* as a lesser work, less steeped in regional culture and damaged by plot elements that aim at commercial success rather than authenticity.

Indeed, *Alburquerque* combines two very standard story lines. One centers on Abrán Gonzalez, a young man who has been raised as part of the working-class Chicano community but who discovers that he is the son of a well-known and wealthy artist who is an Anglo but who has developed a deep sensitivity to New Mexico. After meeting his mother for the first time at the end of her life, he resolves the identity of his father, a quest that takes him to different neighborhoods and individuals representing different facets of the city. He becomes entangled in the second storyline, which involves a three-way contest for mayor between progressive Marissa Martinez, who has the support of barrio residents, along with up-to-date credentials as a battling district attorney; Walter Johnson, who represents the big money of the old Anglo business elite; and Frank Dominic, Hispanic entrepreneur and property developer who wants to bridge the difference as a modern patron, a new *alcalde mayor*. Abrán promises to return to the boxing ring (he was an amateur champion) under the sponsorship of Frank Dominic in exchange for being told his father's identity. Dominic, in turn, hopes his sponsorship will gain him points among Hispanic voters. At the end, all is made clear. Marissa wins the election, and Abrán learns that his father is the well-known Hispanic author Ben Chavez, whom he already knows and respects.

Embedded in the political campaign is Frank Dominic's proposal for a revolutionary land development that will "rebrand" the city as a leisure destination. He wants to promise jobs for the Hispanic barrio, cachet for the North Valley yuppies in their adobe-style houses, development opportunities for the real estate industry, and attractions for tourists. The solution: Acquire rural water rights from nearby Indian pueblos and divert the Rio Grande through downtown in a series of canals and lagoons to create scores of waterside building lots for condos, office buildings, a casino, hotels, a performing arts center. "It was money *and* politics for Dominic. He was aiming to be governor, but he wanted to be mayor first. He wanted to bring in casino gambling and build a Venice on the Rio Grande. . . . Dominic had cooked up a big urban enhancement project. Canals full of Rio Grande water. Casinos. A Disneyland on the river" (58–59). With this scheme, Alburquerque can be Santa Fe and Las Vegas both.[19] At the meeting to roll out the scheme, the architect shows a model of "a desert Venice with beltways of green, ponds, and small lakes, all interconnected by the waterways that crisscrossed the downtown area" (115).

If it were reality rather than fiction, the "El Dorado" plan for Alburquerque would not stand alone. Tucson in the 1990s considered refilling the dry bed of the Santa Cruz River to revitalize downtown. Other Arizonans have successfully promoted development of the amazingly named Scottsdale Waterfront, where flats, shops, and the Fiesta Bowl Museum will hug the bank of the Arizona Canal as it channels irrigation water through the Valley of the Sun. Denver has turned a stretch of the unprepossessing South Platte River into a whitewater park. An investment of $54 million has remade a seven-mile stretch of the North Canadian River into the "Oklahoma River" where rowing and canoeing events attract Olympic athletes from around the globe.[20]

There is something Oklahoma City-like in the ambitions and financial connections of Alburquerque. Exited residents see the scheme as a chance finally to catch up with Dallas and Denver as well as to emulate Las Vegas. The scheme is intended to pull in mobile capital: "The businessmen are dreaming of rich Arabs, Hong Kong investors" (126). Money will flow in from New York and Tokyo with the help of local government in a nice example of the second circuit at work.

Anaya sets up the water scheme in ethnic terms, with the good of the people set against the good of property owners. The real estate juggernaut of which Frank's scheme is one component has two impacts on poor and indigenous communities. Hispanic residents are very much aware of the perils of neighborhood gentrification. The city's wealthy professionals have "discovered rural living and the Alburquerque abode style" and have overwhelmed older Hispanic communities on the north side as they carve out their enclaves. Frank Dominic himself tore down small businesses to make space for his Duke City Plaza office complex, causing one character to muse on the fate of a neighboring city: "Same thing happened in Santa Fe. People with money came to live the Santa Fe style, they bought the downtown barrios and built hotels, shops, condos. The old residents were swept aside, the people gone. . . . If Frank Dominic has his way, the barrio boys will be rowing boats up and down canals that cover the land where they used to live" (80). One of the last paintings by Cynthia Johnson, Abrán's mother, is commentary on gentrification. It shows "the Mexicanos as outcasts in their own land. People in one painting were walking away from the shining city" while "expensive cars, Hollywood faces, and women in the ostentatious Santa Fe style lined the streets. The painting depicted the end of an age" (154–55).

The scheme also impacts nearby Indian pueblos. Frank's scheme depends on buying the water rights that are "the blood of our valley" in the words of old *patron* Manuel Armijo (117). Skeptics doubt that he will ever secure the water, but Frank is confident in his access to Japanese money. "The pueblos are dying and the Hispanic villages up north are withering away" he tells the crowd at the unveiling. "We are promising each pueblo and each land-grant village a percentage of the casinos right off the top" (118). If the pueblos sell, says writer Ben Chavez, "the way of life they hold sacred will be sacrificed. Then they'll have to come into Dominic's city to work for minimum wages, make hotel beds, and hold Indian dances in the casinos for the tourists. The minute you become a tourist commodity, you die" (123).

Anaya hammers at the idea that there is an authentic world and an Anglo world, real world and unreal world, land users and real estate dealers. Hispanic and Indian characters have a deep spiritual connection with the land and the cycles of seasons. The land purifies and renews the spirit, giving extra strength to those who know how to make the connection. Most of the newcomers only see the surface. "There's religion in this earth," says one character, "but when you only come to rent the condo and you don't touch the mud, then you're not connected" (152–53). Looking over the sweeping mountains after riding from a Rio Arriba farm deep into the Sangre de Christo range, Abrán agrees with his newfound friend Lucinda that "this is real, and the world of Frank Dominic unreal" (171).

Almanac of the Dead has its own "El Dorado project," a scheme that sounds like a cross between Venice Beach and Palm Springs. Leah Blue, wife of a crime kingpin, wheels and deals in real estate. Her big development will be Venice, Arizona, where canals will link a chain of lakeside neighborhoods. The whole scheme will require an astounding amount of water. Leah plans to rely on wells run deep into an already depleted aquifer. All she needs is a compliant federal judge to dismiss an Indian water rights claim in Nevada, and she'll have the legal precedent she needs. The judge is happy to offer a favor to his golf buddy Max Blue: "Arne believed in states' rights, absolutely. Indians could file lawsuits until hell and their reservation froze over, and Arne wasn't going to issue any restraining orders against Leah's deep wells either. Max could depend on that" (376). And yes, he could. The judge throws out the last motions for an injunction, and Blue Water Development Corporation is ready to start on hundreds of miles of canals. "Her dream city had been calculated with Arizona's financial collapse and Mexico's civil war in mind. Venice, Arizona, would rise out of the dull desert gravel, its blazing purity of marble set between canals the color of lapis, and lakes of turquoise. . . . Forget Tucson and start over" (662).[21]

In Silko's world, the second circuit of capital has an ugly face. A major purpose of Leah's real estate work is to launder cash from organized crime. Her father and brothers administer huge holdings in California, presumably acquired with dirty money, and the seed money for Leah's enterprise in Arizona comes via the New Jersey mob. Another character, Trigg, considers himself a legitimate businessman because he does not use guns to acquire assets, but he's also laundering money. He is buying downtown Tucson "block by shabby block" and knows how to manipulate zoning laws to turn cheap properties valuable. His real estate plans depend on money siphoned from his commercial blood banks, from detox centers, and then from a business in body parts for medical transplants harvested from murdered winos and cadavers imported from Mexico.

In the complex arc of the novel, the deepest story is that of indigenous peoples who rise against the inequities of five centuries of European conquest. Silko is of mixed Indian, Mexican, and Anglo but is most often identified as an American Indian writer. She grew up with the Laguna Pueblo community while going to school in Albuquerque, graduated from the University of New Mexico, and relocated to Tucson in the 1980s. The novel includes a complex map that locates its characters in different places and parts of North America and traces their connections to Tucson (thus multiplying Silko's own life story). The map and novel chart out an east-west axis along which European Americans move and a north-south axis along which Indian peoples have moved for thousands of years, from the original journeys that peopled the continent to the recent northward migration of Mexican Indians. Individual characters reproduce the movements. Lecha, the Yaqui psychic who is the keeper of the ancient, prophetic almanac that gives the book its title, moves from her native Mexico to the southwestern United States, to Alaska, and back to Tucson via cities like Denver. Leah Blue moves from New Jersey to Tucson and has family connections in California. Because all indigenous America is a single land, revolution in southern Mexico is also revolution in Arizona, and the theme of resistance to conquest underlies the individual story strands that Silko weaves together in what amounts to a prophetic utopian manifesto.[22] It is here that the contrast of real estate and place is most clear: "El Feo [the revolutionary leader] had devised a simple and clear test to reveal whether so-called 'leaders of the people' were true or only impostors sent by the vampires and werewolves of greed. The test was easy: true leaders of the people made return of the land the first priority. No excuses, no postponements, not even for one day . . . the land must be returned to the people whose ancestors had lived on the land for twenty thousand years continuously" (524).[23]

One-Dimensional Region

Silko's novel moves aquatic schemes and fantasies from the satirical to the sobering. Water in the Southwest is about progress as measured in terms as economic development and growth. Water is the determinant of the value of real estate and the future of industries—vital choices in a region where every city has been a land speculation.

As we have seen, water plays a key role in these fictionalized social and economic transitions, entering the plot as developers appropriate it for nonproductive uses (in *Tortilla Curtain* water appears suddenly as a flash flood to take the landscape's own revenge for misappropriation by real estate developers). "Properly," we suppose, water in the arid Southwest is supposed to be productive. It is supposed to nourish life—the natural life or native plants and animals or the ecologically rooted life of indigenous communities engaged in traditional agriculture. It is not supposed to be reduced to a decorative element and amenity. We are not supposed to abstract away its use values in favor of exchange values, to shift it from production to sterile consumption.[24]

But in the novels under discussion the "outsiders" try to do just that in the interest of real-estate investment. Major characters in three of the books want both physically and legally to divert water that "should" nurture crops of beans or water stock on Indian reservations into an amenity and decorative element, while the householders in Arroyo Blanco Estates are presumably very high per capita water users in the midst of their often tinder-dry environment. This capture and abstraction of water are ways in which these authors depict the resource economy as inactive or in decline. The contrast is implicit in *The Tortilla Curtain*, where Los Angeles has no orange groves or celery fields left for Candido to pick and explicit in John Nichols's depiction of Milagro's failing farms that can no longer support its people. Sheriff Bernabé Montoya has six children, every one of whom has moved away to find work, and most other families are in the same situation, which is why Ladd Devine thinks that the lure of tourist industry jobs will win people over. It is explicit and symbolically freighted in *Almanac of the Dead*, where Leah plans to lease inactive Texas oil rigs to drill into deep aquifers. Because Arizona's copper industry has shut down, water is now plentiful; too bad if Leah's deep wells will drain the shallower wells of Indians and small owners. Water, essential for agriculture and for place-based communities, is thus captured by and for the second circuit of capital. Natural flows are tapped and diverted to assist the artificial flows of investment.[25]

These examples are reminders that the authors downplay or ignore the aspects of economic life that theorists like Lefebvre would call the first and third circuits of capital—aspects that are in fact very present in the real

Sunbelt Southwest. The fictional residents of Tucson, Alburquerque, Milagro, and Topanga Canyon may all be captives of capital, but of a very limited sort.

The Sunbelt Southwest has been a manufacturing powerhouse with a prominent role in the first circuit of capital since the early decades of the twentieth century, but readers would not know it from these Sunbelt novels. One of Anaya's mayoral candidates does hope to lure a Japanese electronics plant, but the plant has not been built before the final page. In *Tortilla Curtain* we read nothing of the vast Southern California industrial base with its assembly plants and aerospace giants, with the exception of a clothing sweatshop that América tries to find but cannot locate. Leah and Max's son Bingo runs the vending machines in El Paso and watches over gambling at the horse tracks, but the vast maquiladora industrial complex of El Paso/Juarez does not figure in his activities.

Where the industrial economy does appear in many novels of the Sunbelt Southwest, it comes as industry's end products of physical waste and trash—variations on the polluting coal plants described by Andrew Needham and the human outcasts shipped from urban California to the hinterland in the prison economy that Volker Janssen outlines. Garbage and toxic waste disposal is one of the areas for organized crime in Max Blue's Tucson. Don DeLillo similarly places garbage at the center of the Southwest economy in *Underworld*, where New Yorker Nick Shay finds himself in Arizona and Southern California working for Whiz Co, "a firm with an inside track on the future. The Future of Waste. This was the name we gave our conference in the desert. . . . we were the front-runners, the go-getters, the guys who were ready to understand the true dimensions of the subject."[26] The trope echoes *City of Quartz* (1990), where Mike Davis meditates on the ruins of Fontana, California, which encapsulated the rise and fall of the industrial economy in a mere half-century. So does the scene where Nick visits a desert parking field for abandoned airplanes where the products of the aviation industry, one of the giants of the actual Southwest, are being repainted as a huge art project that almost nobody will see—from economic bang to whimper.

Nor is much made of the universities and research laboratories that give the region a prominent role in the production of knowledge and economic innovation as recipients of third-circuit flows. Arroyo Blanco Estates is not far from UCLA, but presumably no history or literature professor can afford its houses. The University of Arizona provides *Almanac of the Dead* with a student who triples as a federal law enforcement informer and lover of a drug dealer but is otherwise background noise. The University of New Mexico provides an office and back story for literature professor Ben Chavez, and two other characters are taking courses, but it is not an active presence. Kirtland Air Force Base and Sandia Labs rate a mention as the source of new residents who fueled a postwar demand for real estate, but not as active generators of economic change. Dominic plans a performing arts center as part of his development to mollify upper-middle-class voters, but artists are bracketed with gambling as parts of a consumption economy.

As we have seen in the preceding discussion, other information workers are even less productive. They *deal* in information, but they do not create ideas that can expand productive capacities. They are lawyers, judges, politicians, undercover cops, entertainers, artists, gamblers, insurance brokers, and real estate dealers, and none of them appears in a sympathetic light. The "Hollywood nights" reputation of Los Angeles has been around so long that it is American folklore, but pity poor Tucson, which has long struggled to portray itself as more cosmopolitan than upstart Phoenix.[27] In Silko's version, it has "always depended on some sort of war to keep cash flowing" (598). It is a "city of thieves" (610) and "home to an assortment of speculators, confidence men, embezzlers, lawyers, judges, police and other criminals, as well as addicts and pushers, since the 1880s and the Apache Wars." A uranium mine on Laguna lands, a dubious enterprise but undeniably part of the industrial economy, becomes a setting for coke-snorting Hollywood types to shoot a movie and desecrate sacred relics.

So, our analysis leads back to real estate and the second circuit of capital. No one would deny that much of the Sunbelt's growth has involved vast amounts of real estate development out of the simple physical necessity to shelter millions of new residents and house their activities. However, in this imagined Southwest, the second circuit actively supplants the productive economy in the imagined Southwest. Profit comes by devaluing some land to shift value to other land (West Los Angeles suburbs rather than city neighborhoods, new subdivisions rather than old Tucson) or to allow its lucrative redevelopment (as in Alburquerque and Milagro). In the Southwest, the corrupt and corrupting aspects of land development are transparent because these are new cities—or at least places that are new for the dominant Anglo Americans. The social framework of the region is still being *constructed* in a way that Georgia society or New Orleans culture is not. There are few institutional intermediaries to get in the way of deal making or to mask the identities and motives of developers. Government is a tool of capital rather a broker among interest groups. Even in Alburquerque, the city depicted in the greatest practical detail, the narrative highlights power brokers and voters but not the possible intermediary institutions. Certainly, no one is capable or interested in interposing him- or herself between Arroyo Blanco and the homeless immigrants . . . nobody dares to get between Leah and Indian tribal rights . . . no one is capable of mediating between Milagro and Ladd Devine (the state police and Forest Service efforts are comic).

The real estate business in these fictions also plays a central role in the depiction of racial and ethnic divisions. Competition for land is what makes contemporary racial conflict go. Anglos continue their multicentury work of turning place into space, home into real estate. Money trumps tradition, and footloose capital displaces people.

This connection may seem obvious until we contrast the Sunbelt Southeast. This is a region where racial tensions are, if anything, more salient than in the Southwest. However, they are much more deeply tied to questions of family, sex, and miscegenation than they are to land and real estate. In Virginia-born Tom Wolfe's *A Man in Full*, the central character is a bombastic Atlanta real estate developer and there is a conflict in which race is central, but the stories are perpendicular to each other. They overlap, but real estate development is not fundamental to racial relations. In Peter Matthiessen's trilogy about the settlement of the far Gulf Coast of Florida—*Killing Mister Watson* (1990), *Lost Man's River* (1997), and *Bone by Bone* (1999)—the tensions caused by real estate ambitions and racial relations are again independent. Racial tension is part of the background, but it is not central to the overweening ambitions of Ed Watson, who is driven fundamentally by "southern" pride rather than "western" ambition.

This difference among regions connects to the contrasting functions that the concept of a "Sunbelt" has served for different corners of the country.[28] The Southeast is imbued and burdened with its past. From William Faulkner, Robert Penn Warren, and William Styron to the present, writers dealing with the Southeast have struggled with the mythologies of southern history. Echoing *Absalom, Absalom*, for example, Matthiessen's trilogy is about the way that history weighs on a descendent of Ed Watson, who discovers in turn how an earlier history shaped Watson himself. And the southeastern landscape frequently takes on the menace of history itself. Thick, knotted, dark, and dank, it is a place not merely of passive danger but of active menace. The tangled forest of William Faulkner's Mississippi (in "The Bear," for example) is a fictional counterpart to the Virginia wilderness than ensnared so many soldiers in blue and grey. The Everglades and its inhabitants both reach out to kill in Matthiessen's novels, and the jungle grows so rapidly over graves that it is virtually an accomplice in murder. Steamy southern Louisiana is just as menacing in James Lee Burke's novels of crime and moral decay: "The wake off the stern looked like a long V-shaped trench roiling with yellow mud, bobbing with dead logs. . . . I could see cottonmouths coiled on the lower limbs of willow trees, the gnarled brown-green head of a 'gator in a floating island of leaves and sticks, the stiffened, partly eaten body of a coon on a sandbar."[29]

In this context, the concept of a Sunbelt has been a tool for reversing or escaping history, a way for a "backward" region to reposition itself as up-to-date and cutting edge. Outside investment for the Southeast has been a tool of modernization, whether through northeastern industrial capital creating Birmingham and Miami, federal programs like TVA and NASA, headquarters relocations to Atlanta and Charlotte, northern retirees moving to Hilton Head and Fort Myers, or German branch plants in Spartanburg and Greenville. Investment through all three circuits of capital has driven the transformation from "the nation's number one economic problem" to the metropolitan Sunbelt South of the twenty-first century.

Yet history never goes away, even in the Sunbelt South—at least not in Walker Percy's novel *Love in the Ruins* (1971). Writing in the riot-ridden 1960s, Percy imagined a miniature apocalypse for suburban Louisiana at some time around the end of the twentieth century. Society continues to function, but things are falling apart and "the center did not hold." The Catholic Church has splintered. southern states have established diplomatic ties with Rhodesia. Rusting Pontiacs dot the streets of half-abandoned Paradise Estates. Riots have left burned-out motels and shopping malls to be reclaimed by owls, alligators, and moccasins. "Beyond the cypresses, stretching away to the horizon, as misty as a southern sea, lies the vast Honey Island Swamp. . . . Yonder in the fastness of the swamp dwell the dropouts from and castoffs of and rebels against our society: ferocious black Bantus who use the wilderness both as a refuge and as a guerilla base from which to mount forays against outlying subdivisions and shopping malls." The protagonist's challenge is to come to terms with the limits of both individual and social action—with the burdens of sin and history.[30]

In the Southwest, "Sunbelt" has functioned differently, as an add-on and confirmation of an already powerful regional image that has emphasized the chance for Anglo Americans to build communities from scratch. The fictions on which this essay has focused both confirm and contradict that image. They treat the landscape itself as entrancing but not actively menacing. It becomes dangerous only when people make foolish mistakes and get baked in the desert while trying to slip across the border or caught in floods exacerbated by the very real estate development from which they have been profiting. Even Topanga Canyon, for some of James Lee Burke's characters, is a refuge above the fray. It is a place where detective Dave Robicheaux can take his family after a particularly nasty case, in a landscape where "you could see almost every geological and floral characteristic of the American continent tumbling from the purple crest of the Santa Monica Mountains into the curling line of foam that slid up onto the beaches . . . and orange groves whose irrigation ditches looked like quicksilver in the sun's afterglow."[31] When you're visiting from south Louisiana, the landscape is as inspiring as it was once for Delaney Mossbacher.

As in Dave Robicheaux's view, southwestern landscapes and cityscapes are literally more visible than those of the Southeast. In the flatland forests and swamps of the Southeast, you are lucky to see fifty feet through the piney woods or around the next hummock. Atlanta suburbs nestle among forest remnants, shelter in convoluted terrain, and hide in the thick, humid air. In contrast, the Southwest is open, with its cities laid out for all to see from nearby mountains (think El Paso, Tucson, Phoenix, Albuquerque, Salt Lake City, Billings, San Jose, even smoggy Denver). Seeing the city from above is a common trope in writing about Southwestern cities, with their open landscapes and (sometimes) clear air, used by writers as disparate as Yvor Winters and Simone de Beauvoir, Raymond Chandler and Cormac McCarthy.[32]

But the novels under consideration take their readers down from the mountains to the ravines, neighborhoods, and back alleys of the Sunbelt Southwest, where the seemingly empty landscapes are not empty at all. The novels remind us that contests over land and its uses remain central public issues in any region like the Southwest where population is still growing and settlement is still in process. They were the meat of politics in the era of railroad land grants, mining booms, and court battles over Mexican land titles in the nineteenth century. They were the subtext for water allocation politics and conservation politics in the twentieth century. In the twenty-first century, they are the focus of growth management/property rights battles, environmental activism, and community development campaigns.

And in each century, the opportunities and rights of Indian and Hispanic residents have been at issue in the debates. No matter what nineteenth-century Americans imagined, the West was not vacant for the taking, and neither is the Southwest redefined as Sunbelt. What the novels show are the modern methods of dispossession. There is nothing as crude as the rampaging murderers of Cormac McCarthy's *Blood Meridian* (1985) when regional transformation is driven by real estate investors rather than scalp hunters. The novelists personalize that transformation in Kyra, Leah, and the other characters, but the ubiquity of real estate deals and dealing point up the power of the second circuit of capital as the modern Americanizing force. The town of Milagro wins a reprieve, not a permanent victory. In Alburquerque, even progressive mayor Marissa Martinez will end up pushing development plans—just not those of the old growth coalition. People will keep buying in the Los Angeles canyons despite fire and flood. Even Silko ends her novel with a vision of revolution, but not its consummation. The battles are joined but not decided.

PART IV
The Global Sunbelt

Chapter 11

The Marketplace Missions of S. Truett Cathy and Chick-fil-A

Darren E. Grem

With approximately 1,600 restaurant locations in over three dozen states and upward of three billion dollars worth of sales in 2009, Atlanta-based Chick-fil-A has become one of the fastest growing privately owned businesses in America. Famed for its signature fried chicken sandwich and strict, "closed on Sunday" policy, Chick-fil-A purports a singular mission: "to glorify God by being a faithful steward of all that is entrusted to us [and] to have a positive influence on all who come in contact with Chick-fil-A."[1] S. Truett Cathy, a devout Southern Baptist who incorporated Chick-fil-A in 1964 and opened its first restaurant in 1967, played the greatest role in the company's history, although he was not solely responsible for shaping its corporate culture, expansive growth, and broader social influence. Indeed, behind Chick-fil-A lay the history of a region, nation, and world transformed.

In the 1960s and 1970s, as desegregation and suburbanization reoriented social and commercial patterns in the urban South around shopping malls, Cathy transformed Chick-fil-A from a local restaurant into a large-scale corporation. In the 1980s, Cathy threaded his evangelical sensibilities into Chick-fil-A's corporate culture. In doing so, he pitched Chick-fil-A toward the concerns and desires of its mostly suburban customer base via the location of restaurants, "family-friendly" image, advertising, employment policies, and community outreach programs. In the 1990s, as Chick-fil-A increasingly became connected to the world at large, Cathy's sense of cultural and economic mission expanded, affirming the company's transnational growth and the globalization of its conservative perspective on the value of work, faith, and family.

By focusing on Cathy and Chick-fil-A, I do more than tell the story of one businessman's career or historicize the corporation he founded. I also argue that the corporation demands scrutiny as an important site of religious, cultural, and political activism in the Sunbelt's local and global communities.[2] Moreover, I show how the geography of Chick-fil-A's development *inside the Sunbelt* connected to arrangements of culture, capital, and labor *outside the Sunbelt*. That these arrangements stretched—and continue to stretch—from sites in the Sunbelt to specific locales around the globe should move scholars beyond debates over what is or is not the "Sunbelt" and toward a better understanding of the transregional and transnational structures of racial, spatial, political, economic, cultural, and religious power that shape life in a Sunbelt-centered nation and world.

Of Chicken Sandwiches and Shopping Malls

The sixth of seven children, S. Truett Cathy was born to Joseph and Lilla Cathy in rural Putnam County, Georgia, in 1921. When the family farm folded in 1925, Joseph Cathy moved the family to Atlanta, only to experience repeated setbacks in the midst of the Great Depression. As a result, like thousands of other families in the state, the Cathys depended on federal relief during the 1930s, moving into the federally subsidized Techwood Homes before regaining their footing amid the economic revival sparked by World War II. Shortly after returning from wartime service in the army, S. Truett Cathy went into business with his brother Ben Cathy, opening the Dwarf Grill in Hapeville, an industrial community a few miles south of downtown Atlanta. "The Ford Motor Company broke ground for an assembly plant in Hapeville . . . at about the time we located a desirable piece of property nearby," remembered Cathy. "Although not [on] a corner lot," their grill "was next to the corner on a site that gave us a good traffic flow. Industry was moving into that area. I knew we had a chance to work up a good breakfast trade with people going to work, and we could develop a good lunch trade as well."[3]

The economic and racial environment of Hapeville shaped day-to-day business at the Dwarf Grill. In terms of economic standing, Cathy had a mixed clientele. Ford employees filled the Grill during the lunch rush. In the afternoon, working- and middle-class mothers dined with their children, while teenagers from the nearby Hapeville High School kept the place hopping at night. In terms of race, Cathy's restaurant was located in a decidedly white neighborhood. Before the war, the *Fulton County Review* lauded Hapeville as a "98% White" community. The newspaper's assessment was not far off the mark. In 1940, only 85 of Hapeville's 5,059 residents were black. After the war and well into the 1950s, Hapeville's black residential population remained about as minute.[4] Though lily-white, Hapeville nevertheless maintained a segregated economy much like other communities in and around Atlanta. The local Ford plant, nearby airport, and other commercial enterprises adhered to the standards of legal and spatial segregation common in the urban South of the 1940s and 1950s. Regardless of whether Cathy did or did not practice or promote racial segregation at the Dwarf Grill (no hard evidence exists to prove or disprove it), Jim Crow forms of racial exclusion certainly ordered the commercial world inhabited by Cathy.

Although the diner did well in the late 1940s and 1950s, a series of personal and professional tragedies—including Ben Cathy's sudden death in a plane crash in 1949 and the accidental burning down of a second Dwarf Grill in 1960—prompted Cathy to rethink what his business would or could be. He noticed that his chicken entrees often sold well, especially his fried chicken sandwiches. Unfortunately, such items often took a long time to prepare and incurred a higher wholesale cost than cheaper offerings like hamburgers and fries. These problems vexed Cathy until 1961, when he discovered that a food equipment manufacturer had recently developed a relatively cheap pressure fryer, nicknamed the "Henny Penny." With this fryer, the Dwarf Grill reduced cooking time for chicken breasts to roughly the same amount of time as the average quick-serve hamburger. To reduce the cost of raw chicken, Cathy solicited the services of Goode Brothers Poultry Company. Goode Brothers primarily supplied airline companies with boneless, skinless chicken breasts but agreed to sell Cathy any pieces deemed too large for packing in airline trays.[5] Although it is unclear who first contacted whom, Cathy's relationship with Goode Brothers continued for the next few decades. As the chicken processing industry transformed from a peripheral to central industry on the southern economic landscape, Cathy's fortunes would depend on this relationship in more complex (and disconcerting) ways. In the 1960s, however, his connection to the burgeoning chicken industry was relatively straightforward. Goode Brothers supplied him with a cheap source of chicken breasts that he battered, seasoned, fried, topped with a few pickles, inserted in a buttered bun, and sold as the "Chick-fil-A sandwich" (as in "chicken fillet") in restaurants located in a new space, the suburban shopping mall.

The enclosed, climate-controlled mall increasingly became a spatial center of American capitalism in the three decades after World War II. Originally developed as a way to make shopping convenient year-round in northern cities, shopping malls proliferated nationwide as they organized capital and consumers in a contained, safe, and predictable space generally distant from downtown commercial districts. In the urban South as elsewhere, the desegregation of public spaces and downtown businesses encouraged droves of residents and business owners to relocate to the suburbs, with shopping malls serving as important nodes of community and commerce. As a result, malls became paradoxical places. On the one hand, economic standing and automobile ownership, rather than segregation laws, determined access. On the other hand, the creation of capital and value in the space of the shopping mall joined with the suburban migration of money, housing, schools, jobs, and public services to advance a nationwide postwar trend—the bifurcation of metropolitan areas into growing suburban zones and "blighted" central city zones defined by an "urban crisis" of depopulation, declining tax bases, increasing unemployment, higher rates of violent crime, and segregation by race and residence. That poorer people of color—African Americans in particular—living in central city districts often suffered most from such restructurings became one of the most notable aftereffects of "mallification" and the move to a suburban South and nation.[6]

Cathy and his company benefited directly from these complex spatial, racial, and economic restructurings, using the mall as a method for moving into suburban Atlanta and, eventually, into suburban zones outside his native state and region. After officially incorporating Chick-fil-A in 1964, Cathy first entered the mall economy in 1967 when he opened his first "mall unit" at Atlanta's Greenbriar Mall. Built in 1965 as an enclosed regional shopping center, Greenbriar was one of only a few large malls in the

Atlanta vicinity. Located west of downtown, near an exit on the Interstate-285 perimeter after the highway's completion in 1969, it served a wide range of Atlantans. A 1973 report on regional shopping centers ranked Greenbriar third in popularity out of twelve "shopping areas" in Atlanta, with 18 percent of all Atlanta adults visiting it in an average thirty-day period. Approximately one out of four shoppers at Greenbriar was "nonwhite"; in terms of purchasing power, Cathy's first mall customers ranged from middle- to highest-income brackets.[7]

When Chick-fil-A became one of the first quick-serve restaurants in the nation to operate primarily out of a shopping mall, Cathy also revolutionized the fast-food industry. By making cheap, accessible food available to shoppers, Cathy extended the time that shoppers and their families could spend at their local mall, which added value to the mall—via increased revenues—and proved the profitability of fast food inside American shopping malls. Not surprisingly, such payoffs made Cathy's mall units attractive to mall owners. Thus, Chick-fil-A grew by leaps and bounds in the 1970s and 1980s. By 1976, Cathy still maintained the Dwarf Grill in Hapeville but also successfully started up "mall units" of Chick-fil-A at Atlanta's Cumberland Mall, North DeKalb Mall, Perimeter Mall, South DeKalb Mall, and Southlake Mall. With a business model committed to all-mall restaurants, Cathy's company became a fixture in suburban malls in other states, first in South Carolina and North Carolina and then in Texas, Florida, and California. By 1980, Cathy had expanded Chick-fil-A to over one hundred locations. Six years later, this number had risen to 315 mall units in thirty-one states.[8]

Of Sunday Closings and Corporate Ministries

As Chick-fil-A flourished in the particular social and economic space of the suburban shopping mall, it became an explicitly Christian company. Having experienced an evangelical conversion experience at a young age and having been a long-time member and Sunday School teacher in a Southern Baptist church, Cathy had few qualms about wearing his religion on his sleeve. He also strongly believed that religion could and should apply as much on Monday morning as it did on Sunday morning. He was not alone in holding these sentiments. As historians Bethany Moreton and Nelson

Lichtenstein have demonstrated, Sam Walton and other executives at Arkansas-based retailer Walmart likewise built a corporate culture in the 1970s and 1980s well suited to the rural areas and small towns of the South and Midwest by encouraging and appropriating the religious values of their employees and customers. But Walmart was only one of dozens of corporations—and hundreds of small businesses—that trumpeted the benefits of faith-based work, whether that work was in the retail sector or in other branches of a Sunbelt economy that included defense-related industries, technology, media, real estate, agribusiness, food service, oil and petrochemicals, or hospitality and tourism. Indeed, from the 1950s through the 1990s, Sunbelt companies with either evangelical founders or directors included—but were not limited to—Genesco, Eckerd, H-E-B Stores, LeTourneau Technologies, Tropicana Products, Rayco, Buford Television, In-N-Out Burger, Holiday Inn, Days Inn, The Allen Morris Company, Snyder Oil Corporation, Hallmark Electronics, Highland Park Cafeterias, The Medart companies, Wyndham Hotels, PepsiCo, Martin Sprocket & Gear, Westaff, Inc., Pilgrim's Pride, Tyson Foods, Interstate Batteries, Cavan Real Estate Investments, FlowData, Inc., Hobby Lobby, Ukrop's, Kinetic Concepts, SYSCO, World Wide Technology, Comps.com, and eHarmony.com.[9] Like many of these companies, Chick-fil-A was presumably not just in business for business's sake. Indeed, as Chick-fil-A expanded in the 1970s and 1980s, various corporate politics, rituals, and initiatives revealed Cathy's endeavor to make his company a Christian company and, by extension, an active participant in defining and defending relatively conservative stances on work, faith, and family in an increasingly suburban South and nation.

Few corporate policies revealed Cathy's point of view on the value of moral, meritocratic work like Chick-fil-A's Sunday closing. Cathy had abided by this policy since his days as a small restaurant owner in Hapeville. At that time, having a day off made practical sense given the long, labor-intensive hours put in by Cathy and his brother. Moreover, many businesses closed on Sunday well into the postwar period, either due to common custom or local law. In the 1970s and 1980s, however, this policy became a corporate creed intended to mark Chick-fil-A as an upstanding corporate citizen and teach valuable lessons to a nation that Cathy deemed to be in need of entrepreneurial revival and moral renewal.

Paradoxically, the costs of Sunday closing actually reaffirmed its verity as a corporate creed and, in tandem, the notion that anyone who worked with God in mind would receive divine favor. Obviously, closing for a day creates major problems for any enterprise as it cuts potential sales by a seventh, at minimum. For Chick-fil-A especially, Sundays became also high-traffic days as more shopping malls opened their doors on Sundays in the 1970s and 1980s. Not only did Sunday hold more opportunity cost for Cathy than Tuesday or Friday, but shopping mall owners discouraged Sunday closings since they expected the highest sales possible per each unit of mall space they leased or sold. Yet, by acknowledging these potential obstacles to corporate growth and still having profits on the books year after year, Cathy theorized that God was in the mix since, by any other estimation, Chick-fil-A should not have enjoyed continued success. As Cathy later reflected, "God blessed the seventh day and sanctified it, set it aside. It is made for man, not man for it." Such divine decrees, believed Cathy, were granted "not to make life hard but to make it better." By honoring the Sabbath, Cathy "accepted that as a principle and honored God by doing it." In return, "God . . . honored us and the business because of it." Indeed, the Fourth Commandment, like the Bible in general, was a self-evident "formula God has given us for success." By working seven days a week and dismissing such "biblical" business principles, Cathy—along with anyone else—might literally "miss the blessing" that God wished to grant them as an affirmation of their faithfulness.[10]

Sales figures seemed to support Cathy's views, both about Sunday closings and the role that God had to play in the meritocracy of the marketplace. In a 1986 unit-by-unit comparison, Chick-fil-A's mall units performed as well in six days of operation as its nearest competitor, Kentucky Fried Chicken, did in seven days, with both chains averaging $600,000 per unit in yearly sales.[11] Successive years of continually higher sales in the late 1980s and 1990s likewise legitimized Cathy's style of doing business. By pointing to such statistics, Cathy could easily argue that the proof was in his policies. The lack of scandal at Chick-fil-A, which Cathy policed by firing suspicious employees, also seemed to affirm the sanctity of his Bible-based formula for success. If other would-be entrepreneurs, if not the entire American public, imitated such an appreciation for traditionalist values and principled wherewithal, Cathy believed, the economic uplift and cultural redemption of the nation would feasibly result.

Other aspects of Chick-fil-A's corporate culture reflected Cathy's views about how his business was sanctified by God. For instance, when Cathy hired someone, he sought faithful devotion to God and company. In Cathy's imagination, the ideal operator embodied the paradoxical attributes of a fiercely loyal organization man (or woman) *and* an independent entrepreneur. On the one hand, Cathy presumed that "our commitment is going to be like a marriage," a sacred vow of principled, mutually beneficial work "with no consideration given to divorce." On the other hand, Cathy encouraged operators to consider themselves to be self-motivated, pioneering, think-outside-the-box entrepreneurs. As one advertising campaign put it, operators had the potential to "Be Your Own Boss" at Chick-fil-A, presumably unlike other companies in the fast-food business. To attract such operators, Cathy offered a remarkably lenient financial arrangement between them and his company. Since the 1950s, many fast-food owners had made their companies public and grown through franchising, an arrangement that often forced operators to absorb significant start-up costs. Cathy, however, kept Chick-fil-A a private company. He spread ownership among members of the Cathy family and eschewed the traditional style of franchising, allowing any potential operator to open a location with a modest $5,000 investment instead of the tens of thousands of dollars often required of a McDonald's or Wendy's operator. Cathy's company covered the rest of the new location's capitalization and the operator's training, then split any future sales on a fifty-fifty ratio with the operator after he or she remitted 15 percent of gross sales to Cathy. Operators also enjoyed rewards for high sales numbers, from all-expense paid vacations, merchandise, and cash bonuses to free Lincoln Continentals for any operator who raised sales by 40 percent or more in a given fiscal year. Such incentives made Chick-fil-A a popular choice for those seeking to fit into an established corporation while retaining the sense that they made their own futures.[12]

To make good on Cathy's offerings, operators were expected to hire and train equally loyal and driven employees. Though Chick-fil-A restaurants hired mostly teenagers or young adults, Cathy tolerated none of the youthful rebellion, sexual license, surliness, or laziness that conservative Americans condemned as legacies of the 1960s and 1970s. The politics of hair and dress mattered for operators and employees alike. Applicants needed to have a "good general [physical] appearance" and demonstrate, like operators, a "sense of significance" to better their chances of employment at Chick-fil-A. "If a man's got an earring in his ear and he applies to work at one of my restaurants," Cathy told the Associated Press in 2000, "We won't even talk to him. It's not becoming for a man to wear an earring. . . . I can't take that risk."[13] The risk was more than a matter of professional appearance. It was also the risk of condoning such expressions as the new standards of behavior in the fast-food industry specifically and in American life generally.

To counteract these trends, Cathy presented Chick-fil-A as a devoted, hard-working, harmonious, purposeful family—a corporate facsimile of the ideal suburban family. To be sure, the "family" motif in corporate management strategies had precedence long before Chick-fil-A.[14] But in Cathy's estimation, it worked to instill values lost in more recent decades. Thus, Cathy urged all new employees to follow the lead of the unit's operator, who would train them, motivate them, and model for them how they should dress, act, talk, and work their way up the corporate ladder. Various activities promoted these views. In the early 1980s, company policy encouraged Chick-fil-A's employees to sing songs of devotion to the company and their operators. One song, entitled "Movin' On," went:

> We are strong hand in hand.
> We are happy side by side.
> Our hearts are joined together,
> By a sense of family pride.
> Every day is an adventure,
> When you're striving for a goal.
> There's a spirit of excitement,
> When we see the dream unfold.
> CHORUS:
> *Chick-fil-A we're movin' on.*
> *Chick-fil-A we're growin' strong.*
> *We're one big happy family,*
> *That's the way at Chick-fil-A.*
> It's so fun to make our living,
> Doing what we love to do.
> When you're working with your friends,
> Every day is fresh and new.
> We're exploring new horizons.
> Reaching, striving every day.
> And the way we work together,
> Is the pride of Chick-fil-A.[15]

Chick-fil-A rewarded any employees who exemplified such values for their corporate piety, familial devotion, and meritorious work with the symbol of postwar upward mobility—the college scholarship. In the 1970s and early 1980s, Cathy established an incentive program that largely catered to his work force's interests, as well as Cathy's aim to send purposeful, hardworking, morally grounded youngsters to college. Any employee who maintained a "C" average in school and had worked part-time for Chick-fil-A for at least two years could be eligible for a $1,000 scholarship to the school of his or her choice, depending on the manager's recommendation. By 1991, Cathy had given millions of dollars to this scholarship program, with more than 6,500 former employees having received it.[16]

As Chick-fil-A grew and its corporate culture Christianized in the 1980s, the company's public initiatives likewise broadened via the WinShape Foundation. In 1983, Cathy launched the community service nonprofit WinShape Foundation at Berry College, a former junior college turned four-year liberal arts institution in the foothills town of Rome, Georgia. Though not officially linked with any evangelical denomination, Berry College "was holy ground" to Cathy "for God had sanctified it for his purpose." "With God's leading," he thought, "we could not fail." Intended to "Shape Individuals to be Winners," the WinShape Foundation first emerged as an offshoot of Cathy's scholarship program, offering a $10,000 per year scholarship to Berry College for any Chick-fil-A employee who exemplified Cathy's evangelical desire to "equip college students to impact the world for Jesus Christ by following Him and living out His unique calling." By the late 1980s, Cathy had expanded the Foundation to include a foster home for "good children with potential to be winners but who would not have the chance without our program." As WinShape expanded into these avenues, Cathy explicitly cast his foundation as filling a gap in state-run social service programs. "You have other programs for drug addicts, alcoholics, and children with sexual abuse problems," he noted, "But where are the people who will take those who haven't been in trouble, those who want to be winners despite their circumstances?" State services, Cathy believed, did not offer programs for such children and, in fact, often mismanaged those under their care. WinShape, by contrast, functioned as a "ministry" for turning children into "winners" in ways the state never could. Cathy averred that such children could be prepared to stand on their own two feet and make their way in the world, thus proving that the meritocratic American Dream was still available to anyone who—with God in mind—sought after it. To encourage a sense of entrepreneurial drive and moral direction, Cathy also set aside funds for the construction of Camp WinShape at Berry. Much like the backwoods, evangelical revival camps of Cathy's youth, Camp WinShape aimed "to guide . . . children in their moral, spiritual, and physical growth." For Cathy, an entrepreneurial work ethic, combined with a godly respect for authority and morality, was the key to making children "winners." To that end, Camp WinShape staff members strived to teach "Christian stewardship and hard work" through camp programs and curricula.[17]

By the mid-1990s, Cathy's WinShape Foundation had earned him notoriety from Atlanta city officials. Calling Cathy "a great role model for our youth," Atlanta Mayor Bill Campbell commemorated the construction of a twenty-three-foot bronze sculpture downtown, just in time for the arrival of the Olympics in 1996. Featuring an educational theme, the sculpture depicted people lending hands to help others climb an archway constructed of books. An inscription on the sculpture read "No goal is too high if we climb with care and confidence," a fitting tribute, one reporter thought, to "one of America's most responsible corporate citizens." Reflecting on the city's gift, Cathy was demure: "We're also in the people business."[18]

Of Christian Communities and Family Matters

Staying attuned to "the people business" became even more important as Chick-fil-A left the mall market behind. After reaching a saturation point around 1978, mall building in America slowed in the early 1980s.[19] By the 1990s, malls no longer stood as the spatial centers of commerce in metropolitan communities. Stand-alone shopping strips, accessible only by automobile and often anchored by "big box" stores like Walmart, Best Buy, or Home Depot, became more common, challenging the dominance of public shopping malls and encouraging the fuller privatization of American life. In response, Chick-fil-A established free-standing restaurants, following the precedence set by McDonald's, Burger King, KFC, and other fast-food establishments. In 1986, the first free-standing Chick-fil-A unit appeared in Atlanta, and, in 1993, the first "drive-thru-only" restaurant opened in Greenville, South Carolina. By 1994, Chick-fil-A redirected all plans for future expansion away from mall units. Chick-fil-A executives found new "distribution points" in suburban and exurban strip malls, along interstate highways, and at other "alternative sites," including office buildings, universities, grocery stores, hospitals, and high school cafeterias.[20] Chick-fil-A shifted away from malls quickly and thoroughly. By 1987, Chick-fil-A had opened a total of 347 mall units and only one free-standing restaurant. By 1993, however, it had opened 83 additional mall units and 59 free-standing restaurants. By 2000, Chick-fil-A planned to open 65 free-standing restaurants, 30 "licensed outlets" at alternative sites, and only one mall unit.[21]

Chick-fil-A's relocation to these new commercial spaces necessitated an aggressive campaign to create "community support"—in other words, to build a new base of employees and customers. At times, this campaign mirrored the marketing strategies of its competitors in the fast food industry.[22] Like McDonald's, Wendy's, or Burger King, Chick-fil-A regularly supplied local schools with various offerings, from selling Chick-fil-A sandwiches and sides in school cafeterias to sponsoring school fundraisers. In keeping with Chick-fil-A's particular mission to instill meritocratic values in American youngsters, Cathy also started the "Core Essentials" program, a free "educational program available nationwide" that was "designed to give teachers and parents the necessary tools to educate elementary-age children about character and values [such as] honesty, cooperation, and responsibility." If students illustrated real growth in "positive character values," teachers could reward them with a "Value-able Card," redeemable for a free Chick-fil-A kids' meal. Covering twenty-seven values over a three-year period, the program found adoption in over 2,000 schools, including 700 elementary schools, nationwide by 2001. Following his father's lead, Dan Cathy also directed the expansion of entrepreneurial programs in public and private schools, serving on the Georgia state executive board of Junior Achievement, a nonprofit organization devoted to teaching "business ethics" and "showing [students] how to generate wealth and effectively manage it, how to create jobs which make their communities more robust, and how to apply entrepreneurial thinking to the workplace."[23]

Chick-fil-A also sought to build "community support" by ensuring a safe, privatized, "family friendly" experience for anyone coming in contact with the company. Increasingly, free-standing restaurants provided opportunities for family entertainment along with family meals, especially for suburban parents seeking out a secure, predictable recreational environment. Cathy believed that such accoutrements were vital parts of their business strategy and broader social mission. "We believe a positive experience," he suggested, "will lead these children to become lifelong customers of Chick-fil-A." Play-ports—private jungle gyms common at other fast-food establishments—thus became standard fare at free-standing Chick-fil-A locations. Kids' meals also aimed to "reflect our values"—and presumably the values of suburban parents—by including educational toys and literature in each bag, all intended to instill "character traits." Cathy also added the Chick-fil-A Cows in 1994, which he described as "powerful tools" given by God to help the business. Given the importance of mascots for cultivating brand loyalty and a sense of predictable familiarity among children and parents, the Cows became a necessary development to break open the family market. As one Chick-fil-A operator reported, his marketing director used the Cows to plant "seeds for the future by getting involved in children's events," which made "a tremendous difference in our exposure." Most often, this director was accompanied by a life-sized plush cow, which handed out an award at local elementary schools, followed by coupons for free ice cream treats to stand-out students. He had already seen results: "The kids love it."[24]

Unlike its competitors, however, Chick-fil-A's identity as a Christian business also helped it to develop "community support" from like-minded institutions and people in its growth zones. Chick-fil-A's Sunday closing policy made it popular with suburban churches and Christian families, which had tangential benefits for business. "Parents tell me their children sometimes don't understand why we close on Sunday and it gives them an opportunity to explain that Sunday should be set aside for worship and family," Cathy noted, "Many of these conversations occur in the midst of a crowd, and our message gets passed on. That's one-on-one brand building." To develop the brand further, Chick-fil-A's management usually developed close ties with nearby churches and public schools. As one operator in San Antonio, Texas, put it, "[The] key to success . . . is community involvement. If somebody calls and asks for something, we give them something. And if churches and schools don't call us, we call them and make an offer."[25] In some communities, Chick-fil-A offered a "Church Bulletin Night," providing free chicken sandwiches to patrons who brought church bulletins into any participating restaurant. In others, Chick-fil-A became the default sponsor for evangelical youth events—such as Christian music festivals and concerts—and a popular caterer for events at local churches.

Chick-fil-A also became a popular employment option for suburban mothers and fathers interested in managing their children's exposure to unsettling or non-Christian work environments. Though not always from evangelical families, homeschoolers nevertheless served as an important labor pool for Chick-fil-A's recruiters. "They're smart, ambitious, and very driven," observed Andy Lorenzen, a Chick-fil-A representative, "They have a high level of loyalty to the business, are diligent and have a good work ethic." Alexa Mason, a seventeen-year-old homeschooler in Charlotte, North Carolina, "enjoyed the flexible hours" and "great environment" that Chick-fil-A offered, as did her parents, who like many homeschoolers, sought out Chick-fil-A because of its Christian affiliations. Of course, homeschoolers did not make up most of Cathy's work force. One operator claimed that only 10 percent of his employees had been homeschooled.[26] Still, hiring a disproportionate number of homeschoolers lined up with Chick-fil-A's continuing commitment to hire workers of a different background from that of most fast food companies, which helped mark it as a different type of fast food enterprise. "Like its competitors, Chick-fil-A targets high-school students to work the counter," observed business writer Frederick F. Reichheld, "but it goes after the upper end of the class, typically higher achievers and more dedicated workers who have long-term intentions of attending college."[27] Thus, on average, Chick-fil-A's rank-and-file tended to be whiter, more middle class, more educated, and more loyal than those working in the fast food industry in general. (Turnover rates still ranged from about 20–100 percent per year, but nowhere near the industry average of 300 percent per year.) Obviously, Cathy's college scholarship fund continued to attract and keep such workers. But since most did not earn this scholarship, other offerings brought in the job applications. A corporate culture that emphasized the value of middle-class work certainly helped, as did hourly wage rates a few dollars higher than the industry standard of minimum or near-minimum wage. Its Christian affiliations also marked it as a business where, presumably, young suburban workers would not be overworked or undervalued. In short, Chick-fil-A was a fast food environment known to be healthy for suburban youths. It was a place where their parents' moral outlook—whether oriented around conservative evangelicalism or the perceived need for teenagers to have a productive job or just around the notion that hard work pays off in the democratic meritocracy—seemed to flourish and be rewarded in ways unusual in the fast-food industry at large.

In practice, its corporate culture could be more limiting than limitless.

Though Cathy claimed that he expected his operators to "operate on Christian principles" even if he did not "expect every operator to be Christian," Cathy's company tended to attract applicants who agreed with his religious point of view.[28] Non-Christians worked at Chick-fil-A, but the vast majority of operators and employees were Christians. Also, Chick-fil-A often acted like an explicitly evangelical enterprise or at least a vaguely Christian one. As noted before, Chick-fil-A actively drew its corporate policies from this religious perspective, it openly courted the support of Christian churches, and it regularly supported Christian events. Chick-fil-A also allowed room for activities like morning devotionals and prayer meetings, often led by executives or local operators. By bringing religion into the work place, Chick-fil-A, thus, opened the door for religious conflict or outright discrimination. One such conflict occurred during a training session attended by a Muslim manager-in-training named Aziz Latif in November 2000. According to Latif, at this meeting "Everyone said a prayer, one person at a time, to Jesus Christ." When it was Latif's turn, "he didn't say anything. There was an awkward silence. Then eventually the next person started praying to Jesus Christ." The next day, Latif was fired. Chick-fil-A claimed that Latif's termination "was not over a religious issue" but "was based on performance," but a week before his firing, Latif's superiors had apparently praised him as a "great manager" who knew the "operation side of the business very well." Latif sued for reinstatement and damages and later settled with Chick-fil-A on undisclosed terms.[29] Though an isolated case, the episode underscored how Chick-fil-A welcomed and encouraged those holding religious affiliations deemed to be affirmative of Christianity and America's Christian heritage. Those who did not tested the limits of Chick-fil-A's self-touted cosmopolitanism.

Chick-fil-A's identity as a Christian company also dovetailed into Cathy's mission to preserve and protect "traditional" family arrangements in American society. "Next to a person's salvation and the choice of Christ as Master," Cathy once averred, "the most important decision is choosing your mate." Like other cultural and religious conservatives, Cathy emphasized distinct, complementary roles for men and women. Such roles might be implied in his company, but they were explicitly prescribed for marriages: "Father is chairman of the board, president, and chief executive officer in the world's greatest institution—the home. Mother is executive vice president in charge of public relations, bookkeeping, interior decorating, the commissary, infirmary, hospital, and all those things that make a house a home." In sticking to this arrangement, Cathy believed that marital peace would abound, thus resulting in greater productivity on the job.[30] Thus, Cathy funded marriage seminars and implemented an annual "marriage retreat" for his operators, later expanding its availability to the wider public. Sponsored by his WinShape Foundation and run out of a retreat facility at Berry College, Cathy's programs aimed to assist "couples in maintaining and growing their relationships" while "experiencing the presence of God" via "prayer, worship, group discussions, and couple mentoring." Supplemented with materials and funding from the National Institute of Marriage and the Center for Relational Care, both nonprofit Christian marriage organizations, couples paid for general relationship seminars or for more specialized weekend packages. For instance, the "Courageous Hearts" package promoted techniques for "restor[ing] communication and rekindl[ing] affection," the "Prepare to Last" counseled "those considering engagement for a successful Christian marriage," and the "Romantic Adventure" package offered an "exciting retreat for couples who want to increase their passion and have a blast doing it!"[31]

By the 1990s, Donald "Bubba" Cathy had become the foremost spokesman for Chick-filA's promarriage activism. "We need to win back our culture's vision for marriage and family," he told *Philanthropy* magazine in 2007. "Biblical truths do work and can be applied in business, personal, and charitable endeavors. Strategic investing in relational wellness within marriage and family is crucial to the continuity of a healthy and enduring nation." Such a strategy had three goals: first, the equipping of local, grassroots marriage initiatives, whether in churches, schools, or businesses; second, the proliferation of a "sustained national media campaign, in conjunction with the local city marriage initiatives"; third, the funding of premarital education "to help get marriages off to a great start." With the direction of the Marriage CoMission, a seminar series facilitated by "marriage champions from five key sectors of influence in the culture," and the Marriage and Family Legacy Fund, a fund-raising entity that "aligns the donor world with the strategic priorities of the marriage movement," Bubba Cathy believed that his company's "wise investment" would result in incalculable "benefits to individuals, families, and the nation."[32]

Outside partners helped in this campaign. Sometime around 2000, Chick-fil-A began a corporate partnership with Focus on the Family, a Colorado-based conservative lobbying organization founded by Dr. James Dobson. Five years later, Cathy contracted Dobson to supply its restaurants with miniature versions of the organization's *Adventures in Odyssey* series, an "audio drama" for children that "presents exciting entertainment that brings moral and biblical principles to life." Educational CD's inspired by VeggieTales, a Christian cartoon series, and child-oriented games inspired by conservative author William J. Bennett's *The Book of Virtues*, also came along with any kids' meal purchase.[33] In addition, Cathy reportedly held financial or time commitments with other conservative organizations, such as Family First's All-Pro Dad foundation, and a number of conservative parachurch ministries, including the Fellowship of Christian Athletes and Campus Crusade for Christ. Though Cathy publicly asserted that his company would remain nonpartisan during any electoral season (an advertising campaign in 2000 even featured the Cows' universal call for "Donkees and "Elefunts" to "Vote Chikin" because "Itz Not Right Wing or Left"), Cathy's religious and political commitments earned him notoriety from a variety of conservative politicians and organizations. In March 2008, John McCain held a "town hall" meeting at Chick-fil-A headquarters during his run for the Republican Party's nomination, fielding questions from a crowd of about two hundred managers and employees—as well as students involved in Impact 360, a Christian leadership organization sponsored by Chick-fil-A—about his stance on role models, taxes, energy policy, and illegal immigration. The following month, George W. Bush presented Cathy with the President's Call to Service Award, commemorating Chick-fil-A's long record of philanthropy. Afterward, Cathy was also venerated at a lunch hosted by the Marriage and Family Foundation, Marriage Co-Mission, and Family First, all conservative organizations devoted "to strengthen[ing] marriages in America" since "healthy marriages are a keystone to the success of our nation."[34]

Of Marketplace Missionaries and the Global South

National notoriety overlapped with another round of expansions for Chick-fil-A. In the 1990s and early 2000s, restaurants continued to pop up in suburban, exurban, and in other "alternative sites" in the lower Northeast, Midwest, and Southwest, with California serving as the company's most promising venture market. By 2005, Chick-fil-A had eleven restaurants in the Golden State, with the Cathy's planning to double the number of units there by the end of 2006 and double again every two years after that, eventually making California a West Coast bookend to Chick-fil-A's Sunbelt span. "We're making a full assault in growing our brand here," Dan Cathy assured one California reporter.[35]

Having the 2005 Operators Meeting in San Diego symbolized these corporate goals and simultaneously displayed Chick-fil-A's identity as a Christian company. For instance, as Cathy's operators filed into the meeting hall, a soft-rock band provided background music, playing a jazzy, upbeat rendition of a praise song entitled "Lord, I Lift Your Name on High." When the meeting was underway, Mark Miller, Chick-fil-A's vice president for training and development, reiterated Chick-fil-A's corporate mission statement, adding that "good business ethics" always originate in the Golden Rule of Matthew 7:12. Dan Cathy, Chick-fil-A's executive vice president, followed Miller onstage and emphasized similar points, urging the crowd to recognize that the "Bible is [a] blueprint and roadmap" and that they should continually "[be] reminded of God's goodness." "[He] created us for a purpose," expressed Cathy, "[to be] missionaries in [the] marketplace." Stepping aside, Dan Cathy introduced his father, who asked the crowd to have a "time of reflection" on three questions—"Why are we in business? Why are we alive? What are the things we can't change?" According to one operator, such moments made annual meetings like the one in San Diego "like going to a huge revival."[36]

That such meetings potentially included operators from abroad signaled that Chick-fil-A's transnational presence and influence had likewise been growing over the past decade. In 1994, the company opened its first restaurant in Canada and, the following year, began drafting plans for an expansion into the British Isles. In 1995, only a few years after the end of apartheid and one year after the country's first free elections, South Africa became another target market for Chick-fil-A. "There's a real vacuum there and a real pent-up demand," Dan Cathy believed. "The doors are open." With agreements for development assured by South African officials, such as Cape Town's first black mayor William Bantom and President Nelson Mandela, the Cathys planned to open between eighteen and twenty restaurants in South Africa, with another nine to be placed in nine other African countries. But the South African market proved a harder nut to crack than expected, perhaps because the suburban environs that nurtured Chick-fil-A's business model did not exist there. Three of the company's start-up restaurants had closed their doors by the summer of 2001. "We were competing with street vendors," reflected Dan Cathy on the stores' failures.[37] Still, this setback did not fully undercut Chick-fil-A's position in South Africa; nor did it stop its interests in spreading the company's cultural and religious commitments there and elsewhere.

Chick-fil-A's global presence was bolstered in 2005 via WinShape International, which the Cathys founded "to mobilize leaders to transform young adults and communities around the world." Partnered with History-Makers, an evangelical missionary alliance that "Empower[s] Emerging Leaders to Change Nations for God," WinShape International sought to apply the "core values" of the WinShape Foundation and Chick-fil-A via missions projects in nearly two dozen countries. (One list of active projects included China, Bahrain, Abu Dhabi, Ukraine, Jordan, Jamaica, Puerto Rico, South Africa, Colombia, Kenya, Turkey, Romania, Malaysia, Paraguay, Zambia, North Africa, Bangladesh, India, Belize, Haiti, and El Salvador.) WinShape International united Chick-fil-A's corporate purpose with the purposes of evangelical missionaries on the ground, spreading a work ethic that would presumably result in the blessing of "transformed lives" for everyone involved.[38]

That most of WinShape International's programs operated in countries strung throughout the so-called "global South" was not coincidental. As a conceptual model, the global South might be best understood as a collection of countries in sub-Saharan Africa, Central and South America, and Asia that by the 1990s shared—and continues to share—political and economic characteristics roughly similar to the South of Cathy's youth. In the late decades of the twentieth century, the global South increasingly moved beyond economic affiliations with colonialist powers and/or race-based forms of social ordering or segregation. After the collapse of the Soviet Union and the receding of world Communism, the global South also represented areas where transnational capitalist enterprises were having a remarkable impact, rewriting the social, racial, and cultural arrangements of states and people, for better or worse.

Operators who signed up to work with WinShape International certainly saw the global South as fit for Chick-fil-A. Most emphasized both the poverty of the areas they visited and how their experiences abroad moved them beyond their "comfort zone" to consider what they—and Chick-fil-A—might offer to assuage various problems there. During his visit to El

Salvador, operator Tom Balsamides was nearly moved to tears by the sanitary and educational limitations he observed. After his trip, he realized that he "had not truly been at the mountaintop" and "there was more to what I was doing and more to what my purpose was in life." After visiting Zambia, Chick-fil-A consultant Juliet Hall claimed that "God really just opened up my eyes and helped me to see what life was like outside of my bubble here.... Lot of people say it's life changing, but it's soul changing. I'll never be the same from that trip because I saw how inadequate that I was as a giver, as a believer, [and] I'm not doing enough." "This is your opportunity to grow and be blessed beyond your wildest dreams," concluded another operator. Like the short-term missions trips common in many evangelical churches, such visits seemed to result more often in the personal edification of the short-term missionary's faith than in any profound change in the social or economic conditions of their host countries. Still, for many operators, the global South seemed like an environment where the corporate culture and moral mission of Chick-fil-A could be duplicated for the greatest good. Operator Tom Sutton saw "leadership training," based on Chick-fil-A's business model, as the key to uplift and a welcome educational tool. "We're finding that the people are hungry, that the businessmen and women that we come across, that it makes sense to them.... It's actual living proof that we run and operate our restaurants this way," he concluded, "And it's amazing to see the hunger that they have to want to learn more about it." By exporting Chick-fil-A's business model of faith-based entrepreneurialism, the underdeveloped global South might be redeemed by the potential unlocked by Cathy's Sunbelt creed. Promotional videos and pamphlets—which pictured poor, yet affable Latino, African, and Middle Eastern children alongside able-bodied, cheerful adults—seemed to reaffirm that such beliefs were justified, that potential existed amid poverty.[39]

The expansion of Chick-fil-A, either through the company's endeavors or through the internationalization of WinShape, also depended on other forms of interchange between the Sunbelt and the global South. At an undetermined point in either the 1980s or 1990s, Chick-fil-A dropped its affiliation with Goode Brothers Poultry Company, instead receiving its processed chicken meat from other supplies, most notably Perdue Farms, the second largest poultry processor in the United States, and Wayne Farms, the nation's sixth largest vertically integrated poultry processor and a subsidiary of food conglomerate ContiGroup. Like other processors, Perdue Farms and Wayne Farms became industry leaders by specializing in what anthropologist Steve Striffler has termed "the industrial chicken." In plants throughout the economically depressed and deunionized rural South, Perdue Farms and Wayne Farms gained full control over all points of production, from hatcheries to transportation to processing to packaging, marketing, and distribution. Both companies also fully rationalized and specialized the chicken processing line, resulting in a new type of finished chicken, one processed into myriad cuts for wholesale to restaurants, grocery store freezers, and fast food vendors like Chick-fil-A. In Perdue Farms's case, after it bought a 500,000-square-foot plant in Perry, Georgia, in 2004, it supplied Chick-fil-A with nearly 350,000 birds per week for its restaurants.[40]

Despite federal and state prohibitions, both Perdue Farms and Wayne Farms also regularly employed undocumented and illegal workers from Latin and South America to produce their "industrial chicken."[41] Indeed, in Surry County, North Carolina, field researchers for the University of New Hampshire's Carsey Institute found that "80–85% of [Wayne Farms'] work force is Hispanic" with "many employees [living] in a trailer park adjacent to the chicken plant." On occasion, the cost of working at a Wayne Farms plant could be even more severe. In the spring of 2004, a Latino teenager named Augustin Juan arrived for work at a Wayne Farms chicken processing facility in Albertville, Alabama. During the course of his shift, the door to a birdcage became stuck as it moved along a conveyor belt in front of his workstation. According to witnesses, Juan "stepped between two cages to free a stuck cage door when the cages were pushed forward" and, in an instant, the cages crushed Juan to death. After investigating the incident, the U.S. Labor Department's Occupational Safety and Health Administration (OSHA) found no fewer than twenty safety violations warranting citation at the Albertville plant. It recommended $49,500 in fines against the poultry processor, including an additional penalty of $10,000 for an outstanding violation that the company had been previously cited for but had not adequately addressed. Reflecting on the accident and Wayne Farms' liability, OSHA Birmingham area director Roberto Sanchez called for employers to "ensure that employees are not exposed [to] these safety hazards" since "These so-called 'struck-by' accidents are a leading cause of worker deaths in the Southeast." Such labor and safety violations, however, were not the company's only problem. During at least one test period between 1998 and 2005, five of Wayne Farms's seven plants failed federal tests for salmonella contamination. Yet, these violations hardly injured the company's profitability. With a client list that included Chick-fil-A, as well as Campbell's, Zatarain's, Jack in the Box, Costco, Nestlé, and Applebee's restaurants, Wayne Farms posted approximately one billion dollars worth in sales in 2004, with expectations for a "10% annual growth in sales for the next five years."[42]

What worked for the chicken processing industry apparently worked for Chick-fil-A. In 2008, Chick-fil-A's annual sales pushed close to three billion dollars, a 12 percent jump over the previous year. Though facing an economic recession and stiff competition from McDonald's (which produced its own plagiarized version of Cathy's signature sandwich), Chick-fil-A remained one of the fastest growing fast food chains in the country. Reflecting on his company's standing over forty years after its founding, Dan Cathy remarked, "I do think that God has blessed our business."[43]

This explanation, one shared by his father and many of their operators and employees, continues to frame Chick-fil-A's operations and interests. Behind this view stands the sunniest interpretation of recent American history, one that emphasizes the role of enterprising, hardworking, faithful individuals who capitalized on the economic opportunities afforded to them by Sunbelt development. In their own readings of their past, they committed to achieving a God-blessed American Dream, have rightly received its blessings, and have justly been granted authority from above to sponsor a personal and corporate crusade against a past that has presumably undercut the American work ethic, the Christian faith, and the "traditional" family. To be sure, following God's will in this manner has included genuinely beneficial and admirable endeavors, such as WinShape's work with foster children and its commitment to help students with the ever-rising costs of higher education. But as Cathy's evangelicalism moralized the meritocracy of the suburbs and granted it divine sanction, it also ensured that people living and working in places like inner-city Atlanta or the chicken plants of the rural South or the underdeveloped corners in the global South were deemed marketplace sinners in need of conversion to the gospel of Chick-fil-A. This is a message that overlooks and whitewashes much. It is also, however, a powerful one, as evidenced by Chick-fil-A's popularity and proliferation. Currently, new operators sign on to Cathy's management team each month, and new employees sign up to work behind the counters every day but Sunday. The WinShape Foundation's entrepreneurial programs and marriage retreats report record enrollments, and WinShape International now plans additional mission trips throughout the global South. Thus, regardless of the ups and downs of the election cycle, Chick-fil-A's marketplace missions will most likely continue for as long as the chicken plants keep running and its fried chicken sandwiches keep selling. Not only that, they will continue on a corporate missions field that now stretches from the Sunbelt spaces of Chick-fil-A's past to the global South of Chick-fil-A's future.[44]

Chapter 12

Tortilla Politics: Mexican Food, Globalization, and the Sunbelt

Laresh Jayasanker

The National Restaurant Association's Best Menu contest in 1983 signaled the newly surging popularity of Mexican food in the United States. The Association commented that the "full-color photo menu" from second-place winner Monterey House "takes all the guesswork out of ordering. This is particularly useful in a Mexican restaurant where many of the guests may not be familiar with the menu items. To be doubly sure there is no confusion, the menu features a glossary of menu items on the back cover."[1] Located in Houston, Monterey House served the combination plates responsible for popularizing Mexican food in the United States. Its menu initiated diners to the ways of the burrito, explaining that it was "an orgy of brazen beans and coy cheese sensuously stuffed into a clingy covering of tempting tortilla. More cheese is draped seductively over the whole daring concoction." Like the Monterey House diners, those eating at the San Diego-based Carlos Murphy's chain needed assistance with their menu choices. The "Mexican Market" section of its menu advised, "The Hot Ones: This means what it says! Gringos should order with caution. We cannot be held responsible for any tears that come to your eyes." A picture of a fireman drove home the message.

American diners still felt cautious when eating Mexican food in the 1980s, but that would change quickly. In the span of a quarter century, tortillas, the most basic Mexican food, would come to outsell sliced bread in the United States.[2] While Carlos Murphy's offered Irish, Mexican, and BBQ style potato skins in the 1980s, by the mid-1990s a review declared that the "Irish-Mexican cafe," had become "virtually all Carlos, no Murphy."[3] By the time tortillas outpaced sliced bread sales, few menus needed to explain the basics of Mexican food. The cuisine had also expanded beyond its historical base in the Southwest.[4] By the end of the twentieth century, even New Yorkers and Chicagoans had integrated Mexican cuisine into their regular diet. Celebrity chefs Bobby Flay and Rick Bayless popularized haute Mexican and Southwestern cuisine with their popular restaurants, glossy cookbooks, and television shows.[5] Variations on Mexican cuisine appeared all over the world. KFC sold "Mexican Twister" chicken wraps in thousands of outlets across China. GRUMA, the largest tortilla manufacturer in the world, supplied KFC's China branches by shipping tortillas from its plant in Southern California until demand became so great that it built a separate factory in Shanghai.[6]

There is more to the tortilla story than Americans' growing love of tacos and wraps. Changing eating habits accompanied the changing political economy of the Southwest, linking Sunbelt and Mexican patterns of consumption, labor relations, and retail to each other. Corn and wheat cultivated on massive corporate farms in both the U.S. and Mexico and pressed into tortillas in technologically advanced plants found their way to American tables with the help of distribution and retail innovations developed and sold by businesses on both sides of the border. The mass-produced tortilla proliferated in late twentieth-century United States and Mexico on the infrastructure of low taxes, right to work laws, low tariffs, and incentives to attract businesses.

Historians often describe the ascent of the Sunbelt economy in contrast to the Snowbelt or Rustbelt economy. The stories of emergence and decline correspond with geographical migration, as Snowbelters headed southward and westward for the abundant jobs, lower taxes, and business incentives. After the 1960s, however, the Sunbelt increasingly saw migration increase *from* the south too, as Mexican people, ideas, goods, and capital flowed north for the same reasons.[7] First to the Southwest and then increasingly to the old South, Mexican immigrants expanded their economic, cultural, and culinary influence. The emergence of the Sunbelt must, therefore, necessarily consider the impact of Mexican Americans and Mexican companies in the region and the cross-border political and economic exchanges between Americans and Mexicans.

Furthermore, Mexico's leading politicians since the 1980s, the neoliberals, shared the political and economic philosophies of the American Sunbelt policy-makers. Government leaders drawn from the Institutional Revolutionary Party (PRI) worked in constant dialogue with the United States to develop reforms in the 1980s and 1990s. Many of these officials, who were educated in the U.S. or worked for American-based companies, assigned their own vision of the free market for Mexico.[8] Trade liberalization stood at the center of this reform agenda, and beginning in the 1980s, policy-makers on both sides of the U.S.-Mexico border worked progressively to remove restrictions. In the United States, Sunbelt politicians, both Republican and Democrat, led the push for free trade. Meanwhile, neoliberal Mexican leaders privatized state enterprises, deregulated the economy, reprivatized banks, and opened trade and investment to foreign businesses.[9] In contrast to many of its Latin American neighbors, Mexico became much less protectionist over time. Many Mexican business owners vigorously supported free trade too, aiding politicians by means of lobbying and trade associations.[10]

American Sunbelt politicians pushed the North American Free Trade Agreement (NAFTA) as the linchpin of free trade, passing it through Congress in November 1993. Mexico had already opened its market by joining the General Agreement on Tariffs and Trade in 1986, but after NAFTA, cross-border exchanges increased. Direct investment by American firms in Mexico and by Mexican firms in the United States each jumped significantly after NAFTA. The Congressional Research Service estimated that, from 1994 to 2002, U.S. foreign direct investment in Mexico rose from $16.1 billion to $58.1 billion, a 259 percent increase. Similarly, Mexico's foreign direct investment in the United States rose from $2.3 billion to $7.9 billion, a 244 percent increase.[11] Mexico's foreign trade, meanwhile, outpaced all of Latin America from the mid-1980s to 2001.[12] The neoliberal, or free market push (depending on which side of the border you stood), meant greater exchanges of all sorts, whether measured by goods or people moving across the border. The number of business visitors and intracompany transferees crossing the border also rose significantly beginning in the 1980s and continued with NAFTA, signaling greater economic exchanges between the two countries.¹³ And contrary to popular thought, the story of liberalization goes well beyond southward flows of capital and northward flows of labor. Mexican exports have increased three-fold since NAFTA and major Mexican cement, banking, and food companies have pumped capital into American operations too.¹⁴ Those food companies lie at the center of this study.

Tortilla Politics

Here, the tortilla, the "daily bread" and most important foodstuff of Mexico, is a lens onto the new transnational Sunbelt political economy of the United States and Mexico since the 1980s. Five companies that make (or made) tortillas were central to this political economy—GRUMA, Bimbo, Walmart, Archer Daniels Midland (ADM), and El Galindo. GRUMA and Bimbo, both Mexican companies, have grown much more powerful because of the new political order. Bimbo is the largest food company in Mexico, and GRUMA is the largest tortilla maker in the world. Walmart is the largest company in the world and the largest grocer in the United States and Mexico. ADM's global reach in food processing is rivaled by only a few other companies.¹⁵ And El Galindo, a small tortilla manufacturer from Austin, Texas, saw its business contract dramatically on competition with GRUMA, Bimbo, and Walmart.

Tortillas had spread across the world since the 1980s, and GRUMA was the company most responsible for this change, using an American Sunbelt base for its success in the last part of the twentieth century.¹⁶ GRUMA capitalized on the growing Mexican American population in the United States, its ties to the Mexican government, and the liberalization of trade to increase its share of the world tortilla market. GRUMA represented the homogenizing forces that came to dominate the Sunbelt political economy—forces ironically built on the new diversity of increased global trade and migration. Furthermore, the fact that a Mexican company dominated a food business in the United States counters the standard narrative in which American foods such as the hamburger homogenize foreign culture.¹⁷ Mexican food became homogenized not just in Mexico but also across borders in the United States, Europe, and Asia.¹⁸

Food was but one of the globalizing elements after the 1960s. Due to accelerated transportation and communication, global trade and immigration increased overall. Global exports of all goods rose from 12 percent of world gross domestic product (GDP) in 1965 to 22 percent of world GDP in 2000.[19] Furthermore, from 1961 to 2000 the United States admitted over 24 million immigrants, resulting in what one commentator termed a "vast social experiment." More than a fifth of those immigrants came from Mexico, totaling about 5 million people.[20] Added to that were millions of undocumented Mexican immigrants.[21] If globalization, including immigration, was one story of the post-1960s period, the Sunbelt was key to that story, for the region was home to the nation's largest movement of people and goods.[22]

Walmart and GRUMA capitalized on the continued Mexicanization of the Southwest and its business-friendly environment to make it a locus point for globalization.[23] These retail and manufacturing colossuses developed practices to ensure that Americans could get both consistency and diversity in their shopping experiences, practices that became engines of globalization. Walmart, based in Arkansas, and GRUMA, based in Monterrey, Mexico, established patterns that would secure the global dominance of large corporations in the food business by creating one-stop shops for sameness and diversity. At the same time, as tortillas became a staple not just for those Americans with Mexican roots but for people of all ethnicities in the United States, GRUMA extended its reach first through the Southwest and later to the rest of the nation. It used brand-name recognition of its Maseca flour, advertising in Spanish-language newspapers, and distribution in small Mexican grocery stores to woo Mexican American customers.[24] By 2007, 45 percent of GRUMA's overall sales came from the United States. American consumers formed the company's largest market, in part because it had expanded sales beyond a Mexican American base.[25]

Walmart established a retail model that companies replicated the world over. The company learned to work with U.S.-Mexican trade and immigration policies, taking advantage of the borderlands to expand within and beyond it. In the 1990s, Walmart expanded to Mexico and opened new distribution centers to smooth retailing in the country.[26] Millions of consumers shopped in Walmart in Mexico and in the United States as they crossed back and forth.[27] The "big-box" terrain served familiarized and streamlined consumption patterns for migrants who spent considerable parts of their lives on both sides of the border. Both working-class border families and Mexican professionals from Monterrey hunted for bargains at the retailer, whether they were shopping for just the day or planning their move to gated communities in San Antonio. For a time, the Walmart in Laredo, Texas, was the busiest in the United States, fueled by cross-border purchases.[28] In part, because of this international focus, the company became *the* free-enterprise model after the 1980s. Nelson Lichtenstein described Walmart as a "template business setting the standards for a new stage in the history of world capitalism," having been able to "break trade unions, set the boundaries for popular culture, channel capital through the world, and conduct a kind of international diplomacy with a dozen nations."[29] Among the most important of those nations was Mexico. Walmart backed NAFTA in 1993 when it was in danger of failing. As Bethany Moreton has observed, "For a brief but decisive moment in U.S. politics, the key to imagining free trade was Wal-Mart in Mexico."[30] The opening of a massive Walmart store in Mexico City convinced American consumers during the NAFTA debate that Mexicans would buy U.S.-made products en masse. At the time, many Americans feared what Ross Perot described as the "giant sucking sound" of jobs moving southward. When NAFTA passed in November 1993, Sunbelt representatives voted for it in greater numbers than their Midwestern counterparts, where labor unions argued that American manufacturing firms would suffer. About 55 percent of the overall Congress voted for NAFTA, but 63 percent of Sunbelt representatives supported it. In the days leading up to the vote, a *Washington Post* headline called the vote one of "Sun Belt vs. Rust Belt."[31] In committee hearings, Senator John McCain (R-Az.) pointed to major food lobbying associations' support for the bill, such as the National Corn Growers Association and National Cattlemen's Association, explaining that it was the "American zeal for opportunity and competition in the market place that has fared so well throughout its history" and that both the American economy and agriculture will be "the better for" passing NAFTA.[32]

It was no accident that Walmart experienced its greatest growth during the 1990s when legislators put free trade firmly into law. The decade saw stores open at breakneck speed, with goods sourced mainly from cheap manufacturers abroad.[33] Walmart and other large grocery chains sold GRUMA tortillas in increasing proportion, as both the manufacturers and retailers used economies of scale and "free" trade to, freely, squelch competition.[34] Walmart paid workers low wages and resisted unions too. The chain paid around 20–25 percent lower wages than competitors such as Kmart, Target, and Safeway.[35] And, whereas many Snowbelters had moved

South and West for manufacturing jobs in the mid-twentieth century, Walmart replaced those jobs with lower paying retail positions. The real value of those job's wages, notes Lichtenstein, had actually declined since 1970.[36] Walmart, thus, took advantage of and enforced the right-to-work and probusiness environment of the Sunbelt.[37] Mexican Americans constituted a sizeable number of Walmart's employees and a strong portion of its customer base, particularly in Texas, the largest Walmart market.[38] Those customers included the farmworkers who provided cheap food for all consumers. Farmworkers had been on the very bottom of the American economic ladder for decades.[39] Many had come from Mexico because they had been driven off their own farms as companies such as GRUMA, ADM, and Cargill transformed the corn trade across North America. Small farmers could not compete with corporate farms after NAFTA, causing thousands to leave the land for cities in Mexico and the United States.[40]

Those workers (and consumers) moving north became, in part, the basis of GRUMA's successful tortilla empire in the United States, over time deriving more revenue from sales in America than Mexico. Grocers such as Walmart worked in concert with GRUMA, as supermarket chains slowly sought to capture business from the growing population of immigrants and their descendants, while marketing ethnic foods to a wider audience.[41] They did not initially promote some ethnic foods, such as the humble tortilla, to Americans. But even that changed over time, as many "peasant" foods became gourmet so that operators could charge higher prices for them.[42] The chains did not invent ethnic food retailing on their own; consumers *asked* grocers for ethnic foods too and got what they wanted, including tortillas, in the form of tacos, burritos, tostadas, and wraps.

The Tortilla as America's Daily Bread

The tortilla has long been an essential component for Mexican and Central American food, but its production and consumption has grown in the United States and changed in Mexico over the last several decades.[43] In the Southwest and other areas with well-established Mexican-American culinary traditions, inhabitants have consumed tortillas and other border staples for decades.[44] For several decades, most American consumers needed detailed tortilla explanations on menus. At Pepe's, a Mexican restaurant at the tourist-heavy Pier 39 in San Francisco, a 1980 menu explained that tortillas were a "staple" for the Aztecs and that they were served basically "unchanged" there. The menu further advised that diners should enjoy tortillas "in the Mexican fashion; hold the tortilla flat in one hand, butter it, add the hot sauce (sparingly at first), roll and eat," adding, not surprisingly, that they "particularly recommend tortillas with a Frosty Margarita."[45] Across the country in Timonium, Maryland, the Mexican restaurant chain Chi-Chi's offered similar counsel to diners. The back of its menu had a full-page spread titled "Mexican Kitchen Talk." There the basic components of Mexican food were translated—tacos, enchiladas, tostadas, and tamales—along with a pronunciation guide. "TAH-ko—The traditional Mexican 'sandwich,'" appeared with "Tor-TEE-yah—Bread with a Mexican accent—*the* south-of-the-border basic."[46] A cookbook published in 1980 distinguished between Mexican tortillas "made from cornmeal" and the Spanish tortilla, which was an omelet.[47] So, although Americans, particularly in the Southwestern states, had been eating Mexican food for decades, many diners still required instruction.[48]

Twenty years later menus rarely explained tacos or tortillas, for they were already established in the wider American food lexicon.[49] The tortilla, in fact, became a means to explain *other* ethnic cuisines, like foods from Asia. One magazine article extolled the virtues of Indian-fusion dishes generally, even as it recoiled at a recipe for "cinnamon-spiced buffalo meat in a shell of tortilla-like Indian bread, matched with mint and mango chutney and served on mixed greens." The "tortilla" here probably referred to a *chapathi*, a flat, round, whole wheat Indian bread so similar to the tortilla that Indian immigrants in the U.S. were known to buy hand tortilla presses from specialty stores to recreate *chapathis* at home.[50]

Americans without vestiges of Mexican heritage slowly increased their tortilla consumption between the 1970s and 1990s. During the 1970s, tortillas had moved out of a small space in most California supermarkets to a prominent end-of-aisle display. And at many stores, tortillas became so common that grocers simply lumped them them with the rest of the bread.[51] Tom Caron, a director of marketing for one frozen Mexican entrees manufacturer, remarked in 1980 that "The Mexican food category is experiencing in excess of 30 percent growth per year and this growth is going from the Southwest region of the country, into the Midwest and is moving outward."[52] By the 1990s, some grocers, including the Texas supermarket chain H-E-B, featured large tortilla presses within the retail space. An H-E-B vice president explained that his supermarket chain built a press at a majority "Hispanic" San Antonio branch because "around here, tortillas are like bread." The press was enclosed in glass as an attraction for the "kids."[53] Stores that did not primarily serve Hispanic customers built the mechanical presses for that same sense of theater—a machine pumping out soft, hot tortillas, drawing attention with show and scent.

In the United States, tortilla manufacturing primarily operated as a niche ethnic foods industry through the 1980s, existing mostly to serve Mexican American communities in the Southwest. The president of one small gourmet grocery chain in Northern California explained, "we don't sell tortillas to Hispanic people," adding that his chain did not "appeal to the immigrant customer." His stores, however, did sell plenty of tortillas to "Anglo" customers in 12-packs. Hispanic immigrants in the Bay Area, he explained, bought tortillas in 36- and 96-packs at the Safeway, Albertson's, or Costco.[54] Tortillas, thus, filled multiple niche markets by the 1990s. Middle- to upper-class customers, (Anglo, at least in eyes of gourmet grocery store executive) represented the presumably more expensive 12-pack market, while lower-paid Hispanic immigrants represented the 36–96 pack market. Small tortilla plants could make decent profits within this economy. The industry changed radically, however; as more Mexicans immigrated to the United States, more non-Mexicans in the United States ate tortillas,[55] and Mexican food expanded out of regional consumption beyond the Southwest.[56] In Mexico, tortilla production had already shifted from a domestic, labor-intensive activity to one supplanted and supplemented by industrial aid.[57]

This industrial process came to be dominated by GRUMA.

GRUMA and Tortilla Politics

At the beginning of the twenty-first century, GRUMA had become the largest tortilla manufacturer in the world. GRUMA was founded in 1949 by Roberto M. González and his son, Roberto González Barrera in Nuevo Leon but would begin its real ascent in the 1960s after developing more efficient tortilla machines. By the 1990s, González Barrera was on Forbes list of billionaires and the company was rapidly expanding beyond Mexico.[58] According to one estimate, its Mission Foods division alone produced a quarter of all tortillas worldwide.[59] In addition to the Mission Foods brand, in the U.S. GRUMA produced Guerrero tortillas, much of the flour used by major grocers such as H-E-B and Walmart to manufacture their in-house brands, and a large proportion of the tortillas used by major food purveyors such as McDonald's, Taco Bell, and KFC. The company topped tortilla sales in the two largest tortilla markets: Mexico and the United States.[60] The story of GRUMA's ascent is the story of the global Sunbelt. It is a story of how the fates of Mexico and the United States became more closely intertwined in the last half of the century with the help of a new cross-border political order that created (big) business-friendly economic policies.

After its founding, the company slowly increased its share of the tortilla market in Mexico by developing technologies to grind corn more efficiently and cheaply than existing mills. GRUMA's tortilla technology sought to improve on the centuries-old process whereby millions of Mexican women had boiled and ground corn, which they then rolled into tortillas by hand. Millions still do. In this process, women simmer corn in mineral lime overnight to make *nixtamal*. The next morning they grind the corn on a stone to make a dough, or *masa*, which they press flat and then cook over stone griddles at mealtime for fresh tortillas. The process takes hours.[61] In the last half of the nineteenth century, Mexican inventors developed mechanical corn mills. Then, during the twentieth century, inventors developed three industrial technologies that dramatically reduced the tortilla workload. In the 1900s and 1910s, engineers first developed metal rolling presses for the corn dough, and around 1950 new developers made successful mechanical tortilla presses.[62] GRUMA became the leader in the third innovation: *masa harina* (dried corn flour), which requires only water for the finished product.[63] To dry masa, manufacturers boil corn for thirty minutes, blast it with hot air, then package it soon thereafter.[64] Known by GRUMA's trade name, Maseca, the dried flour came to occupy roughly half of tortilla production in Mexico by the early twenty-first century.[65] At the end of the century, the average Mexican consumed around eighteen tortillas per day, or three quarters of a pound's worth, making its production key to any discussion about food and politics in Mexico.[66]

GRUMA controlled about half of the Mexican tortilla market by 2006, but who controlled the other half? Home producers or, more likely, the thousands of local *tortillerias* that dotted the landscape. Some Mexican consumers bought masa from a local mill and took it to a *tortilleria* to make a morning batch. Other consumers bought wet masa from mills to press and cook their own tortillas at home. And still others bought tortillas fresh every morning from local *tortillerias* that ground, cooked, and pressed the tortillas on a daily basis. In comparison to the United States, fewer Mexican consumers bought packaged tortillas, though GRUMA hoped to change that too.[67] GRUMA commented that the tortilla industry in Mexico was "highly fragmented," which meant opportunities for growth.[68] The company continued to push conversion of tortilla production from wet masa to its Maseca brand corn flour, both by large and small tortilla producers, including *tortillerias* and supermarkets that made tortillas in-house.[69]

GRUMA came to dominate the Mexican tortilla landscape in part because of its ties to Mexican political leaders. First, it profited from the dismantling of the National Company of Popular Subsistence (CONASUPO), the Mexican state agency that had subsidized food consumption since the 1960s. CONASUPO had operated partly through a massive network of retail tortilla outlets. The neoliberal government leaders reformed this distribution scheme. When Carlos Salinas de Gortari became president in 1988, he reordered CONASUPO. By the early 1990s, the agency had undergone significant changes and was on the way to privatizing the tortilla trade.[70] His government aided GRUMA by declaring in 1990 that any new growth in the tortilla market must be filled by dehydrated flour, rather than wet masa. At the time, only GRUMA and a state agency produced the dry version.[71] The next president, Ernesto Zedillo, finally eliminated CONASUPO in 1999.

The *New York Times* and other newspapers investigated both the Salinas (1988–94) and Zedillo (1994–2000) administrations for corrupt ties to GRUMA. President Salinas' brother Raul was jailed in 1995 for plotting the assassination of a presidential candidate. As a result of this investigation, his dealings with CONASUPO also came to light, including speculation that he made significant profit from the dismantling process. A congressional investigation found only lesser acts of wrongdoing, but many believed the Zedillo administration had covered up its involvement.[72] Around the same time, another Salinas administration member, Commerce Secretary Jaime Serra Puche, had also coordinated the reorganization of CONASUPO and was a leading figure in NAFTA negotiations with the United States. He enlisted business leaders and organizations to lobby on behalf of free trade.[73] Some observers of Mexican politics charged that Serra Puche acted on behalf of GRUMA by discontinuing the Mexican government's rural corn program, which resulted in a flood of cheap American corn into the Mexican market. Much of that corn was exported to Mexico by the largest privately held firm in the world, Cargill, the American agricultural company.[74] Another congressional investigation examined whether GRUMA had improperly received a $7 million payment from a state agency in the Salinas administration, which then Senior Budget Official Ernesto Zedillo had "acquiesced" to accept.[75] The inquiry eventually cleared the company of wrongdoing, but it raised questions about GRUMA founder Roberto González Barrera's (the "tortilla king") connection to officials in the Mexican government. Carlos Salinas reportedly used Barrera's private plane to leave the country when his brother Raul was jailed.[76] Though it is hard to determine if GRUMA's leadership dealt directly with the Salinas family on the CONASUPO policy, GRUMA certainly benefited from the change.[77] Between 1992 and 2006, the proportion of tortillas made with dry corn flour jumped from about a third to about 48 percent in Mexico, and GRUMA controlled that market.[78]

GRUMA's designs on dominating Mexico's tortilla market worked hand in hand with its American operations. Over time, GRUMA saw that the tortilla markets of the United States and Mexico could be connected quite profitably. American consumers did not share the old Mexican aversion to packaged tortillas, and GRUMA hoped to bring its experience in the United States and the connections between Mexican Americans in the Southwest to Mexico to help its marketing strategies. Jorge Hernandez, a GRUMA sales manager in Los Angeles, went so far as to note, "maybe we can teach Mexicans how to sell tortillas back home."[79] He had reason to believe this: at the end of the 1990s, the company controlled around 82 percent of the American tortilla market.[80]

GRUMA's American tortilla strategy had moved outward from the Sunbelt. The company first entered the American market in 1976, later buying Mission Foods, the largest tortilla maker in the United States. Mission Foods was headquartered in Los Angeles for many years before moving to the Dallas suburbs in 1998 to be closer to GRUMA headquarters in Monterrey, Mexico. It also moved eastward to capture the growing market east and north of the Southwest.[81] GRUMA located most of its plants in California or Texas, including the world's largest tortilla plant in Rancho Cucamonga, California. The company received a grant of $578,000 from the city's redevelopment agency to build there in exchange for supporting 600 jobs at the plant over the next nine years. California Governor Pete Wilson had developed an initiative while in office to recruit and retain businesses in the state, of which the GRUMA plant was one.[82] That plant ran three different processing lines: one for clients such as Taco Bell, another for retailers, and another for tortilla chips. North Carolina also offered incentives to GRUMA. In 1999, GRUMA sought expansion to the East Coast and bought rival tortilla maker Barnes Foods. To entice GRUMA to locate its new facility in Goldsboro, North Carolina, the city and state offered it $400,000 in initial incentives and an annual $200,000 to offset state income tax. GRUMA was expected to provide a $13 million investment in the area and 100 or more jobs, which it did.[83] On top of GRUMA's headquartering its American operations in Texas, the Texas Panhandle sourced most of the company's food grade corn and the company built the world's largest corn flour plant in Plainview, Texas.[84]

The company also adapted to American, European, and Asian markets to increase sales by developing different products. Though Mission represented its largest division, GRUMA bought or created other brands, including the Guerrero label, which was marketed to Mexican Americans rather than the general American population. The company also introduced fat-free, flavored, and low-carbohydrate tortillas.[85] Fast food represented one of the largest growth areas for Mexican food in and beyond in the United States, proving a boon for GRUMA, which contracted with, at one time or another, McDonald's, Taco Bell, and 7-Eleven. GRUMA was Taco Bell's exclusive tortilla provider in the Western region for a time.[86] In gobbling market shares and contracting with large chains, GRUMA gradually bought out competitors in this food-service market. Based in Los Angeles, Candy's Tortilla Factory had derived a quarter of its revenue from sales to Taco Bell but lost its contract. GRUMA then bought Candy's in 1994.[87] GRUMA's rising profits could also be seen in the case of McDonald's, which first offered fajitas and breakfast burritos in 1991 and saw this business grow substantially over time. GRUMA also sought growth in Europe and Asia, typically using its operations in Texas or California as jumping off points for that business.[88]

The much smaller El Galindo tortilla company got caught in the crosshairs of GRUMA's global expansion efforts after the 1980s. By the early twenty-first century, W. Allen Dark owned the Austin, Texas-based company and oversaw manufacturing and distribution of the company's two main products, tortillas and tortilla chips. El Galindo shipped to stores and restaurants around the United States, including in Austin, Dallas, Houston, Georgia, and New Jersey. Whereas it once served a mostly Mexican American clientele, El Galindo shifted to what Dark termed a "niche market" for consumers who wanted "traditional" products. His tortillas fit within the "specialty product" category because, according to Dark, they have "a lot of taste but cost more" than other brands. In addition to corn and flour tortillas, El Galindo manufactured organic and spelt tortillas. In 2004, the organic and spelt versions cost around thirty cents each compared to a few pennies for a common tortilla.[89]

Dark purchased El Galindo in 1996 from the Galindo family, who had run the business for decades. Founded as El Fenix in 1940 by Tomas Galindo, Sr. and his wife Josepha, the small tortilla factory was run by the Galindos with their family in Austin until 1972, when their son Tomas Jr. and daughter-in-law Ernestine bought it, changing the name to El Galindo in 1973.[90] In the early years of the business, the tortilla factory had also featured a gift shop with Mexican potteries and housewares, and Tomas Galindo Sr. was active in the central Texas Mexican American community.[91] The factory sold tortillas to a few local grocery stores, restaurants, and sorority houses but did not distribute widely. It prospered over the years by primarily serving the many Mexicans who came to the U.S. beginning in the 1940s to fill World War II employment shortages, and "as more Mexicans came across the border, [tortilla manufacturing] became good business," said Dark. He explained that, from the 1940s to the 1980s, Mexican food manufacturing consisted of many mom-and-pop operations, of which El Galindo was one.[92] Between the 1970s and the 1990s, Tomas Galindo, Jr., and Ernestine expanded their operations from a six-employee company to over a hundred, selling to many more restaurants and groceries throughout Texas, as Mexican food's popularity surged.[93]

By the 1990s, El Galindo was floundering, however. Ironically, its troubles resulted from the surging popularity of Mexican food. The family had hired W. Allen Dark as a consultant because he specialized in helping "companies in trouble." Later, he purchased the company. He explained that, although "people in California and Texas have always been familiar with Mexican food," that familiarity had spread recently to the rest of the United States, creating a "snowball effect" for Mexican food in the 1990s. Those who "previously wouldn't recognize a Mexican person started eating Mexican food" in that decade, said Dark. Widening consumption necessitated a change in production, and large manufacturers like GRUMA took hold of the tortilla market. In the mid-1990s, Steve Foster, then a vice president for El Galindo, said that major companies were "expanding into new markets" and that McDonald's and Burger King "increase demand" for tortillas "by advertising products like breakfast tacos. People now know there's more things you can do with a tortilla."[94] He added that, as a result, large baking companies entered the tortilla landscape in the United States. W. Allen Dark lamented large producers' ability to pay slotting fees for product placement in grocery stores.[95] The retail market became "tough" then for small companies in the 1990s, said Dark, forcing many out of business. Other small food producers competed by selling directly to restaurants rather than in retail stores, signing contracts for bulk production.[96]

El Galindo's production techniques differed from those of GRUMA and the other big tortilla manufacturers. And even if GRUMA did not directly press tortillas, many other manufacturers used its flour. H-E-B, the largest supermarket chain in Texas, made tortillas in a 20,000 square-foot production facility in Corpus Christi. The tortilla process began there with GRUMA's dry flours, which were added to water. El Galindo and other small manufacturers, such as Sanitary Tortilla Manufacturing Corporation in San Antonio, Texas, instead used the old wet masa process for their tortillas.[97] But H-E-B made its own tortillas using GRUMA flour and also featured GRUMA brand Mission and Guerrero tortillas alongside its store brands on shelves. Though the brand names were different on various packages, consumers were increasingly eating tortillas made from the same Maseca flour.

El Galindo had to turn to niche markets; as a result, its new customers were "mostly Anglo-Saxons in the middle- or upper-income groups." Dark thought Mexican Americans did not buy his higher-priced tortillas because they "don't have the money and will buy a lower-priced product" in bulk, probably made by GRUMA. El Galindo could not compete with the grocery store shelves "loaded with 120-count pack tortillas" and, as a result, had long ago left that business. El Galindo "missed the high-volume market." Ironically, Dark's tortilla business manufactured tortillas more like old Mexican *tortillerias*, but he sold most of those tortillas to non-Mexicans.[98] Instead, Mexican Americans, according to Dark, bought from large producers like GRUMA because they use newer production techniques. Indeed, in 1997, the four largest tortilla manufacturers shipped 57.2 percent of the tortillas in the United States for the billion-dollar-plus industry.[99] As with other aspects of the food industry, the largest operators dominated the tortilla market by the end of the 1990s. These operators dominated from Mexico to the U.S., homogenizing the tortilla as they mainstreamed it. By 2010, El Galindo no longer existed, put out of business by GRUMA.[100] Though many small tortilla manufacturers remained in Texas, most had turned to niche markets for their products.

GRUMA dominated the market by leading tortilla-processing technologies, entering agreements with American agricultural firms and buying up small tortilla producers. GRUMA had long led scientific advances in processing corn and wheat flour, something its management regularly boasted about in corporate reports and interviews.[101] Building on this legacy, it signed an agreement with ADM in 1996, whereby ADM purchased almost a quarter of GRUMA's stock—a proportion it has held since. ADM is among the leaders in corn-, soy-, and seed-oil processing in the world. It markets its high-fructose corn syrup, soy-derived food fillers, animal feed supplements, and other food products in six continents. The deal allowed ADM to increase corn and wheat flour processing in Mexico for the growing corn syrup, white bread, and pastry markets there. For its part, GRUMA gained greater access to the American markets by taking over ADM's corn-milling plants in California and another in Kentucky, to supply the growing Eastern market for tortillas.

GRUMA and ADM took advantage of the cross-border business opportunities offered by NAFTA. Eduardo Livas Cantu, GRUMA's chief executive officer, commented that his company ran its corn-flour business "better than [ADM was] running theirs" and would be better suited to operate mills in the United States for tortillas, concluding, "we are dedicated to corn flour, our mills are newer, and we have a better technology."[102] ADM brought industrial food technologies southward in the form of corn syrup, wheat processing, and livestock feed, and GRUMA brought tortilla technology northward. The collaboration allowed GRUMA to "vertically integrate" its U.S. tortilla operations in short order.[103]

Mexican consumers did not necessarily benefit from GRUMA's rise. After privatization took hold and CONASUPO had been abolished, tortilla prices roughly doubled, for the federal government was no longer subsidizing tortillas for much of the population. GRUMA controlled increasingly larger shares of the tortilla market just as Walmart did the same with groceries. As NAFTA allowed cheap corn from the United States to flood the Mexican market, small farmers in Mexico found it difficult to compete. The rural poor in Mexico became poorer over time, as Mexican farmers were caught in the double vise grip of NAFTA and their countries' neoliberal domestic reforms. Together, these policies meant cheaper agricultural imports, enabled by ADM, GRUMA, and other large firms, whether in the

U.S., Mexico, or elsewhere.[104] Consequently, NAFTA "triggered the most drastic and profound transformation in the history of agriculture in Mexico," said scholars Manuel Ángel Gómez Cruz and Rita Schwentesius Rindermann.[105]

Many of these farmers left the land for the cities of Mexico and the United States, seeking low-wage work in food industries.[106] Their employers included poultry- and pork-processing plants in Alabama, Mississippi, and North Carolina; tortilla factories in Texas and California; and the fruit and vegetable fields that stretched from Florida to California. As NAFTA pushed farmers away from growing corn, they ate fewer tortillas. Though the overall tortilla market in Mexico decreased, GRUMA executives found comfort in the fact that its dry-flour tortillas might supplant the traditional wet masa ones. And even if Mexicans in Mexico did not eat as many tortillas, the American and other foreign markets grew by leaps and bounds.[107]

As the tortilla market boomed in the United States, many small tortilla manufacturers found themselves in dire straits at the precise moment when they should have been profiting. Many blamed GRUMA and other large corporations for their demise. A group of these tortilla manufacturers filed a federal antitrust lawsuit against GRUMA in 2001, charging that it fostered anticompetitive practices in the Southern California, Northern California, Houston, Arizona, and Michigan tortilla markets. The suit alleged that GRUMA entered into marketing agreements with grocers by which it paid slotting fees to "manage or control the placement, location, availability, visibility and promotional activity of competing retail tortillas."[108] The suit further contended that GRUMA attempted to "monopolize" the retail tortilla market in violation of the Sherman Antitrust Act.[109] GRUMA countered that it indeed arranged marketing agreements with stores but that it always received payment in excess of its cost on tortillas. Albertson's, one of the largest grocery chains in California and Texas, testified in the case that it received similar payments from other manufacturers for marketing but that it alone controlled product placement in its stores and was not beholden to GRUMA. GRUMA argued that other tortilla brands could be found in grocery stores, so customers had a number of choices.[110] Bimbo had been named as a codefendant alongside GRUMA in the original suit, but it was dropped before the case went to court. The court dismissed the suit in 2004, ruling that GRUMA had not violated the law.[111] A similar suit was entered in Los Angeles Superior Court in 2004, but it was dismissed the next year. That suit prompted State Senator Liz Figueroa to propose a bill in the California legislature to make retailers inform suppliers of slotting fees and market competition. The bill died, but in its description of GRUMA, it noted that the company controlled "90 percent of the Southern California tortilla market."[112] Her numbers were close. GRUMA indeed dominated many of the biggest urban markets, including Southwestern cities with large Mexican American populations. According to the company, its Los Angeles market share increased from 66 to 85 percent from 1996 to 1999. GRUMA, Walmart, Bimbo, and ADM all achieved dominance in their respective markets by promoting, perfecting, and consolidating the new Sunbelt political and economic order.

Big companies cooperated with other big companies to become bigger companies. Just as GRUMA signed agreements to produce tortillas for McDonald's, Bimbo contracted to bake buns for its burgers, winning exclusive agreements in Mexico in the 1980s and in Venezuela, Colombia, and Peru in 1999.[113] Bimbo needed to become an "export powerhouse and disciple of globalization" to win contracts from big firms such as McDonald's. To supply McDonald's, it had to invest $30 million into research and development before the burger giant would sign on, something a small baker could hardly do.[114] Like GRUMA, it first began American operations in the western United States, building both on its acquisitions of American bakeries and name recognition from Mexican American customers. After establishing a presence in the West, it sought greater market share, trying to take a "proactive role in an industry that [was] consolidating," by buying Weston Foods, Inc., a major baker in the East.[115] By doing this, it became the largest baker in the United States.[116]

As the bread, tortilla, and grocery giants enlarged, many workers and farmers in the United States and Mexico scrambled for decent wages. Delivery drivers for GRUMA in Los Angeles went on strike against the company in August 1996, citing low wages and long work weeks without overtime pay. The drivers, who distributed the Mission and Guerrero brands, had joined the Teamsters Union a few years prior. Their strike garnered local publicity because the Teamster's national president, Ron Carey, spoke at rallies to mobilize support. After seven weeks of strikes, confrontations, and pledges by some politicians to boycott Mission and Guerrero tortillas, GRUMA signed a pay raise of 22 percent for the drivers.[117] Twelve years later GRUMA settled out of court for similar grievances by Teamster's drivers from Los Angeles, paying $2.9 million to the plaintiffs.[118] GRUMA dominated the tortilla market in the biggest Sunbelt city in part by resisting worker demands for higher wages and better working conditions.

To reign over worldwide tortilla consumption, GRUMA capitalized on the Sunbelt political and economic order of free trade, low taxes, business incentives, and anti-unionism. Working from its headquarters in Mexico to its most lucrative market in the United States, GRUMA also pushed, and benefited, from the changes in the Mexican political order. Mexico's neoliberal leaders—many of whom were educated in the U.S. and in constant dialogue with American policy-makers—opened Mexico's banking, agriculture, and manufacturing industries to private investment and supported NAFTA's passage alongside their Sunbelt compatriots. Concurrently, GRUMA supported the dismantling of CONASUPO, the previous system of subsidized tortilla distribution for Mexico. In concert with Walmart, ADM, and other companies that benefited from the opening of trade with Mexico and other countries, GRUMA was able to increase economies of scale and to market its products to a much larger base. It also built on the great demographic and cultural changes in the U.S. since the 1960s, capitalizing on the mass migration of Mexicans to the U.S. and the shift in American eating habits toward more Latin American foods. Ironically, it pushed out long-established family-run tortilla manufacturers in the Southwest, as it developed highly efficient growing, milling, and processing technologies. As GRUMA, Walmart, Bimbo, and other food producers and retailers became bigger, American and Mexican consumers increasingly ate the same foods in Mexico City or Los Angeles—quite often a piece of fast-food meat wrapped in a GRUMA tortilla.

Chapter 13

Latinos in the Sunbelt: Political Implications of Demographic Change

Sylvia Manzano

Contemporary American political discourses frame Latinos pejoratively, focusing on immigration and citizenship status. This charged narrative posed a vexing problem for Republicans in 2008—how to appeal to Latino voters without alienating some segments of their white, conservative base. *Newsweek* noted the McCain campaign's ambivalence to strategically and publicly include Latinos:

> The job of Juan Hernandez is to win John McCain Latino votes. So it may seem odd that the campaign doesn't want its national director of Hispanic outreach to get any press. Repeated *Newsweek* requests to interview Hernandez have been rebuffed or ignored. When a reporter suggested talking to Hernandez at a convention of the National Association of Latino Elected and Appointed Officials, where Hernandez was slated to appear June 28, his name was suddenly removed from the list of scheduled speakers. Here's one possible reason: Hernandez is toxic to many conservatives. "He represents the opposite of everything conservative Republicans stand for," says a GOP strategist who didn't want to be quoted by name on a sensitive topic. Some conservatives have

wanted McCain to deny Hernandez any role in the campaign. But one group's villain is another's hero. Hernandez has good ties to the Latino community; McCain needs those votes, especially in swing states like Florida, New Mexico, Colorado and Nevada. McCain aide Mark Salter calls Hernandez an unpaid volunteer who "doesn't play a role in policy."[1]

Four months later, ten million Latinos voted in the 2008 presidential election, a 25 percent voter turnout increase compared to 2004.[2] Latinos exerted unprecedented national political influence from a Sunbelt base. Their impact on different dimensions of the political environment, including partisan strategies, campaign contributions, and voting trends, was strongest in Florida, Virginia, North Carolina, New Mexico, Colorado, Texas, and Nevada.[3] In a postelection interview, McCain campaign manager Rick Davis noted the importance of incorporating Latinos in a long-term political strategy. "The Republican Party has got to change its attitude versus Hispanics in order to win in the future. Given the really crazy things said on talk radio in the name of the GOP, I don't blame Hispanics for not voting for us. California, Colorado, Texas, Florida—we can't win in these states anymore."[4] Interestingly, Republicans *did* win Texas. Davis articulates a keen awareness that demographic shifts will inevitably surface in the electorate, and winning elections will increasingly require Latino support. Partisan trends in Texas are similar to those in the rest of the country. As journalist Paul Burka succinctly noted, "Republicans are strongest where Texas is not growing; Democrats are strongest where it is growing."[5]

This chapter argues that demographic changes in the Latino population—specifically, size, composition, and geographic distribution—have strong, enduring effects on American politics. Forty-six million Latinos living in the U.S. today may condition the electoral environment and policy agenda as active participants. Increasing population and representation may also spur backlash that makes Latinos political scapegoats. Emergent Latino influence extends beyond the political realm (see Laresh Jayasanker's chapter in this volume) and challenges the traditional, dichotomous geographic, racial, and ideological interpretations of the Sunbelt. Recent Latino political engagement in the region contests long-standing trends and narratives defining Sunbelt influence on national politics, as distinctly conservative. U.S.-born Latinos combine with steady streams of Latin American migration (both largely Mexican origin) to reconfigure political, social, economic, and cultural orientations that do not easily comport with Sunbelt versus Rustbelt or black versus white typologies.[6] Demographic and immigration trends coupled with national political and social forces suggest that Latinos will assert their national influence, as both participants and targets, from a Sunbelt base.

Panethnicity and Heterogeneity

Latino identity in the United States is a function of both shared in-group traits and out-group status. Immigrant experience, residential ethnic density, and Latin American lineage characterized by Catholic traditions and Spanish language heritage link diverse subsets of the Latino population in the U.S.[7] Latino Americans also share ethnic minority status, discrimination experience, and awareness of non-Latino perceptions and responses to the group.[8] It is also true that heterogeneity sharply distinguishes Latinos from other racial and ethnic groups in the United States. Measurable characteristics including national origin, nativity, context of immigration, length of residence/generations in the United States, and regional residence distinguish unique subsets of the broad panethnic group.[9] Thus, it is necessary to specify who the subjects are in any given piece of "Latino" research.

The diverse Latino population is similarly situated along several consequential dimensions of American social, economic, and political life. This study employs a panethnic approach because the topics at hand highlight common political orientations among group members and institutional responses that similarly affect the Latino population. Thus, two dimensions of ethnic identity are addressed: how Latinos see themselves and how non-Latinos approach them. Analysis and references to "Latino" group preferences, behavior, and trends (for example, partisanship, voter turnout, and population size) refer to self-identified classification responses from various survey data sources. Using self-identification measures to define racial and ethnic groups averts bias associated with subjective, author-imposed categorizations. Specific national origin, nativity, and citizenship are noted when the characteristics are pertinent.

The growing presence of Latinos in America demands attention to the consequential nuances associated with this trend. Political prominence and incorporation manifest along different trajectories, depending on regional and demographic contexts. Contemporary Sunbelt dynamics exemplify how various forms of Latino influence affect the political environment. Thus, systematic analysis of Sunbelt Latino politics yields sharp insight on broad-scale American Latino politics. One avenue to influence employs traditional electoral and organizational mechanisms. Group size and long-standing presence in the southwest and Florida facilitate Latino participation and representation.[10] Means to incorporation differ in regions like the south, where Latino populations are relatively new and small. Fewer coalition partners and limited networks direct their political and social participation toward nonelectoral and informal institutions, such as co-ethnic churches and hometown associations.[11] In such demographic contexts, Latinos experience more resistance to incorporation and structural barriers to participation.[12] Ironically, anti-Latino political agendas crafted by non-Latinos contribute to Latino prominence in American politics. Groups and candidates defining themselves relative to Latinos and traits specifically associated with population (for example, foreign born, Spanish dominant, larger median family size, etc.) direct attention to the centrality of ethnic politics in America and, furthermore, identify Latinos as the most salient out-group threat.[13] The rapidly growing Latino population exerts influence as both political actor and policy target, and the Sunbelt has become the hub for this nexus of demographic and political change.

Sunbelt Rising, Latinos *Subiendo*

The Sunbelt has experienced more demographic change than any other region in the country. Average age, birth rates, and immigration make state populations larger, younger, and less white than in years past. If demographics are destiny, then Latinos are indeed destined for political and policy influence. However, Latino population-specific attributes including citizenship status, nativity, national origin, and language ability condition *how* politics and policy incorporates and responds to the demographic shift at hand. Citizenship status and language ability, for example, largely determine viable participation options and venues. At the same time, political culture and institutional structures that influence the region and states apply similarly for Latinos too. For example, unions, ballot initiatives, term limits, and industry priorities that shape local and state policy can be mechanisms to Latino representation or policy targeting.

Scholars must also recognize how immigration trends define the Sunbelt. The region attracts Latino immigrants because numerous industries have provided opportunities for economic mobility in the region. Southern states like Arkansas, North Carolina, Virginia, and Georgia, as well as southwestern cities like Houston, Phoenix, and Los Angeles, have become popular destinations for millions of immigrants from Mexico and Central America.[14] Immigrant men and women fill low-skill labor positions in processing plants, construction, hospitality, and service industries that fuel Sunbelt economic growth.[15] Foreign-born workers from Mexico and other Latin American countries find work in hotels, golf courses, new construction projects, restaurants, salons, homes, and daycares that facilitate and signal prosperity.[16] Immigration streams are potent once established; they become self-perpetuating phenomena that draw more immigrants to the local community.[17] People relocate to the U.S. in clusters that reflect their transnational social networks. No matter where they settle, large foreign-born Latino populations are altering the social, political, and policy agenda. Indeed, fissures in American party politics occur along issues associated with immigration and Latino Americans.

Historic ethnic and racial contexts shape two trajectories of Latino political incorporation. The southwest has been more conducive to Latino empowerment due to their native presence and geographic distribution in the region. Sizeable co-ethnic and citizen populations uniquely facilitated incorporation and empowerment relative to Latinos in other parts of the country. Latinos have always been part of the racial/ethnic politics in the southwest, whether in a brown- white dyad or a more complex multiminority group context. Immigrants to the south are not easily absorbed into black-white schema that largely defines the parameters of southern politics and society. Historian George Sanchez argues that nativism agendas targeting Latinos attempt to keep American racial interpretations framed as dichotomous black-white constructions.[18] As a relatively new minority group, Latinos upset the order of racial politics and do so without entrenched political or social networks to facilitate their incorporation. Southern Latinos are still in the process of establishing community roots and must contend with barriers associated with being a numeric minority population. Limited language ability and local unfamiliarity with Latinos makes the assimilation process especially difficult in the south. Basic community building institutions like public schools, libraries, and churches are not readily available to many parents and newcomers lacking English fluency.

Low share in the population and local electorate translate to few opportunities to elect co-ethnics.

Assimilated and established Latino populations heavily concentrated in the southwest have a qualitatively different influence compared to less resourced southern Latinos. For immigrants to the southwest, there are benefits to residing in places where there is nothing novel about Spanish surnames. Tacitly and directly, co-ethnics facilitate immigrant social, political, and economic incorporation in the country. About half of U.S.-born Latinos are fluent in Spanish; this makes it much easier for new Latino immigrants to engage with their new community. The importance of language cannot be understated. In 2007, the Pew Hispanic Center reported that 46 percent of all Latinos (native and foreign-born) indicated that language was the biggest cause of discrimination.[19] The study noted, "Latinos cite language skills more frequently than immigration status, income, education or skin color as an explanation for discrimination against them." California, Texas, New Mexico, and Arizona have Spanish built into the infrastructure of daily life. Specifically, immigrants to these states can easily find multiple Spanish television and radio outlets, Spanish language religious services reflecting cultural traditions (for example, Catholic masses and churches named for Mexico's patron saint, the Virgin of Guadalupe), bilingual school teachers, and food of their preference outside the ethnic food aisle.

Professional and middle-class Latinos ensure a degree of representation and attentiveness to group needs that is absent in the south. There is a critical mass of Latino voters and elected officials in the region. Depending on the contest and district lines, Latinos may comprise well over 80 percent of the electorate in city and state contests. A tangible policy outcome associated with enduring Latino presence and representation occurs in public schools where funded bilingual education programs have been instituted for decades. In the south, new Latino immigrants lack a comparable co-ethnic buffer, making the challenges associated with undocumented status, English language ability and acclimating to a new country even more difficult. With the exception of the Cuban American population in Florida, Latinos in the south are a relatively foreign, distinct ethnic minority group, lacking direct ties to the area.

The evolution of Mexican American political and social incorporation is well documented; it has been violent and politically explosive at different times.[20] One of the most pervasive tensions in the region is indeed the relationship between Anglos and Mexican Americans. The annexation of Mexican territories after the U.S.-Mexican War created an underclass in what became the southwest United States. With their national identity always in question by non-Latinos, Mexican Americans have struggled since the early nineteenth century against American institutions and laws circumscribing their property, citizenship, and legal rights.[21] Despite their disadvantaged position, the population size and residential ethnic density of Latinos provided avenues to institutional political and social incorporation. In many communities, compact geographic distribution made it possible for Mexican Americans to elect co-ethnics to a wide range of positions, from local governing boards to the United States Congress. Naturally occurring majority-minority districts provided institutional experience and presence long before the Voting Rights Act, and racially gerrymandered districts provided firm protections for legal enfranchisement.

Latino elected officials from the southwest outnumber those from any other region at all levels of government,[22] suggesting future Latino national political figures will likely hail from the region rich with experienced candidates. Large co-ethnic constituencies and electoral bases in the southwest provide benefits that come with political incorporation, including incumbent electoral advantages, long tenures in office, and influential party and committee positions.

There are few Latino elected officials in southern legislatures and local governments. In 2009, southern states elected only 22 (of 242 total) Latino state legislators; 15 of them represent Florida districts. Conversely, six southwest states (Arizona, California, Colorado, New Mexico Nevada, and Texas) account for over half of Latino state legislators in the same period.[23] Southern Latinos have fewer opportunities to participate in formal agenda setting and decision making on any issue by virtue of their diminished representation.

Beyond the explicitly political environment, Latinos exert influence in religious, educational, nonprofit, and business sectors across the southwest, where they occupy leadership positions and have economic clout. For example, the Latino target consumer base for bilingual products and services is widespread; it is not limited to a small and poor segment of the population as is more often the case for southern Latinos. Familiarity with borderland and wider Latin American markets creates entrepreneurial incentives as well. The broader class distribution among Latinos in the southwest (for example, relatively large middle and upper classes, college-educated citizens) has expanded the range of opportunities and access to power. By no means can we suggest that all is equal and cooperative in the southwest. Sharp socioeconomic inequities persist, as they do throughout the country. However, if we use socioeconomic and political representation as a metric of positive outcomes, there is no doubt that Latinos in the southwest are better off than their co-ethnic counterparts in other regions of the country (as noted earlier with respect to legislative representation and language as an access point). In *relative* terms, Latinos have fared well in the region and have institutional and social inroads to continue on an empowerment trajectory.

Demographic Change

The American population grew from 203 million in 1970 to 306 million in 2009, adding over 100 million people. In this time, all racial and ethnic groups have grown in size, but the Latino population has more than tripled, significantly outpacing all other groups. Descriptive demographic and voter turnout data derived from the U.S. Census Bureau call attention to changes in racial diversity and political participation in the Sunbelt. Population trends offer insight into why Latino politics has become central to the region and how this phenomenon will likely influence Sunbelt social and political life for the foreseeable future. Fifteen states are examined for keener understanding of these trends: Alabama, Arizona, Arkansas, California, Colorado, Florida, Georgia, Louisiana, Mississippi, Nevada, New Mexico, North Carolina, South Carolina, Texas, and Virginia.

Sunbelt states, more than any other part of the country, have experienced the most population growth. Demographers expect the region will continue to diversify at a quicker rate than the rest of the country.[24] Growth and diasporas of the Latino population across the American states create a new paradigm of racial and ethnic diversity. Simultaneous trends among Latinos and non-Latinos are responsible for this shift. In the last two decades, relative youth, higher birth rates, and immigration (mostly from Mexico) fueled Latino population increases. White families have become smaller, and the self-identified group is aging more rapidly than other segments in the population.[25] Now the largest minority group in the country, Latinos comprise 15 percent of the national population, compared to less than 5 five in 1970.[26] In raw numbers, this translates to 46.7 million Latinos residing in the United States in 2009. Texas, California, and New Mexico populations are already minority-majority; and a 2008 census report projects that this will be true for the rest of the country by 2042 (54 percent nonwhite nationally).[27] Those Census Bureau estimates also project Latinos will account for 30 percent of the total U.S. population in 2050 and number about 133 million, again tripling in size. The immigrant share of the American population, also concentrated in Sunbelt states, is overwhelmingly of Mexican and Central American origin. We should expect the foreign born population to surpass the peak of the last great waves of immigration in 1890 and 1910.[28] Social and political changes will inevitably accompany the demographic shift already underway.

The Latinization of the population is a modern trend that binds the Sunbelt states regardless of historical antecedents. Since the early 2000s, the Latino population is overwhelmingly clustered in the southern and western regions of the U.S.[29] The largest proportions are in the west at 42 percent, and over one-third (35 percent) reside in the south, but no region has a majority share (defined as 50 percent or more) of the Latino American population. Though sizeable Puerto Rican and Dominican populations are rooted in the Northeast, only 14 percent of the population is located there. The midwest has only 9 percent of the Latino population, largely concentrated in Chicago. The past ten years have marked the most accelerated gains in Latino population. In that time, the south experienced the highest actual numeric gain in Latino population, at 3.7 million, followed by the west at 3.4 million.

Arkansas, Georgia, South Carolina, and North Carolina experienced the largest Latino growth rates during this period. In Virginia, Prince William County (147 percent change) and Loudon County (144 percent change) rank in the top five American counties by Latino growth rate. California, Texas, Arizona, and Florida had the largest net gains in Latino population, owing in large part to the fact that Los Angeles, Houston, Phoenix, and Miami are preferred immigrant destination cities. Five sunbelt states—Georgia, Arizona, Nevada, Texas, and North Carolina—also experienced the largest increase in unauthorized immigrants to the country.[30] Increase in Latino population marks changes in daily life for southern residents, where Spanish language and surnames have not traditionally been part of the social or cultural backdrop. By contrast, Florida, New Mexico, and Arizona can absorb a fair number of Latinos without drastically disrupting the social norms with regard to expected social diversity.

Since the early 1970's the composition of the Sunbelt has changed dramatically. As Figure 13.1 illustrates, whites have lost population, African Americans have remained fairly steady, and Latinos have gained; these are not insignificant proportions. Nationally, white population dropped by 23 percent, and Latinos gained 11 percent. Each Sunbelt state follows this same pattern; it only varies in the magnitude of the increases and decreases. The most striking change occurred in California, which saw the white population drop by over one-third (37 percent) and Latinos increase by nearly a quarter (24 percent).

As previously noted, Latinos are not monolithic; indeed, the wide variation in national origin, language ability, nativity, citizenship status, and immigrant generation influences social and political outcomes. Social scientists often focus on nativity (for example, whether one is native or foreign born) as a variable of interest and often as a proxy measure for other relevant traits because immigration correlates highly with language, citizenship status, education, and other variables important to researchers. About 60 percent are U.S. born, hence citizens by birth. The data reflect both historical trends and modern currents of Latino demography. States with the highest proportion of U.S.-born Latinos are in the southwest. New Mexico claims the largest segment at 84 percent, followed by Colorado, Texas, Arizona, and California. Foreign-born Latinos are the majority of the group population in only five states, all of them in the south: Virginia, Florida, South Carolina, North Carolina, and Georgia. Thus, important in-group differences correlate with region and influence social and political dynamics. Many of the Latino immigrants ultimately become citizens; it would be erroneous to assume that immigrant Latinos are not citizens. The fact remains that all Sunbelt states have a larger proportion of undocumented Latinos than other regions, a demographic reality that poses tremendous social and political pressures. The surge in state policies targeting immigration-related issues and the Spring 2006 immigration protest rallies exemplify how these demographic differences become manifest in the regional political arena.

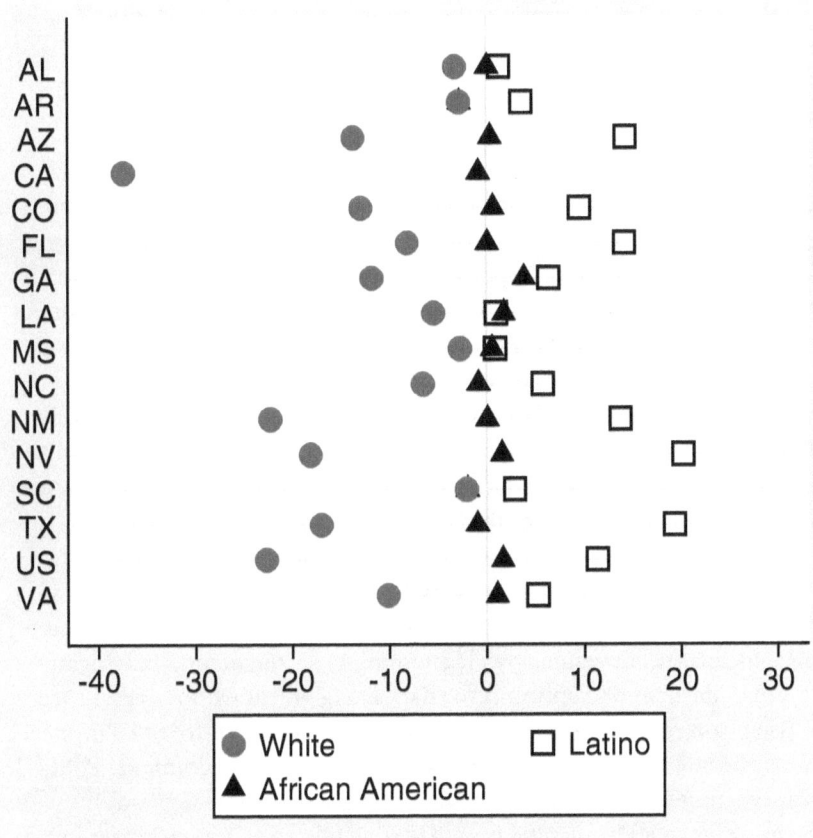

Figure 13.1. Net percent population change, select Sunbelt states 1970–2007. U.S. Census data, 1970–2002.

Direct Political Influence: Participants and Targets

Demographic trends influence national politics in tangible and dramatic ways that are already evident. The impact of Latinos on regional and national politics is not a futuristic projection—it has already happened and continues to develop. Two avenues direct Latino influence on

American politics: (1) they are part of the active electorate and/or participatory public, and (2) they are political targets for campaigns and candidates. Contemporary immigration politics and the 2008 presidential campaign offer opportunities to observe these political dynamics.

Immigration Politics

California of the 1990s epitomized the dual paths of Latino political influence. While targets of an explicitly racialized political agenda, Latinos were also politically mobilized. Republican governor Pete Wilson, with substantial party and private support, spearheaded a series of state ballot initiatives that were widely viewed as hostile toward immigrants and toward Latinos more broadly.[31] Highly controversial, Proposition 187 proposed eliminating all public benefits to immigrants, including public schooling, and called for extensive citizenship-validation procedures.[32] As such, the law would have institutionalized mechanisms for making Latinos a suspect class in the state. Proponents marketed 187 as the "Save Our State Initiative" and "SOS Initiative," implying that California required rescue from immigrants.[33] Governor Wilson included aggressive SOS themes in his reelection bid. In a particularly infamous television ad, the voiceover states, "They keep coming," as images of presumably illegal immigrants run across state highways in broad daylight and sprint in the dark along an anonymous rural road.[34] Wilson won reelection in 1994, and the set of racially controversial propositions passed, though the long-term effects proved more dramatic. Political scapegoating was nonpartisan, as Diane Feinstein's campaign and those of many California Democratic candidates included tough rhetoric on immigration themes.[35] However, the Republican vitriolic approach, making immigrants and immigration central to the party, ultimately realigned partisan politics in the state against them.[36]

The hostile California discourses and policy environment mobilized Latinos, especially immigrants, in unique ways. Research shows the policy threat and harsh racial tones employed in the 1990s mobilized Californians at the polls. Latino voter turnout and Democratic-candidate support increased, while Republicans lost ground with white voters.[37] The ballot measures and strong anti-immigrant rhetoric placed Latinos under social and political attack, producing unanticipated mobilizing effects. Pantoja, Ramirez, and Segura document significantly higher voter turnout among California Latinos that naturalized during this politically hostile time frame.[38]

Barreto, Ramiez, and Woods find Latino voter turnout (both U.S. and foreign born) increased beyond expected increases associated with population size, from 1996 to 2000.[39] Barreto demonstrates California foreign-born Latinos, regardless of naturalization date, turned out to vote at higher proportions than U.S.-born Latinos in 2002, outperforming several segments of the California electorate.[40] Perhaps the most surprising effect is outlined in Bowler, Nicholson, and Segura's 2006 study that finds the racially charged propositions sponsored by the state Republican Party reversed the trend among Latinos *and* Anglos toward identifying with Republicans so much so that they actually shifted party attachments and aligned with Democrats.[41] The reason California is safely in the Democratic column today is because Republican strategists overestimated public taste for harsh, racialized politics. Bowler et al. keenly observe, "Our results raise questions about the long term efficacy of racially divisive strategies for electoral gain."

Latinos tend not to be preoccupied with a "Latino issues agenda." No matter their geographic location, socioeconomic status, nativity or other demographic trait, education remains the priority policy concern.[42] Evidence also suggests the second policy priority for Latinos tends to follow the public mood on national issues such as the economy, the war in Iraq, or health care (the Pew Hispanic Center documents these shifting priorities especially well). It was precisely such race-neutral issues that helped George W. Bush develop inroads with Latinos and capture over 40 percent of their vote in his 1998 campaign for Texas governor and both presidential bids. The caveat here is that when Latinos are met with high-profile campaigns that use their ethnic group as a political target (for example, immigration, English as the official language, bilingual education, proof-of-identification requirements), their policy priorities shift and these "Latino issues" move to the front of the policy salience queue. If the political environment requires it, Latinos will play defense at the ballot box and in other modes of political participation.

The California Republican immigration-centered political agenda of the 1990s offered a preview of the national partisan and ethnic politics that emerged in 2006 and continued well into 2010. Latinos once again entered the cross hairs of partisan political strategy that began as part of the Republican campaign for the 2006 mid-term elections but reverberated through the 2008 presidential race and spilled into the discussion surrounding Sonia

Sotomayor's Supreme Court nomination.⁴³ In December 2005, Representative James Sensenbrenner (R-Wis.) introduced HR 4437, the "Border Protection, Anti-terrorism, and Illegal Immigration Control Act." The bill, which ultimately failed, included several significant provisions: adding 700 miles of fence along the U.S.-Mexican border, increased citizenship status verification efforts, local control of undocumented detainees, and stiff penalties against those assisting or employing undocumented immigrants. Though the Sensenbrenner bill failed in the Senate, HR 6061, which focused exclusively on U.S.-Mexico border fences, was signed into law in October 2006. Many Latinos saw these pieces of legislation and accompanying political rhetoric as a threat that made all Latinos scapegoats for economic, social, cultural, and national security problems.

As the Pew Hispanic Center reported (2007), Latinos felt a chill as immigration rhetoric heated.⁴⁴ The public campaigns around the issues reified "Latino" as a political category despite significant in-group diversity. Enduring national media coverage and consistent immigration issue framing began to link Latinos as an out-group in national politics in a truly unprecedented manner. In contemporary American politics, immigration is specifically politicized around Latinos. Immigration legislation tends to single out ethnic Latinos independent of any other group, a sharp break from previous national trends. Since the 1950s, Latino policy agendas were usually linked to African American political gains and racial equity issues, like voter enfranchisement, affirmative action, and desegregation.⁴⁵ Latino Republicans recognized enforcement-focused immigration policies spelled trouble for the party that was gaining traction with Latino voters (outside California) in recent years. Republican Representative Lincoln Diaz-Balart (R-Fla.) said, "There has been too much of an anti-immigrant tone. When people start to perceive that immigrants are being put in the same category as a threat to national security, it's hard to get your message across."⁴⁶ Typically, immigration enforcement policy is not salient to Cuban American legislators or constituencies because illegal immigration simply does not apply to their case. However, harsh rhetoric conflated distaste for Latinos with immigration policy, and the Cuban American base in the Republican Party was not off-limits. Representative Tom Tancredo (R-Colo.) repeatedly described Miami as a third world country and a harbinger of nefarious national consequences associated with undocumented Latin American immigration.⁴⁷ Republican strategist and advertising executive Lionel Sosa lamented, "Bush's decision to bow to conservative pressure and sign legislation authorizing construction of a 700-mile fence along the U.S.-Mexican border sent a terrible signal."[48]

Latinos, regardless of citizenship status, heard racist commentary that seeped into the 2006 immigration debate and congressional campaigns. Two incumbent House members used representatives from the Minutemen, a vigilante border enforcement organization with documented links to hate groups, at campaign events.[49] Another case in point, Republican congressional candidate Randy Graf ran ads depicting a blonde child walking toward a slowly opening door as the narrator cited crime statistics caused by immigration.[50] Though the party may have mobilized some of their base using this wedge issue, they also mobilized millions of Latinos residing in the United States.

Over three months in the spring of 2006, an estimated 3.5 to 5.1 million people rallied in the streets in over 160 cities in the United States to protest House Bill 4437.[51] The magnitude of this activism was unprecedented; many cities witnessed the largest public demonstrations ever to take place in the area. Over 250,000 people participated in the largest marches held in Phoenix, Houston, Atlanta, Los Angeles, and Chicago. Notably, only one of the megamarch cities is outside the Sunbelt. Smaller cities with relatively small Latino and immigrant populations joined the wave of mass political protest: 10,000 in Charlotte, 3,000 in Birmingham, 15,000 in Tucson, 5,000 in Columbia, South Carolina, and 4,000 in Richmond.[52] The protests underscore the fact that Latino political empowerment may take place outside the voting booth because so many are ineligible voters due to age or citizenship status. Ethnic media, advocacy community groups, and churches demonstrated their extensive networks and organizational skills that mobilized so many, so effectively, so quickly across the country.[53] The mass participation of millions of Latinos of varied citizenship statuses also evidenced their engagement and attention to politics, which is often described as lacking.

Immigration and Latino politics suddenly became a high priority for media and government at every level. Never before had so much print and airtime been devoted to immigration policy and opinion. The extensive coverage and public passions on the issue made it ripe for state and local policy action. State legislatures passed 465 bills dealing with various aspects of immigration policy between 2005 and 2008; 40 percent of these policies passed in fifteen Sunbelt states included for analysis in this chapter.[54] Policy orientation toward immigrants in these various pieces of legislation is a mix of punitive (for example, cutting public benefits) and protective (for example, making in-state tuition available to undocumented students who graduated from in-state high schools) measures. The issue has political traction on both sides and resonates especially with Sunbelt residents.

Since 2006, local governments and candidates increasingly engaged the issue, with several adopting tough enforcement positions as winning campaign issues.[55] In the suburban Dallas community of Carrollton, mayoral candidate (and winner) Ron Branson plainly stated that he would "rid the city of illegal immigrants."[56] From 2006 to 2008, 104 municipal governments entertained a host of ordinances placing disproportionate burden on Latinos. Cities and counties considered laws that would validate citizenship for housing, ban displays of foreign flags, establish English as the official language, and enhance police enforcement procedures to discourage undocumented immigrants from settling in the community.[57] Local immigration regulations represent important resource allocation decisions since substantial local tax dollars absorb the enforcement costs and legal expenses associated with such ordinances.[58]

2008 Presidential Election

Latino influence continued to surface in the 2008 presidential election. At both the primary and general election stage, Latino voters formed a cohesive voting bloc and turned out in record numbers. Campaigns also reflected Latino influence. Hillary Clinton and Barack Obama invested heavily in Latino-targeted messaging and mobilization, and candidates seeking the Republican nomination kept immigration enforcement central to their agenda.

Voter turnout is the standard measure of political influence. It is important to acknowledge that the share of eligible voters varies by group; in 2006 only 39 percent of Latinos were eligible voters, compared to 76 percent of whites and 65 percent of African Americans.[59] Two factors account for this disparity: citizenship and age requirements. A larger share of the Latino population are under eighteen (for example, in 2006, the average age among Latinos was twenty-seven, compared to forty for whites), and, of course, there are larger numbers of noncitizen adults; thus, the pool of eligible voters is relatively small. Even among the eligible electorate, Latino turnout is significantly lower than white and black turnout in the states. Turnout between 1996 and 2006 averaged 66 percent for whites, 57 percent for African Americans, and 47 percent for Latinos in Sunbelt states.[60] Although Latino turnout is low by comparison, it has steadily increased over the last twenty years. The law of large numbers has propelled the trend; as more Latinos age into the electorate or naturalize, their share increases from one election cycle to the next.

This trend points to significant changes on the horizon in American politics. Specifically, when candidates and campaigns seek to expand the electorate (meaning, increase the number of voters in their party and the electorate), Latinos must be a part of that strategy because they represent the largest *potential* electorate. Unlike other groups, Latinos have not reached an average maximum turnout threshold. They are the only segment in the electorate where eligible voter rates *and* turnout continue to rise. White and African American voter turnout rates have essentially peaked in most states and remain relatively stable. Even though the black electorate can grow by a few percentage points, demonstrated partisan loyalties and residence in noncompetitive districts diminish targeted mobilization efforts.[61]

The importance of Latinos in the 2008 presidential campaigns was palpable long before election day. Democrats scheduled the Nevada primary in January to provide Latino voters early influence in the nominating process. Party elites acknowledged that the change was a deliberate, strategic response to actual and perceived gains made by Republicans among Latinos in two previous presidential elections.[62] Candidates Barack Obama and Hillary Clinton aggressively courted the Latino vote, spending over four million dollars on Spanish language ads alone—a dramatic rise from the mere $320,000 spent by all Democrats combined in the 2004 primary.[63] The two candidates also targeted Latino voters in English ads incorporating overt Latino themes. For example, Clinton ran English language television ads with symbolic figures from the Chicano and United Farm Workers movements, Dolores Huerta and a grandson of Cesar Chavez. Obama ads included clips of his most famous speeches with Spanish subtitles. It was not lost on many Latino voters that Obama's campaign rally cry of "Yes, We Can" is the English translation of the United Farmer Workers slogan "Sí Se Puede."[64]

New Mexico governor and Democratic candidate Bill Richardson bowed out of the primary early in the 2008 campaign. As the race between Obama and Clinton tightened, his political influence rose. Political journalists anticipated Richardson's endorsement, claiming his was the most important Latino endorsement available.[65] Obama created a campaign event out of the Richardson endorsement that dominated the national news cycle for days—yet another indicator that Latino politics had arrived.[66] The Sunbelt governor was on the campaign trail for Obama for the rest of the 2008 campaign season, focusing on Latino voter mobilization.

Conversely, Republican primary candidates played a game of "quien es el mas macho" on immigration enforcement throughout the primary season. The 2008 Republican presidential primary employed an approach strikingly similar to the 2006 congressional races and California in the 1990s with Pete Wilson at the helm. Immigration was the centerpiece of the party platform with tough policy prescriptions and rhetoric to match. Mitt Romney, Rudolph Giuliani, Mike Huckabee, Tom Tancredo, and Fred Thompson consistently and loudly castigated John McCain for his efforts at comprehensive immigration reform in the Senate.[67] Each Republican primary debate included several questions on immigration enforcement and border control, which was not the case in Democratic forums. Clearly, the candidates ascertained this was a winning issue for the party. This approach failed the party on two counts: first, the most moderate candidate on immigration policy, John McCain, won the nomination; and second, they reinforced the unfriendly image that the GOP had developed from the heat of the 2006 marches.

In terms of party preference, Latinos have certainly trended toward Democrats, but they have demonstrated a willingness to cross party lines in various electoral contests. Their partisanship is less cohesive compared to African Americans or white voters. Figures 13.2 and 13.3 illustrate trends in presidential vote choice among Latinos, African Americans and whites. The data in Figure 13.2 plot the average share Democratic presidential candidates won in 1996, 2000, and 2004 in select states.[68] Figure 13.3 plots the share Obama won from the various groups in 2008. These illustrations show Latino partisan preferences in relationship to other groups at two important junctures. The 1996–2004 period does not include national anti-immigrant rhetoric and policy positions associated with the Republican Party, while 2008 is characterized by polarizing immigration politics.

Both figures illustrate degrees of racially polarized voting in the Sunbelt. Across the states, African Americans and Latinos are more supportive of Democratic candidates than are whites. The gap between black and white voters is much wider than the gap between Latinos and either group. Indeed, the graphic presentation shows that Latinos fall, as a moderate bloc,

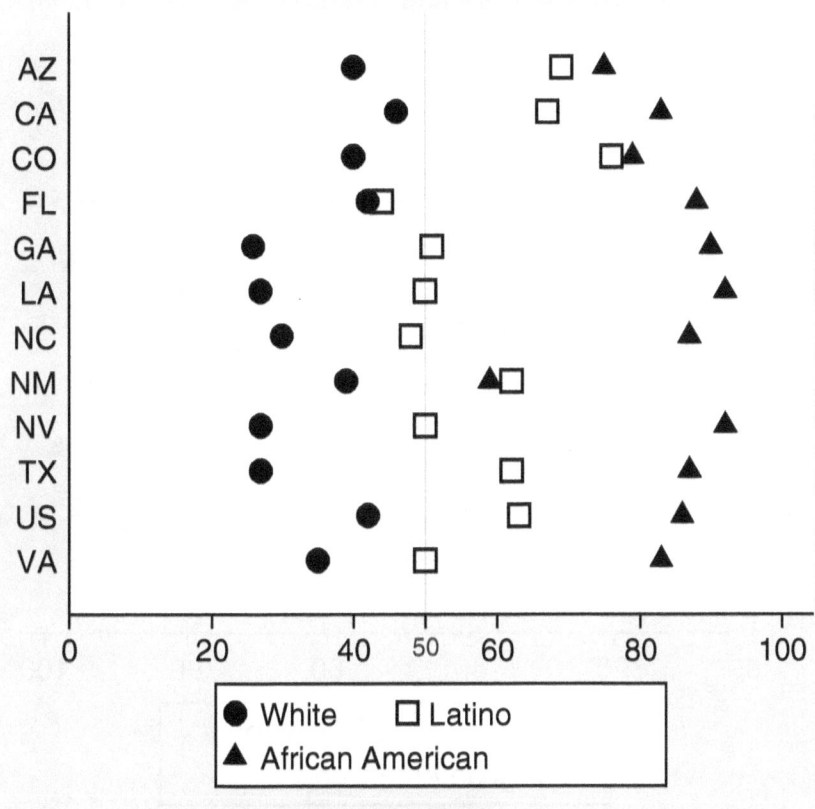

Figure 13.2. Percent vote for Democratic presidential candidate, select Sunbelt states 1996–2004. National Election Pool, 2000, 2004.

between the stronger political orientations asserted by white and black voters. Sunbelt Latinos were slightly closer to white partisan preferences than to African Americans during the 1996–2004 era but aligned closer to blacks in the 2008 election. Latino voters have sided with Democratic candidates at higher rates than whites but are a less cohesive bloc than African Americans.

It is also important to recall that the winner-take-all structure of the electoral college makes even smaller shares of large groups (for example,

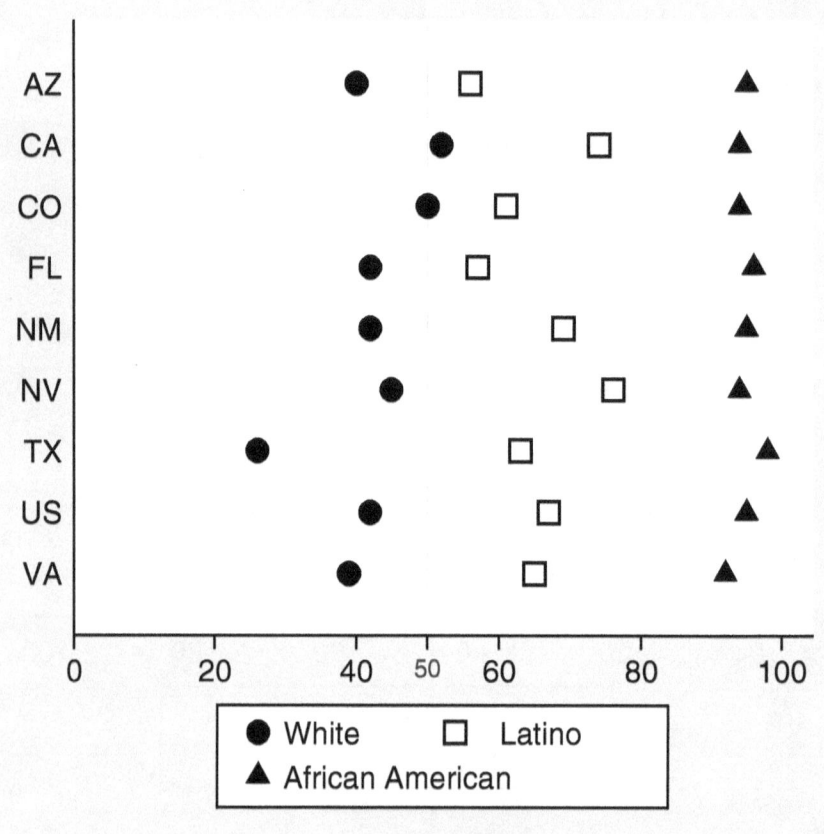

Figure 13.3. Percent vote for Barack Obama, select Sunbelt states 2008. National Election Pool, 2008.

one-third of the Latino vote in a competitive state can change the outcome) important to the calculus of winning. Comparing Figures 13.2 and 13.3, it is clear that Latinos supported Obama at a much higher rate than they had supported previous Democratic candidates.[69] The significance of minority support for Obama lies in the fact that he won the presidency despite losing the majority of the white vote. Only 43 percent of the white electorate voted for Obama. Obama's ascent to the presidency, thus, resulted from supermajorities of Latino, black, and other nonwhite voter turnout, which represented critical margins to his victory.

The introduction to this essay noted that the McCain campaign was anxious about Latino mobilization for fear that the party base would conflate outreach efforts with immigration politics. McCain ran several ads during the primary season asking for a more respectful tone on immigration discourse and acknowledging Latino military contributions.[70] Yet the campaign lacked vigorous strategies to educate voters on McCain's "Latino-friendly" record and was not as developed as the Obama (or Bush, for that matter) Latino effort.

In the general election, Obama's campaign aggressively pursued the Latino vote even though the political winds were already in his favor. A pointed Obama Spanish language ad titled "Dos Caras" (Two Faces) reminded Latino voters how the conservative movement used immigration to express racist, explicitly anti-Latino sentiments. The voiceover begins the ad saying, "They want us to forget the insults we've put up with, the intolerance," an image of Rush Limbaugh then appears with his recent quotes, "Mexicans are stupid and unqualified" and "Shut your mouth or get out." The announcer continues, "They made us feel marginalized in a country we love so much."[71] McCain's moderate positions could not erase the perception that Republicans are hostile or unwelcoming to Latinos. Party leaders and advocates have, perhaps unwittingly, contributed to a deep archive of audio and video footage that attests to that point.

A week before election day, NBC's Chuck Todd prophetically declared the importance Latino voters would have on election day. Describing trends in preelection polling in Sunbelt states, he wrote, "Obama's dominance among Hispanics in the west is proving to be the difference maker in Colorado, Nevada and New Mexico. In addition, the increased numbers of non-Cuban Hispanics in Florida, as well as the growing Hispanic population in North Carolina and Virginia, could be the tipping voting group in those three states."[72] He was correct on all counts, as Obama handily carried 67 percent of the Latino vote and went on to win each of the states referenced. Florida, New Mexico, Colorado, and Nevada saw Latinos vote in cohesive fashion, surfacing as an important member in the electoral coalition. North Carolina and Virginia showed that Latinos can influence outcomes outside the southwest despite their small share of the electorate. In North Carolina, Obama won by about 14,000 votes, and estimates show about 26,000 of his total votes came from foreign-born Latinos. Similar trends emerged in

Virginia, where the margin of victory was about equal to the number of immigrant Latino voter support in the state.[73]

Looking Forward

The new configuration of Sunbelt politics surfaced in 2008; it is a politics characterized by incorporation and tension. The campaign environment included Latino elected officials and attended to diversity within the population (for example, targeting Latinos in both English and Spanish). The national electorate and Sunbelt states in particular saw the highest rates of Latino voter turnout ever. At the same time, resistance to the demographic shifts also emerged. Immigration policy provided a political cover for candidates and citizens to voice spiteful commentary directed at Latinos.[74] Latino political power and incorporation are not necessarily synonymous with large population or Democratic control (whether local or national) because Latinos remain underrepresented in consequential authority positions in American institutions including politics, business, industry, and education.

Coalitions

The partisan middle ground can be advantageous for developing a broad base of political coalition partners. Recall voting distribution figures showing that Latinos have not voted in polar opposition to black or white voters. That is to say, Latinos are not extreme partisans or ideologues. The immigration protest politics in 2006 illustrated that Latinos have strong political allies within their ethnic group and beyond. Citizens, U.S.- and foreign-born alike, participated, as did Latinos of many national origin groups; and in California, substantial support came from Asian-American immigrant and community-based organizations.[75] Political solidarity emerged across diverse groups that may not have been threatened by the House resolution but found the policy and political environment so distasteful that it mobilized their participation.

Because Latinos and African Americans are similarly situated in terms of socioeconomic status and racial marginalization, there is reason to expect their shared partisanship and policy preferences may translate into support for similar candidates and policies. The number of viable minority candidates has increased, and multiracial coalitions in several cities, including Houston, San Antonio, and Los Angeles, have elected African Americans and Latinos to office even in contexts where there are no racially gerrymandered districts.[76] Racial diversity may serve to further the political empowerment of multiple minority groups, but associated multiracial coalitions may be fragile if political agendas and campaigns emphasize one group's interests over another.

We have already seen public opinion split over Latino policy issues. Because millions of Latinos reside in the Sunbelt, issues like bilingual education, English as the official language, and public services for immigrants are likely to remain agenda items of interest for advocates and opponents alike. The noncitizen population raises new questions regarding political representation and institutional discrimination in a region that has a long history and mixed record of dealing with these issues. It remains to be seen whether different groups and the institutions that represent them in state and local contexts will adopt long-term political strategies and policy approaches that resist or accommodate the changes at hand. The implications of historical forces converging with demographic trends will have substantial effects on the political and social life of Latinos and other groups alike that will continue to transform not only regional but also national politics.

Partisan Possibilities

The future of Latino empowerment and influence will develop as a function of group traits and behaviors that make them distinctive. According to political scientist Thomas Schaller, collective Latino influence on politics emanates from size and projected population growth, issue cohesiveness, electoral volatility, and geographic distribution.[77] Group size and projected growth provide avenues to elect co-ethnics and place group-specific issues on the political agenda if necessary. Larger populations also attract attention from candidates and elected officials that need a majority of the electorate to support them to keep their jobs and pursue their political ambitions. Second, Latinos are politically cohesive on a subset of issues that resonates with their shared heritage, including opposition to official English, support for bilingual education programs, and advocacy of national immigration policy that includes a pathway to citizenship.[78] If Republicans continue to define themselves as tough immigration opponents, they are conceding the Latino vote. Most Latinos favor Democrats, though most Cuban Americans favor Republicans, but loyalties are not especially strong. In any given national or statewide election, Latinos split their vote about 70–30 across the two parties. Most often, a 60–40 or 70–30 split of the group vote forces both parties to address the group's interests during the campaign in substantive (policy positions) and symbolic (campaign budget and time allocation) terms. Latinos become more powerful in some ways because, as one party pursues a larger share of their vote, the other party must attempt to retain its base of voters. Finally, concentrated distribution in geographic units can facilitate political empowerment. Campaigns, candidates, and elected officials can communicate and mobilize Latinos efficiently when they are clustered in regions where there is a sense of common local issues. Residential ethnic density also means large Latino electorates are influential in multiple districts (for example, city councils, state legislatures, and congressional districts), thus amplifying their institutional influence.

Right now, Latinos certainly look like Democratic voters because the party courted them aggressively during the very long party primary and because the Republican Party essentially conceded their vote. Latinos may continue to vote Democratic because early political experiences have enduring effects on political behavior and millions of Latinos have been baptized into politics in a racially hostile environment fostered by Republican appeals on immigration issues—whether in 1994 in California or 2008 across the nation. The buoyancy of the Obama campaign could also have an enduring positive impact for the Democrats. Depending on how the parties decide to approach Latino constituencies, it is entirely feasible that immigration issues could shape the Latino vote for generations, akin to the manner in which the civil rights agenda solidified the Democratic vote among African Americans. Additional in-group trends reported by the 2008 National Election Pool show additional favor toward Democrats: among Latinos aged 19–29, Obama received 76 percent of the vote. He also picked up 57 percent of the Latino vote in Florida, which had been solidly Republican for three decades.

Mobilization and courtship must continue if Democrats want to make Latinos a permanent segment of their coalition, though. Latinos are willing to cross party lines in favor of candidates who make a concerted effort to mobilize their votes or make their policy preferences a high priority; they have demonstrated their partisan malleability in the past: 67 percent of Latinos voted for the Democratic presidential candidate in 2008, but there are contextual election-specific factors that should be acknowledged. The Democrats had a highly appealing candidate, and Republican partisan baggage on immigration was difficult for even their most moderate candidate to avoid. There are trends that favor Democrats, but it is not empirically evident that the strong Obama support is transferable to the Democratic Party at large. U.S.-born Latinos represent the most obvious segment of the population to help Republicans win back votes but would require extensive strategic repair within the GOP that reaches beyond "*amigo* politics."

Between 2006 and 2009, unique political events provided unusual opportunities for both parties and their representatives to address Latinos as part of national platform politics. The 2006 immigration marches, 2008 presidential election, and 2009 nomination of Sonia Sotomayor to the U.S. Supreme Court were major events in Latino American life that further solidified Latinos as a political entity. As central characters in these stories, Latinos received more news coverage than usual and, accordingly, followed these events with more attention to news and politics.[79] Partisan responses to the marches and immigration policy were addressed earlier in this chapter. Democrats emerged as the more Latino-friendly party, but some of that perception may simply be attributable to relative Republican-branded commentary. At all three junctures, Republican candidates, elected officials, media surrogates, and party supporters expressed relatively consistent commentary that questioned Latino patriotism, citizenship, and ability to compete on par with whites in school and employment.[80] On the other hand, Democrats have attempted to accommodate proponents of stiff immigration policy, too. When New York Democratic Senator Chuck Schumer announced he was consulting with television anti-immigration activist Lou Dobbs on immigration reform policy to include many perspectives on the issue, the Latino blogosphere quickly voiced strong disapproval. Those sentiments echoed in various media outlets, especially on Spanish language radio and online forums.[81] The future of Latino participatory politics is not quite evident. Traditionally low voter turnout rates suggest that Latinos are comfortable choosing "none of the above" instead of the lesser of two evils. But more Latino elected officials and candidates out of either party could be the solution to advance party politics beyond immigration and cultural discourses.

Currently, the national and regional political environments are in transition, adjusting to the reality that Latinos are a permanent and expanding segment in the electorate and citizenry. In the 1980s panethnic Latino identity politics was roundly dismissed as a meaningless categorization that did not resonate across the various Hispanic national origin groups in the United States.[82] This is no longer true. Existing commonalities in cultural heritage (specifically Spanish, Catholicism, and immigrant experience) loosely link Latinos of all backgrounds. Latino American identity is reinforced by shared referents and experiences, many linked to apolitical regional figures and institutions. Watching Jorge Ramos and Maria Elena Salinas deliver the nightly news on Univision, listening to music by Juanes and Maná, and rooting for Jets Quarterback (and Los Angeles native) Mark Sanchez further define a panethnic American Latino experience. Experiences with and perceptions of non-Latinos also give meaning to the panethnic construction. This combination of in-group linkages and out-group perceptions gives rise to a new national panethnic Latino politics agenda that is most evident in the Sunbelt.

Recent political events and projected trends suggest that more similarities than differences among Latinos will facilitate their incorporation in different facets of American society. The stable of Latino political talent is rich in the southwest and Florida, and there are enough eligible co-ethnics in the electorate to advance at least a few political careers. Latino officials from Sunbelt states have provided advocacy and representation to co-ethnic immigrants in the south and southwest who may lack formal (for example, disenfranchised nonvoters) or substantive (for example, elected officials not representing their interests) opportunities for representation.[83] We can surmise what national Latino politics will look like by revisiting Sunbelt trends in incorporation, resistance, and response. Traditional Sunbelt interpretations hold that regional economic, political, and religious trends strengthen the GOP and assert conservative agendas; the evidence presented here suggests otherwise. Demographic change and the political response to these changes have emboldened and empowered the Latino community in ways that tend to favor Democrats, but there is no guarantee of partisan loyalty. The Sunbelt remains a dynamic region that will continue to transform national political, social, and economic life, but it will do so with a distinctive Latino influence in the years ahead.

Notes

Introduction

1. Tape of E. V. Hill Sermon at National Prayer Congress, Dallas, 1976, Tape 13, Collection 176, Billy Graham Evangelistic Association, Billy Graham Center Archives (BGCA), Wheaton College, Illinois.
2. Tape 4, Collection 176, BGCA.
3. Ibid. This introduction is drawn from Darren Dochuk, *From Bible Belt to Sunbelt: Plain-Folk Religion, Grassroots Politics, and the Rise of Evangelical Conservatism* (New York: Norton, 2010), chap. 13.
4. For a more extensive historiographical treatment of Sunbelt terminology and literature, see David R. Goldfield, "The Rise of the Sunbelt: Urbanization and Industrialization," in John B. Boles, ed., *A Companion to the American South* (Malden, Mass.: Blackwell, 2002), 474–93.
5. Kevin Phillips, *The Emerging Republican Majority* (New Rochelle, N.Y.: Arlington House, 1969).
6. Kirkpatrick Sale, *Power Shift: The Rise of the Southern Rim and Its Challenges to the Eastern Establishment* (New York: Random House, 1975), 6.
7. Ibid., 5–7
8. Here we are drawing from Raymond A. Mohl, "The Transformation of Urban America Since the Second World War," in Raymond A. Mohl, Robert Fisher, Carl Abbott, Roger W. Lotchin, Robert B. Fairbanks, and Zane I. Miller, *Essays on Sunbelt Cities and Recent Urban America* (College Station: Texas A&M University Press, 1990), 20.
9. "Born Again! The Year of the Evangelicals!" *Newsweek*, October 25, 1976, 76.
10. Carey McWilliams, "The Evangelical Bloc," draft of article for *The Nation*, Evangelicals Folder, Box 46, Carey McWilliams Papers (CWP), Special Collections, University of California, Los Angeles.

11. Wayne King, "Federal Funds Pour into Sunbelt States," *New York Times*, February 9, 1976, 1.

12. Bernard L. Weinstein and Robert E. Firestine, *Regional Growth and Decline in the United States: The Rise of the Sunbelt and the Decline of the Northeast* (New York: Praeger, 1978).

13. David C. Perry and Alfred J. Watkins, eds., *The Rise of the Sunbelt Cities* (Beverly Hills, Calif.: Sage, 1977), 9.

14. For helpful overview of these two volumes, see Goldfield, "The Rise of the Sunbelt."

15. Richard M. Bernard and Bradley R. Rice, eds., *Sunbelt Cities: Politics and Growth Since World War II* (Austin: University of Texas Press, 1983).

16. See, for instance, Carl Abbott, *The New Urban America: Growth and Politics in Sunbelt Cities* (Chapel Hill: University of North Carolina Press, 1981); in comparison, Richard Bernard, ed., *Snowbelt Cities: Metropolitan Politics in the Northeast and Midwest Since World War II* (Bloomington: Indiana University Press, 1990); David R. Goldfield, *Cotton Fields and Skyscrapers: Southern City and Region, 1607–1980* (Baton Rouge: Louisiana State University Press, 1982); Roger Lotchin, ed., *The Martial Metropolis: U.S. Cities in War and Peace* (New York: Praeger, 1984); Randall M. Miller and George E. Pozzetta, eds., *Shades of the Sunbelt: Essays on Ethnicity, Race, and the Urban South* (New York: Greenwood Press, 1988).

17. For a helpful overview of these questions, see Carl Abbott, "Sunbelt and Snowbelt Cities," in David Goldfield, ed., *Encyclopedia of American Urban History* (Thousand Oaks, Calif.: Sage, 2007), 780–82.

18. Howard N. Rabinowitz and David R. Goldfield, "The Vanishing Sunbelt," in Raymond A. Mohl, ed., *Searching for the Sunbelt: Historical Perspectives on a Region* (Knoxville: University of Tennessee Press, 1990), 231.

19. Urban historians who began researching the peculiar social, economic, cultural, racial, and political dimensions of single southern cities found unity in the underlying theoretical and historiographical elements of Goldfield's work, which posited (and protected) a distinctively regional character for southern urbanization, even as this concept became more problematic. Over time, Goldfield would soften this position slightly, as developmental trends in the 1990s pointed to the nationalization of the southern metropolitan pattern, yet he would only budge a bit: "amid the bagel shops and coffee boutiques, there are still elements of regional culture that persist in religion, food, music, political culture, and gender relations. The main difference . . . is that the urban South has now become the regional arbiter of these cultural attributes in much the same way that our national metropolitan culture has pervaded every corner of the country." Goldfield, "The Rise of the Sunbelt," 476–77.

20. James C. Cobb, *The Selling of the South: The Southern Crusade for Industrial Development, 1936–1990* (Urbana: University of Illinois Press, 1993); Bruce J. Schulman, *From Cotton Belt to Sunbelt: Federal Policy, Economic Development, and the Transformation of the South, 1938–1980* (New York: Oxford University Press, 1991).

21. The literature dealing with conservatism (or neoliberalism) in a Sunbelt context is expanding rapidly, so much so that it is impossible here to make note of every major work in the field. This historiography will emerge in the text and notes of the essays that follow. For our purposes, however, it is worth mentioning a few *recent works of history* that are critical to our understanding of *Sunbelt conservatism*: Joseph Crespino, *In Search of Another Country: Mississippi and the Conservative Counterrevolution* (Princeton, N.J.: Princeton University Press, 2007); Donald Critchlow, *The Conservative Ascendancy: How the GOP Right Made Political History* (Cambridge, Mass.: Harvard University Press, 2007); Matthew Dallek, *The Right Moment: Ronald Reagan's First Victory and the Decisive Turning Point in American Politics* (New York: Free Press, 2000); Dochuk, *From Bible Belt to Sunbelt*; Robert Goldberg, *Barry Goldwater* (New Haven, Conn.: Yale University Press, 1995); James Gregory, *The Southern Diaspora: How the Great Migrations of Black and White Southerners Transformed America* (Chapel Hill: University of North Carolina Press, 2005); Kevin Kruse, *White Flight: Atlanta and the Making of Modern Conservatism* (Princeton, N.J.: Princeton University Press, 2005); Matthew Lassiter, *The Silent Majority: Suburban Politics in the Sunbelt South* (Princeton, N.J.: Princeton University Press, 2006); Lisa McGirr, *Suburban Warriors: The Origins of the New American Right* (Princeton, N.J.: Princeton University Press, 2001); Steven Miller, *Billy Graham and the Rise of the Republican South* (Philadelphia: University of Pennsylvania Press, 2009); Bethany Moreton, *To Serve God and Wal-Mart: The Making of Christian Free Enterprise* (Cambridge, Mass.: Harvard University Press, 2009); Michelle Nickerson, *Mothers of Conservatism: Women and the Postwar Right* (Princeton, N.J.: Princeton University Press, forthcoming); Kim Phillips-Fein, *Invisible Hands: The Making of the Conservative Movement from the New Deal to Reagan* (New York: Norton, 2009); Jonathan Schoenwald, *A Time for Choosing: The Rise of Modern American Conservatism* (New York: Oxford University Press, 2001). For a more thorough overview, see Darren Dochuk, "Revival on the Right: Making Sense of the Conservative Moment in American History," *History Compass: An Online Journal* 4 (July 2006): 975–99.

22. Abbott, *The New Urban America*, esp. 8.

23. Kevin Starr, *Golden Dreams: California in an Age of Abundance, 1950–1963* (New York: Oxford University Press, 2009), 420.

24. Amy L. Scott, "Remaking Urban in the American West: Urban Environmentalism, Lifestyle Politics, and Hip Capitalism in Boulder, Colorado," in Jeff Roche, ed., *The Political Culture of the New West* (Lawrence: University Press of Kansas, 2008), 253–55. On "counterculture libertarians," see also Andrew G. Kirk, "Free Minds and Free Markets: Counterculture Libertarians, Natural Capitalists, and an Alternative Vision of Western Political Authenticity," in Roche, ed., *The Political Culture of the New West*, 281–309.

25. For an elaborated analysis of space as a landscape of economic and social production, see Henri LeFebvre, *The Production of Space*, trans. Donald Nicholson-Smtih (Oxford: Blackwell, 1991).

26. Dolores Hayden, *The Power of Place: Urban Landscapes as Public History* (Cambridge, Mass.: MIT Press, 1995), 18.

27. Edward L. Ayers and Peter S. Onuf, "Preface," in Edward L. Ayers, Patricia Nelson Limerick, Stephen Nissenbaum, and Peter S. Onuf, eds., *All Over the Map: Rethinking American Regions* (Baltimore: Johns Hopkins University Press, 1996), vii; C. Van Woodward, *The Burden of Southern History*, 3rd ed. (1960; Baton Rouge: Louisiana State University Press, 1993), vii.

28. Thank you to the Metropolitan History Workshop at the University of Michigan for calling our attention to the importance of frontier ideology in the emergence of the Sunbelt.

29. For more on Del Webb and Sun City, see John M. Findlay, *Magic Lands: Western Cityscapes and American Culture after 1940* (Berkeley: University of California Press, 1992), chap. 4, "Sun City, Arizona: New Town for Old Folks," 160–214.

30. Tamara Jenkins, *The Savages*, 113 min., Fox Searchlight Pictures, Los Angeles, 2008; Wim Wenders, *Paris, Texas*, 147 min., Road Movies Filmproduktion, Berlin, 1984; Duncan Tucker, *Transamerica*, 103 min., Belladonna Productions, IFC Films and the Weinstein Company, 2005; Michael Arndt, Jonathan Dayton, Valerie Faris, *Little Miss Sunshine*, 101 min., Fox Searchlight Pictures, 2006.

31. See Panel on Policies and Prospects for Metropolitan and Nonmetropolitan America, President's Commission for a National Agenda for the Eighties, *Urban America in the Eighties: Perspectives and Prospects* (Washington, D.C.: U.S. Government Printing Office, 1980); "John Herbers, "Experts Do Not Expect Energy Problems to Halt Population Shift Away from Cities," *New York Times*, June 9, 1980, A18; John V. Lindsay, "Shaping Urban Policy," *New York Times*, February 5, 1981, A23; George Will, "Good Regional Rivalries," *Dallas Times Herald*, January 1, 1981.

32. See Edward Ayers, "What We Talk About When We Talk About the South," in Ayers et al., *All Over the Map*, 62–82; and Matthew D. Lassiter and Joseph Crespino, "Introduction," in Lassiter and Crespino, eds., *The Myth of Southern Exceptionalism* (New York: Oxford University Press, 2009).

33. James Cobb, *Away Down South: A History of Southern Identity* (New York: Oxford University Press, 2005), 2.

34. For studies of the West as region, see William Cronon, George Miles, and Jay Gitlin, eds., *Under an Open Sky: Rethinking America's Western Past* (New York: Norton, 1992); Patricia Nelson Limerick, *The Legacy of Conquest: The Unbroken Past of the American West* (New York: Norton, 1987); Patricia Limerick, "Region and Reason," in Ayers et al., *All Over the Map*, 83–104; Limerick, Clyde A. Milner II, and Charles E. Rankin, *Trails: Toward a New Western History* (Lawrence: University Press of Kansas, 1991). See also Robert Johnston, "Beyond 'the West': Regionalism, Liberalism, and the Evasion of Politics in the New Western History," *Rethinking History* 2, 2 (1998): 239–77. Johnston argues that, in their efforts to reconceptualize their field, New Western historians reessentialized "the West" into a region united by classically liberal virtues:

"market-oriented, property-obsessed, avarice-driven, radically individualist and monolithically capitalist" (240).

35. Limerick, "Region and Reason," 102–3.

36. See Lassiter, *The Silent Majority*, and Kruse, *White Flight*.

37. Robert Alan Goldberg, "The Western Hero in Politics: Barry Goldwater, Ronald Reagan, and the Rise of the American Conservative Movement," in Roche, ed., *The Political Culture of the New West*, 14.

38. See R. Douglas Hurt, "Agricultural Politics in the Twentieth-Century American West" and Karen R. Merrill, "The Illusions of Independence: Texas Oilmen and the Politics of Postwar Petroleum," in Roche, ed., *The Political Culture of the New West*, 51–73, 74–96.

39. See Goldberg, "The Western Hero in Politics," 13–52; and Rick Perlstein, *Before the Storm: Barry Goldwater and the Unmaking of the American Consensus* (New York: Hill and Wang, 2001), 17–20.

40. "Moral geography" is loosely drawn from Simon Schama, *The Embarrassment of Riches: An Interpretation of Dutch Culture in the Golden Age* (New York: Vintage, 1997), chap. 1.

41. Randal C. Archibold, "Arizona Enacts Stringent Law on Immigration," *New York Times*, April 23, 2010.

42. Ibid.

43. Paul Coro, "Phoenix to Wear 'Los Suns' Jerseys for Game 2 vs. Spurs," *Arizona Republic*, May 4, 2010.

44. "Sarah Palin's Nevada Tea Party Speech: No Time to Retreat; 'It's a Time to Reload,'" *Los Angeles Times*, March 27, 2010.

Chapter 1. Sunbelt Boosterism: Industrial Recruitment, Economic Development, and Growth Politics in the Developing Sunbelt

Epigraph: Kevin P. Phillips, *The Emerging Republican Majority*, 2nd ed. (Garden City, N.Y.: Anchor, 1970), 442.

1. Phillips, *The Emerging Republican Majority*, 437, 438, 440, 438.

2. Carl Abbott, *The New Urban America: Growth and Politics in Sunbelt Cities* (Chapel Hill: University of North Carolina Press, 1981), esp. 8.

3. On the disparity in economic development see James C. Cobb, "Cracklin's and Caviar: The Enigma of Sunbelt Georgia," *Georgia Historical Quarterly* 58 (1984): 19–39; Gavin Wright, *Old South, New South: Revolutions in the Southern Economy Since the Civil War* (New York: Basic Books, 1986), 239–75.

4. James C. Cobb, *Industrialization and Southern Society, 1877–1984* (Lexington: University Press of Kentucky, 1984), 5–51; Wright, *Old South, New South*, 81–239; Gerald Nash, *The Federal Landscape: An Economic History of the Twentieth-Century West* (Tucson: University of Arizona Press, 1993), 3–55; Elizabeth Tandy Shermer,

"Creating the Sunbelt: The Political and Economic Transformation of the Sunbelt" (Ph.D. dissertation, University of California, Santa Barbara, 2009), chaps. 1–3; James C. Cobb, *The Selling of the South: The Southern Crusade for Industrial Development, 1936–1990* (Urbana: University of Illinois Press, 1993), 5–64; Bruce Schulman, *From Cotton Belt to Sunbelt: Federal Policy, Economic Development, and the Transformation of the South, 1938–1980* (New York: Oxford University Press, 1991), 3–63; Roger W. Lotchin, "The Origins of the Sunbelt-Frostbelt Struggle: Defense Spending and City Building," in Raymond Mohl, ed., *Searching for the Sunbelt: Historical Perspectives on a Region* (Knoxville: University of Tennessee Press 1990), 47–68, esp. 50–64.

5. David Kennedy, *Freedom from Fear: The American People in Depression and War, 1929–1945* (Oxford: Oxford University Press, 1999).

6. Wright, *Old South, New South*; Gerald D. Nash, *The American West in the Twentieth Century: A Short History of an Urban Oasis* (Albuquerque: University of New Mexico Press, 1977).

7. Schulman, *From Cotton Belt to Sunbelt*, esp. xii; Wright, *Old South, New South*, 1–17, 239–74, esp. 16; Ira Katznelson, Kim Geiger, and Daniel Kryder, "Limiting Liberalism: The Southern Veto in Congress, 1933–1950," *Political Science Quarterly* 109 (Summer 1993): 283–306, esp. 285; Richard Lowitt, *The New Deal and the West* (Bloomington: Indiana University Press, 1984), 81–99, 218–28, 99.

8. Shermer, "Creating the Sunbelt," chaps. 3–4; Jordan Schwarz, *The New Dealers: Power Politics in the Age of Roosevelt* (New York: Knopf Doubleday, 1994), 59–108.

9. Cobb, *Industrialization and Southern Society*, 5–50; Wright, *Old South, New South*, 156–239; Thomas A. Scott, "Winning World War II in an Atlanta Suburb: Local Boosters and the Recruitment of Bell Bomber," in Phillip Scranton, ed., *The Second Wave: Southern Industrialization from the 1940s to the 1970s* (Athens: University of Georgia Press, 2001), 1–23; Jack J. Claiborne, *Crown of the Queen City: The Charlotte Chamber from 1877–1999* (Charlotte: the Chamber, 1999), 53–68.

10. Amy Bridges, *Morning Glories: Municipal Reform in the Southwest* (Princeton, N.J.: Princeton University Press, 1997), 99–101, n 6.

11. Paul A. C. Koistinen, *Arsenal of World War II: The Political Economy of American Warfare, 1940–1945* (Lawrence: University Press of Kansas, 2004), esp. 52–54; Abbott, *The New Urban America*, 102–4.

12. Shermer, "Creating the Sunbelt," chaps. 3–8.

13. Ibid., chaps. 6–7; John D. Strasma, *State and Local Taxation of Industry: Some Comparisons* (Boston: Federal Reserve Bank of Boston, 1959), unpaginated appendix.

14. John F. Due, "Studies of State-Local Tax Influences on Location of Industry," *National Tax Journal* 14 (June 1961): 163–73; Strasma, *State and Local Taxation of Industry*, 13–16, esp. 16.

15. Bridges, *Morning Glories*, 52–174; Abbott, *The New Urban America*, 123–45.

16. Ronald H. Bayor, "Models of Ethnic and Racial Politics in the Urban Sunbelt South," in Mohl, ed., *Searching for the Sunbelt*, 105–23, esp. 105–8; Richard M. Bernard, "Metropolitan Politics in the American Sunbelt," in ibid., 69–84, esp. 73–76;

Ronald H. Bayor, *Race and the Shaping of Twentieth-Century Atlanta* (Chapel Hill: University of North Carolina Press, 1996); Clarence N. Stone, *Regime Politics: Governing Atlanta, 1946–1988* (Lawrence: University Press of Kansas, 1990); Bridges, *Morning Glories*, 29–62, 125–50; Abbott, *The New Urban America*, 123–25, 144–45; Claiborne, *Crown of the Queen City*, 56–57.

17. Mary Ellen Glass, *Nevada's Turbulent '50s: Decade of Political and Economic Change* (Reno: University of Nevada Press, 1981), 41; Shermer, "Creating the Sunbelt," chaps. 5–6.

18. Shermer, "Creating the Sunbelt," chap. 6; Advisory Commission on Intergovernmental Relations, *State-Local Taxation and Industrial Location: A Commission Report* (Washington, D.C., Government Printing Office, 1967), 31–48; Meg Jacobs, *Pocketbook Politics: Democracy and the Market in Twentieth-Century America* (Princeton, N.J.: Princeton University Press, 2003), 179–261.

19. Elizabeth Tandy Shermer, "Counter-Organizing the Sunbelt: Right to Work Campaigns and Anti-Union Conservatism, 1943–1958," *Pacific Historical Review* (February 2009): 81–118.

20. Shermer, "Creating the Sunbelt," chap. 7.

21. Kenneth Jackson, "Metropolitan Government Versus Political Autonomy: Politics on the Crabgrass Frontier," in Kenneth Jackson and Stanley Schultz, eds., *Cities in American History* (New York: Knopf, 1972), 442–62; Abbott, *The New Urban America*, 54–55, 172–84; Bridges, *Morning Glories*, 152–59; Matthew D. Lassiter, *The Silent Majority: Suburban Politics in the Sunbelt South* (Princeton, N.J.: Princeton University Press, 2006), 52–54, 128, 297–98.

22. Shermer, "Creating the Sunbelt," chaps. 7, 8; Margaret Pugh O'Mara, *Cities of Knowledge: Cold War Science and the Search for the Next Silicon Valley* (Princeton, N.J.: Princeton University Press, 2005).

23. Western Management Consultants, Inc., *The Economy of Maricopa County, 1965 to 1980: A Study for the Guidance of Public and Private Planning Made Possible by the Financial Support of Government and Business Sponsors* (Phoenix: Western Management Consultants, Inc., 1965), 122–24; Advisory Commission on Intergovernmental Relations, *State-Local Taxation and Industrial Location*, 71–76; Michael I. Luger and Harvey Goldstein, *Technology in the Garden: Research Parks and Regional Economic Development* (Chapel Hill: University of North Carolina, 1991), 76–99; O'Mara, *Cities of Knowledge*, 216–17; Cobb, *Industrialization and Southern Society*, 108.

24. Peter Wiley and Robert Gottlieb, *Empires in the Sun: The Rise of the New American West* (New York: Putnam, 1982), esp. 165.

25. Shermer, "Creating the Sunbelt," chaps. 5–8; "Electronics Industry in Arizona," n.d., pp. 1–2, Folder 1, Box 4, Paul Fannin Papers (Arizona State Library, Archives, and Public Records, Phoenix) (hereafter Fannin); James A. Rork, "Establishments in Arizona Providing Products and Services Directly Involved in or Allied to Aerospace and Electronics Industries," December 1963, p. 2, Folder 1, Box 4; "Arizona State Board of Technical Registration," [1962], p. 1, Folder 1, Box 4; James Rork to

Paul Fannin, December 2, 1963, p. 1, Folder 2, Box 4; L. J. Crampton and Paul W. De Good, Jr., *Industrial Location Survey: A Study of the Reasons Why Manufacturing Establishments Have Selected Sites in the State of Colorado Between 1948 and 1957* (Boulder: University of Colorado Press, 1957), 1–11, esp. 1; Joe Bassi, "Where Earth Met Sky: The Creation of Boulder, Colorado, as a City of Scientific Knowledge Production, 1945–1965" (Ph.D. dissertation, University of California, Santa Barbara, 2009).

26. Frank Snell interview by Kristina Minister, April 26, 1988, audiotape, side 1, tape 10, Chamber Centennial Oral History Interviews (Greater Phoenix Chamber of Commerce, Phoenix) (hereafter Chamber Oral).

27. Shermer, "Creating the Sunbelt," chap. 3.

28. Frank Snell interview by Kristina Minister, April 26, 1988, audiotape, side 1, tape 10, Chamber Oral; Shermer, "Creating the Sunbelt," chaps. 3–4.

29. Elizabeth Tandy Shermer, "Origins of the Conservative Ascendancy: Barry Goldwater's Early Senate Career and the De-Legitimization of Organized Labor," *Journal of American History* 95 (December 2008): 678–709, esp. 686–96; Robert Alan Goldberg, *Barry Goldwater* (New Haven, Conn.: Yale University Press, 1995), 47–48; Barry M. Goldwater, "Scaredee-Cat," *Phoenix Gazette*, June 23, 1939, page number missing from clipping, frame 79, Scrapbook CD 1, Personal and Political Papers of Senator Barry M. Goldwater (Arizona Historical Foundation, Tempe) (hereafter Goldwater); Barry M. Goldwater, "A Fireside Chat with Mr. Roosevelt," June 23, 1938, no page number on clipping, frame 94.

30. Shermer, "Origins of the Conservative Ascendancy," 686–89; Shermer, "Creating the Sunbelt," chaps. 3–6; Howard Pyle, "Making History: Good, Bad, and Indifferent," March 6, 1985, p. 7, typescript, Folder 6, Box 12, Oral History Collection (Arizona Historical Foundation, Tempe); Ruth Adams interview by G. Wesley Johnson, September 29, 1978, 19, Phoenix History Project (Arizona Historical Society, Tempe) (hereafter PHP); Nancy Anderson Guber, "The Development of Two-Party Competition in Arizona" (M.A. thesis, University of Illinois, 1961); Ross R. Rice, "The 1958 Election in Arizona," *Western Political Quarterly* 12 (January 1959): 266–75; J. E. Woodley to Howard Pyle, October 9, 1950, Folder 33, Box 74, Howard Pyle Collection (Department of Archives and Special Collections, Arizona State University, Tempe) (hereafter Pyle).

31. Michael Francis Konig, "Toward Metropolis Status: Charter Government and the Rise of Phoenix, Arizona, 1945–1960" (Ph.D. dissertation, Arizona State University, 1983), 53; Dix Price interview by G. W. Johnson, October 18, 1978, 17–19, PHP; Eli Gorodezky interview by Karen Smith, June 28, 1978, transcript, 12–14, PHP; Brent Whiting Brown, "An Analysis of the Phoenix Charter Government Committee as a Political Entity" (M.A. Thesis, Arizona State University, 1968), 33–36, 99–117; Shermer, "Creating the Sunbelt," chap. 5.

32. Gorodezky interview, pp. 14–18, 21–22; Newton Rosenzweig, Dick Smith, and Dorothy Theilkas to Friend of Charter Government, December 11, 1963, Folder 13,

Box 2, Phoenix City Government Records (Arizona Historical Society, Tempe); Mrs. Leslie [Margaret] Kober interview by S. Laughlin, June 18, 1976, transcript, 12–13, PHP; Newton Rosenzweig interview by Minister, side 2, tape 4, Chamber Oral.

33. The Smoke Screen," *Arizona Republic*, November 6, 1949, n.p., frame 8, Scrapbook CD 5, Goldwater; "Be Sure You Vote in the City Primary Tomorrow," postcard, frame 15, Goldwater; Orren Beaty, "Ballot Due on Changes in Charter," *Arizona Republic*, November 8, 1949, unattributed clipping, frame 12, Goldwater; Konig, "Toward Metropolis Status," 60, 202–3; Goldberg, *Barry Goldwater*, 79–80; quoted in Matthew Gann McCoy, "Desert Metropolis: Image Building and the Growth of Phoenix, 1940–1965" (Ph.D. dissertation, Arizona State University 2000), 113–14.

34. Shermer, "Creating the Sunbelt," chaps. 3–4, 6–8.

35. Board of Directors, Minutes of Meeting, March 15, 1954, p. 2, volume labeled "1953–1954," Board of Directors Records (Greater Phoenix Chamber of Commerce, Phoenix) (hereafter PCoC); Board of Directors, Minutes of Meeting, July 21, 1947, pp. 1–3, October 20, 1947, pp. 5–6, bound volume labeled "1947–1948"; Frank Snell interview by G. Wesley Johnson, December 7, 1978, p. 6, PHP; Allen Rosenberg interview by Kristina Minister, March 28, 1989, audiotape, side 2, tape 11, Chamber Oral; Patrick C. Downey interview by K. Trimble, July 8, 1978, transcript, pp. 6–10, PHP; Board of Directors, Minutes of Meeting, July 11, 1949, p. 4, volume labeled "1949–1950," PCoC.

36. Board of Directors, Minutes of Meeting, October 20, 1947, pp. 5–6, bound volume labeled "1947–1948," PCoC; C. E. Van Ness, "1948–49: A Great Year of Accomplishment," *Phoenix Action!* 4 (May 1949), 1–2; William S. Collins, *The Emerging Metropolis: Phoenix, 1944–1973* (Phoenix: Arizona State Parks Board, 2005), 41–43; Benjamin J. Taylor, *Arizona Labor Relations Law* (Tempe: Bureau of Business Research Services, College of Business Administration, Arizona State University, 1967), 17–24.

37. "Inventory Tax Cut," *Phoenix Action!* 8 (January 1953): 1; Gerald Whitney Stone, "A Study of Business Tax Burdens in the Southwest" (M.A. thesis, Arizona State University, 1969), 1–2, 36–50.

38. Stone, "A Study of Business Tax Burdens in the Southwest," 1–2; Advisory Commission on Intergovernmental Relations, *State-Local Taxation and Industrial Location*, 31–48.

39. Western Management Consultants, *The Economy of Maricopa County, 1965 to 1980*, 122–24; Advisory Commission on Intergovernmental Relations, *State-Local Taxation and Industrial Location*, 71–76; Ernest J. Hopkins and Alfred Thomas, Jr., *The Arizona State University Story* (Phoenix: Southwest Publishing, 1960), 245–94; Shermer, "Creating the Sunbelt," chaps. 7, 8.

40. Shermer, "Creating the Sunbelt," chaps 7, 8; Hopkins and Thomas, *The Arizona State University Story*, 288–90; D. E. Noble, "Motorola Reports Phoenix Progress," March 29, 1957, Office of the President Records (Department of Archives and Special Collections, Arizona State University, Tempe), vol. 234, 7–9; "State College at

Tempe Foundation," April 17, 1956, ibid., 229: 1–2; "Summary of Engineers Registered in the Graduate School at Arizona State College," Office of the President Records, ibid., 427: Daniel E. Noble to Governor Fannin, December 5, 1963, p. 3, Folder 2, Box 4, Fannin.

41. Quoted in Shermer, "Creating the Sunbelt," 479–80.

42. Milton MacKaye, "The Cities of America: Phoenix," *Saturday Evening Post*, October 18, 1947, 36–37, 88–95, esp. 37, 90.

43. *Wall Street Journal*, March 9, 1953: Carter Henderson, "Phelps Dodge, Profile" (11); "Squaw Dress Builds a $4 Million Industry" (11); "Giant Valley Bank Gets Even Bigger By Swallowing Fastest Growing Rival" (10); "Meet Arizona Highways, Unique State Publication" (11); "'It's a Homer!'—for Mesa, Phoenix, Tucson Chambers of Commerce" (11); "State's Tenth-Largest City Is Planned for Cactus Patch near New Copper Mine" (11); "Porters' Saddle-Shop-Under-Canvas Grows into Flourishing Retail Chain" (10); John F. Bridge, "States of the Union" (10); "Arizona's Dude Ranchers Ride a Golden Roundup" (11); "Life in the Desert Suits the Ranching Tuckers Just Fine—No Traffic" (10); "A $20 Million Boast" (18); "Cactusland Cotton" (1); "Cactus Needles" (11); "City Dwellers' Yearning for Wide Open Spaces Gets Sympathy in Wickenburg" (11).

44. Bradford Luckingham, *The Urban Southwest: A Profile History of Albuquerque, El Paso, Phoenix, Tucson* (El Paso: Texas Western Press, 1982), 80–86; Mark Adams and Gertrude Adams, *A Report on Politics in El Paso* (Cambridge, Mass.: Joint Center for Urban Studies of the Massachusetts Institute of Technology and Harvard University, 1963), V-26–V-27; quoted in Bradford Luckingham, *Phoenix: The History of a Southwestern Metropolis* (Tucson: University of Arizona Press, 1989), 187.

45. Blake L. Johnson to Boyd H. Gibbons, Jr., June 28, 1963, Folder "Chambers of Commerce Out-ofState [sic]—Misc.," Box 315, Governor's Files (Arizona State Library, Archives, and Public Records, Phoenix).

46. Ernest Jerome Hopkins, *Financing the Frontier: A Fifty Year History of the Valley National Bank* (Phoenix: Valley National Bank, 1950), 200–204, 268–70; Walter R. Bimson, "Talk Before Convention of General Insurance Agents of Arizona," October 15, 1948, p. 1, Folder 238, Box 29, Valley National Bank Collection (Arizona Historical Society, Tempe).

47. Keith Monroe, "Bank Knight in Arizona," *American Magazine* (November 1945): 24–25, 116–12, esp. 24, 25, 122.

48. "Meet President Bimson," *Banking: Journal of the American Bankers Association* (October 1960): 1–7, Folder 6, Box 1, Valley National Bank Collection (Arizona Historical Society, Tempe); "Surtax or Chaos: Valley Bank Official," *Arizona Republic*, April 7, 1968, 1-F, 6-F; Carl Bimson, "Handling Loans to Small Business," *Burroughs Clearing House*, January 1945, 18–20, 37–39, Folder 934, Box 68, Valley National Bank Collection; Carl Bimson, "A Banker's Participation in Public Affairs," February 12, 1960, in Bimson, *Addresses of Carl A. Bimson*, vol. 9 (self-published, 1960), Arizona

Historical Foundation (Tempe); Bimson, "Paying Our Way," May 17, 1960, in ibid.; Bimson, "Westward Ho!," May 20, 1960, in ibid.

49. Goldberg, *Barry Goldwater*, 100–104; Rick Perlstein, *Before the Storm: Barry Goldwater and the Unmaking of the American Consensus* (New York: Hill and Wang, 2001), 26–27; Barry Goldwater to Mr. Robert Goldwater and Mr. William E. Saufley, January 30, 1954, Folder: "Saufley, William E. (Goldwater Store Manager), 1939–1958 (1 of 3)," Personal Correspondence, Goldwater.

50. "Union Leadership Assailed by G.O.P.," *New York Times*, October 25, 1955, 25; Joseph A. Loftus, "Mitchell Urges Amity to Labor"; Loftus, "Broad State Rule over Labor Urged in Senate Debate," *New York Times*, November 22, 1955, 27; Damon Stetson, "Taft Act Proposal Labeled Tyranny," *New York Times*, May 4, 1954, 27.

51. Anthony V. Baltakis, "Agendas of Investigation: The McClellan Committee, 1957–1958" (Ph.D. dissertation, University of Akron, 1997), 7–28; David Witwer, *Corruption and Reform in the Teamsters Union* (Urbana: University of Illinois Press, 2003), 157–211; U.S. Congress, Senate, Select Committee on Improper Activities in the Labor or Management Field, *Investigation of Improper Activities in the Labor or Management Field*, 85 and 86 Cong., February 26, 1957–September 9, 1959, pts. 1–58; Goldberg, *Barry Goldwater*, 121–25; Perlstein, *Before the Storm*, 27–39.

52. Barry Goldwater to Mr. Lloyd Jones, May 3, 1956, Folder: "Republican Policy Committee, 1952–1956," Box 7, Goldwater; Joseph A. Loftus, "Kohler Hearings Hit Three Ways," *New York Times*, March 16, 1958, esp. E9; Robert F. Kennedy, *The Enemy Within* (Westport, Conn.: Greenwood Press, 1982), 266; "Reuther Warns of Tough Bargaining," *Los Angeles Times*, January 23, 1958, esp. 9; *Congressional Record*, 85 Cong., 2 sess., vol. 104, 1958, pt. 3: 2887.

53. Shermer, "Origins of the Conservative Ascendancy"; Everett McKinley Dirksen to Barry Goldwater, September 11, 1959, Folder "Dirksen, Everett McKinley, 1952–1969," Box "M," Personal, Alpha Files, Goldwater; Robert S. Ball, "Goldwater in Fray as GOP's New Taft," *Detroit News*, January 25, 1959, esp. 20-A; Goldberg, *Barry Goldwater*, 132–34; Perlstein, *Before the Storm*, 41–45.

Chapter 2. Strom Thurmond's Sunbelt: Rethinking Regional Politics and the Rise of the Right

1. *Los Angeles Times*, November 29, 1961, 2; November 30, 1961, 26.

2. *Washington Post*, September 28, 1961, A4; *Chicago Tribune*, October 7, 1961, N6; *New York Times*, October 7, 1961, 6; P. W. Gifford to John Stennis, November 13, 1961, Folder Interview/ Major Mayer, Box 65, Series 4, John C. Stennis Papers, Mississippi State University (hereafter JCSP).

3. *Chicago Tribune*, Dec. 3, 1961, 1; Program, Survival U.S.A., December 3, 1961, MF 45, Box 12—Reel 022.0001.pdf, p. 55, Barry Goldwater Papers, Arizona Historical Foundation, Arizona State University.

4. *Charleston News and Courier*, December 2, 1961.

5. *Los Angeles Times*, February 8, 1962, 16; February 11, 1962, F2; February 28, 1962, A1.

6. For such speculation, see E. W. Kenworthy, "Fulbright Becomes a National Issue," *New York Times Magazine*, October 1, 1961, 21.

7. Robert Sherrill, *Gothic Politics in the Deep South: Stars of the New Confederacy* (New York: Grossman, 1968).

8. Numan V. Bartley, *The Rise of Massive Resistance: Race and Politics in the South During the 1950s* (Baton Rouge: Louisiana State University Press, 1969), 185; Neil McMillen, *The Citizens' Council: Organized Resistance to the Second Reconstruction, 1954–1965* (Urbana: University of Illinois Press, 1969), 191–92. Recent literature has provided a more complex portrait of southern anticommunism yet still sees it as unique from anticommunism outside the region. See Jeff Woods, *Black Struggle, Red Scare: Segregation and Anti-Communism in the South, 1948–1968* (Baton Rouge: Louisiana State University Press, 2004); George Lewis, *The White South and the Red Menace: Segregationists, Anticommunism, and Massive Resistance, 1945–1965* (Gainesville: University Press of Florida, 2004). For an example of a recent work that reads white Southern anticommunism as not merely derivative of yet still implicated in white racism, see Christopher Myers-Asch, *The Senator and the Sharecropper: The Freedom Struggles of James O. Eastland and Fannie Lou Hamer* (New York: New Press, 2008).

9. Lisa McGirr, *Suburban Warriors: The Origins of the New American Right* (Princeton, N.J.: Princeton University Press, 2001), 14–15. For an example of the common view regarding the distinction between southern conservatives and non-southern anticommunist conservatives, see Donald T. Critchlow, *The Conservative Ascendancy: How the GOP Right Made Political History* (Cambridge, Mass.: Harvard University Press, 2007), 47, 66.

10. Matthew Dallek, *The Right Moment: Ronald Reagan's First Victory and the Decisive Turning Point in American Politics* (New York: Oxford University Press, 2004); Michelle Nickerson, *Mothers of Conservatism: Women and the Postwar Right* (Princeton, N.J.: Princeton University Press, forthcoming); Daniel Martinez HoSang, *Racial Propositions: Ballot Initiatives and Making of Postwar California* (Berkeley: University of California Press, 2010).

11. For more on this variety, see Anthony Badger, "The South Confronts the Court: The Southern Manifesto of 1956," *Journal of Policy History* 20, 1 (2008): 126–42.

12. McGirr, *Suburban Warriors*; Kevin Kruse, *White Flight: Atlanta and the Making of Modern Conservatism* (Princeton, N.J.: Princeton University Press, 2005); Matthew D. Lassiter, *The Silent Majority: Suburban Politics in the Sunbelt South* (Princeton, N.J.: Princeton University Press, 2006); Robert O. Self, *American Babylon: Race and the Struggle for Postwar Oakland* (Princeton, N.J.: Princeton University Press, 2003); Darren Dochuk, *From Bible Belt to Sunbelt: Plain-folk Religion, Grassroots Politics, and the Rise of Evangelical Conservatism* (New York: W.W. Norton, 2010).

13. *Charleston News and Courier*, May 11, 1948; *New York Times*, September 5, 1948.

14. Kevin P. Phillips, *The Emerging Republican Majority* (New Rochelle, N.Y.: Arlington House, 1969), 218.

15. A perfect example is provided in Tami J. Friedman, "Exploiting the North-South Differential: Corporate Power, Southern Politics, and the Decline of Organized Labor After World War II," *Journal of American History* 95, 2 (2008): 323–48.

16. Ann Mathison McLaurin, "The Role of the Dixiecrats in the 1948 Election" (Ph.D. dissertation, University of Oklahoma, 1972), 84.

17. Glen Jeansonne, *Leander Perez: Boss of the Delta* (Baton Rouge: Louisiana State University Press, 1977).

18. *Charleston News and Courier*, September 21, 1948.

19. Kari Frederickson, *The Dixiecrat Revolt and the End of the Solid South, 1932–1968* (Chapel Hill: University of North Carolina Press, 2001), 169. Fredrickson points to the Dixiecrats' skimpy campaign budget to suggest that if oil interests were, in fact, the drivers behind the party's finances, they were parsimonious backers at best (169). Surely it was difficult to solicit funds for a candidate who announced so late in the campaign and who was such a political long shot. Regardless of the dollar amount that oil companies actually gave, however, their interest was representative of the fact that southern conservative economic forces were looking for alternatives to traditional New Deal Democratic leadership. They would eventually find it in the progrowth, antiunionism of the GOP Sunbelt conservatism.

20. Alexander Heard, *A Two-Party South?* (Chapel Hill: University of North Carolina Press, 1952), 159.

21. Thomas Sancton, "White Supremacy—Crisis or Plot?" *The Nation*, July 24, 1948, 97.

22. Samuel Lubell, *The Future of American Politics*, 3rd ed. rev. (New York: Harper and Row, 1965), 106–30.

23. Vernon Burton, "In My Father's House Are Many Leaders: Can the Extreme Be Typical?" *Proceedings of the South Carolina Historical Association* (1987): 23–32. Also see Orville Vernon Burton, *In My Father's House Are Many Mansions: Family and Community in Edgefield, South Carolina* (Chapel Hill: University of North Carolina Press, 1985).

24. Quoted in Mary Beth Reed and Barbara Smith Strack, *The Savannah River Site at Fifty* (Washington, D.C.: Department of Energy; Stone Mountain, Ga.: New South Associates, 2002), 57. For more on the Savannah River site's impact on the local area, see Kari Frederickson, "The Cold War at the Grassroots: Militarization and Modernization in South Carolina," in Matthew D. Lassiter and Joseph Crespino, eds., *The Myth of Southern Exceptionalism* (New York: Oxford University Press, 2009), 190–209.

25. Reed and Strack, *The Savannah River Site at Fifty*, 184.

26. Thurmond quoted Charles Daniel, owner of Daniel Construction Company;

see interview with Strom Thurmond by Jack Bass, February 1, 1974, A-0166, Southern Oral History Program Collection #4007, Southern Historical Collection, Wilson Library, University of North Carolina at Chapel Hill.

27. For more on postwar southern industrial recruitment, see Friedman, "Exploiting the North-South Differential," 323–48; and James C. Cobb, *The Selling of the South: The Southern Crusade for Industrial Development, 1936–1990* (Urbana: University of Illinois Press, 1993).

28. Rivers quoted in Bruce J. Schulman, *From Cotton Belt to Sunbelt: Federal Policy, Economic Development, and the Transformation of the South, 1938–1980* (New York: Oxford University Press, 1991), 146–47; see 135–73 more generally on the role of defense spending in Sunbelt growth.

29. Nadine Cohodas, *Strom Thurmond and the Politics of Southern Change* (New York: Simon and Schuster, 1993), 236.

30. The opinion was that of South Carolina industrialist Roger Milliken, a major contributor to a variety of postwar conservative causes. See Stephen Shadegg to Barry Goldwater, February 16, 1962, Folder Shadegg, Stephen, Box S-Y, Subseries Correspondence, Series I, Personal, Barry Goldwater Papers.

31. Strom Thurmond to Pinckney Estes Glantzberg, April 18, 1961, Folder Un-American Activities I (Communism), Folder I; January 2, 1961–April 28, 1961, Box 36, Subject Correspondence 1961 Series, Strom Thurmond Papers, Strom Thurmond Institute, Clemson University (hereafter STP). Thurmond turned down a position on the Birch Society board; see Cohodas, *Strom Thurmond*, 326.

32. Jonathan M. Schoenwald, *A Time for Choosing: The Rise of Modern Conservatism* (New York: Oxford University Press, 2001), 45–48; Rosalie M. Gordon, *Nine Men Against America: The Supreme Court and Its Attack on American Liberties* (New York: Devin-Adair, 1958); W. Cleon Skousen, *The Naked Communist* (Salt Lake City, Utah: Ensign, 1958); J. Edgar Hoover, *Masters of Deceit: The Story of Communism in America and How to Fight It* (New York: Holt, 1958).

33. Schoenwald, *Time for Choosing*, 55–56.

34. National Council of Churches of Christ in the United States of America, *Operation Abolition: Some Facts and Some Comments* (New York: Department of Religious Liberty, National Council of Churches, 1961).

35. Strom Thurmond to Dr. C. J. Maddox, March 14, 1961, Folder: Walker Related, 18–1, November 1961–December 1961, Box 25, Special Preparedness Investigating Subcommittee Series, STP.

36. Strom Thurmond to Mr. William H. Beattie, May 15, 1961, Folder Un-American Activities I (Communism), Folder II; May 1, 1961–June 25, 1961, Box 36, Subject Correspondence 1961 Series, STP.

37. "Digest of Senator Strom Thurmond's Actions Against the Conspiracy to Muzzle Military Anticommunist Statements and Seminars," August 17, 1961, Folder: Prep Sub Muzzling 1961, Box 3, Series 43, JCSP.

38. *Los Angeles Times*, January 31, 1961, 23; *Chicago Tribune*, February 1, 1961, 10; *New York Times*, April 8, 1962, E5.

39. Schoenwald, *Time for Choosing*, 100–101, 105–7.

40. For the full text of the memo, see Congressional Record—Senate, August 2, 1961, 14395–97; Ralph McGill, "The Incredible Generals," Folder Un-American Activities 1–5, Folder XV, Box 41, Subject Correspondence 1961 Series, STP.

41. *New York Times*, February 10, 1995, A1; Randall Bennett Woods, *Fulbright: A Biography* (New York: Cambridge University Press, 2006).

42. Congressional Record—Senate, August 2, 1961, 14395–97; *Chicago Tribune*, July 22, 1961, 6.

43. *New York Times*, June 18, 1961, 1.

44. *New York Times*, July 21, 1961, 1; *Washington Post*, July 21, 1961, A15.

45. *New York Times Magazine*, October 1, 1961, 21.

46. Strom Thurmond to J. William Fulbright, July 21, 1961; J. William Fulbright to Strom Thurmond, July 21, 1961, Folder Un-American Activities 1–5, Folder I, Box 39, Subject Correspondence 1961 Series, STP.

47. Alberta Lachicotte, *Rebel Senator: Strom Thurmond of South Carolina* (New York: Devin-Adair, 1966), 162–63.

48. *New York Times*, July 22, 1961, 12. Also see Thurmond to Fulbright, July 21, 1961; J. Fulbright to Thurmond, July 21, 1961.

49. *Chicago Tribune*, July 22, 1961, 6.

50. *Congressional Record*, Senate, August 2, 1961, 14398.

51. Strom Thurmond to Dan Smoot, August 23, 1961, Folder Un-American Activities 1–5 (Fulbright Note Muzzling the Military), Folder VII, August 23–August 25, 1961, Box 40, Subject Correspondence 1961 Series, STP.

52. Billy James Hargis to Strom Thurmond, August 31, 1961, Folder Un-American Activities 1–5, Folder IX, Box 40, Subject Correspondence 1961 Series, STP.

53. Phoebe Courtney to Strom Thurmond, October 2, 1961, Folder Un-American Activities 1–5, Folder XV, Box 41, Subject Correspondence 1961 Series, STP.

54. Richard D. Morphew to Strom Thurmond, August 24, 1961, Folder Un-American Activities 1–5, Folder VIII, Box 40, Subject Correspondence 1961 Series, STP; Richard D. Morphew to Harry Dent, September 21, 1961, Folder Un-American Activities 1–5, Folder XII, Box 40, Subject Correspondence 1961 Series, STP.

55. Jim Kendall to John Stennis, August 30, 1961, Folder Prep Sub Muzzling 1961, Box 3, Series 43, JCSP.

56. *Los Angeles Times*, October 5, 1961, 7.

57. For examples of the letters Russell received, see Folders 7 and 8, Box 130, Series IX—Legislative, Richard Russell Papers. For the link between the letters and the John Birch Society, see Richard W. Edmonds to Richard Russell, December 3, 1961, Folder 7, Box 130, Series IX—Legislative, Richard Russell Papers. Also see MGW to BABS, November 7, 1961, Folder 8, Box 130, Series IV—Legislative, Richard Russell Papers, University of Georgia.

58. *New York Times*, September 21, 1961, 20.
59. Lachicotte, *Rebel Senator*, 174.
60. *Washington Post*, September 22, 1961.
61. *New York Times*, September 22, 1961, 8.
62. *Evening Star*, September 8, 1961, A-15.
63. *New York Times*, April 24, 1995, B11.
64. *New York Times*, March 15, 1962, 15.
65. Strom Thurmond to John Stennis, November 6, 1961, Folder: Prep Sub-Muzzling, Box 3, Series 42, JCSP.
66. *Chicago Tribune*, November 21, 1961, A2.
67. *Los Angeles Times*, November 21, 1961, B5.
68. *Washington Post*, December 9, 1961, A13.
69. *Time*, February 2, 1962; *Christian Science Monitor*, January 27, 1962, 9; *Los Angeles Times*, January 26, 1962, B1.
70. *Chicago Tribune*, January 31, 1962, 8.
71. *New York Times*, February 1, 1962, 1; *Chicago Tribune*, February 1, 1962, 4.
72. *New York Times*, February 2, 1962, 1.
73. *Washington Post*, February 9, 1962, A12. At a televised news conference on February 9, one reporter asked Thurmond if he saw parallels between McCarthy and himself. Thurmond dismissed the question as one more attempt by "left-wing liberal newspapers" who wanted to "degrade this investigation." *Chicago Tribune*, February 10, 1962, 3.
74. *Christian Science Monitor*, February 10, 1962.
75. Robert A. Caro, *The Years of Lyndon Johnson*, vol. 3, *Master of the Senate* (New York: Knopf, 2002), 370–82.
76. "Statement by Senator John Stennis in Ruling on Plea of Executive Privilege," February 8, 1962, and John Stennis to Richard B. Russell, February 15, 1962, Folder Armed Services Special Committee, Box 129, Subseries D, Series IX, Richard Russell Papers, University of Georgia.
77. John Stennis, Memorandum for James Kendall, April 7, 1962, Folder 43 Prep Sub Memos 1962, Box 3, Series 43, John C. Stennis Papers, Mississippi State University.
78. *Washington Post*, June 9, 1962, A2; *New York Times*, June 9, 1962, 11.
79. Memorandum on Executive Meeting of Special Senate Preparedness Subcommittee, June 14, 1962, Folder Memoranda June 14, 1962; n.d., Box 13, Special Preparedness Investigative Subcommittee Series, STP.
80. Jim Kendall, Memorandum to Senator Stennis, July 25, 1962, Folder Senator's Memos Re Cold War, Box 65, Series 4, John C. Stennis Papers, MSU; John Stennis, untitled memo, August 10, 1962, Folder: Thurmond, Strom Hon., Box 8, Series 28, JCSP.
81. *Chicago Tribune*, August 21, 1962, 23; "Strom Thurmond Report to the People," August 20, 1962, Folder Thurmond, Strom Hon., Box 8, Series 28, JCSP.

82. *New York Times*, September 3, 1962, 1; *New York Times*, October 2, 1962, 38.
83. *Chicago Tribune*, September 7, 1962, 3.
84. *Los Angeles Times*, September 13, 1962, A4.
85. *Chicago Tribune*, December 3, 1962, B18.
86. *Christian Science Monitor*, October 25, 1962, 10; *New York Times*, October 26, 1962, 7.
87. *Chicago Tribune*, October 26, 1962, 15.
88. *John Birch Society Bulletin*, December 1962, 23.
89. Edward Hunter, "Letter to Contacts," October 25, 1962, Folder Friendly Organizations Folder II January–October 1962; n.d., Box 9, Special Investigative Subcommittee Series, STP.
90. *Washington Post*, February 22, 1962, D24.
91. *Washington Post*, February 15, 1962, A2.
92. *New York Times*, March 8, 1962, 1.
93. *Chicago Tribune*, April 2, 1962, C8, and July 9, 1962, B8.
94. *New York Times*, January 15, 1965, 16.

Chapter 3. Big Government and Family Values:
Political Culture in the Metropolitan Sunbelt

1. Dan Balz and Ronald Brownstein, *Storming the Gates: Protest Politics and Republican Revival* (Boston: Little, Brown, 1996); Earl Black and Merle Black, *The Rise of Southern Republicans* (Cambridge, Mass: Harvard University Press, 2002).
2. John F. Stacks, "Good Newt, Bad Newt," *Time*, December 25, 1995; "Republican Contract with America" (1994), http://www.house.gov/house/Contract/CONTRACT.html.
3. *New York Times*, August 1, 20, November 10, 1994.
4. Peter Applebome, *Dixie Rising: How the South Is Shaping American Values, Politics, and Culture* (New York: Harcourt Brace, 1996), 23–55; Thomas Allan Scott, *Cobb County, Georgia, and the Origins of the Suburban South: A Twentieth-Century History* (Marietta, Ga.: Cobb Landmarks and Historical Society, 2003).
5. "Cobb County: Historical Population Profile," GeorgiaInfo, Digital Library of Georgia, http://georgiainfo.galileo.usg.edu/countypop/cobbpop.htm; State of Georgia, Office of Planning and Budget, Census Data Program, http://www.gadata.org/; Robert E. Lang and Patrick A. Simmons, "'Boomburbs': The Emergence of Large, Fast-Growing Suburban Cities," in Bruce Katz and Robert E. Lang, eds., *Redefining Urban and Suburban America: Evidence from Census 2000* (Washington, D.C.: Brookings Institution Press), 1: 110–12.
6. "Cobb Fact Book 1994," *Marietta Daily Journal*, July 31, 1994; *New York Times*, August 1, 1994.
7. Matthew D. Lassiter, *The Silent Majority: Suburban Politics in the Sunbelt South*

(Princeton, N.J.: Princeton University Press, 2006); Earl Black and Merle Black, *Politics and Society in the South* (Cambridge, Mass.: Harvard University Press, 1987).

8. On the backlash thesis, see Dan T. Carter, *The Politics of Rage: George Wallace, the New Conservatism, and the Transformation of American Politics* (New York: Simon & Schuster, 1995). On Sunbelt conservatism, Lisa McGirr, *Suburban Warriors: The Origins of the New American Right* (Princeton, N.J.: Princeton University Press, 2001), which draws too sharp a distinction between southern racial conservatism and western ideological conservatism; see esp. 14–15.

9. Kevin P. Phillips, *The Emerging Republican Majority* (New Rochelle, N.Y.: Arlington House, 1969), 26, 278; Kirkpatrick Sale, *Power Shift: The Rise of the Southern Rim and Its Challenge to the Eastern Establishment* (New York: Random House, 1975); McGirr, *Suburban Warriors*, 271–72.

10. Bruce J. Schulman, *From Cotton Belt to Sunbelt: Federal Policy, Economic Development, and the Transformation of the South, 1938–1980* (New York: Oxford University Press, 1991); Ann Markusen, Peter Hall, Scott Campbell, and Sabina Deitrick, eds., *The Rise of the Gunbelt: The Military Remapping of Industrial America* (New York: Oxford University Press, 1991); Margaret Pugh O'Mara, *Cities of Knowledge: Cold War Science and the Search for the Next Silicon Valley* (Princeton, N.J.: Princeton University Press, 2005).

11. On the John Birch Society in California, see McGirr, *Suburban Warriors*; Michelle Nickerson, *Mothers of Conservatism: Women and the Postwar Right* (Princeton, N.J.: Princeton University Press, forthcoming).

12. Matthew D. Lassiter and Kevin M. Kruse, "The Bulldozer Revolution: Suburbs and Southern History Since World War II," *Journal of Southern History* 75, 3 (August 2009): 691–706; John B. Judis and Ruy Teixeira, *The Emerging Democratic Majority* (New York: Scribner, 2002).

13. On suburban residential segregation, see Kenneth T. Jackson, *Crabgrass Frontier: The Suburbanization of the United States* (New York: Oxford University Press, 1985).

14. *Dallas Morning News*, December 19, 1994.

15. James V. Carmichael, Speech to the Cobb Chamber of Commerce, February 3, 1966, Folder 24, Box 63, James V. Carmichael Papers, Special Collections and Archives, Robert W. Woodruff Library, Emory University (hereinafter Carmichael Papers).

16. Joseph B. Hosmer, "Combing Georgia for 40,000 Workers," *Atlanta Constitution Magazine*, March 1, 1942; "Georgia Gives Bell a Big Southern 'Howdy!'" *Bell Ringer* (April 1942), Folder 7, Box 65, Carmichael, Speech to Cobb Chamber of Commerce, Feb. 3, 1966, Folder 24, Box 63, Carmichael Papers; *Atlanta Journal*, September 27, 28, 1945; Scott, *Cobb County*, 109–78.

17. James C. Cobb, *The Selling of the South: The Southern Crusade for Industrial Development, 1936–1980* (Baton Rouge: Louisiana State University Press, 1982).

18. James V. Carmichael, Speech at Confederate Memorial Day, 1941, Folder 15, Box 62, Carmichael Papers.

19. *Atlanta Journal*, September 28, 1945; *Marietta Journal*, October 26, 1945, in Folder 10, Box 65, Carmichael Papers.

20. Cobb County Carmichael for Governor Club, *The Carmichael Advance* (July 1946), Folder 12, Box 65, Carmichael Papers. Also see Numan V. Bartley, *The Creation of Modern Georgia*, 2nd ed. (Athens: University of Georgia Press, 1990), 201–7.

21. James V. Carmichael, Commencement Speech to Emory University, 1950, Folder 23, Box 62, Carmichael Papers.

22. Lockheed Aircraft Corporation, "Facts About Lockheed in Georgia," Lockheed Aircraft Corporation, "Lockheed Has a Great Future," Folder 174, Vertical Files, Georgia Room, Cobb County Public Library [hereinafter VF-CCPL]; *Lockheed Southern Star*, September 15, 1951, Folder 14, Box 65, Carmichael Papers; *Marietta Daily Journal*, October 8, 1959, February 2, 1961; "Cobb County, Georgia: An Area of Industrial Potential," *Manufacturers Record* (Jan. 1958), 23–38; Scott, *Cobb County*, 211–33.

23. Cobb County Chamber of Commerce, "Welcome to Marietta," n.d. [early 1950s], "Travel Scenic and Historic Route 41," n.d. [early 1950s], "Folks Like to Live in Cobb County, Georgia," n.d. [early 1950s], Folder 199, VF-CCPL.

24. Cobb County Chamber of Commerce, "Cobb County, Georgia—1959," "Cobb County, Georgia—1960," Folder 199, VF-CCPL.

25. "Where the Growth Is," *Time*, June 19, 1964.

26. James V. Carmichael, "The South in Transition," April 11, 1964, Folder 14, Box 63, Carmichael Papers.

27. *Cobb Daily News*, n.d. [c. 1967], in Folder 174, VF-CCPL; *Marietta Daily Journal*, Sept. 30, 1966; *Atlanta Journal-Constitution*, May 24, 2001; Scott, *Cobb County*, 387–469; Cobb County Chamber of Commerce, "Here's What Your Chamber Will Do in 1965," Folder 200, VF-CCPL; Johnny Isakson Interview, May 22, 1992, Georgia Government Documentation Project, Special Collections Department, William Russell Pullen Library, Georgia State University [hereinafter GGDP].

28. Cobb County Board of Commissioners, "Your Cobb County," n.d. [late 1960s], Folder 202, VF-CCPL.

29. *Cobb Daily News*, July 7, 1969, Folder 174, "Salute to Lockheed," *Marietta Daily Journal*, n.d. [late 1960s], Folder 180, VF-CCPL; Erwin Knoll, "The Education of Henry Durham," *The Progressive* (1972).

30. "The Lockheed Bailout Battle," *Time*, August 9, 1971; Cobb County Chamber of Commerce, "Cobb County Georgia" 1976, Folder 202, VF-CCPL.

31. Cobb County Chamber of Commerce, "Cobb County Proudly Salutes Our Partners in Progress," October 4, 1976, Folder 174, "Salute to Lockheed," *Marietta Daily Journal*, n.d. [late 1960s], Folder 180, "Lockheed-Georgia: The First Thirty Years," *Marietta Daily Journal*, May 10, 1981, Folder 178, VF-CCPL.

32. Peter Overby, "White-Picket Welfare: What Would the Suburbs Be Without Federal Money?" *Common Cause Magazine* (Fall 1993); *Marietta Daily Journal*, April 16, 2006.

33. Cobb County Chamber of Commerce, "Here's What Your Chamber Will Do

in 1965," Folder 200, "1980 Program of Work," Folder 202, *Impact* (May 1977), Folder 206, VF-CCPL. On corporate politics, see Kimberly Phillips-Fein, *Invisible Hands: The Making of the Conservative Movement from the New Deal to Reagan* (New York: Norton, 2009); Bethany Moreton, *To Serve God and Wal-Mart: The Making of Christian Free Enterprise* (Cambridge, Mass.: Harvard University Press, 2009), 125–221.

34. Cobb County Chamber of Commerce, "1981 Annual Report," *Impact* (December 1984), folder 203, VF-CCPL; Reagan administration, "America's New Beginning: A Program for Economic Recovery," February 18, 1981, http://www.presidency.ucsb.edu/ws/index.php?pid=43427.

35. "Armed Forces Week, May 9–16: Peace Through Strength," *Marietta Daily Journal*, May 13, 1982, Folder 177, VF-CCPL.

36. "So Proudly We Hail," Armed Forces Day: Open House and Air Show, May 17, 1980, Folder 177, VF-CCPL.

37. "Lockheed-Georgia: The First Thirty Years," *Marietta Daily Journal*, May 10, 1981, Folder 178, "Congratulations to Lockheed on the New C-5B," *Marietta Daily Journal*, July 11, 1985, Folder 176, VF-CCPL.

38. Cobb County Chamber of Commerce, *Impact* (June 1980), Folder 207, VF-CCPL.

39. James V. Carmichael, Speech to the Cobb Chamber of Commerce, Feb. 3, 1966, Folder 24, Speech to Southern Businessmen, n.d. [mid-1960s], Folder 30, Box 63, Speech to Commonwealth Club of San Francisco, July 16, 1963, Folder 9, Box 62, Carmichael Papers.

40. James V. Carmichael, Speech Introducing Richard Nixon, September 1960; Harvard Business School Club of Atlanta, Press Release, October 11, 1960, Folder 29, Box 62, Statement by National Independent Committee for President Johnson and Senator Humphrey, n.d. [1964], Folder 1, Box 46, Carmichael Papers.

41. On California, see McGirr, *Suburban Warriors*; Rick Perlstein, *Before the Storm: Barry Goldwater and the Unmaking of the American Consensus* (New York: Hill and Wang, 2001).

42. *Atlanta Constitution*, August 27, 1960; *New York Times*, August 27, 1960; Theodore White article about Nixon's visit to Atlanta in *Saturday Review* (September 1960), in Folder 4, Box 66, Carmichael Papers; Lassiter, *The Silent Majority*, 225–50.

43. Atlas of U.S. Presidential Elections, USelectionatlas.org.

44. Isakson interview, GGDP; Kevin M. Kruse, *White Flight: Atlanta and the Making of Modern Conservatism* (Princeton: Princeton Univ. Press, 2005); *1970 Census of Population and Housing*; *1990 Census of Population and Housing*; Cobb County Chamber of Commerce, "1972 Cobb County," Folder 201 (CC: Chamber of Commerce 1970–1975), "Cobb County, Georgia," 1976, Georgia Department of Industry and Trade, "Cobb County: Economic Development Profile," 1979, Folder 202, VF-CCPL; "Nativity and Place of Birth," State of Georgia Census Data Program, http://www.gadata.org/information_services/Census_Info/1990NATIVITY.htm.

45. Numan V. Bartley and Hugh D. Graham, *Southern Elections: County and Precinct Data, 1950–1972* (Baton Rouge: Louisiana State Univ. Press, 1978), 92–119; Atlas of U.S. Presidential Elections, USelectionatlas.org; Scott, *Cobb County*, 493–512.

46. The voting patterns of Cobb residents who previously lived in Atlanta challenge the direct connection between "white flight" and Republican conversion in Kruse, *White Flight*, 205–66.

47. Walter Herron, Letter to Supporters, October 21, 1962, Biographical Sketch, 1962, Folder 1, Box 46, Carmichael Papers.

48. Isakson interview, GGDP; Roy Eugene Barnes Interview, October 5, 1990, GGDP.

49. *Marietta Daily Journal*, November 3, 1976, January 13, 1986; *Atlanta Journal-Constitution*, November 13, 1986; Scott, *Cobb County*, 513–34.

50. Barnes Interview, GGDP; Buddy Darden, News Release, n.d. [mid-to-late 1980s], *Atlanta Constitution*, Nov. 9, 1988, Folder 26, VF-CCPL.

51. *Marietta Daily Journal*, May 20, 1993, May 18, 2003; Joe Mack Wilson Interview, April 1, 1988, GGDP.

52. Scott, *Cobb County*, 493–512; on the broader GOP surge at the local level in the South, see Black and Black, *Rise of Southern Republicans*.

53. Isakson Interview, Barnes Interview, Wilson Interview, GGDP.

54. *Marietta Daily Journal*, February 28, 1971; *1970 Census of Population and Housing*; *1980 Census of Population and Housing*; Cobb County Chamber of Commerce, "Facts and Figures about Cobb County," March 6, 1964, "Facts and Figures about Cobb County," Januray 1973, Folder 205, VF-CCPL. On African American history before World War II, see Patrice Shelton Lassiter, *Generations of Black Life in Kennesaw and Marietta, Georgia* (Charleston, S.C.: Arcadia Publishing, 1999).

55. Cobb County Chamber of Commerce, "Who's Who in Cobb County Business," May 1969, Folder 200, Cobb County Board of Commissioners, "A Report to the People of Cobb County," 1974, Folder 300, VF-CCPL.

56. James V. Carmichael, Speech to the Cobb Chamber of Commerce, February 3, 1966, Folder 24, Box 63, Carmichael Papers; Ronald H. Bayor, *Race and the Shaping of Twentieth-Century Atlanta* (Chapel Hill: University of North Carolina Press, 1996), 191–95; *New York Times*, August 13, 1989.

57. Cobb County Chamber of Commerce, "1972 Cobb County: Membership Directory and Buyer's Guide," Folder 201, VF-CCPL.

58. Cobb County Board of Commissioners, "Your Cobb County," n.d. [late 1960s], Cobb County Chamber of Commerce, "1979: Program of Work," Folder 202, Special Section on Six Flags Amusement Park, *Marietta Daily Journal*, March 28, 1973, Doug Monroe, "Happy 20th Six Flags," *Inside Cobb* (Summer 1987), 24–30, Folder 187, VF-CCPL; Cobb County Board of Commissioners, "Cobb County Welcomes You!" *Marietta Daily Journal*, July 30, 1972.

59. Cobb County Chamber of Commerce, "Cobb County, Georgia—1960," Folder 199, VF-CCPL.

60. Similar versions of this image appear in Cobb County Chamber of Commerce, "Cobb County, Georgia—1959," "Cobb County, Georgia—1960," Folder 199, VF-CCPL; "Cobb County, Georgia: An Area of Industrial Potential," *Manufacturers Record* (January 1958), 31.

61. *Marietta Daily Journal*, September 4, 1993, September 30, 1995, May 20, 1996, March 18, 2001, January 12, 2003; First Baptist Church of Marietta, "In His Name We Build," 1959, Folder 212, VF-CCPL.

62. "Roswell Street Baptist Celebrating 50 Years," *Marietta Daily Journal*, September 5, 1993, Folder 225, VF-CCPL. On Eastside Baptist, *Atlanta Journal-Constitution*, April 27, 2000.

63. Roswell Street Baptist Church, "Reach Out," *Marietta Daily Journal*, n.d. [1970], "Roswell Street Baptist Celebrating 50 Years," *Marietta Daily Journal*, September 5, 1993, Folder 225, VF-CCPL; *Marietta Daily Journal*, September 4, 1993; *Atlanta Journal-Constitution*, April 27, 2000.

64. Kevin M. Kruse, "Beyond the Southern Cross: The National Origins of the Religious Right," in Matthew D. Lassiter and Joseph Crespino, eds., *The Myth of Southern Exceptionalism* (New York: Oxford University Press, 2010), 286–307; Matthew D. Lassiter, "Inventing Family Values," in Bruce Schulman and Julian Zelizer, eds., *Rightward Bound: Making America Conservative in the 1970s* (Cambridge, Mass.: Harvard University Press, 2008), 13–28. On gay rights and the Religious Right, see especially Darren Dochuk, *From Bible Belt to Sunbelt: Plain-folk Religion, Grassroots Politics, and the Rise of Evangelical Conservatism* (New York: W.W. Norton, 2010). On Price and Carter, see *Marietta Daily-Journal*, March 14, 1976.

65. "Roswell Street Baptist Celebrating 50 Years," *Marietta Daily Journal*, September 5, 1993, Folder 225, VF-CCPL; Price quoted in *Atlanta Journal-Constitution*, April 27, 2000.

66. *New York Times*, January 23, 1992; *Atlanta Journal-Constitution*, October 25, 1988, March 8, 1990; *Marietta Daily Journal*, November 5, 1990, May 20, 1996; miscellaneous "social problems" clippings in Folder 398, VF-CCPL.

67. *Atlanta Journal-Constitution*, February 15, 1996.

68. *Atlanta Journal-Constitution*, November 20, 1986; *Marietta Daily Journal*, November 4, 2000, January 4, 2002. On the Ten Commandments, see *Atlanta Journal-Constitution*, June 9, 1994. On the arts controversy, see *Christian Science Monitor*, September 8, 1993; *Washington Post*, September 26, 1993; *Marietta Daily Journal*, May 12, 1994.

69. "Court Rejects Colorado's Antigay Amendment," *Christian Century* (June 5, 1996).

70. *Marietta Daily Journal*, June 17, 1994, June 7, 2006 (on Clinton's policy); *Washington Post*, September 26, 1993; *Atlanta Journal-Constitution*, July 30, 1993; *New York Times*, August 12, 1993; William A. Henry III, "Price and Prejudice," *Time*, June 27, 1994; David Deitcher, "The Gay Agenda: Attempts by Conservative Groups To

Suppress Gay and Lesbian Art," *Art in America* (April 1994), http://findarticles.com/p/articles/mi_m1248/is_n4_v82/ai_15105639.

71. *Atlanta Journal-Constitution*, August 11, 1993, May 26, June 9, 1994; *New York Times*, August 29, 1993, August 1, 1994 (Tucker McQueen quotation); *Marietta Daily Journal*, June 3, 1994. Otis Brumby quoted in *Dallas Morning News*, December 19, 1994. Lebow and the Marietta Interfaith Alliance in *Atlanta Journal-Constitution*, May 26, June 9, 1994.

72. *Atlanta Journal-Constitution*, July 29, 1994; Pat Hussain and Jon-Ivan Weaver, *Olympics Out of Cobb Spiked!* (Atlanta: Hussain/Weaver, 1996).

73. *New York Times*, May 1, 1994; *Marietta Daily Journal*, October 28, 1994.

74. *Marietta Daily Journal*, June 3, 1994.

75. *New York Times*, June 24, 1999; *Atlanta Journal-Constitution*, June 28, 2001.

76. *New York Times*, June 23, 1994; *Marietta Daily Journal*, June 27, 1994, March 29, August 23, 1995.

77. *Atlanta Journal-Constitution*, June 23, 1994; *Marietta Daily Journal*, June 27, 1994.

78. *Atlanta Journal-Constitution*, May 21, 22, June 3, October 13, 1988, October 9, 1994, November 15, 1998; Isakson Interview, GGDP.

79. "Mr. Speaker," Series on Newt Gingrich in *Atlanta Journal-Constitution* (January 1995); *Marietta Daily Journal*, September 14, 1991, October 3, 1996; *New York Times*, October 29, 1992, August 30, 1995; *Dallas Morning News*, December 19, 1994. Voting returns from Georgia Secretary of State Elections Division, http://www.sos.ga.gov/elections/.

80. *Atlanta Journal-Constitution*, November 9, 1994; Georgia Secretary of State Elections Division, http://www.sos.ga.gov/elections/.

81. *New York Times*, November 10, 1994; Mark Hosenrall, "How Normal Is Newt?" *Newsweek*, November 7, 1994.

82. Overby, "White-Picket Welfare"; Stacks, "Good Newt, Bad Newt"; Joan Didion, *Political Fictions* (New York: Knopf, 2001), 167–90; Michael Moore and Kathleen Glynn, *Adventures in a TV Nation* (New York: Harper Paperbacks, 1998), 163–72.

83. Georgia Secretary of State Elections Division, http://www.sos.ga.gov/elections/.

84. Georgia Secretary of State Elections Division, http://www.sos.ga.gov/elections/; Barnes Interview, GGDP; Roy Barnes, "State of the State Address," Feb. 8, 2001, http://www.dlc.org/ndol_ci.cfm?contentid=3021&kaid=104&subid=116.

85. U.S. Census Bureau, "American FactFinder," http://factfinder.census.gov; State of Georgia Census Data Program, http://www.gadata.org/; *Marietta Daily Journal*, January 30, July 17, 2007; Andrew Wiese, "African-American Suburbanization and Regionalism in the Modern South," in Lassiter and Crespino, eds., *Myth of Southern Exceptionalism*, 210–33; "Special Report: Hispanics in Cobb," *Marietta Daily Journal*, October 11, 1998; "La Identidad Cambiante de Cobb (The Changing Face of Cobb)," *Marietta Daily Journal*, August 24, 2003.

86. Clippings about "Latinos" in Folder 398, Folder 338A, VF-CCPL.

87. *New York Times*, September 23, 1990, June 3, 2000; *Marietta Daily Journal*, January 20, 2001, November 4, December 4. 2004, July 21, 2007; *Atlanta Journal-Constitution*, November 28, 2002.

88. *Marietta Daily Journal*, December 4, 21, 2005, January 23, 2007; http://davidscott.house.gov/.

89. Results of 2008 presidential election at Cobb County Board of Elections and Registration, http://www.cobbelections.org/. Also see Judis and Teixeira, *Emerging Democratic Majority*.

90. *New York Times*, June 3, 2000.

91. *Atlanta Journal-Constitution*, June 25, July 30, August 7, 12, 20, 1998; *Marietta Daily Journal*, July 2, 2001, August 27, 2002; *New York Times*, June 3, 2000; Georgia Log Cabin Republicans, "The GOP Primary Runoff Results," 1998, http://www.lcrga.com/news/98101401.shtml.

Chapter 4. Religion and Political Behavior in the Sunbelt

1. Byron Shafer, *The End of Realignment? Interpreting American Electoral Eras* (Madison: University of Wisconsin Press, 1991); Warren E. Miller and J. Merrill Shanks, *The New American Voter* (Cambridge, Mass.: Harvard University Press, 1996); Jeffrey M. Stonecash, *Class and Party in American Politics* (Boulder, Colo.: Westview, 2000).

2. V. O. Key, *Southern Politics* (New York: Knopf, 1949).

3. John H. Fenton, *Politics in the Border States* (New Orleans, La: Hauser Press 1957); John H. Fenton, *Midwest Politics* (New York: Holt, Rinehart and Winston, 1966); Duane Lockard *New England State Politics* (Princeton, N.J.: Princeton University Press, 1966).

4. Nicole Mellow, *The State of Disunion: Regional Sources of Modern American Partisanship* (Baltimore: Johns Hopkins University Press, 2008), 18–23.

5. David E. Campbell, ed., *A Matter of Faith: Religion in the 2004 Presidential Election* (Washington, D.C.: Brookings Institution, 2007); James L. Guth, Lyman A. Kellstedt, Corwin E. Smidt, and John C. Green, "Religious Influences in the 2004 Presidential Election," *Presidential Studies Quarterly* 36, 2 (2006): 223–42.

6. See John C. Green, *The Faith Factor: How Religion Influences American Elections* (Westport, Conn.: Praeger, 2007); Earl Black and Merle Black, *Divided America: The Ferocious Power Struggle in American Politics* (New York: Simon & Schuster, 2007); Mellow, *The State of Disunion*; Mark Silk and Andrew Walsh, *One Nation, Indivisible: How Regional Differences Shape American Politics* (Lanham, Md: Rowman & Littlefield, 2008).

7. See Mellow, *The State of Disunion*, especially chap. 3.

8. Kevin B. Phillips, *The Emerging Republican Majority* (Garden City, N.Y.: Anchor Books, 1969); Jerry Hagstrom, *Beyond Reagan: The New Landscape of American Politics* (New York: Norton, 1988).

9. For example, John Egerton, *The Americanization of Dixie: The Southernization of America* (New York: Harper's Magazine Press, 1974).

10. Mark A. Shibley, *Resurgent Evangelicalism in the United States: Mapping Cultural Change Since 1970* (Columbia: University of South Carolina Press, 1996).

11. Respectively Charles Reagan Wilson and Mark Silk, eds., *Religion and Public Life in the South: In the Evangelical Mode* (Walnut Creek, Calif.: Altamira, 2005); William Lindsey and Mark Silk, eds., *Religion and Public Life in the Southern Crossroads: Showdown States* (Walnut Creek, Calif.: Altamira, 2005); Wade Clark Roof and Mark Silk, eds., *Religion and Public Life in the Pacific Region: Fluid Identities* (Walnut Creek, Calif.: Altamira, 2005); Jan Shipps and Mark Silk, eds., *Religion and Public Life in the Mountain West: Sacred Landscapes in Tension* (Walnut Creek, Calif.: Altamira, 2004).

12. Key, *Southern Politics*; Daniel J. Elazar, *American Federalism: A View from the States* (New York: Crowell, 1966).

13. William M. Lunch, *The Nationalization of American Politics* (Berkeley: University of California Press, 1987); Byron Shafer and William J. M. Claggett, *The Two Majorities: The Issue Context of Modern American Politics* (Baltimore: Johns Hopkins University Press, 1995); Raymond A. Mohl, ed., *Searching for the Sunbelt: Historical Perspectives on a Region* (Knoxville: University of Tennessee Press, 1990).

14. Guth et al., "Religious Influences in the 2004 Presidential Election"; Corwin E. Smidt, Lyman A. Kellstedt, and James L. Guth, eds., *The Handbook of Religion and American Politics* (New York: Oxford University Press, 2009).

15. Lyman A. Kellstedt, John C. Green, James L. Guth, and Corwin E. Smidt, "Grasping the Essentials: The Social Embodiment of Religion and Political Behavior," in John C. Green, James L. Guth, Corwin E. Smidt, and Lyman A. Kellstedt, eds., *Religion and the Culture Wars: Dispatches From the Front* (Lanham, Md,.: Rowman & Littlefield, 1996), 176.

16. Paul Kleppner, *The Third Electoral System, 1853-1892: Parties, Voters, and Political Cultures* (Chapel Hill: University of North Carolina Press, 1979).

17. Martin B. Bradley, Norman M. Green Jr., Dale E. Jones, Mac Lynn, and Lou McNeil, *Churches and Church Membership in the United States, 1990* (Atlanta: Glenmary Research Center, 1992).

18. Dale E. Jones, Sherri Doty, Clifford Granmich, James E. Horsch, Richard Houseal, Mac Lynn, John P. Marcum, Kenneth M. Sanchagrin, and Richard H. Taylor, *Religious Congregations and Membership in the United States, 2002* (Nashville, Tenn.: Glenmary Research Center, 2002).

19. Barry A. Kosmin and Seymour P. Lachman, *One Nation Under God: Religion in Contemporary American Society* (New York: Harmony Books, 1993).

20. Green, *The Faith Factor*.

21. Because of the limited number of cases for some periods, especially in the American National Election Studies, we are often hampered in the comparisons we can make for smaller religious groups or for particular states. For subregional analysis,

we have divided the Sunbelt into the Old South, Florida, Texas, the Southwest (Colorado, New Mexico, Arizona, Nevada), and California. Although the size of state samples permits us to look separately at Florida, Texas, and California, there are also good theoretical reasons to expect that, if there are distinctive state political cultures within the Sunbelt, they might well appear in these large and electorally critical states.

22. The Landscape Survey data became available for dissemination in late 2009. We were allowed to use the data for this chapter before general distribution. We thank Greg Smith of the Pew Forum on Religion & Public Life for his technical assistance and Professor John C. Green of the University of Akron for his advice.

23. See Pew Forum on Religion and Public Life, *U.S. Religious Landscape Survey* (Washington, D.C.: Pew Forum, 2008) for a comprehensive report on the findings.

24. We have included Nevada and Colorado in the Southwest, as well as Arkansas, Oklahoma, and Tennessee in the South, as Sunbelt states in order to cast our net broadly. Given the lack of consensus about the conceptual definition of the Sunbelt, this decision seems defensible.

25. Michael Hout and Claude S. Fischer, "Why More Americans Have No Religious Preference: Politics and Generations," *American Sociological Review* 67 (2002): 165–90.

26. Other religious changes in the Sunbelt should be noted. Latter-day Saints and adherents of non-Christian faiths have multiplied, albeit from a low base. At the same time, evangelical Protestants and the unaffiliated have enjoyed modest growth, while Anglo Catholics have suffered a slight decline. Finally, a big religious story in the Sunbelt, as elsewhere, is in the precipitous drop in the proportion of mainline Protestants (data not shown).

27. In the 1992–96, 2000–2004, and 2007 periods, we have much larger numbers of respondents and can focus on Latino Protestant/Catholic differences. In 1992–96, we find Latino Protestants 3 percentage points more Republican than Latino Catholics in both the non-Sunbelt and Sunbelt. For 2000–2004, the comparable figures are 2 percent in the non-Sunbelt and a sizable 12 percent in the Sunbelt. The latter may have been due to the candidacy of George W. Bush, whose Texan background and evangelical faith appealed to Latino Protestants. In the 2007 Landscape Survey, again, Latino Protestants were more Republican than Latino Catholics—12 percent more in the non-Sunbelt and 9 percent in the Sunbelt. This remained the case in 2008 where the disparity between Protestants and Catholics reached 20 percent in the non-Sunbelt and 28 percent in the Sunbelt.

28. David Burner, *The Politics of Provincialism: The Democratic Party in Transition, 1918–1932* (New York: Knopf, 1968); Kleppner, *The Third Electoral System*.

29. Differences between Latino Protestants and Catholics can be noted in the last three periods.

30. Given the rapid increase in the Latino population in the Sunbelt, regional dependence on "minorities" by the Democratic Party is almost certainly going to increase in the future.

31. Small numbers make Latino Protestant and Catholic comparisons hazardous except in 2004 when Sunbelt Protestants gave Bush three-quarters of their votes, while Sunbelt Catholics gave Bush only 37 percent.

32. Alan Wolfe, *One Nation After All: What Middle-Class Americans Really Think About* (New York: Viking, 1998).

33. Mellow, *The State of Disunion*, 47, suggests that free trade is a "defining" Sunbelt issue. She calls the Sunbelt region "trade-dependent."

34. For the Sunbelt Caucus, http://www.opencongress.org/wiki/Congressional_Sunbelt_Caucus; http://www.ou.edu/special/albertctr/archives/sunbelt.htm.

35. Cf. Mohl, ed., *Searching for the Sunbelt*.

36. Mellow, *The State of Disunion*.

Chapter 5. From the Southwest to the Nation: Interracial Civil Rights Activism in Los Angeles

1. Charles Wollenberg, *All Deliberate Speed: Segregation and Exclusion in California Schools, 1855–1975* (Berkeley: University of California Press, 1976).

2. This material comes from Shana Bernstein, *Bridges of Reform: Interracial Civil Rights Activism in Twentieth-Century Los Angeles* (New York: Oxford University Press, forthcoming). *Race* and *ethnicity* are slippery terms; I use *ethnoracial*, which encompasses both race and ethnicity and underscores the categories' historical constructedness. For more, see David Hollinger, *Postethnic America: Beyond Multiculturalism* (New York: Basic Books, 1995); and Michael Omi and Howard Winant, *Racial Formation in the United States: From the 1960s to the 1990s*, 2nd ed. (New York: Routledge, 1994).

3. On *Plessy*, see Michael J. Klarman, *From Jim Crow to Civil Rights: The Supreme Court and the Struggle for Racial Equality* (New York: Oxford University Press, 2004).

4. Gilbert G. González, *Chicano Education in the Era of Segregation* (Philadelphia: Balch Institute Press, 1990), 28. See also Christopher Arriola, "Knocking on the Schoolhouse Door: *Mendez v. Westminster*—Equal Protection, Public Education, and Mexican Americans in the 1940s," *La Raza Law Journal* 8 (1995): 166–207; Kevin R. Johnson, "*Hernández v. Texas*: Legacies of Justice and Injustice," UC Davis Law, Legal Studies Research Paper 19 (November 2004), http://ssrn.com/abstract=625403 (accessed February 23, 2010); and Richard Valencia, "The Mexican American Struggle for Equal Educational Opportunity in *Mendez v. Westminster*: Helping to Pave the Way for *Brown v. Board of Education*," *Teachers College Record* 107 (March 3, 2005): 389–423.

5. Arriola, "Knocking," 194–96; Mario T. García, "Americans All: The Mexican American Generation and the Politics of Wartime Los Angeles, 1941–1945," *Social Science Quarterly* 65 (June 1984): 278–89, 281–83; González, *Chicano Education*, 154; and untitled document, Fred Ross, late 1946 (?), Folder 1, Box 8, Fred Ross Papers,

Department of Special Collections, Green Library, Stanford University (hereafter Ross).

6. The 1950 population was 1,970,358. U.S. Census Bureau, *A Report of the Seventeenth Decennial Census of the United States Census of Population: 1950*, vol. 2: *Characteristics of the Population, Part 5: California* (Washington, D.C.: Government Printing Office, 1952), 10, 54. There were 25,502 Japanese and 171,209 African Americans (179, 100). Mexicans were approximately 157,067. Census Bureau, *U.S. Census of the Population: 1950—Special Reports: Persons of Spanish Surname*, vol. 4: *Special Reports Part 3, Chapter C* (Washington, D.C.: Government Printing Office, 1953), 3C-43. The closest number available for Jews is approximately 250,000 in 1948. Max Vorspan and Lloyd P. Gartner, *History of the Jews of Los Angeles* (San Marino, Calif.: Huntington Library, 1970), 225. See following notes.

This study speaks to scholarship that generally aggregates non-southern movements as northern. See Jacqueline Dowd Hall, "The Long Civil Rights Movement and the Political Uses of the Past," *Journal of American History* 91, 4 (March 2005): 1233–63; Thomas Sugrue, *Sweet Land of Liberty: The Forgotten Struggle for Civil Rights in the North* (New York: Random House, 2008), xxvii; and Jeanne Theoharis, "Black Freedom Studies: Re-imagining and Redefining the Fundamentals," *History Compass* 4, 2 (2006): 363n24.

7. Martha Biondi, *To Stand and Fight: The Struggle for Civil Rights in Postwar New York City* (Cambridge, Mass.: Harvard University Press, 2003); Wendell E. Pritchett, "A Local and National Story: The Civil Rights Movement in Postwar Washington, D.C.," *History Now: American History Online* 8 (June 2006), http://www.historynow.org/06_2006/historian3.html; and Stuart Svonkin, *Jews Against Prejudice: American Jews and the Fight for Civil Liberties* (New York: Columbia University Press, 1997).

8. It began during the 1930s; see Bernstein, *Bridges*.

9. Edward J. Escobar, *Race, Police, and the Making of a Political Identity: Mexican Americans and the Los Angeles Police Department, 1900–1945* (Berkeley: University of California Press, 1999), 207–29, 281–84; and Eduardo Obregón Pagán, *Murder at the Sleepy Lagoon: Zoot Suits, Race, and Riot in Wartime L. A.* (Chapel Hill: University of North Carolina Press, 2003).

10. Luis Álvarez, *The Power of the Zoot: Youth Culture and Resistance During World War II* (Berkeley: University of California Press, 2008); Escobar, *Race*; Mauricio Mazón, *The Zoot-Suit Riots* (Austin: University of Texas Press, 1984); and Pagán, *Murder*.

11. Josh A. Sides, "Working Away: African American Migration and Community in Los Angeles from the Great Depression to 1954" (Ph.D. dissertation, UCLA, 1999), 80–81; Ric Dias, "Cold War Cities in the American West," in Kevin Fernlund, ed., *The Cold War American West, 1945–1989* (Albuquerque: University of New Mexico Press, 1998), 71.

12. The Los Angeles population increased from 1,504,277 in 1940 to 1,970,358 in 1950. Census Bureau, *Sixteenth Census of the United States 1940. Population*, vol. 2:

Characteristics of the Population, Part 1: United States Summary and Alabama-District of Columbia (Washington, D.C.: Government Printing Office, 1943), 132; Census Bureau, *A Report of the Seventeenth Decennial Census, Part 5: California*, 10, 54.

13. The only census figures for the 1940 Japanese population are for the county, from which I extrapolated; Los Angeles county's Japanese population decreased from 1.3 percent of the general population in 1940 to 0.89 percent in 1950 (36,866 to 36,761). Census Bureau, *Sixteenth Census*, vol. 2, *Characteristics of the Population, Part 1*, Table 25,568; and Census Bureau, *A Report of the Seventeenth Decennial Census, Part 5: California*, 179. The total county population in 1940 was 2,785,643 and in 1950, 4,151,687. See Census Bureau, *Sixteenth Census of the United States 1940. Population*, vol. 1, : *Number of Inhabitants* (Washington, D.C.: Government Printing Office, 1943), 122;. Census Bureau, *A Report of the Seventeenth Decennial Census, Part 5 California*, 56.

14. The African American population grew over 268 percent, from 63,774 to 171,209. Census Bureau, *Sixteenth Census*, vol. 2: *Part 1: United States Summary and Alabama-District of Columbia*, 629; Census Bureau, *A Report of the Seventeenth Decennial Census, Part 5: California*, 100.

15. The Mexican population grew by 46 percent, from 107,680 to 157,067. Approximately 250,000 Mexican-descent people resided in Los Angeles County by 1945. The 1940 and 1950 population figures are estimates, since the census did not categorize this population separately but rather alternated between categorizing Mexicans as whites and "other races." The only information is the 1940 census "Spanish-mother tongue population" (107,680) and the 1950 census "Spanish-surnamed population" (157,067). Census Bureau, *Sixteenth Census of the United States, 1940, Population: Nativity and Percentage of the White Population, Mother Tongue* (Washington, D.C.: U.S. Government Printing Office, 1943), 34; Census Bureau, *U.S. Census of the Population: 1950—Special Reports: Persons of Spanish Surname*, vol. 4, *Special Reports Part 3, Chapter C* (Washington, D.C.: U.S. Government Printing Office, 1953), 3C–43.

16. Jews in Los Angeles increased from 1941 (130,000) to 1945 (150,000), and again to 1948 (250,000). Vorspan and Gartner, *History*, 225.

17. Vorspan and Gartner, *History*, 242; Milton A. Senn, "A Study of Police Training Programs in Minority Relations," August 7, 1950, Folder 1, Box 5, Ross. Census numbers and other official estimates counted 171,209 African Americans, 25,502 Japanese, 157,067 Mexicans, and 250,000 Jews in 1948: 603,778 of the city's total population of 1,970,358, or 30 percent. See previous notes.

18. John W. Dower, *War Without Mercy: Race and Power in the Pacific War* (New York: Pantheon, 1986); Mary L. Dudziak, *Cold War Civil Rights: Race and the Image of American Democracy* (Princeton, N.J.: Princeton University Press, 2000). On Los Angeles discrimination's negative international wartime attention, see Bernstein, *Bridges*.

19. Minutes, Meeting of December 2, 1942, Folder 6, Box 4, Manuel Ruíz Papers,

Department of Special Collections, Green Library, Stanford University. See too Bernstein, *Bridges*.

20. Sleepy Lagoon Defense Committee, *The Sleepy Lagoon Case*, (n.p.), ca. 1944, in David G. Gutiérrez, *Walls and Mirrors: Mexican Americans, Mexican Immigrants, and the Politics of Ethnicity* (Berkeley: University of California Press, 1995), 128. See, too, Bernstein, *Bridges*. On Double V campaigns, see Ronald Takaki, *Double Victory: A Multicultural History of America in World War II* (Boston: Little, Brown, 2000).

21. Only 16,000 of 87,000 were Mexican American. "The Latin One-Eighth," *Los Angeles Daily News*, July 1, 1949; and Robin Fitzgerald Scott, "The Mexican American in the Los Angeles Area, 1920–1950: From Acquiescence to Activity" (Ph.D. dissertation, University of Southern California, 1971), 296–97. See, too, Katherine Underwood, "Pioneering Minority Representation: Edward Roybal and the Los Angeles City Council, 1949–1962," *Pacific Historical Review* 66 (August 1997): 399–425; and Underwood, "Process and Politics: Multiracial Electoral Coalition Building and Representation in Los Angeles' Ninth District, 1949–1962" (Ph.D. dissertation, University of California San Diego, 1992).

22. Anthony P. Ríos, "Application for Funds to United Steelworkers of America," approximately 1953, CSO Folder, Box 9, Edward Roybal Collection, Special Collections, Charles Young Research Library, UCLA (hereafter Roybal); and Scott, "The Mexican American," 299.

23. On Bloody Christmas, see Edward J. Escobar, "Bloody Christmas and the Irony of Police Professionalism: The Los Angeles Police Department, Mexican Americans, and Police Reform in the 1950s," *Pacific Historical Review* 72 (May 2, 2003): 171–99, 171–72.

24. Albert Camarillo, *Chicanos in California: A History of Mexican Americans in California* (San Francisco: Boyd & Fraser., 1984), 81–82.

25. Danny Feingold, "Common Threads," *Los Angeles Times*, October 21, 1998.

26. Ríos, "Application for Funds to United Steelworkers of America," Roybal; and Scott, "The Mexican American," 299.

27. "The Latin One-Eighth," *Los Angeles Daily News*, July 1, 1949.

28. Linda M. Apodaca, *Mexican American Women and Social Change: The Founding of the Community Service Organization in Los Angeles, an Oral History*, Working Paper Series 27 (Tucson: University of Arizona, 1999); Maria Linda Apodaca, "They Kept the Home Fires Burning: Mexican American Women and Social Change" (Ph.D. dissertation, University of California Irvine, 1994); Camarillo, *Chicanos*, 80–82; Margaret Rose, "Gender and Civic Activism in Mexican American Barrios in California: The Community Service Organization, 1947–1962," in Joanne Meyerowitz, ed., *Not June Cleaver: Women and Gender in Postwar America, 1945–1960* (Philadelphia: Temple University Press, 1994); and Scott, "The Mexican American," 294–99. Some have acknowledged but not explored the significance of the CSO's multiracial roots. See Kenneth C. Burt, "The Battle for Standard Coil: The United Electrical Workers, the Community Service Organization, and the Catholic Church in Latino East Los

Angeles," in Robert W. Cherny, William Issel, Kieran Walsh Taylor, eds., *American Labor and the Cold War: Grassroots Politics and Postwar Political Culture* (New Brunswick, N.J.: Rutgers University Press, 2004), 118–40; Rosina Lozano, "The Struggle for Inclusion: A Study of the Community Service Organization in East Los Angeles, 1947–1951" (B.A. thesis, Stanford University, 2000); Stephen J. Pitti, *The Devil in Silicon Valley: Northern California, Race, and Mexican Americans* (Princeton, N.J.: Princeton University Press, 2003), 242n.5; Pitti, "Quicksilver Community: Mexican Migrations and Politics in the Santa Clara Valley, 1800–1960" (Ph.D. dissertation, Stanford University, 1998), 438, 439–41; and Underwood, "Process," 18, 99–100.

29. Rodolfo Acuña, *Anything but Mexican: Chicanos in Contemporary Los Angeles* (New York: Verso, 1996), 45; Scott Kurashige, *The Shifting Grounds of Race: Black and Japanese Americans in the Making of Multiethnic Los Angeles* (Princeton, N.J.: Princeton University Press, 2008), 232, 233, 243, 268–69, 272–75, 280–81; Deborah Dash Moore, *To the Golden Cities: Pursuing the American Jewish Dream in Miami and L. A.* (New York: Free Press, 1994), 56, 58–60; George J. Sánchez, "'What's Good for Boyle Heights is Good for the Jews': Creating Multiracialism on the Eastside During the 1950s," *American Quarterly* 56, 3 (September 2004): 633–61; Josh Sides, *L. A. City Limits: African American Los Angeles from the Great Depression to the Present* (Berkeley: University of California Press, 2003); and Vorspan and Gartner, *History*.

30. CSO/Industrial Areas Foundation, Southern California Division, Program, 1949, 2, Folder 11, Box 5, Ross.

31. Lawrence I. Hewes, Jr., *Race Relations on the West Coast*, September 1946, 3, Carton 6, John Anson Ford Collection, Huntington Library, San Marino California (hereafter Ford).

32. On Alinsky, see P. David Finks, *The Radical Vision of Saul Alinsky* (Ramsey, N.J.: Paulist Press, 1984), 34–45; and Sanford D. Horwitt, *Let Them Call Me Rebel: Saul Alinsky—His Life and Legacy* (New York: Knopf, 1989), 127–29, 222–35. On Ross, see Pitti, *Devil*, 149–50.

33. Fred Ross, Report, February 20, 1948, Folder 1, Box 2, Ross.

34. Fred Ross, Minutes of the Meeting of the Subcommittee on Agencies, February 14, 1949, Subcommittees Agencies—Minutes 1947–1950 Folder, Section AII, Series III, The Jewish Federation Council of Greater Los Angeles' Community Relations Committee Collection, Urban Archives Center, Oviatt Library, California State University, Northridge (hereafter CRC).

35. Ríos, "Application for Funds to United Steelworkers of America," Roybal.

36. CSO, Minutes, October 29–30, 1955, 28, Folder 4, Box 5, Ross.

37. CSO, Memo, 1955, Folder 10, Box 11, Ross; and CSO, National CSO Executive Board Meeting Minutes, July 17, 1955, CSO Folder, Box 9, Roybal.

38. Ibid.

39. Ross to Alinsky, September 26, 1947, Folder 1, Box 2, Ross.

40. Carmen Medina to Ida A. Siegel, August 19, 1949, Folder 12, Box 5, Ross.

41. Ralph Guzman to Rabbi Magnin, February 25, 1950, Subcommittee: CSO, 1949–1950 Folder, Section AII, Series III, CRC.

42. The CRC provided $7,500 of the CSO's $10,500 1948 funding. CSO, Memo, April 18, 1951, Folder 6, Box 5, Ross; CRC, Minutes, August 30, 1948, Subcommittees: Agencies—Minutes 1947–1950 Folder, Section AII, Series III, CRC; CRC, Minutes, July 14, 1949, Subcommittee: CSO 1949–1950 Folder, Section AII, Series III, CRC.

43. Various files in Box 7, Ross.

44. Memo, August 13, 1948, Minutes July–December 1948, Folder, AII, Series III, CRC.

45. 400,000 of 4,000,000 unemployed Americans were in California, with 250,000 in Los Angeles. Governor Earl Warren to Fred Herzberg, November 10, 1949, Employment 1949 Folder, Section 3C, Series III, CRC and Reverend Clayton D. Russell, Report, August and November 1949, Employment 1949 Folder, Section 3C, Series III, CRC.

46. Mr. Howard Holtsendorf, "Red Letter Dates for Unity," Council for Civic Unity, 1945, Folder 5, Box 13, Series II, CRC.

47. American Council on Race Relations, *The Problem of Violence: Observations on Race Conflict in Los Angeles*, Carton 6, Ford.

48. CSO/Industrial Areas Foundation, Southern California Division, Program, 1949, 2, Folder 11, Box 5, Ross.

49. Conference on Watts Community Situation, February 15, 1949, Housing: Watts Community Program (1947–1949) Folder, Section 3C, Series III, CRC.

50. ACRR, *The Problem of Violence*, Ford.

51. CRC, Memo, September 6, 1949, Memos from Exec Office Staff Nov-Dec 1949 Folder, Section AII, Series III, CRC.

52. CRC, Meeting Minutes, July 14, 1949, Subcommittee: CSO 1949–1950 Folder, Section AII, Series III, CRC.

53. Ross, Report, February 20, 1948, Folder 1, Box 2, Ross.

54. CRC, Meeting Minutes, February 14, 1949, Subcommittees: Agencies—Minutes 1947–1950 Folder, Section AII, Series III, CRC.

55. CSO/Industrial Areas Foundation, Southern California Division, Program, 1949, 4, Folder 11, Box 5, Ross.

56. On postwar red-baiting, see Bernstein, *Bridges*.

57. Ross to Alinsky, November 16, 1947, Folder 1, Box 2, Ross.

58. Ross to Alinsky, September 26, 1947, Folder 1, Box 2, Ross.

59. Ross to Alinsky, November 16, 1947.

60. Herman Gallegos to Rev. John [Ralph] Duggan, August 5, 1982, Unfiled material, Box 14, Hermán Gallegos Papers, Department of Special Collections, Green Library, Stanford University (hereafter Gallegos). I thank Gina Marie Pitti for sharing this source. On the Catholic Church and CSO's relationship, see Burt, "The Battle for Standard Coil."

61. Leonard Bloom, Memo to Herzberg attached to Minutes of the Committee

on Agencies, July 14, 1949, Subcommittee: CSO 1949–50 Folder, Section AII, Ser. III, CRC.

62. Ross, Report, February 1948, Folder 1, Box 2, Ross.

63. Leonard Pitt, Joseph Roos Oral History Interview, December 18, 1979, January 7, January 28, February 14, 1980, CRC, 55–8.

64. Fred Herzberg to Philip Lerman, February 5, 1948, Displaced Persons: Corr January–April 1948 Folder, Section 3C, Series III, CRC.

65. Eric L. Goldstein, *The Price of Whiteness: Jews, Race, and American Identity* (Princeton, N.J.: Princeton University Press, 2006); Matthew Frye Jacobson, *Whiteness of a Different Color:* European Immigrants and the Alchemy of Race (Cambridge, Mass.: Harvard University Press, 1998); Mae Ngai, *Impossible Subjects: Illegal Aliens and the Making of Modern America* (Princeton, N.J.: Princeton University Press, 2003); and Svonkin, *Jews Against Prejudice*.

66. On postwar Jews' interests in avoiding attention as Jews, see Peter Novick, *The Holocaust in American Life* (Boston: Houghton Mifflin, 1999).

67. Pitt, *Joseph Roos*, CRC, 55.

68. "Argument in the Matter of the Citizens' Advisory Committee," August 1, 1948, Tenney, Jack B.: Corresp 1948 Folder, Section 3C, Series III, CRC.

69. Fred Herzberg to Davis McEntire, August 25, 1947, and McEntire to Herzberg, August 8, 1947, in Inter-group Relations: American Council on Race Relations corresp. May–Oct 1947 Folder, Section 3C, Series IV, CRC.

70. Adrienne L. McLean, *Being Rita Hayworth: Labor, Identity, and Hollywood Stardom* (New Brunswick, N.J.: Rutgers University Press, 2004); Clara E. Rodríguez, *Heroes, Lovers, and Others: The Story of Latinos in Hollywood* (Washington, D.C.: Smithsonian Books, 2004).

71. Arriola, "Knocking," and González, *Chicano Education*. On the 1930 census, see Camarillo, *Chicanos*, 201. For more on Mexican Americans and whiteness, see Neil Foley, "Becoming Hispanic: Mexican Americans and the Faustian Pact with Whiteness," in Foley, ed., *Reflexiones 1997: New Directions in Mexican American Studies* (Austin: University of Texas Press, 1998).

72. ACRR, *The Problem of Violence*, Ford.

73. Tony Serrato (CSO Civil Rights Committee), inter-office memo, June 1949, Folder 1, Box 5, Ross.

74. Personnel Policy Board of the Secretary of Defense, "Policy Regarding 'Race' Entries," Memo to Secretary of the Army, Navy, Air Force, April 15, 1950, Folder 1, Box 5, Ross. See also files in Folder 26, Box 4, Ross.

75. See, too, Mario García, *Mexican Americans: Leadership, Ideology, and Identity, 1930–1960* (New Haven: Yale University Press, 1989), 74.

76. See, for instance, Svonkin, *Jews Against Prejudice*.

77. Foley, "Becoming Hispanic;" Neil Foley, "'Over the Rainbow': *Hernandez v. Texas, Brown v. Board of Education,* and Black v. Brown," in Michael A. Olivas, ed., *"Colored Men" and "Hombres Aquí": Hernandez v. Texas and the Emergence of Mexican*

American Lawyering" (Houston: Arte Público Press, 2006): 111–21; Thomas A. Guglielmo, "Fighting for Caucasian Rights: Mexicans, Mexican Americans, and the Transnational Struggle for Civil Rights in World War II Texas," *Journal of American History* 92, 4 (March 2006): 1212–37; Craig A. Kaplowitz, *LULAC, Mexican Americans, and National Policy* (College Station: Texas A&M University Press, 2005); and Nancy MacLean, *Freedom Is Not Enough:* The Opening of the American Workplace (Cambridge: Cambridge University Press, 2006). See, too, Gabriela F. Arredondo, *Mexican Chicago: Race, Identity, and Nation, 1919–1939* (Urbana: University of Illinois Press, 2008); and Arredondo, "Navigating Ethno-Racial Currents, Mexicans in Chicago, 1919–1939," *Journal of Urban History* 30, 3 (March 2004): 399–427. For disagreement on Texas Mexicans' whiteness strategy preventing alliances with African Americans, see Emilio Zamora, *Claiming Rights and Righting Wrongs in Texas: Mexican Workers and Job Politics During World War II* (College Station: Texas A&M University Press, 2009).

78. Bernstein, *Bridges,* especially chaps. 4 and 5.

79. Ibid., especially chas. 4, 5, and 6.

80. Arriola, "Knocking," 194–96; Mark Brilliant, "Color Lines: Civil Rights Struggles on America's 'Racial Frontier,' 1945–1975" (Ph.D. dissertation, Stanford University, 2002), 88–89; Brown Foundation for Educational Equity website, http://brownvboard.org/research/opinions/347us483.htm, accessed February 23, 2010; Valencia, "The Mexican American Struggle," 407.

81. Stan Oftelie, "Murder Trial Obscured 1946 O.C. Integration Landmark," *Santa Ana Register,* August 22, 1976, in González, *Chicano Education,* 28; Valencia, "The Mexican American Struggle," 402, 417.

82. "Segregation in Schools as a Violation of the XIVth Amendment," *Columbia Law Review* 47 (March 1947): 325–27, 326–27.

83. "Segregation in Public Schools—a Violation of 'Equal Protection of the Laws,'" *Yale Law Journal* 56 (1947): 1059–67, 1060.

84. Ibid., 1066–67.

85. Robert R. Alvarez, Jr., "The Lemon Grove Incident: The Nation's First Successful Desegregation Court Case," *Journal of San Diego History* 32 (Spring 1986): 2; Arriola, "Knocking;" González, *Chicano Education,* 28; Johnson, "*Hernández v. Texas*"; Valencia, "The Mexican American Struggle."

86. Quintard Taylor, *In Search of the Racial Frontier: African Americans in the American West, 1528–1990* (New York: Norton, 1998), 270; Howard Holtsendorf, in "Red Letter Dates for Unity," Council for Civic Unity, 1945, Folder 5, Box 13, Series II, CRC.

87. Greg Robinson and Toni Robinson, "Korematsu and Beyond: Japanese Americans and the Origins of Strict Scrutiny," *Law and Contemporary Problems* 68, 2 (2005): 29–55, esp. 40–41, http://law.duke.edu/journals/ (accessed December 21, 2009).

88. Thomas L. Griffith to Roy Wilkins, March 14, 1945, Los Angeles, Calif, 1945

Folder, Box C14, Group II, NAACP Papers, Library of Congress (hereafter NAACP LOC). See too Taylor, *In Search*, 270.

89. See Lawrence B. de Graaf, Kevin Mulroy, Quintard Taylor, eds., *Seeking El Dorado: African Americans in California* (Los Angeles: Autry Museum of Western Heritage with University of Washington Press, 2001), 32–37; Sides, *L. A. City Limits*, 99–100; Sides, "Working Away," 237.

90. Lawrence de Graaf, Judge Loren Miller Interview, "Negroes in Los Angeles During the Depression," April 29, 1967, 23, CSU Fullerton Oral History Program.

91. Loren Miller, *The Petitioners: The Story of the Supreme Court of the United States and the Negro* (New York: Pantheon, 1966), 326–27.

92. Los Angeles Branch NAACP, news release, "NAACP Sponsored Case Strikes Death-Blow to Race Restrictive Covenants; District Court of Appeals Here Upholds Property Rights," August 14, 1952, "Los Angeles, Calif, 1952," Box C16, Group II, NAACP LOC. See, too, Miller interview, CSU Fullerton Oral History Program, 23; Douglas Flamming, *Bound for Freedom: Black Los Angeles in Jim Crow America* (Berkeley: University of California Press, 2005), 369; Toni Robinson and Greg Robinson, "The Limits of Interracial Coalitions: *Méndez v. Westminster* Reexamined," in Nicholas De Genova, ed., *Racial Transformations: Latinos and Asians Remaking the United States* (Durham, N.C.: Duke University Press, 2006): 94–119; and Sides, *L. A. City Limits*, 100–101.

93. Bernstein, *Bridges*.

94. The victories in housing and education were significant achievements that delegitimated aspects of segregation's legal basis. Nevertheless, the liberal civil rights agenda that emerged from these struggles and triumphed in mid-century legislation and court cases did not fulfill the hopes of many minorities; they did not ensure equality. For more on liberalism's limitations, see N. D. B. Connolly, "Sunbelt Civil Rights," and Daniel Martinez HoSang, "Racial Liberalism and in the Rise of the Sunbelt West," both in this volume.

Chapter 6. Sunbelt Civil Rights: Urban Renewal
and the Follies of Desegregation in Greater Miami

In addition to the contributors to this volume, the author would like to thank Shani Mott, Marcus Allen, Reanna Ursin, Tara Bynum, Kelly Baker Josephs, Ray Mohl, Brett Gadsden, Andrew Kahrl, Robert Henderson, David Freund, Kelly Quinn, and participants in the University of Maryland's African American Political Culture Workshop for their thoughtful comments on earlier drafts of this chapter.

1. Rick Perlstein, *Nixonland: The Rise of a President and the Fracturing of America* (New York: Scribner, 2008), 295; Eric Tscheschlok, "Long Time Coming: Miami's Liberty City Riot of 1968," *Florida Historical Quarterly* 74, 4 (Spring 1996): 440–60.

2. "'68 Miami Rioting Held Untied to GOP Parley," *Washington Post*, February 12, 1969, A3.

3. Irene V. Holliman, "From Crackertown to Model City? Urban Renewal and Community Building in Atlanta, 1963–1966," *Journal of Urban History* 35, 3 (March 2009): 369–86, 370.

4. Thomas J. Sugrue, *Sweet Land of Liberty: The Forgotten Struggle for Civil Rights in the North* (New York: Random House, 2009), 519–24; Volker Janssen, "Sunbelt Lock-Up: Where the Suburbs Met the Super-Max," this volume.

5. John T. Woolley and Gerhard Peters, The American Presidency Project (on-line), Santa Barbara: University of California (hosted), Gerhard Peters (database), http://www.presidency.ucsb.edu/ws/?pid=25968, accessed April 5, 2009.

6. Raymond A. Mohl, "Race and Space in the Modern City: Interstate-95 and the Black Community in Miami," in Arnold R. Hirsch and Raymond A. Mohl, eds., *Urban Policy in Twentieth-Century America* (New Brunswick, N.J.: Rutgers University Press, 1993), 100–158.

7. Lisa McGirr, *Suburban Warriors: The Origins of the New American Right* (Princeton, N.J.: Princeton University Press, 2001); Robert O. Self, *American Babylon: Race and the Struggle for Postwar Oakland* (Princeton, N.J.: Princeton University Press, 2003), esp. chap. 4; Matthew D. Lassiter, *The Silent Majority: Suburban Politics in the Sunbelt South* (Princeton, N.J.: Princeton University Press, 2006); Kevin M. Kruse, *White Flight: Atlanta and the Making of Modern Conservatism* (Princeton, N.J.: Princeton University Press, 2005); see also Daniel Ho Sang's essay in this volume, "Racial Liberalism and the Rise of the Sunbelt West."

8. William G. Grigsby, "Housing Markets and Public Policy," in John Q. Wilson, ed., *Urban Renewal* (Cambridge, Mass.: MIT Press, 1966), 28.

9. "Housing Statistics, June 1960–June 1964," Folder, National Urban League Papers, Part III, Box 73, Library of Congress, Washington, D.C. (hereafter LOC).

10. Andrew Weise, *Places of Their Own: African American Suburbanization in the Twentieth Century* (Chicago: University of Chicago Press, 2005), 168–84.

11. N. D. B. Connolly, "By Eminent Domain: Race and Capital in the Building of an American South Florida" (Ph.D. dissertation, University of Michigan, 2008), esp. chap. 8.

12. Miami City Planning Board, *Report of City Planning Board of Miami Relative to New Railway Terminal* (1940), 14; Harland Bartholomew and Associates, City Planning Consultants, Saint Louis, Missouri, "A Preliminary Report upon Population, Land Uses and Zoning, Miami Beach, Florida" (1940); Joseph Heathcott, "The City Quietly Remade: National and Local Agendas in the Movement to Clear the Slums, 1942–1952," *Journal of Urban History* 34, 2 (January 2008): 221–42, 224.

13. Miami City Planning Board, *Report* (1940), 14; Robert A. Caro, *The Power Broker: Robert Moses and the Fall of New York* (New York: Knopf, 1974).

14. Miami Chamber of Commerce, "Meeting minutes of the Industrial Development Committee, July 8, 1942," *Committee Meetings Minutes vol. 2 (1941–1946)*,

Greater Miami Chamber of Commerce collection, Charles W. Tebeau Library, Historian Association of Southern Florida, Miami (hereafter HASF).

15. Elizabeth Tandy Shermer, "Counter-Organizing the Sunbelt: Right-to-Work Campaigns and Anti-Union Conservatism," *Pacific Historical Review* 78, 1 (2009): 81–118, esp. 86–87, 94–96.

16. David M. P. Freund, *Colored Property: State Policy and White Racial Politics in Suburban America* (Chicago: University of Chicago Press, 2007); Homer Hoyt, *The Structure and Growth of Residential Neighborhoods in American Cities* (Chicago: University of Chicago Press, 1939); Marc A. Weiss, *Richard T. Ely and the Contribution of Economic Research to Home Ownership and Housing Policy* (Boston: MIT Center for Real Estate Development, 1989).

17. Raymond A. Mohl, "Whitening Miami: Race, Housing, and Government Policy in Twentieth-Century Dade County," *Florida Historical Quarterly* 79, 3 (Winter 2001): 319–45; Connolly, "By Eminent Domain."

18. Charles E. Connerly, *"The Most Segregated City in America": City Planning and Civil Rights in Birmingham, 1920–1980* (Charlottesville, University of Virginia Press, 2005).

19. Edward Braynon, interviewed by Stephanie Wanza, August 6, 1997, 28; Tell the Story Collection, Black Archives History and Research Foundation of South Florida, Miami (hereafter BA); "An Abstract of Title for Realty Securities Corp. to Lots 8, 9, 10, 11, 40, 41, 42, & 43 of Block 10 of Railroad Chops [sic] Colored Addition. From Security Abstract Company, Incorporator, Abstracts Prepared, Money Loaned and Invested, 33 N.E. First Avenue, Miami, Dade County, Florida, No 25056;" "Neighborhoods and Communities" collection, Box 3, BA.

20. HOLC Security Map Area descriptions "Musa Isles and Allapattah Section, Miami Florida, Security Grade C;" HOLC Security Map Area descriptions "South of 62nd Street from N.W. 17th Ave. to N.E. 4th Ct., Miami, FL, Security Grade D," Record Group 207, National Archives II, College Park Maryland (hereafter NA); Office of the Miami City Clerk, Resolution 19821, February 19, 1947, *Resolutions and Minutes of the City Commission, 1921–1986*, Box 28; Resolution 18747, March 7, 1945, *Resolutions and Minutes of the City Commission, 1921–1986*, Box 31; Resolution 17802, April 29, 1942, *Resolutions and Minutes of the City Commission, 1921–1986*, Box 28, State Archives of Florida, Tallahassee (hereafter SAF); *Miami Herald*, August 1, 1947; *Miami Tropical Dispatch*, August 9, 1947; Black Archives History and Research Foundation of South Florida, Narratives, "Railroad Shop," Neighborhoods and Communities Collection, Box 3, BA; Braynon, "Tell the Story," 29.

21. For a case of similar displacements in the 1940s South, see Ronald H. Bayor, *Race and the Shaping of Twentieth-Century Atlanta* (Chapel Hill: University of North Carolina Press, 1996), 58; C. Fraser Smith, *Here Lies Jim Crow: Civil Rights in Maryland* (Baltimore: Johns Hopkins University Press, 2008), 1–2.

22. "Still Unsettled," *Miami Times*, January 22, 1949, 4; Correspondence from Elizabeth Virrick to Malcolm Wiseheart, March 7, 1949, Elizabeth Virrick Collection,

"Correspondence, Memos, etc., 1949–1967" Folder, Box 1, HASF; Raymond A. Mohl, "Elizabeth Virrick and the 'Concrete Monsters': Housing Reform in Postwar Miami," *Tequesta* 51 (2001): 5–37, 11.

23. Carita Swanson Vonk, *Theodore R. Gibson: Priest, Prophet, and Politician* (Miami: Little River Press, 1997), 39.

24. Mohl, "Elizabeth Virrick and the 'Concrete Monsters'," 17.

25. For similar action in Brooklyn's Brownsville neighborhood, see Wendell E. Pritchett, "Race and Community in Postwar Brooklyn: The Brownsville Neighborhood Council and the Politics of Urban Renewal" *Journal of Urban History* 27, 4 (May 2001): 445–70, 451.

26. Thelma Vernell Anderson Gibson with Helen Lawrence McGuire and Howard Carter, Sr., *Forbearance: The Life Story of a Coconut Grove Native* (Homestead, Fl.: Helena Enterprises, 2000), 140.

27. Gibson, *Forbearance*, 94–95.

28. "Voice of America to Tell Grove's Slum Clearance Work," *Miami Herald*, December 14, 1950; letter from Elizabeth Virrick of the Coconut Grove Citizen's Committee to Carroll Seghers II of the Black Star media company, December 20, 1950, Elizabeth Virrick Collection, Box 14, HASF.

29. Southern Regional Council, "Roots of Racial Tension," 2.

30. Financial records and client information about one company in particular, Bonded Collection Agency, is available at the Black Archives History and Research Foundation of South Florida, Miami. On landlord profits, see David Harvey, *The Urbanization of Capital: Studies in the History and Theory of Capitalist Urbanization* (Baltimore: Johns Hopkins University Press, 1985), esp. chap. 3.

31. Connolly, "By Eminent Domain," esp. chap. 6.

32. Art Green, "Landlord and Tenant Legislation in the Florida Legislature—1971," Bonded Rental Agency, Inc., Collection, BA.

33. James Russell, "Slum Property Owners Block Blight Removal," *Miami Herald*, Bonded Rental Agency, Inc., Collection, "Newspaper Clippings on Housing, 1960 and back to 1952," BA; Green, "Landlord and Tenant Legislation in the Florida Legislature—1971;" "Interview with Mayor Haydon Burns of Jacksonville, Florida: March 13, 1957, Record Group 100, Series 226, Records of Florida Advisory Commission on Race Relations, 1957–1961, Box 3, "Housing" Folder, SAF.

34. Correspondence from Don Shoemaker, *Miami Herald* editor, to James S. Knight, July 30, 1959, Don Shoemaker Papers, Special Collections, University of North Carolina, Chapel Hill.

35. *Miami Herald*, April 17, 1950.

36. *New Orleans Times-Picayune*, November 10, 1957, quotation in U.S. Congress, House Committee on Government Relations, *Federal-State-Local Relations: Dade County (Florida) Metropolitan Government*, Hearings before a Subcommittee of the Committee on Government Operations, House of Representatives, 85th Cong., 1st sess., November 21–22 (Washington, D.C.: Government Printing Office, 1957), 5;

Housing and Home Finance Agency, "Summary of the Workable Program for Urban Renewal for Metropolitan Dade County, Florida," October 28, 1958, 3, Slum Clearance Folder 1, Box 81, "WTVJ" Collection, HASF.

37. Bonded Collection Agency, "25 Years of Property Management and Community Service" (1959), 18, "Bonded Rental Agency, Inc.," Collection, BA. *Miami News*, October 15, 1974.

38. *Miami Times*, September 3, 1949.

39. Section 421.02 of Florida State Statutes cited in the proceedings of the Miami City Commission; Office of the Miami City Clerk, Resolution 20354, "A Resolution Authorizing the City Manager to Make a Survey of Sanitary and Slum Conditions in the Downtown Colored Area for the Purpose of Eliminating the Said Conditions and Establishing a Low Cost Housing Project in the Said Area," December 12, 1947, *Resolutions and Minutes of the City Commission, 1921–1986*, Box 35, SAF.

40. Federal Housing Administration interoffice correspondence from A. L. Thompson, racial relations advisor, to Herbert C. Redman, zone commissioner, July 12, 1948, 9, Record Group 207, Housing and Home Finance Agency Race Relations Program 1946–1958 Collection, "Miami, Florida" Folder, Box 750, NA.

41. Planning Board of the City of Miami, Slum Clearance Committee, and Dade County Health Department, *Dwelling Conditions in the Two Principal Blighted Areas: Miami, Florida* (Miami: Planning Board of Miami, 1949), 68; Reinhold P. Wolff and David Gillogly, *Negro Housing in the Miami Area: Effects of the Postwar Building Boom* (Coral Gables: Bureau of Business and Economic Research, University of Miami, 1951), 5.

42. "Starting Points for Discussion" (c. 1960), 1, 4, Record Group 100, Series 226, Records of Florida's Advisory Commission on Race Relations, 1957–1961, Box 8, "Florida Communities—Miami" Folder, SAF.

43. "Governors Advisory Commission on Race Relations" Record Group 100, Series 226, Records of Florida's Advisory Commission on Race Relations, 1957–1961, Box 1, "Commission Minutes" Folder, SAF; Letter from Saul Silverman, staff assistant, Florida's Governor's Office, to the staff of *Phylon Quarterly*, December 29, 1960, Record Group 100, Series 226, Records of Florida's Advisory Commission on Race Relations, 1957–1961, Box 4, "Phylon Periodicals" Folder, SAF; Herbert Hill, "Recent Effects of Racial Conflict on Southern Industrial Development," *Phylon* 20, 4 (Winter 1959): 319–26.

44. Robert C. Weaver, "Class, Race, and Urban Renewal," *Land Economics* 36, 3 (August 1960): 235–51.

45. Wendell E. Pritchett, *Robert Clifton Weaver and the American City: The Life and Times of an Urban Reformer* (Chicago: University of Chicago Press, 2008).

46. Correspondence from Miami Mayor Robert King High to Cody Fowler, chairman of Governor's Commission on Race Relations, March 31, 1960; "Memorandum for Leaders in Dade County Area," October 17, 1960; "An Ordinance Creating a Community Relations Board . . ." (1960), 1; Record Group 100, Series 226, Records of

Florida's Advisory Commission on Race Relations, 1957–1961, Box 8, "Florida Communities—Miami" Folder, SAF.

47. *Miami Times*, December 31, 1992.

48. "Slum Clearance Path Cleared," *Metro Bulletin*, November 27, 1959, 1; *Grubstein v. Urban Renewal Agency*; *Miami Herald*, November 20, 1959.

49. Nancy Raquel Mirabal, "Telling Silences and Making Community: Afro Cubans and African Americans in Ybor City and Tampa, 1899–1915," in Lisa Brock and Digna Castañeda Fuertes, eds., *Between Race and Empire: African Americans and Cubans before the Cuban Revolution*, (Philadelphia: Temple University Press, 1998), 49–69; precedent for the *Grubstein* ruling had been set in *Adams v. Housing Auth. of Daytona Beach*, 60 So. 2d 663 (Fla. 1952).

50. For discussions of the racial uses of the blight discourse, see Wendell E. Pritchett, "The 'Public Menace' of Blight: Urban Renewal and the Private Uses of Eminent Domain," *Yale Law & Policy Review* 21, 1 (2003): 1–52. Some historians have elected to take urban renewal's color-blind language at face value, suggesting any claims blacks make about the intentionality of "Negro Removal" simply represent an attempt to secure reparations; see Milan Dluhy, Keith Revell, Sidney Wong, "Creating a Positive Future for a Minority Community: Transportation and Urban Renewal Politics in Miami," *Journal of Urban Affairs* 24, 1 (2002): 75–95.

51. Office of the Miami City Clerk, Resolution 19821, February 19, 1947; Office of the Miami City Clerk, Resolution 17802, April 29, 1942, *Resolutions and Minutes of the City Commission, 1921–1986*, Box 28, SAF.

52. Metropolitan Dade County Advisory Board and Planning Department, *Preliminary Land Use Plan and Policies for Development*, 1961, 34, "Metro Land Use Plan" Folder, Box 50; "Within recent months . . . ," "Slum Clearance" Folder 2; Box 81; Miami-Dade Chamber of Commerce, "The 53rd Dinner of the Miami-Dade Chamber of Commerce . . ." (1960), "Magic City Center Plan" Folder, Box 46, "WTVJ" collection, HASF.

53. James Russell, "Your Money's Ending Slums—But Not Here," *Miami Herald*, December 15, 1957, 1A.

54. Heathcott, "The City Quietly Remade," 227; Andrew R. Highsmith, "Demolition Means Progress: Urban Renewal, Public Policy, and State-Sanctioned Ghetto Formation in Flint, Michigan," *Journal of Urban History* 35, 3 (March 2009): 348–68, 354–55.

55. *Miami Times*, March 2, 1957, cited in Raymond A. Mohl, "The Interstate and the Cities: Highways, Housing, and the Freeway Revolt" (Washington, D.C.: Poverty and Race Action Council, 2002), 79.

56. "Eliminate Miami's Slums, Then Beautify: Mrs. Range," August 29, 1967, "Slum Clearance" Folder 1, Box 81, WTVJ Collection, HASF.

57. Sonny Wright, interviewed by Electra Ford, August 30, 1997, 22, Tell the Story Collection, BA; T. Willard Fair, quoted in Lawrence Hott and Tom Lewis, *Divided Highways* (Public Broadcasting Service, 1997).

58. "The Urban League Financial and Personnel Report of 1969," prepared by Talmadge Willard Fair, April 30, 1969, "Miami (Fla.), Urban League of Greater, April 1969–June 1982" Folder, National Urban League Papers, Part III, Box 341, LOC.

59. Wright Interview, 22; Miami-Metro News Bureau, "Press Release," June 8, 1961, 2, "Negroes-Miami" Folder, Box 62, WTVJ Collection, HASF; *Miami Times*, August 26, 1966; Opal King, interviewed by Stephanie Wanza, August 20, 1997, 39, Tell the Story Collection, BA.

60. Roberta Thompson, interviewed by Electra R. Ford, August 29, 1997, 19; George Littlefield, interviewed by Devoune Williams, August 12, 1997, 14; Leome Culmer, interviewed by Stephanie Wanza, August 13, 1997, 16; all in Tell the Story Collection, BA.

61. Planning Department Research Division Report, 1982, *Growth and Change: The Black Population of Dade 1950–1980* in Office of Black Affairs, *Blueprint for the 1980s, Part II*, 27, 31, "Government" Box, BA.

62. Marian Shannon, interviewed by Yvonne Daly, August 15, 1997, 14; Rachel Williams, interviewed by Electra R. Ford, August 19, 1997, 21; Genevieve Lockhart, interviewed by Yvonne Daly, August 13, 1997, pp. 10–20; all in Tell the Story Collection, BA.

63. Dorothy Graham, interviewed by Stephanie Wanza, August 5, 1997, p. 22, Tell the Story Collection, BA.

64. Range, 33; Williams, 21; Edward McKinney, interview by Stephanie Wanza, August 30, 1997, 39; all in Tell the Story Collection, BA; *Miami Herald*, November 20, 1966.

65. Planning Board of the City of Miami, The Slum Clearance Committee, and the Dade County Health Department, *Dwelling Condition in the Two Principle Blighted Areas* (1950), 41; "Statement of Bernard J. Dyer," *Oversight of Federal Housing and Community Development Plans in the State of Florida*, Hearing before the Subcommittee on Housing of the Committee on Banking and Currency, House of Representatives, 92nd Cong., 1st sess., Miami, October 8, 1971 (Washington, D.C.: Government Printing Office, 1971), 218–19.

66. *Miami Report*, Appendix IV; Al Featherstone, testimony before Florida Commission on Human Relations, public hearing regarding the "Miami Crisis" of June 13–19, 1970, Miami, July 1, 1970, 4, Files of the Florida Commission on Human Relations, Record Group 891, Series 382, Box 1, SAF.

67. See, for instance, James Robert Saunders and Renae Nadine Shackleford, *Urban Renewal and the End of Black Culture in Charlottesville, Virginia: An Oral History of Vinegar Hill* (Jefferson, N.C..: McFarland, 1998).

68. In his discussion of the suburban origins of America's shifting political center, Matthew Lassiter argues that regional distinctiveness—in political, demographic, and economic terms—ceased to matter in direct proportion to the suburbanization of the South, North, and West in the postwar period; Lassiter, *The Silent Majority*.

69. Andrew Weise, "African American Suburbanization and Regionalism in the

Modern South," in Matthew D. Lassiter and Joseph Crespino, eds., *The Myth of Southern Exceptionalism* (New York: Oxford University Press, 2009), 210–11.

70. Lisa Lekis, "A Study of the Demographics, Needs, Unmet Needs and Services Available to the Black Community, Broward County, Florida" (Community Service Council of Broward County, Inc., August 22, 1980), 32.

71. http://www.miamiherald.com/multimedia/news/houseoflies/; http://takeback theland.org/, last accessed December 14, 2009; George Packer, "The Ponzi State," *New Yorker*, February 9, 2009, 81.

72. http://business.theatlantic.com/2009/06/whats_wrong_with_florida_and_california.php, accessed December 14, 2009.

73. Marc A. Weiss, "The Origins and Legacy of Urban Renewal," in J. Paul Mitchell, ed., *Federal Housing Policy and Programs: Past and Present* (New Brunswick, N.J.: Center for Urban Policy and Research 1985), 253–76. See also Arnold R. Hirsch, *Making the Second Ghetto: Race and Housing in Chicago* (Chicago: University of Chicago Press, 1983, 1998); Raymond A. Mohl, "Making the Second Ghetto in Metropolitan Miami, 1940–1960," *Journal of Urban History* 21, 3 (May 1995): 395–427.

Chapter 7. Racial Liberalism and the Rise of the Sunbelt West:
The Defeat of Fair Housing on the 1964 California Ballot

1. Kevin Phillips, *The Emerging Republican Majority* (New Rochelle, N.Y.: Arlington House, 1969), 440–50.

2. "California: Proposition 14," *Time*, September 25, 1964, 23.

3. Phillips, *The Emerging Republican Majority*, 446.

4. Ethan Rarick, *California Rising: The Life and Times of Pat Brown* (Berkeley: University of California Press, 2005), 255–71.

5. The Kennedy Order of November 20, 1962, covered all FHA and VA financed mortgages made after that date, as well as all public housing and urban renewal projects. John Denton, *Apartheid American Style* (Berkeley, Calif.: Diablo Press, 1967), 9.

6. *Shelley v. Kraemer*, 334 U.S. 1 (1948).

7. "Human Relations," vol. 1, no. 1, 1964, Box 169, Folder 2, Alexander Pope Collection.

8. Jack Lagguth, "Figures Tell of Segregation," *Valley Times*, February 28, 1963.

9. "Negroes Raise Civil Rights War Chant in Westside Mass Meeting," *Westwood Hills Citizen*, July 11, 1963, Folder 7, Box 111, American Civil Liberties Union of Southern California Collection (hereafter ACLU).

10. "Owner Agrees to Integrate Torrance Tract," *Los Angeles Times*, July 13, 1963.

11. "Brown Calls on Aides to Save Housing Act," *Los Angeles Times*, October 29, 1963.

12. Robert O. Self, *American Babylon: Race and the Struggle for Postwar Oakland* (Princeton, N.J.: Princeton University Press, 2003), 265.

13. Ibid.
14. Denton, *Apartheid American Style*, chap. 1.
15. Cited in Thomas Casstevens, *Politics, Housing and Race Relations: California's Rumford Act and Proposition 14* (Berkeley: Institute of Governmental Studies, University of California, 1967), 58.
16. See Rutledge memorandum, 12, Box 168, Folder "Housing: Prop 14," ACLU. Local referendums or initiatives opposing antidiscrimination measures were also being supported by the NAREB in Berkeley in 1963 and in Detroit and Seattle in 1964, but all observers agreed that California would be a singularly important arena for this debate. Denton, *Apartheid American Style*, 19–22.
17. Rarick, *California Rising*, 261–70.
18. *California Real Estate Magazine*, May 1963, 19. A 1965 assessment of the Proposition 14 debate written by the National Committee Against Discrimination in Housing suggested that CREA had been planning the strategy for an initiative amendment for several years.
19. California Secretary of State, "Proposed Amendments to the Constitution, General Election, November 3, 1964" (1964), 13.
20. The legal analysis is cited from "A Legal Opinion on Prop 14 and a Description of Its Effects on the Constitution and the Laws of the State of California," n.d., Box 29, Folder 1, California Democratic Council Collection, Southern California Library for Social Studies and Research, Los Angeles (hereafter CDC-SCL).
21. One of the main campaign spokespersons for the CHP, William Shearers, was a regular contributor to the White Citizens Council of America. See NAACP flyer in Box 105, Folder 61, Records of the National Association for the Advancement of Colored People, Region I, Bancroft Library, UC Berkeley (hereafter NAACP-UCB). Reference to the assessment of realtors, Memorandum Bill Becker to Governor Brown, November 6, 1963, carton 1, California Federation for Civic Unity Papers, Bancroft Library, UC Berkeley (hereafter CFCU).
22. Cited in Casstevens, *Politics, Housing and Race Relations*, 49.
23. "Realtor's News," n.d., Box 17, Folder "Rumford," Marie Koenig Papers, Huntington Library, San Marino, California (hereafter MKP).
24. See, for example, closed minutes, Southwest Realty Board, January 20, 1964, Box 26, Folder 12, Loren Miller Papers, Huntington Library, San Marino, California (hereafter LM).
25. "Apartment Association Kickoff Rally Memo, December 3, 1964," Box 26, Folder 12, LM.
26. The CREA estimated that it collected nearly one million signatures in total, including those gathered for a supplemental filing. See *California Real Estate Magazine*, March 1964, 5.
27. At one point, Dr. Nolan Frizzelle, president of the California Republican Assembly, was quoted as saying that "the essence of freedom is the right to discriminate." Such candid expressions, however, rarely appeared in official campaign literature of

statements of the CHP, and Frizzelle was quickly condemned by other Proposition 14 supporters. See Kurt Schuparra, *Triumph of the Right: The Rise of the California Conservative Movement, 1945–1966* (Armonk, N.Y.: M.E. Sharpe, 1998), 105.

28. "Statement of Policy," adopted June 4, 1963, by the NAREB and June 22, 1963, by CREA, Box 26, Folder 12, LM.

29. "Director's Minutes," *California Real Estate Magazine*, August 1963, 16, 18.

30. "Decision on Housing Initiative," *Los Angeles Times*, February 2, 1964. The majority of major daily newspapers in Northern California came out against the initiative. See *Casstevens, Politics, Housing and Race Relations*, chap. 4.

31. "Property Owners Bill of Rights" pamphlet, published by CREA, Box 17, Folder "Rumford," MKP.

32. Ibid.

33. "Yes on 14" pamphlet, Box 17, Folder "Rumford," MKP.

34. California Secretary of State, "Proposed Amendments to the Constitution, General Election, November 3, 1964," 18–19.

35. "Proposition 14: The Cases for and Against," *Los Angeles Times*, September 20, 1964.

36. Ibid.

37. Cheryl I. Harris, "Whiteness as Property," *Harvard Law Review* 106, 8 (1993): 1714.

38. California Secretary of State, "Proposed Amendments to the Constitution, General Election, November 3, 1964," 18.

39. CREA pamphlet, "Property Owners Bill of Rights."

40. *Realtor News*, Folder: "Rumford," Box 17, MKP.

41. L. H. Wilson speech at the Changing Peninsula Forum, Part III, February 20, 1964, "Proposition 14 Campaign Materials," Institute of Governmental Studies (hereafter IGS), UC Berkeley.

42. Cited in "No on Prop 14 Alameda County," press release, October 12, 1964, "Proposition 14 Campaign Materials," IGS.

43. "Rockefeller Backs Housing Law," *Bay Area Independent*, February 1, 1964, Box 104, Folder 1, NAACP-UCB.

44. On church-based activism on behalf of Proposition 14, see Darren Dochuk, *From Bible Belt to Sunbelt: Plain-Folk Religion, Grassroots Politics and the Rise of Evangelical Conservatism* (New York: Norton, 2010); Matthew Dallek, *The Right Moment: Ronald Reagan's First Victory and the Decisive Turning Point in American Politics* (New York: Free Press, 2000); Lou Cannon, *Governor Reagan: His Rise to Power* (New York: PublicAffairs, 2003).

45. Casstevens, *Politics, Housing and Race Relations*, 57; Ronald Reagan's "A Time for Choosing" address, October 27, 1964, http://www.reagan.utexas.edu/archives/reference/timechoosing.html, accessed October 1, 2009.

46. "Stenographers Reports" May 7, 1964, and May 28, 1964, Box 16, Los Angeles

County Chamber of Commerce Papers. See also minutes, Board meetings January 19, 1964–December 17, 1964, Box 35.

47. "Fight on Housing Law Hit," *Palo Alto Times*, November 19, 1963; "News from CAP 14," Newsletter 10, October 2, 1964, "Proposition 14 Campaign Materials," IGS.

48. Earle Vaughan, "Facing the Inevitable Changes," *Apartment Journal*, October 1963, Carton 1, CFCU.

49. Cited in Rutledge memorandum, 8, Box 198, Folder "Housing: Prop 14," ACLU.

50. Belford Gardens letter, November 26, 1963, Box 26, Folder 12, LM.

51. Minutes, CDC statewide convention in Long Beach, December, 1963, Box 29, Folder 1, CDC-SCL.

52. Casstevens, *Politics, Housing and Race Relations*, 62.

53. On "responsible liberalism," see Martin J. Schiesl, *Responsible Liberalism: Edmund G. "Pat" Brown and Reform Government in California 1958–1967* (Los Angeles: Edmund G. "Pat" Brown Institute of Public Affairs, 2003).

54. Lucien Haas, oral-history interview, conducted 1989 by Carlos Vasquez, UCLA Oral History Program, for the California State Archives State Government Oral History Program," 135.

55. CDC memorandums, Box 29, Folder 1, CDC-SCL.

56. Brown speech to the women's group on August 20, 1964, Box 29, Folder 1, CDC-SCL. Brown spent much of the fall condemning Goldwater as an extremist as well, declaring that there was "the stench of fascism in the air." Cited in Rarick, *California Rising*, 288.

57. California secretary of state, "Proposed Amendments to the Constitution, General Election, November 3, 1964" (California Secretary of State: Sacramento), emphasis original.

58. Anderson's speech excerpted in October 9 press release by CAP14, Box 29, Folder 1, CDC-SCL.

59. See generally, Jerry Gonzalez, "A Place in the Sun: Mexican American Identity, Race, and the Suburbanization of Los Angeles, 1940–1980" (Ph.D. dissertation, University of Southern California, 2008).

60. Various materials related to Hollywood involvement in CAP 14, Box 29, Folder 1, CDC-SCL.

61. See "Press Release: United Civil Rights Committee," n.d., Box 116, Folder "1964 United Civil Rights Committee," ACLU. Example of MAPA flyers, Box 9, Folder 20, Eduardo Quevedo Papers, Stanford University (hereafter EQ)

62. Flyer, "Eliminating Housing Discrimination in California," Box 27, Folder 14,CDC-SCL.

63. CORE leaflet, Box 5, Folder 7, Max Mont Collection, Urban Archives Center, California State University Northridge (hereafter MM).

64. "Report on Operation of NAACP Headquarters for No on Proposition 14," November 16, 1964, Box 5, Folder 21, MM.

65. Carta Editorial, vol. 2, no. 6, August 20, 1964, p. 3, MO224, Box 54, Folder 8, Ernesto Galaraza Papers, Stanford University (hereafter EG).

66. Carta Editorial, vol. 2, no. 10, October 29, 1964, Box 9, Folder 20, EG.

67. "A Manual for the 'Constitutional Amendment-No!' Campaign," February 5, 1964, 2. California Committee for Fair Practices. Box 4, Folder 20, "Campaign Manual & Organization," MM.

68. Becker to Max Mont et al., April 10, 1964, Box 5, Folder 1, MM.

69. Excerpted from release "Clergy and Christian Social Relations Chairman of the Episcopal Diocese of Los Angeles: Fact Sheet on Proposed Initiative to Cancel the Rumford Fair Housing Act," Box 16, Folder "Housing," MKP.

70. "The Church Says No on Proposition 14," Council of Churches in Northern and Southern California, Box 16, Folder "Housing," MKP.

71. Brown's comments, widely quoted in the press, were seized upon by the CHP, which charged that the governor was resorting to desperate scare tactics. See CHP pamphlets, Box 17, Folder "Rumford," MKP.

72. From ACLU fundraising letter to supporters, February 1, 1964, MKP.

73. See daily news releases from CAP14, October, 1964, Box 29, Folder 1, CDC-SCL.

74. For an excellent case study of such activity, see Becky M. Nicolaides, *My Blue Heaven: Life and Politics in the Working-Class Suburbs of Los Angeles, 1920–1965* (Chicago: University of Chicago Press, 2002).

75. Gathered from data cited in Casstevens, *Politics, Housing and Race Relations*, 56, 68.

76. Ibid., 68–74.

77. Los Angeles County election returns, California Democratic Council report, Box 29, Folder 1, CDC-SCL.

78. Richard Kline, "Richard Kline: Governor Brown's Faithful Advisor. Oral History Interview, Conducted by Eleanor Glaser" (Sacramento: California State Government Oral History Program, 1977), 18–19.

79. Haas, oral history interview, 134–35.

80. African Americans constituted 1.06 percent of the total population of West Los Angeles in 1950 and 1.75 percent in 1960. "A Comparative Statistical Analysis of Population by Race for Incorporated Cities of Los Angeles County, 1950–1956–1960," Box 169, Folder 3, Alexander Pope Papers, Huntington Library.

81. *Mulkey v. Reitman*, 64 Cal.2d 877 (1966).

82. Petition for a Writ of Certiorari to the Supreme Court of the State of California, *Mulkey v. Reitman*, August 25, 1966, William French Smith, Counsel for petitioners. (Smith was retained to represent apartment owners who had evicted tenants after the passage of Proposition 14).

83. "Reasons Given for Size of Reagan and Yorty Votes," *Los Angeles Times*, June 12, 1966.
84. Bill Boyarsky, *The Rise of Ronald Reagan* (New York: Random House, 1968), 205.
85. Lee Edwards, *Reagan: A Political Biography* (San Diego: Viewpoint Books, 1967), 156. "Reagan Assails Rumford Act Study in Hard Attack on Brown," *Los Angeles Times*, October 13, 1966.
86. Boyarsky, *The Rise of Ronald Reagan*, 205.
87. Phillips, *The Emerging Republican Majority*, 441.
88. Boyarsky, *The Rise of Ronald Reagan*, 203; Cannon, *Governor Reagan*, 201–4.
89. Mike Davis, *City of Quartz: Excavating the Future in Los Angeles* (New York: Vintage, 1990), 153.
90. For a detailed account of these ballot measures, see Daniel Martinez HoSang, *Racial Propositions: Ballot Initiatives and the Making of Postwar California*, American Crossroads (Berkeley: University of California Press, 2010).

Chapter 8. Sunbelt Lock-Up: Where the Suburbs Met the Super-Max

1. "Patents: A Prison That Looks like a Suburb Enclosed in Barbed Wire," *New York Times*, October 3, 1994; Lorna Rhodes, *Total Confinement: Madness and Reason in the Maximum Security Prison* (Berkeley: University of California Press, 2004), 36–37.
2. Michael Flamm, *Law and Order: Street Crime, Civil Unrest, and the Crisis of Liberalism in the 1960s* (New York: Columbia University Press, 2005), 148–50.
3. Rebecca McLennan, "The New Penal State: Globalization, History, and American Criminal Justice," *Inter-Asia Cultural Studies* 2, 3 (December 2001): 407–19, 413; Jonathan Simon, "Rise of the Carceral State," *Social Research* 74, 2 (Summer 2007): 471–508.
4. Michael Meranze, *Laboratories of Virtue: Punishment, Revolution, and Authority, 1760–1835* (Chapel Hill: University of North Carolina Press, 1996), 136; Louis P. Masur, *Rites of Execution: Capital Punishment and the Transformation of American Culture, 1776–1865* (New York: Oxford University Press, 1991).
5. Eric Avila, *Popular Culture in the Age of White Flight: Fear and Fantasy in Suburban Los Angeles* (Berkeley: University of California, 2006), 142. This hypothesis is inspired by the work of David Garland, *The Culture of Control: Crime and Social Order in Contemporary Society* (Chicago: University of Chicago Press, 2001), 77–79.
6. Rebecca McLennan, *The Crisis of Imprisonment: Protest, Politics, and the Making of the American Penal State, 1776–1941* (Cambridge: Cambridge University Press, 2008). Emphasizing the continuity between slavery and imprisonment are Loïc J. D. Wacquant, *Les Prisons de la misère* (Paris: Liber, 1999); Wacquant, "From Slavery to Mass Incarceration: Rethinking the 'Race Question' in the U.S.," *New Left Review* 13

(2002): 41–60; Christian Parenti, "The 'New' Criminal Justice System: State Repression From 1868 to 2001," *Monthly Review* 53, 3 (2001): 19; Kim Gilmore, "Slavery and Prison: Understanding the Connections," *Social Justice* 27, 3 (2000): 195–212; Robert P. Weiss, "Humanitarianism, Labour Exploitation, or Social Control? A Critical Survey of Theory and Research on the Origin and Development of Prisons," *Social History* 12, 3 (1987): 331–50; Timothy Gilfoyle, "The Tombs and the Experience of Criminal Justice in New York City, 1838–1897," *Journal of Urban History* 29, 5 (2003): 525–54; Rebecca McLennan, "Imprisonment's 'Square Deal': Prisoners and Their Keepers in the 1920s New York," *Journal of Urban History* 28, 5 (2003): 597–619; Charles Bright, *The Powers That Punish: Prison and Politics in the Era of the "Big House," 1920–1955* (Ann Arbor: University of Michigan Press, 1996); Alex Lichtenstein, *Twice the Work of Free Labor: The Political Economy of Convict Labor in the New South* (New York: Verso, 1996); Peter Wallenstein, *From Slave South to New South: Public Policy in Nineteenth-Century Georgia* (Chapel Hill: University of North Carolina Press 1987).

7. Robert T. Chase, "Building Tenders, Slaves of the State, and Jail House Attorneys: The Evolution of a Prison-Made Civil Rights Movement," in *Race, Labor, and the City*, special issue, *Labor: Studies in Working-Class History of the Americas* 7, 3 (2010); Norwood Henry Andrews III, "Sunbelt Justice: Politics, the Professions, and the History of Sentencing and Corrections in Texas Since 1968" (Ph.D. dissertation, University of Texas, 2007); Robert Perkinson, *Texas Tough: The Rise of America's Prison Empire* (New York: Metropolitan Books, 2010).

8. Judith Johnson, "For Any Good at All: A Comparative Study of State Penitentiaries in Arizona, Nevada, New Mexico, and Utah from 1900 to 1980" (Ph.D. dissertation, University of New Mexico, 1987); John Aubrey Douglass, "Earl Warren's New Deal: Economic Transition, Postwar Planning, and Higher Education in California," *Journal of Policy History* 12, 4 (2000): 473–512, esp. 475, 480, 487; Public Service Broadcast by Governor Earl Warren, ABC Network, December 6, 1949, Folder F3717:1374, Speeches, 1948–1957, Department of Corrections Records, California State Archives (hereafter CSA).

9. Alexander Pisciotta, *Benevolent Repression: Social Control and the American Reformatory-Prison Movement* (New York: New York University Press, 1994); Bright, *The Powers That Punish*, 248–249; Jonathan Simon, *Poor Discipline: Parole and the Social Control of the Underclass, 1890–1990* (Chicago: University of Chicago Press, 1993), 62; "Prison Labor—Past and Future," in *Proceedings of American Prison Association, St. Paul, Minnesota, October 2–7, 1938* (New York: American Prison Association 1939), 327–29; James B. Jacobs, *Stateville: The Penitentiary in Mass Society* (Chicago: University of Chicago Press, 1978); McLennan, *Crisis of Imprisonment*; Richard A. McGee, *Riots and Disturbances in Correctional Institutions* (Washington, D.C.: American Prison Association, 1952); Austin H. McCormick, "Behind the Prison Riots," *Annals of the American Academy of Political and Social Science* 293 (1954): 18–19; Gresham M. Sykes,

The Society of Captives: A Study of a Maximum Security Prison (Princeton, N.J.: Princeton University Press, 1958).

10. Vernon Fox, "Reputational Rankings of American Prison System," *Indian Journal of Social Research* 5, 3 (1964): 279–88, 280–82. Only Missouri and Wyoming broke the pattern.

11. John Irwin, *Prisons in Turmoil* (Boston: Little, Brown, 1980), 56, 61; Blake McKelvey, *American Prisons: A History of Good Intentions* (Montclair, N.J.: P. Smith, 1977), 324; Flamm, *Law and Order*, 17–19.

12. Maury Maverick, "Pennsylvania Penal Program Viewed by the Prison Industries Division of the War Production Board," *Prison Journal* 23, 4 (December 1943): 379–93, 385, 387; Negley Teeters, "The Loss of Civil Rights of the Convicted Felon and Their Reinstatement," *Centennial Issue: Police, Jails, Civil Rights, Prison Journal* 25, 3 (July 1945): 77–87, 79, 81; *Coffin v. Reichard* 143 F.2d 443 (1944); McLennan, *Crisis of Imprisonment*, 116–18.

13. Christopher Smith, "Black Muslims and the Development of Prisoners' Rights," *Journal of Black Studies* 24, 2 (December 1993): 131–46, 138.

14. Milton Burdman to Director McGee, August 16, 1960; Folder F3717:588, Incidents in Folsom, 1949–1960, Correctional Program Services, Department of Corrections Records, CSA; A.B. 61/40 Islamic Literature, April 4, 1961, Folder F3717:1387, Administrative Bulletins 1961, Corrections Administration, CSA.

15. Lawrence E. Wilson to Walter Dunbar, May 15, 1962, Folder F3717:383, Asst. Dir. Investigation Files on National Emancipation Proclamation Centennial Observance Committee of Philadelphia 1962, Corrections Administration, CSA; Asst. Dir. to Walter Dunbar, March 15, 1963, and San Quentin Ass. Warden L. S. Nelson to Walter Dunbar, March 6, 1963, Folder F3717:379, Asst. Dir. Investigation Files, Muslim Assassination Plot, 1963, CSA; Steve Estes, *I Am A Man! Race, Manhood, and the Civil Rights Movement* (Chapel Hill: University of North Carolina Press, 2005), 88; Walter Dunbar to Lt. Robert Gray, Intelligence Section, Indiana State Police, March 29, 1966, 2, Folder F3717:378, Asst. Dir. Investigation Files, Muslim Correspondence, 1961–1968, Corrections Administration, CSA.

16. James C. Cobb, "The Sunbelt South: Industrialization in Regional, National, and International Perspective," in Raymond A. Mohl (ed.), *Searching for the Sunbelt: Historical Perspectives on a Region* (Athens: University of Georgia Press, 1993), 25–46, 35.

17. Bayard Rustin, "The Watts 'Manifesto' and the McCone Report," *Commentary* 41, 30 (1966): 29–35, 32.

18. Thomas Sugrue, *The Origins of the Urban Crisis: Race and Inequality in Postwar Detroit* (Princeton, N.J.: Princeton University Press, 2005).

19. John M. Findlay, *Magic Lands: Western Cityscapes and American Culture After 1940* (Berkeley: University of California Press, 1992); Josh Sides, *L. A. City Limits: African American Los Angeles from the Great Depression to the Present* (Berkeley: University of California Press, 2003).

20. Avila, *Popular Culture in the Age of White Flight*.

21. William J. Wilson, "The Cost of Racial and Class Exclusion from the Inner City," *Annals of the American Academy of Political and Social Science* 501 (1989): 8–25; Loïc J. D. Wacquant, "Deadly Symbiosis: When Ghetto and Prison Meet and Mesh" *Punishment & Society* 3 (2001): 95–133. For expert testimony from the McCone Commission, see California Governor's Commission on the Los Angeles Riots, vol. 17: Reports of Consultants (Los Angeles, 1965).

22. Quoted in Richard A. Berk, Harold Brackman, and Selma Lesser, *A Measure of Justice: An Empirical Study of Changes in the California Penal Code, 1955–1971* (New York: Academic Press, 1977), 138.

23. Polls indicated that Americans increasingly connected crime in the streets with riots. James Q. Wilson, "The Urban Mood," *Commentary* 48, 4 (1969): 52–61.

24. McLennan, "The New Penal State," 414; Folder: Juvenile Delinquency, Box 73, Correspondence Unit, 1968, Administration, Ronald Reagan Gubernatorial Records, Ronald Reagan Presidential Library, National Archives and Records Administration, Simi Valley, Calif. (hereafter RRPL); Folder State Prisons, Box 62, Correspondence Unit, 1968, RRPL; Brinton H. Stone on February 26, 1968, Folder: Riots June (2 of 2), Box 83, Administration 1968, RRPL; *Reynolds v. Sims*, 377 U.S. 533 (1964); Totton J. Anderson and Eugene C. Lee, "The 1966 Election in California," *Western Political Quarterly* 20, 2 (June 1967): 535–54.

25. Thomas E. Cronin, Tania Z. Cronin, and Michael E. Milakovich, *U.S. v. Crime in the Street* (Bloomington: Indiana University Press, 1981), 60, 69; Bert Useem and Peter Kimball, *States of Siege: U.S. Prison Riots, 1971–1986* (New York: Oxford University Press, 1987), 15; Flamm, *Law and Order*, 68, 170, 148–50; Parenti, "The 'New' Criminal Justice System," 19; Lisa McGirr, *Suburban Warriors: The Origins of the American Right* (Princeton, N.J.: Princeton University Press, 2002), 188, 204; Robert W. Winslow, ed., *Crime in a Free Society: Selections from the President's Commission on Law Enforcement and Administration of Justice* (Belmont, Calif.: Dickenson, 1968), 361; Diana R. Gordon, *The Justice Juggernaut: Fighting Street Crime, Controlling Citizens* (New Brunswick, N.J.: Rutgers University Press, 1990), 200–201; Jennifer Mittelstadt, *From Welfare to Workfare: The Unintended Consequences of Liberal Reform, 1945–1965* (Chapel Hill: North Carolina Press 2005).

26. Michael Flamm, *Law and* Order, 148–50; Dan Baum, *Smoke and Mirrors: The War on Drugs and the Politics of Failure* (Boston: Back Bay Books, 1997).

27. "Riots and Crime," President's Commission on Law Enforcement and Administration of Justice, *Task Force Report: Crime and Its Impact—An Assessment* (Washington, D.C.: Government Printing Office, 1967), 116–22, 116.

28. Johnny Urdaburn, "Chino: A City of Men C.I.M. U.S.A," *Pioneer News*, June 1966, 11–13, in Folder F3717:1839, California Institution for Men (Chino) Newsletters, 1966, Institutions, Publications, Department of Corrections Records, CSA.

29. Nicholas Horrok, "New Breed Of Convict: Black, Angry and Radical," *San Jose Mercury*, September 26, 1971, 58; Allen F. Breed, *The Significance of Classification*

Procedures to the Field of Correction, in United States President's Commission on Law Enforcement and Administration of Justice Report (Washington, D.C.: Government Printing Office, 1967); David A. Ward, "Evaluative Research for Corrections," in Lloyd Ohlin, ed., *Prisoners in America* (New York: Columbia University Press, 1973), 184–206, 200–201. Phoenix, Denver, Houston, Nashville, Memphis, Birmingham, Atlanta, Miami, Tampa, Jacksonville, and Columbia (South Carolina) all witnessed riots between 1964 and 1968.

30. "Folsom Prison Lock-Up Is Over," *San Francisco Chronicle*, November 24, 1970, 3; Eric Cummins, *The Rise and Fall of California's Radical Prison Movement* (Stanford, Calif.: Stanford University Press, 1994); Useem and Kimball, *States of Siege*; *Nolan v. Fitzpatrick*, 451 F.2d 454 (1st Cir. 1971), established a prisoner's right to communicate with the press. *National Prisoners Reform Ass'n v. Sharkey*, No. 4884 (D.R.I. April 28, 1972), granted prisoners the right to freedom of association. In 1972, *Cruz v. Beto*, 405 U.S. 319, the court held that "Federal courts sit not to supervise prisons but to enforce the constitutional rights of all 'persons' which include prisoners." *Morrissey v. Brewer*, 408 U.S. 471 (1972), and *Wolff v. McDonnell*, 418 U.S. 539 (1974), significantly broadened prisoners' due process rights against administrative changes to their sentences under the indeterminate sentencing guidelines. James B. Jacobs, "Macrosociology and Imprisonment," in David F. Greenberg, ed., *Corrections and Punishment* (Beverly Hills: Sage, 1999) 89–107, 96.

31. Scott Christianson, "Correctional Law Developments: Prison Labor and Unionization—Legal Developments," *Criminal Law Bulletin* 14, 3 (1978): 243–47; Ronald M. Berkman, *Opening the Gates: The Rise of the Prisoners' Movement* (Princeton, N.J.: Princeton University Press, 1977), 68. Unions successfully pushed the "conception of a prisoner as a citizen in a temporarily reduced legal status." Irwin, *Prisons in Turmoil*, 105; "Note on Bargaining in Correctional Institutions: Restructuring the Relationship Between the Inmate and the Prison Authority," *Yale Law Journal* 81 (1972): 726–57; Frank Browning, "Organizing Behind Bars," *Ramparts* 10 (1972): 40–45. See *Sprouse v. Federal Prison Indus., Inc.*, 480 F.2d 1 (5th Cir. 1973); *Harris v. Yeager*, 291 F. Supp. 1015 (D.N.J. 1968), and *Pennsylvania ex rel. Raymond v. Rundle*, 339 F.2d 598 (3d Cir. 1964). Prisoners had no legal claim to wages at all, the court stated in *Holt v. Sarver*, 309 F. Supp. 362 (E.D. Ark. 1970).

32. Ruth Gilmore, *Golden Gulag: Prisons, Surplus, Crisis, and Opposition in Globalizing California* (Berkeley: University of California Press, 2007), 88–101.

33. Next to Texas, court-ordered reform took place in Alabama, Arkansas, Mississippi, South Carolina, Tennessee, New Mexico, Alaska, Delaware, and Rhode Island. Malcolm M. Feeley and Edward L. Rubin, *Judicial Policy Making and the Modern State: How the Courts Reformed America's Prisons* (New York: Cambridge University Press, 1998), 41; Chase, "Hidden Economy Under Chained Hands," 11; Wilbert Rideau and Billy Sinclair, "Prisoner Litigation: How It Began in Louisiana," *Louisiana Law Review* 45 (May 1985): 1061–76.

34. 503 F. Supp. 1265 (S.D. Tex. 1980).

35. Sheldon Ekland-Olson, "Crowding, Social Control, and Prison Violence: Evidence from the Post-Ruiz Years in Texas," *Law & Society Review* 20, 3 (1986): 389–422, esp. 390; Andrews, "Sunbelt Justice"; Mark Colvin, "The 1980 New Mexico Prison Riot," *Social Problems* 29, 5 (June 1982): 449–63.

36. Gilmore, *Golden Gulag*, 107–11.

37. Franklin E. Zimring, Gordon Hawkins, and Sam Kamin, *Punishment and Democracy: Three Strikes and You're Out in California* (New York: Oxford University Press, 2001), 200, 232; Garland, *Culture of Control*, 15, 142–43, 145.

38. The rich body of scholarship on Sunbelt conservatism conveys a sense of the white middle class's hardened sense of mission in response to its sense of violation and victimization since the 1960s. Paul Wright, "Victims 'Rights' as a Stalking-horse for State Repression," in Tara Herivel and Paul Wright, eds., *Prison Nation: The Warehousing of America's Poor* (New York: Routledge, 2003), 60–64; Marie Gottschalk, *The Prison and the Gallows: The Politics of Mass Incarceration in America* (New York: Cambridge University Press, 2006); Peter Dreier, "America's Urban Crisis: Symptoms, Causes, Solutions," *North Carolina Law Review* 71 (June 1993): 1351–1400, 1367; Alan Booth et al., "Correlates of City Crime Rates: Victimization Surveys Versus Official Statistics," *Social Problems* 25, 2 (December 1977): 187–97, 196; Raymond J. Michalowski and Michael A. Pearson, "Punishment and Social Structure at the State Level: A Cross Sectional Comparison of 1970 and 1980," *Journal of Research in Crime and Delinquency* 27, 1 (February 1990): 52–78, 52.

39. Edward J. Blakely and May Gail Snyde, *Fortress America: Gated Communities in the United States* (New York: Brookings Institution Press, 1997), 40. States at the forefront of prison expansion have also seen the most dramatic growth in gated communities. Mona Lynch, *Sunbelt Justice: Arizona and the Transformation of American Punishment* (Stanford, Calif.: Stanford Law Books, 2010); Katherine Becket and Steve Herbert, "Dealing with Disorder: Social Control in the Post-Industrial City," *Theoretical Criminology* 12, 1 (2008): 5–30; Steven Flusty, *Building Paranoia: The Proliferation of Interdictory Space and the Erosion of Spatial Justice* (Los Angeles: Los Angeles Forum for Architecture and Urban Design, 1994); Susan Christopherson, "The Fortress City: Privatized Spaces, Consumer Citizenship," in Ash Amin, ed., *Post-Fordism: A Reader* (Oxford: Blackwell Publishing, 1994), 409–27; Garland, *Culture of Control*, 153–55, 262; Flamm, *Law and Order*, 170; Gilmore, *The Golden Gulag*, 107.

40. Michele Hoyman and Micah Weinberg, "The Process of Policy Innovation: Prison Sitings in Rural North Carolina," *Policy Studies Journal* 34, 1 (2006): 95–112, 97–98; Volker Janssen, "When the 'Jungle' Met the Forest: Public Work, Civil Defense, and Prison Camps in Postwar California," *Journal of American History* 96, 3 (December 2009): 702–26; Gregory Hooks, Clayton Mosher, Thomas Rotolo, and Linda Lobao, "The Prison Industry: Carceral Expansion and Employment in U.S. Counties, 1969–1994," *Social Science Quarterly* 85, 1 (March 2004): 37–55, 37; Gilmore, *The Golden Gulag*, 148–66; Roger W. Lotchin, "The Origins of the Sunbelt–Frostbelt Struggle: Defense Spending and City Building," in Mohl, ed., *Searching for the Sunbelt*, 47–68.

41. Peter T. Kilborn, "Rural Towns Turn to Prisons to Reignite Their Economies," *New York Times*, August 1, 2001, A1. For the origins of California's CCPOA, see Volker Janssen, *Convict Labor, Civic Welfare: Prisons and Rehabilitation in Mid-Twentieth-Century America* (Oxford: Oxford University Press, forthcoming).

42. Alison Tarmann, "Fifty Years of Demographic Change in Rural America," Population Reference Bureau, January 2003; Amy K. Glasmeier and Tracey Farrigan, "The Economic Impacts of the Prison Development Boom on Persistently Poor Rural Places," *International Regional Science Review* 30, 3 (July 2007): 274–99, 275, 294; Kenneth M. Johnson and Calvin L. Beale, "The Rural Rebound: Revival of Rural America," *Wilson Quarterly* 22, 2 (Spring 2002): 16–34, 2; Hooks et al., "The Prison Industry," 37.

43. Joseph T. Hallinan, *Going up the River: Travels in a Prison Nation* (New York: Random House, 2001).

44. Gilmore, *The Golden Gulag*, 158; Daniel Glaser, "Politicalization," *American Journal of Criminology* 6, 9 (1972): 8–10, 20–22, 37; Folder F3717:1780, Camps U.S.F.S. 1951–1954, 1959–1963, Sierra Conservation Center, Box California Conservation Camp Services, Department of Corrections Records, CSA; James Williams, former NAACP president, to Department of Corrections, February 2, 1973, Folder F3717:1780, Sierra Conservation Camp, Correspondence, 1972–76, Department of Corrections Records, CSA.

45. Tarmann, "Fifty Years of Demographic Change in Rural America" 5 percent of the population moving to rural counties between the census of 1980 and 1990 were actually prisoners. Christian Parenti, *Lockdown America: Police and Prisons in the Age of Crisis* (London: Verso, 1999), 211–13; Matthew R. Engel, "When a Prison Comes to Town: Sting, Location, and Perceived Impacts of Correctional Facilities in the Midwest" (Ph.D. dissertation, University of Nebraska, 2007), 55–146; Sarah Lawrence and Jeremy Travis, *The New Landscape of Imprisonment: Mapping America's Prison Expansion*. Research Report (Washington D.C.: Urban Institute, Justice Policy Center April 2004), 3, 32.

46. Lawrence and Travis, *The New Landscape of Imprisonment*, 32.

47. Ibid., 19–30.

48. Gilmore, *Golden Gulag*, 68–69.

49. The efforts of low-income Americans to rise to the living standards previous generations had achieved in the New Deal welfare state are discussed in Louise Lamphere, *Sunbelt Working Mothers: Reconciling Family and Factory* (Ithaca, N.Y.: Cornell University Press, 1993); Michael E. Lewyn, "Are Spread Out Cities Really Safer?" *Cleveland State Law Review* 41 (1993): 279–95 ; Jane Jacobs, *The Death and Life of Great American Cities* (New York: New Library, 1993), 32.

50. Luis Suarez Villa, "Regional Inversion in the United States: The Institutional Context for the Rise of the Sunbelt Since the 1940s," *Tijdschrift voor Economische en Sociale Geografie* 93, 4 (September 2002): 424–42, 430. I have assembled the data on northern versus Sunbelt prison development in this essay from the Prison Census,

2000, 1998, U.S. Census Bureau, 2000, Table P37; and data from Prison Policy Initiative at http://www.prisonersofthecensus.org. I have included California, Nevada, Utah, Colorado, New Mexico, and Arizona in the region of the Southwest since they share certain characteristics in postwar economic development. For the South, I included Texas, Oklahoma, Arkansas, Louisiana, Alabama, Mississippi, Tennessee, Georgia, Florida, North Carolina, and South Carolina. Even though Virginia, Maryland, and Delaware share many features of the Sunbelt South, their metropolitan interconnection with Washington, D.C., prompted me to exclude them.

51. Stanley Mosk, "The Secure Court: Justice in Violent Times," *The Nation*, November 2, 1970, 431–34; Roy D. King, "The Rise and Rise of the Supermax: An American Solution in Search of a Problem," *Punishment & Society* 1, 2 (October 1999): 163–86, 175.

52. Garland, *Culture of Control*, 142.

53. Jeremy Travis and Michelle Waul, *Prisoners Once Removed: The Impact of Incarceration and Reentry on Children, Families, and Communities* (Washington, D.C.: Urban Institute Press 2004); Rose Heyer and Peter Wagner, "Too Big to Ignore: How Counting People in Prisons Distorted Census 2000," April 2004, Prison Policy Initiative: http://www.prisonersofthecensus.org/toobig/.

54. Jeff Manza and Christopher Uggen, *Locked Out: Felon Disenfranchisement and American Democracy* (New York: Oxford University Press, 2006), 74, 79, 80, 248, 275, A.2.1, A3.2, A.3.3, A.3.4, A8.1. Manza's calculations assume a disproportionally lower voter turnout of 13.6 percent among former felons, but a propensity to vote Democratic of 68.9 percent.

Chapter 9. Sunbelt Imperialism: Boosters, Navajos,
and Energy Development in the Metropolitan Southwest

1. Sociologists Harvey Molotch and John Logan have coined the phrase "growth machine" to describe an "apparatus of interlocking progrowth associations and governmental units," such as newspapers, chambers of commerce, real estate developers, and corporations, that aimed to use metropolitan growth to make "great fortunes out of place." John Logan and Harvey Molotch, *Urban Fortunes: The Political Economy of Place* (Berkeley: University of California Press, 1987), 32, 53. For examples of Sunbelt histories influenced by Logan and Molotch's work, see Kevin Kruse, *White Flight: Atlanta and the Making of Modern Conservatism* (Princeton, N.J.: Princeton University Press, 2005); and Matthew Lassiter, *The Silent Majority: Suburban Politics in the Sunbelt South* (Princeton, N.J.: Princeton University Press, 2006).

2. For a similar treatment of the spatial organization of politics, see Robert Self, *American Babylon: Race and the Struggle for Postwar Oakland* (Princeton, N.J.: Princeton University Press, 2003), 28.

3. For the limited power of the local state, see Paul Peterson, *City Limits* (Chicago:

University of Chicago Press, 1981); and Philip Ethington, "Mapping the Local State," *Journal of Urban History* 27, 5 (2001): 686–702.

4. On the importance of federal housing, transportation, and defense policies in creating the Sunbelt, see Lassiter, *The Silent Majority*; and Ann Markusen, Peter Hall, Scott Campbell, and Sabina Deitrick, *The Rise of the Gunbelt: The Military Remapping of Industrial America* (New York: Oxford University Press, 1991).

5. On Sunbelt development as neoliberalism, see Nancy MacLean, "Southern Dominance in Borrowed Language: The Regional Origins of American Neoliberalism," in Jane Lou Collins, Micaela Di Leonardo, and Brett Williams, eds., *New Landscapes of Inequality: Neoliberalism and the Erosion of Democracy in America* (Santa Fe, N.M.: School of Advanced Research Press, 2008), 21–38; and Bethany Moreton, *To Serve God and Wal-Mart: The Making of Christian Free Enterprise* (Cambridge: Harvard University Press, 2009).

6. For New Deal energy resource policy, see Martin Melosi, *Coping with Abundance: Energy and Environment in Industrial America* (Philadelphia: Temple University Press, 1985). For the TVA's effect on the South, see Bruce Schulman, *From Cotton Belt to Sun Belt: Federal Policy, Economic Development, and the Transformation of the South*, 2nd ed. (Durham, N.C.: Duke University Press, 1994, 91–93. For details on the Indian Recovery Act, see Lawrence Kelly, *The Assault on Assimilation: John Collier and the Origins of Indian Policy Reform* (Albuquerque: University of New Mexico Press, 1982).

7. For quotation, see Peter Iverson, *Barry Goldwater: Native Arizonan* (Norman: University of Oklahoma Press, 1998), 180–81.

8. For Lewis's role in termination, see Donald Fixico, *Termination and Relocation: Federal Indian Policy, 1945–1960* (Albuquerque: University of New Mexico Press, 1986), 94–102.

9. For two important examples, see Paul Rosier, "'They Are Ancestral Homelands': Race, Place, and Politics in Cold War Native America, 1945–1961," *Journal of American History* 92 (March 2006), 1300–1326; and Kenneth Philp, *Termination Revisited: American Indians on the Trail to Self-Determination* (Lincoln: University of Nebraska Press, 1999). For the political history of termination, see Fixico, *Termination and Relocation*.

10. For details of Orme Lewis's life and career, see the biographical note in the finding aid of the Orme Lewis Papers, Arizona Historical Foundation, Tempe, Arizona (hereafter OLP). The description of Lewis and Roca as a "modern corporate firm" is from "Lewis and Roca: Corporate Representation in Arizona," manuscript in author's possession. For the work of Lewis and Roca in *Arizona v. California*, see Norris Hundley, *Water in the West: The Colorado River Compact and the Politics of Water in the American West* (Berkeley: University of California Press, 1975).

11. This characterization of Phoenix's economy comes from Writers Project of the Works Progress Administration in Arizona, *Arizona: A State Guide* (New York: Hastings House, 1940).

12. For details of these changes, see Bradford Luckingham, *Phoenix: A History of a Southwestern Metropolis* (Tucson: University of Arizona Press, 1989), 136–76.

13. For details of these structural changes and the broader campaign they were part of, see Andrew Needham, "Power Lines: Urban Space, Energy Development, and the Making of the Modern Southwest" (Ph.D. dissertation, University of Michigan, 2006), chap. 1; and Amy Bridges, *Morning Glories: Municipal Reform in the Southwest* (Princeton, N.J.: Princeton University Press, 1997).

14. For a history of Arizona's right-to-work law, see Michael Wade, *Bitter Issue: The Right to Work Law in Arizona* (Tucson: Arizona Historical Society, 1976).

15. Robert Collins, *More: The Politics of Economic Growth in Postwar America* (New York: Oxford University Press, 2000); and Lizabeth Cohen, *A Consumer's Republic: The Politics of Mass Consumption in Postwar America*. For an emphasis on military spending, sometimes referred to as "military Keynesianism," see Roger Lotchin, *Fortress California, 1910–1961: From Warfare to Welfare* (New York: Oxford University Press, 1992).

16. The classic treatment of the idea of efficiency in conservation policy is Samuel Hays, *Conservation and the Gospel of Efficiency* (Cambridge, Mass.: Harvard University Press, 1959).

17. For details of the "Arizona Navy" and the early disputes between Arizona and California over the Colorado River, see Norris Hundley, *The Great Thirst: Californians and Water* (Berkeley: University of California Press, 1993), 225–27.

18. See Karen Merrill, *Public Lands and Political Meaning: Ranchers, the Government, and the Property Between Them* (Berkeley: University of California Press, 2002).

19. Arizona's basis to claim 18 percent of the power from Hoover Dam lay in the Colorado River Compact of 1922, which apportioned water and power between the states. The Compact allowed states to utilize resources over their apportionment if they were not being utilized by other states. In the case of Hoover Dam, these details gave California utilities an outsized ability to utilize the river, as they alone possessed sufficient capital to build transmission lines. The 1930 agreement over Hoover Dam power distribution, in addition to giving Southern California Edison and the LADWP control over the dam's power plant, required utilities to build their own power lines to connect their isolated regional systems to Boulder Dam. Central Arizona utilities simply did not have the capital resources or the technical capacity to build the 500 miles of transmission lines necessary to connect with Boulder Dam. Hundley, *Water in the West*, 219–27, 231–32.

20. The Boulder Dam Power Transmission Association of Arizona, "Boulder Dam Power for Arizona," 1, Bureau of Reclamation Project Files, Hoover Dam, Box 42, RG 75, National Archives and Records Administration, Denver, Colorado.

21. Richard White, *The Organic Machine* (New York: Hill & Wang), 51.

22. "Dream Homes by the Dozens," *Arizona Highways* (February 1954): 12–18.

23. Transmission Association of Arizona, "Boulder Dam Power for Arizona," 4.

24. Ibid., 5.

25. On the economics and politics of natural gas transmission, see Richard Vietor, *Contrived Competition: Regulation and Deregulation in America* (Cambridge, Mass.: Belknap Press of Harvard University Press, 1994).

26. For details of electric utilities in Phoenix during the 1930s and 1940s, see Needham, "Power Lines," chaps. 4 and 5.

27. Canz, quoted in the *Arizona Republic*, July 28, 1941, 1.

28. Kim Phillips-Fine, *Invisible Hands: The Making of the Conservative Movement from the New Deal to Reagan* (New York: Norton, 2009), 119.

29. Darwin Aycock Oral History, Phoenix History Project, Arizona Historical Society, Tempe.

30. Quote from Phillips-Fine, *Invisible Hands*, 119.

31. On this matter, see particularly Goldwater's support for the Submerged Lands Act of 1953, which granted states jurisdiction over development of the first three miles of offshore lands, in Iverson, *Barry Goldwater*, 83.

32. For a contemporary description of the "land freedom" movement, see Jean Bogeman, "Season for Plunder: I. The Public Domain," *New Republic*, March 23, 1953, 13–16.

33. David Berman, *Arizona Politics and Government: The Quest for Autonomy, Democracy, and Development* (Lincoln: University of Nebraska Press, 1998), 51. For Goldwater's Senate campaign, see Robert Goldberg, *Barry Goldwater* (New Haven, Conn.: Yale University Press, 1995), 92–99.

34. Orme Lewis, "Use is the Essence of Conservation," *Pacific Fisherman* 52, 1 (January 1, 1954): 1.

35. Orme Lewis testimony, "Hearing before the Committee on Interior and Insular Affairs, United States Senate, 83d Congress, February 5, 1953" (Washington, D.C.: Government Printing Office, 1953).

36. Lewis, "Use Is the Essence of Conservation."

37. Clyde Kluckhohn and Dorothea Leighton, *The Navajo* (Cambridge, Mass.: Harvard University Press, 1946), 1.

38. For details of these policies, see Richard White, *The Roots of Dependency: Subsistence, Environment, and Social Change Among the Choctaws, Pawnees, and Navajos* (Lincoln: University of Nebraska Press, 1983), chaps. 12–13.

39. Peter Iverson, *Diné: A History of the Navajos* (Albuquerque: University of New Mexico Press, 2002), 182–90.

40. Kluckhohn and Leighton, *The Navajo*, 24. For conditions on the Navajo Reservation following World War II, see Philp, *Termination Revisited*, 50–56; Iverson, *Diné*, 188–90.

41. Kluckhohn and Leighton, *The Navajo*, 295.

42. William Warne, testimony before the House Committee on Public Lands. U.S. House Committee on Public Lands, Subcommittee on Indian Affairs, *Navajo and Hopi Rehabilitation*, 81st Cong., 1st sess., April 18, 19, 22, May 16–18, 1949, (hereafter *Navajo and Hopi Rehabilitation* hearings), 9.

43. For the evolution of modernization theory, see Michael Latham, *Modernization as Ideology: American Social Science and "Nation Building" in the Kennedy Era* (Chapel Hill: University of North Carolina Press, 2000).

44. A 1947 BIA study of Navajo industrialization by Max Drefkoff, a Chicago-based industrial consultant, recommended the creation of both twelve industrial villages where Navajos would engage in the light manufacturing of consumer goods and commercial cooperatives to spread consumer society onto the reservation. Drefkoff's recommendations were abandoned after attacks on his plan as the "Sovietization" of the Navajo tribe. See Max Drefkoff's report, "An Industrial Program for the Navajo Indian Reservation: A Report to the Commissioner of Indian Affairs," January 1948, Box 18, Folder 28, Theodore Hetzel Papers, Fort Lewis College, Durango, Colorado. For the attacks on Drefkoff in the 1948 *Los Angeles Times*, see "Attempt to 'Sovietize' Navajo Tribe Told," April 28; "Navajo Sovietization Plan Would Wipe out Traders on Reservation," April 30; "Indian Sheep Business Factor in 'Soviet' Plan," May 1.

45. Warne, *Navajo and Hopi Rehabilitation* hearings, 20.

46. James Preston, assistant secretary of the interior, *Navajo and Hopi Rehabilitation* hearings, 73.

47. Rep. John Murdock, Arizona, *Navajo and Hopi Rehabilitation* hearings, 33.

48. Preston, *Navajo and Hopi Rehabilitation* hearings, 75.

49. Warne, *Navajo and Hopi Rehabilitation* hearings, 32, 33.

50. Rosier, "'They Are Ancestral Homelands'," 1300–1301.

51. For quote, see Goldberg, *Barry Goldwater*, 124.

52. Philp, *Termination Revisited*, 75.

53. Ibid., 75–77.

54. Navajos' deep mistrust of the BIA emerged largely from stock reduction, in which officials seized and killed large numbers of sheep, goats, and horses, frequently before their owners' eyes. These actions were especially galling given the central place of sheep in Navajo spirituality. Navajos widely perceived these actions as not for the benefit of the Navajo range but for nearby white stockholders or other interests. As Richard White argues, such suspicions were largely correct, as much of the impetus for stock reduction emerged from fears that run-off from Navajo land would shorten the life span of Lake Mead and thus harm Southwestern economic development. White, *Roots of Dependency*, 312.

55. Rosier, "'They Are Ancestral Homelands'," 17.

56. Joe Duncan, *Navajo and Hopi Rehabilitation* hearings, 100.

57. Eric Meeks, *Border Citizens: The Making of Indians, Mexicans, and Anglos in Arizona* (Austin: University of Texas Press, 2007).

58. Joe Duncan, *Navajo and Hopi Rehabilitation* hearings, 58.

59. Don Dedera, "Walter Reed Bimson: Arizona's Indispensable Man," *Arizona Highways* (April 1973): 24–29.

60. Walter Bimson, "Remarks for Broadcast, Paradise Inn," Box 34, Folder 306, Valley National Bank Papers, Arizona Historical Society, Tempe, Arizona (hereafter VNB).

61. House Committee of Interior and Insular Affairs, *Survey Report of the Bureau of Indian Affairs*, Committee Print 14, January 26, 1954 (Washington: Government Printing Office, 1954), 4.

62. Orme Lewis to Walter Bimson, September 17, 1953; Walter Bimson to Orme Lewis, October 14, 1953, both Box 35, Folder 317, VNB.

63. George Kirsch, *Mineral Resources, Navajo-Hopi Indian Reservations, Arizona-Utah: Geology, Evaluation, and Uses* (Tucson: University of Arizona Press, 1954–55).

64. Stanford Research Institute, "A Preliminary Study of Economic Feasibility of Generating Electricity from Northern Arizona Coal, Prepared for Arizona Public Service Company," April 1955, Archives of the Stanford Research Institute, Stanford, California, quotes executive summary, 25.

65. Lewis to Bimson, January 13, 1955, Box 34, Folder 310, VNB.

66. "Tribal Chairman Sees Bright Future," *Navajo Times*, September 9, 1959.

67. Map from United States, Department of the Interior, *Southwest Energy Study* (Washington, DC: Government Printing Office, 1971).

68. Quote and photo from "Western Utilities Intend to Develop Facilities Jointly," *Wall Street Journal*, September 23, 1964, 2. The initial members of WEST Associates were Arizona Public Service, El Paso Electric, Nevada Power, Public Service Company of New Mexico, Public Service Company of Colorado, San Diego Gas and Electric, Sierra Pacific Power, Southern California Edison, Tucson Gas and Electric, and Utah Power and Light. Later the same day, the Los Angeles Department of Water and Power joined; later that year so did Burbank (Calif.) Public Service, Glendale (Calif.) Public Service, Pasadena Municipal Light and Power, and the Imperial Irrigation District. For the press conference announcing WEST, see Gene Smith, "10 Utilities in 9 Western States Map a $10.5 Billion Expansion," *New York Times*, September 23, 1964, 67; "Western Utilities Intend to Develop Facilities Jointly," *Wall Street Journal*, September 23, 1964, 2; "Utilities Plan Massive Growth," *Navajo Times*, October 1, 1964, 1.

69. Many Mules' Daughter interviewed in *Diné Baa-Hani* (Ft. Defiance, New Mexico), October 1970, 1.

70. "They're Just Saying That," *Diné Baa-Hani*, September 1970.

71. Peter MacDonald, "Indian Tribes Must Get Fair Return for Resources," *Navajo Times*, April 22, 1976.

72. Scott Barker and Chloe White, "TVA Ash Spill: Workers Cleaning Up; Rebuilding Infrastructure," *Knoxville News Sentinel*, December 24, 2008, http://www.knoxnews.com/news/2008/dec/24/tva-ash-spill-crews-mount-round—clock-cleanup, accessed April 4, 2009.

Chapter 10. Real Estate and Race: Imagining the Second Circuit of Capital in Sunbelt Cities

Page references to the four novels discussed in this essay are to the following editions: Rudolfo Anaya, *Albuquerque* (Albuquerque: University of New Mexico Press,

1992); T. Coraghessan Boyle, *The Tortilla Curtain* (New York: Viking, 1995); Leslie Marmon Silko, *Almanac of the Dead* (New York: Penguin, 1992); John Nichols, *The Milagro Beanfield War* (New York: Ballantine, 1996). I want to acknowledge the late Howard Rabinowitz, my predecessor as a history major at Swarthmore College and as a graduate student of John Hope Franklin and Richard Wade at the University of Chicago. As a faculty member at the University of New Mexico, Howard delved deeply into the history of Albuquerque and taught us much of what we know about its recent development. He also introduced me to *The Milagro Beanfield War* sometime in the mid-1970s.

1. The Amazon.com sales ranks on December 21, 2008, were 7,907 for Boyle, 38,966 for Silko, 65,881 for Nichols, and 143,404 for Anaya.

2. John E. Loftis, "Community as Protagonist in John Nichols' *The Milagro Beanfield War*," *Rocky Mountain Review of Language and Literature* 38, 4 (1984): 201–13.

3. One critic likens it to a spider web and another calls it a "web of quests." Caren Ire, "The Timeliness of *Almanac of the Dead*, or a Postmodern Rewriting of Radical Fiction" (239); Janet Powers, "Mapping the Prophetic Landscape in *Almanac of the Dead*" (263), both in Louise K. Barnett and James L. Thorson, eds., *Leslie Marmon Silko: A Collection of Critical Essays* (Albuquerque: University of New Mexico Press, 1999).

4. These are not the only possibilities for this analytical approach. Real estate and its developers figure in novels of the Southwest that are as different as James Cain's noir melodrama *Mildred Pierce* (1941), Thomas Pynchon's extravagant fantasy *The Crying of Lot 49* (1966), and the Arizona-based mysteries of J. A. Jance. Real estate development also played a major role in novels from earlier eras as discussed in George Henderson, *California and the Fictions of Capital* (Philadelphia: Temple University Press, 1998).

5. For the claims that cities make on their environments, see Carl Abbott, "Land for Cities, Scenery for City People: Managing Urbanization in the American Grain," in James Foster and William Robbins, eds., *Land in the American West* (Seattle: University of. Washington Press, 2001), 77–95.

6. Henri Lefebvre, *La Révolution urbaine* (1970), trans. *The Urban Revolution* (Minneapolis: University of Minnesota Press, 2003) and *La Production de l'espace* (1974), trans. *The Production of Space* (Cambridge: Blackwell, 1991). Lefebvre's ideas were adapted into English language theory by geographer David Harvey and have since been used and elaborated by many other critical sociologists. See Harvey, *The Urbanization of Capital: Studies in the History and Theory of Capitalist Urbanization* (Baltimore: Johns Hopkins University Press, 1985); Mark Gottdiener, "A Marx for Our Time: Henri Lefebvre and *The Production of Space*," *Sociological Theory* 11 (March 1993): 129–34; Gottdiener, *The Social Production of Urban Space* (Austin: University of Texas Press, 1985); Joe R. Feagin, "The Secondary Circuit of Capital," *International Journal of Urban and Regional Research* 11 (1987): 171–92; Feagin, *The New Urban Paradigm: Critical Perspectives on the City* (Lanham, Md.: Rowman and Littlefield, 1998).

7. The investments to enhance the productivity of human capital can be positive (education, social welfare programs, medical insurance) or negative (repression of labor organizations, inculcation of hegemonic value systems, imprisonment of criminals).

8. Lefebvre's work was part of an effort by European social theorists to update Marxist analysis to account for the revival of capitalist economies from the ruin of World War II. Jürgen Habermas, Manuel Castells, David Harvey, and others tried to formulate an intellectual foundation for progressive social action in the era of the German economic miracle, swinging England, and the general modernization of Western Europe. In Lefebvre's case, his seminal *La Révolution urbaine* appeared two years after the political upheavals and failed rebellions of 1968. Even though the context for his work was far removed from the Sunbelt, his ideas have proved robust enough to be useful on both sides of the Atlantic.

9. Feagin, "Secondary Circuit of Capital," 186.

10. Tom Wolfe, *A Man in Full* (New York: Farrar Straus and Giroux, 1998); Jonathan Franzen, *The Twenty-Seventh City* (New York: Farrar Straus and Giroux, 1988).

11. "Vulturine" because corrupt Anglo and Mexican society thrives on death and its products both figuratively and literally—it is not a pleasant book.

12. "Ever since I learned how to drive the same year they invented cars," storms Onofre, "I been parking where I wanted to park and nobody ever made me pay money to do it . . . and I'll be goddamned if I'll start now" (59).

13. See Sharon Zukin, *Loft Living: Culture and Capital in Urban Change* (Baltimore: Johns Hopkins University Press, 1982); Neil Smith, *The New Urban Frontier: Gentrification and the Revanchist City* (New York: Routledge, 1996); Janet Abu-Lughod, ed., *From Urban Village to East Village: The Battle for New York's Lower East Side* (Cambridge: Blackwell, 1994).

14. John Nichols, "The Case for a Social Ecology," in *Dancing on the Stones: Selected Essays* (Albuquerque: University of New Mexico Press, 1993), 93.

15. Poor feckless Herbie is not really necessary to the novel, but he's lots of fun. In 1974, many of the novel's audience had just finished VISTA or Peace Corps stints or were considering them, and Herbie confirmed our worst nightmares about how we might appear in the communities we were sent to help.

16. The novel appeared at the same time as Robert Coles, *The Old Ones of New Mexico* (Albuquerque: University of New Mexico Press, 1973), which celebrated the cultural continuity and endurance of the rural people of Hispanic New Mexico.

17. One of the models for *The Tortilla Curtain* is Sinclair Lewis's 1922 novel *Babbitt*: Delaney Mossbacher and George F. Babbitt both deal in words as writer and real estate salesman; both are inordinately proud of their expensive automobiles; opening scenes take the reader through the wonders of the most up-to-date houses and neighborhood, with Arroyo Blanco Estates on its canyon rim as the latest version of Babbitt's Oriole Heights on its rise overlooking Zenith; and each suffers a mid-life crisis.

18. Richard Etulain, *Reimagining the Modern American West: A Century of Fiction, History, and Art* (Tucson: University of Arizona Press, 1996), 153.

19. "He was going to put Alburquerque on the map . . . Create a city to rival Las Vegas" (59).

20. Katie Thomas, "Revival of a River Alters a City's Course in Sports," *New York Times*, April 22, 2008.

21. Silko wrote in the aftermath of the savings and loan crisis of the late 1980s, which hit Arizona particularly hard.

22. An insightful reading of the novel as prophetic manifesto is in William Katerberg, *Future West: Utopia and Apocalypse in Western Science Fiction* (Lawrence: University Press of Kansas, 2008). He places the book in the contexts of post-frontier fiction and utopian science fiction.

23. A multiracial group of veterans are also reclaiming the land by creating a camp on the outskirts of Tucson. El Feo believes that city people will easily identify true leaders because "true leaders would immediately seize all vacant apartments and houses to provide shelter for all the homeless" (524).

24. The standard narrative of the Los Angeles water system and its effects on the Owens Valley epitomizes this understanding. In the film *Chinatown*, even the orange groves are morally suspect because they are not planned to be permanent. I have not included the film as a one of my texts because it is presented as historical fiction rather than a contemporary story.

25. We can also presume that the same pools of Eastern and international capital that finance these fictional real estate developments (whether funneled through mafia rackets, the entertainment industry, or ordinary banks) also bought the state and corporate bonds that built real California prisons and Navajo Reservation power plants.

26. Don DeLillo, *Underworld* (New York: Scribner's, 1997), 282.

27. Michael Logan, *Desert Cities: The Environmental History of Phoenix and Tucson* (Pittsburgh: University of Pittsburgh Press, 2006).

28. Carl Abbott, "New West, New South, New Region: The Discovery of the Sunbelt," in Raymond Mohl, ed., *Searching for the Sunbelt: Historical Perspectives on a Region* (Knoxville: University of Tennessee Press, 1990), 7–24.

29. James Lee Burke, *In the Electric Mist with Confederate Dead* (New York: Avon, 1994), 182–83.

30. Walker Percy, *Love in the Ruins: The Adventures of a Bad Catholic at a Time near the End of the World* (1971; New York: Picador, 1999), 15, 18. Percy presents his ideas about sin and history within a social satire, trying not to be self-righteous about his serious messages.

31. Burke, *In the Electric Mist*, 369.

32. Examples come from Yvor Winters, "A View of Pasadena from the Hills," Simone de Beauvoir, *America Day by Day*, Raymond Chandler, *The Little Sister*, and Cormac McCarthy, *Cities of the Plain*.

Chapter 11. The Marketplace Missions of S. Truett Cathy and Chick-fil-A

1. The most recent, unofficial company statistics are available at "Chick-fil-A," http://en.wiki pedia.org/wiki/Chick-fil-A and "Chick-fil-A Crosses $3 Billion Sales Mark," *QSR Magazine* (December 10, 2009), http://www.qsrmagazine.com/articles/news/story.phtml?id = 9832.

2. For other explorations of the corporation's public influence in postwar American life, see Elizabeth Fones-Wolf, *Selling Free Enterprise: The Business Assault on Labor and Liberalism, 1945–1960* (Urbana: University of Illinois Press, 1995); D. Michael Lindsay, *Faith in the Halls of Power: How Evangelicals Joined the American Elite* (New York: Oxford University Press, 2007), esp. 161–207; Alice O'Connor, "Financing the Counterrevolution," in Bruce J. Schulman and Julian E. Zelizer, eds., *Rightward Bound: Making America Conservative in the 1970s* (Cambridge, Mass.: Harvard University Press, 2008), 148–68; Kimberly Phillips-Fein, *Invisible Hands: The Making of the Conservative Movement from the New Deal to Reagan* (New York: Norton, 2009); and Bethany Moreton, *To Serve God and Wal-Mart: The Making of Christian Free Enterprise* (Cambridge: Harvard University Press, 2009).

3. S. Truett Cathy, *It's Easier to Succeed Than to Fail* (Nashville: Thomas Nelson Publishers, 1989), 43; S. Truett Cathy, *Eat Mor Chikin: Inspire More People* (Decatur: Looking Glass Books, 2002), 12–34; On diners in other locales that attempted, to a certain extent like Cathy's, to play "host to everyone," see Andrew Hurley, *Diners, Bowling Alleys, and Trailer Parks: Chasing the American Dream in the Postwar Consumer Culture* (New York: Basic Books, 2001), 43–57.

4. Teri Peitso, "King of the Malls," *Business Atlanta* (February 1986): 28; *Fulton County Review*, August 2, 1940, 4; U.S. Census Bureau, *Sixteenth Census of the United States: 1940*, vol. 2, no. 2 (Florida–Iowa) (Washington, D.C.: Government Printing Office, 1941),Table 30, 359; *Seventeenth Census of the United States: 1950*, vol. 2, pt. 11 (Georgia), Table 39, 11–84; *Eighteenth Census of the United States: 1960*, vol. 1, pt. 12 (Georgia), Table 21, 12–62.

5. Cathy, *It's Easier to Succeed*, 52–67; Cathy, *Eat Mor Chikin*, 75–79; "Chick-fil-A Growing Strong," *Athens Banner-Herald*, February 15, 1981, 8-C; "Creating the Original Chick-fil-A Sandwich," http://www.truettcathy.com/pdfs/CreatingOriginalChickenSandwich.pdf.

6. Lizabeth Cohen, "From Town Center to Shopping Center: The Reconfiguration of Community Marketplaces in Postwar America," *American Historical Review* 101, 4 (October, 1996): 1050–81. On the importance of racial segregation and discrimination in metropolitan development outside the South, see Thomas J. Sugrue, *The Origins of the Urban Crisis: Race and Inequality in Postwar Detroit* (Princeton, N.J.: Princeton University Press, 1998); and Robert O. Self, *American Babylon: Race and the Struggle for Postwar Oakland* (Princeton, N.J.: Princeton University Press, 2003).

7. "A Study of Greenbriar Mall in Metropolitan Atlanta" (Atlanta: Atlanta Journal and Constitution Research and Marketing Department, 1973), 5, 8–10, 16.

8. "Chick-fil-A Inc.," in *Telephone Directory, Greater Atlanta, GA., White Pages* (Atlanta: Southern Bell Telephone and Telegraph Company, 1976, 1986). For more on the demographics of Atlanta area malls during Chick-fil-A's early years, see Borden D. Dent, "Trade Area Analysis of Atlanta's Regional Shopping Centers" (Atlanta: Department of Geography, Georgia State University, 1978), 18–19, 31–32, 34–50; and "Shopping Centers" (Atlanta: *Atlanta Journal-Constitution*, 1978) 46–47, 51, 53; Cathy, *Eat Mor Chikin*, 118; Peitso, "King of the Malls," 28, 38. In 1983, the company reported that it was opening more downtown restaurants, starting in Atlanta and Houston. Still, for the most part throughout the 1980s, its growth continued mostly in the suburbs and almost exclusively in shopping malls. Thomas Oliver, "Chick-fil-A Has Strategy for Downtown," *Atlanta Constitution*, October 21, 1983, D-1.

9. Moreton, *To Serve God and Wal-Mart*, 49–172; Nelson Lichtenstein, *The Retail Revolution: How Wal-Mart Created a Brave New World of Business* (New York: Metropolitan Books, 2009), 53–84. For more on the varieties of postwar corporate evangelicalism, see Darren E. Grem, "The Blessings of Business: Corporate America and Conservative Evangelicalism in the Sunbelt Age, 1945–2000" (Ph.D. dissertation, University of Georgia, 2010).

10. Cathy, *It's Easier to Succeed*, 69–70, 78.

11. D. M. Levine, "Old-Time Religion Guides Chick-fil-A; Bible Sets Tone for Cathy," *Nation's Restaurant News* (January 1, 1986), http://findarticles.com/p/articles/mi_m3190/is_v20/ai_40832 23/; Cathy, *Eat Mor Chikin*, 111–12; "Are Customers Hungry for Old Fashioned Values in Today's Quick-Service Restaurant Era?" (November 20, 2002), http://knowledge.emory.edu/article.cfm?articleid=598.

12. Cathy, *It's Easier to Succeed*, 135–43, 127–31, 160; Cathy, *Eat Mor Chikin*, 97–100; Renee Gibson, "Chick-fil-A Chief at Home in Rome," *Rome News-Tribune*, April 17, 1989, 4; Nancy J. White, "Truett Cathy Helps the Lord Run Chick-fil-A," *Atlanta Constitution*, May 30, 1985, 1-C, 7-C. For an example of Chick-fil-A's advertising campaign toward potential operators, see "Be Your Own Boss," *Wall Street Journal*, November 19, 1987, 39.

13. "Chicken Chain Won't Hire Men with Earrings," *Associated Press State and Local Wire*, February 2, 2000, accessed via LexisNexis.

14. See Julie Kimmel, *The Corporation as Family: The Gendering of Corporate Welfare, 1880–1920* (Chapel Hill: University of North Carolina Press, 2002).

15. Cathy, *Eat Mor Chikin*, 111; Cathy, *It's Easier to Succeed*, 133.

16. Lewis Grizzard, "Chicken Man," *Atlanta Journal-Atlanta Constitution, Atlanta Weekly*, November 28, 1982, 66; Marc Rice, "Chick-fil-A Founder Uses Spiritual Principles in Business, Personal Life," *Athens Daily News*, September 23, 1991, 4-A.

17. Cathy, *Eat Mor Chikin*, 134–39; William J. Ventura II, "The Personal Values Communicated by Truett Cathy and Their Effect on the Culture of Chick-fil-A: A Quantitative Case Study" (Ph.D. dissertation, Regent University, 2006), 94; "Move Over, Colonel Sanders: The Chick-fil-A Fast Food Empire Espouses Christian Principles," *Canadian Business and Current Affairs, Western Report* (October 10, 1994), n.p., accessed via LexisNexis.

18. "Chick-fil-A Sculpture Takes Shape," *Atlanta Journal-Constitution*, December 10, 1994, C-10. "'Climb with Care and Confidence' Scholarship Sculpture Reflects Spirit of Emerging Atlanta," *PR Newswire*, October 23, 1995, accessed via LexisNexis.

19. Arthur Asa Berger, *Shop 'til You Drop: Consumer Behavior and American Culture* (Lanham, Md.: Rowman and Littlefield, 2005), 100–101.

20. "Greenville Chosen as Site for Chick-fil-A's First Drive-Thru-Only Restaurant in the Nation," *PR Newswire*, March 11, 1993, accessed via LexisNexis; Chris Roush, "Chick-fil-A Seeks Nontraditional Sites as Growth Strategy Turns Aggressive," *Atlanta Constitution*, December 23, 1994, C-1; Susannah Vesey, "Fast (and Closer) Food," *Atlanta Constitution*, July 14, 1993, E-1.

21. Jim Osterman, "Chick-fil-A Hops into Easter with 'Taste' Promotion," *Adweek*, Southeast Edition, March 30, 1987, 6; "Chick-fil-A Cranks Up Expansion," *Atlanta Constitution*, February 13, 1993, C2; "Chick-fil-A Takes a Strong Step Forward," *QSR Magazine* (January 26, 2000), http://www.qsrmagazine.com/articles/news/story.phtml?id=3079.

22. On the importance of youth marketing in the fast food industry, see Eric Schlosser, *Fast Food Nation: The Dark Side of the All-American Meal* (New York: HarperCollins, 2001), 42–49.

23. "Chick-fil-A to Sign More Schools for Value-Based Curriculum," *Nation's Restaurant News* (May 14, 2001): 14; on Junior Achievement, see http://www.ja.org/about/about.shtml. On Dan Cathy's seat on the Georgia state board, see "Junior Achievement of Georgia: Board of Directors List," http://www.ja.org/nested/georgia/boardlist1.pdf; for an example of Junior Achievement's curriculum, see *Excellence Through Ethics: Guide for Volunteers and Teachers* (Colorado Springs: Junior Achievement, 2002).

24. Cathy, *Eat Mor Chikin*, 156, 153.

25. Ibid., 153, 155.

26. Robert J. Grossman, "Home is Where the School Is," *HR Magazine*, November 2001: 58–65; Nahal Toosi, "Atlanta-Based Chick-fil-A Chain Seeks Home-school Students as Employees," *KnightRidder/Tribune Business News*, August 8, 1998, http://www.accessmylibrary.com/coms2/summary_0286–5591332_ITM.

27. Frederick F. Reichheld, *Loyalty Rules: How Today's Leaders Build Lasting Relationships* (Boston: Harvard Business Press, 2001), 78.

28. Judith H. Dobrzynski, "Chicken Done to a Golden Rule: Fast-food Chain Treats Its Employees as Family," *New York Times*, April 3, 1996, D-1.

29. Ron Ruggless, "Muslim Sues Chick-fil-A over On-the-job Prayer," *Nation's Restaurant News* (November 4, 2002): 1, 80; Caroline Wilbert, "Former Worker Sues Chick-fil-A," *Atlanta Journal-Constitution*, October 23, 2002; "Muslim Sues Chick-fil-A After Firing," *Atlanta Journal-Constitution*, October 23, 2002, D-4; Emily Schmall, "The Cult of Chick-fil-A," *Forbes*, July 23, 2007, 83.

30. To that end, Cathy and WinShape affirmed the work of Life Innovations, Inc., which published regular research reports on how companies might benefit from

supporting "marriage and family wellness." For an example of their work, see Matthew D. Turvey and David H. Olson, "Marriage & Family Wellness: Corporate America's Business?" (Minneapolis: Life Innovations, 2006).

31. Sharon Jayson, "Chick-fil-A Offers Marital Advice on the Side," *USA Today*, June 22, 2006, 1-D; on WinShape's marriage programs, see http://www.winshape.org/marriage/.

32. "Building and Strengthening Healthy Families," *Philanthropy* (October 1, 2007), http://www.philanthropyroundtable.org/article.asp?article=1498&paper=1&cat=149.

33. On *Adventures in Odyssey*, see http://www.whitsend.org/. Kristina Buchthal, "The Ten-Minute Manager's Guide to . . . Being Child-Friendly," *Restaurants and Institutions* (February 15, 2006): 20; Erica Noonan, "Southern Christian Chicken Maker Chick-fil-A Comes North," *The Associated Press State and Local Wire*, October 19, 1998, accessed via LexisNexis.

34. Aaron Gould Sheinin, "McCain: 'Strong Role' for Perdue," *Atlanta Journal-Constitution*, March 7, 2008, B-1, B-4; Joni B. Hannigan, "McCain Visits Chick-fil-A Offices," *Baptist Press*, March 10, 2008, http://www.bpnews.net/printerfriendly.asp?ID=27586; "Chick-fil-A Founder S. Truett Cathy Honored at the White House For His Life-long Commitment to Volunteer Service," *PR Newswire*, April 15, 2008, accessed via LexisNexis.

35. Nancy Luna, "Poised to Rule the Roost," *Orange County Register*, February 24, 2006, http://www.charochickensanclemente.com/news/OCRruleTheRoostArticle.pdf; Nancy Luna, "Chickfil-A Puts Faith in Etiquette," *Orange County Register*, April 14, 2006, http://www.highbeam.com/doc/1G1-144496676.html.

36. I reconstructed this scene via notes taken by an eyewitness at the meeting. See Ventura, "The Personal Values Communicated by Truett Cathy," 282–87, 246. Concerning the praise song, Ventura's record of the event details it as "You Came from Heaven to Earth." He might have only recorded a portion of the song's lyrics, which are probably from "Lord, I Lift Your Name on High" (Maranatha Praise, 1989), a Christian worship song written by Rick Founds and regularly sung in evangelical churches and youth groups.

37. Zach Coleman, "Chick-fil-A Follows in Tracks of Big Chains Overseas," *Atlanta Business Chronicle*, May 23, 1997, http://www.bizjournals.com/atlanta/stories/1997/05/26/newscolumn2.html; Chris Roush, "Something to Crow About," *Atlanta Journal-Constitution*, September 28, 1995, E-1; Mark Hamstra, "Chick-fil-A Targets S. Africa for 1st Expansion Effort," *Nation's Restaurant News*, December 4, 1995, 54; Scott Barancik, "Chicken with a Conscience," *St. Petersburg Times*, October 23, 2002, http://www.sptimes.com/2002/10/23/Business/Chicken_with_a_consci.shtml.

38. See the video and testimonials online at http://www.winshape.org/international/.

39. Ibid.

40. Steve Striffler, *Chicken: The Dangerous Transformation of America's Favorite*

Food (New Haven, Conn.: Yale University Press, 2005), 15–71; Ling Li, *Supply Chain Management: Concepts, Techniques, and Practices* (Singapore: World Scientific, 2007), 296–97.

41. Perdue Farms and Wayne Farms, of course, were not the only companies to do this. For a fuller account on the connections between industrial food and immigration, see Leon Fink, *The Maya of Morganton: Work and Community in the Nuevo New South* (Chapel Hill: University of North Carolina Press, 2003).

42. Julie Ardery, "Mayberry Shake-Up: Economic and Ethnic Change Comes to Surry County, North Carolina," *Reports on Rural America* 1, 1 (2006): 18 (Durham: Carsey Institute, University of New Hampshire); Shelly Howell, "News Shorts," *Meat Processing*, September 28, 2004, http://www.meatnews.com/index.cfm?fuseaction=article&artNum=8262; "OSHA Cites Alabama Poultry Processor Following Fatal Accident, Agency Proposes $59,500 in Penalties" OSHA Region 4 News Release Number 04-1853-ATL (206), http://www.osha.gov/pls/oshaweb/owadisp.show_documentp_table=NEWS_RELEASES&p_id=11036; Ahmed El Amin, "Top Poultry Processors Faulted for High Salmonella," *Food Production Daily* (July 6, 2006), http://www.foodproductiondaily.com/Quality-Safety/Top-poultry-processors-faulted-for-highSalmonella-rates; Ann Bagel, "All Things Unequal," *Poultry*, October/November, 2005, 36; Client list and quote from http://en.wikipedia.org/wiki/Wayne_Farms and http://www.foodprocessingtechnology.com/projects/wayne/.

43. "Chick-fil-A Tops Its Own Sales Record, Despite Economic Crisis," *QSR Magazine* (January 29, 2009), http://www.qsrmagazine.com/articles/news/story.phtml?id=7982; Giannina Smith, "Chicken Fight: McDonald's Looks to Challenge Chick-fil-A," *St. Louis Business Journal*, May 13, 2008, http://www.bizjournals.com/stlouis/stories/2008/05/12/daily33.html; "Not All Businesses Suffering: Christian-Owned Chick-fil-A Profits Up in 2008," *Black Christian News*, February 7, 2009, http://www.blackchristiannews.com/news/2009/02/not-all-businesses-suffering-chick-fil-a-profits-upin-2008.html.

44. The contributors to this volume have been instrumental in shaping and refining this essay. I thank them for their comments and critiques, along with the encouragement and assistance of James C. Cobb, Bethany Moreton, Pamela Voekel, Clayton Howard, and John H. Hayes.

Chapter 12. Tortilla Politics: Mexican Food, Globalization, and the Sunbelt

1. *Great Menus: 1983* (Washington, D.C.: National Restaurant Association, 1983).

2. Jim Kabbani, executive director, Tortilla Industry Association, telephone interview with the author, February 20, 2009. Tortilla sales surpassed sliced sliced-bread sales in 2008.

3. "Familiar Mexican Fare Awaits at Carlos Murphy's, *Virginian-Pilot* (Norfolk), August 7, 1994.

4. Jeffrey M. Pilcher, "Tex-Mex, Cal-Mex, New-Mex, or whose Mex? Notes on the Historical Geography of Southwestern Cuisine," *Journal of the Southwest* 43, 4 (2001): 659–80.

5. In 1991, Flay opened Mesa Grill restaurant in New York. "Bio" at Bobby Flay Web site, http://www.bobbyflay.com (accessed April 2, 2009). Bayless opened Frontera Grill in 1987 and Topolobampo in 1989 in Chicago. "About Rick Bayless," www.rickbayless.com (accessed February 26, 2010). Both chefs sold packaged foods and cooking utensils.

6. GRUMA opened a tortilla plant in Shanghai to fill Asian demand and reduce pressure on its Rancho Cucamonga, California, facility. KFC had more than 1,500 locations in China when the Shanghai plant opened, which was to distribute outside of China also. "Wrapping the Globe in Tortillas," *Business Week*, February 26, 2007, 54; Mission Foods Press Release, "Mission Foods Opens Plant in China," November 2006, http://www.missionmenus.com/News.aspx (accessed April 2, 2009; Lu Haoting, "Mexican Mission," *China Business Weekly*, July 10, 2006.

7. The Sunbelt also had a vibrant and growing relationship with Asia in the late twentieth century, whether in the form of mass migration from Asian countries or cross-Pacific investment by Asian and American companies.

8. Mexican President Carlos Salinas de Gortari (1988–94) earned a Ph.D. in political economy and government at Harvard. President Ernesto Zedillo earned a Ph.D. in economics from Yale. President Vicente Fox Quesada (2000–2006) was not a PRI member, but he was president of Coca-Cola Mexico and a board member on the United States-Mexico Chamber of Commerce.

9. Juan M. Rivera and Scott Whiteford, "Mexican Agriculture and NAFTA—Prospects for Change," in Juan M. Rivera, Scott Whiteford, and Manuel Chávez, eds., *NAFTA and the Campesinos: The Impact of NAFTA on Small-Scale Agricultural Producers in Mexico and the Prospects for Change* (Scranton, Pa.: University of Scranton Press, 2009), xv-xvi.

10. Strom C. Thacker, *Big Business, the State, and Free Trade: Constructing Coalitions in Mexico* (New York: Cambridge University Press, 2000), 1–11.

11. J. F. Hornbeck, "NAFTA at Ten: Lessons from Recent Studies," *Congressional Research Service Report for Congress*, February 13, 2004, 3, at www.fpc.state.gov.

12. Rivera and Whiteford, "Mexican Agriculture and NAFTA," in Rivera et al., *NAFTA and the Campesinos*, xii-xvi.

13. Douglas S. Massey, Jorge Durand, and Nolan J. Malone, *Beyond Smoke and Mirrors: Mexican Immigration in an Era of Economic Integration* (New York: Russell Sage, 2002), 78–82.

14. Rivera and Whiteford, "Mexican Agriculture and NAFTA," xii–xvi; Marla Dickerson and Jerry Hirsch, "Investment Money Pours in from Mexico," *Los Angeles Times*, May 5, 2007.

15. Grupo Bimbo, *Annual Report 2005*, 3. On the claim that it is the largest tortilla manufacturer in the world, see GRUMA, "This is GRUMA," http://www.gruma.com/

vIng/Acerca/acerca_esto.asp (accessed June 12, 2008); Walmart became the largest grocer in the United States in 2003, according to Tom Weir, "Wal-Mart's the 1," *Progressive Grocer*, May 1, 2003, 35. Other estimates place it as the largest grocer by 2002. Walmart was the largest supermarket chain in Mexico by 2001. See Rita Schwentesius and Manuel Ángel Gómez, "Supermarkets in Mexico: Impacts on Horticulture Systems," *Development Policy Review* 20, 4 (2002): 492; Archer Daniels Midland, *Annual Report 2008*.

16. On the global expansion of Mexican food, see Jeffrey M. Pilcher, "Eating Mexican in a Global Age: The Politics and Production of Ethnic Food," in Warren Belasco and Roger Horowitz, eds., *Food Chains: From Farmyard to Shopping Cart* (Philadelphia: University of Pennsylvania Press, 2009), 158–77.

17. Reinhold Wagnleitner and Elaine Tyler May, ed., *"Here, There and Everywhere": The Foreign Politics of American Popular Culture* (Hanover, N.H.: University Press of New England, 2000); Benjamin Barber, *Jihad vs. McWorld* (New York: Ballantine, 1995); George Ritzer, *The McDonaldization Thesis: Explorations and Extensions* (Thousand Oaks, Calif.: Sage, 1998), esp. 84–87. James L. Watson offers a counterargument in *Golden Arches East: McDonald's in East Asia* (Stanford, Calif.: Stanford University Press, 1997).

18. This chapter builds on work in Laresh Jayasanker, "Sameness in Diversity: Food Culture and Globalization in the San Francisco Bay Area and America, 1965–2005" (Ph.D. dissertation, University of Texas, 2008).

19. Timothy Taylor, "The Truth About Globalization," *Public Interest* (Spring 2002); 25. Mexico was the third-largest source of imports to the United States each year from fiscal years 1990 to 2007, as measured by dollar value. Only the European Union (consisting of multiple countries) and Canada sent a larger amount in those years. Mexico grew from the sixth-largest export destination for American goods in fiscal year 1990 to the second largest in 2007. See Economic Research Service, U.S. Department of Agriculture, "Top 15 U.S. Export Destinations, by Fiscal Year, $U.S. Value," and "Top 15 Import Sources, by fiscal year, $U.S. value," http://www.ers.usda.gov/Data/FATUS (updated December 11, 2007, accessed June 13, 2008).

20. Quote from Christopher Jencks, "Who Should Get In, Part I," *New York Review of Books*, December 20, 2001. Officially, 24,248,500 immigrants entered the United States between 1961 and 2000; Mexico sent 4,999,495. Immigration and Naturalization Service, *2001 Statistical Yearbook of the Immigration and Naturalization Service: Tables Only* (Washington, D.C.: Government Printing Office, 2002), 6–9. Liberalization of American immigration law in 1965 created this surge.

21. The INS estimated that, in 1996, about 2.7 million illegal immigrants from Mexico resided in the United States. Immigration and Naturalization Service, *2000 Statistical Yearbook of the Immigration and Naturalization Service* (Washington, D.C.: Government Printing Office, 2002), Table N.

22. The nation's population shifted to the Sunbelt in the last half of the twentieth century. In 1900, northeastern and midwestern cities dominated the list of the ten

largest cities in the nation, but by 2000, southern and western cities such as Phoenix, San Diego, Los Angeles, Houston, and Dallas were on the list. The three largest states in the Sunbelt—California, Texas, and Florida—saw their populations increase dramatically and immigration was a major part of the surge. Frank Hobbs and Nicole Stoops, *Demographic Trends of the 20th Century*, Census 2000 Special Reports, November 2002, http://www.census.gov/prod/2002pubs/censr-4.pdf (accessed January 4, 2007), 16–37, 49, A1-A6; U.S. Census Bureau, *The Foreign-Born Population: 2000*, Census 2000 Brief, December 2003, http://www.census.gov/prod/2003pubs/c2kbr-34.pdf (accessed June 14, 2008).

23. Globalization reconfigured the South too. See Raymond A. Mohl, "Globalization, Latinization, and the Nuevo New South," *Journal of American Ethnic History* 22, 4 (2003): 31–66.

24. GRUMA, *Annual Report 2007*, 5–17; GRUMA, *Form 20-F for Fiscal Year Ended 1999*, 12–13; Rick Wartzman, "A Push to Probe Buying Habits in Latino Homes," *Wall Street Journal*, August 5 1999.

25. GRUMA, *Annual Report 2007*, 3. That year, 33 percent of GRUMA's net sales were in Mexico.

26. Charles R. Handy and Suchada Langley, "Food Processing in Mexico Attracts U.S. Investments," *Food Review* 16, 1 (U.S. Dept. of Agriculture) (January–April 1993):20–24.

27. Jayasanker, "Sameness in Diversity," chap. 2. European companies first introduced the superstore, but Walmart spread its form more widely.

28. Allen R. Meyerson, "Lines Shift in Border War for Mexican Shopper," *New York Times*, April 25, 1994; Aïssatou Sidimé, "Mexican Nationals Call San Antonio Home," *San Antonio Express-News*, July 17, 2008.

29. Nelson Lichtenstein, "Wal-Mart: A Template for Twenty-First-Century Capitalism," in Lichtensteim, ed., *Wal-Mart: The Face of Twenty-First Century Capitalism* (New York: New Press, 2006), 4.

30. Bethany Moreton, *To Serve God and Wal-Mart: The Making of Christian Free Enterprise* (Cambridge, Mass.: Harvard University Press, 2009), 253.

31. Kenneth J. Cooper, "House Approves U.S-Mexico Canada Trade Pact on 234 to 200 Vote, Giving Clinton Big Victory," *Washington Post*, November 18, 1993; Moreton, *To Serve God and Wal-Mart*, 248–63. Kenneth J. Cooper and Peter Behr, "Sun Belt vs. Rust Belt: Trade Pact Debate Causes Regional Conflict," *Washington Post*, November 6, 1993. The full vote on NAFTA was 61–38 in the Senate and 234–200 in the House. I calculated the Sunbelt percentage using Alabama, Arizona, California, Florida, Georgia, Louisiana, Mississippi, New Mexico, North Carolina, South Carolina, Texas, and Virginia. The Sunbelt vote was 16–8 in the Senate and 109–64 in the House. In the Senate, 9 Republicans and 7 Democrats voted for the bill, and in the House, 52 Republicans and 57 Democrats voted yes. In the House, the Sunbelt representatives that voted "no" were overwhelmingly in the Democratic Party. Notable

congressional members voting "yes" included Newt Gingrich (R-Ga.), Nancy Pelosi (D-Calif.), Phil Gramm (R-Tex.) and J. J. Pickle (D-Tex.).

32. Statement of Senator John McCain, Senate Committee on Commerce, Science, and Transportation, *Hearings on Agricultural Trade with Mexico*, 103rd Cong., 1st sess., July 22, 1993, 68–74, 70.

33. Anthony Bianco and Wendy Zellner, "Is Wal-Mart too Big?" and "The Long Arm of Bentonville, Ark.," *Business Week*, October 6, 2003, http://www.businessweek.com/magazine/content/03_40/b3852001_mz001.htm, accessed August 15, 2010.

34. The discussion about Walmart, free trade, and antitrust is voluminous. See, for example, Barry C. Lynn, "Breaking the Chain: The Antitrust Case Against Wal-Mart," *Harper's*, July 2006; Steve Lohr, "Discount Nation: Is Wal-Mart Good for America?" *New York Times*, December 7, 2003; Lichtenstein, *Wal-Mart*.

35. Lichtenstein, *Wal-Mart*, 13–15, gives an overall 25 percent lower wage than competitors. Bianco and Zellner, "Is Wal-Mart too Big?" and "The Long Arm of Bentonville, Ark.," *Business Week*, October 6, 2003 estimate Wal-Mart's labor costs as 20 percent lower than unionized grocers.

36. Lichtenstein, "Wal-Mart," 15.

37. See Elizabeth Tandy Shermer's article in this volume and her "Counter-Organizing the Sunbelt: Right-to-Work Campaigns and Anti-Union Conservatism, 1943–1958," *Pacific Historical Review* 78, 1 (2009): 81–118.

38. "Hispanic Communities Fact Sheet," and "Texas Community Impact," www.walmartstores.com (accessed July 12, 2009).

39. On labor and Walmart, see Lichtenstein, "Wal-Mart." Walmart's wages are high in Mexico relative to other retailers, in part because unions there have been successful in securing wage increases. See Chris Tilly, "Wal-Mart and Its Workers: NOT the Same All over the World," *Connecticut Law Review* 39, 4 (May 2007): 1805–23. On farmworkers in the United States, see Daniel Rothenberg, *With These Hands: The Hidden World of Migrant Farmworkers Today* (Berkeley: University of California Press, 1998).

40. Chris Tilly and Marie Kennedy, "Supply, Demand, and Tortillas," *Dollars and Sense*, Spring 2007. One estimate had just Cargill, GRUMA, ADM, Minsa, Arancia Corn Products, and Agroinsa controlling 70 percent of the corn import and export trade to Mexico in 2007. Oxfam International, "Double-Edged Prices," Oxfam Briefing Paper, October 2008, http://www.oxfam.org.uk/resources/policy/conflict_disasters/downloads/bp121_food_price_crisis.pdf (accessed February 3, 2009), 19.

41. Jayasanker, "Sameness in Diversity," chap. 2; Marilyn Halter, *Shopping for Identity: The Marketing of Ethnicity* (New York: Schocken Books, 2000); Donna Gabaccia, *We Are What We Eat: Ethnic Food and the Making of Americans* (Cambridge: Harvard University Press, 1999).

42. One example of the changing use of tortillas in the United States is Karen Howarth, *Gourmet Tortillas: Exotic and Traditional Tortilla Dishes* (Santa Fe, N.M.: Clear Light Publishers, 2000), 2–9. Howarth's cookbook included orange tortillas with

Montmorency cherries, lavender tortillas with garlic chives, and sunny-side-up fried rice over tortillas.

43. The discussion below owes a great debt to the work of Jeffrey M. Pilcher, especially ¡Que Vivan los Tamales! Food and the Making of Mexican Identity (Albuquerque: University of New Mexico Press, 1998).

44. The tortilla was eaten in what are now the southwestern states of the United States before European conquest and when Spain and Mexico controlled those lands, Jeffery M. Pilcher, "Tex-Mex, Cal-Mex, New-Mex, or whose Mex?" *Journal of the Southwest* 43, 4 (2001): 659–80; Sophie Coe, *America's First Cuisines* (Austin: University of Texas, 1994), 145–48.

45. Menu, Pepe's, Pier 39, San Francisco, 1980, Alice Statler Library, City College of San Francisco (hereafter CCSF), Folder: Calif—San Francisco, Ethnic/Mexican.

46. Menu, Chi-Chi's, Timonium, Maryland, Copyright 1980, taken by customer on September 21, 1983, New York Public Library, Rare Books Division, Humanities and Social Sciences Library, Main Branch, New York, NY, #1983–0007.

47. Elizabeth Paulucci, *Cookbook from a Melting Pot* (New York: Grosset & Dunlap, 1981), 221–24, 221.

48. A newspaper story about Mexican restaurants in San Francisco from 1923 makes unfettered reference to tortillas, mole, and chilies without explaining what they are. Perhaps this was due to high Mexican immigration rates during the 1920s. See "Spanish-Mexican" by Robert H. Willson, from *San Francisco Examiner*, December 2, 1923, in Robert H. Willson, George Hodel, and Emilia Hodel, *Foreign Nationalities in San Francisco* (San Francisco: n.p., 1951), San Francisco History Center, San Francisco Public Library. Taco stands were common in Southern California during the 1950s. Andrew F. Smith, "Tacos, Enchiladas, and Refried Beans: The Invention of Mexican-American Cookery," paper presented at Oregon State University, 1999, http://food.oregonstate.edu/ref/culture/mexico_smith.html (accessed November 26, 2006). Both Anglos and Mexican-Americans in Tucson had high consumption levels of "packaged, prepared tortillas" in the 1980s. Melanie Wallendorf and Michael D. Reilly, "Ethnic Migration, Assimilation, and Consumption," *Journal of Consumer Research* 10, 3 (1983): 292–302.

49. Menu, La Festa, San Bruno, California, circa 1990s, CCSF, Folder Ethnic-Mexican; Menu, Acapulco Restaurants, Inc., 1991 (the chain listed 48 California locations, mostly in the southern region); menu of Chipotle chain at http://www.chipotle.com/#flash/food_menu (accessed September 3, 2007).

50. Sri Devi Rangaraj, Olympia Fields, Illinois, telephone interview with the author, April 5, 2004.

51. The trade magazine *Progressive Grocer* shows the progression of tortillas from the "impulse-buy" category to a regular purchase for both Mexican and non-Mexican customers. See "QFI Helps Sales with an Ethnic Case," *Progressive Grocer*, January 1973, 94; Robert Dietrich, "As Easy as ABC: An Independent Brings Scanning to the Inner City," *Progressive Grocer*, September 1981, 123. In this article, Paul Kodimer,

president of ABC Markets in South Central Los Angeles, said that tortilla sales had recently "gone wild" in his store. See also "Taco and Tortilla Chips Offered," *Progressive Grocer* (February 1972): 126, about how Wise Foods, a snack food manufacturer, first added tortilla chips to its product line. Tortilla chips were first listed as a separate food category in *Progressive Grocer* in its July 1978 issue. A typical story from a restaurant trade magazine in 1982 said, "Mexican cuisine has also been growing in popularity this year. A long-time favorite of the western states, its ethnic dishes are quickly becoming accepted nationwide." Elyse Cuttler, *NRA News*, December 1982.

52. Tom Caron was director of marketing for Happy Joe's Foods, a division of Tony's Pizza Service that manufactured frozen Mexican entrees. Quote in Mary Ann Linsen, "Three Hot Specialty Departments Where Grocery Is Growing," *Progressive Grocer*, October 1980, 129.

53. Marjorie Wold, "H-E-B's New Look: From Salsa to Sushi" *Progressive Grocer*, September 1991, 86–88. Quote from Paul Madure, vice president, store development, H-E-B. The Tianguis chain, owned by Von's in Southern California, also built these presses in the 1990s. Marian Burros, "Supermarkets Reach out to Hispanic Customers," *New York Times*, July 18, 1990.

54. David Bennett, founder and president, Mollie Stones, Inc., interview with the author, July 28, 2006.

55. Mexicans were the predominant immigrant group eating tortillas in the United States. After the 1970s, immigrants from Guatemala and El Salvador also consumed tortillas in large numbers.

56. Linsen, "Three Hot Specialty Departments Where Grocery Is Growing," 129. Del Monte Foods introduced a line of frozen burritos in 1981, Advertisement, C20, *Progressive Grocer*, October 1981. See also Robert McCarthy, "Consumer Watch: Supermarkets Listen for That Resounding 'Ole,'" *Progressive Grocer*, August 1982, 32.

57. Jeffrey M. Pilcher catalogs the move from homebound, labor-intensive tortilla making to GRUMA's industrial dominance by the 1990s in "Industrial *Tortillas* and Folkloric Pepsi: The Nutritional Consequences of Hybrid Cuisines in Mexico," in Warren Belasco and Philip Scranton, eds., *Food Nations: Selling Taste in Consumer Societies* (New York: Routledge, 2002), 222–29; and *¡Que Vivan los Tamales!*, 99–111. See also "About GRUMA: Timeline," http://www.gruma.com/vIng/Acerca/acerca_historia.asp (accessed August 25, 2007).

58. Pilcher, *¡Que Vivan los Tamales!*, 105; "About GRUMA: Timeline."

59. Mission Foods Corporation, "About Us," http://www.missionmenus.com/pressroom (accessed April 11, 2009).

60. GRUMA Annual Reports and 20-F statements, years 1999–2007.

61. Pilcher, *¡Que Vivan los Tamales!*, 101.

62. Ibid, 101–5. As with many inventions, there were fits and starts with these new technologies before they were widely adopted.

63. Pilcher, "Eating Mexican in a Global Age," in Belasco and Horowitz, eds., *Food Chains*, 160–61.

64. Patrice Duggan, "Tortilla Technology," *Forbes*, April 29, 1991.

65. GRUMA, *Annual Report 2006*, 11.

66. Tim Duffy, "Mexico Tortilla Deregulation Doesn't Boost Sales," *Wall Street Journal*, June 8, 1999.

67. Robert Donnelly, "Tortilla Riddle," *Business Mexico*, October 1, 1999.

68. GRUMA, *Annual Report 2001*, 1.

69. GRUMA, "Fourth Quarter 2008 Results," February 18, 2009, at http://www.gruma.com/Documentos/seccion_6/Categoria_448/4Q08-GRUMA.pdf (accessed February 22, 2009), 4.

70. Antonio Yunez-Naude "The Dismantling of CONASUPO, a Mexican State Trader in Agriculture," *World Economy* 26, 1 (January 2003): 97–122.

71. Anthony DePalma, "How a Tortilla Empire Was Built on Favoritism," *New York Times*, February 15, 1996.

72. Enrique C. Ochoa, *Feeding Mexico: The Political Uses of Food since 1910* (Wilmington, Del.: Scholarly Resources, 2000), 208–20.

73. Thacker, *Big Business, the State, and Free Trade*, 135–61.

74. Agrarian protesters have battled the Mexican government intermittently since the signing of NAFTA. The revision to the Mexican Constitution in December 1991 had also ended the requirement for state distribution of land. See "The Dismantling of CONASUPO, a Mexican State Trader in Agriculture," *The World Economy* 26, 1 (January 2003): 97–122. Kenneth Edward Mitchell, *State-Society Relations in Mexico* (Burlington, Vt.: Ashgate, 2001), 1–4, 37–40, 68–83. On the general progression of food policy and the conflict that emerged from privatization, see Ochoa, *Feeding Mexico*, 208–20. On Cargill see John Ross, "Tortilla Wars," *The Progressive*, June 1, 1999.

75. Quote in Anthony DePalma, "Graft Inquiry in Mexico Ties Zedillo to Disputed Payment," *New York Times*, July 5, 1996. See also DePalma, "How a Tortilla Empire Was Built on Favoritism." Then CEO of GRUMA, Eduardo Livas, Jr., disputed DePalma's allegations in a letter to the *New York Times* in "Mexico Tortilla Maker Won No Favors," February 21, 1996. See also Mitchell, *State-Society Relations in Mexico*, 48–83.

76. Ross, "Tortilla Wars."

77. Scott Kilman and Joel Millman, "ADM, Showing New Interest in Mexico, Agrees to Buy 22% Stake in Gruma SA," *Wall Street Journal*, August 23, 1996; Donnelly, "Tortilla Riddle."

78. José J. Yordán and Michael J. Mauboussin, "Grupo Industrial Maseca, S.A. de C.V. (GIMSA): 1993 Fourth Quarter and Full-Year Results" (New York: CS First Boston, 1994), 4; GRUMA, *Annual Report 2006*, 11.

79. Quoted in Joel Millman, "Mexican Tortilla Firms Stage U.S. Bake-Off," *Wall Street Journal*, May 10, 1996.

80. GRUMA, *Annual Report 1999*, 3.

81. Trey Garrison, "GRUMA Corp. Relocating to Metroplex," *Dallas Business Journal*, March 6, 1998.

82. "Owner Participation Agreement" between Rancho Cucamonga Redevelopment Agency and GRUMA Corporation Foods, Inc., January 18, 1996 (in possession of author), and e-mail correspondence with Tony Le-Ngoc, redevelopment analyst II, Rancho Cucamonga Redevelopment Agency, February 2, 2010. Though Governor Wilson sought to keep businesses in California, he likely was not personally involved in the Rancho Cucamonga plant deal. See also David Bacon, "Taking on the Tortilla King," September 22, 1996, at http://dbacon.igc.org/strikes/o6tortil.htm (accessed January 12, 2010), but this gives the wrong figure of $400,000 for locating the plant in the city.

83. Joel Millman, "Foreign Firms also Outsource—to the U.S.," *Wall Street Journal*, February 23, 2004.

84. GRUMA built another tortilla facility in Panorama City, California, in 2008 that was about the same size as its Rancho Cucamonga plan. Dickerson and Hirsch, "Investment Money Pours in from Mexico"; GRUMA, *Form 20-F, Fiscal Year Ended 1999*, 14–15; Millman, "Mexican Tortilla Firms Stage U.S. Bake-Off"; Rick Wartzman, "Southern California Sees a Low-Tech Boom," *Wall Street Journal*, January 25, 1999.

85. GRUMA, *Annual Report 2004*, 22.

86. Trey Garrison, "GRUMA Corp. Relocating to Metroplex," *Dallas Business Journal*, March 6, 1998. In 1991, one estimate had GRUMA providing a third of Taco Bell's tortillas. See Duggan, "Tortilla Technology." See also "Mission Possible," *Snack Food and Wholesale Bakery*, July 1998, 18–21.

87. "Mission Foods Parent in Move to Purchase Candy's," *Milling and Baking News*, April 19, 1994.

88. Matt Moffett, "U.S. Appetite for Mexican Food Grows, Cooking Up Hotter Sales for Exporters," *Wall Street Journal*, February 5, 1992; "Mexico: Maseca to Invest US$1bil in Asia over Five Years," *El Economista* (Mexico), March 8, 2006.

89. All quotes from W. Allen Dark (president and owner, El Galindo, Austin, Texas), telephone interview with the author, February 9, 2004. Confirming Dark's estimate, a 90-tortilla package of Mission Foods Brand corn tortillas sold for $2.79 at an Austin, Texas, H-E-B in February 2004.

90. S. A. Eckert, "The Good That Can Come When You're 'Not Too Good to Do Anything'," *Nation's Business*, October 1990, 14–15.

91. Galindo Family Papers, ca. 1867–1950, Benson Latin American Collection, General Libraries, University of Texas at Austin.

92. W. Allen Dark interview, February 9, 2004.

93. On the Galindo family history and the company, see also Susanna Person, "Tortilla Cos. Press On," *Austin Business Journal*, October 6–12, 1995, in Austin History Center, Austin Public Library, AF Food F2500 (10), El Galindo, Inc.; Eckert, "The Good That Can Come When You're 'Not Too Good to Do Anything'"; "After Surviving War, Man Turned Family Business into Tortilla Giant," oral-history interview of Tomas Galindo from September 2001 conducted by Antonio Gilb, U.S. Latinos and Latinas & WWII Oral History Project, University of Texas at Austin, http://www.lib

.utexas.edu/ww2latinos/template-stories-indiv.html?work_urn = urn%3Autlol%3Aww latin.135&work_title = Galindo%2C + Thomas, accessed August 25, 2007; Pam Stephenson, "'Tortilla Lady' Learned Hard Work in Pflugerville," *Community Impact Newspaper* (Pflugerville, Tex.), September 9, 2006, http://impactnews.com/round-rock-pflugerville/history/279-tortill a-lady-learned-hard-work-in-pflugerville, accessed July 19, 2010; Richard Zelade, "Masa Marketing," *Texas Monthly*, May 1989, 132–141.

94. Steve Foster, vice president of sales and marketing for El Galindo, Austin, Texas, quoted in Person, "Tortilla Cos. Press On."

95. El Galindo was not a party in the lawsuit detailed below.

96. W. Allen Dark interview, February 9, 2004. Data from the Census Bureau confirms Dark's suspicion. The number of tortilla producers increased from 1997 to 2002 (the only two years for which the bureau surveyed tortilla manufacturers), but the shipment value of the small firms (1 to 4 employees) paled in comparison to that of the large firms (250 to 999 employees). U.S. Census Bureau, *Tortilla Manufacturing: 2002* (Washington, D.C: Government Printing Office, 2004), 4.

97. Patricia Sharpe, "Round and Round," *Texas Monthly*, April 2001, http://www.texasmontly.com (accessed February 5, 2004).

98. All quotes in this paragraph from W. Allen Dark, interview with the author, February 9, 2004.

99. Percentage of four largest manufacturers from J. Michael Harris, Phil Kaufman, Steve Martinez, and Charlene Price, *The U.S. Food Marketing System, 2002*, 65. Total value of shipments was $1.11 billion, from U.S. Census Bureau, *Tortilla Manufacturing*, 1997 Economic Census, Manufacturing Industry Series (Washington, D.C.: Government Printing Office, 1999), 7.

100. After several telephone calls and visits to tortilla businesses and grocers in the Austin, Texas, area, I could not find El Galindo or its tortillas. W. Allen Dark's personal Web site stated that he was "winding up operations" for El Galindo in May 2009, http://www.linkedin.com/pub/w-allen-dark/13/834/873 (accessed January 14, 2010).

101. Naresh Nakra, president and CEO of GRUMA USA, boasted that the Rancho Cucamonga facility would be the most technologically advanced in the world when the company was finishing it in 1996. Jay Sjerven, "Tortilla Industry: Capacity to Increase, But at a Slower Pace," *Milling and Baking News*, January 30, 1996.

102. Quote in Kilman and Millman, "ADM, Showing New Interest in Mexico." On the relationship between GRUMA and ADM, see GRUMA Corporate Web site, "Investor Relations: Basic Questions," http://www.gruma.com/vIng/Relacion/relacion_preguntas.asp?idEmpresa = 1 (accessed February 22, 2009); Archer Daniels Midland Company, *2008 Annual Report*, 5–6; "ADM Discloses Probe By Mexico on Pricing Of Synthetic Lysine," *Wall Street Journal*, February 14, 1997; "ADM's Mexican Deal: Far from Corny," *Crossborder Monitor*, November 13, 1996.

103. Quote from GRUMA, *Form 20-F, Fiscal Year Ended 2003*, 21.

104. Rivera and Whiteford, "Mexican Agriculture and NAFTA," Rivera et al., eds., *NAFTA and the Campesinos*, xix. American grain producers enjoyed greater subsidies and technological advantages, meaning corn yields measured 8.55 tons per hectare in the U.S. as compared to 2.50 tons per hectare in Mexico. See Manuel Ángel Gómez Cruz and Rita Schwentesius Rindermann, "NAFTA's Impact on Mexican Agriculture: An Overview," in *NAFTA and the Campesinos*, 4.

105. Cruz and Rindermann, "NAFTA's Impact on Mexican Agriculture," 14.

106. David Bacon, "Displaced People : NAFTA's Most Important Product," and Sergio Zermeño, "Desolation: Mexican Campesinos and Agriculture in the 21st Century," *NACLA Report on the Americas*, September/October 2008; Tim Duffy, "Mexico Deregulation Doesn't Boost Sales," *Wall Street Journal*, June 8, 1999.

107. Estimates vary concerning the decline in tortilla consumption, but reports consistently show a decline from 2000 to 2008. Price increases and alternative foods are typically cited as reasons. "Tortilla Consumption Continues to Decline in Mexico but Grows Steadily Overseas," *SourceMex Economic News and Analysis on Mexico*, June 23, 2004; "Agriculture Groups Offer Mixed Opinions on Pending Elimination of Corn Tariffs Under NAFTA," *SourceMex Economic News and Analysis on Mexico*, December 12, 2007. For GRUMA's ascent, see Annual Reports, 1990–99.

108. *El Aquila Food Products v. Gruma Corp.*, 301 F. Supp. 2d 612 (S.D. Tex. 2003), 6. For background, see Marla Dickerson, "Small Tortilla Makers Lose Antitrust Suit Against Rival," *Los Angeles Times*, January 6, 2004.

109. *El Aquila Food Products v. Gruma Corp.*

110. Ibid., 12–13, 18.

111. *El Aquila Food Products. v. Gruma Corp*; see also Joel Millman, "Mexican Retailers Enter U.S. to Capture Latino Dollars," *Wall Street Journal*, February 1, 2001. The case was dismissed on appeal in 2005. See *El Aguila Food Prods. Inc. v. Gruma Corp.*, 131 Fed. Appx. 450 (5th Cir. 2005).

112. Bill No. SB 582, April 11, 2005, Senate Committee on Business, Professions and Economic Development.

113. "Mexican Firm Wins McDonald's Contract," *National Post* (Canada), August 4, 1999.

114. Joel Millman, "New Export Tiger Isn't Asian; It's Mexico," *Wall Street Journal*, May 9, 2000.

115. Grupo Bimbo Press Release (Web cast), "Transaction Overview: A Transformative Opportunity," December 2008, http://www.grupobimbo.com/relacioninv/uploads/presentations/GB%20Webcast%20Final%20Web.pdf (accessed January 14, 2010).

116. Grupo Bimbo Press Release, "Grupo Bimbo Completes and Closes Weston Foods, Inc. Acquisition," January 22, 2009, http://www.bimbobakeriesusa.com/about_us/media_center.php?id=1143 (accessed March 31, 2009).

117. Sonia Nazaro, "Teamsters Head Assails Tortilla Company at Rally," *Los Angeles Times*, August 19, 1996; Bacon, "Taking on the Tortilla King"; Christopher

David Ruiz Cameron, "Labor Law and Latcrit Identity Politics: The Labyrinth of Solidarity: Why the Future of the American Labor Movement Depends on Latino Workers," *University of Miami Law Review* 53 (July 1999): 1090–91.

118. GRUMA, *Annual Report 2008*, 51.

Chapter 13. Latinos in the Sunbelt: Political Implications of Demographic Change

1. Jessica Ramirez and Holly Bailey, "Why Won't Juan Come to the Phone: McCain's Hispanic Outreach Chief Is Both Loved and Loathed," *Newsweek*, July 19, 2008, 28.

2. Mark H. Lopez, *The Hispanic Vote in 2008* (Washington, D.C.: Pew Hispanic Center, 2008).

3. Matt A. Barreto, Loren Collingwood, and Sylvia Manzano, "A New Measure of Group Influence in Presidential Elections: Assessing Latino Influence in 2008," *Political Research Quarterly* (2010), OnlineFirst, August 4, 2010, DOI:10.1177/1065912 910367493.

4. Nicholas Tabor, "The Campaign 08 Lesson: Don't Piss Off Letterman," *National Journal*, December 11, 2008.

5. Paul Burka, "Two-Party Animal," *Texas Monthly*, December 2008, 16.

6. Tomás R. Jiménez, *Replenished Ethnicity: Mexican Americans, Immigration, and Identity* (Berkeley: University of California Press, 2009).

7. F. Chris Garcia and Gabriel R. Sanchez, *Hispanics and the U.S. Political System: Moving into the Mainstream* (Upper Saddle River, N.J.: Pearson Prentice-Hall, 2008); Felix Padilla, *Latino Ethnic Consciousness: The Case of Mexican Americans and Puerto Ricans in Chicago* (Notre Dame, Ind.: University of Notre Dame Press, 1985).

8. Padilla, *Latino Ethnic Consciousness*.

9. John Garcia, *Latino Politics in America: Community, Culture, and Interests* (Lanham, Md.: Rowman & Littlefield, 2003).

10. Rodney Hero, *Latinos and the U.S. Political System: Two-Tiered Pluralism* (Philadelphia: Temple University Press, 1992).

11. S. Karthick Ramakrishnan and Irene Bloemraad, *Civic Hopes and Political Realities* (New York: Russell Sage Foundation, 2008).

12. Daniel J. Hopkins, "Politicized Places: Explaining Where and When Immigrants Provoke Local Opposition," *American Political Science Review* 104, 1 (2010): 40.

13. See, e.g., Samuel Huntington, *Who Are We? The Challenges to America's National Identity* (New York: Simon & Schuster, 2004).

14. U.S. Census Bureau, 2010 Statistical Abstract, Table 40, Native and Foreign-Born Population by Place of Birth and State: 2008, http://www.census.gov/compendia/statab/2010/tables/10s0040.pdf, released October 22, 2009.

15. Abraham T. Mosisa, "Foreign-Born Workforce, 2004: A Visual Essay,"

Monthly Labor Review (July 2006): 48–55; U.S. Department of Labor Statistics, "Foreign Born Workers: Labor Force Characteristics—2009," March 19, 2010.

16. Arthur D. Murphy, Colleen Blanchard, and Jennifer A. Hill, *Latino Workers in the Contemporary South* (Athens: University of Georgia Press, 2001).

17. Douglas Massey, "Why Does Immigration Occur? A Theoretical Synthesis," in Charles Hirschman, Philip Kasinitz, and Josh DeWind, eds., *The Handbook of International Migration: The American Experience* (New York: Russell Sage Foundation, 1999), 34–52.

18. George J. Sanchez, "Face the Nation: Race, Immigration, and the Rise of Nativism in Late Twentieth Century America," *International Migration Review* 31, 4 (Winter 1997): 1009–30.

19. Shirin Hakimzadeh and D'Vera Cohn, *English Usage Among Hispanics in the United States* (Washington, D.C.: Pew Hispanic Center, November, 2007), 4.

20. Benjamin H. Johnson, *Revolution in Texas: How a Forgotten Rebellion and Its Bloody Suppression Turned Mexicans into Americans* (New Haven, Conn.: Yale University Press, 2005); David Lorey, *The U.S.-Mexican Border in the Twentieth Century: A History of Economic and Social Transformation* (Wilmington, Del.: Scholarly Resources Press, 1999); Hero, *Latinos and the U.S. Political System*; David Montejano, *Anglos and Mexicans in the Making of Texas: 1836–1986* (Austin: University of Texas Press, 1987); Mario Barrera, *Race and Class in the Southwest: A Theory of Racial Inequality* (South Bend, Ind.: University of Notre Dame Press, 1979).

21. Garcia and Sanchez, *Hispanics and the U.S. Political System*.

22. National Association of Latino Elected Officials, *National Directory of Latino Elected Officials, 2007* (Los Angeles: NALEO Educational Fund, 2007).

23. National Conference of State Legislatures, "Legislator Demographics: Latino Legislators," 2009, http://www.ncsl.org/Default.aspx?TabId=14766, accessed February 8, 2010.

24. U.S. Census Bureau, "Hispanics in the United States," 1–25, population estimates, July 1, 2000 to July 1, 2006, release date February 8, 2008, http://www.census.gov/population/www/socdemo/hispanic/hispanic_pop_presentation.html.

25. Jeffery S. Passel and D'Vera Cohn, *U.S. Population Projections 2000–2050* (Washington, D.C.: Pew Hispanic Research Center, February 2008).

26. The Census has varied widely in its methodology to track Latino population over time. In the interest of consistency, the data analyzed here begin with 1970. The Census first asked a separate ethnicity question, apart from racial categories, meant to count the Latino population beginning in 1970. Campell Gibson and Kay Jung, "Historical Census Statistics on Population Totals by Race, 1790 to 1990, and by Hispanic Origin, 1970 to 1990, for the United States, Regions, Divisions, and States," September 2002, http://www.census.gov/population/www/documentation/twps0056/twps0056.html.

27. U.S. Census Bureau News, "An Older and More Diverse Nation by Mid-Century," August 14, 2008, http://www.census.gov/newsroom/releases/archives/population/cb08-123.html.

28. Passel and Cohn, *U.S. Population Projections 2000–2050*.

29. U.S. Census Bureau. Percent Change in Hispanic or Latino Population: 2000 to 2006 by Region and State. Population Estimates, July 1, 2000 to July 1, 2006, released Feburary 8, 2008, http://www.census.gov/population/www/socdemo/hispanic/hispanic_pop_presentation.html.

30. U.S. Department of Homeland Security, "Estimates of the Unauthorized Immigrant Population Residing in the United States: January 2008," released February 2009, http://www.dhs.gov/xlibrary/assets/statistics/publications/ois_ill_pe_20 08.pdf.

31. Adrian D. Pantoja, Ricardo Ramirez, and Gary M. Segura, "Citizens by Choice, Voters by Necessity: Patterns in Political Mobilization by Naturalized Latinos," *Political Research Quarterly* 54, 4 (December 2001): 729–50. Proposition 227 called to cease state funding for bilingual education; Proposition 209 to rescind affirmative action policies in state institutions; and Proposition 187: called to end all public benefits to immigrants, including elementary school; it also indicated penalties for those who did not assist in validating citizenship in various public venues, including teachers, medical professionals, and others.

32. Philip Martin, "Proposition 187 in California," *International Migration Review* 29, 1 (Spring 1995): 255–63.

33. Jewelle Taylor Gibbs and Teiahsha Bankhead, *Preserving Privilege: California Politics, Propositions, and People of Color* (Westport, Conn.: Praeger, 2001).

34. Shanto Iyengar and Jennifer McGrady, *Media Politics: A Citizen's Guide* (New York: Norton, 2007).

35. Daniel HoSang, *Racial Propositions: Ballot Initiatives and the Making of Postwar California* (Berkeley: University of California Press, 2010).

36. Pantoja, Ramirez, and Segura, "Citizens by Choice, Voters by Necessity"; Shaun Bowler, Stephen P. Nicholson, and Gary M. Segura, "Earthquakes and Aftershocks: Tracking Partisan Identification amid California's Changing Political Environment," *American Journal of Political Science* 50, 1 (2006): 146–59.

37. Ibid.

38. Pantoja, Ramirez, and Segura, "Citizens by Choice, Voters by Necessity."

39. Matt A. Barreto, Ricardo Ramirez, and Nathan D. Woods, "Are Naturalized Voters Driving the California Latino Electorate? Measuring the Effect of IRCA Citizens on Latino Voting," *Social Science Quarterly* 86, 4 (2005): 792–811.

40. Matt A. Barreto, "Latino Immigrants at the Polls: Foreign-Born Voter Turnout in the 2002 Election," *Political Research Quarterly* 58, 1 (March 2005): 79–86.

41. Bowler, Nicholson, and Segura, "Earthquakes and Aftershocks," 146.

42. Evidence from several national surveys shows that education priorities have held constant over the last two decades. See, for example, the 2006 Latino National Survey, Luis R. Fraga, John A. Garcia, Rodney Hero, Michael Jones-Correa, Valerie Martinez-Ebers, and Gary M. Segura, *Latino National Survey, 2006* [Computer file], ICPSR20862-v4 (Ann Arbor, Mich.: Inter-University Consortium for Political and Social Research, distributor, May 2010); the Harvard Kaiser 1999 Survey of Latinos,

Henry J. Kaiser Family Foundation, *National Survey of Latinos in America* (Menlo Park, Ca.: Washington Post/Kaiser Family Foundation/Harvard University Survey Project, 1999); and the 1989 Latino National Political Survey, Rodolfo de la Garza, Angelo Falcon, F. Chris Garcia, and John A. Garcia, *Latino National Political Survey, 1989–1990* [Computer file], ICPSR06841-v3 (Ann Arbor, Mich.: Inter-University Consortium for Political and Social Research, distributor, 1998).

43. Mark Croomer, "The GOP's Lost Opportunity: Immigration Approach Alienated Latinos," *Washington Times*, December 18, 2008; Paul Kane and Perry Bacon, Jr., "GOP Senators Seem Unconcerned About Hispanic Backlash over Sotomayor Opposition," *Washington Post*, August 4, 2009.

44. Pew Hispanic Center, *National Survey of Latinos: As Illegal Immigration Issue Heats Up, Hispanics Feel a Chill* (Washington, D.C.: Pew Hispanic Center, December 2007).

45. Garcia and Sanchez, *Hispanics and the U.S. Political System*.

46. Kathy Kiely, "Republicans Lose Ground Among Hispanic Voters," *USA Today*, November 9, 2006.

47. Sean Alfano, "GOP Rep. Calls Miami 'Third World Country'," CBSnews.com, November 30, 2006.

48. Kiely, "Republicans Lose Ground Among Hispanic Voters."

49. David Holthouse, "San Diego Minutemen Linked to White Supremacists," Southern Poverty Law Center Hatewatch, August 7, 2007; Southern Poverty Law Center, "Nazis, Racists Join Minutemen Project," April 22, 2005.

50. As of February 2010, the ad was archived under the name "Open Borders 2" at Randy Graf's Youtube channel, http://www.youtube.com/user/VoteGraf. Key word searches in both Google and YouTube for "Randy Graf open borders 2" typically generate the video file.

51. Xóchitl Bada, Jonathan Fox, Elvia Zazueta, and Ingrid García, "Immigrant Marches, Spring 2006," Mexico Institute, Mexican Migrant Civic and Political Participation, Woodrow Wilson International Center for Scholars, 2006.

52. Xóchitl Bada, Jonathan Fox, Elvia Zazueta, and Ingrid García of the Mexico Institute at the Woodrow Wilson Center for International Scholars provided the most comprehensive database on the 2006 marches. Their data collection is archived at the Wilson Center Web site.

53. Matt A. Barreto, Sylvia Manzano, Ricardo Ramirez, and Kathy Rim, "Mobilization, Participation, and Solidaridad: Latino Participation in the 2006 Immigration Protest Rallies," *Urban Affairs Review* 44, 5 (May 2009): 736–64.

54. National Conference of State Legislatures, *2009 Latino Legislators* (National Conference of State Legislatures, 2010)

55. S. Karthick Ramakrishnan and Tom Wong, "Immigration Policies Go Local: The Varying Responses of Local Governments to Undocumented Immigration," manuscript, archived at http://www.law.berkeley.edu/files/RamakrishnanWongpaper final%281%29.pdf.

56. Stephanie Sandoval, "Survey: Carrollton Residents Don't Want Immigration Regulation Cost to Affect Services, Taxes," *Dallas Morning News*, February 9, 2009.

57. Kim Cobb, Susan Carroll, and Chase Davis, "Small Towns Clamping Down: Fear, Frustration Prompt 'Raging Fire' of Ordinances Against Illegal Immigrants," *Houston Chronicle*, November 19, 2006; Jill Esbenshade, *Division and Dislocation: Regulating Immigration Through Local Housing Ordinances*, Immigration Policy Center Special Report (Washington, D.C.: Immigration Policy Center, July 2007).

58. Esbenshade, "Division and Dislocation." With few exceptions, immigration regulation and enforcement fall under federal jurisdiction, thus making local ordinances ripe for lawsuits and fairly easily overturned. Thus the symbolic weight of these policies frequently motivates their placement on the city list of priorities.

59. Pew Hispanic Center. "The Latino Electorate: An Analysis of the 2006 Election," July 24, 2007, http://pewhispanic.org/files/factsheets/34.pdf.

60. U.S. Census Bureau. Population (P20) Characteristic and Detailed Tables: http://www.census.gov/hhes/www/socdemo/voting/publications/p20/index.html, Table 4A: Reported Voting and Registration by Race, Hispanic Origin and Age for States, November 1996, release date August 17, 1998; http://www.census.gov/hhes/www/socdemo/voting/publications/p20/1996/tab4A.txt, Table 4: Reported Voting and Registration by Race, Hispanic Origin and Age for States, November 1998, release date July 19, 2000; http://www.census.gov/hhes/www/socdemo/voting/publications/p20/1998/tab04.txt. Table 4A: Reported Voting and Registration by Race, Hispanic Origin and Age for States, November 2000, release date February 27, 2002; http://www.census.gov/hhes/www/socdemo/voting/publications/p20/2000/tab04a.pdf. Table 4A, Reported Voting and Registration by Race, Hispanic Origin and Age for States, November 2002, http://www.census.gov/hhes/www/socdemo/voting/publications/p20/2002/tab04a.pdf, release date July 28, 2004, Table 4A: Reported Voting and Registration by Race, Hispanic Origin and Age for States. November 2004; http://www.census.gov/hhes/www/socdemo/voting/publications/p20/2004/tables.html, release date May 25, 2005, Table 4B: Reported Voting and Registration by Race, Hispanic Origin and Age for States, November 2006; http://www.census.gov/hhes/www/socdemo/voting/publications/p20/2006/tables.html, release Date: July 1, 2008.

61. Kevin A. Hill, "Does the Creation of Majority Black Districts Aid Republicans? An Analysis of the 1992 Congressional Elections in Eight Southern States," *Journal of Politics* 57, 2 (May 1995): 384–401; David Lublin, *The Paradox of Representation: Racial Gerrymandering and Minority Interests in Congress* (Princeton, N.J.: Princeton University Press, 1999).

62. Will Lester, "Colorado Bids for Early Voting Spot," Associated Press, July 21, 2006; Adam Nagourney, "Democrats Shake Up Nominating Calendar," Associated Press, August 19, 2006.

63. Adam. J. Segal, "Total 2004 Spanish Language Television Ad Spending by Market and Campaign," *Hispanic Voter Project*, February, 2006, archived at http://advanced.jhu.edu / academic / government / hvp / Total%202004%20Spanish-Language

%20TV%20Ad%20Spending%20by%20Market%20and%20Campaign.pdf; Segal, "Initial Findings: Spanish Language Advertising in the 2008 Presidential Campaign," presented at the "Understanding the Latino Vote in 2008" Conference at the Center for Politics and Governance at LBJ School of Public Policy at University of Texas at Austin, April 2009, archived at http://advanced.jhu.edu/media/files/government/Adam%20J%20Segal%20Hispanic%20Voter%20Project%20at%20Johns%20Hopkins%20University.pdf.

64. YouTube channel "Political Realm" archives many of these ads at http://www.youtube.com/user/PoliticalRealm. Additionally, YouTube searches on "Nuestra Amiga," "Sueño Americano," and "John McCain Memorial Day Spanish" provide links to Spanish ads by the viable 2008 candidates.

65. Jose Antonio Vargas, "Richardson's Choice," *Washington Post*, January 29, 2008.

66. For example, Jeff Zeleny, "Richardson Endorses Obama," *New York Times*, March 21, 2008; Lynn Sweet, "Richardson, in Endorsing Obama Says Obama Rejects the Politics of Pitting Race Against Race," *Chicago Sun-Times*, March 21, 2008; Jonathan Weisman, "Richardson Throws Support to Obama," *Washington Post*, March 21, 2008.

67. Brendon Farrington and Libby Quaid, "Thompson Proposes Immigration Crack Down," *USA Today*, Associated Press, October 24, 2007; Sarah Wheaton, "New Romney Ad Hits McCain on Immigration," *New York Times*, December 29, 2007.

68. Data for Figures 13.2 and 13.3 are collected from the National Election Pool and Voter News Service datasets collected in 1996, 2000, 2004, and 2008. National Election Pool, Edison Media Research, and Mitofsky International, *National Election Pool General Election Exit Polls, 2008* [Computer file], ICPSR28123-v1 (Ann Arbor, Mich.: Inter-University Consortium for Political and Social Research [distributor], 2010); National Election Pool, Edison Media Research, and Mitosky International, *National Election Pool General Election Exit Polls, 2004* [Computer file], ICPSR version (Somerville, N.J.: Edison Media Research/New York: Mitofsky International [producers], 2004; Ann Arbor, Mich.: Inter-University Consortium for Political and Social Research [distributor], 2005); Voter News Service, *Voter News Service General Election Exit Polls, 2000* [Computer file], ICPSR version (New York: Voter News Service [producer], 2000; Ann Arbor, Mich.: Inter-University Consortium for Political and Social research [distributor], 2002). Voter News Service, *Voter News Service General Election Exit Polls, 1996* [Computer file], ICPSR version (New York: Voter News Service [producer], 1996; Ann Arbor, Mich.: Inter-University Consortium for Political and Social research [distributor], 1997).

69. Only states with data available for multiple racial groups are included in Figure 13.3.

70. As of February 2010, these ads were located searching for "Symbols of Hope" and "En Nuestro Lado?" at the McCain YouTube channel, http://www.youtube.com/user/JohnMcCaindotcom.

71. As of February 2010, these ads were located searching for "Dos Caras" at the Obama campaign YouTube channel, http://www.youtube.com/user/BarackObama dotcom.

72. Chuck Todd, "Hispanics Could Put Obama over the Top," NBC News, October 27, 2008, http://www.msnbc.msn.com/id/27403090.

73. Robert Parel and Associates, Immigration Policy Center Fact Sheet, "Latino New American Voters Wield Influence in New States," November 12, 2008.

74. Examples of anti-Latino affect expressed in cultural and immigration frames are used by interest group ads. These ads ran during the campaign and remain part of online mobilization on these issues. English: http://www.youtube.com/watch?v=3W7 srmHLclw; unauthorized voting allegations.

75. Barreto et al., "Mobilization, Participation, and Solidaridad."

76. For example, Lee Brown, an African American, was Houston's mayor (1997–2004) despite the fact that blacks comprise only 25 percent of the population. He handily won the Latino vote even when a viable Latino candidate was on the ballot in 2001. Another black elected official, Art Hall, was elected to two terms on the San Antonio City Council from a white and Latino majority district.

77. Thomas Schaller, "Obama and the Hispanic Vote," War Room, October 28, 2008.

78. Several items from the 2006 Latino National Survey capture this sentiment.

79. National Association of Hispanic Journalists, *Network Brownout Report* (Washington, D.C; NAHJ, 2006); Pew Research Center Publications: Project for Excellence in Journalism, "Hispanics in the News: An Event Driven Narrative," December 2009, archived at http://www.journalism.org/analysis_report/hispanics_news; Mark Jurkowitz, "Sotomayor and Race Drive the News," Pew Research Center Publications: Project for Excellence in Journalism, June 2, 2009.

80. Examples about all three instances abound. The Southern Poverty Law Center and Media Matters have compiled the most comprehensive and accessible data on these issues. Former Representative Tom Tancredo, a regular on the television and talk radio circuit, often referred to the Latino vote as the "illegal vote" during the 2008 election season. Voices on the right including U.S. senators described Sonia Sotomayor as an underqualified beneficiary of affirmative action (Charlie Savage, "Sotomayor Confirmed by Senate, 68–31," *New York Times*, August 7, 2009). Former presidential candidate Pat Buchanan repeatedly said she was not intelligent enough to be on the court and mocked her English language ability (Jamison Fosser, "Look Who Pat Buchanan's Hanging Out With," *Media Matters for America*, June 11, 2010).

81. Sampling some well-established Latino readership blogs, the response was unanimously negative. Latina Lista ran the story with the headline "Sen. Schumer's Talk with Lou Dobbs on Immigration Reform Does Little to Inspire Hope Among Latinos." The MigraMatters headline read, "Schumer Reaches Out to Dobbs: This Is Insanity."

82. For example, Peter Skerry, "E Pluribus Hispanic?" in F. Chris Garcia, ed.,

Pursuing Power: Latinos and the Political System (South Bend, Ind.: University of Notre Dame Press, 1997), 16.

83. Examples include the immigrant protections and benefits policies initiated by Latinos in state legislatures, as well as their efforts to kill restrictive and punitive policies, as with HR 4437.

Contributors

Carl Abbott is Professor of History at Portland State University.

Shana Bernstein is Assistant Professor of History at Southwestern University.

N. D. B. Connolly is Assistant Professor of History at Johns Hopkins University.

Joseph Crespino is Associate Professor of History at Emory University.

James L. Guth is Professor of Political Science at Furman University.

Darren E. Grem is a Postdoctoral Research Fellow at the Yale Center for Faith and Culture at Yale University.

Daniel Martinez HoSang is Assistant Professor of History at the University of Oregon.

Volker Janssen is Associate Professor of History at California State University, Fullerton.

Laresh Jayasanker is Assistant Visiting Professor at Carroll University.

Lyman A. Kellstedt is Professor Emeritus of Political Science at Wheaton College.

Matthew D. Lassiter is Associate Professor of History at the University of Michigan.

Sylvia Manzano teaches Political Science at Texas A&M University.

Andrew Needham teaches History at New York University.

Elizabeth Tandy Shermer teaches History at Loyola University Chicago.

Index

Page numbers in *italics* represent tables and figures.

Abbott, Carl, 11, 24, 32, 265–89
abortion issue, 105, 132–36, *133–34t*
Abrams, Charles, 169, 179
African Americans: Black Protestant political behavior, 113, 115–19, *116–17*, *124t*, 125, *127* 128–29, 132; Democratic identification, *124t*, 125; Democratic presidential vote choice, 132, 352–55, *353t*, *354t*; history of segregation and exclusion in California, 190–91; history of segregation and suburban containment in Miami, 165, 181–82, 184–86; Los Angeles mid-1960s race relations and urban unrest, 223–26; and Mexican Americans, 160–61; political positions, *133–34t*, 135; political party coalitions, *127t*, 128–29; postwar civil rights activism in Southern California, 150–51; poverty in postwar South, 168–69; Sunbelt population growth/change, 108, 344, *345f*; voter turnout, 350–51. *See also* civil rights activism and interracial collaboration; fair housing legislation; urban renewal and neighborhood reform
Ahkeah, Sam, 257
Aiken, South Carolina, 65–66
AiResearch (Phoenix), 50, 52, 249
Albany, Georgia, 35
Albuquerque, New Mexico, 39
Alburquerque. See Anaya
Alcoa (Phoenix), 246, 249

Alexander, Holmes, 74
Alinsky, Saul, 149, 152
Almanac of the Dead. See Silko
American Bankers Association Small Business Commission, 53
American Civil Liberties Union (ACLU), 161, 207
American Correctional Association, 220
American Council of Race Relations (ACRR), 142, 149, 152, 156; *The Problem of Violence*, 152
American Federation of Labor (AFL), 148
American Jewish Congress, 159, 204
American Legion, 50, 59
American Magazine, 53–54
American National Election Studies (ANES), 114, 119–21, 385n21
American Prison Association, 236
American Religious Identification Project (2001), 114
Anaya, Rudolfo, 266–67, 278. *Alburquerque*, 24, 266–68, 272, 278–81, 284, 286; *Bless Me, Ultima*, 278
Anderson, Glenn, 204
Anderson, Thelma, 174
anticommunist conservatism and rise of Right, 10–11, 19, 58–81; Cold War, 64–81; Dixiecrats and proto-Sunbelt, 60–64, 79; Fulbright memo, 61, 68–72; grassroots mobilization, 19, 61; HUAC hearings,

anticommunist conservatism and rise of Right (*continued*)
  67–68; John Birch Society, 66–67, 69–70, 72, 79; National Prayer Congress (1976), 1–3, 6; New Right thesis, 20, 84; oil/gas interests, 63–64, 373n19; rising Republican Party, 80–81; Savannah River Site, 65–66; Senate muzzling hearings (1961), 58–59, 61, 71–81; Thurmond crusade, 19, 58–61, 68, 70–81, 376n73
Anti-Communist Liaison, 79
Apartment Association of Los Angeles, 195
Archer Daniels Midland (ADM), 319–22, 331, 333
Arizona: Goldwater and businessmen-politicians, 33, 45, 54–57; immigration law, 26–28; Latino growth, 343–44; Republican Party, 242, 250–51; water and developers' plans, 279. *See also* Phoenix; Phoenix boosters
Arizona Bankers Association, 54
Arizona County Assessors Association, 49
Arizona Public Service (APS), 259–61, 262
Arizona Republic, 250
Arizona School of Mines, 259
Arizona State University (ASU), 50–51
Arkansas, 343
Arlington County, Virginia, 107
Aronovitz, Abe, 174, 180
Atlanta, Georgia: civil rights era, 93; early malls and Chick-fil-A, 296–97; and New South, 92–93; 1996 Olympics, 104, 303; postwar business elite and voter registration, 39; postwar population growth, 83; postwar suburban expansion, 94–95; Republican politics, 1960s, 93–94; Summerhill riot (1966), 165; WinShape Foundation, 303. *See also* Cobb County
Atlanta Constitution, 87
Atomic Energy Commission, 65
Austin, Texas, 36
Ayers, Edward, 14

Babbitt. *See* Lewis, Sinclair
Bailey, Lester, 150–51
Balsamides, Tom, 312
Barnes, Roy, 96–98, 107
Barnes Foods, 328
Barr, Bob, 106, 108
Barreto, Matt A., 347

Barrett, Ernest, 90
Barros v. Jackson (1953), 11
Bartholomew, Harold, 169–70
Baudrillard, Jean, 271
Bayless, Rick, 317, 428n5
Beale, Calvin L., 231
Becker, William, 201, 206–7
Bell Aircraft Corporation, 87
Bennett, William J., *Book of Virtues*, 309
Bernard, Richard M., and Bradley R. and Rice, *Sunbelt Cities: Politics and Growth Since World War II*, 8
Bernstein, Shana, 21, 141–63, 239
Berry College, 302, 308
Bimbo (tortilla manufacturer), 319–22, 332, 333
Bimson, Carl, 53, 54
Bimson, Walter, 53–54, 242–44, 258–61
Black Belt, 62–63
Black Muslims, 222–23
Bless Me, Ultima. *See* Anaya
Blood Meridian. *See* McCarthy, Cormac
Bloom, Leonard, 154
The Book of Virtues. *See* Bennett
boosterism and postwar business climate, 9, 12, 19, 31–57, 65–66, 247; anti-liberal rhetoric, 33–34, 37–38, 54; business-driven municipal reform, 38–39; businessmen-politicians/Anglo economic elite, 33–34, 38–57, 65–66, 241–42, 246–48, 250; campaigns for political office, 39, 46–48; commodities-based economy, 32–33; confronting dwindling tax revenues, 40–42; effects of demobilization, 33, 37; electronics and aerospace, 43, 48–51, 88–92; and energy development, 240–64; and Goldwater, 33, 45, 54–57, 242, 244, 250–51, 255; higher education and technology/science hubs, 41–42, 50–51, 284–85; industrial recruitment, 33–34, 39–40, 42–51, 242; New Deal, 9, 33–37, 39–40, 44–45, 242–44, 247, 250–53; Phoenix, 33–34, 42–57, 240–64; probusiness tax legislation, 39–40, 49–50; right-to-work/antiunion statutes, 40, 45, 49, 54–56, 65, 250; state legislatures, 39–40; suburb annexation policies, 41; tax-code initiatives, 47–48, 49; Thurmond and South Carolina, 65–66. *See also* energy development

Border Protection, Anti-terrorism, and Illegal Immigration Control Act (HR 4437), 348–49
Boulder, Colorado, 43
Boulder Dam Power Transmission Association of Arizona, 248–49
Bowler, Shaun, 347
Boyle, T. Coraghessan, 266–67, 274–75; *The Tortilla Curtain*, 24, 266–68, 272, 274–78, 283, 284, 421n17
Branson, Ron, 350
Braynon, Edward, 171
Brevard County, Florida, 107
Brewer, Jan, 26, 28
Brooks, Preston, 64
Brown, Edmund (Pat), 11–12; and fair housing legislation, 189–90, 193, 201–11, 405n56; law-and-order issue and 1966 campaign, 225
Brown, Jerry, 11, 32, 225, 227
Brown, Willie, 211
Brown v. Board of Education of Topeka (1954), 60, 141–42, 144, 150–51, 159–61, 173
Bryant, Anita, 101
Buchanan, Pat, 444n80
Bureau of Indian Affairs (BIA): Bimson and reorganization of, 242, 258–61; and Indian leasing policy, 259–61; and Navajo mineral resources, 259–61; Navajo Reservation and economic development, 253–61, 264, 418nn44,54; paternalism, 243; and energy policies, 250
Bureau of Land Management, 250
Bureau of Reclamation, 243, 247–48, 250
Burka, Paul, 336
Burke, Arleigh, 68, 79
Burke, James Lee, 24, 287–88
Burton, Vernon, 65
Bush, George H. W., 107
Bush, George W.: Anglo Catholic supporters, 132; and Cathy, 309; evangelical supporters, 131, 309; Justice Department and Miami's black population, 187; and Latino voters, 347; 2000 election and Florida felony voting laws, 239
Buzhardt, Fred, 77
Byrne, Bill, 104
Byrne, Shannon, 104

California: Chick-fil-A restaurants, 309–10; city planners of Progressive Era, 170; Latino population, 145–46, 343–44, 347, 388n6, 389n15; Mexican food producers, 327–28; Mexican restaurants, 322–23, 432n48; postwar business boosters, 43–44, 53; postwar housing crisis, 151, 161–63, 208–10; postwar housing segregation, 151, 161–63, 190–91, 208–10; presidential election (1964), 188, 209; prison system/penal ideology, 23, 220–28; race relations and urban unrest (1960s), 223–26; racial politics and conservatism, 60–61, 93; regional exceptionalism, 10; Republican anti-immigration environment, 346–48, 440n31; Republican identification, 120t, 121; school desegregation struggles, 141–42, 144, 150, 159–61; Social Democrats and civil rights movement, 11; Sunbelt liberals, 11–12; Three Strikes Law, 229; Thurmond speaking tour, 58–59, 74; urban historians and, 9–10. *See also* civil rights activism; fair housing legislation; Los Angeles
California Apartment Owners' Association, 193
California Committee for Fair Practices, 206
California Correctional Peace Officers Association (CCPOA), 231
California Council of Churches, 204, 207
California Democratic Council (CDC), 201, 202
California Department of Corrections, 221, 227. *See also* prisons and penal ideology
California Labor Federation, 204
California Real Estate Association (CREA), 190–98, 200–201
California Supreme Court, 210–12
California Teachers Association, 204
Campbell, Bill, 303
Campus Crusade for Christ, 1, 309
Cannon Electric Company (Phoenix), 51
Canz, Sylvan, 249
CAP 14 (California campaign to defeat Proposition 14), 201–10; billboard campaign, 202–3; and civil rights groups, 201, 204–6; and Democrats, 201–2, 204; and white voters, 206–8
Carey, Ron, 333
Cargill, 322, 327
Carlos Murphy restaurant chain, 316, 317

Carmichael, James V., 87–89, 92–93, 95, 99
Caron, Tom, 323
Carroll, Joseph F., 79
Carter, Jimmy, 6, 15–16, 95–96, 101, 131
Carter, Robert, 159–60
Catholic Americans: Anglos, 113, *116–17t*, 118, 122, *123t*, 125, *127t*, *130t*, 131–32, *133–34t*, 135, 386n26, 387n31; Latinos, 113, *116–17t*, 118, 122–26, *123–24t*, *127t*, 128–29, *133–34t*, 135, 386n27, 386n30; political issue positions, *133–34t*, 135; political party identification, 122–25, *123–24t*, 125, 386n27; postwar interracial collaboration, 154; presidential electoral decisions, *130t*, 131–32, 387n31; regional party coalitions, 126, *127t*, 128–29, 386n30
Cathy, Ben, 294–95
Cathy, Dan, 304, 310–11, 314
Cathy, Donald "Bubba," 308
Cathy, S. Truett, 25, 293–309. *See also* evangelical marketplace missions
CBS Reports, 80
Center, Tony, 106
Center for Relational Care, 308
Central Arizona Power and Light Company (CALAPCO), 249
Charleston News and Courier, 59
Charlotte, South Carolina, 35–36
Charter Government Committee (CGC, Phoenix), 39, 46–48
Chicago Tribune, 74, 78
chicken processing industry, 295–96, 312–14
Chick-fil-A. *See* evangelical marketplace missions
Childs, Marquis W., 76
Chinatown (film), 422n24
Christian Coalition, 102, 105–6, 109
Cisneros, Harry, 32
Citizens' Committee for Latin American Youth, 146–47
Citizens' Council of America, 72
City of Quartz. *See* Davis, Mike
Civil Rights Act (1957), 60, 79, 179
civil rights activism and interracial collaboration in postwar Southern California, 21, 141–63, 190–91; Community Relations Committee, 149–59; Community Services Organization (CSO), 147–59; Eastside neighborhood, 149, 152; ethnoracial diversity, 143–47, 388n6; fears of neighborhood violence, 151–53; first interracial committees, 146–47; Guzman incident and military racial classifications, 157; housing desegregation struggles, 161–63, 190–91, 395n94; impact on national politics, 161–63, 395n94; Jewish American community, 147, 148–59; postwar racial tensions, 146–59; red-baiting, 153–54; and Rumford Act, 190; school desegregation struggles, 141–42, 144, 150–51, 159–61, 395n94; Sleepy Lagoon case, 144, 146, 147; "Zoot Suit" riots, 144–47, 151. *See also* fair housing legislation
civil rights in Sunbelt, 174–75. *See also* civil rights activism; fair housing legislation; urban renewal and neighborhood reform
Cleland, Max, 105
Clinton, Bill, 82–83, 187
Clinton, Hillary, 350, 351
Cobb, James C., 9, 17
Cobb Citizens Coalition, 103
Cobb County, Georgia, and Sunbelt conservatism ascendancy, 20, 82–109; anti-gay rights resolution (1993), 102–4; bipartisan electoral politics, 90, 93–94, 95–98, 107–8; boosters, 86–92; Carmichael and metropolitan New South miracle, 92–93, 99; challenging three models of political change, 20, 84–85; culture wars/moral crusades and family values, 86, 99–104, 106; federal investment, 91, 106–7; Gingrich and "Republican Revolution," 82–86, 104–7; grassroots conservatives and civil rights era, 93, 97; late 1990s, 109; Lockheed-Georgia Company and Cold War aerospace industry, 88–91, 92; Marietta Bell Bomber Plant, 86–87, 100; nationalistic and militaristic political culture, 90–92; neighborhood zoning and residential segregation, 98–99; and New Right thesis, 20, 84; population growth and demographic trends, 83–84, *83t*, 107–8; postwar defense spending, 85, 87–92; postwar suburban expansion, 94–95, 97–98; property rights movement, 85–86, 99; Protestant worship, 99–100; and proto-Sunbelt nexus, 88–89; Reagan security and economic programs, 91–92; Religious Right thesis, 20, 84, 100–106; Republican ascension, 82–86, 93–98, 104–9; "Southern Strategy" thesis, 20, 84;

Index   453

working-class/white-collar neighborhoods, 94–95
Cobb County Chamber of Commerce, 88–92, 98–99, 104
Coffin v. Reichard (1944), 222
Cold War: anticommunism and Sunbelt conservatism, 64–81; Cobb County, 85, 86–92; Cuban Missile Crisis, 78–79; HUAC hearings, 67–68; Lockheed-Georgia and aerospace industry, 88–91, 92; Reagan security and economic programs, 91–92; red-baiting, 153–54; Savannah River Site, 65–66; Senate muzzling hearings (1961), 58–59, 61, 71–81; Soviet-U.S. ideological battles and racial discrimination in LA, 146. *See also* anticommunist conservatism
Coles, Robert, *The Old Ones of New Mexico*, 421n16
Collins, LeRoy, 178–80
Colorado: Colorado Springs gay rights referendum, 102; Latino voters and 2008 election, 355; U.S.-/foreign-born Latinos, 344
Colorado River Compact (1922), 416n19
color-blind conservatism, 18, 21
Columbia Law Review, 160
Commission for a National Agenda for the Eighties, 15–16
Committee for Home Protection (CHP), 193, 195–98, 200
Common Cause, 106–7
Community Service Organization (CSO, Los Angeles), 147–59
Congressional Research Service, 318
Congress of Industrial Organizations (CIO), 148
Congress of Racial Equality (CORE), 191, 201, 205
Connolly, N. D. B., 21–22, 27, 164–87
ContiGroup, 312
Cooper v. Pate (1964), 222
Coordinating Council for Latin American Youth (CCLAY), 146–47
Council for Civic Unity, 153
Courtney, Kent and Phoebe, 72
Cousins, Tom, 90
Coverdell, Paul, 107
Crespino, Joseph, 14, 19, 58–81
Crime in a Free Society. See Winslow
Criswell, W. A., 1–3, 28
Cuba, 78, 179–80; Cuban Missile Crisis, 78–79

Cuban Americans, 348, 358
Cullen, H. R., 63
Culmer, Leome, 184
Curtis, Carl, 71

Dallas, Texas: National Prayer Congress (1976), 1–3, 6, 10; postwar business-driven reform, 39
Daniel, Charles, 65; Daniel Construction Company, 65
Darden, George (Buddy), 97, 106
Dark, W. Allen, 328–30
Davis, Mike, 9–10, 212, 278, 284; *City of Quartz: Excavating the Future in Los Angeles*, 9–10, 284; *Ecology of Fear: Los Angeles and the Imagination of Disaster*, 278
Davis, Rick, 336
Dawes Act, 243
DeLillo, Don, *Underworld*, 284
Democratic Party: California urban crisis and law-and-order issue, 225–26; coalition patterns, 125–29, *127t*, 386n30; Cobb County electoral politics, 93–98, 107–9; fair housing campaigns, 189, 201–2, 204; immigration reform policy, 359; Latino electorate, 122–25, *123–24t*, 132, 350–56, *353f*, *354f*, 358–59; liberal and Social Democrats, 3, 11–13; New Democratic centrism and Blue Dogs, 126; nineteenth-century politics, 113; party affiliation, 119–21, *120t*; party identification by religious affiliation, 122–25, *123–24t*, 386n27; presidential vote by religion, 132; regional religious coalitions, 125–29, *127t*; Southern Democrats, 61–62, 80, 95–96; state trends in presidential vote, 352–55, *353f*, *354f*; 2008 presidential election, 350–56, *354f*, 358–59
Denton, Jeremiah, 32
Denver, Colorado, 234, 279
desegregation. *See* housing segregation; school desegregation; urban renewal
Deukmejian, George, 227
Diaz-Balart, Lincoln, 348
Dirksen, Everett, 56
Dixiecrat Party, 61–64; economic issues, 62–64; name, 62; 1948 presidential campaign, 61–64, 79; oil and gas interests, 63–

Dixiecrat Party (*continued*)
64, 373n19; and proto-Sunbelt, 60–64, 79; Thurmond and, 60–64, 79
Dobbins Air Force Base (Georgia), 88, 92
Dobbs, Lou, 359
Dobson, James, 308–9
Douglas, Helen Gahagan, 149–50, 157
Douglas, Melvyn, 149–50
Drefkoff, Max, 418n44
Dukakis, Michael, 107
Duncan, Joe, 256–57
Dupont Corporation, 65
Dymally, Mervyn, 206–7

East Cobb, Georgia, 95, 96; East Cobb Civic Association, 109
Ecology of Fear. See Davis, Mike
Eden in Jeopardy. See Lillard
Edgefield, South Carolina, 64–65
Edwards, Willard, 74, 78
Eisenhower, Dwight D.: appointment of Lewis to Interior Department, 251–52; and Cold War anticommunism, 67; Goldwater criticism of, 54–55; New South supporters, 93; 1952 election and Arizona electoral votes, 250
El Paso, Texas, 52–53
The Emerging Republican Majority. See Phillips
eminent domain and slum clearance, 170–75, 177–80
energy development, 23–24, 240–64; and Arizona Republican Party, 242, 250–51; Bimson and BIA reorganization, 242, 258–61; booster-led "growth machines," 241–42, 414n1; Bureau of Reclamation, 243, 247–48, 250; "business-oriented government," 250–51; city limits and natural resource policies, 241–42; federal "growth liberalism policies," 246–48; Goldwater, 242, 244, 250–51, 255; Indian leasing policy, 259–62; Indian policy and resource development on reservations, 243–45; Indian policy and state jurisdiction, 255–58; Indian policy of "termination," 244, 255–58; "land freedom," 243, 251–52, 257–58; Lewis and Department of the Interior, 242–46, 251–53, 257–58; "metropolitan growth politics," 246–48; New Deal natural resource policies, 242–44, 250–53;

Phoenix electrical utilities, 249–50; private utilities/public power, 252–53, 262–63
Equal Rights Amendment (ERA), 101
evangelical Christians: and Bible Belt revival of 1970s, 6; and 1976 National Prayer Congress gathering, 1–3, 6; political issue positions, *133–34t*, 135; political party identification, 122, *123t*, 125; presidential vote (1960–2008), *130t*, 131; regional party coalitions, 126–29, *127t*; religion and political behavior, 113, 115, *116–17t*, 119, 122, *123t*, 125, 126–29, *127t*, *130t*, 131, *133–34t*, 135, 386n26; Sunbelt companies with evangelical founders/directors, 297–98; traditional family/domestic roles, 307–8; WinShape International and missions in Global South, 311–12, 314–15. *See also* evangelical marketplace missions
evangelical marketplace missions of S. Truett Cathy and Chick-fil-A, 24–25, 293–315; Christian corporate culture, 302–3, 308, 311–12, 314–15; as Christian evangelical company, 297–310, 314–15; Christian family arrangements, 307–8; Christian operators and employees, 299–302, 305–7, 314–15; college scholarship program, 302, 306; "Core Essentials" program, 304; early "community support" campaigns, 304–5; early restaurant business, 294–95, 297; early shopping malls and all-mall business model, 296–97, 299, 303–4, 424n8; entrepreneurial programs in schools, 304; expansions in 1990s and early 2000s, 309–15; family-friendly entertainment, 304–5; free-standing and "drive-thru-only" restaurants, 303–4; homeschoolers and, 305–6; incorporation (1964), 296–97; kids' meals and educational toys, 305, 309; mascot, 305; non-Christian employees, 307; outside partnerships, 308–9; poultry suppliers and chicken processing, 295–96, 312–14; promarriage activism, 308; and Republican Party, 309; South African restaurants, 310–11; suburban churches and Christian family patrons, 305; Sunday closing policy, 298–99, 305; transnational presence, 310–12, 314–15; 2005 Operators Meeting in San Diego, 310, 426n36; WinShape Foundation, 302–3, 308, 311–12, 314–15; WinShape International and missions in Global South, 311–12, 314–15

Fair, T. Willard, 183
Fair Employment Practices Commission (FEPC, California), 190, 208, 211
Fair Employment Practices Committee, 60
fair housing legislation and 1964 California ballot, 22, 188–213, 223–24; and apartment owners, 195, 200; billboard campaign, 202–3; and Brown administration, 189–90, 193, 201–11, 405n56; CAP 14, 201–10; Committee for Home Protection (CHP), 193, 195–98, 200; CREA, 190–98, 200–201; debate in LA Chamber of Commerce, 199–200; Democrats and, 201–2, 204; election and aftermath, 188–89, 208–13; "forced housing" rhetoric, 198; grassroots approaches, 194–95, 200, 212; history of housing segregation and racial exclusion in California, 190–91, 223–24; "homeowners' rights" rhetoric, 193, 210–11, 213; NAACP, 197, 201, 204–5; neighborhood and homeowner associations, 194–95, 212; property rights language, 193–94, 196–98; Proposition 14 ballot initiative, 193–201, 208, 223–24; and racial liberalism, 189; Reagan and, 199, 211–12; Republicans and Proposition 14, 198–99; rights-based language and emerging liberal civil rights discourse, 195–98, 200–201, 210; ruling on Proposition 14 constitutionality, 210–12; Rumford Housing Act, 189–92, 193–98, 206–10, 223
faith-based entrepreneurialism. See evangelical marketplace missions
Falwell, Jerry, 101
Family First, 309
Fannin, Paul, 56
fast food industry, 303–4, 312–14. See also evangelical marketplace missions
Faulkner, William, 286–87
Feagin, Joe R., 270
Federal Bureau of Investigation (FBI), 67
Federal Highway Administration, 246
Federal Housing Administration (FHA), 170, 177, 186, 246
Federal Reserve Bank of San Francisco, 53
Feinstein, Diane, 346
Fellowship of Christian Athletes, 309
Fernandez, Antonio, 256
Fernandez, Juan, 335–36
Figueroa, Liz, 333

Firestine, Robert E. See Weinstein
first circuit (manufacturing and industry), 269, 283–84
First Presbyterian Church (Marietta, Georgia), 100
First United Methodist Church (Cobb County, Georgia), 104
Flay, Bobby, 317, 428n5
Flint, Michigan, 182
Florida: evangelicals and Republican presidential vote, 131; felony voting laws and 2000 election, 239; Latino population, 343–44; Latino voters and 2008 election, 355, 358; Republican identification, 120t, 121; statistics on prisoners in rural counties, 232–33. See also urban renewal and neighborhood reform
Florida Supreme Court, 180–81
Focus on the Family, 308–9
Foster, Steve, 329–30
Four Corners Power Plant, 262
Fox Quesada, Vicente, 428n8
Frank, Leo, 87
Franklin, E. J., 191
Franzen, Jonathan, *The Twenty-Seventh City*, 270
Frederickson, Kari, 373n19
Freedom Forum (Dallas), 59
Fulbright, J. William, 61, 69–72; memo, 61, 68–72
Fulton County Review, 295

Galindo, Tomas, Sr., 329
El Galindo (tortilla manufacturer), 319–22, 328–31
Gallegos, Herman, 154
Garland, David, 238
gay rights: Cobb County resolution (1993), 102–4; Colorado Springs referendum (1992), 102; Religious Right moral crusades and, 101–4; Sunbelt opinion on, 132–36, 133–34t
General Agreement on Tariffs and Trade, 318
General Electric, 51
General Motors, 182
Georgia: Latino population, 343–44; population growth and demographic trends, 83–84, 83t. See also Atlanta; Cobb County; evangelical marketplace missions
Germinal. See Zola

Gibbons, Sam, 176
Gibson, Theodore, 172–75, 183
Gingrich, Newt, 82–86, 104–7
Giuliani, Rudolph, 352
Glenmary Research Center surveys, 113
globalization, 24; Global South and marketplace missions, 309–15; NAFTA, 318–19, 321, 331–32, 334, 430n31; Sunbelt political economy and trade liberalization, 318–19, 321, 326, 331–32, 334; trade and world GDP, 319–20, 429n19. *See also* tortilla politics
Goldberg, Robert Alan, 17
Goldfield, David R., 9, 10, 362n19
Goldfield, Robert, 9, 14
Goldwater, Barry, 11, 54–57; and anticommunism, 68, 78–80; antilabor message, 45, 54–56; antiliberal politics and rise to prominence, 45, 54–57; anti–New Deal message, 54–55, 250–51; and "business-oriented government," 250–51; cowboy imagery and Western persona, 18; and Eisenhower administration, 54–55; 1952 election as junior senator, 242, 250; and energy development, 250–51, 255; and Fulbright memo, 71; and Kennedy administration, 68, 78; land management/natural resource policies, 244, 251, 255; 1958 reelection campaign, 56; 1964 Republican campaign, 56–57, 59, 94, 188, 209; *Phoenix Gazette* editorials, 45; and postwar Phoenix business elite, 33, 45, 54–57, 250–51; Proposition 14, 199; and Reuther, 55–56; and Senate muzzling hearings, 74–75, 80–81; and Thurmond crusade, 59, 71, 79–81
Gómez Cruz, Manuel Ángel, 332
González, Roberto M., 324
González Barrera, Roberto, 324, 327
Goode Brothers Poultry Company, 295–96, 312
Goodyear Aviation, 246, 249
Gordon, Rosalie M., *Nine Men Against America: The Supreme Court and Its Attack on American Liberties*, 67
Graduate Center of the City University of New York, 114
Graf, Randy, 349
Graham, Dorothy, 185
Graham, Frank, 64

Grem, Darren E., 24–25, 293–315
"growth liberalism," 246–48
Grubstein v. Urban Renewal Agency of the City of Tampa (1959), 180–81
GRUMA (tortilla manufacturer), 25, 317, 319–22, 324–34; in China, 317, 428n6; dismantling of CONASUPO, 25, 326–27, 331, 334; Maseca flour, 320, 325, 330; Mission Foods division, 324–25, 327–28, 333; and NAFTA, 331–32; sales and global dominance, 320, 322, 326–34; and Salinas/Zedillo administrations, 326–27; and small tortilla producer antitrust suit, 332–33; tortilla/masa flour technology, 325–26, 331; and Walmart, 321–22, 325
Guth, James L., 20–21, 110–38, 240
Guzman, Ralph, 151, 157

Haas, Lucien, 201–2, 209–10
Hall, Juliet, 312
Hargis, Billy James, 71–72, 79–80
Hayden, Delores, 14
Hayden, Tom, 11, 32
Heard, Alexander, 63–64
H-E-B (Texas supermarket chain), 323–25, 330
Helms, Jesse, 11, 32
Hernandez, Jorge, 327
Herron, Warren, 96
Herzberg, Fred, 151–53, 155–56
High, Robert King, 179–80
Hill, E. V., 1–3, 28
HistoryMakers (evangelical missionary alliance), 311
Hodges, Luther, 42
Hoffa, Jimmy, 74
Holden, Martha, 202
Holden, Marvin, 201
Holifield, Chet, 157
Homestead Act, 251
Hoover, J. Edgar, 67
Hoover Dam, 248–49, 416n19
Hope IV project, 187
HoSang, Daniel Martinez, 22, 188–213, 223
House Armed Services Committee, 65–66
House Science and Astronautics Committee, 75
House Sunbelt Caucus, 136
House Un-American Activities Committee (HUAC), 67–68

Housing Acts of 1949 and 1954, 173
Housing and Home Finance Agency, 179
housing segregation: Cobb County zoning, 98–99; discriminatory federal lending, 170–72, 190–91; and FHA mortgage programs, 170; Miami city planners, 169–70; postwar Southern California, 151, 161–63, 190–91, 208–10; restrictive covenants and occupancy clauses, 161–62, 172–73, 190–92; and Rumford Act, 189–92; *Shelley v. Kraemer*, 11, 162, 172–73, 191–92; urban renewal in Greater Miami, 164–87. *See also* fair housing legislation
Houston, Texas: Latino-African American coalitions, 357, 444n76; real estate development and second circuit of capital, 270
Huckabee, Mike, 352
Huerta, Dolores, 351
Humble Oil Company, 63
Humphrey, Hubert, 94
Hunter, Edward, 79

IBM, 42
Ickes, Harold, 252
immigration and Sunbelt: Arizona law, 26–28; California ballot initiatives and anti-immigration environment, 346–48, 440n31; House bill 4437 and U.S-Mexico border legislation, 348–49; Latino population trends and demographic changes, 119, 317–18, 320, 339, 342–45, *345f*, 429nn20–21, 439n26; local governments and regulations, 350, 442n58; Mexican immigration since 1961, 317–18, 320, 429nn20–21; Republican anti-immigration politics, 346–50, 352, 355, 359, 444n80; South/Southwest, 339; 2006 debate, 348–50, 356; unauthorized/undocumented, 320, 343–44, 429n21
Impact 360 (Christian leadership organization), 309
Independent American, 72
Indian Renewal Act (IRA), 243
Indian reservations: energy development and state jurisdiction, 255–58; and "land freedom," 243, 251–52, 257–58; leasing policies, 259–62; natural resource policies, 243–45; policy of "termination," 244, 255–58; prison building, 231–32. *See also*

Navajo Reservation and postwar energy development
Industrial Areas Foundation, 149, 152
In re Ferguson (1961), 222–23
Institutional Revolutionary Party (PRI, Mexico), 318
Irwin, John, 222
Isakson, Johnny, 96, 98, 104, 105–7, 109

Janssen, Volker, 23, 217–39, 268, 284
Japanese American Citizens League (JACL), 158, 161
Javits, Jacob, 78
Jayasanker, Laresh, 25, 316–34
Jewish Americans: Democratic presidential vote (1960–2008), 132; in-between status, 155–58; interracial civil rights activism in postwar Los Angeles, 147–59, 152, 155–56; party identification, *124t*; political positions, *133–34t*, 135; postwar LA population, 143, 145, 388n6; religion and political behavior in Sunbelt, *116–17t*, 118, *124t*, 132, *133–34t*, 135
Jewish Labor Committee, 201
John Birch Society, 97; Cold War anticommunism and New Right, 66–67, 69–70, 72, 79; and defeat of fair housing on 1964 California ballot, 202; rise of southern Republicanism, 85
Johnson, Booker T., 223
Johnson, Lyndon: and Austin business boosters in New Deal era, 36; New South supporters, 93, 131; 1964 election in California, 188, 209; task force report on war on poverty, 226; and Thurmond, 66, 80; Vietnam War policies, 70, 80
Johnston, Olin, 64
Johnston, Robert, 14, 364n34
Jones, Paul, 261, 263
Jordon, Frank, 195
Juan, Augustin, 313
Junior Achievement (nonprofit organization), 304

Katerberg, William, 422n22
Keating, Kenneth B., 78
Kellstedt, Lyman A., 20–21, 110–38, 240
Kennedy, Robert, 74, 226
Kennedy administration: and Cuban Missile Crisis, 78; executive order for fair housing

Kennedy administration (*continued*)
  legislation, 191; and Fulbright memo, 68; and Senate muzzling hearings, 19, 58–59, 68, 76, 81
Kentucky Fried Chicken, 299, 303, 317, 325, 428n6
Key, V. O., *Southern Politics*, 110
Khrushchev, Nikita, 67
Kido, Saburo, 159
Kilgallen, Dorothy, 65
King, Martin Luther, Jr., 223
King, Wayne, 6
Kingston Fossil Plant accident (2008), 264
Kline, Richard, 201, 209
Kluckhohn, Clyde, 253–54
Kodimer, Paul, 432n51
Korean War, 76, 88, 90
Kosmin, Barry, 114
Ku Klux Klan, 175

"land freedom," 243, 251–52, 257–58
land management. *See* energy development; real estate and landscape
Lassiter, Matthew, 14, 20, 36, 82–109, 401n68
Latif, Aziz, 307
Latinos in Sunbelt, 25–26, 335–60; and anti-immigration politics, 346–50, 352, 355, 359, 444n80; and California ballot initiatives, 346–48, 440n31; coalition-building with African Americans, 356–57, 444n76; Cobb County, 108; Cuban Americans, 348, 358; and Democratic Party, 122–25, *123–24t*, 132, 350–56, *353f*, *354f*, 358–59; direct political influence, 335–36, 345–56, 358–59; elected officials, 341; ethnic identity and self-identification measures, 337; immigration trends, 119, 317–18, 320, 339, 342–45, 429nn20–21; Latino Republicans, 122–25, *123–24t*, 125, 348–49, 358, 386n27; low-skill labor, 339; panethnicity and heterogeneity, 337–38, 360; political incorporation, 339–41; political issue positions, *133–34t*, 135; party coalitions, 126, *127t*, 128–29, 386n30; as political participants/targets, 338, 345–50; political party identification, 122–25, *123–24t*, 386n27; population trends, 119, 317–18, 320, 339, 342–45, *345f*, 429nn20–21, 439n26; professional and middle-class, 340; race-neutral priorities, 347; religion and political behavior, 113, *116–17t*, 118, 122–25, *123–24t*, 126, *127t*, 128–29, *133–34t*, 135, 386n27, 386n30; and Republican Party, 122–25, *123–24t*, 335–36, 346–50, 352–56, 358–59, 386n27; Sotomayor nomination, 347–48, 359, 444n80; Spanish language, 340; 2008 presidential election, 335–36, 350–56, *354f*, 358–59, 444n74; unassimilated/assimilated populations, 340; undocumented workers, 313; U.S.-/foreign-born, 344; voter turnout, 336, 346–47, 350–51, 359–60. *See also* tortilla politics
Law Enforcement Assistance Administration (LEAA), 225, 226
Lawrence, Willis D., 75
League of Women Voters, 182
Lebow, Steven, 103
Lee, Laurence, 251
Lefebvre, Henri, 269–70, 283–84, 421n8; *La Production de l'espace*, 26; *La Révolution urbaine*, 269, 421n8
Lewis, Orme, 242–46, 251–53, 257–58; campaign to register Arizona migrants, 251; and Department of the Interior, 242, 251–53, 257–58; and early Phoenix, 245–46; and Indian policies, 243–44, 252, 257–58, 260; and "land freedom," 243, 252, 257–58
Lewis, Sinclair, *Babbitt*, 421n17
Lichtenstein, Nelson, 297–98, 321, 322
Lillard, Richard G., *Eden in Jeopardy: Man's Prodigal Meddling with His Environment—The Southern California Experience*, 12
Limbaugh, Rush, 355
Limerick, Patricia Nelson, 17
literature. *See* real estate and landscape
Littlefield, George, 184
Little Miss Sunshine (film), 15
Livas Cantu, Eduardo, 331
Lockheed Corporation, 88, 90
Lockheed-Georgia Company, 88–91, 92
Logan, John, 414n1
Lorenzen, Andy, 306
Los Angeles, California: African American population, 143, 145–46, 388n6, 389n14; Chamber of Commerce debate over fair housing, 199–200; Japanese population, 143, 145–46, 388n6, 389n13; Jewish population, 143, 145, 388n6; Mexican descent/origin population, 145–46, 388n6, 389n15;

postwar population and ethnoracial diversity, 145–47; race relations and mid-1960s unrest, 223–26; Topanga Canyon and Boyle's *Tortilla Curtain*, 274–78; urban historians, 9–10. *See also* civil rights activism; Watts riots
Los Angeles Daily News, 148
Los Angeles Department of Water and Power (LADWP), 248, 262–63, 416n19
Los Angeles Times, 196
Love in the Ruins. See Percy
Lowe, Floyd, 200
Lubell, Samuel, 64

MacArthur, Douglas, 76
MacDonald, Peter, 264
MacFarland, Ernest, 250
MacKaye, Milton, 52
Maddox, Lester, 95
A Man in Full. See Wolfe
Many Mules' Daughter, 263
Manza, Jeff, 239
Manzano, Sylvia, 25–26, 335–60
Marcus, David, 160
Marietta, Georgia, 86–87, 94–95, 98, 100
Marietta Baptist Church, 100
Marietta Daily Journal, 84, 88, 91, 103
Marietta Interfaith Alliance, 103–4
Marriage and Family Foundation, 309; Legacy Fund, 308
Marriage CoMission (Christian promarriage seminar series), 308–9
Marshall, Thurgood, 159–60, 162
Maslow, Will, 159
Mason, Alexa, 306
Masters of Deceit (Hoover), 67
Matthiessen, Peter, 24, 286–87
McCain, John, 27, 131; Anglo Catholic supporters, 132; Arizona immigration efforts, 352; evangelical supporters, 131, 309; Latino voters and 2008 election, 335–36, 352, 355; and NAFTA, 321
McCarthy, Cormac, 288–89; *Blood Meridian*, 289
McCarthy, Eugene, 226
McCarthy, Joseph, 73, 75–76, 376n73
McClellan Committee, 55–56
McCone Commission (Los Angeles), 224
McDonald, Larry, 97
McGirr, Lisa, 60–61, 167

McGovern, George, 95
McGucken, Joseph T., 154
McNamara, Robert, 70, 75–76
McWilliams, Carey, 6, 10, 11
Media Matters, 444n80
Mellow, Nicole, *The State of Disunion*, 110
Mendez v. Westminster School District (1946), 11, 141–42, 144, 150, 159–61
Mexican American Political Association (MAPA), 204–6
Mexican Americans: ambiguous racial status and census categorizations, 156–58; anti-Mexican sentiment in wartime Los Angeles, 144–47; campaign to defeat Proposition 14, 201, 204–6; immigration since 1961, 317–18, 320, 429nn20–21; interracial civil rights activism in postwar Southern California, 147–59. *See also* Latinos
Mexico: free trade/trade liberalization agendas, 318–19, 321, 326, 331–32, 334; GRUMA dismantling of CONASUPO, 25, 326–27, 331, 334; immigrants since 1961, 317–18, 320, 429nn20–21; NAFTA, 318–19, 321, 331–32, 334, 430n31; neoliberal politicians, 25, 318, 326, 334, 428n8; Salinas/Zedillo administrations, 326–27; Walmart expansion, 320–21, 431n39. *See also* tortilla politics
Miami. *See* urban renewal
Miami Herald, 176, 182, 186
The Milagro Beanfield War. See Nichols
Miller, Loren, 144, 150, 159, 161–62
Miller, Mark, 310
Millner, Guy, 105, 107
Minutemen, 349
Mohl, Raymond A., *Searching for the Sunbelt: Historical Perspectives on a Region*, 8
Molotch, Harvey, 414n1
Mondale, Walter, 96
Monroe, Keith, 53–54
Mont, Max, 201, 205–7
Monterey House (Houston restaurant), 316
Moore, Michael, 107
Moral Majority, 101
Moreton, Bethany, 297–98, 321
Morphew, Richard, 72
Moses, Robert, 169–70
Moskowitz, Andrei, 217–18
Motorola (Phoenix), 50–52, 246

Mouer, Benjamin, 247
Mulkey v. Reitman (1966), 210
Mundt, Karl, 71
municipal reform, 38–39
Murdock, John, 254
Murphy, George, 198
muzzling hearings. *See* Senate Armed Services muzzling hearings

The Naked Communist. See Skousen
The Nation, 6, 64
National Association for Real Estate Boards (NAREB), 192–93, 403n16
National Association for the Advancement of Colored People (NAACP): and campaign for fair housing on 1964 California ballot, 197, 201, 204–5; and interracial civil rights struggles in mid-century LA, 144, 150–51, 158, 161–62, 191; Legal Defense and Educational Fund, 159; and slum clearance/urban renewal in Miami, 173–74, 183
National Castings Company, Capitol Foundry Division, 51
National Cattlemen's Association, 321
National Company of Popular Subsistence (CONASUPO), 25, 326–27, 331, 334
National Corn Growers Association, 321
National Election Pool (2008), 358
National Institute of Marriage, 308
National Prayer Congress (Dallas, 1976), 1–3, 6, 10
National Reclamation Association, 35
National Rifle Association, 106
National Security Council Report 68 (NSC-68), 63
National Security Policy (1958), 69, 70
National Survey of Religion and Politics (NSRP), 114, 121, 135–36
National Survey of Religious Identification (1990), 114
National Urban League, 173, 183–84
Native Americans. *See* Indian reservations; Navajo Reservation; real estate and landscape
natural resource policies, 241–44, 250–53; Goldwater and, 244, 251, 255; and Indian leasing policy, 259–62; and Indian reservations, 243–45. *See also* energy development

Navajo-Hopi Rehabilitation Act (1950), 255–57, 259–60
Navajo Reservation and postwar energy development in Arizona, 241, 253–64; BIA and, 253–61, 264, 418nn44, 54; Department of Interior and, 253–54; impoverishment, 253; Indian leasing policy and electrical utilities/energy resources, 259–62; mineral resources, 259–61, 263; modernization theory and education/training, 253–55; Navajo-Hopi Rehabilitation Act, 255–57, 259–60; state jurisdiction, 255–58; termination policy, 244, 255–58; Tribal Council, 256–57, 260–61; tribal critiques and energy development, 256–57, 263–64, 418n54; WEST consortium of private utilities, 262–63. *See also* energy development
Needham, Andrew, 23–24, 240–64, 268, 284
Neil, Lilly, 256
neoliberalism: and metropolitan growth politics, 247; Mexico, 25, 318, 326, 334, 428n8
Nevada: Latino population growth, 343–44; Latino voters and 2008 election, 355
New Deal: agencies, 242–43; energy development and natural resource policies, 242–44, 250–53; prison reforms, 221; and Sunbelt business climate, 9, 33–37, 39–40, 44–45, 242–44, 250–53; and West's institutionalized racism, 35
New Mexico: and Anaya's *Alburquerque*, 278–81; Latino population, 344; Latino voters and 2008 election, 355; and Nichols's *Milagro Beanfield War*, 272–74; prison reforms, 228
New Orleans Times-Picayune, 176
New Right thesis, 20, 84. *See also* anticommunist conservatism
Newsweek, 6, 106, 335
New Western historians, 17, 364n34
New York Times, 6, 80, 217, 221, 326
Nichols, John, 266–67, 272; *The Milagro Beanfield War*, 24, 266–68, 272–74, 283, 421n16
Nicholson, Stephen P., 347
Nine Men Against America. See Gordon
Nixon, Richard: and Cobb County Lockheed-Georgia, 90; and Goldwater, 56; New South supporters, 93–95, 131; 1968 campaign, 31, 164, 226; Southern Strategy,

167; and Thurmond, 80; and urban crisis-crime connection, 226
North American Free Trade Agreement (NAFTA), 318–19, 321, 331–32, 334, 430n31
North Carolina: Latino population, 343–44; Latino voters and 2008 election, 355–56; prisons, 231; Research Triangle and corporate investment, 42; tortilla manufacturers, 328

Oakland Tribune, 194–95
Obama, Barack, 28; and Arizona immigration law, 26; Cobb County voters, 109; Latino voters, 350–56, *354f*; 2008 election, 109, 125, 131, 163, 350–56, *354f*, 358–59
Occupational Safety and Health Administration (OSHA), 313
Ohio Bankers Association, 54
oil industry and 2010 Gulf oil spill, 27
The Old Ones of New Mexico. See Coles
Olens, Sam, 109
Olympics Out of Cobb, 104
Olympic Summer Games (1996), 104, 303
O'Mara, Margaret Pugh, 41
Onuf, Peter, 14
Operation Abolition (HUAC film), 67
Overseas Weekly, 68–69

Palin, Sarah, 27–28
Pantoja, Adrian D., 346
Paris, Texas (film), 15
Parker, William, 223
Parkland riot (Louisville, 1968), 165
Peabody Coal and Black Mesa mine, 262
Pepper, Claude, 64
Percy, Walker, *Love in the Ruins*, 287
Perdue Farms, 312–14
Perez, Leander, 63
Perot, Ross, 107, 321
Perry, David C., 7–8
Pew Forum on Religion and Public Life, U.S. Religious Landscape survey, 114–15, 121
Pew Hispanic Center, 119, 340, 347, 348
Philanthropy magazine, 308
Phillips, Kevin, 31–32; on Black Belt and Thurmond Dixiecrat campaign, 62–63; and long-term political alignment, 188–89, 212–13; *The Emerging Republican Majority*, 4–5, 31–32, 188–89, 213; on race and Reagan 1966 gubernatorial campaign, 211–12; and Sunbelt concept, 4–10, 15, 28, 31–32, 84, 188–89; on white identity and California centrist political culture, 212
Phoenix, Arizona, 33–57, 240–64; growth and search for power resources/utilities, 245–50, 416n19; Phoenix miracle and national attention, 51–53; "prototypical Sun Belt city," 33–34, 42–51. *See also* Phoenix boosters
Phoenix boosters: antiunion legislation, 45, 49, 54–56; Arizona State University engineering program, 50–51; booster-led "growth machines," 241–42, 414n1; businessmen-politicians/Anglo economic elite, 33–34, 43–51, 241–42, 246–48, 250; Chamber of Commerce, 33–34, 44–51, 53–54, 57, 241, 246, 258; Charter Government Committee and campaigns for office, 39, 46–48; City Council, 246, 250; Democratic Party, 46–47; electronics and aerospace enterprises, 43, 48, 49–51; energy development, 241–50; federal development of water and power resources on Colorado River, 247–49, 416n19; Goldwater, 33, 45, 54–57, 242, 250–51, 255; Indian policies, 243–45, 255–58; Industrial Development Committee, 48–49; industrial recruitment efforts, 46, 47, 48–51, 242; "metropolitan growth politics" in opposition to federal "growth liberalism," 246–48; and New Deal, 45–46, 242–44, 250–51; and postwar business climate, 33–34, 42–57; Republican Party, 46, 47; tax-code initiatives, 47–49
Phoenix Gazette, 45
Phoenix Suns (basketball team), 26–27
Pinchot, Gifford, 247
Plessy v. Ferguson (1896), 142, 160
population trends and Sunbelt, 429–30n22; African Americans, 108, 344, *345f*; Cobb County and Georgia, 83–84, *83t*, 107–8; Latinos, 119, 317–18, 320, 339, 342–45, *345f*, 429nn20–21, 439n26; Los Angeles ethnoracial diversity, 145–47. *See also* immigration
Power Shift. See Sale
presidential election: (1952), 250; (1960), 93–94, 131; (1964), 94, 188, 209; (1968), 94, 164, 226; (1972), 95, 131; (1976), 1, 6,

presidential election (*continued*)
95–96, 101, 131; (1980), 3, 96, 131; (1984), 96, 131; (1988), 107, 131; (1992), 131; (1996), 131; (2000), 131, 239; (2004), 131

presidential election, 2008: Cobb County vote, 109; evangelical vote, 131; Latino electorate, 335–36, 350–56, 358–59, 444n74; Obama voters, 109, 125, 131, 163, 350, 352–56, *354f*, 358–59; Republican anti-immigration rhetoric, 352, 355

presidential electoral decisions and religion (1960–2008), 129–32, 130t

President's Commission for a National Agenda for the Eighties, 15–16

President's Commission on Law Enforcement and Administration of Justice (1968), 225

Preston, James, 254

Price, Nelson, 100–104

prisons and penal ideology, 23, 217–39; California, 23, 220–28; census-based funding and political representation, 231, 233, 238–39; civil rights activism, 239; comparing Sunbelt and North, 235–38, *236f*, *237f*, *238f*; converging discourse on urban and penal crisis, 224–26; convict lease system, 220, 235; death sentences and executions, 237–38; early legal victories, 222; felony voting laws, 239; history, 217–28; LA race relations and urban unrest of mid-1960s, 223–26; law-and-order discourse and "tough-on-crime" initiatives, 219, 224–26, 229–30; legal contests of 1970s, 227–28; methods for determining prison sites, 231; metropolitan prisons, 233–34; militarized supermax prison industrial complex, 219, 236–37, *237f*; modernization and modern carceral landscape, 217–20, 228–39; new carceral capacity, 235–36, *236f*; overcrowding, 227–28; postwar welfare state, 220–21; pre–World War II South, 220, 235; prison building and corrections industry, 219, 227–28, 230–39; prisoners' rights movement, 219, 222–23, 226–28, 239, 411n30; prison riots of late 1960s, 226; private prisons, 237, *238f*; "punitive segregation," 238; reforms, 220–22, 228; rehabilitation/treatment model, 219, 221–25, 227, 232; rural communities and isolated prisons, 230–33, 238–39; sentencing,

225, 227–29; spatial-political landscapes, 218–20; suburbs and prisons, 23, 217–20, 229–30, 234–35; Texas, 220, 228, 232–33, 235–36, 237

The Problem of Violence. See ACRR

Procunier, Raymond, 226

La Production de l'espace. See Lefebvre

Progressive Grocer, 432–33n51

property rights movement: and Republican ascension in Sunbelt South, 85–86, 99; urban renewal/slum clearance in Greater Miami, 167–68. See also fair housing legislation and 1964 California ballot

Proposition 13 (California), 27

Proposition 14 (California). See fair housing legislation and 1964 California ballot

Proposition 187 (California), 346–47

Protestant Americans: African American, 113, 115–18, *116–17t*, 119, *124t*, 125, *127t*, 128–29, 132, *133–34t*, 135; Cobb County, 99–100; Latinos, *116–17t*, 118, 122–25, *123–24t*, 126, *127t*, 128–29, *133–34t*, 135, 386n27, 386n30; Mainline, 113, 115, *116–17t*, 119, 122, *123t*, 125–26, *127t*, *13*; political positions, *133–34t*, 135; presidential electoral decisions, *130t*, 131–32; regional party coalitions, 126–29, *127t*. See also evangelical Christians

Public Service Company of New Mexico, 262

Pulliam, Eugene, 44–45

Pyle, Howard, 244, 250

Rabinowitz, Howard N., and Robert Goldfield, "The Vanishing Sunbelt," 9

Ramirez, Ricardo, 346, 347

Ramos, Jorge, 360

Reagan, Ronald, 6, 11, 187; California law-and-order issue, 224–25; cowboy imagery and Western persona, 18; Goldwater and 1964 election, 188, 211; New South supporters, 91–92, 96; 1966 California gubernatorial campaign, 211–12, 225; 1980 presidential election, 3, 96; Proposition 14 and defeat of fair housing on 1964 California ballot, 199, 211–12; "A Time for Choosing" Speech, 1964 Republican National Convention, 199

real estate and landscape in Sunbelt Southwest, 24, 265–89; Anaya's *Alburquerque*,

Index 463

24, 266–68, 272, 278–81, 284, 286; "authentic" connections to land, 271–72, 281; capital and community in fictional communities, 24, 271–82; contrasting with Sunbelt Southeast, 271, 286–89; and first circuit of capital (manufacturing and industrial economy), 269, 283–84; Hispanic traditions, 274; land as place/ commodity, 269–71, 276, 282; land conversion and indigenous claims, 268; land/landscape and racial conflict, 267–68, 285–89; Lefebvre's second circuit of capital, 269–71, 280–86, 289, 421nn7–8; outside investment, 273–74, 283, 422n25; rootlessness of Anglo cities, 271; water issues, 272–73, 279–84, 422n24. *See also* Boyle, *The Tortilla Curtain*; Nichols, *The Milagro Beanfield War*; Silko, *Almanac of the Dead*
Reeves, D. W., 262
regional concept and Sunbelt, 5, 6–18, 32, 110–12, 240–41. *See also* Sunbelt studies
regional exceptionalism, 10, 16–17
Regional Growth and Decline in the U.S. See Weinstein
Reichheld, Frederick F., 306
religion and political behavior in Sunbelt, 20–21, 110–38; data sources, 20, 113–14, 385n21; ethnoreligious theory and nineteenth-century politics, 112–13; "nationalization" hypothesis and American political history, 137; partisanship/party identification by religion, 122–25, *123–24t*; party affiliation, 119–21, *120t*; political issue positions, 132–36, *133–34t*; presidential electoral decisions, 129–32, *130t*; regional explanations, 135–37; regional religious Democratic/Republican coalitions, 125–29, *127t*; religious composition of the Sunbelt, 115–19, *116–17t*, 386nn24,26; religious/political conservatism, 111, 135–38; and "religious tradition," 112–13; summary and implications, 136–38. *See also* African Americans; Catholic Americans; evangelical Christians; evangelical marketplace missions; Jewish Americans; Latinos in Sunbelt; Protestant Americans
Religious Right, 100–106; and conservative political culture in Cobb County, 84–86, 100–106; culture wars/moral crusades and family values, 100–104, 106; Religious Right thesis and political change in modern America, 20, 84. *See also* evangelical Christians; evangelical marketplace missions
Religious Roundtable, 101
Reno, Nevada, 39
Republican National Convention: (1964), 199; (Miami Beach, 1968), 164–67
Republican Party: anti-immigration politics and rhetoric, 346–50, 352, 355, 359, 444n80; coalition patterns, 126–28; Cobb County, 82–83, 93–98, 104–9; and conservatism's ascendancy in metropolitan Sunbelt South, 82–86, 93–98, 104–9; and fair housing on 1964 California ballot, 198–99; and Latino electorate, 335–36, 346–50, 352–56, 358–59; Latino Republicans, 122–25, *123–24t*, 348–49, 358, 386n27; and nascent Religious Right, 84–86, 104–5; nineteenth-century politics and ethnoreligious groups, 113; Nixon's "new road to progress," 165–67; party affiliation, 119–21, *120t*; party identification by religious affiliation, 122–25, *123–24t*, 386n27; presidential vote by religion, *130t*, 131–33, 387n31; regional religious coalitions, 125–29, *127t*; "Republican Revolution" of Gingrich and Religious Right, 82–86, 104–7; Thurmond's party switch and anticommunist crusade, 80–81; 2008 election, 335–36, 352–56, 358. *See also* Goldwater
Republican Senate Campaign Committee, 54, 56
Research Triangle Foundation, 42
Reserve Officers Association, 66
restrictive housing covenants, 161–62, 172–73, 190–92
Reuther, Walter, 55–56
La Révolution urbaine. See Lefebvre
Reynolds v. Sims (1964), 225
Rhodes, John, 260
Rice, Bradley R. *See* Bernard
Richardson, Bill, 351–52
"right-to-work" legislation, 40, 49, 250
Rindermann, Rita Schwentesius, 332
Ríos, Tony, 150
Rivers, Mendel, 65–66
Robertson, Pat, 102, 105
Roca, Paul, 245

464 Index

Rockefeller, Nelson, 188, 199
Romney, Mitt, 352
Roos, Joe, 154–56
Roosevelt, Franklin D., 36–37
Ross, Fred, 149–50, 153–54
Roswell Street Baptist Church (Marietta, Georgia), 100–102, 104
Roybal, Edward, 147, 149–50, 153–54
Ruiz v. Estelle (1980), 228
Rumford, William Byron, 190
Rumford Fair Housing Act, 189–92, 206–10, 223; attempts to roll back, 193–98. *See also* fair housing legislation
Rusk, Dean, 78
Russell, James, 176
Russell, Richard, 61, 72–73, 76–77, 79, 80
Rustin, Bayard, 223–24

Sale, Kirkpatrick, 4–10, 15, 28; *Power Shift*, 5
Salinas, Maria Elena, 360
Salinas de Gortari, Carlos, 326, 428n8
Salt River Project, 249, 262–63
San Antonio, Texas, 39, 59
San Bernadino Chamber of Commerce, 53
Sanchez, George, 339
Sanchez, Mark, 360
Sanchez, Roberto, 313
Sancton, Thomas, 64
San Diego, California, 43, 310
San Fernando Valley Fair Housing Council, 191
San Jose, California, 36
Saturday Evening Post, 52, 56, 93
The Savages (film), 15
Savannah River Site (Aiken, South Carolina), 65–66
Schaller, Thomas, 357
school desegregation, 141–42, 144, 150–51, 159–61, 395n94
Schulman, Bruce, 9
Schumer, Chuck, 359
Scott, Amy, 12
Scott, David, 108–9
Scottsdale, Arizona, 279
Scripto Company (Atlanta), 93
Searching for the Sunbelt. See Mohl
second circuit of capital in Southwest cities, 269–71, 280–86, 289, 421nn7–8; fiction and, 269–71, 280–86, 289; financial system, 270; and first circuit, 269, 283–84;

real estate, 269–70, 285–86, 421n7; water issues, 272–73, 279–80, 281, 282–84, 422n24
segregation. *See* housing segregation; school desegregation
Segura, Gary M., 346, 347
Self, Robert, 192
Senate Armed Services Committee muzzling hearings (1961), 19, 58–59, 61, 71–81; final report, 78–79; and Fulbright memo, 61, 68–72; legacy, 78–81; and Thurmond, 19, 66, 79–81
Senate Foreign Relations Committee, 76; Fulbright and, 69–70; Thurmond and, 66
Senate Select Committee on Improper Activities in the Labor or Management Field (McClellan Committee/Senate Rackets Committee), 55–56
Sensenbrenner, James, 348
Serra Puche, Jaime, 326
Shannon, Marian, 185
Shelley v. Kraemer (1948), 11, 162, 172–73, 191–92
Sherman Antitrust Act, 332
Shermer, Elizabeth Tandy, 19, 31–57
Sherrill, Robert, 60
shopping malls and postwar American capitalism, 296–97, 299, 303–4
Silicon Valley, 41–42
Silko, Leslie Marmon, 266–67, 282. *Almanac of the Dead*, 24, 266–68, 272, 281–85, 289, 421n11, 422nn21–23
Sineath, Charles, 104
Skousen, W. Cleon, *The Naked Communist*, 67
Sleepy Lagoon Defense Committee (SLDC), 147
slums: and black poverty in postwar South, 168–69; building of, 175–76; eminent domain and slum clearance, 170–75, 177–80. *See also* urban renewal and neighborhood reform
Smathers, George, 64
Smith, William French, 210
Smith, Willis, 64
Smoot, Dan, 71
Smyrna, Georgia, 89, 94–95
Social Security Administration, 246
Sosa, Lionel, 348–49
Sotomayor, Sonia, 347–48, 359, 444n80

Index   465

South Africa, 310–11
South Carolina: Latino population growth rates, 343, 344; Savannah River Site, 65–66; Thurmond and Aiken community, 65–66
Southern Baptist Convention, 101
Southern California Edison, 248, 262, 416n19
Southern Christian Leadership Conference, 1
Southern Manifesto (1956), 60, 61
Southern Politics. *See* Key
Southern Poverty Law Center, 444n80
Southern Regional Council, 175
"Southern Strategy," 20, 84, 167
Soviet Union, 67, 78, 146
St. Louis, Missouri, 182
Stanford Research Institute, 259
Stanford University, 41–42
Starr, Kevin, 12
State Bar of California, 204
The State of Disunion. *See* Mellow
States' Rights Democratic Party, 61–62. *See also* Dixiecrat Party
Stennis, John, 61, 72–77, 79–80
Striffler, Steve, 313
suburbs: Cobb County postwar expansion, 94–95, 97–99; crime, 229–30, 235; law-and-order discourse/tough-on-crime initiatives, 229–30; mortgage crisis, 234–35; postwar Sunbelt business climate and suburb annexation, 41; prisons, 23, 217–20, 229–30, 234–35; riots of the late 1960s, 164–67; shopping malls, 296–97, 299, 303–4, 424n8; urban renewal and black suburbanization, 165, 170–72, 173–74, 184–87. *See also* urban renewal and neighborhood reform
Sumner, Charles, 64
Sunbelt Caucus (House), 136
Sunbelt Cities. *See* Bernard
Sunbelt conservatism. *See* anticommunist conservatism; Cobb County
Sunbelt studies, 1–28; as "conceptual region," 14–18, 110–11, 240–41; definitions, 13, 15, 235; geographic boundaries, 8–9; new urban forms and organization of metropolitan space, 7–8; New Western historians and myths of "westernness" and frontier, 17–18, 364n34; origins of Sunbelt, 4–13, 31–32; Phillips and, 4–10, 15,

28, 31–32, 84, 188–89; place/place making, 14–16; political-economic space/space making, 14, 16; and popular 1970s Sunbelt storyline/narrative, 6–8; as postindustrial, poststructural region, 5; questions about usefulness of, 6–13, 15, 32, 112; regional concept, 5, 6–18, 32, 110–12, 240–41; regional exceptionalism, 10, 16–17; regional mythologies, 16–17; Sale and, 4–10, 15, 28; social science research, 7–9; urban historians, 8–9, 362n19
Sun City retirement communities, 15
Survey Research Center, University of Akron, 114
"Survival U.S.A." (Memphis), 59
Sutton, Tom, 312
Sylvester, Arthur, 77

Taft-Hartley Act (1947), 40, 55
Tancredo, Tom, 348, 352, 444n80
Teamsters, 55, 333–34
Tea Party and resurgent grassroots Right, 27–28
Tennessee Valley Authority (TVA), 243–64
termination, Indian policy, 244, 255–58
Texas: evangelicals and Republican presidential vote, 131; Latino population, 343–44; Latino voters and 2008 election, 336; prison system/penal ideology, 220, 228, 232–33, 235–36, 237; Republican identification, *120t*, 121; tortilla manufacturers, 328; Walmart in, 322
Thompson, Fred, 352
Thornal, Campbell, 180
Thurmond, Strom, 19, 58–81; and Aiken, South Carolina, 65–66; anti-civil rights efforts, 60; anticommunist crusade, 19, 58–61, 68, 70–81, 376n73; and Dixiecrats, 60–64, 79; failed 1950 Senate campaign, 64–65; and Fulbright memo, 70–72; influence in military affairs, 66; military service, 66; and 1957 Civil Rights Act, 60, 79; 1948 presidential campaign, 61–64; party switch to Republican, 80; Senate muzzling hearings, 19, 58–59, 61, 71–78, 79–81; and Southern Manifesto, 60, 61; Sunbelt conservatism and rise of Right, 19, 58–81
Tillman, "Pitchfork" Ben, 64
Time magazine, 56, 89, 106, 189
Todd, Chuck, 355
The Tortilla Curtain. *See* Boyle

tortilla politics (Mexican food, globalization, and Sunbelt), 25, 316–34; ADM, 319–22, 331, 333; antitrust lawsuit against GRUMA, 332–33; Bimbo, 319–22, 332–33; dismantling of CONASUPO, 25, 326–27, 331, 334; ethnic food retailing, 322, 324, 330; food menu explanations for American diners, 316, 322–23; foreign direct investment, 318–19; free trade/trade liberalization agendas, 318–19, 321, 326, 331–32, 334; El Galindo, 319–22, 328–31; grocers/supermarket chains, 322–24, 432–33n51; GRUMA, 25, 317, 319–22, 324–34; major tortilla producers, 319–22, 436n96; NAFTA, 318–19, 321, 331–32, 334, 430n31; popularity of Mexican food in U.S., 316–17, 322–24, 428n5; Sunbelt political economy and globalization, 318–22; tortilla consumption and sales, 317, 322–24, 330, 431n42, 432–33n51, 433n55, 437n107; tortilla presses, 323–24; Walmart, 319–22, 325, 333, 428–29n15, 431n39; Walmart expansion to Mexico, 320–21, 431n39
Tower, John, 11, 32, 78
Transamerica (film), 15
Truman, Harry S, 62, 70, 76, 256
Tucson, Arizona: and Silko's *Almanac of the Dead*, 281–82, 285; water and developer plans, 279
TV Nation, 107
The Twenty-Seventh City. See Franzen

Underworld. See DeLillo
unions: Eisenhower administration, 45; Goldwater antilabor message, 45, 54–56; postwar antiunion business boosters, 40, 45, 54–56, 65, 250; prisoners' rights movement, 226–27; "right-to-work" legislation, 40, 49, 250; Taft-Hartley Act, 40, 55; Teamsters and Senate Rackets Committee, 55–56; Thurmond and, 65
United Auto Workers (UAW), 55–56
United Civil Rights Committee, 204–5
United Prisoners Union (California), 227
University of Arizona, 50, 284–85
University of Colorado, 43
University of New Hampshire Carsey Institute, 313
University of New Mexico, 278, 282, 285
Unruh, Jesse, 11
Unruh Civil Rights Act, 201

urban renewal and neighborhood reform in Greater Miami, 21–22, 164–87; and black middle-class homeowners, 182, 184–85; black suburbanization, 165, 170–74, 184–87; "blight" (term), 181; Central Negro District, 165, 181–82, 184–86; Coconut Grove, 172–75; Coconut Grove Citizens' Committee for Slum Clearance, 172–75, 177; Collins mayoral administration, 178–80; committee approaches, 179–80; Edison Center suburb and racial violence, 175; elite black support, 183; eminent domain and slum clearance, 170–75, 177, 178–80; Florida Supreme Court and 1959 *Grubstein* ruling, 180–81; history of black housing segregation and suburban containment, 165, 181–82, 184–86; interstate highway development, 166, 181–86; landlords and tenement owners, 175–78, 185–86; Liberty City riots and 1968 GOP Convention, 164–67; Liberty City suburbs, 165, 171–72, 186; "Magic City Center Plan," 181–82; Miami City Commission, 171, 175; Overtown, 165, 176, 178, 183–86; postwar federal housing policies, 170–72; progressive liberal reformers, 167–68, 187; property rights movement, 167–68; and public housing projects, 177; Railroad Shop, 171, 181; relocation and displacement, 181–86; slum problems/solutions in other cities, 182–83; and tourism, 174–75
U.S. Air Force, 88, 89–90
U.S. Army Reserves, 66
U.S. Census: census-based funding and political representation for rural communities, 231, 233, 238–39; data and Sunbelt as analytical category, 13; data on Latino population, 342–43, 439n26
U.S. Chamber of Commerce, 243, 251
U.S. Department of Agriculture, Economic Research Service, 231
U.S. Department of Commerce, Business Advisory Committee, 53
U.S. Department of Defense: and Cold War anticommunism, 19, 68, 70, 75–76; Fulbright memo and 1961 directive, 70; McNamara and 1961 Senate muzzling hearings, 75–76
U.S. Department of Housing and Urban Development, 179

U.S. Department of State: Cuban Missile Crisis, 79; McCarthy hearings, 75–76
U.S. House. *See* House
U.S. Senate. *See* Senate
U.S. Supreme Court: *Brown v. Board of Education*, 60, 141–42, 144, 150–51, 159–61, 173; and Cold War anticommunism, 67; *Mendez v. Westminster School District*, 11, 141–42, 144, 150, 159–61; *Plessy v. Ferguson*, 142, 160; postwar rulings regarding prisoners' rights, 222; *Reynolds v. Sims*, 225; *Shelley v. Kraemer*, 11, 162, 172–73, 191, 192; Sotomayor nomination, 347–48, 359, 444n80
Utah International, 261

Valley National Bank (Phoenix), 53, 242, 258
Vance, Cyrus, 75
"The Vanishing Sunbelt." *See* Rabinowitz and Goldfield
Vaughan, Earle, 200
VeggieTales (Christian cartoon series), 309
Vietnam War, 70, 80, 90
Virginia: Latino population, 343, 344; Latino voters and 2008 election, 355–56
Virrick, Elizabeth, 173–75
voter turnout: African American, 350–51; Latino, 336, 346–47, 350–51, 359–60; 2008 presidential election, 336, 350–51

Walker, Edwin, 19, 58–59, 68–69, 72, 80
Wallace, George, 94, 95–96
Wall Street Journal, 52
Walmart, 298, 303; expansion to Mexico, 320–21, 431n39; and GRUMA tortillas, 321–22, 325; Mexican American employees and customer base, 322; and NAFTA, 321; sales and retail model, 320–21; tortilla production and Sunbelt political economy, 319–22, 333, 428–29n15; workers' lower wages, 321–22
Walton, Sam, 298
Warne, William, 254, 255
Warren, Earl, 221
Washington Post, 71–73, 321
water resources: federal development on Colorado River, 247–49, 416n19; landscape and real estate in Southwest cities, 272–73, 279–84, 422n24
Waters, Maxine, 230

Watkins, Alfred J., 7–8
Watts riots (Los Angeles, 1965), 165, 223–26
Wayne Farms, 312–14
Weaver, Robert, 169, 179, 181
Webb, Del, 15
Weinberger, Caspar, 198
Weinstein, Bernard L., and Robert E. Firestine, *Regional Growth and Decline in the U.S.: The Rise of the Sunbelt and the Decline of the Northeast*, 7
Weise, Andrew, 169, 186–87
Welch, Robert, 67, 79–80
Western Energy Supply and Transmission Associates (WEST), 262–63, 419n68
Weston Foods, 333
White, Richard, 248, 418n54
White, William S., 73
Williams, Rachel, 185
Wilson, Joe Mack, 97, 98
Wilson, L. H., 193, 195, 198
Wilson, Pete, 327, 346, 352
WinShape Foundation: Camp WinShape, 303; and Chick-fil-A Christian corporate culture, 302–3, 308, 311–12, 314–15; college scholarship program, 302; pro-marriage seminars and retreats, 308, 425n30; and social services, 302–3
WinShape International, 311–12, 314–15
Winslow, Robert W., *Crime in a Free Society*, 225
Wirin, A. L., 161
Wolfe, Tom, *A Man in Full*, 24, 270, 286
Woods, Nathan D., 347
Woodward, C. Vann, 17
World War II: and Cobb County, 86–87, 90; Phoenix electrical shortages, 249–50; production and defense industry employment, 36–37, 86–87, 145, 151; Southern California racial tensions, 144–47; Thurmond service, 66
Wright, Sonny, 183
Wysong, Gordon, 103, 109

Yale Law Journal, 160
Yorty, Samuel, 211, 223
Young, Andrew, 11, 32
Young Americans for Freedom, 80

Zedillo, Ernesto, 326, 428n8
Zola, Émile, *Germinal*, 273

Acknowledgments

The work of this volume has been incredibly exciting, fun, and rewarding. We are grateful to everyone who helped bring this to publication, from the call for papers to the final copyedits. We are especially indebted to the Clements Center for Southwest Studies at Southern Methodist University (SMU), the research institution that provided most of the funding for this project. We benefited enormously from the Clements Centers program of workshops and symposia that brought our scholars together for discussion, revision, and public presentation of their work. For the organizational assistance and moral support throughout this project we would like to thank especially Andrea Boardman, RuthAnn Elmore, Sherry Smith, David Weber, and Benjamin Johnson. We are also very grateful for the generous financial support from the Center.

We were also fortunate to be sponsored by the Huntington-USC Institute for California and the West, which hosted the preliminary workshop and symposium at the Huntington Library in San Marino, California. For the wonderful hospitality, accommodations, and publicity, we would like to thank Robert Ritchie, William Deverell, Susie Krasnoo, Carolyn Powell, Jenny Watts, and Erin Chase.

Sunbelt Rising would have been infinitely more frustrating if not for the quick and abiding support of our editor Robert Lockhart at the University of Pennsylvania Press. As novices to this kind of project, we are so grateful for the responsive, informed, and enthusiastic guidance we found in Bob. We also want to thank Alison Anderson, Chris Bell, Julia Rose

Roberts, and Sandra Haviland for ably directing this volume through every stage of production.

At risk of making significant omissions, we would nevertheless like to thank others who contributed to this project, including the History Department at Purdue University and the School of Arts and Humanities at the University of Texas Dallas for institutional support. We have also bent the ear and relied on the work of colleagues Jeff Roche, Robert Johnston, and Benjamin Johnson for our thoughts about region. Matthew Lassiter, a contributor to this volume, pointed us to some additional sources for use in our introduction and, most importantly, invited us to present portions of our own research on the Sunbelt and a draft of this introduction to the Metropolitan History Group at the University of Michigan. The experience proved to be instructive and incredibly enriching.

We want to thank our outstanding contributors. Though they impressed us from the start, our essay writers dazzled us with the work they put into the numerous drafts they submitted for this volume and the public presentations they made at SMU and the Huntington Library. The sense of camaraderie among contributors was special. We are thrilled with the way rookie Sunbelt scholars, whose first-rate work will change the field in the coming years, and veteran Sunbelt scholars (most notably Carl Abbott), whose exemplary work has already defined it for a generation, were able to come together in rigorous, spirited engagement, both of the scholarly and social kind. We feel mentored by all of them. Finally, we would like to thank our families: Debra Dochuk, Benjamin Johnson, and Tobias Johnson, the most supportive companions in our Sunbelt adventures.

www.ingramcontent.com/pod-product-compliance
Lightning Source LLC
Chambersburg PA
CBHW030103010526
44116CB00005B/78